FILAMENTS

FILAMENTS

Theological Profiles

SELECTED ESSAYS ✳ VOLUME 2

DAVID TRACY

The University of Chicago Press   Chicago and London

The University of Chicago Press, Chicago 60637
The University of Chicago Press, Ltd., London
© 2020 by The University of Chicago
All rights reserved. No part of this book may be used or reproduced in any
manner whatsoever without written permission, except in the case of brief
quotations in critical articles and reviews. For more information, contact the
University of Chicago Press, 1427 East 60th Street, Chicago, IL 60637.
Published 2020
Printed in the United States of America

29 28 27 26 25 24 23 22 21 20   1 2 3 4 5

ISBN-13: 978-0-226-56732-7 (cloth)
ISBN-13: 978-0-226-60845-7 (e-book)
DOI: https://doi.org/10.7208/chicago/9780226608457.001.0001

The University of Chicago Press gratefully acknowledges the
generous support of the Divinity School at the University
of Chicago toward the publication of this book.

Library of Congress Cataloging-in-Publication Data
Names: Tracy, David, author.
Title: Filaments : theological profiles : selected essays, volume 2 / David Tracy.
Other titles: Theological profiles
Description: Chicago ; London : University of Chicago Press, 2020. |
Includes bibliographical references and index.
Identifiers: LCCN 2019045330 | ISBN 9780226567327 (cloth) |
ISBN 9780226608457 (ebook)
Subjects: LCSH: Theology. | Theology — History.
Classification: LCC BR85 .T692 2020 | DDC 230/.2 — dc23
LC record available at https://lccn.loc.gov/2019045330

♾ This paper meets the requirements of ANSI/NISO Z39.48-1992
(Permanence of Paper).

To Mary Weber Gerhart
indispensable aid and friend

A noiseless patient spider,
I mark'd where on a little promontory it stood isolated,
Mark'd how to explore the vacant vast surrounding,
It launch'd forth filament, filament, filament, out of itself,
Ever unreeling them, ever tirelessly speeding them.

And you O my soul where you stand,
Surrounded, detached, in measureless oceans of space,
Ceaselessly musing, venturing, throwing, seeking the spheres to connect them,
Till the bridge you will need be form'd, till the ductile anchor hold,
Till the gossamer thread you fling catch somewhere, O my soul.

WALT WHITMAN

CONTENTS

INTRODUCTION

This second volume of *Selected Essays* gathers writing on some significant theologians, philosophers, and religious thinkers. The range of theological choices in this volume can also, metaphorically, be named "fragments," in harmony with the understanding of fragment as "frag-event" (as described in *Fragments*, the companion to this volume), or "filaments," Walt Whitman's brilliant metaphor in the epigraph to this volume. Whitman's filaments are thrown out from the speaking self to some others (ancient, medieval, modern, and contemporary) in order to "catch somewhere, O my soul." I hope that readers will find at least some of the fragments chosen for this volume helpful for their own intellectual and soulful journeys.

The thinkers are arranged in rough chronological order, from choices in ancient theology (Augustine), through medieval (William of St. Thierry), to early modern (Martin Luther and Michelangelo), and modern and contemporary (Bernard Lonergan, Karl Rahner, Reinhold Niebuhr, Paul Tillich, et al.). The essay on each thinker is, I trust, sufficiently self-explanatory as not to need a summary. I will instead make a few remarks, mainly on the context of the individual thinker. Most of these essays result from lectures at conferences. In each case, however, the invitation was a welcome chance to write about an admired thinker.

Some essays in the first volume of this two-volume set could have been included in this volume, especially the long sections in the essays on Infinity that interpret the incomparable Plotinus and the unique Gregory of Nyssa (Augustine's older contemporary). The modern thinkers of volume 1 (René Descartes, François Fénelon, Jeanne Guyon, and Blaise Pascal) could likewise be in this volume, but they seemed to fit more naturally in volume 1. By no means are all the major theologians interpreted here: many (Origen, Gregory Nazianzen, Boethius, Anselm, Bernard, Hildegard of Bingen, Abelard, the Victorines, Thomas Aquinas, Bonaventure, Duns Scotus, John Calvin, Teresa of Ávila, Friedrich Schleiermacher, Rudolf Bultmann, Karl Barth, Hans Urs von Balthasar, and several others) are mentioned but not discussed at length. However, this volume on some basic thoughts of certain thinkers may serve as a partial initiation into that pluralistic and ambiguous history of Christian theology.

Most texts, like all individuals, are complex, plural, and ambiguous, containing truth and falsehood, good traits and bad, and—if spiritual—holy and unholy dimensions. After careful interpretation, most major texts, especially classics, describe a real but elusive unity. As in volume 1, the philosophical and theological approach here is justly described as hermeneutical. Hermeneutics, as I argued in several essays in volume 1, is grounded in the reality of conversation with a genuine Other—not a projected other of my own beliefs and attitudes but the other as Other. The claim of the Other, whether in person, text, event, or symbol, must rule all conversation. One enters a conversation (here with the texts of theological, philosophical, and artistic thinkers) with the fundamental effort to understand that otherness on its own terms.

These essays, therefore, are largely exercises in a hermeneutics of recovery—that is, an attempt to render accurate the complex, plural, and ambiguous realities of the texts and the particular individuals who wrote them in highly specific historical contexts. A hermeneutics of recovery is not, *pace* Friedrich Schleiermacher and all Romantic hermeneutics, an exercise in trying to reexperience the felt experience of the Other. Hermeneutics is not empathy but conversation with a focus on the truth and meaning of another's claim to one's attention. Hermeneutics of recovery, thus understood fundamentally as conversation, can employ any method that aids in that enterprise of recovered meaning from either the contemporary present or from the past, that foreign country.

A full hermeneutics does not confine itself to a hermeneutics of recovery. Just as in conversation, when clarification or correction is believed necessary, different kinds of argument enter. Included in such arguments are disclosures of conscious errors (e.g., a fundamentalist reading of Genesis; patriarchy as exposed by feminist criticism). Hence the second form of hermeneutics is necessary: a hermeneutics of critique (e.g., Voltaire, Diderot, and the other *philosophes*).

However, not all hermeneutical problems with the complexity, plurality, and ambiguity of texts, authors, and interpreters alike are conscious errors that can be spotted and corrected by the appropriate argument. In fact, there are more unconscious than conscious realities afoot in texts and persons alike — those unconsciously hidden but systemically functioning, treacherous distortions that part 4 of this volume describes: sexism, racism, classism, imperialism, anti-Semitism, Islamophobia, and all the other fatal "isms" that inflict themselves upon us and which it is our responsibility to admit and to attempt to heal through various hermeneutics of suspicion informed by diverse critical theories.

There is yet another issue that demands attention in the arts, the sciences, philosophy, and theology. That issue is the existence, in the modern period, of unfortunate splits: that is, distinctions become fatal separations, and polarities become binary oppositions. In modern rationality, as distinct from classical reason, three splits between once distinct but not separate realities have proved devastating to much modern understanding: first, the separation of passion and reason to the impoverishment of both; second, the separation of form and content so that the many earlier forms of thought (narrative, rhetoric, poetics, aphorisms, praise, prayer) have been widely ignored as proper forms for modern thought, where only the form of conceptual proposition is honored; third, the modern separation of theory and practice, in contrast to ancient and medieval thought as well as to contemporary Buddhist thought, wherein theory and practice are distinct but not separate.

Much modern theology has also been affected by these three modern, fatal separations. In theology itself, the two worst splits in modern thought are the separation of spirituality and theology (related to all three more general separations cited above) and the separation of theology and ethics (related especially to the split of theory and praxis).

The historical separation of theology and spirituality, as Hans Urs von Balthasar rightly insisted, has proved tragic for both theology proper and the now-separate discipline of spirituality. Theology without spirituality is existentially too thin and too removed from its biblical, liturgical, and patristic grounding sources and from the rich resources of contemporary Christian traditions of spirituality and piety, both personal and communal.

At the same time, spirituality as a discipline on its own, without a relationship to rigorous theological theory, philosophy, and social science, is ever in danger of becoming a free-floating sentimentality. Without strict theoretical theology and philosophy, spirituality can become all too *ad hoc* as a captive of ever-shifting attitudes of the reigning culture. But without spirituality, theoretical theology can lose its own ground in the prophetic, existential faith that grounds all three radical monotheisms.

Judaism, Christianity, and Islam are in their origins prophetic faiths directed by the command of the transcendent God of the Bible and the Qur'an to existential trust in God's promises and in fidelity to that God through ethical-political-existential actions. Each of the great radical monotheisms participates in its fundamental event of God's self-revelation.

In Judaism, faith exists as gift and command, existential trust in and loyalty to God. God's decisive actions in the history of Israel have disclosed a just and caring God and evoked the exceptional commitment of Jews through the centuries to justice, even amid their own terrifying sufferings in history, culminating in the Shoah. This profoundly ethical, monotheistic Jewish faith is grounded in God's revelations to biblical Israel and his law, kept alive and ever new in post-biblical rabbinic Judaism.

In Christianity, existential faith and loyalty are determined by God's decisive self-revelation in the event and person of Jesus Christ, who reveals God as, in essence, Love (1 John 4:8, 16). That grace of a divine love empowers Christians to struggle for love and social justice, especially for the poor, the oppressed, and the marginalized. For Christians, moreover, the essence of God as Love inevitably leads to a Trinitarian understanding of the loving God that deepens its radical monotheism.

In Islam, the revelatory event evoking existential faith as both gift and command is to be found not in the history of a people, not in a specific individual, but in a text, the sacred Qur'an and the profound ethical-political personal and communal actions the Qur'an prescribes for all Muslims—hence Islam's remarkable ability to found and sustain so many Islamic law–governed communities. Moreover, the uncompromising Islamic insistence on the oneness of God (*tawhid*) makes clear that the very same God is present in all three monotheisms: Yahweh of the Hebrew Bible and later Judaism; God as the one God of Trinitarian relational love in Christianity; God as the one Allah as testified to by Muhammad as the seal of the prophets. The same God of Judaism, Christianity, and Islam remains the same one God of all three radical monotheisms, along with different emphases in the three radical monotheisms: the just and compassionate God of Judaism; the God of love and justice in Christianity; the God of justice and mercy in Islam.

For any interpretation of any one of these classic religious traditions, an interpreter—even one who is principally interested in the later philosophic and theological developments in each tradition—must acknowledge that each of them is, in its origin and grounding, a prophetic religion evoking existential faith and ethical-political acts for the Other (the neighbor). An interpreter may choose to follow the mystical trajectories that each prophetic tradition has produced in order to show the prophetic, mystical character of its theologies (e.g., liberation theologies) and its spiritualities (e.g., Sufism, Kabbalah, Christian mysticism).

To confine my comments for the moment to Christianity, my own tradition: in the multicultural, centuries-old traditions of Christianity, many diverse aesthetic and social justice traditions emerged, as they did in each of the monotheisms (in art—mainly aniconic in Judaism and Islam; mainly iconic in Christianity). Furthermore, there is truth to Alfred North Whitehead's generalizing and only slightly exaggerated observation comparing Buddhism and Christianity: Christianity was a religion in search of philosophy and found one; Buddhism was a philosophy in search of a religion and found one. Christianity, like its parent religion, biblical Judaism, and its later sibling religion, Islam, is in its origins a profoundly prophetic religion calling for existential trust (faith) and fidelity to God's ethical-political commands regarding specific actions in history for love and justice, especially for the most disadvantaged among us.

That Christian prophetic faith very soon also cultivated philosophical-theological expressions of its faith related to reason in its many forms (initially, various Platonisms served a major role; later, Aristotle; now, any number of valuable philosophies—phenomenology, hermeneutics, process, some forms of analytical philosophy, neo-Thomism, etc.). As the history of the best Christian theology demonstrates, there is no good reason to separate theology and spirituality. In Catholicism, Neo-Scholasticism for centuries unfortunately did encourage that separation. Unlike Neo-Scholasticism, the high Scholasticism of the medievals did not separate theology and spirituality. Consider, for example, Thomas Aquinas's theology—in the two great summas, the *Summa Contra Gentiles* and especially the *Summa Theologiae*.

In fact, for any attentive reader Thomas Aquinas's *Summa Theologiae* includes a theological culmination of the two centuries of intense work actualizing all the technical elements developed by the Scholastics. The *Summa Theologiae* is theoretically constructed in terms of those prior Scholastic achievements from Anselm forward, as well as saturated from the very beginning on God (*Prima Pars*), through its lengthy Christian anthropology (2.1 and 2.2) on the natural and theological virtues to guide a Christian life, to the final, unfinished third part (*Tertia Pars*) on Christology and the sacraments. Thomas Aquinas was a theoretical genius in both theology and philosophy and a spiritual master (Jean-Pierre Torrell, the most distinguished living scholar of Thomas Aquinas, does not hesitate to name him a spiritual master in the second volume of his study of the life and works of Thomas Aquinas, *Initiation à saint Thomas d'Aquin: Sa personne et son oeuvre*).

Only Thomas Aquinas himself had the right to state, following what clearly seems to have been a powerful mystical experience, that all he had written was straw (what straw!) and he would write no more. Clearly, therefore, Thomas Aquinas, like Bonaventure or Friedrich Schleiermacher or Karl Rahner, and most major theologians from the earliest days of theology (the *Logos* theologians) until today, distinguished but did not separate spirituality and theology.

In addition, Thomas Aquinas cannot be charged (as, alas, many theologians and philosophers can be, as Ellen K. Wondra has observed) with separating theology and ethics. Once again, the *Summa Theologiae* is the best evidence for this nonseparation. The longest part of the *Summa* by far is the second part (*Pars Secunda*), with its two extensive sections, wherein an Aristotelian virtue ethics is transformed into an explicitly Christian ethics. Even interpreters like myself, who are most interested in and concerned with Thomas's brilliant and corrigible discussion of God as one and triune (in *Prima Pars*), cannot ignore the fact that his Christian ethics is the subject of the most lengthy discussion in the entire *Summa*.

In conclusion, none of the theologians, philosophers, social scientists, or artists interpreted in the essays of this volume can be accused of splitting theology or philosophy from spirituality, or theology or philosophy from ethics. Unfortunately, there are many theologians and philosophers who all too readily separate them. For example, in philosophy, many interpreters of Ludwig Wittgenstein's philosophy read it as solely a philosophy of logic and language separated from his profound ethical and spiritual concerns. Many of Wittgenstein's analytical followers may separate his ethical and religious reflections as mere *obiter dicta*, but Wittgenstein himself, more Viennese than Cantabrigian, never did; even his work on logic and language was also an ethical-spiritual work.

In the essays that follow, each of the five parts includes introductory comments, largely on the historical context of each major thinker interpreted. In place of a longer introduction to the whole volume, such individual introductions seem more fitting for such a diversity of thinkers and issues.

Part 1

ANCIENTS, MEDIEVALS, MODERNS

AUGUSTINE OF HIPPO

The first two essays in this section are on that singular colossus of Western theology and philosophy, Augustine of Hippo. More recently, a younger generation of Eastern Orthodox theologians happily have abandoned the earlier, purely polemical attitude of so many of their Orthodox predecessors toward Augustine.

From Augustine's day until our own, Augustinian theology has largely defined the basic frameworks of all Western theology, whether Catholic, Anglican, Lutheran, Reformed, or radical Reformation and/or Free Church. The Catholic, Anglican, and much of Liberal Protestant traditions, with some notable exceptions (e.g., Blaise Pascal), have been largely formed by Augustine's nature-grace paradigm (more exactly, grace-nature-grace paradigm), with its emphasis on Augustine's philosophical and theological reflections on intellect and love, in continuity with the pure gratuity of divine grace (especially in his brilliant early dialogues and his interpretation of the Gospel and letters of John in his greatest theological work, *De Trinitate*). The classic Protestant Reformation theologians, especially Luther, Calvin, and Müntzer, as well as others, hold to Augustine's sin-grace paradigm (more accurately, grace-sin-grace paradigm), which rejects any continuity between fallen human nature and divine grace, especially as found in the late Augustine's anti-Pelagian writings and his *City of God*. These late writings, like *Confessions*, include both the nature-grace paradigm and the sin-grace paradigm in creative tension.

The first essay on Augustine was occasioned by the welcome invitation of Susan Schreiner who, with Willemien Otten, organized the conference on Augustine and the volume of essays *Augustine Our Contemporary*. This essay, an account of Augustine's anthropology, is one of five essays on Augustine I have published over the years. It is intended to address the split in the reception of Augustine between those theologians, largely Catholic, Anglican, and several modern Liberal Protestant (e.g., process theologians), who hold that the nature-grace paradigm is Augustine's fundamental theological framework, and those largely (but not solely) Reformation theologians, from Luther and Calvin through Kierkegaard and Barth, who hold to the sin-grace paradigm as Augustine's fundamental theological framework.

In this first essay, I hold that the primary (never the exclusive) theological framework for interpreting Augustine requires both paradigms to understand the whole of Augustine. For my part, the nature-grace paradigm is the more fundamental one, the more inclusive Augustinian paradigm. However, that nature-grace paradigm can function as genuinely inclusive only if it also dialectically includes the increasing importance in the late, anti-Pelagian Augustine of the sin-grace paradigm. In the course of this attempted retrieval of the "whole" Augustine, I also argue critically, even suspiciously, against Augustine's peculiar and fatal notion of "original" sin, transmitted through sexual intercourse as a deadly legacy to Western theology and, more widely, to Western culture's troubled and confused interpretation of human sexuality. I argue that Augustine's profound — indeed unique — insight into the dark side of the pervasive evil and the resulting suffering of the human condition is better interpreted as sometimes human evil and sometimes, more accurately, as tragic, since, *contra* the late Augustine, human beings are not responsible for all evil and suffering. A good deal of human suffering is innocent suffering occasioned by the pluralistic, complex, ambiguous character of nature and the tragic actuality of the human situation. Human sin, both personal and inherited, is indeed as extensive and deadly as the genius of Augustine saw with such frightening clarity. However deeply damaged as human beings are in both mind and will, it is important to stress, again, that they are *not* responsible for *all* evil. A tragic consciousness (which Augustine clearly possessed but refused to make theological use of) is a more adequate model for understanding many of the complexities of the human situation.

Part of the inherited tragedy of Western culture can be laid at Augustine's door. In Augustine's peculiar interpretation, original sin is fatally linked with human sexuality, which, from Augustine's view, transmits original, or, more accurately (as in Eastern Christianity), "inherited" sin. On human sexuality, the Pelagian Julian of Eclanum, although unable to understand Augustine's Dostoevsky-like profound understanding of the dark side of human beings, was able to cut Augustine's link between sexuality and Augustine's all-too-original notion of "original" sin.

The second essay, on Augustine's Christomorphic theocentrism, addresses the highly controverted issue in Augustine scholarship of whether Augustine's theology is more accurately described as theocentric or Christocentric. This essay argues that Augustinian theology is, at its heart, profoundly theocentric (i.e., a Trinitarian monotheism, classically articulated in Augustine's magnificent theological work, *De Trinitate*). At the same time, Augustine's theocentrism, precisely as Trinitarian, is formed as such by the form (*morphe*) of Jesus Christ. Augustine's theocentrism is, therefore, an unmistakably Christomorphic one. If Augustine had a stronger pneumatology than he did, his fuller position would be *both* Christomorphic *and* spiritus-dynamic. As it stands, Augustine's theology is one of the most powerful Christomorphic theocentrisms in the entire history of Western theology. This is surely one of Augustine's most important contributions to all Christian theology, which must always be theocentric — as Thomas Aquinas stated with characteristic clarity and precision in his description of theology as the study of God and all things as related to God.

Hans Urs von Balthasar acutely observed that in Western Christian theologies (unlike in Eastern Orthodox theologies), a tragedy was the fact that, in both Catholic Scholastic and Protestant scholastic theologies, spirituality (or, in the Reformed tradition, piety) was separated from theology. The fourteenth-century, late Scholastic theologians, especially the nominalists, who had little theological use for metaphysics, made logic and grammar the main philosophical conversation partners with theology. Logic and grammar became, as in Martin Luther, the only philosophical tools that theology should employ. Metaphysical understandings of God and humankind were idols strongly—even violently—to be rejected. In modern Scholasticism, spirituality was no longer intrinsic to theology, as it had been in Alexander of Hales, Thomas Aquinas, Bonaventure, Meister Eckhart, Marguerite Porete, and Duns Scotus—that is, from the confessional era forward to the centuries-long reign of diverse Neo-Scholasticisms in both Catholic and Protestant theologies. In the Catholic context, spirituality became not a distinct dimension of a common theological project, but a separate, basically practice-oriented discipline given such names as ascetic-mystical theologies or "spiritual theology"—now ironically kept distinct from the now purely theoretical and Scholastic theologies.

This move in theology away from spirituality was an intellectual and spiritual disaster for both late Scholastic and later Neo-Scholastic theologies, which reigned supreme in Catholic theology for centuries. Fortunately, there were some notable exceptions (Newman, the Tübingen school) before the great generation of *ressourcement* theology (de Lubac, Daniélou, Bouyer, Congar, Balthasar, et al.) and the equally important rethinking of the positions of Thomas Aquinas's magisterial Scholastic theology as both theoretical and deeply spiritual (Chenu), and as a retrieval of Aquinas's position as a full conversation partner with modern philosophy and theology (especially in German transcendental philosophy and theology in Maréchal, Rahner, Coreth, et al.) and Anglo-American empirical (not empiricist) philosophy and theology (Bernard Lonergan).

That enormously fruitful time in Catholic theology in the early and mid-twentieth century led to the major religious and theological event of modern Christianity: the reforming Second Vatican Council. The theological generations after "the great generations" continued that Vatican II reforming tradition in two major forms, perhaps best represented in two Catholic journals, both with an international editorial board and both publishing in several languages: the earlier progressive journal *Concilium* (Karl Rahner, Yves Congar, Edward Schillebeeckx, Hans Küng, Johann Baptist Metz, Elisabeth Schüssler Fiorenza, Gustavo Gutiérrez, Leonardo Boff, Lisa Soule Cahill, Gregory Baum, Mary Collins, Nicholas Lash, Maria Clara Bingemer, David Tracy, Jon Sorbino, et al.); and the equally excellent, more traditional journal *Communio*

(Hans Urs von Balthasar, Joseph Ratzinger, Henri de Lubac, Louis Bouyer, Jean Daniélou, Avery Dulles, Jean-Luc Marion, Corinne Marion, Jean-Yves Lacoste, Jean-Louis Crétien, Jean-Robert Armogathe, Rémi Brague, et al.).

The theological differences between the two journals can sometimes be quite acute but more usually, in my judgment at least, they can be read as complementary. Among other commonalities, both journals have reunited theology (and philosophy) with "spirituality": in *Concilium*, for the most part, in a more prophetic (mystical-political) way, oriented to social justice and full liberation; in *Communio*, in a more traditionally ecclesial retrieval of the rich and pluralistic Catholic tradition. However, these are different emphases, not exclusivities: the more progressive theologians of *Concilium* also love and retrieve aspects of the great tradition and are also deeply ecclesial, if often in a more critical manner (e.g., *Concilium* includes feminist, womanist, and *mujerista* theologies and the various contextual forms of liberation, political, and public theologies across global Catholicism). The more traditional theologians and philosophers of *Communio* also strongly affirm the modern Catholic social justice tradition, from Pope Leo XIII's *Rerum Novarum* to Pope Francis's encyclical *Laudato Si'* on ecology. Although there are still some Neo-Scholastic theologians who, in effect, continue to separate theology and spirituality, they are now a vociferous minority, unheralded by either the *Concilium* or the *Communio* theologians.

Moreover, in historical studies of the history of Catholic theology before Vatican II, the majority of historical work on medieval theology concentrated on the two-century-long, complex, and deeply impressive development of Scholasticism in the groundbreaking scholarship of Joseph Lottin, Martin Grabmann, and, above all, the inestimable Étienne Gilson—whose work still illuminates the intrinsic intellectual greatness of the high Scholasticism of Thomas Aquinas, that theologian of exceptional lucidity who knew instinctively how to distinguish (not separate) in order to unite. In the same century, Bonaventure cultivated works that were both theoretical (i.e., high Scholastic) and profoundly spiritual (e.g., in his remarkable *Itinerarium mentis in Deum* [*The Mind's Road to God*]).

In the post-Gilson era of medieval study, today's historians of medieval theology, still happily informed by Gilson's magisterial studies, continue to study Scholastic theology as it developed over several centuries, from the proto-Scholasticism of Anselm through that unique, logical master of Scholastic theory, Duns Scotus. At the same time, historians of medieval theology now devote even more scholarly attention to the three non-Scholastic forms of medieval theology: namely, monastic theology (especially in the twelfth century); humanistic theologies (e.g., Alain de Lille), and lay mystical theologies, especially the once-ignored but now-central female mystical theologians, such as Hildegard of Bingen, Mechthild of Magdeburg, Angela of Foligno, Marguerite Porete, and several others.

WILLIAM OF ST. THIERRY

To demonstrate a medieval theology that is principally monastic while also including mystical-theological and even some early Scholastic work, I have chosen William of St. Thierry to study how philosophy, theology, and spirituality could be united into a powerful and believable theology in the late twelfth century.

William of St. Thierry created a complex theology, at once rigorously intellectual and deeply spiritual. In my judgment, William is even more worthy of contemporary theological attention than his friend and mentor, the deeply influential Bernard of Clairvaux, one of the best poetic and experiential theologians of the entire tradition. William shows the remarkable strength of monastic theology.

MARTIN LUTHER

The next essay is on Martin Luther, under the title "Martin Luther's *Deus Theologicus.*" There are very few theologians of whom one can justly state that they are both religious geniuses *and* theological geniuses. Martin Luther, that explosive figure, was a member of that small number in the history of Christian theology—a number that begins with three New Testament texts that express the Christian religion in theological form at its best: the Gospel and First Epistle of St. John, so rightly held by mystics, metaphysicians, and contemplative theologians as the deepest theological Christic vision, and St. Paul's Epistle to the Romans, that dense, magnificent synthesis of the many major elements of Paul's distinctive dialectical theology of Christ Crucified, whereby the Christian lives in Christ (i.e., paradoxically, with fear and trembling in Christ Crucified). It is no surprise that Martin Luther loved and wrote so well on both Romans and Galatians as well as the Gospel of John. Indeed, if all we had left of Christian theology were the Gospel of John and Paul's Epistle to the Romans, we would possess most of what we need to understand Christianity.

There are many aspects of Luther to consider, from his understanding of justification through grace by faith, to his law of the cross, and forward. There are, of course, also many troubling writings of Luther, above all his disgraceful writings on the Jews and the peasants as well as many of Luther's writings on Renaissance popes. Most of those Renaissance popes deserved Luther's sharp, polemical criticism but not the unjust title "Anti-Christ." These are serious flaws in Luther. Nevertheless, the exceptionally passionate and powerful — indeed, magnificent — theology of Martin Luther and his honest, earthy, flamboyant personality fully deserve a name to be rarely used: Martin Luther was both a religious and theological genius.

For my part, as the essay on Luther in this book argues, it is Luther's original, commanding understanding of the Hidden God (in both forms) that I cannot but find unique, persuasive, and in need of close attention by all serious Christians and all those curious to know how Christians understand God to be named both as Incomprehensible (e.g., as Infinite, as in volume 1 of my *Selected Essays, Fragments*), and as Hidden in suffering, pain, and negativity. For Luther, the Infinitely Loving, Trinitarian One is best revealed as the doubly hidden God in the cross of Jesus Christ.

MICHELANGELO BUONARROTI

In late 2017, a distinguished curator of fashion of the New York Metropolitan Museum of Art, Andrew Bolton, contacted me. He explained that he was organizing a large exhibit for May–October 2018 entitled "Heavenly Bodies: The Catholic Imagination and the Arts of Fashion." He also informed me that he had been influenced for the structure of the exhibit, to some extent, by my earlier book, *The Analogical Imagination: Christian Theology and the Culture of Pluralism* (1981).

Andrew Bolton invited me to contribute a preface to the two volumes to be published by the Yale University Press on the exhibit. At first, I turned down his request since, as I explained, I am ignorant of the history of fashion, including the role of fashion in the Catholic tradition. He understood my refusal and informed me that he had already found a scholar of fashion to contribute an essay on that topic. He invited me only to summarize certain aspects of my reading of the Catholic imagination in *The Analogical Imagination* — a book he had clearly read with some care.

I agreed to write the prefatory essay on the Catholic imagination as an analogical imagination in theology and the arts. However, unlike my late good friend Andrew Greeley, I do not believe that only the Catholic theological and artistic imagination is an analogical one. To be sure, I do agree fully with Andrew Greeley that the Catholic imagination is indeed fundamentally an analogical imagination. Moreover, for its full effect, the Catholic analogical imagination must *always* include some necessary dialectical negations within the analogies. As the Fourth Lateran Council (1215) asserted about theological analogy, the greater the similarity, the greater the dissimilarity in any proper analogy between the Infinite, Incomprehensible God and our finite selves.

In fact, beside the strongly analogical and sacramental imagination of Catholicism, there are other theological analogical imaginations: for example, in the Anglican tradition (in the writings of George Herbert, John Donne, T. S. Eliot, Richard Hooker, F. O. Maurice, William Temple, Rowan Williams, John Milbank, Sarah Coakley, et al.); or in Orthodox art and theology, especially Russian Orthodox (in Andrei Rublev, Dostoevsky, the later writings of Tolstoy, Soloviev, Bulgakov, et al.). Furthermore, the work of several Liberal Protestant artists, philosophers, and theologians is, basically, analogical in character (e.g., Friedrich Schleiermacher, Ralph Waldo Emerson, Samuel Taylor Coleridge, Emily Dickinson, William James, Alfred North Whitehead, Charles Hartshorne, John Cobb, and many others). In fact, Christian theological, analogical imaginations are not alone: a good deal of modern Jewish philosophy and theology has often constituted itself in analogical terms: for example, in the writings of Moses Mendelssohn, Hermann Cohen, Martin Buber, Franz Rosenzweig, Paul Mendes-Flohr, Susan Shapiro, and others.

The Catholic imagination therefore is by no means alone among analogical theologies and visions of life. To be sure, the centuries-old Catholic theological tradition has produced many rich and pluralistic forms of a Catholic theological imagination: early Augustine, for example; also Boethius, John Scotus Eriugena, Anselm, William of St. Thierry, Hildegard of Bingen, Bernard of Clairvaux, Mechthild of Magdeburg, Abelard and Héloïse, Thomas Aquinas, Bonaventure, Duns Scotus, René Descartes, Jeanne Guyon, François Fénelon and many, many more, including such contemporary Catholic analogical theologians as Karl Rahner, Bernard Lonergan, Hans Urs von Balthasar, Adrienne von Speyr, Erich Przywara, Henri de Lubac, Louis Bouyer, Hans

Küng, Edward Schillebeeckx, Gustavo Gutiérrez, Maria Clara Bingemer, Francis Schüssler Fiorenza, Joseph Komonchak, and many others. Anyone who has read any one of these Catholic theologians will know two things about them: first, each theologian is quite different, even, at times, oppositional to the others on substantive theological grounds; and second, each has produced a unique form of the Catholic analogical imagination, always including some distinct, necessary dialectical moments encompassed by the analogies. In the arts as well there exists a plurality of Catholic analogical artists. One finds diverse forms of Catholic analogical art, century after century: in music (Palestrina, Mozart, Olivier Messiaen, et al.); in painting (Fra Angelico, Massacio, Botticelli, Giotto, Piero della Francesca, Leonardo da Vinci, Raphael, Caravaggio, Bernini, Rubens, et al.); in literature (Dante, Chaucer, Calderón, Racine, Corneille, Ben Jonson, Gerard Manley Hopkins, Flannery O'Connor, Claudel, Péguy, Waugh, Graham Greene, Muriel Spark, Mary Gordon, and hundreds more); and in fashion (e.g., the papal vestments that the Vatican has loaned to the Metropolitan Museum of Art for Andrew Bolton's exhibit).

In sum (*pace* my late good friend Andrew Greeley): Catholicism is not the *only* great tradition bearing an analogical imagination. At the same time, I join Andrew Greeley (and Andrew Bolton) in affirming that most traditional Catholic art, as well as Catholic literature and painting (e.g., Georges Henri Rouault), are products of the Catholic religiously sacramental and analogical imagination.

The brief essay on Michelangelo in this volume serves, therefore, as a preface to the New York Metropolitan Museum's "Heavenly Bodies" exhibit. To make the discussion of the Catholic imagination more concrete, I have included an interpretation of one of the greatest Catholic artists of the centuries-long Catholic tradition: Michelangelo Buonarroti. Michelangelo—like Dante, Raphael, Caravaggio, and Bernini; like Racine or Calderón, Mozart or Rubens—is one of those rare artists who are not merely good but great, not merely talented but an unrivaled genius. Moreover, Michelangelo's work cannot be fully understood without studying the contextual religious and theological underpinnings embedded in his art in a fashion similar to those of other great artists: Bach's Lutheranism, Rembrandt's Reformed vision, Milton's complex form of Puritanism, Dostoevsky's Russian Orthodoxy; Tolstoy's brilliant personal version of Christianity, and so on. Unfortunately, whenever most art historians interpret Michelangelo, they tend not to interpret either Michelangelo's Neoplatonic philosophy or his quite original version of an Augustinian-Dantean theology. Michelangelo's theology deeply *in*forms, even *trans*forms Michelangelo's unique artistic vision in sculpture, architecture, paintings, and drawings. Fortunately, there are some notable exceptions to the relative silence of most historians of art on Michelangelo's art (the inestimable Edgar Wind, Kenneth Clark, Ingrid Rowland, John O'Malley, and a few others).

Unfortunately, the silence of most art historians on the influence of Michelangelo's theology on his art is more than equaled by the resounding silence of most historians of theology on Michelangelo as a distinct, indeed, original Catholic theologian of the too-little-studied sixteenth-century Catholic Reform movement that included Cardinals Contarini and Pole; theologians like Egidio of Viterbo; and the only Italian, sixteenth-century poet as accomplished as Michelangelo himself, the superb poet and beloved friend of Michelangelo, Vittoria Colonna.

Michelangelo was undoubtedly not only, as all admit, one of the supreme artists of Western culture; he was also an artist deeply informed in philosophy (Neoplatonism learned in his youth) and theology (Augustine, Dante, and the nascent Catholic Reform movement of Contarini, Pole, Vittoria Colonna, and others). To understand Michelangelo fully, one needs scholars in art, in Neoplatonic philosophy, *and* in theology, such as that brilliant *rara avis* John O'Malley. Otherwise Michelangelo's amazing forms of a Catholic analogical imagination will remain forever misidentified. The essay in this volume is a brief attempt to encourage scholars in both art history and the history of theology to provide a fuller artistic, religious, philosophical, and theological accounting of that uniquely great artist, Michelangelo Buonarroti.

CHAPTER I

AUGUSTINE OUR CONTEMPORARY

The Overdetermined, Incomprehensible Self

There are three explicit elements in Augustine's account of the self's interiority: first, intelligence-in-act; second, will as both basic energy-love and free choice; and third, sin, which can becloud the intelligence and entrap the will. There is also a fourth element in the self that is not explicit in Augustine but often haunts his texts: tragedy—that is, some mysterious, inherited necessity causing intense suffering. Together these four elements constitute Augustine's unique model of an overdetermined self.

The first two elements, intelligence and will, are best interpreted through the traditional Catholic nature-grace paradigm. The third element, sin, is best read through the classical Reformed sin-grace paradigm. The fourth element, tragedy, can now be read through what deserves the name "tragedy-grace paradigm." Sometimes the four elements clash with, or even fragment, each other.

Sometimes they tentatively harmonize. There is finally a unified self in Augustine but never a permanently stable self: *cor inquietum*. Precisely through his troubled, restless complexity, Augustine, more than any other ancient Western Christian thinker on the self, remains our contemporary. Part of Augustine's genius was to understand the head and the heart together, never apart. It is necessary first to distinguish each element on its own, however, before one can realize that Augustine's self is penultimately overdetermined and ultimately incomprehensible (i.e., theologically as the *imago dei* of the Incomprehensible God).[1]

AUGUSTINIAN INTELLECTUAL INTERIORITY: THE JOURNEY WITHIN

Augustine, concerned throughout his life with the relation of transient time to eternity, usually preferred temporal metaphors. Surprisingly, however, he chose principally spatial metaphors for understanding our inwardness, our interiority. We can move *upward* (to God) only by moving *within*. When we move *within* we find an inner, cave-like — in fact, abyss-like — space. Eventually we will find, if we travel (temporal) that inner route (spatial) rightly, that we are not alone in our own private space. For Augustine, every self is a unique individual self, but not a private self. In modern terms, there is no purely autonomous self, although, as Paul Tillich sharply formulated it, for the Christian, there is a theonomous (*not* heteronomous) self. Each self, for Augustine, is unique, and its very uniqueness is constituted by relationships through intellect and love to all others and, above all, to God through Christ in the Spirit. Especially in *Confessions*, Augustine believed that he displayed the self discovering through its most inner point — the *acies mundi* — the eternal, changeless Truth. More accurately, for Augustine, it is not so much that we discover God in ourselves as that we find ourselves in God. We are *in* God *with* others. Once again, Augustine

---

1. On the *imago dei*, Augustine is original: he shifts the theological understanding of the *imago* from the Greek emphasis on Christ alone as the *imago* to a Trinitarian *imago* (i.e., to the Father through Christ in the Spirit). As Trinitarian, the *imago* in human beings becomes memory-understanding-will (love). It is, therefore, not accurate to describe and criticize Augustine's *imago* as a mere psychological analogy. It is a theological (i.e., Trinitarian) analogy that yields triads, especially memory-understanding-will (love) in human beings. See Augustine 1991a, esp. 298–303 and 383–88. On the Christomorphic character of Augustine's Trinitarian theocentrism, see Tracy 2008.

ANCIENTS, MEDIEVALS, MODERNS

here prefers *spatial* metaphors even to describe our *temporal*, transient selves, grounded in the timeless, eternal God.

Augustine probably learned the philosophical-theological potentialities of the journey inward from Plotinus and Porphyry. As early as *De libero arbitrio* (Augustine 1956, 2.7.7–2.15.35), Augustine follows Plotinus's advice of moving within himself: classically, he describes the inward journey in the first nine books of *Confessions*.[2] Largely through spatial and temporal metaphors and rhetorical tropes, as much as through rhetorical topical arguments, Augustine confesses God (*confessio* as testimony-witness in prayer) while also confessing his graced and sinful journey to God; then he confesses to himself and to his readers (especially, but not solely, his fellow Christian readers). Augustine keeps moving within until he arrives at the reflections on time (Book 10) and the theological speculations on creation and the created order (Books 11, 12, and 13). Only later in his life, in the more serene sea of contemplation in the final books of *De Trinitate*, does the restless, Augustinian, inward-directed soul come to full contemplative, loving peace and joy by proposing that we search *within* our own deepest graced inwardness — memory, understanding, and will-love — as grounded in the Trinity of infinite intelligence and infinite love: Father, Son, Spirit.

In the splendidly serene Plotinus, as well as in the more anxious Porphyry, the intellectually and morally purified soul on its "journey within" leaves what Augustine, too, will call the "region of dissimilarity" for the highest region available to the self under its own powers: the realm of *nous*, pure intelligence-in-act. There, for Plotinus, the soul must wait for the ultimate possibility (*not* necessity — it may not happen), for the magnetic, radiant Other Power of ultimate reality, the One Good, to draw the self home.

In the realm of *nous*, the intellectually purified, contemplative soul rests and struggles no more. In its earlier, rigorous intellectual and moral exercises of purification, the soul has struggled to reach the realm Aristotle describes as contemplation. For Aristotle, although not for Plato, thought-thinking itself is the ultimate reality as the source and goal of all reality. For Plotinus, in the realm of *nous*, the soul, Odysseus-like, reaches its own natural home. But the

---

2. For *Confessions*, I use the fine, three-volume text and commentary by James J. O'Donnell (1992). Volume 1 is the text and introduction; this volume will be cited parenthetically in the text. For an English translation, see Augustine 1991b.

Plotinian self's truest home is the Ultimate Reality beyond *nous*—the realm of the One and the Good, from which all reality emanates-radiates—to which the self's entire ascent of accelerating intellectual and moral purification is directed, and by which the self is magnetically drawn ever upward.

Plotinus brilliantly unites Plato's Good beyond Being of *Republic* to the one of *Parmenides* to become the Plotinian One Good as our final end, just as it is our source. The contemplative, indeed mystical Plotinian experience of the Good is one that, Porphyry informs us, Plotinus himself experienced only four times during his years with Porphyry (Porphyry 1966, 1:71). Plotinus's mystical experience of the One Good is necessarily transient, yet it does permanently affect the soul-self with a sense of lasting peace, joy, and serenity. Eventually the Plotinian One emanates-radiates impersonally the soul *back* to the realm of *nous* to begin its return descent through all the lower levels of reality, only to begin to ascend anew. Plato was taken in *Republic* to a vision of the Good beyond Being and, in *Symposium*, to the appearance—suddenly—of the beautiful itself. Aristotle, in the view of most Platonists, never reached Plato's Good beyond Being and beyond intelligence. For all post-Plotinus Platonists (later named Neoplatonists), Plotinus, like Plato, had been gifted with the contemplative-mystical vision of the One Good. Some Platonists (e.g., Iamblichus) added theurgy and sacred texts—even magic—to Plotinus's more austere inward journey. Clearly the Plotinian inner journey appealed to Augustine, philosophically Platonist and newly baptized. Now a Christian, Augustine began his Plotinus-like journey within. The self Augustine found in his own journey within was quite different from the Plotinian self. Above all, Augustine in his graced journey moved within to discover not the emanating generous (but unintelligent and unloving) impersonal Good of Plotinus, but the all-intelligent, all-loving, creating, sustaining, redeeming God of the Bible—the God disclosed, in Paul as in Augustine, only in and through Christ ("I no longer live but Christ lives in me": Gal. 2:20).

In *De Trinitate*, the true destiny of Augustine's graced intellectual and loving self can be described not only with the ancient idea of the self as microcosm but also with the biblical idea of the self as *imago dei*. The human being as divine *imago* was probably first experienced by Augustine in a mystical and uniquely dialogical vision he shared with Monnica at Ostia. The Augustinian "drive" from rhetoric, dialectic, and dialogue as the preparatory routes to the highest experience of intelligence-in-act—contemplation—was initiated in his Cassiciacum dialogues. Shortly before that time of *otium* (leisure with friendship and dialogue), Augustine's Christian Platonist contemplative spirit had been released when he first heard the allegorizing sermons of Ambrose. Ambrose's Origenist sermons freed Augustine from despising many biblical texts as too vulgar in their literal sense. Christian Platonists at Milan, especially the bishop, Ambrose, showed Augustine how an allegorical exegesis of the Bible could reveal meditative and contemplative readings of the Scriptures to complement the literal-historical sense of the texts.

Full contemplative intensity came later for Augustine — at its highest in *De Trinitate*. Indeed, the amazing accomplishment of *De Trinitate*, theologically the most profound of Augustine's texts, is that its doctrinally Christian vision (for the importance of the Nicene doctrine, see Ayres 2010, 142–71) — that is, Augustine's Trinitarian, Christological, and Pneumatological interpretation of the Christian vision — was originally inspired by his introspective reading of Paul alongside his interiorized (journey-within) reading of Plotinus from the time of his two conversions: his intellectual conversion (God is pure spirit, not matter), occasioned by reading some books of the Platonists (probably Latin translations of parts of both Plotinus and Porphyry); and his Christian conversion proper, leading up to his baptism (along with his son, Adeodatus) by Ambrose (387). Augustinian contemplation is a profound experience of the participation of the soul's memory, understanding, and will in God's Trinitarian, very own tri-personal Godhead.

THE SELF AS AWAKE: INTELLIGENCE-IN-ACT

Late in his life, Augustine received a letter from a recently converted Christian young man with an intellectual dilemma that he hoped the then internationally famous Christian thinker, Bishop Augustine of Hippo, might resolve. This youthful intellectual — bright, honest, with all the idealism of youth — informed Augustine that he had spent most of his intellectual life reading the philosophers. He was close to giving up in skeptical despair before God's grace caught him up into the truth, that is, the Christian faith. Hence his question to Augustine: Now, on the other side of faith, should he give up philosophy altogether? Does it bear any further use? Perhaps he expected that the famous Catholic bishop, the greatest living defender of the faith, would encourage his desire to abandon argument and philosophy altogether for faith alone. This expectation was to be sharply disappointed. The old bishop wrote back a resounding "No."

Augustine wrote his young correspondent words that Plotinus or, for that matter, Kant, could well have written: *Intellectum valde ama* (Augustine 1895–1923, 2:704–22). Faith was, of course, the revelation of the final truth for Augustine. However, faith must always seek understanding of itself, its intellectual internal and external coherence; faith as reasonable trust must *always* be ready to give reasons for its hope to itself and to outside critics. Faith released a new knowledge and a new, powerful desire always to know more — redirecting, enriching, but never abandoning the employment of all the usual forms of reason. *Fides quaerens intellectum.*

Popular religion, for Augustine, should also become a philosophical religion. Like Origen before him, Augustine believed that the truths revealed by faith made Christianity the true philosophical religion: philosophy for all people, not only for a philosophical elite. For Christian thinkers, popular religion and philosophic religion were not contraries but partners in the same community, grounded in faith. Augustine's earlier, more purely philosophical religion (seen in the dialogues) gradually yielded to a Christian theology that was orthodox, daring, philosophical, and biblical, and, at times, erroneous (e.g., on double predestination). At still other times (e.g., in the debates on the origin of the soul), Augustine, after great efforts and with characteristic intellectual honesty, decided not to decide (Augustine 1913, 303–419).

Since the groundbreaking work of Pierre Hadot (1995) on the role of spiritual exercises in ancient philosophy, it is clear that no one can understand Augustine's diverse uses of reason without realizing that for Augustine, as for his philosophical and theological contemporaries, intellectual exercises like mathematics (especially numbers, for Augustine) and dialectics are not only intellectual exercises (as for most moderns) but also spiritual exercises. This Augustine learned, both intellectually and spiritually, from "some books of the Platonists." Through enacting Platonic dialectic, dialogue, and contemplation, Augustine learned several important intellectualist truths that he never abandoned: God is pure spirit; intellect is spirit, not matter; and the soul is embodied, but as soul (i.e., spirit); it is as accurate to say "ensouled body" as "embodied soul." As the later, more Aristotelian Scholastics would say, one must learn to distinguish — but not separate — soul and body, matter and form, mind and the senses. Above all, the theologian must learn the singular philosophical insight of the intellectualist Platonists on the purely spiritual nature of God and the soul — an insight not shared by materialist Stoics, Epicureans, and Skeptics, or even by some Christian theologians (e.g., Tertullian).

Augustine's reading of the books of "some Platonists" has rightly been described as an "intellectual conversion,"[3] a crucial component in his explicitly Christian conversion (*"Tolle, lege"*) in the garden at Milan. Through the Platonists, Augustine now grasped that his former Manichean- and Stoic-influenced, materialist understanding of God and the soul was erroneous.

The shift in Augustine's new Platonist understanding of the soul-mind led him to hold that the true power of the intellect reaches beyond the senses and matter to the purely intelligible world of mathematics, dialectic, metaphysics, and theology. Mind (*mens*), as intelligence-in-act, is able, through its various reasoning processes, to understand the intelligible forms of sensuous, bodily, spatial, and temporal realities, as well as the ideas or forms of such purely intelligible realities as forms or ideas of the mind itself, and to attain, in its highest moments of graced contemplation, some understanding of the supreme Forms or Ideas, which are, Christianly construed, Ideas in the mind of God.

For the philosophically mature Augustine, the mind — through its exercises of attentive intelligence-in-act — was capable of producing both a genuine *scientia* of bodily, sensuous things and a *sapientia*, or wisdom, about the first principles of reason. At the limit, the mind, through its finite participation in divine infinite intelligence, could, through both apophatic and cataphatic analogous theological understanding, come to an always inadequate but real and partial understanding of God as the Incomprehensible One — incomprehensible as infinite intelligence-in-act and infinite love. Moreover, a theological understanding of God's incomprehensibility can lead a Christian thinker to realize that the human being, by its very *imago dei* participation in the incomprehensible loving God, is itself, in its own finite way, *also* incomprehensible, as manifested in its distinctive and amazing human powers of intelligence and love. Completely unlike the infinite God, however, finite human intelligence and love as

---

3. This does not mean, *pace* Alfaric et al., that Augustine's real conversion was to Platonism, as Augustine makes clear in *Confessions*. This important intellectual conversion needed prayer, scripture reading, and baptism in order to become a full Christian conversion. Amid the vast literature on the topic of Augustine and Platonism, see Crouse (2000, 37–50) and Reale (1995).

finite can become, through sin (original and personal), as we shall see later, also negatively incomprehensible—a smoldering abyss of self-enclosed and self-deluding egocentricity.

Both the depth of Augustine's philosophical and theological acuity (e.g., on the nature of *memoria*) (Wills 1999, 88–97) and the range of the forms of intellect that he mastered are amazing. Throughout his life, Augustine engaged in argument in both rhetorical and dialectical forms: in dialogue with friends; in fierce polemical arguments when he thought them appropriate (perhaps too often); and above all in the contemplative intelligence-in-act embedded in his Plotinus-like journey within. Like Plotinus or, for that matter, like Gautama Buddha (whose very name means Awakened One), Augustine understands intelligence-in-act as an awakening. Augustine helps his readers to be attentive, to awaken from their customary, everyday slumbers and self-occlusion. Reason, for Augustine, is an always awakening intelligence-in-act.

This Augustinian intellectualist self should not lead one to downplay the important role of will or love. The desire for the Good drives the desire to know, not the reverse. Without abandoning his intellectualism, Augustine also never lost his artist's instinct for being able to think through image and metaphor. Nor did he lose his erotic, passionate instinct for the cognitive role of affect, feeling, emotion, and will. At heart, Augustine was a rhetorician—indeed, the best Latin rhetorician of his day, and the best rhetorical theologian of *any* day. Gregory Nazianzen, his contemporary and another major rhetorical theologian, was his only Greek rival as a rhetorical theologian. Even the wisely allegorical sermons and treatises of Ambrose, even the sermons of the golden-mouthed John Chrysostom, and finally even Gregory Nazianzen's brilliant rhetorical and lyrical theological élan were no match for the many-sided, protean Augustine.

Augustine's native talent for rhetoric, combined with his Latin literary education, trained him to possess a second self—an artistic-rhetorical-poetic self. Well educated in a Roman, literary, rhetorical tradition, although mostly self-taught in philosophy, Augustine, the former professor of rhetoric, never abandoned his call, even after his intellectualist, Platonic discovery of a purely intelligible world available to reason not through rhetoric, but only through mathematics, dialectics, metaphysics, and contemplation.

There are, to be sure, better dialectical and theoretical theologians than Augustine (e.g., the ever-lucid Thomas Aquinas). And there are greater contemplative theologians than Augustine, especially in the Greek tradition (e.g., Origen, Gregory of Nyssa, Dionysius the Areopagite, Maximus the Confessor). However, no other rhetorical theologian, however accomplished—Gregory Nazianzen, Bernard of Clairvaux, Teresa of Ávila, Blaise Pascal, Søren Kierkegaard, John Henry Newman—can capture such sudden, unexpected moments of lightning brilliance in metaphor and irony, in image and concept, in narrative and theory.

Most of Augustine's arguments (save a few more strictly metaphysical arguments on God) are, in both the Ciceronian and Aristotelian senses, usually *topical* arguments in rhetoric and dialectic: that is, as Aristotle clearly states, arguments on contingent matters, which might be other than they are, not necessary ones. Some postmodern thinkers (Julia Kristeva, Jean-François Lyotard, Jacques Derrida), with characteristic postmodern emphasis on the rhetoric of the tropes rather than on their topics, highlight just how radically rhetorical Augustine often is—tropically, not only topically. Like those of the postmoderns, Augustine's tropes often control his topics, not the reverse. Augustine—like Plato himself, far more than later Platonists, such as Pascal, Kierkegaard, Newman, and Simone Weil—was that rarity: a major philosopher-theologian, expert in analyzing and developing abstract concepts (e.g., time, will, memory, creation, sin, grace), who was also a major artist. Augustine, like Plato and unlike most philosophers and theologians, was more like the great philosophical artists (Aeschylus, Sophocles, Lucretius, Hildegard of Bingen, Dante, Donne, Goethe, Dostoevsky, Eliot), who could think not only through concepts but also through images (*carthago-sartago*, the "cave" of memory, the "abyss" of the will, the "weight" of love). Augustine often enacted his arguments narratively—for example, through the Virgilian musical rhythms that served as an undertow in *Confessions*, or the outbursts of lyricism in his wondrous commentaries on Psalms, through the sustained Roman gravitas of *City of God*, through the almost baroque contemplative leaps of *De Trinitate*, indeed, through all the registers of the Latin language with Tacitean lucidity and precision—the Ciceronian rolling thunder of his cumulative sentences, and his proto-Romantic, restless sensibility breaking through his impeccable late-antique Latin prose. Save for his polemical works, content in Augustine always finds itself only in and through form.

As a natural and trained rhetorician, Augustine was language-intoxicated (Burton 2007). He swam in all the major linguistic streams: metaphor and irony; metonymy, narrative, paradox, didacticism; rhetoric, dialectic, dialogue. Augustine never stopped believing that intelligence-in-act is one of our greatest gifts and must never be disparaged.[4] Only intelligence-in-act can be trusted to awaken us and keep us awake. Intelligence in all its forms, for Augustine, acknowledges that all is grace, including its own stunning powers and its greatest power — its ability to acknowledge its own limits, not through its flaws but through its very strength. *Intellectum valde ama.*

THE SELF AS WILL AND LOVE: WILL AS ENERGY, WILL AS FREE CHOICE

Augustine is the first philosopher to elaborate a full-fledged concept of will as central for understanding the self (Dihle 1982). And yet there is no systematic definition of will in this unique philosopher of will. In fact, Augustine uses "will" (*voluntas, arbitrium*) in different ways. Faithful to his own restless will, as described in *Confessions*, Augustine's plural understandings of will are differently articulated depending on context: will as free choice and consent, free will, will as energy, the will's basic energy as love, the two wills or loves at war in history, as in each of us (*caritas* and *cupiditas*).

Many discussions of Augustine's concepts of the will have been distracted by trying to render into a single, coherent statement his different, sometimes conflicting reflections on "free will," from his early work *De libero arbitrio* to his later, bleak understanding of the "bondage of the will." In *The Retractions*, Augustine strongly maintained that Pelagius and Julian of Eclanum had no right to appeal to his early discussion of free will as evidence against his later reflections on the bondage of the will (Augustine 1968). Appearances to the contrary notwithstanding, the old Augustine insisted that he still held to his earlier *De libero arbitrio* affirmation of free will. In fact, however, Pelagius and Julian were not without a point. It is unclear how, exactly, Augustine could render other than roughly and paradoxically coherent his earlier strong insistence on the freedom of the will and his later equally strong position on the bondage of the will.

At the same time, Julian's polemic against Augustine failed to understand Augustine's deeper philosophical and theological reflections on the energy of reality itself as will, and that universal energy as ultimately "will as divine love."

---

4. This pervasive interiority can be seen as early as the dialogue of Augustine on reason itself (see Augustine 1986a, 3–98).

Moreover, Augustine understood "the will" to possess a conflictual, abysmal dimension that Pelagius's and Julian's untroubled, easily unified, strongly moralistic notion of the self did not, perhaps could not, grasp. Jane Austen would probably have dismissed the view of the passionate, conflicted self in the Brontë sisters as so much romantic nonsense; Vladimir Nabokov never could accept Dostoevsky's irredeemably conflictual self. American ego-psychologists never seem to be within shouting distance of understanding Jacques Lacan's brilliant and persuasive interpretation of Freud's radical uncovering of an always-already split conflictual self. The ego-psychologists domesticated an abysmal truth of the Freudian self just as some Christian philosophers and theologians (e.g., Malebranche) domesticated Augustine's disturbing portrait of the always split self. John Dewey never understood why some of his fellow liberal theorists found Reinhold Niebuhr's still politically liberal but far bleaker, Augustinian, *City of God*–inflected portrait of both self and history in *The Nature and Destiny of Man* (vols. 1 and 2) far more realistic than Dewey's own more benign secular view of self and history alike; hence, the ironic paradox of "atheists for Niebuhr." As William James observed in *The Varieties of Religious Experience*, healthy-minded souls and sick souls are destined to misunderstand one another (classically and fatally Pelagius and Augustine).

A modern analogy: To use classical psychoanalytic terms, there is no unconscious for Pelagius, whereas the will as the unconscious force driving us forward for good and ill is omnipresent in Augustine. Simultaneously, the unconscious for Freud, like the will driving as energy for Augustine, is a realm of depth. For Augustine, the embodied will is the space of the many unconscious affects, feelings, emotions, and desires constituted both by the will itself as the energy-power of love (*eros* and *agape*) (for references, see Tracy 2005) and by the constant to-and-fro movements of its own restlessness and ambivalence. The primal will in Augustine, like the unconscious in Freud, is fully alive, manifesting a *fascinans et tremendum* power-energy underlying and driving the conscious will. It is ultimately not impossible to affirm both the conscious freedom of the will and the unconscious bondage of the will, although their multiple interactions, like the interactions of the superego, ego, and id in the later Freud, are so intertwined as to need some adjective like Freud's fine adjectival choice — "overdetermined" — to describe our motives. *Overdetermined*, indeed, is the most accurate adjective I know to describe Augustine's self as abyss.

One of Augustine's sharpest portraits is his picture of the unstoppable power of the will: "*Pondus meum, amor meus*" (*Confessions* 13.9.10) — my weight is my love; my desire, my affects, emotions, feelings, and moods; my unconscious, preconscious, and conscious will is my weight—a weight that can draw me up like a flame or hurl me down like a gravity-laden falling rock. Love-will is the affective weight that pulls me to itself, often against my conscious will and intention. When "in" love, we simultaneously feel liberated, more alive, more intelligent, and in bondage to the beloved object. As Lady Caroline Lamb is supposed to have cried out in the moment she first saw Lord Byron across a filled reception-hall: "That face is my fate." Indeed it was, with disastrous results for both Lady Caroline and Byron. Augustine, unlike Pelagius and other moralists, would not have been surprised.

The will as affects, moods, and choices (rational and irrational) can become so habitual as to become a second nature: a habitual evil (vice) or a habitual good (virtue). As Aristotle sharply pointed out, it is as difficult for a habitually good person of virtue to do evil as for a habitually evil person to do good.

We live in boxes within boxes within boxes, where the outermost box—choice as freedom of the will—is actual enough but fragile, and is often hostage to our vices-habits-addictions (our second nature) and to the fundamental and largely preconscious—even unconscious—powers of desire, more than we want to believe. Most of us are relatively helpless in freeing ourselves from authentic addictions (drugs, alcohol, smoking, etc.) solely on our own. Addictions literally take over the self. Addictions are the exact negative opposite of Paul's great cry of liberation: "No longer I but Christ lives in me!" (Gal. 2:20). At the same time, for Augustine, God's grace lives in the ever-flowing grace of the human desire for the Good. Even at our most perverse, other-denying, other-destructive, and self-destructive moments, we can suddenly have experiences, times out of time, that serve as epiphanic "hints and guesses" (Eliot) of the Good or God, drawing us unconsciously forward.

Even more than Plato in *Symposium*, Augustine dramatically portrayed the power of beloved objects to attract us like a magnet: the beautiful physical bodies of others; the spirit-filled intellects of beautiful souls; the night sky; the North African sun; the harvest thick in the fields; the gentle sea breezes from the Mediterranean on a summer's day in Hippo that become a sudden, violent storm; the haunting emptiness of the desert; the fecundity of the rainy season. More realistically than Plotinus, the more body-conscious and affect-laden Augustine demonstrated over and over just how strongly our five basic loves—for God, neighbor, self, mind, body—have allowed us to experience the desire for the Good deep within us driving us as God's own magnetic grace in us, of which we may remain unconscious. Authentic loves, desires, and affections leap upward like a flame to *agapic* wisdom. The thrill of beauty in the arts — music especially, for Augustine — frees us to experience, however transiently, the beautiful as goodness and truth. Augustine, so alive to his own and others' shifting moods, affects, and will, was, in one way, a kind of romantic *avant la lettre*. He was, for example, so disturbed to discover music's power over him that he briefly considered banning it. For Augustine, the deepest reality in us is the affect-laden will-desire for the Good, which ultimately, as divine providence, determines all reality, despite all the swerves of chance, fate, and fortune. Nature-grace is ultimately deeper and more powerful than sin-grace, joy than sorrow, peace than conflict, yes than no.

For Augustine, the will for the Good is, as much as for Dante, the most powerful force in our lives and in the cosmos itself. Above all, will as love is the most basic energy in human reality, as it is in reality itself, because love is the very reality of God in Godself: God is Love (see Augustine's commentary on the First Letter of John) (Augustine 1986a, 501–8). Even understanding is driven by love; love's affections contain understanding. The desire for the Good (will-love) drives what Bernard Lonergan named the pure, detached, unrestricted, disinterested desire to know. Affections, for Augustine, are not some pleasant addition to or distraction from understanding. Like Heidegger, whose early work up to and including *Sein und Zeit* was deeply influenced by Augustine (Heidegger 1995, 160–299), Augustine held — contrary to many Platonists — that affects, morals, and feelings bore cognitive value. For Augustine, intellectual attention must always be paid to our affects, our feelings, our desires — in a word, our will. The will, with or without conscious choice, cannot but keep on willing. Love, like faith and hope, drives understanding. *Fides quaerens intellectum* is simultaneously *Amor quaerens intellectum*, as some medieval Augustinians made explicit: Gregory the Great, in *Amor ipse notitia est*, and William of St. Thierry in *Amor ipse intellectus est*.

In Augustine the intelligent, conscious, deliberative will is, by nature, free in its choices. Therefore, the will in its freedom of choice does not merely choose but also consents to its choice. And yet rumbling, sometimes thundering beneath all choice, sometimes suddenly flashing out of nowhere, the unconscious will wills. To repeat: the will wills; the will cannot *but* will. The will as preconscious desire and unconscious inexorable energy cannot stop willing. In Augustine, we can best understand the ultimately Real less by reflecting on the external cosmos than by turning inward into a *tremendum et fascinans* discovery of the abyss of the self, where eventually we find the will in all its conflictual complexity willing: "The human being is a vast deep. . . . The hairs of our heads are easier by far to number than are our feelings and the movements of the heart" (*Confessions* 4.14.22).

Unfortunately, Augustine knew only partly the highly original readings of his more optimistic Greek contemporary, Gregory of Nyssa, for whom the self's will is a stretching out (*epectasis*) in never-ending, loving contemplation and reaching toward God. Via *epectasis*, Gregory daringly affirms, the will continues even after this life (we experience not eternal rest, therefore, but eternal *epectasis*). If Augustine had known Gregory's brilliant notion of the contemplative will as always-already *epectasis* stretching out forever in even more *epectasis*,[5] one wonders if this uniquely Nyssan reading might have given Augustine a way to interpret his ineradicable restlessness — as a constant stretching out of mind and will-love for more of God's infinite gift-grace of love. Restlessness is, to be sure, often negative, as it was for Augustine, but it can also be a positive affect, as it was for Gregory of Nyssa.

Augustine's account of will, however, did not include Gregory of Nyssa's *epectasis* or, for that matter, the more positive reading of the will adopted by most Greek Christians (with a few exceptions, such as Macarius). At the same time, Augustine's portrait of the will, unlike that in so many modern accounts of the will (above all, Nietzsche's), is, like that of the Greeks and unlike Nietzsche's, always purposeful. For Augustine, even in choosing the wrong object of love, a person still purposively wills the good.

The contrast between will in Augustine and Nietzsche clarifies both. Nietzsche's will is a driving, endless energy, a power without beginning, without end, without purpose. Will, for Augustine, is likewise, before and beyond intelligence, the driving energy of all reality, but Augustine's will is fully purposeful as the love of God that, for the Christian, is the source and end of all reality.

Nietzsche, the most influential philosopher of the will in modernity, in his various artistic enactments of will as Will to Power, found it impossible not to attack violently Augustine's radically opposed Christian notion of will as love. For both thinkers, will as pure energy is reality; for both, will is power; but that power, for Augustine, is not the purposeless energy of Schopenhauer and

---

5. A modern interpreter can see, following Jean Daniélou's classic analysis of *epectasis*, that *epectasis* is very like the notion of spiritual exercise described by Pierre Hadot (1995).

Nietzsche or the *Liebestod* of Wagner and other Romantics, but the engifted, gracious, other-driven and other-directed "love of God and love of neighbor" that in *De doctrina christiana* Augustine dares to make the working canon (perhaps the canon within the canon) for interpreting all Scripture. Not surprisingly, almost all Nietzsche's references to Augustine are negative. And yet, given that Augustine was Nietzsche's unwelcome predecessor on the centrality of will as the energy driving all reality, Nietzsche might well have written of Augustine what he wrote about one of the most authentic heirs of the Augustinian model of the conflicted self *grandeur et misère* in the modern period, Blaise Pascal: "Whatever else be true, Pascal is in all our blood." More than any thinker on the will prior to Nietzsche, Augustine, the first major philosopher of will, is in the blood of all of us, philosophers and theologians alike, whether, with Pascal, we affirm or, with Nietzsche, reject his portrait of the will.

In Western Christianity itself, Augustine's interpretation of the will as love had profound consequences. Recall only the most famous heirs of Augustine's interpretation of will as love: Gregory the Great, Bernard of Clairvaux, William of St. Thierry, the Victorines, all the love mystics; Bonaventure (*"bonum diffusivum sui"*), Dante (*"L'amor che move il sole e l'altre stelle"*), the Love-saturated Teresa of Ávila, who called *Confessions* her second scripture; John Donne ("[Lord, unless] you enthrall me, [I] never shall be free, / Nor ever chaste, except you ravish me"); Pascal (*"Le coeur a ses raisons que la raison ne connaît point"*); George Herbert (in his classic poems on love); Søren Kierkegaard (in his extraordinary *Works of Love*); Simone Weil (in her *agapic*, mystical experience occasioned by reading George Herbert's poem "Love"); and Pope Benedict XVI (in his theologically acute encyclical, *Deus Est Caritas*). The list of Augustinians writing on love could easily be extended. In fact, the Augustinian synthesis on love as *caritas* has served as the now-familiar Western Christian Catholic *caritas* synthesis, wherein *agape* transforms but does not reject *eros*. More than any other theologian, Augustine so defines the classical Catholic Christian understanding on love that Anders Nygren's brilliant but wrong-headed 1930 attack on Augustine's *caritas* synthesis (Nygren 1982, 136; Burnaby 2007; Burnaby 1954–55, 1:85–92) occasioned critical responses from almost every major theologian of two generations, whatever their other differences: Karl Barth, Rudolf Bultmann, Paul Tillich, William Temple, Karl Rahner, Hans Urs von Balthasar, Bernard Lonergan, Werner Jeanrond, as well as several philosophers, including Max Scheler, Hannah Arendt, and Paul Ricoeur.

Intelligence-in-act and will-as-love: these two central realities are so interwoven in Augustine that they can be distinguished but never separated. Nevertheless, another reality — sin — enters this Augustinian interweaving of intelligence and love to darken, wound, and becloud knowledge as it twists the will from its natural desire to love the Good into something defined by false loves. Sin, both personal and original, invades and at times overwhelms the convalescent Augustinian self. The will becomes not only weak and fragile (as the will always was for Augustine), but also sinful. In the "region of dissimilarity," the will as love becomes twisted almost beyond recognition, as it is distorted more and more by unending false desires become unbreakable addictions (see Bonner 2007 for a persuasive reading and the myriad relevant references). Even before the Pelagian controversy, Augustine began to fear that something was awry about the self, however intelligent, however loving. Reading Paul, in what came to be known as the Augustinian "introspective" manner, Augustine believed that Paul confirmed his own fears in words that seemed to be directly addressed to him: "The good that I would do, that I do not; the evil I would not do, that I do" (Rom. 7:19).

Without Augustine's ever abandoning the nature-grace model (the intelligent-loving self described thus far), another Augustinian element in the self surfaced more and more: a self not just positively constituted by its love for neighbor and through its love for God, and thereby also by a love for one's authentic loving self, but a self now sinking, as in quicksand, into an inescapable solidarity-in-sin with others — the self finding very crowded company as it sinks, the *massa peccati*.

THE SIN-SATURATED SELF: SIN AND GRACE IN AUGUSTINE

As scholars of early modernity have argued, the sixteenth century was profoundly influenced by Augustine both in the Renaissance (e.g., in Petrarch, Ficino, Erasmus, Montaigne, Shakespeare) and in the Protestant and Catholic Reformations. That conflict-ridden century ("early modernity") should be read not only as a fierce conflict of interpretations of how to read Scripture, especially Paul, properly, but also as an equally intense conflict about how to read Augustine rightly: Is Augustine on the self best understood through the Renaissance (both Catholic and secular) paradigm of nature-grace in continuity with the medievals? Or is he better understood through the sixteenth-century Protestant Reformers and the seventeenth-century Jansenist paradigm of sin-grace? Both paradigms can justly appeal to important texts of Augustine. In *Confessions*, for example, the primary paradigm is nature-grace (or graced human nature as intelligence-in-act and will-love). Confession, for Augustine, is principally testimony and praise to God for all his gifts (intelligence, love, friendship, learning, etc.) and only secondarily confession of Augustine's own sins to God as well as to the community, to himself, and to any reader of the text. In sum, the theocentric priority (Tracy 2008) in Augustine's *Confessions* is the exact opposite of the anthropocentric, indeed egocentric, model initiated in modernity by Rousseau's *Confessions*. Sin-grace often interrupts the nature-grace continuities of Augustine's narrative: "The enemy held my will; and of it he made a chain and bound me. Because my will was perverse it changed to lust, and lust yielded to become habit, and habit not resisted became necessity. They were like links hanging one on another—which is why I have called it a chain—and their hard bondage held me bound hand and foot" (*Confessions* 8.5.10). This is the Augustine who attracted Martin Luther in his even more radical sin-grace reading of the bondage of the will.

The paradigm of nature-grace for most medieval and High Renaissance thinkers and artists, before the more sin-grace-infused works of the later Michelangelo (the *Last Judgment*, the unfinished sculptures), illuminated the continuities they found between our nature as intelligence-in-act and affective loving will as both *eros*-love and God's *agapic* grace (e.g., in Marsilio Ficino, Raphael, and the early Michelangelo). Indeed, as Karl Rahner well observed, the graced nature of intelligence-in-act and will-as-love is our concrete actuality; what we often call "nature" is merely a useful abstraction (a "remainder concept," in Rahner's phrase). The classical Protestant Reformers, however, especially that explosive religious and theological genius Martin Luther, as well as the more humanist, more systematic reformers, but hardly less radical John Calvin, rejected the traditional medieval and contemporary Renaissance humanist paradigm of nature-grace for understanding the human situation as well as for reading Augustine himself in favor of the sin-grace paradigm, which alone could probe the radicality of the sin-saturated self (bondage for the will, self-delusion for the intellect). Both Luther and Calvin believed Augustine's anti-Pelagian texts on the sinful self were the most important formulation of Augustine's model of the self, as well as the most accurate reading of our existential state since St. Paul himself in Romans and Galatians. For Luther, and even more for Calvin, the intellect was a very useful tool for logical analysis, for formulating arguments against opponents, and (for Calvin and Melanchthon) for a theological ordering of the principal theological *topoi* into a coherent, Lutheran and Reformed systematic theology. On strictly theological — that is, existentially salvific — matters, however, reason was powerless. Luther held that, on strictly theological matters, "the whore reason" (especially Aristotle) was useless. Analogously, on the will, Martin Luther, in his famous polemic against the Catholic Reformer and humanist Desiderius Erasmus, violently insisted on the total bondage of the will against Erasmus's defense of free will.

Paradoxically, the more humanistically (logically and rhetorically) educated John Calvin went even further than Luther by claiming that, however useful reason clearly was for many purposes, unaided metaphysical reason, especially in its Scholastic ("sophistical") versions, was basically useless on questions of understanding the nature and attributes of God. Indeed, Calvin once stated that, on these matters, reason was nothing other than "a factory for making idols." Far more radically than Calvin himself, the later seventeenth-century Reformed theologians at the Synod of Dort denounced Arminius's defense of free will and proclaimed their own doctrine of the total depravity of the will, double predestination, and irresistible grace as central beliefs of the Reformed (or Calvinist) tradition. It should be emphasized, however, that Calvin himself was not necessarily a Calvinist at the Synod of Dort. In fact, Calvin's own principal theological emphasis, despite his affirmation of the "terrible decree" of double predestination, was not the same as that of the Synod of Dort but was a theological portrait of God as gracious and loving sovereign Father (Steinmetz 1995 and 2001), even given the mystery of the "terrible decree" of predestination, which was to be not understood but held in faith.

Augustine's own understanding of the sin-saturated self deepened with the years. As early as 397, Augustine analyzed the weak and sin-inflected will in his responses to the questions of Simplicianus. A sense of the will's actual bondage became far more radicalized in his later anti-Pelagian writings. Originally, Augustine responded nonpolemically to Pelagius's lucid, if rather complacent, moralistic analysis of the will, its freedom, and its rather facile ability to be reformed through moral effort. Modern "moral rearmament" is a Pelagian banner. Pelagius was an impressive moral reformer (Bonner 1972; repr. in Bonner 1987). He believed the self had a weak will that needed grace, of course, but above all, moral strengthening through moral self-discipline aided by grace. Augustine and Pelagius never met personally. Unfortunately, Augustine was away at a conference of bishops when Pelagius tried to visit him on his way to Jerusalem. Pelagius and Augustine did, however, correspond and did read each other's work. Their first correspondence shows a polite, restrained dialogical disagreement that only later became a disastrous polemical fight to the death. Pelagius, an empirical and British moral reformer, was a favorite of Christian aristocratic circles in Rome. Augustine, on the contrary, was neither principally a moral reformer nor a favorite of Roman aristocratic circles. Augustine was a passionate Latin African beyond the moral horizon of these circles.[6] Augustine was a radically religious and theological genius who would have no truck with Pelagius's position, which inevitably seemed to him at best naive, at worst perverse and heretical. Why, Augustine pointedly demanded of Pelagius, did the church baptize infants if there is no original sin?

In reading Pelagius's responses to Augustine, one cannot avoid the impression that Pelagius never really grasped what — or whom — he was dealing with: an Augustine whose portrait of a sinful self was so conflicted that, once examined by a journey within, sin revealed abyss upon abyss in the self, wherein an ineradicably conflicted, self-trapped ego could never be saved — or even diagnosed properly — by any Pelagian moral self-reform. As Peter Brown well observed, Pelagius and many other contemporaries of Augustine were as shocked by and uncomprehending of Augustine's unnerving vision of a seething, untamable, conflicted self as Sigmund Freud's contemporary Viennese psychologists and moral reformers were by Freud's discovery of an unconscious (Brown 2000, 368), which shattered their much easier psychologies of the self and its discontents as so many toys.

In the last years of his long life, Augustine had to deal not with the very decent, well-mannered, polite, if evasive, moral reformist Pelagius, but with a new generation of far more fierce Pelagians. Julian of Eclanum, a south Italian aristocratic bishop, was a celebrated young dialectician and committed Pelagian moralist (for a defense of Julian, see Lössl 2001). Indeed, Julian, like Pelagius, was an admirable ethical Christian — for one example, Julian contributed most of his personal wealth to the poor of Sicily. In many ways, Julian, like Pelagius in an earlier generation, was an admirable moral Christian reformer of a familiar type that still exists today. What Julian preached for was Christian moral reform as outlined by Pelagius. What Julian preached against was Augustine.

---

6. The tone of Augustine's initial criticisms of Pelagius does not demonstrate the violent polemics that eventually took over, especially when Julian of Eclanum entered the controversy. For Augustine on Pelagius himself, see "Against Two Letters of the Pelagians," "On Grace and Free Will," and "On Rebuke and Grace" in Augustine 1971, 374–492.

Even more than Pelagius himself, Julian of Eclanum found repulsive Augustine's depiction of a human being as so ridden with sin that no combination of "just enough" grace and "just enough" moral self-discipline would solve the problem.

As in so many polemical exchanges, the increasingly violent polemics between Julian and Augustine displaced any hope of dialogical argument. Neither Augustine nor Julian was at his best in these bitter, brittle exchanges. Julian, a first-rate dialectician, used his argumentative skills very well, but he also made some mean-spirited, *ad hominem* attacks on the elderly Augustine — telling Augustine, for example, to go back to his Punic donkeys as "the Punic Aristotle" and leave civilized Christians (i.e., Italian Romans) at peace. Julian's ultimate insult, however, was not ethnic but deeply theological: over and over, Julian tormented Augustine with the unnerving charge that the old Augustine was no longer a Christian but had returned to his Manicheanism through his relentlessly pessimistic reading of the human condition, especially of human sexuality. For Julian, the bizarre Augustinian reading of original sin as transmitted through the sexual intercourse of our parents sounded too much like a Manichean detestation of flesh, sex, and, at the limit, matter itself.

Julian was not without a point, but it was not one that Augustine would ever grant. Augustine did not need his extreme views on sexuality to defend his complex, perhaps overdetermined theological view of the human condition. But Augustine would not retreat. The tragedy deepened: the more Julian attacked Augustine for excessive statements on our sin-saturated, guilt-ridden, concupiscent self, the more Augustine responded with even more excessive statements, not (as his admirers like myself still wish he had done) by moderating some of his judgments, especially on sexuality, while still maintaining his basic vision of the overdetermined will.

Julian's combination of dialectical skill and *ad hominem* insults provoked the now elderly and exhausted Augustine into a fury, at times almost a frenzy, as he flailed out at Julian, never once moderating even some of his in fact extreme and unnecessary positions, but instead making them yet more radical and provocative.[7] Did Augustine really need to insist upon double predestination? Did

---

7. This increasingly polemical stance against Julian of Eclanum begins in two letters against the Pelagians and lasts until the very end of the unfinished work against Pelagius in *Opus Imperfectum*. See "The Spirit and the Letter," "Nature and Grace," and "The Deeds of Pelagius," in Augustine 1997, 150–202, 225–75, 336–81.

ANCIENTS, MEDIEVALS, MODERNS

he need his humanly repulsive teaching that infants who died without baptism are damned? Did he need to declare that his position on original sin in human-kind can be demonstrated by the (masculinist) observation that, in the sexual act, a human being loses reason, the characteristic that distinguishes him from all the other animals (since a male cannot control his erections as Augustine believed Adam apparently did before the Fall). In the sexual act, for Augustine, a human being become merely another animal bereft of reason's control of the passions. Above all, did he need to hold that original sin was transmitted sexually — a position with devastating effects to this day on the attitude of some Christians to sexuality.

And yet, and yet these famous, late Augustinian outbursts were not the only moments of Augustine's later life. Indeed, when one reads the recently discovered letters and sermons of Augustine,[8] one can easily agree with Peter Brown that the elderly Augustine was not just the shrill anti-Pelagian polemicist of legend, or even the angry old bishop Peter Brown himself had earlier portrayed. In fact, to his pluralistic congregation at Hippo, Augustine was always deeply pastoral — compassionate yet just; strong but gentle; above all, pastorally under-standing of human fragility and the all-too-human need for consolation. As refugees poured into Hippo during the last twenty years of Augustine's life after the Vandal seizure of Rome (410 CE), and as the barbarian armies ad-vanced mercilessly across North Africa, ever closer to Hippo, the pastor-bishop Augustine at the very end of his life did all he could to comfort and to protect his people. The people of Hippo were justly terrified of the future. The old Augustine (who died as the Vandals were laying siege to Hippo) refused to leave his people for safety elsewhere, as some other North African bishops did.

Whatever else was true of the old Augustine, he never lacked courage — physical or moral. The old Augustine remained at the end of his bishopric as he was at the beginning: sometimes stern but always compassionate for all his parishioners, especially for the poor and the marginalized. Concurrently, the late Augustine remained a fierce polemicist, especially against Julian of Eclanum. As with Augustine's earlier, deeply unfortunate, and seemingly atypical appeal to coercion against the Donatists, as well as the accelerating bitterness of his fierce exchanges with Julian demonstrated, Augustine was altogether too

---

8. On the importance of the recently discovered sermons (by François Dolbeau) and letters (by Johannes Divjak) for reinterpreting the pastoral, nonpolemical character of Augustine in his later years, see "Epilogue," in Brown 2000, 440–513.

uncompromising a person ever to be sentimentalized in his old age as anything remotely like a mellow old man.

Fierce polemicist he remained. At the same time, Augustine was too good a pastor in his unflagging pastoral activity for his people to have his last days remembered only for his slash-and-burn, take-no-prisoners polemical exchanges with Julian. Not only did Augustine develop an overdetermined model of the self; he was himself an overdetermined character. Taken as a whole—early, middle, and late—Augustine is something like a character out of Dostoevsky. Over the years, Augustine seemed unconsciously to display the polyphonic voices and multiple selves of all the Karamazovs—Ivan, Dimitri, Alyosha, and even at times the repulsive father Karamazov (for Mikhail Bakhtin on Dostoevsky, see "Dostoevsky's Poetics," in Clark and Holquist 1984, 238–52).

Augustine, like Dostoevsky, forces his attentive reader into facing several ordinarily unacknowledged, because undesirable, actualities about the self. A concealed part of the incomprehensible self for Augustine is an abyss that many may prefer not to notice or even to hear about. In an analogous manner, Virginia Woolf elicits what can happen to non-Russian readers when they first read the great unnerving Russian novels (Woolf 1987, 341–44). As Woolf discerningly observes in reading Dostoevsky and Tolstoy, we feel we are entering an unknown and disturbing world. Our familiar landmarks, indeed the very floor beneath us, can seem to give way. Tectonic shifts occur in our increasingly unsteady psyches. We no longer know ourselves. We are no longer just fragile; we are fractured. We are now besieged not just by the strictly philosophical "limit questions" of modern Western thought (Kant et al.) but also by what the Russians name "the accursed questions"—the unavoidable, perhaps unanswerable questions that most human beings experience in some period of their lives, especially in the boundary situations of life (profound anxiety; a sense of nothingness that can suddenly descend on us; our fierce grief at the illness and death of those we love; our confused fear at our own illness, our inevitable dying, our encroaching death [Tolstoy's Ivan Ilyich]; our intractable guilt; our poisonous ennui, an honest sense of powerlessness).

"Who am I?" "Is my life or any life worth living?" "How can God exist when there is so much suffering?" "Whence evil?" Virginia Woolf wisely remarked that neither Dickens nor the Brontës, splendid as they are, prepared us for the altogether strange, disturbing world of the Russian novel. Woolf is surely correct: we can never be quite the same again after reading Dostoevsky, Tolstoy, Gogol, Chekov. Nor can anyone ever be quite the same after reading Augustine on the conflicted, overdetermined self. One may ultimately reject Augustine's view of the self. Many thinkers do. Just as many (e.g., Vladimir Nabokov) reject the extremity of Dostoevsky's vision of the conflicted, twisted self. However, after such revelations, what peace? Rejection of Augustine's view is fully possible, but the full, complex, conflicted, ambivalent, unnerving power of Augustine's portrait of our overdetermined selves—both highly intelligent and deluded, both loving and hate-filled, both sinful and tragic—haunts most of Augustine's careful readers. Did Augustine allow nature-grace to yield to sin-grace as the paradigm by which to understand the self? I think not; but the readings of Luther, Calvin, Jansen, and others do articulate realities that cannot be set aside or ignored in Augustine's texts on the self. If a tornado is headed this way, it does not help to hope it proves a refreshing summer wind.

Another Augustinian, Søren Kierkegaard, rightly argued that one can understand what a Christian means by sin as a fundamental disorientation of the self (*not* sins as moral fault) only if one first understands what a Christian means by grace. Augustinian sin is not a collection of moral faults, as in Pelagius's thought; rather, sin for Augustine is a twisted disorientation of the whole self. Sin for Augustine is not a temporary state of moral weakness but a state of being: a full-fledged, perverse, addictive disorientation of the self. If the human situation were less conflicted and overdetermined than Augustine argues it is, Pelagius's austere moralism might well suffice. Moral reforms, like better, more rigorous arguments, should always be welcome and are always needed. But neither argument nor moral reform is sufficient when dealing with or even diagnosing the deepest, most twisted, unconscious actuality of the self. For such actuality, one needs a radical hermeneutics of suspicion, including that of the greatest Christian hermeneut of suspicion, Augustine of Hippo (for the concept of a "hermeneutics of suspicion," see "Interpretation as Exercise of Suspicion," in Ricoeur 1970, 32–36).

In the analogous philosophical language of contemporary critical theory (e.g., that of Jürgen Habermas), the Augustinian notion of sin is a description not of conscious error but of an unconscious, systemically functioning distortion in the self. The self-deluded (not merely erroneous) self's liberation cannot be achieved through any self-healing of intellect (better arguments) or will (moral self-reform). As the Japanese Pure Land Buddhists insist, our situation is such that only some Other Power—for the Christian, God's grace—can free us. A psychotic is not liberated by further rational argument or by further dialogue with family and friends. A psychotic needs, as we say, professional help. It matters relatively little whether our self-delusions are caused by actions of our recent selves or, as is more likely, by some childhood or youthful trauma, genetic condition, or even life itself (*sunt lacrimae rerum*; Virgil, *The Aeneid*). Critical theorists can spot systemic distortions in an individual (classical psychoanalytic theory) or, at the limit, in whole cultures (ideology-critique, genealogical analysis, feminist theories, queer theories). Sexism, racism, classism, elitism, homophobia, and so on are more likely to be unconscious systemic distortions than conscious errors. Critical theories have been forged to find ways (unlike traditional theories) not only to understand the self but also to help emancipate it from its unconscious systemic distortions.

Like secular critical theories, Augustine's theological model of the self can accurately be called a theological critical theory. His paradigm of grace-sin helps one to understand aspects of the self that the nature-grace paradigm on its own does not. It is impoverishing for nature-grace theologians to ignore Augustine's sin-grace paradigm, his uniquely theological critical theory, even if, like myself, these theologians believe that the nature-grace paradigm is the foundational model of the Christian self, within which the sin-grace paradigm must dialectically be incorporated. But theologians of the nature-grace paradigm can unintentionally ignore the fury and power of sin in the self and in all history—foolishly, and, at the limit, fatally so. Pelagius, I repeat, was an admirable moralist; Julian, a brilliant dialectician. However, moralism and dialectics alike can regrettably evaporate once exposed to any deep and conflictual vision of sin-evil such as that proposed by the old Augustine, even amid his polemical fury and bizarre exaggerations.

THE FOURTH ELEMENT: THE IMPLICITLY TRAGIC SELF IN AUGUSTINE

All the elements outlined earlier are necessary for any adequate interpretation of the self in Augustine. However, there is another element in Augustine, an element admittedly more implicit than explicit, a matter of his unthematized but ever-present sensibility—in more Augustinian language, a matter of affect, mood, and sensibility. This further element—a tragic sensibility—was the implied but not explicit element Augustine needed to complete his model of the self and to correct some of his misfirings in blaming all evil and suffering on human beings.

In addition to (not in replacement of!) employing the nature-grace paradigm for understanding intelligence and will, and the sin-grace paradigm for understanding the depth of sin, I propose a tragedy-grace paradigm to complete Augustine's rich, polyphonic, and conflictual (in a single word, overdetermined) understanding of that ultimately incomprehensible reality, the human self. Through the three paradigms, the human self is viewed as penultimately overdetermined; that very overdetermination, moreover, leads one to the threshold of the self's understanding of itself, as much as, at that limit, it evokes the ultimate incomprehensibility of the self: the self's participation, even divinization, in the incomprehensibility of God's self. The Augustinian self is ultimately a mystery to itself; to understand that mystery as mystery, an interpreter needs help from all four paradigms.

One reason that an interpreter needs the addition of a tragedy-grace paradigm to understand the Augustinian self fully is this: as important as the issue of radical evil is for understanding humankind after the horrors of the last century, as well as the massive, global suffering of whole peoples and classes in this century, evil alone is not the only topic that needs theological attention (Evans 1982).

Human beings, other animals, and Earth itself are afflicted even more by suffering than by outright evil-sin; much of that enormous suffering has been caused by human evil, indeed sin, but much of it has not been thus caused. Sometimes evil just happens: volcanoes erupt; there are floods, tsunamis, earthquakes, the inexplicable suffering and death of infants and children, even ordinary, inexorable adult illness, dying, and death—all these so-called "natural" evils cause enormous suffering to human beings, as to all sentient beings. These realities are named *natural evils* only because we do not cause them; nature does. But they so affect *us* with suffering that we can name them natural evils but not sins. We call them "evils" in the same way we call some undesirable (to us) plants "weeds," but only because we do not want them in *our* gardens. So-called natural evils would be better named natural afflictions; that is, intense sufferings caused not by sin or by God but by nature itself. Nature impersonally and indifferently follows its own inexorable laws. Alternatively, as human-caused climate change now so afflicts us (Pope Francis, *Laudato Si'*), nature has been so interfered with by human beings that some recent floods, forest fires, and even hurricanes bear all the marks of human evil-sin. Nature is experienced by us as, on the one hand, wondrous and awesome, and, on the other hand, as brutal, even seemingly cruel and indifferent toward us. Most natural afflictions and sufferings, however, can be accorded neither to God as "acts of God" nor to human sin.

Augustine, more than any other ancient thinker, uncovered the uncanny human tendency to evil and the stark actuality of evil and sin in history and ourselves. This actuality is obvious to all but the inextricably Pollyannaish. A tragic consciousness uncovers sin (e.g., the vile murders of a brother's children at the bloody origin of the House of Atreus). However, a tragic consciousness is just as concerned to uncover the enormous suffering caused less by personal sin than by some mysterious necessity—whether fate, fortune, chance, or providence. Personal sin may be a subsidiary but not the principal cause of such overwhelming suffering and excessive punishment as that of Oedipus, Orestes, Phaedra, Cassandra, Pentheus, and others. Much of the enormous suffering in human existence seems deeply inappropriate, at times even obscene, to blame on human evil (e.g., the Lisbon earthquake immortalized by Voltaire's *Candide*; the terrifying tsunami in Japan in 2011; the unjust fate of Spartacus and so many others throughout history: Shakespeare's Lear, Cordelia, and Desdemona). Suffering, even more than evil-sin, demands philosophical and theological attention today, at a time when even increasing natural "evils" or afflictions cause so much suffering, and when massive global suffering abounds through the tragic injustice operative in many social, economic, and political structures (see my essay "Incarnation and Suffering: On Rereading Augustine" [Tracy 2012]).

Most contemporary Christian thinkers (including Reinhold Niebuhr, Paul Ricoeur, and Joseph Ratzinger—perhaps the three most prominent Augustinian thinkers of the last century) have been reluctant, as was Augustine, to use the categories of tragedy to rethink what a demythologized Augustinian "original sin" might mean for a contemporary understanding of the self. However, after so many modern and postmodern rereadings of the philosophical import of the ancient Greek tragedies, why not take tragedy with full seriousness—more exactly, take seriously a paradigm of tragedy-grace—to help explicate a sensibility implicit in many of Augustine's texts, and then use that tragedy-grace paradigm not, of course, to replace the sin-grace paradigm, but to partly correct and complement it? Evil and sin are intractably real, causing overwhelming suffering; so are tragic necessity (fate, chance, fortune) and its attendant suffering.

Augustine avoided the category *tragedy*, despite what clearly seems to have been his own tragic sensibility, because he rejected the notion of a fate not controlled by an omnipotent God. There is also the historical fact (fate): Augustine (like most of his contemporaries) probably did not know the texts of Aeschylus or Sophocles. However, Augustine knew and loved Virgil, the greatest writer of lament in the West to this day, very well indeed. Augustine also knew Homer indirectly well enough: Homer, the father of the ancient tragic form, about which Aeschylus reportedly said that he and all later tragedians lived on the crumbs dropped from that bounteous Homeric table. As Simone Weil brilliantly wrote in one of the classic essays of the twentieth century, "The Iliad, or The Poem of Force" (Weil [1945] 1977, 153–83), Homer was the first Greek thinker to enact as the true hero of tragedy the reality of force, that force in life itself with which every human being, victor or victim of the back-and-forth shifts of history or the vagaries of nature, must one day deal. Unlike Weil, with her extreme anti-Roman viewpoint, Augustine knew that Virgil's *Aeneid* was a truly worthy successor of Homer's *Iliad* and *Odyssey*. Virgil famously continued Homer's tale with the tale of the escaped Trojan, Aeneas, wandering purposefully toward the new Troy, Rome. *Aeneid* is not, as too often read, simply a triumphal epic to honor Augustus Caesar (see Johnson 1976). To be sure, it is partially that. Far more, however, *Aeneid* is the greatest tragic lament in Western literature; it displays the terrible tragic price to be paid by both victors (Aeneas-Rome) and victims (Dido-Carthage). Virgil incarnates the authentic Greek, now also Roman, tragic vision: suffering comes not just from our own evil actions but also from some strange necessity in reality itself: "*Sunt lacrimae rerum.*" Augustine himself knew this Virgilian truth well, as witnessed by a Virgilian tonality of the entire *Confessions*, the gravitas in lament in *City of God*, and in his powerful commentaries on the psalms of lamentation.

Fate was a dangerous category for Augustine's purposes since, for the tragedians, fate, chance, and fortune (a curious combination of fate and chance), unlike providence (a biblical and Stoic category that Augustine accepts), are not controlled by the gods, even by the high god Zeus. Augustine, as a Christian, believed that only a doctrine of divine providence was an appropriate theological category for describing what happens to us, whether we will it or not, since all reality (even fate, if such there be) is ultimately controlled providentially by the biblical God, all-powerful, all-knowing, and all-loving. Augustine, therefore, rejects the category of fate. In Greek tragedy, after all, the gods, even

Zeus, are very powerful but they are not all-powerful; they do not control fate. Zeus is not Yahweh. Yahweh, for Augustine, is all-powerful or is not God at all (*Deus sine Deo*).

Nevertheless, Augustine presents something like a Christian tragic sensibility with the categories of providence and predestination, not fate. What might this mean? Why otherwise did Augustine so love Virgil, whose tragic lament is embedded in the very rhythms and many of the images of *Confessions*, if he lacked a tragic sensibility so attuned to Virgil? One example: Augustine is troubled in *Confessions* that he had been so moved as a student whenever he read Virgil's account of Dido's tragic suffering when Aeneas cruelly abandoned her on the shores of North Africa (Augustine 1991b, 81). In retrospect, the now-Christian Augustine feared that his youthful, vicarious experience of dramatic and poetic lament for a "merely" fictional character may have been wrong. And yet, Augustine himself echoed this very same Virgilian tragic lament when he confessed his own guilt for first deceiving and then cruelly abandoning his mother Monnica on the same Carthaginian shore where Aeneas had abandoned Dido. That Virgilian tragic lament spoke to Augustine's own sensibility toward his action as not just a sin but also a necessity demanded at the time — that is, a tragic necessity.

Augustine's sensibility, in my judgment, was unmistakably a tragic one, focused not only on sin but also on a tragic necessity: thus his own initial attraction to the Manicheans and their ineradicable sense of our tragic fate; thus his own increasingly dark vision of the human condition, exploding in full force in his late anti-Pelagian writings. Augustine's reading of original sin does insist on the guilt of its inheritors, but it also suggests something very like a tragic necessity wreaking itself on all human beings. What kind of tragic vision was Augustine's? Virgilian, certainly, and biblical as well, deeply influenced by his two favorite biblical works, the Psalms — especially, of course, the poignant tones of the psalms of lamentation — and the epistles of Paul, with Paul's sense of the paradoxical reality that we can understand the truth of God only through Jesus Christ and Him crucified, the sinless but divinely, tragically fated Jesus the Christ.

Even if one attends only to the classical tragedies of the ancient Greeks — that is, to Aeschylus, Sophocles, and Euripides — it is impossible to claim that any single definition can apply to all Greek tragedies. In fact, most philosophical definitions of tragedy are generalizations from one preferred tragedy: *Oedi-*

pus Rex for Aristotle and Freud; Aeschylus's *Oresteia* for Nietzsche and Arendt; Sophocles's *Antigone* for Hegel and Lacan; Euripides's *Hippolytus* for Seneca and Racine; and Homer's *Iliad* for Simone Weil.

In post-Kantian German philosophy, tragedy became a major issue for philosophers — from Goethe, Schiller, Friedrich and August Schlegel, and Novalis to Hegel, Schelling, Schopenhauer, Kierkegaard, and Nietzsche, as well as, in modern German contemporary philosophy, Scheler, Heidegger, Adorno, Jaspers, Benjamin, Gadamer, and Arendt. The German philosophical world was shaken by Greek tragedy in a way analogous to the way the medieval theological paradigm of nature-grace was shaken by the new sin-grace emphasis of the Reformation.

Most of these German philosophers so taken with tragedy were Lutheran in heritage. Indeed, as Friedrich Nietzsche, himself the descendant of three generations of Lutheran pastors, once ironically noted, "German philosophy was born in Lutheran parsonages." Not only the Latins but also the Greek Christian theologians, with the possible exception of Gregory Nazianzen, found little to no theological interest in the ancient Greek tragedies. No Greek Christian Father (again, except possibly Nazianzen) found that Greek tragedy, unlike Greek philosophy, was either a resource for or a challenge to their contemplative theologies. Like the early Augustine of the *Dialogues* of Cassiciacum and Thagaste, the Greek theologians were far more optimistic about the self, especially the self's intuitive understanding and contemplative powers, as well as the self's freedom of will. As Jaroslav Pelikan argued, the Greek theologians, surrounded by an ever-darkening Hellenistic culture where fate reigned supreme, emphasized freedom of the will to fight cultural fatalism (Pelikan 1974, 216–52). The major situational problem for the Greek theologians contemporary to Augustine, therefore, was the opposite to that for Augustine; he faced the Pelagians, for whom an excessive belief in the freedom of a relatively unimpeded will denied the Christian belief in inherited sin (which the Greeks never denied, but which they believed was better understood as a weakened and wounded will rather than Augustine's more radical picture). The Pelagians also ignored the tragic sense of the ancient tragedians as well as the affirmation of fate in the Roman Stoics (e.g., Marcus Aurelius).

The nature-grace paradigm, with its relative optimism about the self, flourished in Eastern Christian thought. Indeed, a relatively optimistic account of the freedom of the will continued in Orthodox theology until the modern Russian theologians (especially Soloviev and Bulgakov) developed their speculative theologies of history, which, faithful to the tragic character of so much Russian history, included undeniably tragic, not only sinful, elements. Although the Russian Orthodox Vladimir Lossky articulated a deeply impressive apophatic theology, neither he nor his successors (both the non-apophatic John Zizioulas and the apophatic Christos Yannaras) took to heart any Augustinian—for that matter, any Dostoevskian—portrait of an irretrievably split self (see the consistently negative appraisals of Augustine in Zizioulas 1985; Yannaras 2007). Indeed, Lossky and his successors mostly rejected both Augustine and Dostoevsky. On the contrary, Sergius Bulgakov—influenced by Dostoevsky and, even more, by his own sense of the seemingly unending tragic disruptions of Russian history, culminating in his own experience of exile and the even worse fate of his theological colleague Pavel Florensky in the violently anti-Christian Bolshevik Revolution—understood tragedy theologically. The exiled Russian philosopher Nikolai Berdyaev also created a Christian tragic and apocalyptic philosophy of religion and was even willing to speak of tragedy in God (Berdyaev 1935, 1952).

Scholars over the past several decades have frequently analyzed the role of socioeconomic-political factors informing the peculiar religious intensity and haunting tragic sense of late-antique North African Christians—Tertullian, Cyprian, Tyconius, Augustine, Donatists, Manicheans, Stoics, and Catholics alike. A passionate, tragic North African sensibility never disturbed the more contemplative Christian Alexandria or Cappadocia or Constantinople. The difference between North African and Greek theology is somewhat analogous to that between modern British analytical philosophy and modern, although not contemporary, German philosophy. In the latter case, as noted earlier, most German philosophers found themselves philosophically challenged by ancient tragedy. Even the later Kant, by the time of the *Third Critique*, discovered that the philosophical problem of freedom and necessity had become far more complex and existential than he had once hoped it would prove to be in the first two *Critiques*. The categories of the *sublime* and *symbol* disclose an openness to the modern tragic sense as sublime (a favorite, post-Kantian Romantic trope). Even more of a sense of radical evil invaded Kant's late thought. In *Religion within the Limits of Reason Alone*, for example, Kant's newly articulated sense of radical evil disturbed but did not displace his moral rationalism (Kant 1960). However, more than Kant admitted, his own late sense of the problem of radical evil effectively unhinged the limits within which both religion and tragedy were earlier supposed to live. The terror erupting in the French Revolution (which Kant, unlike Fichte, continued to defend) influenced the more sober tone, occasionally touched by a genuine historical tragic sense, in Kant's brilliant late essays on history, especially "On the Impossibility of All Attempted Philosophical Theodicies" (1791).

Neither Goethe nor Schiller nor the early Romantics (Friedrich and August Schlegel and Novalis) needed lessons on the importance of tragedy for understanding the human situation philosophically. They were all both philosophers and tragedians, either in drama or in reflection. August Schlegel, for example, insisted on the philosophical importance of Shakespeare's tragedies before any English philosopher had really noticed. The first major German philosophical breakthrough on the relationship of tragedy and philosophy, however, was accomplished by Hegel.[9] He was the first philosopher for whom the fact that reason had a history was a major issue for reason itself. Hegel's contextual-historical turn in philosophy likewise meant that the blatant tragedies of history (a "slaughter-bench," as Hegel described it) must be taken into account by philosophy. The deepest history — the history of *Geist* itself — must transform all prior philosophical, religious, and artistic understandings of the self, as of all reality, in order to form new dialectical models of the self. For Hegel, in *Phenomenology of Spirit*, the philosopher as philosopher must trace the history of the major forms of art, religion, and philosophy. For this new, historicized philosophy or philosophical history, one of the most important historical, aesthetic, moral, religious, and implicitly philosophical forms, Hegel argued, was Greek tragedy.

In consequence, post-Kantian German philosophical understandings of tragedy became both more capacious and more challenging than Kant's tentative steps. Post-Hegelian and post-Nietzschean philosophers up to Benjamin, Heidegger, Gadamer, and Arendt (although, curiously, not Habermas), have found it important to correlate their philosophy critically with one or another Greek tragic vision. It is distinctive of many modern German idealist and post-idealist existential, phenomenological, and hermeneutical German philosophers to take classical Greek tragedy, as well as that of such modern tragedians as Shakespeare and Calderón, or Goethe and Schiller, with critical philosophi-

---

9. Beistegui 2000, 11–56; see also other essays in *Philosophy and Tragedy*. The other, later major German philosophical reading of tragedy is, of course, that of Friedrich Nietzsche.

cal seriousness. Additionally, Walter Benjamin rediscovered the uniqueness and import of the formerly overlooked, seventeenth-century, German Lutheran baroque form of tragedy, *Trauerspiel* (Benjamin 1998).

In the contemporary period, some major Russian (Berdyaev), Polish (Kolakowski), and Iberian philosophers (both the Basque Miguel de Unamuno and the Castilian Ortega y Gasset) took tragedy with full philosophical seriousness (Unamuno 1954). The Iberian philosophers, faithful to the uniquely Iberian, Catholic, tragic sensibility as seen in Calderón, were the principal Western philosophers besides the Germans to make tragedy a major philosophical and theological issue. In the mid-twentieth century, some French philosophers (Sartre, Camus, Marcel) wrote philosophical tragic dramas; since that earlier existentialist period, however, French philosophers have been largely silent on tragic themes, especially in the more aleatory French postmodern thought, in which chance, not fate, is a predominant category. In Anglophone philosophy, only a few analytical philosophers (Bernard Williams, Martha Nussbaum, Stanley Cavell) have made tragedy a philosophically important concern. In the culture of the United States, the secularized Calvinism deeply formed by the earlier Calvinist culture of explicit predestination (e.g., in Jonathan Edwards), became fate in the tragic novels of Nathaniel Hawthorne and Herman Melville, and later in those of Henry James, William Faulkner, Ernest Hemingway, and others, but did not much affect most American philosophers, who have remained Emersonian, not Edwardian, in their nontragic sensibilities.

Ironically, modern Christian theologians have paid less attention to tragedy than have the philosophers. In fact, most modern theologians have accorded very little attention to tragedy as a form that might help inform, reform, and transform, and in turn be transformed by, one or another theological vision of salvation. To be sure, Christianity ultimately offers a nontragic vision (indeed, as Dante rightly insisted, Christianity is theologically a *commedia*). However, the hopeful Christian resurrection vision of peace and joy is grounded in the unignorable primordial Gospel passion narratives: the tragic reality of horrifying suffering (indeed affliction) of Jesus in Gethsemane, his capture, torture, and crucifixion — the most disgraceful and painful of deaths for the lowest of criminals of the ancient Roman world. Paul's dialectical, paradoxical theology speaks the truth: Christians believe only in the God revealed in "Jesus Christ and Him crucified" (1 Cor. 2:2). When one recalls that the central Christian symbol since about the fifth century is the cross (so unlike the serene symbol of the sitting, peaceful Buddha), one must ask, Why did the first theologians and their successors, so wise in their use of Greek philosophy to help them think through Christianity as a philosophical religion, at the same time ignore the great potential of Greek tragedies in helping to articulate a Christian theology of the cross and a theology of suffering? Fortunately, some modern Christian theological voices did break the puzzling silence on the possible import of the classical Greek tragic visions for a religion grounded in the crucified one: those of Søren Kierkegaard, Simone Weil, Karl Barth, Sergei Bulgakov, Reinhold Niebuhr, Hans Urs von Balthasar, Donald MacKinnon, Jon Sobrino, James Gustafson, Rowan Williams, Lawrence Bouchard, Wendy Farley, and a few others. From the very beginning of Christian theology, the huge majority of theologians have turned solely to philosophy and almost never to tragedy to help articulate the fuller complexities of Christian self-understanding.

Here is a thought experiment: What if early Greek theologians, from Justin Martyr (second through third centuries) through Dionysius the Areopagite (probably sixth century), had taken the Greek tragedies as seriously as they wisely took Greek philosophy? Greek Orthodox theology would not have had to wait for the modern Russian Orthodox theologians, as well as the theologically informed novelist Fyodor Dostoevsky (see Rowan Williams 2011) and the religious philosopher of tragedy Nikolai Berdyaev, to learn how fruitful sustained attention to Greek tragedy can be for Christian theology.

Theology can also illuminate and be illuminated by the tragic (not only sinful) elements in many biblical stories — the stories of Hagar and Ishmael, the narratives of Saul, David, Solomon, even Moses. A complex, conflictual story of tragic necessity also skulks along in the biblical prophets' terror-ridden responses to the divine, unhinging calls to prophesy in Isaiah, Jeremiah, Ezekiel, and others. Classical prophets seem to be both exceptionally graced and exceptionally tragic figures — note, for example, the Lamentations of Jeremiah; the fate of John the Baptist; the cries of Montanus, Maximilla, and Priscilla; and Muhammad's terrified initial resistance to his prophetic calling. Furthermore, does Greek tragedy not have affinities with the laments in the book of Lamentations, including the daring lamentations toward God, still a far more prominent tradition in Judaism than in Christianity, just as the theological employment of fate is far more prominent in Islamic theology than in most Christian theology? That strange, unnerving biblical book Ecclesiastes ("Vanity, vanity, all is vanity") could have been written by Euripides. Even more unexpectedly for the Bible, Job's terrifying cry, beyond lamenting against divine injustice, bears all the power of the decimated Theban cry of revolting injustice at the revolting actions of the god Dionysus in *Bacchae*.

In the New Testament, the Gospel of Mark displays strong elements of tragedy, where only the mad and the demons rather than the confused, unimpressive disciples of Jesus seem to understand the divine power of this strange, doomed, apocalyptic prophet. In Mark, Jesus's resurrection, to be sure, is affirmed as in the other Gospels. At the same time, in Mark alone, the original ending of the Gospel is strange and incomplete: the women at the tomb flee, weeping and confused, while the male disciples have absented themselves altogether. Even the more sanguine Luke will change geography itself to ensure that his gospel narrative carries Luke's Jesus to the city of Jerusalem and his divinely predestined fate.

In the Gospel of Matthew, an increasingly sober, even tragic sense of inevitability takes over the narrative as it unfolds, always relating word and action, Jesuanic discourse and the crowd's disheartening, constant misunderstandings and rejections, until the final discourse, Matthew 25, before the passion itself begins. Matthew leads his readers from the most optimistic Christian discourse ever written (the incomparable Sermon on the Mount, a call to a fully Christian life, which, as Tolstoy bitterly observed, no Christian church has ever dared to live), to the deeply moving, still demanding, almost desperate cry of Matthew 25 (the Magna Carta of all liberation theologies) — if you will do nothing else, at least listen and live the most important Jesuanic call of all, the call to pay attention above all to the outcasts, the rejected, the forgotten: Feed the poor, give drink to the thirsty, clothe the naked, visit the sick and the imprisoned. In sum, wake up and fight the suffering and injustice all around you. As Augustine himself would later write in *De doctrina christiana*, the sole hermeneutical key to the whole Scripture is "love of God and love of neighbor."

The whole Christian Bible ends, after all, with the apocalyptic-tragic, often too-violent cries of the persecuted Christian community in Asia Minor in Revelation. Greek tragedy could have been helpful to aid the earliest theologians in their sometimes unsteady readings of central aspects of these biblical texts and many others — the Exodus, the Babylonian Exile, the two destructions of the Temple — as surely as Greek mysticism and the Greek philosophy of *eros* helped Philo, Origen, and Gregory of Nyssa in their enriching readings of the Song of Songs and the Gospel and letters of John. The Jewish theologian Philo and the

Christian theologian Gregory of Nyssa created Platonically influenced mystical readings of Moses. Could not their brilliant, contemplative, and mystical treatises on Moses's ascent of Mt. Sinai have been well complemented by a second, different reading — one more influenced by Greek tragedy on the descent of an elated Moses down Mt. Sinai with the Decalogue, only to find an unwelcoming, ungrateful people worshipping a golden calf? The full story of Moses bears triumph and joy, but also unmistakably tragic components: Moses's murder of an Egyptian official; God's near murder of Moses himself; Moses's unending, even tragic difficulties with his people, whose relentless complaints sometimes burst forth in fierce fury at their leader; and, above all, the fact that Moses (like the later Martin Luther King Jr.) was a prophet destined never to reach the promised land himself.

Here is a second thought experiment, this time for Latin theology. What if the passionate and often pessimistic North African Latin theologians had developed a Christian theological vision with the aid of a tragedy-grace paradigm,[10] together with Augustine's unique rendering of the nature-grace paradigm on intelligence and will-love, as well as the sin-grace paradigm on the abyss of sin? Virgil, the *Iliad*, and the many suggestive biblical passages cited earlier were available, even if Aeschylus and Sophocles apparently were not, although it is possible (not probable) that Euripides may have been available through Seneca. If Augustine had allowed himself to incorporate his own innate tragic sense into his theology, as well as he articulated his joyful, contemplative orientation with the aid of Platonist philosophy and his unique and North African sense of unconscious and conscious sin, he might well have added an explicitly tragic element to his complex model of the self. As the more pastoral Augustine sometimes hints in his letters and sermons, some human situations may be described more accurately as tragic than as sinful. Augustine, the pastor of his beleaguered people, never insinuates (like some contemporary Christian fundamentalist preachers) that floods or storms, earthquakes or barbarian invasions, are the people's fault. An Augustine influenced, Christian theological transformation of Greek, Latin, and biblical tragic senses happened much later: first,

---

10. There is a need for a full study of Augustine on fate and necessity — for example, in *City of God*, in his criticism of Cicero in book 5 (chaps. 8, 9, and 10), and in his polemical response, in book 2 (chaps. 9, 10, and 11), to Julian of Eclanum, who had accused Augustine of still remaining — in his "Against Two Letters of the Pelagians" — Manichean and fatalistic (see Augustine 1984, 188–96, 394–95).

in early modernity, in great Christian tragic artists such as Calderón, Milton, Racine, and Corneille; in philosophers such as Pascal; and, in later modernity, in such Christian thinkers as Péguy, Kierkegaard, Simone Weil, and T. S. Eliot. Christian artists, more than Christian theologians, have sensed that tragedy can illuminate the Christian paradoxical human situation to the point at which a paradigm of tragedy-grace should be added to nature-grace and sin-grace.

Indeed, most modern theologians, as much as the earliest theologians, have kept their distance from tragedy. Jonathan Edwards is the outstanding eighteenth-century exception. Kierkegaard and Newman are the major nineteenth-century Christian exceptions. Theologians have too often and too facilely contented themselves with easy declarations that Christianity is "beyond tragedy" (Reinhold Niebuhr). That is indeed true (as attested by the resurrection), but it is crucial that what Jesus Christ endured *before* the resurrection be understood and not lost, even in order to understand the resurrection itself. Christianity, after all, is, as I have said before, a religion whose foundational narrative is the passion narrative and whose foundational symbol is the cross. When a theology moves beyond philosophy, it does so only by passing *through* philosophy. So, too, should any theological move beyond tragedy be only *through* tragedy, not around it. Analogously, the only powerful forms of postmodern thought are those that have seriously gone through modernity rather than, as is sometimes the case, used *post*modernity as an excuse to return with unearned ease to *pre*modernity. Theologians should be as willing to go through the raging river of tragedy as they have been willing to go through the "fiery brook" of philosophy and critical theory.

A few Christian theologians have so dared. Outstanding is the late Anglican theologian Donald MacKinnon (1968, 100), who, despite his unjust comments on Plato, justly wrote,

> There is a sense in which Christian theology may be much more than it realizes the victim of the victory won in the person of Plato by the philosophers over the poets, and in particular the tragedians. It is true that Aristotle sought to modify the significance of this victory; but he failed to reverse it. . . . I wish to ask the question whether in fact the theme of the work of Christ may not receive effective theological treatment when it is represented as tragedy. This I say remembering the supreme significance of the resurrection, but also continually recalling the extent to which in popular apologetic understanding the resurrection has

been deformed through its representation as in effect a descent from the Cross, given greater dramatic effect by a thirty-six-hour postponement.

Original or inherited sin for Augustine served as the surest explanation of the mystery of iniquity — the mystery that always most tortured him. But against Augustine's official teaching, why could this inherited necessity not be read as a tragic inheritance, not personal sin (which should always involve personal consent)? Is it plausible to claim, with Augustine or not, that there is some mysterious inherited evil in which we all participate and through which we all must suffer, even though we are not personally responsible for the origins of this mysterious inheritance? Augustine's penetrating sense of some strange and powerful inherited evil afflicting humanity can, however, also be read, *contra* Augustine, as an inherited, necessary, tragic evil but not as sin. Inherited evil, along with an inevitable inclination toward evil, is not as such (i.e., before one acts upon it) sinful. That inevitable aspect of our situation is better described as tragic, not sinful.

This Augustine would not allow. Since God cannot be responsible for causing (as distinct from permitting) evil, he concluded, in effect, that human beings must be responsible for all evil. This Augustinian conclusion is probative only if no third possibility is given (*tertium non datur*). *Sed tertium datur.* A sense of tragic necessity is that third possibility: an element, as noted earlier, that is present in the Bible alongside powerful biblical portraits of sin.

There is an intellectually skeptical and existentially dark side to Augustine, where sin and tragic necessity seem to coexist uneasily side by side. Perhaps, left to himself, Augustine might have become, as Ronald Knox (1961, 202) ironically observed about Pascal, the village atheist. But grace caught Augustine, and he became and remained for life a hopeful, often joyful and contemplatively peaceful Christian to the end. Like Pascal, however, Augustine also never fully lost his other, tragic, sensibility. Augustine was a Christian convalescent; he was never fully healed, never a serene and joyful mystic in the manner of Dionysius the Areopagite.

As for Greek tragedy itself, in spite of many modern misunderstandings that tragedy characteristically ends without any hope, the fact is that among the Greek tragedies that have survived, about half end in a "hopeless" mood, and half end with hope. Despite common linguistic usage, "tragic" does not mean "hopeless." Augustine may have been able, therefore, to strengthen, not weaken, his Christian hope, his incarnational theology of the cross and resurrection, and his nonapocalyptic eschatology if he had allowed himself to include a tragic element in his model of the intelligent, loving, willing, sinful, and implicitly tragic self.

One can further clarify the implicit tragic aspects in Augustine's portrait of the self by comparing his vision of the self to certain aspects of those of the three classical Greek tragedians whose texts (tragically!) Augustine did not know. Clarification through contrast is always a promising intellectual exercise. Who among the ancients, other than Euripides (e.g., 1959b, 4:397–454), is as penetrating as Augustine on how our affects and passions can so becloud and take over our minds that we reach the point of impenetrable self-delusion? Euripides, the child of the Athenian intellectual revolution of the Sophists and Socrates, believed that reason does indeed enlighten and liberate human beings from superstition and obscurantism. But Euripides was no optimistic rationalist: reason, even philosophical reason, can at times turn human beings into self-satisfied, arrogant monsters programmed for a tragic fall. Intelligence, Euripides thought, can rarely suppress or even deflect the passions away from blindness and self-delusion. In *Bacchae* (Euripides 1959a, 4:543–608), Euripides's greatest work, Pentheus, the young rationalist and self-satisfied king of Thebes, bearing all the hubris of youth and power, is driven by the orgiastic god Dionysus, the god at once of ecstatic joy and revolting cruelty, to insanity and merciless destruction. Dionysus cruelly manipulates Pentheus's vanity and his deeply repressed and confused erotic passions. Euripides, like Augustine, believed that the passions can so disorient our intellects that even our positive *eros* can shift suddenly into a pathway of tragic self-destruction. So it is in Euripides's *Hippolytus* with Phaedra's inappropriate but irresistible tragic erotic love for her unknowing stepson, who has his own repressions to afflict him. The Euripidean tragic strain in Augustine shows itself in his brilliant (and very non-Platonist) focus on the passions—how passion can easily dislocate, even destroy, reason (*pondus meum, amor meus*). A Euripidean tragic strain is alive in Augustine in his penetrating observations on the power of feeling, emotion, affect, and mood over our best intentions and most brilliant thoughts. Still, Augustine's tragic view of the human situation is ultimately less comparable to that of Euripides than are those of Aeschylus and Sophocles.

Augustine's awesome vision of the power of inherited original sin possesses a more Aeschylean gravitas than the Euripidean lament over disordering passions. Aeschylus, like Augustine, possessed an innate sense that evil can be inherited as a result of some aboriginal ancestral crime. For Augustine himself, this inheritance was original sin. That sin included humanity's tragic solidarity in a universal and inescapable, inherited — that is, original, at the origin — ancestral sin, for which Adam's and Eve's descendants are somehow also to be held responsible and guilty. For Augustine all humankind is now in the House of Atreus. In the last play of *Oresteia*, Aeschylus dramatizes the hope that, through their dialectical and dialogical reasoning on justice, human beings, by using reason in the polis — if they act with the aid of the Olympian gods, especially Athena, goddess of wisdom — can hope to understand justice enough to found a court of law and thereby break the unending cycle of revenge in the doomed House of Atreus.

In the final play of Aeschylus's trilogy, *Eumenides*, human beings, with the inestimable aid of the Olympian gods, may persuade the gods of blood, earth, and family — the Furies — to partake of the new tentative order of justice. This hope, moreover, for law as justice, not revenge, is a solid one for Aeschylus. This hope is theologically grounded (Aeschylus 1959, 1:166–71, esp. lines 881–1047): for Aeschylus Zeus is ultimately just. Human beings will therefore discover a tragic, not philosophical, wisdom: despite all appearances to the contrary, Zeus is just; life, in consequence, despite its evils, its injustices, its sufferings, is meaningful and hopeful. We learn this Aeschylean wisdom, however, only through tragic suffering "drop by drop even in sleep." Profound suffering purifies both mind and heart to be open to receive tragic wisdom. This classical, Aeschylean tragic wisdom can be found in Augustine, whose tragic wisdom was, of course, theologically transformed by his Christian vision into Christian *agapic* wisdom through suffering, a process of which the cross reminds all Christians. Neither dolorism nor fatalism accurately invokes either the Aeschylean or the Augustinian tragic theology of suffering. Aeschylus thought that the story of the House of Atreus needed three plays to enact its truth dramatically, while Sophocles and Euripides believed that a single play was sufficient. For Augustine, the foundational Christian story of suffering and unlimited hope is the story in the four Gospels, not one, the story of Jesus of Nazareth as the Christ through whom one understands that God is infinite love and intelligence, infinite justice and mercy. The traumas described by Aeschylus and Augustine are radically different, yet both include a similar sense of tragic necessity (Orestes in the *Oresteia*, Jesus in the Synoptic Gospels), and a wisdom through suffering in the Gospel of John and the letters of Paul. Despite their radical differences, the stories of the Bible can, at times, be illuminated in classical Aeschylean terms — as those exceptional Augustinians, John Milton and Jean Racine, demonstrated. Unsurprising is the fact that two of the greatest Christian tragic dramatists, the revisionary Puritan, John Milton, and the revisionary Jansenist, Jean Racine, were both Augustinian. Almost despite himself, Augustine communicates a Christian tragic sensibility to readers — although more, alas, to Christian artists than to Christian theologians and philosophers.

Both Euripidean and Aeschylean tragic notes, therefore, can be found in Augustine's implicitly tragic Christian vision. However, there is also something peculiarly Sophoclean in Augustine's overdetermined model of the self. Augustine could have written his own (to be sure, Christianly transformed) version of Sophocles's greatest ode — his ode to humankind as *deinos*:[11] that is, as a paradoxical wonder, shining in intelligence and joyful strength, while at the same time sharply damaged and twisted. *Deinos* is a Sophoclean word for the abyss of wonder that is the human self.

Oedipus is both highly intelligent and self-deluded: both well-intentioned toward others (his entire city, for whose sake he is willing to die), and ineradicably egocentric; both innocent and responsible. Sophocles implies that not only Oedipus but every human being is a *deinos*. Some human beings, like Oedipus, refuse to live according to the human measure (the Sophoclean heroes, *daimons*). Oedipus is determined to know the truth about his origins, whatever the horrendous consequences. No one — the prophet Teresias, his wife, the warning Chorus — can stop Oedipus before it is too late. It was always too late for Oedipus. *He must know.* Sophoclean daimonic heroes are mortals who cannot but go beyond the mortal human measure into a realm closer to that of the immortal gods.[12] The heroes are no longer "human, all too human" — they are *daimons*.

Antigone, too, refuses the human measure. She "lives for love, not for hatred."[13] She lives by the code of the gods for justice, not the reasonable political code of the city. It matters not at all to Antigone that the ruler of her polis, Creon, has threatened death to anyone who disobeys his decree that Antigone's brother, a traitor to the city, will not be buried and, therefore, will be disgraced

---

11. The ode referring to *deinos* in *Antigone* (Sophocles 1956, lines 332–40), spoken by the Chorus, begins with "πολλὰ τὰ δεινὰ κοὐδὲν ἀνθρώπου δεινότερον πέλει" (many wonders there be, but naught more wondrous than man).

12. This is my own reading of the controverted issue of the exact meaning of Sophocles's notion of the hero as *daimon*.

13. "My nature is for mutual love, not hate" (Sophocles 1956, line 523).

in death as in life. Antigone will not—cannot—obey this unjust law. She lives for love through justice—the ancient justice, that of the gods. She is fully prepared to go to her death in obedience to another, higher law—the ancient law of the gods that one must bury one's own family members. Antigone is not in any simple sense an obviously good person like Shakespeare's Cordelia. Rather, Antigone, like Oedipus and all Sophoclean heroes, has obvious flaws: her unattractive stubbornness, for example, which ambiguously lies within her admirable and unrelenting sense of justice. Moreover, Antigone treats her weaker sister Ismene cruelly, with unwarranted contempt. She ignores the loving feelings of her fiancé, Haemon. And yet Hegel was right to call Antigone the most beautiful (i.e., morally admirable) figure in our literature. As a daimonic hero who must live beyond the finite measure, Antigone could not but live as she did, no matter what the consequences, just as Oedipus could not continue living until he knew the terrible truth of his own origins, no matter what the consequences.

All Sophoclean heroes are mortals who, faithful to their daimonic natures, must go beyond the human limit, beyond the finite measure appropriate for humanity. Sophocles seems to believe that the best human hope for understanding human beings in the cosmos is to turn away from stories of ordinary mortals and to turn to the uncanny stories of those larger-than-life figures, the daimonic heroes. Only by attending to the unnerving stories of these daimonic heroes, Sophocles seems to hold, can human beings hope to find some glimpse into the "accursed questions." Is Zeus ultimately just? Is human life—finite, measured, and mortal—ultimately meaningful? Or is it all, ultimately, absurd? Sophocles believed we cannot learn enough by telling the stories of ordinary mortals, even exceptional ones like the impressive characters of Aeschylus and Euripides. Only the stories of the Sophoclean daimonic heroes—inevitably tragic because of their irresistible drive to go beyond the human measure—may give us some clue to our place in the universe.

Unlike Aeschylus, Sophocles is not entirely sure that Zeus is indeed just. In some tragedies, Sophocles enacts a hope that Zeus is just. In other tragedies, he clearly does not. After displaying an unrelenting drama of horror and injustice, *Trachiniae* concludes with the uncanny, seemingly hopeless line "there is / nothing here which is not Zeus" (Sophocles 1959, 2:325, lines 1277–78). *Oedipus Tyrannus* ends without hope, but *Oedipus at Colonus* ends with great hope in the form of tragic wisdom, with the suffering hero Oedipus becoming an official *daimon* to be honored at his new shrine at Colonus (the shrine where

Sophocles was a priest for the cultic rituals). Unlike Euripides, Sophocles does clearly believe in the gods and, in some but not all of his plays, believes they are just.

As a deeply committed Christian, Augustine always had graced hope. And yet the self portrayed by Augustine is in some ways very like a Sophoclean *deinos* (so intelligent, so strange), and sometimes like a Sophoclean *daimon*. As we have seen, in the first place, Augustine's self is as intelligent as Augustine himself so clearly was: in discursive rhetorical arguments, in dialogues, in meditation and speculation, and finally in divinizing contemplation with moments of profound, intuitive, theological vision. In the second place, as we have also seen, Augustine's self is always active in affect, emotions, will, and love. The self of Augustine is *deinos*. In the third place, Augustine's understanding of the self also finds itself unable to escape its own self-created prison, its God-denying, other-rejecting, intelligent and loving, self-destructive ego (later named by Martin Luther the self *curvatus in se*). In other words, Augustine's fully positive, intelligent and loving "nature-grace" self is simultaneously a self darkened in intelligence, twisted in will, ever restless and mood-shifting, addicted to its sins, and poisoned by some evil, fate-like, inherited necessity. Both Augustine's nature-grace paradigm and his sin-grace paradigm are fundamental for understanding the complex Augustinian self. Augustine's self bears not only all the characteristics of Sophocles's human being as *deinos*, but also bears, at its extreme limit, the excessive character of a *daimon* (both saint and sinner; Luther's *simul iustus et peccator*). Human beings are capable of the extremes of good (note the importance, for Augustine, of the story of the daimonic saint, Anthony, as a Sophoclean, hero-like monk in the desert—a choice of life clearly beyond the human measure) and evil (as in Augustine's own portrayal of his youthful, Iago-like love of evil for evil's sake in his famous youthful, pointless theft of pears with his friends).

Contrary to his explicit theological intentions, Augustine does in fact implicitly render tragedy, as Milton and Racine did explicitly centuries later, as not only a nature-grace version of the self, not only a sin-grace version, but also, I believe, a Christian tragic version. If Augustine had known Greek tragedy, he would, of course, have theologically transformed the Euripidean, Sophoclean, and Aeschylean tragic elements, as did Calderón, Milton, Racine, Eliot, and other later Christian tragedians, into a distinctly Christian tragic vision, just as he had earlier transformed Platonist philosophy into a Christian contemplative theology. In my judgment, the Latins, unlike the Greeks, produced no great tragedians save the incomparable Virgil and the tragedian *manqué*, Augustine of Hippo. Seneca, usually cited as the greatest Latin tragedian, hardly qualifies: Seneca dramatizes a violent, sensationalized, somewhat Euripidean vision without the precarious tragic balance that Euripides maintained in his best plays and Seneca almost never did. By contrast, Augustine's vision — at once resolutely and explicitly Christian — is also implicitly tragic.

And yet something else — something uncanny — may likewise be the case. Perhaps Augustinian theology, almost alone among ancient Christian theologies and almost alone among modern theologies, was also a theology betraying the few traces of ancient Greek tragedy still alive in Augustine's day of theatrical decadence. Perhaps. At any rate, the authentic greatness of Augustine's complex theological model of the self is that it included both the classical Christian nature-grace and the sin-grace paradigms to understand dimensions of the self. In its overdetermined and ultimately incomprehensible way, Augustine's model of the self is also open to a tragedy-grace paradigm if one would understand its full complexity, plurality, and ambiguity, as well as its real, if elusive, unity. Augustine's understanding of the self is an uncanny one: a self ultimately (i.e., theologically) an incomprehensible *imago dei* of the incomprehensible Trinitarian God in Godself. And yet that same self is penultimately comprehensible only as an overdetermined self — dazzlingly intelligent and loving, constituted by will as energy and will as choice — as well as a graced, sinful, tragic self.

The history of the reception of Augustine has usually consisted in highlighting one or, at most, two of these four major elements as the master key to Augustine's understanding of the self. This will no longer serve. It is time to recover the complete Augustinian, overdetermined portrait of the self. Partial, indeed partisan, readings, however valuable in their historical context, and however insightful they remain for grasping one or the other central element in the self of Augustine, no longer satisfy. For all their brilliance and permanent value, the classical readings of Augustine on the self are not adequate interpretations of the multiple, sometimes conflicting, insights on the self uniquely enacted in our history by Augustine of Hippo in both his thought and his life. *Sui generis* is a phrase that seems to have been invented to describe Augustine: our contemporary, with his incomparable portrait of the self — penultimately overdetermined and ultimately incomprehensible.

REFERENCES

Aeschylus. 1959. *The Eumenides*. Translated by Richard Lattimore. In *Complete Greek Tragedies*, vol. 1, edited by David Grene and Richard Lattimore, 4 vols. Chicago: University of Chicago Press.

Augustine. 1895–1923. *Epistle 120*. In *S. Aureli Augustini Hipponiensis episcopi Epistulae*, edited by Alois Goldbacher. Vol. 34 of *Corpus Scriptorum Ecclesiasticorum Latinorum*. Vindobonae, Austria: F. Tempsky.

———. 1913. *De anima et eius origine libri quattuor*. Edited by Karl Franz Urba and Joseph Zycha. In vol. 60 of *Corpus Scriptorum Ecclesiasticorum Latinorum*. Vindobonae, Austria: F. Tempsky.

———. 1956. *De libero arbitrio libri tres*. Edited by William M. Green. Vol. 74 of *Corpus Scriptorum Ecclesiasticorum Latinorum*. Vindobonae, Austria: Hoelder-Pichler-Tempsky.

———. 1968. *The Retractions*. Translated by Mary Inez Bogan. Fathers of the Church Series, vol. 60. Washington, DC: Catholic University of America Press.

———. 1971. *Saint Augustine: Anti-Pelagian Writings*. Translated by Peter Holmes, Robert Ernest Wallis, and Benjamin B. Warfield. Vol. 5 of *A Select Library of the Nicene and Post-Nicene Fathers of the Christian Church*. Grand Rapids, MI: W. B. Eerdmans.

———. 1984. *The City of God*. Translated by Henry Bettenson. London: Penguin.

———. 1986a. "Homily VII." In *Homilies on the First Letter of John*, in *Saint Augustine: Homilies on the Gospel of John, Homilies on the First Epistle of John, Soliloquies*, translated by H. Browne. Vol. 7 of *A Select Library of the Nicene and Post-Nicene Fathers of the Christian Church*. Grand Rapids, MI: T & T Clark and W. B. Eerdmans.

———. 1986b. *Soliloquiorum libri duo*. Edited by Wolfgang Hörmann. Vol. 89 of *Corpus Scriptorum Ecclesiasticorum Latinorum*. Vindobonae, Austria: Hoelder-Pichler-Tempsky.

———. 1991a. *The Trinity [De Trinitate]*. Translated by Edmund Hill. Hyde Park, NY: New City Press.

———. 1991b. *Confessions*. Translated by Henry Chadwick. Oxford: Oxford University Press.

———. 1992. *Confessions*. Commentary by James J. O'Donnell. 3 vols. Oxford: Clarendon Press.

———. 1997. *Answer to the Pelagians*. Translated by Roland J. Teske. In vol. 23 of

The Works of Saint Augustine: A Translation for the 21st Century. 23 vols. Hyde Park, NY: New City Press.

Ayres, Lewis. 2010. *Augustine and the Trinity*. Cambridge: Cambridge University Press.

Beistegui, Miguel de. 2000. "Hegel, or The Tragedy of Thinking." In *Philosophy and Tragedy*, edited by Miguel de Beistegui and Simon Sparks. London: Routledge.

Benjamin, Walter. 1998. *The Origin of German Tragic Drama*. Translated by John Osborne. London: Verso.

Berdyaev, Nicholas. 1935. *The Fate of Man in the Modern World*. Translated by Donald A. Lowrie. London: SCM Press.

———. 1952. *The Beginning and the End*. Translated by R. M. French. London: G. Bles. Orig. pub. as *Essai métaphysique eschatologique*. Paris: Aubier, 1946.

Bonner, Gerald. 1972. *Augustine and Modern Research on Pelagianism*. Villanova, PA: Augustinian Institute of Villanova University.

———. 1987. *God's Decree and Man's Destiny: Studies on the Thought of Augustine of Hippo*. London: Variorum Studies.

———. 2007. *Freedom and Necessity: St. Augustine's Teaching on Divine Power and Human Freedom*. Washington, DC: Catholic University of America Press.

Brown, Peter. 2000. *Augustine of Hippo: A Biography*. Berkeley: University of California Press.

Burnaby, John. 1954–55. "The *Retractationes* of St. Augustine: Self-criticism or Apologia?" In *Augustinus Magister: Congrès internationale augustinien, Paris, 21–24 September 1954*. 3 vols. Paris: Institut d'Études augustiniennes.

———. 2007. *Amor Dei: A Study of the Religion of St. Augustine; The Hulsean Lectures for 1938*. London: Wipf and Stock Publishers.

Burton, Philip. 2007. *Language in the Confessions of Augustine*. Oxford: Oxford University Press.

Clark, Katerina, and Michael Holquist. 1984. *Mikhail Bakhtin*. Cambridge, MA: Harvard University Press.

Crouse, Robert. 2000 "Paucis Mutatis Verbis: St. Augustine's Platonism." In *Augustine and His Critics: Essays in Honour of Gerald Bonner*, edited by Robert Dodaro and George Lawless. London: Routledge.

Dihle, Albrecht. 1982. *The Theory of the Will in Classical Antiquity*. Berkeley: University of California Press.

Euripides. 1959a. *Bacchae*. Translated by William Arrowsmith. In vol. 4 of *Complete Greek Tragedies*, edited by David Grene and Richard Lattimore, 4 vols. Chicago: University of Chicago Press.

———. 1959b. *Electra*. Translated by Emily Townsend Vermeule. In vol. 4 of *Complete Greek Tragedies*, edited by David Grene and Richard Lattimore, 4 vols. Chicago: University of Chicago Press.

Evans, G. R. 1982. *Augustine on Evil*. Cambridge: Cambridge University Press.

Hadot, Pierre. 1995. *Philosophy as a Way of Life: Spiritual Exercises from Socrates to Foucault*. Edited by Arnold I. Davidson, translated by Michael Chase. Oxford: Blackwell.

Heidegger, Martin. 1995. "Augustinus und der Neuplatonismus." In *Phänomenologie des religiösen Lebens, Gesamtausgabe* 2.60.2. Frankfurt am Main: Klostermann.

Johnson, W. R. 1976. *Darkness Visible: A Study of Virgil's "Aeneid."* Berkeley: University of California Press.

Kant, Immanuel. 1960. *Religion within the Limits of Reason Alone*. Translated by Theodore M. Greene and Hoyt H. Hudson. New York: Harper and Brothers.

Knox, Ronald A. 1961. *Enthusiasm: A Chapter in the History of Religion, with Special Reference to the XVII and XVIII Centuries*. Oxford: Oxford University Press.

Lössl, Josef. 2001. *Julian von Aeclanum: Studien zu seinem Leben, seinem Werk, seiner Lehre und ihrer Überlieferung*. Supplements to vol. 60 of *Vigiliae Christianae*. Leiden: Brill.

MacKinnon, Donald M. 1968. *Borderlands of Theology and Other Essays*. Philadelphia: J. B. Lippincott.

Nygren, Anders. 1982. *Eros and Agape*. Translated by Philip Watson. London: SPCK Publishing.

Pelikan, Jaroslav. 1974. *The Spirit of Eastern Christendom (600–1700)*. In vol. 2 of *Christian Tradition: A History of the Development of Doctrine*. Chicago: University of Chicago Press.

Porphyry. 1966. "On the Life of Plotinus and the Order of His Books." In *Plotinus*, translated by A. H. Armstrong. 7 vols. Cambridge, MA: Harvard University Press.

Reale, Giovanni. 1995. *Aurelio Agostino: Natura del Bene*. Milan: Vita e Pensiero.

Ricoeur, Paul. 1970. *Freud and Philosophy: An Essay on Interpretation*. Translated by Denis Savage. New Haven, CT: Yale University Press.

Sophocles. 1956. *Antigone*. In *Sophocles*, translated by F. Storr. Cambridge, MA: Harvard University Press.

———. 1959. *Women of Tracchis*. Translated by Michael Jameson. In vol. 2 of *Complete Greek Tragedies*, edited by David Grene and Richard Lattimore, 4 vols. Chicago: University of Chicago Press.

Steinmetz, David. 1995. *Calvin in Context*. Oxford: Oxford University Press.

———. 2001. *John Calvin: Writings on Pastoral Piety*. Edited and translated by Elsie Anne McKee. New York: Paulist Press.

Tracy, David. 2005. "The Divided Consciousness of Augustine on Eros." In *Erotikon: Essays on Eros, Ancient and Modern*, edited by Shadi Bartsch and Thomas Bartscherer. Chicago: University of Chicago Press.

———. 2008. "Augustine's Christomorphic Theocentrism." In *Orthodox Readings of Augustine*, edited by Aristotle Papanikolaou and George Demacopoulos. Crestwood, NY: St. Vladimir's Seminary Press.

———. 2012. "Incarnation and Suffering: On Rereading Augustine." In *Godhead Here in Hiding: Incarnation and the History of Human Suffering*, edited by Terrence Merrigan and Frederik Glorieux. Vol. 234 of *Bibliotheca Ephemeridum Theologicarum Lovaniensium*. Leuven, Belgium: Peeters.

Unamuno, Miguel de. 1954. *The Tragic Sense of Life*. Translated by J. E. Crawford Flitch. New York: Dover Publications.

Weil, Simone. (1945) 1977. "The Iliad, or The Poem of Force." In *The Simone Weil Reader*, edited by George Panichas. Wakefield, RI: Moyer Bell.

Williams, Rowan. 2011. *Dostoevsky: Language, Faith and Fiction*. Waco, TX: Baylor University Press.

Wills, Garry. 1999. *St. Augustine*. London: Weidenfeld and Nicolson.

Woolf, Virginia. 1987. "The Russian View." In *The Essays of Virginia Woolf, 1912–1918*, edited by Andrew McNeillie. San Diego: Harcourt Brace Jovanovich.

Yannaras, Cristos. 2007. *Person and Eros*. Translated by Norman Russell. Brookline, MA: Holy Cross Orthodox Press.

Zizioulas, John. 1985. *Being as Communion: Studies in Personhood and the Church*. Crestwood, NY: St. Vladimir's Seminary Press.

CHAPTER 2

AUGUSTINE'S CHRISTOMORPHIC THEOCENTRISM

INTRODUCTION: AUGUSTINE IN FRAGMENTS?

In an essay on Wittgenstein and Nietzsche, Erich Heller (1965, 376–92) developed an interesting dual metaphor: understanding some thinkers is like climbing Mont Blanc; understanding other thinkers is like exploring an ancient city like Rome. First, Mont Blanc: the journey can be tedious, sometimes through detours, always tough. But once you have managed to reach the summit, you know exactly where you are. The surrounding territory lies before you as a clear, ordered, coherent panorama. Heller's philosophical examples for this mountain imagery are nicely chosen: Aristotle and Kant. One can easily add theological examples: Thomas Aquinas, Gregory Palamas, John Calvin — difficult, disciplined, impressive, orderly, coherent panoramic thinkers all.

On the other hand, a never-completed understanding of an ancient city is a good metaphor to understand a very different kind of thinker: Plato, Pascal, Simone Weil, Wittgenstein, Nietzsche, Gregory of Nyssa, Martin Luther, and, surely, Augustine. Years of studying the texts of Augustine is indeed like getting to know an ancient, crowded, labyrinthine city—a city like Rome, with layer after layer of history, with individual neighborhoods often defining an era (for example, Renaissance Rome manifests itself in the Via Giulia and a few Renaissance palaces here and there—all surrounded by Baroque and Risorgimento and contemporary times). One never really knows a city like Rome. One can take walk after walk for years; one can study interminable books of history, art, philosophy, and theology; and one can consult ancient, medieval, Renaissance, Baroque, Risorgimento, and contemporary maps. Despite all that work, any honest explorer of Rome (even a native) is always unsure if one has really understood Rome. One is never quite sure where one is in relationship to the ever-shifting whole named Rome. In my judgment, Heller's city metaphor seems particularly appropriate for those very rare thinkers who are also great artists or, if you prefer, those very rare artists who are also major thinkers: Luther, Nietzsche, Kierkegaard, Pascal, Newman, and Gregory Nazianzen, surely; but especially Plato and Augustine. The thought of these thinker-artists will never yield to a Mont Blanc panorama.

After great and sustained labor, one may believe that one has reached something like an adequate vision of the basic set of distinctions, definitions, and ordering structures that constitute the great work of an Aristotle, a Thomas Aquinas, a Descartes, a Kant, a Whitehead, a Lonergan. Does anyone wish to announce that she has understood all the fragments, resolved all the seeming contradictions, unfolded all Augustine's tropes and topics in his often astounding, late-antique Latin rhetoric? Augustine is a singular writer: both thinker and artist, rhetorician and dialectician, alternately gently dialogical and fiercely polemical, contemplative, and a full-time pastor. Karl Jaspers states that no great thinker was ever as busy with the world's business as Nicholas of Cusa; he forgot Augustine.

Reading Augustine will always disclose new alleys, new diggings (in Augustine's case, newly discovered sermons and letters!), new readers, ever-new admirers and detractors, and new methods of scholarship to shift an emphasis for interpreting Augustinian texts. For example, there is an important difference in understanding Augustine on God, in addition to the emphasis on Augustine's Platonism, from the Courcelle (1968) period of scholarship of the 1950s to the present scholarly insistence that *De Trinitate* can be adequately interpreted only by noting the importance of Augustine's defense of Nicaea against the Latin Homoiusians (*inter alia*, Ayres 2002, 51–76). As with revisions in understanding any ancient, but still thriving, city—Jerusalem, Athens, Rome, and so on—every new scholarly advance complicates but rarely effaces former readings. There is much work still to be done by scholars, literary critics, literary theorists, philosophers, and theologians on the fascinating, debatable, exact relationships of Augustine to Plotinus and Porphyry. In the multiple texts of Augustine and in the texts of his many admirers and critics from his own time until today, Augustine has always remained both a famous and a controversial thinker through the avalanche of conflicting receptions of fragments of his work through the centuries. *Confessions* is the one Augustinian text every educated person in our culture has probably read. Even those contemptuous of other Augustinian texts may well agree with Ludwig Wittgenstein that Augustine's *Confessions* is "perhaps the most serious book ever written."

In the various texts of Augustine, we find a lasting city but not a very stable one. Which text, which fragment, of the enormous oeuvre is most worth attention now? All educated persons enter "Città Augustiniana" in their youth through *Confessions*. Most then journey on to *City of God*. The more philosophically and theologically inclined eventually turn to Augustine's third classic work, *De Trinitate*. Any one of these texts is clearly worth a lifetime or two of scholarly study and hard philosophical and theological reflection. After prolonged study of Augustine's three great classics, however, you will still not be on a mountaintop to envisage the vast Augustinian panorama. Petrarch, after climbing Mount Ventoux with Augustine's *Confessions* in hand, hoped that by rereading *Confessions* on that mountaintop he might finally see clearly the Augustinian vision. In vain: Augustine, I repeat, is not a mountain but an ancient city. Like all of us, Petrarch did see a rich part of Augustine's view (Stock 2001, 71–86). However, again like all of us, Petrarch glimpsed only one part of that crowded city. Augustine is a teaming, overcrowded metropolis. He is not a clean, well-lighted place.

Theological students must also labor with Augustine's polemical texts, those very influential—perhaps, dare I suggest, too influential—texts: against the Skeptics, the Manicheans, the Donatists, the Arians, the Pelagians, and, in *City of God*, even against the formerly honored Platonists. And yet, alongside these polemical texts, there exist also the more serene, the deeply dialogical, mostly nonpolemical early writings from Augustine's leisure years at Cassiciacum and Thagaste. Those early dialogical writings are not only fascinating in themselves; they are also deeply suggestive of the kind of dialogues Augustine may well have continued to write if he had not been forced to leave his life of contemplative leisure (*otium*) and his companions, both at Cassiciacum and in his rural retreat at his home in Thagaste. For Augustine was, in effect, coerced into a bishopric and its enormous pastoral duties. The time of dialogues with like-minded companions was over. His pastoral life as priest, then as bishop, had begun.

Once Augustine became a baptized Christian, this classically trained rhetorician realized he did not know the Bible at all well. His childhood memories on Christianity were of catechesis and Monnica's lessons. As an adult, he held to a dismissive "cultured despiser" view of the Bible, compared to Virgil, Horace, and Cicero. The Platonist allegorical sermons of Ambrose of Milan freed Augustine to read the Bible with new and eager eyes. Moreover, the books of "some Platonists" freed Augustine from his earlier materialistic view of the world. Thus altered, the newly baptized Augustine was ready to become more and more a biblical theologian. One result of Augustine's turn to the Bible has been to lead many contemporary interpreters (myself, among them) to find certain of his biblical commentaries far more important theologically than his more polemical works (La Bonnardière 1986): the sermons, the sermon-commentaries, initially the commentaries on Paul, then the sermon-commentaries on First John and the Sermon on the Mount, the commentaries on Genesis, and his incomparable commentary on the Psalms. In these sermons and biblical commentaries, Augustine's passionate intelligence and full rhetorical genius are ablaze.

Augustine, the thinker and artist, therefore, does not yield to a single vision, from the beginnings of his writings at Cassiciacum through his *Retractions* and his anti–Julian of Eclanum texts at the end. In that sense, even when we possess many full Augustinian texts, what we possess are, in fact, fragments of some larger whole, at once elusive and overdetermined. In Augustine, even the entire texts themselves have become fragmentary: sometimes complementing one another; sometimes merely stranded next to one another like sunken ruins; and sometimes seeming to contradict one another. For example, it is not easy or perhaps even desirable to try to render coherent all Augustine's positions on free will.[1] There are still other fragments in Augustine's texts that are more like verbs than like nouns. Such fragments are not merely fragments of a larger whole, by means of which, as with the German Romantics, nostalgia is evoked for some lost whole (in this case, some lost totality called "true" Augustinianism). Rather, as Walter Benjamin (1999) demonstrated (in his case, principally Trauerspiel, Kabbalistic texts, Kafka, Baudelaire, Proust, nineteenth-century Paris), there are certain texts that, even when we possess the whole text, are intrinsically fragmentary in their explosive power to shatter any temptation of totality or some final, once-and-for-all, "true" interpretation. Only period pieces yield to a once-and-for-all interpretation. Classics never. There are Augustinian fragments (perhaps more accurately named *frag-events*) that dissolve, implode, or explode to manifest unforeseen new meanings not easily assimilable to other fragments.[2] All true readers of Augustine live for a while with one or another fragment—sentences, metaphors, images, at times whole texts.

Some Augustinian images and phrases (frag-events) from *Confessions* have haunted his readers for centuries: "*pondus meum, amor meus*" (my weight is my love; 13.9.10); "*sero te amavi*" (late have I loved you; 10.27.38); "*quaerebam quod amarem, amans amare*" (I searched for something to love, in love with loving; 3.1.1); and, most unforgettably, the Augustinian strain that has haunted Western cultures for centuries: "*tu excitas, ut laudare te delectet, quia fecisti nos ad te et inquietum est cor nostrum, donec requiescat in te*" (you move us to delight in praising you, for you formed us for yourself and our hearts are restless until they find rest in you; 1.1.1).

If one views Augustine's texts through the metaphor of an ancient, layered, overcrowded city, one also may understand better how certain famous longtime visitors (tourists need not apply!) to the "Città Augustiniana" tended to embrace one fragment, one neighborhood—the one that exploded for them as the central theological clue they had long sought. Thomas Aquinas loved Augustine with a purity of mind peculiar to that serene thinker. As one example, Thomas sharpened the more intellectualist moments in Augustine's Trinitarian analogy of God (Lonergan 1967). On the contrary, Cornelius Jansen stated

---

1. Note, for example, the seeming contradictions between the early text *On Free Will* and the later, bleaker, anti-Pelagian *Bondage of the Will* (Defarrari 1968, 32–41).

2. See the introduction to volume 1 of my *Selected Essays*, *Fragments* (2020), and the first chapter there, "Fragments: The Spiritual Situation of Our Time."

that he read most of Augustine "several" times, but he read the anti-Pelagian writings thirty(!) times. Calvin also read the anti-Pelagian writings with unyielding attentiveness. Hans Urs von Balthasar read *De vera religione* even more than *Confessions* as a less subjective, crucial Augustinian text that, for Balthasar, discloses how Augustine found true religion in Christianity's disclosive, beautiful forms (Balthasar 1984, 93–112). Bernard Lonergan read Augustine's early dialogues over and over before he turned to Thomas Aquinas in *Verbum: Word and Idea in Aquinas*; then Lonergan composed his own unique cognitional theory in *Insight* (Liddy 1993, 50–74). Reinhold Niebuhr insisted that his entire Christian theological ethics (which Niebuhr named Christian realism) was really a modern version of *City of God*. So it was. Martin Heidegger's youthful work in his Augustine seminars underlies, more than Heidegger admitted, much of the structure of *Being and Time*: not only "fallenness" but also *Befindlichkeit* is ultimately Augustinian *affectus*; Heidegger's appeals to the cognitive power of mood (*Stimmung*) are Augustinian (Van Buren 1994, esp. 158–96; Coyne 2015).

This very partial list could easily be expanded. Diverse, often conflicting receptions of Augustine in philosophy and Western Christian theology are not the exception but the rule. For the moment, I cite these familiar examples only to suggest that, hermeneutically, the reception of Augustine (*pace* all pure historicists) is sometimes as important for understanding Augustine as are readings determined solely by Augustine's historical context (Gadamer 1989, 171–265). Furthermore, Augustine's dialectical arguments are embedded in and transformed by a rhetoric of both the topics and the tropes. Many postmodern rhetoricians (e.g., Paul de Man, Jacques Derrida, Jacques Lacan, Michel Foucault, Julia Kristeva) prefer the radical, unstable irony of the tropes to the more stable irony of topical arguments. All careful readers can find both kinds of rhetoric in text after text of Augustine. It is fascinating how protean the reception of Augustine continues to be: the last work of the proponent of postmodernity, Jean-François Lyotard, is an unfinished manuscript on Augustine (Lyotard 2000); the too-often-ignored fact that Augustine was a North African theologian writing in a colonial outpost of the Roman Empire has made him newly fascinating to postcolonial critics.[3] On the other hand, despite the efforts of some contemporary interpreters, I fail to see how Augustine's views

---

3. See the interesting essays in Fux, Roessli, and Wermelinger 2003.

on women (*De Trinitate* is an exception) are anything other than a typical, fourth-century, masculinist ideology.[4]

When one states that Augustine was a great fragmentary writer, one means, among other things, that Augustine was not a writer with a single, unchanging theological vision (as, for example, Evagrius was; as Irenaeus seems to have been). Peter Brown nicely stated that, even after Augustine's conversion, he never felt fully healed: Augustine was always a Christian in convalescence. One can justly add to Brown's apposite comment that, intellectually, Augustine, in his philosophical and theological thinking, as much as in his artistic imagination, was never at rest. He was always rethinking his theological vision, always *inquietum*. Except for *De Trinitate* and some biblical commentaries, most of his writing is occasional. In *Retractions*, Augustine tried to render his thought more coherent than it probably was. The plural and complex imagination of Augustine can be viewed not as a defect but as an advantage. Most major postmodern artists and thinkers are more bricoleurs than systematic thinkers. They tend to build their final vision (if one emerges) by collating ever-changing fragments into diverse, collage-like texts. Among modern poets, think of Emily Dickinson and Gerard Manley Hopkins: both fragmented the English langage to express their poetic vision with greater accuracy. Think of that propagandist of modernist fragmenting literature, with his *Cantos* or fragments. Indeed, most major modernist poets are a stark contrast to the rarer modern poetic visionaries of a single, commanding vision: Blake, Rimbaud, Wordsworth, Whitman. The difference between the fragmentary artist or thinker and the artist of a single vision is not at all a difference of quality. It is a difference of temperament, a difference of historical context, and a difference of genre: lyric poetry is not epic; a haiku is not an ode. In fact, visionary poets with a single commanding vision often do not seem to fare well in fragmented and fragmentary modernity:[5] Rimbaud very early abandoned poetry altogether; Wordsworth and Whitman, in later life, kept adding to and revising their original vision until they almost ruined it. Most modern artists have a similar fragmentary stance, most famously, Pablo Picasso That is why, after all, we find it necessary to speak of early and late Wittgenstein; early and late Heidegger; early and late Karl Barth; early and late Karl Rahner, and others.

---

4. For a contrary, subtle view, see Børresen 1981.

5. For the concept *fragmentary* as distinct from *fragment*, see Blanchot 1992 and Hart 2004 (67–87). For my own view of the fragment, see chapter 1, "Fragments," in volume 1 of my *Selected Essays, Fragments.*

As contemporary receptions — often intellectual revivals — demonstrate, the thinkers of an ever-elusive, fragmentary vision disclosed in a work always-in-process can seem more helpful in our fragmented and fragmentary day: note the distinct philosophical retrievals of Plato's Good beyond Being in Emmanuel Levinas and Iris Murdoch; note also the surprising new turn in many Western theologians to Gregory of Nyssa; and note some new ways that Martin Luther is now interpreted — from traditional grace-sin perspectives to the *unio Christi* (even deification!) interpretations of Luther by the new Finnish school (Braaten and Jenson 1998). No reading of any great classic can ever prove definitive. Classic texts are at best fragmentary. Period pieces are all too unitary.

AUGUSTINE'S THEOCENTRISM AND CHRISTOMORPHISM

In some event, epiphany, or manifestation, or through the "hints and guesses"[6] afforded by fragments of life, art, and religion affecting our lives deeply, one can become more receptive to naming the Real anew: the Void, the Open, Being, the One, Creativity, the gods, the Good, God.[7] Today many major thinkers (not only the radically monotheistic Christians, Jews, and Muslims) find that the Real somehow discloses itself as itself for our naming and understanding it (revelation). The only name that we can create through reason alone for the Real is a name at the limits of the possible, that is, at the limits of reason (e.g., God as a limit-concept for Kant). Some modern philosophers persuasively argue for the reasonableness of belief in naming the Real as God (e.g., the careful analytical studies of Alvin Plantinga, and the more constructive naming of God in process thinkers like John Cobb, Franklin Gamwell, Schubert Ogden, et al.).

Other philosophers, modern, ancient, and medieval, argue for the reasonableness of naming the Real as the impersonal Good beyond Being (Murdoch), or as the Open (Heidegger), or as the Void (Nietzsche), or as Creativity (Whitehead and Hartshorne), or as the gods (Hölderlin), or as *Esse Ipsum Subsistens* (Thomas Aquinas and Étienne Gilson), or as *Ipsum Intelligere* (Thomas Aquinas and Bernard Lonergan), or as the One (Plotinus). But very few contemporary thinkers, on the basis of reason alone, presume to name the Real at

---

6. The phrase is from T. S. Eliot's *Four Quartets* (1968, 30).

7. I analyze these namings of the Real in the forthcoming *This Side of God*.

all. The Real must somehow disclose itself (revelation) for our acknowledgment (faith) and philosophical-theological naming. Not only biblical thinkers realize this. For example, Nietzsche insisted that his ultimate name for the Real—will to power as eternal return—is a result, in Nietzsche's own language, of both "revelation" and "inspiration" (a word Nietzsche says he is surprised to use). Indeed, Nietzsche names the exact places (Genoa and Sils-Maria) and the exact times that the revelation of eternal return happened (a large stone on the exact spot at Sils-Maria memorializes it—or, in the fine German word, *ein Denkmal*, a time and place to think).

It is also the case that the later Heidegger dared to name the Real the Open by thinking meditatively, that is, receptively, with certain thinkers (the pre-Socratics), certain works of art (Rilke, Hölderlin, the Greek temple, van Gogh's and Cézanne's paintings). Even more so, I believe, the later Heidegger learned to name the Real through the radical Open described in the classic way of Taoism. Moreover, Other Power revealing itself in the ever-repeated name Amida in Pure Land Buddhism is a lucid candidate for the Real. Plato's "the Good beyond Being" cannot be arrived at through dialectical effort on its own but must happen, must be given, not achieved, just as in *Symposium* the Beautiful Itself also happens "suddenly."

By means of such events or happenings, the Real manifests itself for naming. In Augustine, as for the Jewish middle Platonist Philo before him and Thomas Aquinas after him, there is one great exception to the Real disclosing itself as impersonal Void, or Open, or the Good, followed by our philosophical labor to name that disclosure more fully through philosophy and theology (*fides quaerens intellectum*). As Philo acutely claimed, the Real as God discloses Godself by name in Exodus 3:14, at least in the Septuagint Greek (Philo) and Latin (Augustine, Thomas Aquinas, et al.) translations of the original Hebrew. "*Ego sum qui sum*" (I am who am) is one such Latin translation of the Hebrew *ehye asher ehye*. The Septuagint Greek and Latin translations of Exodus 3:14 are not errors, as some exegetical purists claim, although they are only two possible translations of the original Hebrew naming of God (LaCocque and Ricoeur 1998, 307–30).

The truest naming of God for Augustine, however, is not Exodus 3:14, nor the Plotinian One Good. For Augustine, God reveals Godself decisively through Christ in both creation and redemption. As Love, God is the Trinity of the loving, distinct, and interrelated divine persons (*persona, prosopa*) of Father, Son, Holy Spirit. For Augustine, to so name God as Love (and therefore, the Ultimate Real) occurred to him not principally through personal mystical experience in the garden (*Tolle, lege*) at Milan and with Monnica at Ostia[8] but through faith (as gift) in the revelation (as given) of Jesus Christ. One can reformulate Augustine's point this way: God is Love (1 John 4:16) only by naming Jesus of Nazareth the Christ. The Jesus affirmed in the Christian confessions is not "the historical Jesus," that is, the Jesus constituted by modern historical-critical methods. Rather the Jesus confessed as the Christ by Christians is the actual Jesus, the unsubstitutable, historical person Jesus of Nazareth whose words, actions, and sufferings are narrated in the four Gospels and in the confessions of St. Paul and all the early Christian communities. For the Christian, only by naming Jesus the Christ can one find God a decisive name — the same God named in the Tanakh as Yahweh; the same God later named as Allah in the holy Qur'an. Through faith in Jesus the Christ, the Christian names the One God as Love-Trinity. In Augustine's own words, to name God truly (i.e., as Trinitarian love) is possible only by confessing through Jesus Christ the man (*per Christum hominem*) to Christ as God (*ad Christum divinum*). In Augustinian Christology, the Form Christ gathers all other forms to name God: *per Christum hominem ad Christum divinum*. Augustine's theology is theocentric through and through. At the same time, Augustine's theocentrism is constituted through his emphatic Christomorphism, theologically focused on Christ as Mediator and *totus Christus* as theologically including Christ's church.

Even those theologians who do not admire Augustine's wondrous *De Trinitate* as much as I do must admit that to understand the heart of Augustine's theology in its full-fledged theocentrism, we are very fortunate to possess not only the fragments of several other Trinitarian reflections throughout Augustine's oeuvre, but also his one, fully systematic treatise on God in God's Trinitarian oneness: on the Real, the Trinitarian monotheism wherein God is Love, that God is Trinity. This Trinitarian theocentrism is in Augustine profoundly Christomorphic. For Augustine, only through the Form of forms, the incarnate Mediator, Jesus Christ, do Christians adequately learn to name God as Love, as Triune.

And yet there remains a problem in understanding Augustine's Christology: namely, that, unlike in his treatise on God, *De Trinitate*, Augustine did

---

8. For a balanced account of the debate on whether Augustine had mystical experiences at Milan and in Ostia with Monnica, see McGinn 1991, 228–38.

not write a single, systematic treatise on Christology. In terms of the later genre of systematics, Augustine is not really a systematic theologian. He is more like Luther than like Calvin or Melanchthon; more like Bernard of Clairvaux than like Thomas Aquinas or even Bonaventure, who is at times a systematic — even a Scholastic — theologian (e.g., in the *Breviloquium*). Nevertheless, Augustine's Christology is the central Form of his entire theology. Christology throughout the work of Augustine informs and transforms all his theology: on God, on creation, on grace, on eschatology, on ecclesiology, on anthropology.

Furthermore, a similar search is needed to gather all the fragmentary texts in Augustine's scattered texts on the Spirit (e.g., TeSelle 1999, 434–37). Otherwise, we erroneously accuse Augustine (as has been done too often) of Christomonism. It is the case that Augustine, like Western theology in general, lacked a fully developed ontological as distinct from a profound devotional doctrine of the Holy Spirit of the kind that one finds in the Eastern Christian tradition from Basil of Caesarea forward. But this typical Western underdevelopment of the full theology of the Spirit has yielded in recent years to several Western highly developed pneumatologies (e.g., Roger Haight). Augustine was not a Christomonist. The Christ-saturated Augustine, as his *Enarrationes in Psalmos* shows, is also a Spirit-saturated theologian. It is true that Augustine needed to learn far more than he ever did (his Greek was not fluent) from his Cappadocian older contemporaries in order to develop a fuller objective and subjective doctrine of the Holy Spirit. At the same time Augustine did possess a clear and strong doctrine of the Spirit in multiple texts.

Augustine's underdeveloped pneumatology is a real lack in his theology, as in most Western theology until recently. At the same time, one finds in the theocentric-Christomorphic Augustine one of the most impressive Christologies of the Incarnate Mediator in all Christian theology, even though Augustine's Christology unfortunately was never expressed systematically in a single treatise. Perhaps the fact that Augustine did not devote a major single treatise to Christology as he did to the Trinity has caused his Christology to be undervalued in many histories of doctrine and histories of theology by being read as simply one more admirable but not notably original Neoplatonic Christology of mediation. Augustine's Christology is indeed a Mediator Christology, but also far more than that. To see how this is the case demands appealing to several Augustinian texts, images, metaphors, arguments — in sum, to many different fragments of Augustine's Christology scattered throughout his oeuvre. Only then can one appreciate the richness and complexity of Augustine's actual

Christology. Only then—*per Christum hominem ad Christum divinum* and, I presume to add, *per Christum divinum ad Deum Trinitatem* (through Christ as God to God as Trinity)—can we grasp Augustine's naming of the Real as the Triune, the One God who is Love and, as Love, is also the mutual, loving, communal relationships of Father, Son, and Holy Spirit.

CHRISTOLOGICAL FRAGMENTS

In histories of doctrine and histories of theology, Augustine's Christology is usually described as a traditional Mediator Christology. In terms of the Person of Christ, Augustine's Christology is often further described as Chalcedonian *avant la lettre*: Augustine died in 430 CE; Ephesus occurred in 431 (he had been invited); Chalcedon in 451. The descriptions of Augustine's Christology as Christ the Mediator are, of course, accurate. Without the technical terms of Chalcedon, Augustine's understanding of the Person of Christ was proto-Chalcedonian (i.e., One Divine Person in two natures). Augustine always held to the definition of Nicaea. In fact, Augustine, in fidelity to Ambrose in the strong, anti-Arian position of Ambrose, also consistently (most notably in the early anti-Arian books of his *De Trinitate*) stood fast against the characteristically Latin Arian position. There can be no doubt that Augustine held a strong Nicene Christology and a strong Mediator Christology.

▪ But should that be the end of a discussion of Augustine's Christology? On the one hand, there is no single Augustinian treatise on Christology; on the other hand, Christology is the most pervasive reality in all his works. Christ the Mediator for Augustine is Christ the Incarnate God-man, above all Christ the Form of both true God and true human being. As the Form of Forms, Christ informs all reality, transforms all theology. Christ the Form is not only incarnational but, as in Augustine's too-often-ignored theology of the cross (for example, in the *Enarrationes in Psalmos*), is also Christ as Cruciform Form. Augustine, in the Psalms commentary-sermons, even dares to speak of *Deus crucifixus*. The cruciform Christ form not only informs and transforms all theology (in harmony with the kenotic incarnation), but also shatters and fragments any Christology that may be tempted to remain only a traditional Mediator Christology. Jesus Christ the Mediator, Christ the Form of Forms, Christ the kenotic Incarnate God, Christ the Fragmenting Cruciform, Christ the Risen One, are the indispensable foundations of Augustine's Christology. That complex Christological structure, however, is not Augustine's whole Christological edifice. His fuller Christological position can be built up only by gathering the varied Christological fragments in Augustine's early, middle, and late works. Fortunately, Basil Studer's classical scholarly work (1997) has gathered together the more important Christological fragments to aid any theological attempt to formulate Augustine's full Christology.

The exact nature of Christ as Mediator for Augustine continues to attract scholarly attention. Given the Platonist understandings of the notion of mediation in Augustine, early and late, Augustine's Christology of Christ as Mediator is directly related to both Nicaea and to Platonism. As it happens, Augustine's largely Platonist formulation of the category of mediation is more important in the development of the pre-Chalcedonian Christology of the Person of Christ than earlier scholars like Adolf von Harnack (who tended to elide the Christology of Christ's Person as God-human mediating incarnation to the soteriological work of Christ as mediator of salvation) noticed. Indeed, in the last three decades, the precise relationship of the Augustinian Christology on the Person of Christ as Mediator to the debates within Neoplatonism from Porphyry through Iamblichus, as well as later to Proclus in the sixth century, has admitted renewed scholarly attention. This can be seen, for example, in the work of Giovanni Reale (1994). Reale's thesis is persuasive to me: post-Plotinus, the major theoretical difficulty for all Neoplatonic thinkers was the philosophical need to determine the forms of mediation necessary to allow the Plotinian One to emanate to the many. In Reale's reading, the pagan Neoplatonists kept complicating emanation by multiplying the forms of mediation from the Plotinian One Good to the many (including from Iamblichus through theurgy).

On the other hand, for Reale Augustine's strategy — as an explicitly Christian Platonist — was the exact opposite: Augustine argued persuasively in Christian theological Neoplatonic terms that Jesus Christ, the God-man as the Mediator, was the only mediation needed. Unlike Iamblichus and the pagan Neoplatonists after Plotinus, Augustine, through his Christology of Christ, the One Mediator, simplified the Platonic issue of mediation rather than further complicating the Neoplatonic problem of too many mediations from the overflowing, emanating, impersonal One Good of Plotinus. Augustine could thus simplify the problem since, as a Christian, he held to a kenotic, personal God who so loves the world that God the Father with the Spirit sends the Son as the divine love itself by means of creation (not emanation) and salvation by

Jesus Christ as Mediator. Christ bestows God's kenotic love to creatures who have sinfully soiled the gifted (kenotic) love of God in creation. In that theological sense (Harrison 2000), humans are wounded and deeply damaged but nevertheless have not lost their essence as *imago dei*. God's love, both ecstatic and kenotic, is rendered present in and through the ultimate, singular, sufficient mediation—namely, the personal Mediator Jesus Christ, the Incarnate God-Man. The "pagan" Neoplatonists complicated the problem of mediation by ever more mediations of emanation. Augustine solved the problem of mediation for Christian Platonists through Christ the One Mediator.

As noted earlier Pierre Hadot's (1995) works have demonstrated, all the ancient philosophers and theologians (whether Stoic, Epicurean, Aristotelian; whether pagan, Jewish, or Christian Platonist) held that philosophy-theology was never a purely theoretical discipline, as it usually is in modernity. Theory and practice were rarely divorced in ancient thought, as they regrettably are for many, probably most, philosophers in modern Western philosophy and theology. Some scholars hold that this separation of practice and theory (philosophy as a way of life; philosophy as a theory of life) began when Western medieval theology moved from the monasteries to the universities. Yet this claim needs more nuanced distinction. As the Scholastics rightly insisted, distinctions are not separations. For example, Thomas Aquinas, for whom Augustine always remained the principal theological authority, developed many fine distinctions on theological and philosophical issues that were not separations at all, including the distinction, not separation, between theory and practice. Moreover, Thomas's major contemporary at the University of Paris, Bonaventure, another Augustinian, correlated the new Franciscan spirituality of creation to traditional Augustinian interiority as well as to the achievements of high Scholasticism. As a result, in Bonaventure's more Scholastic works and even more so in his other works (especially his classic *Itinerarium mentis in Deum*), Bonaventure's medieval theology does not separate theory from practice, spirituality from theology. Unfortunately, however, certain fatal separations did occur in later Western philosophy and theology, from the nominalists of the late medieval period through the strangely eclectic, sixteenth-century theoretical philosophy of Suárez to much modern philosophy, including the Suárezian Thomism of much modern Western Neo-Scholasticism. The Suárezian influence in the Neo-Scholastics was fortunate for law but mostly unfortunate for philosophy and theology. In fact, Neo-Scholasticism, the once all-powerful, modern Catholic philosophical and theological force, seemed to believe, as Bernard Lonergan once observed, in clear and distinct ideas — and very few of them.

Paradoxically, the Neo-Scholastics were far less interested in Augustine than Descartes was. For them, Augustine was an "inspiring" but rhetorical thinker. In separating philosophy (or theology) as theory from philosophy or theology as a way of life, most modern Western thought lost the concern with specific spiritual practices so characteristic of all the ancient schools. Even more importantly, "modern" theology ignored what Bernard McGinn names a third form of medieval theology — the lay theologies often written in the vernacular, especially by medieval female mystics. By way of contrast, in Eastern Christian thought, with its contemplative character and its liturgical and cosmic character, the fatal, modern Western theological separation of theory and practice rarely occurred; on the other hand, in some Orthodox theology, this separation does occur in neo-Palamite terms. The sustained contemporary Western Christian interest in Orthodox theology, since the French Catholic theologians of *ressourcement* (such as Daniélou, de Lubac, Congar, the Swiss Balthasar, et al.), is partly due to the need, among Western theologians, to learn how Orthodox theology, even in modernity, managed not to separate theory from practice, nor theology from spirituality.

The fact of the separation of theory and practice and the attendant loss of a contemplative moment in much Western theology has also occasioned, in my judgment, serious repercussions in modern Western theological interpretations of Augustine's theology of Christ as Mediator. For example, the problem of many modern Catholic theological readings of Augustine had a difficulty directly the opposite of Liberal Protestant near-reductions of Christ's person to Christ's work. In fact, many Catholic theologians interpreted Augustine's Christology as almost exclusively concerned with Christ's person (the Mediator) and its proleptic relationship to Chalcedon. Among Catholic interpreters, soteriological concerns, the main focus of Liberal Protestant interpreters since Harnack, were quietly shifted to Augustine's ontological theology of grace and his ecclesiology.

Fortunately, in our day there has been a remarkable shift of emphasis in contemporary Augustinian scholarship away from Augustine's relationship to his theoretical side of Neoplatonism to his more doctrinal (that is, Nicene) concerns, as well as a new emphasis on the richer Christology to be found in Augustine's biblical commentaries and sermons. This new emphasis in Augustine can be found in his commentaries and sermons *De sermone Domini in monte*

(*On the Sermon of the Mount*), *In evangelium Ioannis tractatus* (*Tractates on the Gospel of John*), *Tractatus in epistolam Ioannis* (*Tractates on the First Epistle of John*), as well as Augustine's Christological readings of the Old Testament, not only in the more familiar Augustinian readings of Paul for a theology of grace but, even more so, in Augustine's development of his fuller Mediator Christology of the person *and* the work of Christ, especially in his *Enarrationes in Psalmos* (*Expositions of the Psalms*). In addition, recent scholarly attention to Augustine's sermons and letters (aided, of course, by the discovery of further sermons and letters and the hope, with the aid of modern technology, for yet more discoveries) has enriched interpretations of Augustine's Christology as Christ the Mediator. Christ's mediatorship in Augustine is more complex than many earlier modern Catholic, and most modern Protestant, or modern Orthodox readings had acknowledged.

In sum, thanks to contemporary Augustinian scholarship, all theologians have been driven to reread the relevant polemical works (especially the Latin anti-Arianism works) and to reread with more scriptural and doctrinal eyes the three classic Augustinian texts — *Confessiones, De civitate Dei,* and *De Trinitate.* Theologians also now read, often for the first time, the many letters, sermons, and the biblical commentaries to understand the more complex contours of Augustine's Christology. There are multiple ways to illuminate not only Christ's person as Mediator but also Christ's work. In Augustine, Christ is both the way to God and the homeland longed for.[9] In still other texts, we can find Augustine interpreting Christ as both the external and the interior teacher as well as Christ as both the physician and the medicine taken. In addition, in one of Augustine's most striking metaphors for the church, the church is the hospital where we receive the Mediator-physician's several medicines (the Sacraments, preaching, spiritual counseling, and actions guided by the *ordo caritatis*).

Augustine as bishop learned the Bible more fully in order to preach to his people and to transform himself Christianly. It is also important to remember that Augustine's sermons were preached to a very mixed congregation, including ordinary people — among them, the largely illiterate congregation of provincial Hippo. One can observe this crowded pastoral side of Augustine in the older but still very informative work of Frederik van der Meer, *Augustine the Bishop* (1961). More recently, one can also observe Augustine the pas-

---

9. For Christ as both way and homeland, see Madec 1989.

tor in the appendix to the revised edition of Peter Brown's biography, *Augustine of Hippo* (Brown 2000, 441–73). In a characteristically modest moment of scholarly self-correction, Brown comments that the newly discovered sermons and letters of the old Augustine in his episcopal role as caring, compassionate pastor for his people call into serious question the harsher portrait of the late Augustine that he (Peter Brown) held in the first edition. Augustine was certainly harsh and extreme in his late polemical controversies with Julian of Eclanum. Julian himself, to be sure, was just as fierce and polemical in return. In my judgment (*pace* Jansenius and Calvin), the dispute between the elderly Augustine and the young Julian is, on the whole, not a happy sight. In the same time period, however, in sermon after sermon, in pastoral action after action for his people (including legal juridical work for a good part of his everyday life, such as serving as a judge of family disputes over property), Augustine showed his pastoral rather than polemical side. In the sermons we possess, unlike his anti-Pelagian treatises, Augustine did not seem to preach double predestination to his people. As his sermons and commentaries make clear, Augustine distinguished but never separated his understanding of Christ's person from Christ's work. The key is Augustine's almost mantra-like description of the Christian way to God: *per Christum hominem ad Christum divinum* (Studer 1997, 43–47).

A typical quotation from the sermons:

> Now because Christ is himself truth and life with the Father, the Word of God, of which it says The life was the light of men (Jn 1.4); so because he is with the Father life and truth, and because we didn't have any way of getting to the truth, the Son of God, who is always in the Father truth and life, became the way by taking to himself a man. Walk along the man, and you arrive at God. You go by him, you come to him: Don't look for a way to come to him by, apart from him. After all, if he had refused to be the way, we would always be going astray.
>
> So he became the way; by which you could come to him. I'm not telling you, "Look for the way"; the way itself has come to you; get up and walk.[10]

Christ as both true God and true human being is more and more portrayed frequently by Augustine as radically humble — that is, kenotic. God entered

---

10. *Sermons*, 141, 411 (*Sermons on the New Testament* 3.4.94A–147A), in Augustine 1992.

our darkness in the flesh of Jesus Christ. The great hymn of Paul in Philippians sings the Word's kenotic, humble, compassionate movement, from the "form of God" to the "form of a slave." At the same time, Augustine, in his sermons and biblical commentaries, deliberately traveled beyond Paul's relative lack of attention to the teachings, ministry, and life of the Jesus of the four Gospels.

On the doctrinal-symbolic level of theology, therefore, Augustine joined a Pauline kenotic reading of the incarnation to Paul's theology of the cross in order to articulate the central doctrinal-symbolic dialectic of Christian faith: incarnation-cross-resurrection. It is this tripartite Christological doctrinal complex that led Augustine's Pauline kenotic theology to his further, more narratively detailed Christology in the Gospels. We find God by following the way of the Incarnate God-man, Jesus the Christ. The all-important mediating way of Christ the Mediator became clearer and clearer for Augustine through the narrated details of the life of Jesus in the Gospels. Eventually, for Augustine, the Gospels and the Psalms, even more than Paul, spell out how we may move *per Christum hominem ad Christum divinum*. As early as the dialogue with his son Adeodatus, *De Magistro*, Augustine discovered one aspect of this *"per-ad"* motif: Jesus was the teacher who became the interior teacher of the Christian way. Furthermore, as the influence of Paul's Philippians imprinted itself on Augustine's mind, he increased his attention to the affections and, therefore, to the centrality of the Christian virtues of humility and *caritas* for the Christian way, Christologically construed. Augustine, unlike most Platonists, believed that the "affections" counted intellectually. Remarkably, the Platonist Augustine prayed to God not for less but for more affections!

Augustine strongly held that if one follows the way of the narrated Jesus of the Gospels, one follows the way of one "like us in all things save sin" — the Jesuanic way of compassionate suffering and joyous, vulnerable, humble, kenotic love for others. In Augustine's theology, any Christian graced by God in Christ is graced to live the way of Jesus. For Augustine, no Christian disciple should expect or desire a purely tranquil life of ancient *apatheia*. Despite a lifelong commitment to contemplation, which continued every evening in his small monasterium next to his episcopal cathedral, Augustine did not finally wish for a life of *apatheia* — that noble ancient ideal, whether Stoic or Platonist, as well as for some ancient Christians (e.g., Evagrius). To repeat: Augustine had once hoped to live, converse, and write with his friends at Cassiciacum and at his rural hometown Thagaste. After Augustine became priest and bishop, all that changed. Without abandoning the ideal of contemplative interiority, Augustine modified that contemplative ideal considerably (presumably at great personal price). He did so not for his own sake but in order to serve his people every day, all day before returning to the monastery-like companionship of his priestly colleagues. Later Christians named this now-familiar Christian spiritual way "contemplation-in-action." Through his dual love of the contemplative ideal and of ceaseless pastoral activity in the world, Augustine was one of the earliest Christian proponents of this option. *Pondus meum, amor meus.*

Moreover, in his Psalms commentaries, and sermons, Augustine states (in his commentary on Psalm 140:7) that two texts provide the key for understanding all Scripture:[11] Paul, as Saul, hearing the voice saying "Why do you persecute me?" and Matthew 25, on the test beyond all beliefs in doctrines, the final Christian test of action for others, above all the poor, the oppressed, the marginal, the hungry, the naked, the mad, the possessed, the imprisoned.

In his ever-developing Christology, Augustine consistently believed that we are led by Jesus Christ as Mediator, teacher, and healer — at times to become "deified" (Augustine is relatively sparse in his use of this familiar Eastern Christian language), more often to become adopted sons and daughters of Christ by discipleship *per Christum hominem ad Christum divinum.* One final, surprising — perhaps even shocking — fragment in Augustine's fuller Christology: Augustine was often driven to dark Christological reflections, where he dares, like St. Paul, to speak of *Deus crucifixus*; only through the afflicted, human Jesus (*per Christum hominem*) does the *Christum divinum* emerge. The form of Christ is cruciform; the cruciform shatters and fragments all Christian complacency, including Augustine's earlier, more sanguine Mediator Christology.

CONCLUSION: THE INEXORABLE CHRISTOLOGICAL DRIVE OF AUGUSTINE

Augustine's Christology — at least the very abbreviated version I have formulated and articulated above — can be fully comprehended only by gathering the many Augustinian Christological fragments into a tentative interpreted unity. Of course, this is only a beginning. Even if my readings of Augustine's Christology are persuasive, these interpretations would only serve to initiate a study

---

11. *Enarrationes in Psalmos,* 140.7 (*Expositions of the Psalms, 121–150,* III/20), in Augustine 2004, 306.

of Augustine's full Christology. Above all, we need extended theological reflection on how, exactly, Augustine's *per Christum hominem ad Christum divinum* Christology, allied to his pneumatology, leads to naming of the Real as the Trinitarian God who is Love.

There remain some further implications of Augustine's Christology for contemporary thought. First, Augustine's Christology implicitly addresses the Void named by so many contemporary thinkers as their principal concern. What other early Christian thinker was so obsessed with the Void-producing question, *unde malum*? (Evans 1982). Julian of Eclanum was erroneous and unjust to sneer that the elderly Augustine was still a Manichean. Augustine had abandoned the Manichean anti-body, antimarriage, antireproduction positions. Unlike every Pelagian, then or now, Augustine stared into the nihilistic abyss of evil, the ultimate Void. To be sure, Augustine, good Platonist as he was, interpreted evil ontologically as *privatio boni*. However, unlike some other Platonists, Augustine's incorporation of evil as *privatio boni* did not remove the existential sting of the Void-Abyss opened by the never-ending question for Augustine: *unde malum*?

From another, much more positive, angle on the Void, the endless abyss of the cavern of *memoria* — surely one of Augustine's greatest philosophical discoveries (Garry Wills) — can be read as a positive reading of the Void-Abyss, analogous to Zen Buddhism's even more positive portrait of the Void. Augustine, too, wants us to let go to — that is, to understand and will — the abyssal, void-like cavern of our memory. On the other hand, Augustine's increasingly angry and, at times, almost desperate rhetoric in his angry exchanges with Julian of Eclanum suggests that some deep sense of the existential void of evil, and not just the Platonic concept of evil as the ontological nonbeing (*privatio boni*), never left Augustine.

Augustine's fury at the Pelagian moralistic refusal to understand the depth of the void of evil and thereby our never-ending need for God's grace sounds, Bolero-like, louder and louder in his final anti-Pelagian writings. Augustine has always and will always appeal to anyone who cannot entirely silence a deep sense of the Void, even in the midst of a ineradicable faith in God's grace: Luther with his two senses of the hidden God; Pascal with his sense of the silence of infinite space; Paul Tillich with his belief that a sense of meaninglessness, a sense of the void, is now the principal concern of many Christians. An Augustinian sense of Void emerges both positively, through his discovery of the cave-abyss of *memoria* at the heart of our inwardness (another example of the nature-grace typology in Augustine), as well as negatively, through his over-riding sense of the power of evil in us and the ineluctable power of the question *unde malum*? (an especially powerful example of the sin-grace typology in Augustine). Augustine will always be a natural conversation partner for anyone, believer or nonbeliever, who possesses any powerful experience of the actuality of the Void. Augustine knew that we could be saved only by God's grace — the only Other Power strong enough to save us from the negative Void within and without, that nihil we self-destructively seem unable not to seek (*non posse non peccare*).

Nor is Augustine irrelevant to a Heideggerian option on naming the Real as the Open. For all the Romantics and, in a strikingly new way, for the later Heidegger, the power of the Real as the Open is disclosed by every great work of art. After *Being and Time*, Heidegger abandoned Augustine and moved to a new mode of contemplative thinking (Heidegger called it meditative thinking as distinct from calculative thinking). Heidegger's later philosophical thought — no longer Christian but still religious through and through — certainly was not grounded in God, as Augustine's always was, nor did Heidegger's later thought rest in the Void of *Being and Time* (i.e., Death replaces God as our destiny). The Void of Death — the end of all possibility for *Dasein* — must be personally appropriated resolutely. The Real for the Heidegger of *Being and Time*, more than he admitted perhaps even to himself, was the Void opened up to authentic *Da-sein* to be appropriated as the Real of one's own death, as Jacques Lacan, that Augustinian *manqué*, saw more clearly than Heidegger himself did. After his further, Nietzsche-inflected work on the Void, the later Heidegger emerges; his late turning to the Real as the Open manifested and hidden through the artwork, the "clearing," and ultimately, I believe, through a Western Heideggerian form of Taoism and Zen Buddhism.

What if Heidegger had continued his reading of Augustine after *Being and Time*? What if he had read, among other Augustinian texts, the Genesis commentaries for their disclosure of what he sought: an Open disclosing the goodness of the infinite differences of each and every reality — for Augustine, each real being created by a kenotic loving Creator God? Of course, Heidegger did not continue to read Augustine. Even if he had, Heidegger post Nietzsche probably would not have found Augustine persuasive at all. After all, God was as dead for Heidegger as for Nietzsche, from Heidegger's famous Nietzsche interpretation forward. Nevertheless, the contemporary discussion on the best name for the Real — the Void, the Open, Creativity, the Good, the gods,

God—would have been greatly enhanced, I suggest, if the full complexity of Augustine's Christomorphic theocentrism were more fully comprehended by the once-Augustinian Heidegger. Given the enormous influences of Heidegger (along with Nietzsche himself) in postmodern thought, a continued Augustinian moment could have been very fruitful for later postmodernity. At the same time Augustine is still present in myriad different forms in several secular postmoderns—Lacan, Kristeva, Derrida, and Lyotard, among them—but never as deeply and pervasively as in the early Heidegger (Coyne 2015).

Despite Augustine's reputation in our culture as "pessimistic," Augustine's final word is more accurately described as hopeful, rather than either optimistic or pessimistic. Optimism and pessimism, if they are virtues at all, are purely natural ones. Optimism and pessimism are attitudes largely dependent less on choice than on one's temperament, one's society, and one's personal and historical fate. It is perhaps impossible not to be pessimistic after all the evil, the slaughters, the horrors, the totalitarian ideologies of the twentieth century. Augustine was what William James (1985, 71–139) named "a sick soul" (restless, conflicted, convalescent). In that sense, Augustine was a natural pessimist. However, Augustine never was—save possibly at Cassiciacum—what James named the alternative human type: a "healthy-minded" optimist.

In his Christian conversion, Augustine turned (or more accurately, as he would insist, was turned by God's grace) from his natural, sick-souled temperament to a usually joyous faith working through love and hope. After Augustine's acceptance of priestly and episcopal duties, with their inevitable exposure to life's struggles, joys and sorrows, good and evil, whatever earlier optimism was present at Cassiciacum retreated into the cave of his memory. Existentially, Augustine was never fully cured; he was always convalescent. Intellectually, Augustine was always restless. At the same time, Augustine discovered in Christianity what he most needed: a faith that, as gift, bestowed upon his restless soul a genuine, transforming hope. Christian hope is neither optimism nor pessimism. Christian faith should empower one to act compassionately for others, as Jesus is narrated to have done (a major concern of Augustine's sermons). A faith that grants hope on behalf of the hopeless is always worth honoring. Augustine's hard-won, graced hope, his frequent joy, his realistic view of a complex, ambiguous world is his greatest gift. And yet even hope is not Augustine's final word. A large part of the greatness of Augustine's sermons and commentaries on the Psalms is that in Augustine, as in the Psalms themselves (more than any other biblical book), one finds all the affects of life itself: lamentations, jubilation, thanksgiving, praise, wonder, teaching, anger, mercy, faith, hope, love. Without his Christian conversion, Augustine, the most varied, the most affect-laden of great thinkers, may have found himself torn into a thousand pieces. In the Psalms (the leitmotif of *Confessions* as well), Augustine found a home. In Augustine's reading of the Psalms and the First Letter of John, as well as well as in his classical *Confessions*, it becomes clear that Augustine's hope was accompanied by the rarest of experiences, authentic joy: not a facile, fleeting happiness but inexplicable joy — an experience as rare and gifted as faith, love, and hope. Joy, like love, like hope, like faith, cannot be achieved. It happens, or it does not. It is given; it is grace.

I will end with a passage from Augustine's wondrous work on the Psalms. Here Augustine recalls (perhaps from memories of his own rural youth) the wordless chant of workers in the field, the chant then named *jubilum*:

> Do not worry, for he provides you with a technique for singing. Do not go seeking lyrics, as though you could spell out in words anything that will give God pleasure. Sing to him in jubilation. This is what acceptable singing to God means: to sing jubilantly. But what is that? It is to grasp the fact that what is sung in the heart cannot be articulated in words. Think of people who sing at harvest time, or in the vineyard, or at any work that goes with a swing. They begin by caroling their joy in words, but after a while they seem to be so full of gladness that they find words no longer adequate to express it, so they abandon distinct syllables and words, and resort to a single cry of jubilant happiness. Jubilation is a shout of joy; it indicates that the heart is bringing forth what defies speech. To whom, then, is this jubilation more fittingly offered than to God who surpasses all utterance? You cannot speak of him because he transcends our speech; and if you cannot speak of him, yet may not remain silent, what else can you do but cry out in jubilation, so that your heart may tell its joy without words, and the unbounded rush of gladness not be cramped by syllables? Sing skillfully to him in jubilation.[12]

An amazing memory that resounds in the cavern of Augustine's *memoria*: the word-saturated rhetorician here remembers not words but a time when he be-

---

12. *Enarrationes in Psalmos*, 32 (*Expositions of the Psalms, 1–32*, III/15), in Augustine 2000, 401. I was first alerted to this wonderful quotation some years ago in the chapter on Augustine titled "The Clamour of the Heart" in Williams 1979. For an excellent reflection on Augustine's spirituality, see the introduction to Mary Clark's edition of Augustine (1984).

came silent in order to listen to the Christian *jubilum* of others. Augustine listens not only in hope but in a quiet, moving joy. A joyful Augustine — that's a side of him that even Peter Brown did not quite notice. Augustine's move in naming God is ultimately beyond all language of predication into the language of praise and prayer and, ultimately, a jubilating, wordless joy, that cicada-like humming beyond speech: *Per Christum hominem ad Christum divinum; per Christum divinum ad Deum Trinitatem.*

REFERENCES

Augustine. 1984. *Augustine of Hippo: Selected Writings in the Classics of Western Spirituality*. Edited by Mary T. Clark. New York: Paulist Press.

———. 1992. *The Works of Saint Augustine: A Translation for the 21st Century*. Translated by Edmund Hill. Brooklyn, NY: New City Press.

———. 2000. *Expositions of the Psalms, 1–32*. Translated by Maria Boulding. Hyde Park, NY: New City Press.

———. 2004. *Expositions of the Psalms, 121–150*. Translated by Maria Boulding. Hyde Park, NY: New City Press.

Ayres, Lewis. 2002. "The Fundamental Grammar of Augustine's Trinitarian Theology." In *Augustine and His Critics*, edited by Robert Dodaro and George Lawless. London: Routledge.

Balthasar, Hans Urs von. 1984. *The Glory of the Lord: A Theological Aesthetics*. Vol. 2. San Francisco: Ignatius Press.

Benjamin, Walter. 1999. *The Arcades Project*. Translated by Howard Eiland and Kevin McLaughlin. Cambridge, MA: Belknap Press.

Blanchot, Maurice. 1992. *The Infinite Conversation*. Translated by Susan Hanson. Minneapolis: University of Minnesota Press.

Børresen, Kari Elisabeth. 1981. *Subordination and Equivalence: Nature and Role of Women in Augustine and Thomas Aquinas*. Translated by Charles H. Talbot. Washington, DC: University Press of America.

Braaten, Carl E., and Robert W. Jenson, eds. 1998. *Union with Christ: The New Finnish Interpretation of Luther*. Grand Rapids, MI: W. B. Eerdmans.

Brown, Peter. 2000. *Augustine of Hippo: A Biography*. Rev. ed. Berkeley: University of California Press.

Clark, Mary T., ed. 1984. *Augustine of Hippo: Selected Writings in the Classics of Western Spirituality*. New York: Paulist Press.

Courcelle, Pierre. 1968. *Recherches sur les "Confessions" de saint Augustin*. Paris: Éditions de Boccard.

Coyne, Ryan. 2015. *Heidegger's Confessions: The Remains of Saint Augustine in "Being and Time" and Beyond*. Chicago: University of Chicago Press.

Defarrari, Roy Joseph, ed. 1968. *The Fathers of the Church: A New Translation*. Washington, DC: Catholic University of America Press.

Eliot, T. S. 1968. *Four Quartets*. London: Faber and Faber.

Evans, Gillian R. 1982. *Augustine on Evil*. Cambridge: Cambridge University Press.

Fux, Pierre-Yves, Jean-Michel Roessli, and Otto Wermelinger, eds. 2003. *Augustinus Afer: Saint Augustin, africanité et universalité; Actes du colloque international, Alger-Annaba, 1–7 avril 2001*. Fribourg, Switzerland: Éditions Universitaires.

Gadamer, Hans-Georg. 1989. *Truth and Method*. 2nd rev. ed. Translated by Joel Weinsheimer and Donald G. Marshall. New York: Crossroad.

Hadot, Pierre. 1995. *Philosophy as a Way of Life: Spiritual Exercises from Socrates to Foucault*. Edited by Arnold I. Davidson. London: Blackwell.

Harrison, Carol. 2000. *Augustine: Christian Truth and Fractured Humanity*. Oxford: Oxford University Press.

Hart, Kevin. 2004. *Postmodernism: A Beginner's Guide*. Oxford: Oneworld.

Heller, Erich. 1965. "Ludwig Wittgenstein." In *Encounters: An Anthology from the First Ten Years of "Encounter" Magazine*, edited by Stephen Spender, Irving Kristol, and Melvin J. Lasky. New York: Simon and Schuster.

James, William. 1985. *The Varieties of Religious Experience*. Cambridge, MA: Harvard University Press.

La Bonnardière, Anne-Marie, ed. 1986. *Bible de Tous les Temp*. Vol. 3. *Saint Augustin et la Bible*. Paris: Beauchesne Éditeur.

LaCocque, André, and Paul Ricoeur. 1998. *Thinking Biblically: Exegetical and Hermeneutical Studies*. Translated by David Pellauer. Chicago: University of Chicago Press.

Liddy, Richard M. 1993. *Transforming Light: Intellectual Conversion in the Early Lonergan*. Collegeville, MN: Liturgical Press.

Lonergan, Bernard. 1967. *Verbum: Word and Idea in Aquinas*. Edited by David B. Burrell. Notre Dame, IN: University of Notre Dame Press.

Lyotard, Jean-François. 2000. *The Confession of Augustine*. Translated by Richard Beardsworth. Stanford, CA: Stanford University Press.

Madec, Goulven. 1989. *La patrie et la voie: Le Christ dans la vie et la pensée de saint Augustin*. Paris: Desclée.

McGinn, Bernard. 1991. *The Foundations of Mysticism: Origins to the Fifth Century*. New York: Crossroad.

Reale, Giovanni. 1994. *Agostino: Amore assoluto e "terza navigazione."* Milan: Vita e Pensiero.

Stock, Brian. 2001. *After Augustine: The Meditative Reader and the Text*. Philadelphia: University of Pennsylvania Press.

Studer, Basil. 1997. *The Grace of Christ and the Grace of God in Augustine of Hippo: Christocentrism or Theocentrism?* Translated by Matthew J. O'Connell. Collegeville, MN: Liturgical Press.

TeSelle, Eugene. 1999. "Holy Spirit." In *Augustine through the Ages*, edited by Allan D. Fitzgerald. Grand Rapids, MI: W. B. Eerdmans.

Tracy, David. 2020. *Fragments: The Existential Situation of Our Time*. Vol. 1 of *Selected Essays*. Chicago: University of Chicago Press.

Van Buren, John. 1994. *The Young Heidegger: Rumor of the Hidden King*. Bloomington: Indiana University Press.

van der Meer, Frederik. 1961. *Augustine the Bishop: The Life and Work of a Father of the Church*. Translated by Brian H. Battershaw and G. R. Lamb. London: Sheed and Ward.

Williams, Rowan. 1979. *The Wound of Knowledge: Christian Spirituality from the New Testament to St. John of the Cross*. Cambridge: Cowley.

CHAPTER 3

TRINITARIAN THEOLOGY AND SPIRITUALITY

*Retrieving William of St. Thierry
for Contemporary Theology*

TOWARD A TRINITARIAN THEOLOGY CENTERED ON LOVE

As many theologians have observed, the separation of theology from spirituality has been a tragedy for both theology and spirituality (McIntosh 1998, 39–90). Moreover, Pierre Hadot (1995), distinguished scholar of ancient Western philosophy, argued that most modern philosophers do not even notice that they consistently misread ancient philosophical texts — Platonist, Aristotelian, Stoic, Epicurean, and Academic-Skeptical alike. Moderns misread the ancients because they have lost the ability to relate philosophical theory to a way of life. For all the ancient philosophers, theory (in the compartments of logic, physics, ethics) was always on behalf of a way of life. Every day an ancient philosopher would practice the spiritual exercises of her or his school (e.g., the Platonist

Hypatia, the Stoic Marcus Aurelius, the Epicurean Lucretius) to assure that one's way of life and one's theory were indivisible.

In the medieval period, many theologians and philosophers moved to the university. In many ways, of course, this move from the rural monasteries or the urban canonries (e.g., the Victorines) and to the urban universities was a boon for theology: greater clarity and precision; a drive to system; and a more differentiated theoretical and practical consciousness. By the thirteenth century, many more theoretically inclined, scholastic university theologians (e.g., Thomas Aquinas) distinguished but did not separate theory and way of life, theology and philosophy, theology and spirituality, but they did highlight theories in their intellectualist, university emphases. Bonaventure was a partial exception, since some of his works were situated in the new scholastic emphasis of the University of Paris where he taught, as did Thomas Aquinas. Other theological works of Bonaventure (e.g., the religious classic *Itinerarium*) were written in a directly spiritual way, reminiscent of the great spiritual theologies of the twelfth century. In the fourteenth century, however, the division between theology and spirituality became a separation: implicitly in the brilliant logic and conceptualist theology of Duns Scotus; explicitly in William of Ockham and the nominalists, who, however much they wanted theology to be more related to spiritual experience, in fact separated even more strongly theology and philosophy alike from spirituality. After the fourteenth century, *word* (*nomen*) was separated from its traditional reference to reality in an increasingly influential epistemological nominalism. By the fifteenth and sixteenth centuries, neither the humanists of the Renaissance nor the Protestant Reformers could bear the nominalist — and, more generally, the Scholastic — stranglehold of theology. The humanists (e.g., Erasmus and Ficino) produced theologies with affinities to the humanist theological works of the twelfth century. The Reformers produced works, at times, reminiscent of the spiritual theologies of experience of the twelfth century. For example, both Martin Luther and John Calvin admired Bernard of Clairvaux's theology of experience.

The modern philosophical division of theory and way of life would have been as unintelligible to most ancient philosophers as it is to contemporary Buddhist and Taoist thinkers in Asia. Two centuries before the nominalists, however, monastic, mystical, and humanist theologians in the twelfth century presciently feared the emerging separation of theology and spirituality, philosophy and way of life. Bernard of Clairvaux, that colossus who bestrode the entire twelfth century, seemed, with all his formidable energies and convictions, to be everywhere at once. Bernard, with a monastic vision and a complex, indeed sometimes troubling personality, interfered in secular and monastic affairs alike: he dominated his era as much as Athanasius of Alexandria had dominated his. Like Athanasius, Bernard was restless, energetic, brilliant, unyielding, and often intransigent and inflexible about new ways of thinking (e.g., Abelard).

Bernard was a rhetorician of exceptional talent and, at times, a poet of genius. To read Bernard's paradoxical life (as often outside his monastery as within it) is to find a character both serene and pugnacious.[1] Bernard's genuine greatness can scarcely be doubted. But like many larger-than-life figures, the great theologian of love seemed to possess a surprising talent for unchecked anger and rage: his unjust attacks on Peter the Venerable at Cluny; his preaching for the disastrous Second Crusade (which, as he later acknowledged, was a resounding failure); his relentless attacks on Peter Abelard (with an increasing rhetorical fierceness proportionate to his own failure to understand Abelard's dialectical method or his theological and philosophical program). Bernard hounded Abelard until their partial reconciliation at Cluny.

Moreover, as the historian of theology Willemien Otten (2004, 1–78) reminds us, the famous twelfth-century Renaissance included not only the new monastic theologies of experience and love of Bernard and William of St. Thierry. Nor did it include only harbingers of the great Scholastics of the following century. Rather, as Otten argues, the twelfth-century Renaissance was also a humanist renaissance in a new world enacting humanist poetry, philosophy, and theology alike (William of Conches, Alan of Lille, Peter Abelard, Héloïse d'Argenteuil). This humanist theology was a new mode of theologizing: neither merely a signal of the emerging triumph of Scholastic theology, nor only a profoundly visionary theology like that of the amazingly versatile Hildegard of Bingen, nor only a monastic theology of experience and love (themselves partially humanistic in the emphasis on experience [*ut experiar*] for theology and their possible connections to the love poetry of the troubadours of Provence). The new humanist theologies were based on a humanist recovery of *conversatio* and a central affirmation of the intellectual and affective dignity of a humanity construed as in conversation with both *natura* and God. The twelfth-century Renaissance was a century of rich diversity in forms

---

1. On the controversy on his person, see Bredero 1996. On his theology, see Gilson 1940.

of theology: monastic, mystical, emerging Scholastic, humanist. Although my focus here is on the greatest of the monastic theologians, William of St. Thierry, one must always remember that his theology too was only one fragment in the twelfth-century pluralistic mosaic. Between them, the two Cistercian friends, Bernard of Clairvaux and William of St. Thierry, largely defined twelfth-century monastic theology.

Bernard's many admirers (among them Bonaventure, Martin Luther, and John Calvin) sensed that, in Bernard's work and person, theology and spirituality were never separated. For all his controversial actions, Bernard made major and enduring contributions to theology, indeed to Western culture as a whole. First, Bernard's theological turn to experience was both needed and prescient. Second, by placing love, not reason, as the central reality for the Christian theologian to try first to experience (*ut experiar*) and then to understand (*ut intelligam*), Bernard appropriated and rethought Augustine's love emphasis anew for the twelfth-century love-obsessed age.

William took up both of these Bernardine themes, transformed them, and worked them into a highly original theology of the Trinity, grounded in an experienced spirituality of love and reason for a new Trinitarian theology—an existential direction that many philosophers and theologians may learn from, even today. William's theology was a reasoned, contemplative theology, grounded in an experience of divine love as articulated in three stages of the theologian's spiritual and intellectual journey. In his unique Trinitarian theology, William expressed a theology of deeply interdependent love-knowledge made possible *through* Christ *in* the gift of love of the Holy Spirit, the *unitas Spiritus*. Many later theologians—from William's contemporary Richard of St. Victor to Bonaventure, to François Fénelon, Jeanne Guyon, Blaise Pascal, Friedrich Schleiermacher, Karl Rahner, Hans Urs von Balthasar, and the later work of Bernard Lonergan—would also follow a love-centered direction for theology, a few even a Trinitarian theology centered in love. William formulated a linked theological and spiritual way to clarify how the New Testament's deepest belief, "God is Love" (Tracy 2010, 131–62), is the first Christian way of saying God is One God constituted by three divine Persons.

REASON TRANSFORMED BY FAITH AND LOVE

William lacked Bernard's genius for a passionately poetic way to articulate the singular richness of the experience of faith become love. And yet, William also held that faith was a new and richer form of reason. William learned from Bernard to make theology more experiential and more love-centered. However, William more than compensated for his lack of Bernard's poetic-rhetorical genius by becoming a more careful, methodical, and systematic theologian than Bernard ever was. William, like Bernard and their common mentor Augustine, insisted that love drives knowledge, not the reverse; that our *affectus* (dispositions, affects, feelings) was as important for a theologian to analyze as reason; that faith transforms reason into a new *ratio fidei*;[2] that eventually faith becomes love and evokes the most expansive and rich forms of this transformed reason: meditation and contemplation. At stage three, love and reason alike are transformed together into loving wisdom (*sapientia*). For William, therefore, both a spiritual and theological analysis of the experience of love was needed in order to develop an adequate Trinitarian theology, grounded in the experience of love fully interdependent with the many forms of reason.

For William, a spirituality of love demanded a new Trinitarian theology as much as a Trinitarian theology needed a spirituality embedded in the graced experience of divine love. William's major spiritual works (*Nature and Dignity of Love, Commentary on the Song of Songs, Mirror of Faith, Golden Epistle*)[3] focus principally upon the new spirituality of divine love through describing various stages of a lifelong, ascetic-mystical spiritual journey. By contrast, in his more speculative theological works (especially *Enigma of Faith*), William

---

2. William of St. Thierry 1959b (*Speculum fidei* 50, par. 31): "Rationalitas enim, sicut dictum est, in seipsa inquieta et improba, ubi ratiocinandi habet facultatem, fidem sepius aggreditur, etsi non studio contradicendi sed natura ratiocinandi; non ut illi velit occurrere sed quasi illam sibi concurrere. Nam sicut solet agere in rebus humanis humana ratio, quasi per mediam credendi necessitatem irrumpere nititur in rerum divinarum cognitionem; set tamquam aliunde ascendens, offendit, impingit, labitur, donec revertatur ad ostium fidei; ad eum qui dixit: *Ego sum ostium*, et humiliata sub jugo divine auctoritatis, quanto humilius tanto securius ingrediatur. Sed in aliis non sentit temptationem negligentia magnitudo, in aliis rationis hebetudo, in aliis illuminate fidei concepta certitudo."

3. See Jacques-Paul Migne's *Patrologia Latina* (1841–55) for *De natura et dignitate amoris* (184:379–408); *Expositio super Cantica Canticorum* (180:475–546); *Speculum fidei* (180:365–87); *Aenigma fidei* (180:397–440); *Epistola ad Fratres de Monte Dei* [*Epistola aurea*] (184:307–54).

produces a methodical, systematic, speculative Trinitarian theology, correlative to the spiritual journey described in his other works. William's speculative theology is logically coherent, speculatively and dialectically daring, especially in *Enigma of Faith*. William's theology is designed not only to allow an experience of divine love (*Mirror of Faith* emphasizes *ut experiar*). In the companion work, *Enigma of Faith*, William developed a strict Trinitarian theology of *ut intelligam* (in *Aenigma fidei* [1959a]). William's full Trinitarian theology analyzes the radical interdependence, harmony, almost unity of love and reason, with love as primary.

One of the extraordinary conversations in the history of Christian theology and spirituality (like the conversation of Gregory of Nyssa and his sister Macrina on her deathbed; like the mystical conversation of Augustine and Monnica in the garden at Ostia) was the days-long conversation in the infirmary of Clairvaux between Bernard and William on the Song of Songs. In reading their two quite distinct commentaries on that favorite text of most mystical theologians from Origen onward, one senses both the profound similarities of Bernard and William (theology must be grounded in an experienced life of graced love) and their equally profound differences. The poetic-rhetorical language of Bernard moves to heights of rich expression worthy of Gregory Nazianzen, Augustine of the *Confessions*, John of the Cross in his splendid poetry, Teresa of Ávila in her lustrous autobiography, Pascal in the *Pensées*, or the Friedrich Schleiermacher of the *Speeches*, Søren Kierkegaard in *Diary of a Seducer*, or the John Henry Newman of the *Plain and Parochial Sermons*. The more rigorous, more philosophical and speculative language of William moves to a slower rhythm, more like Gregory of Nyssa's *Contra Eunomium*, Schleiermacher's *Glaubenslehre*, or Newman's *Grammar of Assent*. Whatever happened in the conversation of Bernard and William in the infirmary in those precious few days when illness freed both monks to share their thoughts on divine love, thereafter each of them seemed liberated to write two of the greatest commentaries on the Song of Songs in the history of Christian mystical writings on the Song.

Both Bernard and William developed penetrating spiritual theologies. Only William, however, developed a Trinitarian theology appropriate to what both had discovered in the experience of divine love in the Song of Songs (Matter 1990). One way to clarify how this shared experience of divine love also became, in William, an original theology of the Trinity, is to focus on faith, because for William, faith, decisively and uniquely, transforms both reason and love, only to be transformed itself by pure love, united to contemplative reason.

Like many medieval theologians, William held to a distinction between the *imago dei* and the *similitudo dei*, based on a Latin reading of Genesis: "Let us make human beings in our image and likeness" (Bell 1984; Brooke 1980). For William, the *imago dei* is damaged in us but not lost. As human beings, we retain what the *imago* gives each person as pure gift: an openness to and capacity for God. We never entirely lost the *imago dei*. After the Fall, however, human beings have lost the *similitudo dei*. Like Adam and Eve before us, all human beings since the Fall have lost Eden. They must now take refuge as best they can in the disturbing, fragmented *regio dissimilitudinis*, an arresting metaphor that William found in both Origen and Augustine.

Both our intellects and our wills have been wounded (*vulnus*) by our inherited and personal sin. We wander aimlessly in the labyrinth of the *regio dissimilitudinis*. Through God's grace, we are still open to God through the *imago dei* in our souls (Augustine's *memoria, intellectus, voluntas*).[4] The human question to itself is unavoidable: How can we fallen ones recover the *similitudo dei* to ensure the proper functioning of our wounded reason and our misdirected desire?

The answer for William, as for the Christian tradition generally, lies in first acknowledging that we are certainly not self-authored, nor can we cure ourselves. We are finite creatures of the infinite Creator God. We are also fallen creatures who are saved through Christ in the Spirit as the Scripture, the liturgy, and the prayers of ordinary Christians manifest. We are saved only through God's redeeming grace, given to us through the birth, teaching, ministry, death, and resurrection of Jesus the Christ, true God (the Second Person of the Trinity, the eternal Son of the eternal Father) and true man (the Word made flesh and like us in all things save sin).

William shared in much of the Christian humanistic optimism of his age: we have never lost the *imago dei*; all creation including nature and body is good; we possess free will; in our reason is an infinite desire to know and, by that fact, we are open to knowing God; our desire to know and all our other desires are grounded in desire for the Good. In sum: for William, we have never lost our openness to and capacity for God (our *imago dei*); our reason, our freedom of will, our human dignity are all intact. This is William's form of a pervasive,

---

4. Augustine, *De Trinitate*, in Jacques-Paul Migne, *Patrologia Latina* (1841–55), 42:819–1098, esp. 11.10 to 12.19.

twelfth-century theological optimism shared with his even more optimistic and more fully humanistic colleagues (Alan of Lille, William of Conches, Peter Abelard) in that exciting age of the twelfth-century Renaissance.

However, unlike the more optimistic and humanistic thinkers of his day (especially Abelard), William's humanism was far more mitigated or, perhaps, more nuanced. William never abandoned Augustine's basic theological anthropology on our fallen state, but his basic theological position had more affinity with the early Augustine of the "dialogues," focused on grace transforming nature, rather than the later Augustine's sin-grace, anti-Pelagian emphasis. William never conceived our fallen state in the later radical terms of Luther, Calvin, Jansen, or the later Augustine himself. Like twelfth-century Christian theologians in general, William never speaks such Augustinian language that we humans are so fallen that we are a *massa damnata*. William never uses the most antihumanistic teaching of all Augustine's later, desperate teachings against the Pelagians: double predestination. In sum, William was never the kind of radical, pessimistic, late Augustinian that John Calvin or Cornelius Jansen later became. William always enunciated and consistently defended the human dignity of reason open to God. He always defended both God's grace and a graced free will. But William was never a full-fledged humanist. Even after William began to read and learn from Origen, he never swerved into full-fledged Origenism. Origen was far more optimistic in his anthropology than not only the later Augustine but even the mature Augustine (e.g., in *Confessions*) ever was. William did indeed drink deeply at Origen's well: most deeply in William's later use of Origen's three stages of the spiritual journey (William 1983). Even then, however, William maintained the more Augustinian rather than Greek portrait of humanity, the more tragic-realistic humanism of the mature (not the late) Augustine. Abelard's perhaps too-optimistic and humanistic reading of the use of dialectic in theology, insofar as William understood it (see below), frightened him to the depths of his Augustinian soul.

Like Thomas Aquinas and Bonaventure in the following century, William learned more from Augustine than from any other prior theologian. However, either consciously or unconsciously, William as a child of the more optimistic and more humanistic twelfth-century Renaissance, articulated a basically Augustinian anthropology but never with the profoundly pessimistic turn of the later Augustine. For William, free will is more lucidly analyzed and defended than it was in Augustine. For William, when we receive the gift-grace of the self-manifestation of God in the Word made flesh, we also receive the gift of faith, which we freely accept or reject. Faith, therefore, is both grace from God attendant to the grace of the revelation of the Incarnate Word itself, and an action of our own genuine free will. In principle, William agreed with the ancient tradition: God created us without ourselves (we are not self-authored; we are finite creatures of a loving Infinite Creator), but chooses not to save us without our consent (we are justified by Christ's grace through faith and a graced will; we are sanctified through the work of the Holy Spirit working in and with us).

Faith, therefore, is the decisive, unique, irreplaceable moment for the beginning of the full healing of the *imago dei* in us, and an ever-deepening spiritual restoration of the *similitudo dei* in us, for our graced and free journey of sanctification. Faith is the all-important, necessary beginning of that restoration. Without faith, our reason, otherwise strong, struggles in vain to reach God and cannot even acknowledge its own limit. Without faith, our desire sinks into vanity, our loves attach themselves not to God's Infinite Love and to love of neighbor in love for each other through our love of God. Rather, we stumble with our restless, disoriented, confused desires. We move in the dark with our loves dragging us along by their energy and weight (*amor meus, pondus meum*; Augustine, *Confessions* 13.9.10), after another foolishly loved improper object (fame, money, power). Even proper objects of love become disoriented: every person becomes an object, every desire is unconsciously trapped in its own deluded self-love, not a subject for our love; so we cannot even love ourselves truly; every other person is not allowed to be an Other but only a target for possession; nature exists only to be used as our instrument, not as a proper object of our awe and love; God is loved, if at all, only for our own possible merit, not for the pure love of God in Godself. Like all the Cistercians, especially Aelred of Rievaulx, William cherished the grace of friendship. But he also knew that even the great gift of friendship could be tempted to live only for itself (*egoisme à deux*) rather than being, as it is constituted to be, a further healing of our natural egotism and a further sanctifying of our journey with our friends to friendship with God.

Without faith, the soul (senses, intellect, will, desire) is an unfathomable and harrowing mystery to itself. At crucial points, William's anthropology seems less twelfth-century Renaissance, that is, straightforwardly optimistic and humanistic, than Augustinian and tragic in orientation. Nevertheless, tragic humanism is also one of the classical forms of Western orientation.[5] William's passionate insistence that we are a complete mystery to ourselves resonates not only with the famous portrait of Pascal on the human state as tragically-humanistically constituted by both *grandeur et misère*. At times, in reading William, one hears echoes of what is to come: Nietzsche's unsettling question to all optimistic humanists in the preface to his *Genealogy of Morals*: "We are unknown to ourselves, we knowers — and with good reason. We have never sought ourselves — how could it happen that we should ever *find* ourselves; . . . who are we really? . . . Each as furthest from himself applies to all eternity" (Nietzsche 1967, 15). William combines a tragically humanistic portrait of our situation with an enormous capacity to show a way forward to healing, to a pure love of God and neighbor, to a contemplative wisdom. It is that tragic, humanistic spirituality, once transformed into more contemporary terms, that gives one hope for a way forward in our theological time: a time that shares the rich diversity of theologies of the twelfth century, but not the relatively untroubled, nontragic humanism of the simple, admirable optimism about reason's powers in Abelard and William of Conches.

For William of St. Thierry, faith comes first as an external force (1959b, 48, par. 27). Faith happens to us; it is not our own achievement. Faith is first external to us, touching us from outside and calling us to freely accept its truth. At the beginning, faith is healing but mostly exterior; it is not yet interior to us. This first faith — "simple faith," William names it — is nevertheless, for all Christians, including intellectual elites like William himself, the decisive beginning of our later understanding of ourselves and all reality, especially, of course, the reality of God and all things related to God, the object of theology, as Thomas Aquinas insisted. Indeed, as William acutely declares, the first, strictly theological discovery of faith is grace. The first discovery of faith is, therefore, that it happens to us by means of some Other — not self — Power, some external force that faith as faith can acknowledge as God's own force, God's gift, grace, Other Power, touching us. Faith happens to us either suddenly, as in Paul's conversion, or more likely gradually as, through faith, we learn to understand ourselves, reality, and God anew, and to love God and all others as other, not only the friend but also the neighbor, even the enemy.

---

5. Augustine's anthropology can be read as a classical, Christian, tragic humanism (see chap. 1 in this volume).

After William's "conversion" to the monastic life—first Benedictine, then Cistercian, along with a love for the Carthusians, to whom his last text, the famous *Epistola aurea* is addressed—his understanding and experience of faith deepened beyond "simple faith" through the carefully structured ascetic, liturgical, and prayerful practices of the monastic life. Indeed, the greatest part of William's last text, *Golden Epistle*, discusses the nature and necessity of asceticism for novices to the monastery. United to monastic ascetic practices for interiorizing faith are the sacraments, especially the Eucharist, where, at times, reason can become contemplative joy in the eucharistic presence of God, meditative communal and private prayers, and meditative readings (*Lectio divina*) of the Scripture.[6]

Faith becomes less external and more internal as these spiritual practices take hold. Faith frees the understanding (*intellectus*) to discern spiritual realities. Gradually, the spiritual novice learns to read the Scriptures morally and spiritually in order to make their treasures her own. At this point, a second stage of the relationship of faith and reason quite naturally takes hold in the rhythm of the spiritual journey. William calls this second stage of reason's spiritualizing journey *ratio fidei*: that is, faith in its creative power of illumination transforms ordinary reason—natural reason—into a new, richer form of reason than natural reason possesses on its own. William calls this transformed reason *ratio fidei*.

William's concept of *ratio fidei* is different from what he understands (mostly incorrectly) as Abelard's more humanist and more rationalist position on faith and reason for theology (on which see below). More surprisingly, William's *ratio fidei* is also different from Anselm's earlier position on theology as *fides quaerens intellectum* (Anselm 1965; Evans 1989, 37–49). The differences of content between the theologies of Anselm and William are less important than their important differences in method. For Anselm, as much as for William, the theological journey begins in faith. However, for Anselm, theology proper begins as faith seeks understanding (*fides quaerens intellectum*) through all the instruments of natural reason (dialogue, dialectic, logic).

Anselm insists, unlike William of St. Thierry and, in this case, more like William of Conches and Abelard, on the importance of the extensive use of

---

6. Although William is best known as a Cistercian, it is important to remember that he was a Benedictine for fifteen years and learned *Lectio divina* there.

dialectic, logic, and dialogue (reason in its natural forms) in theology. Anselm also encourages (here far more like William of St. Thierry than like William of Conches or Abelard) the theological acknowledgment that reason is employed in theology, within the encompassing context of meditative prayers and readings, as well as contemplative reason (*sapientia* as distinct from *scientia*). As the endless conflict of interpretations on the so-called ontological argument in Anselm demonstrates, comprehending the full complexity of Anselm's position on theology as *fides quaerens intellectum* is a difficult hermeneutical task — far more difficult than it at first seems. On the one hand, Anselm accords a full theological role to *intellectus* — that is, to logic, metaphysics, dialectic, and contemplation. For example, the so-called ontological argument (Hick and McGill 1967; Olivetti 1990) and all Anselm's other arguments are indeed genuine arguments and are to be judged as such. Anselm's logical and dialectical arguments can, in principle, be abstracted from his larger text and judged strictly as arguments, as they are in Thomas Aquinas, Bonaventure, Descartes, Kant, Hegel, Hartshorne, and many other philosophers and theologians, especially the analytical and process philosophers of today.

Anselm may have accepted William's later formulation, but he himself does not speak of a new kind of transformed reason (*ratio fidei*), which theology, unlike philosophy, employs. On the other hand, Anselm's arguments, again in all his theological texts, including the *Monologion* and the *Proslogion*, are situated within an encompassing context of Benedictine prayer (often textually included), meditation, and contemplation, as such interpreters as Anselm Stolz, Karl Barth, and many other theological interpreters have correctly insisted. Unlike William's model, Anselm's theological model (like Augustine's before him) of *fides quaerens intellectum* is not nearly as clear as it first seems and is still unclear to many interpreters. Perhaps both William of St. Thierry and Peter Abelard sensed the latent ambiguity in Anselm's formulation of *fides quaerens intellectum* and opted for clearer theological models. Whatever the case may be, that magnificent theologian and philosopher, Anselm of Canterbury, did not provide a model for William of St. Thierry in his distinct use of reason in theology: for William, reason's principal but not sole use in theology was as *ratio fidei*.

William's theological method is notably different from Anselm's. Natural or ordinary reason is no longer accorded the high place it had in Anselm, although William continues to use logic and dialectic when he needs them. Reason, for William of St. Thierry, has been so transformed by faith that it now functions as a more than natural reason. In that sense, for William, ordinary reason (e.g., logic, dialectic, dialogue) will continue to be used by the theologian when needed but will not define the more expanded range of reason opened by faith. For William, *ratio* has now been transfigured into a richer *ratio fidei*. *Ratio fidei* therefore elicits new rational powers of discernment of spiritual realities (in the Scripture, the liturgy, the prayers of all Christians), new hermeneutical possibilities of meditative reading, ultimately discerned to be new, speculative, contemplative reasoning. William's concept of *ratio fidei* is ultimately understood to be driven by the love that faith itself becomes in the second stage.

In the second stage of William's spiritual and intellectual journey, therefore, *ratio fidei* yields to what might be named (although William himself does not so name it) *ratio amoris*.[7] This final transformation of reason culminates in what William, recalling Gregory the Great, famously claimed: "*Amor ipse intellectus est*." With the power of *ratio fidei*, the intellect (*intellectus, ratio*) can now discover that it itself is inexorably driven by a deeper desire than its powerful, indeed unrestricted, desire to know: the desire for the Good — that is, the authentic love of God.

In sum, for William, *fides* produces *ratio fidei*. *Ratio fidei* discerns spiritual realities. A key example of William's use of *ratio fidei* is his insistence that philosophical categories like *person* and *substance* cannot be directly applied to the mystery of the Trinity, traditionally three persons in one substance. William did use Boethius's second definition of person,[8] rather than Boethius's more widely used first definition (*subsistens distinctum in natura intellectuali*), but he changed it into a more explicitly theological Trinitarian category. *Ratio fidei*, for William, can and should transform philosophical categories into theological categories. In contemporary theological terms, William's *ratio fidei* has more affinity to an *analogia fidei* (Karl Barth) or to an *analogia caritatis* (Hans Urs von Balthasar) than to an *analogia entis* (Boethius, Thomas Aquinas, Karl Rahner). William's use of his map for the spiritual journey in three stages is consistent. In the second stage, *ratio fidei* progresses through its spiritual exercises and becomes meditative, for example, by meditating on sensible images of the life of Christ in the Gospels (here like the future use of images in the spiritual exer-

---

7. William 1959b (*Speculum fidei* 62, par. 46): "Tu ergo, o fidelis anima, cum in fide tua natura tripidanti ingeruntur occultiora mysteria; aude et dic, non studio occurrendi, sed amore sequendi. *Quomodo fiunt ista?* Questio tua oratio tua sit, amor sit, pietas sit, et humile desiderium; non in sublimibus scrutans Dei majestatem, sed in salutaribus Dei salutarium nostrorum quaerens salutem."

8. For a discussion of the two definitions of *person* in Boethius, see Chadwick 1981, 190–203.

cises of Ignatius Loyola). As the soul moves to its third stage of deeper love and understanding, *ratio fidei* yields to its own transformation into *ratio amoris*. Thus begins the final stage of the journey, within which contemplative wisdom (the gift of the Spirit's love) harmonizes and integrates reason and love in the soul. In this final stage of its journey, *ratio fidei* becomes more speculative, more contemplative. *Scientia* yields to *sapientia*. *Sapientia* is the wisdom-love that can now be tasted (*sapiens*). When faith was an external force in stage one, it touched the soul. Now that faith has been so interiorized by its journey through all three stages, it has become a pure love of God. Love-reason now tastes (*sapiens*) its newfound pure love and contemplative reason (*sapientia*). Rarely have the "spiritual senses" first enunciated by Origen been so well developed as in William's sensual description of the soul's journey from faith touching a soul to the soul tasting love and reason, now united in *sapientia*.

At this point of contemplative wisdom, William retrieves and gives even deeper meaning to Gregory the Great's aphorism, "*Amor ipse notitia est*,"[9] which William reformulates as "*Amor ipse intellectus est*." The meaning of "*Amor ipse intellectus est*" can be fully understood, however, only by recalling William's version of the three stages of the spiritual-theological life. In stages one and two, the searching soul moves from simple faith to *ratio fidei*, akin to ancient Christian *gnosis* in Clement of Alexandria and Origen.[10] Just as faith transforms reason into *ratio fidei*, so too faith, as it becomes more and more interior to the self, yields to love. As the spiritual life continues, faith working through love becomes pure love, delight in God for Godself. Pure love continues to expand and continues to transform reason to prepare for the reception of a new form of loving contemplation made possible by the gift of the Holy Spirit as the *unitas Spiritus* of the Trinity itself to the soul. Just as natural reason has been sublated into *ratio fidei*, *ratio fidei* is sublated into love (*ratio amoris*). Pure love has been sublated by the Spirit into the grace of the *unitas Spiritus*. This gift-grace of the Spirit allows the soul, now restored, not only as *similitudo dei* but also as *imago Trinitatis*, to participate *in* the Spirit and therefore in the inner life of the Trinity. In the Trinity, the Spirit is the eternal bond of love of Father and Son. Moreover, through their eternal, divine, loving relationships, the Father, Son,

---

9. For an analysis of Gregory the Great on love and knowledge, see McGinn 1994, 34–80. Gregory's *amor ipse notitia est* is a major motif in both Gregory's *Moralia in Job* and *Expositiones: In Canticum canticorum, In librum primum Regum* (Gregory 1963, 144).

10. See the discussion of William's relationship to ancient Christian *gnosis* in Bouyer 1958, 120–24.

and Spirit are not merely united and harmonized, but are also one through the bond of the Spirit who is Love. The Trinitarian constant of Love is manifested in the Spirit who lovingly relates the Loving Father and the Beloved Son.

"AMOR IPSE INTELLECTUS EST"

As with Bernard, love is primary for William. Unlike Bernard, whose style is more poetic-rhetorical than dialectical, and whose theological-spiritual interests are more directly pastoral-affective than speculative, William methodically works out the relationship of reason and love. William reached a unique and still underappreciated understanding of how, in effect, the New Testament proclamation "God is Love" means God is Triune.

For William, love, like understanding-knowledge, begins with faith. As with reason, so with desire-love: we live, as Adam did after the Fall, in a *regio dissimilitudinis* with our confused minds and our disordered desires. Our problem in this labyrinthine region of dissimilarities is harrowing: we find ourselves in a space of colliding acts of understanding and desire, where the differences are so marked that anarchy can prevail in both our reason and our will. The harder we try to escape this region of ever-increasing dissimilarities, the more we find ourselves sinking as if in quicksand. Sometimes we think we see, mirage-like, a possible door out: for example, through love of another, that can often prove to be another dissimilarity; we do not really love the other as Other but want only to possess her or him.

William's unyielding portrait of our lostness in the *regio dissimilitudinis* can, at times, remind one of Franz Kafka's *Das Schloss* (1981): in the radical confusion of constant dissimilarities in our fallen state, there is, we believe, a door of relief, one in fact constructed only for me, but that door is now and forever closed upon me. Our own powers are delusory. We possess, like Kafka's K., a knowledge incapable of understanding its own limits. Our natural desire for the Good finds itself trapped by false loves, insatiable desires, and infinite hunger for release from the region of dissimilarity. However, what we seem unable to admit to ourselves is the devastating fact that, with only our own powers of reason and love, there is no exit.

Not only are we weary, wandering, and unable to understand ourselves, we are also unable to love properly. Our knowledge cannot reach God. We are an insoluble puzzle to ourselves. Our *affectus* (feeling, dispositions, loves) cannot rightly love God or others (the neighbors) or even the self. As Augustine taught William, our sin-laden affections possess a deceptive gravitational attraction to false loves. Our sin-laden minds can become, as another Augustinian, Martin Luther, memorably said, a factory for manufacturing idols. Our loves, restless, wandering, confused, and self-deluding, flail about with false love after false love, only to become more and more trapped in themselves (as Luther memorably said, "*curvatus in se*").

In these portraits of bleak, tragic reality in our lives in the fallen *regio dissimilitudinis*, William challenged the humanistic optimism of his day as much as Augustine had challenged his fellow Platonists, and as Freud would later challenge his optimistic colleagues in psychology by his terrifying portrait of the power of the Unconscious.[11]

As with knowledge, so too can love be liberated to its true course only by grace and the spiritual journey. We recover our *similitudo dei* by grace and by a graced, free commitment to undertaking the stages of the spiritual life. We slowly convalesce through ascetic, liturgical, meditative, and, finally, contemplative love. At last, we sense again the presence of a healed *imago dei* and a sanctified *similitudo dei*, by which we can at last begin to understand and love God and every neighbor properly. As a final result of our spiritual and intellectual journey, we learn to answer the earlier question shared by the Russian novelists and all tragic realists with Augustine, Pascal, Nietzsche, Kierkegaard, and Kafka: Who am I?

God's loving, justifying grace answers that otherwise unanswerable question. Grace comes to us through Christ and faith in him. We receive that gift free *through* the Incarnate Word *in* the Spirit. The will and its affections, like the understanding they drive us toward, begin to heal as they are strengthened and focused by this simple faith. Faith, originally an exterior power, works internally as strongly in the will as it does in the understanding. Faith redirects the affections, the soul's weight, upward to the flame of love. In the first stage of healing following God's gift of faith, love is guided by *ratio fidei* to learn to read the Scriptures more meditatively, more interiorly. For example, we learn to understand one of William's most frequently cited scriptural texts: "We can love because God first loved us" (1 John 4:19).

---

11. On the terrifying character of Freud's unconscious, see Lacan 2006, 671–746. On the analogy of Augustine and Freud, see Brown 1967, 261.

The new *ratio fidei* not only helps our understanding but also heals our drives, desires, and affections. Love makes us understand and love the Scriptures, the liturgy, and ancient theological texts. For William, an attentive, loving faith helps us become attuned (Heidegger's *Befindlichkeit*) to the Scriptures, the liturgy, the community, and the texts of the earlier classical theologians. The writings and persons of the Fathers, the Mothers, the teachers of the early church are central for William of St. Thierry: above all the indispensable Augustine and the more optimistic Greek fathers — Origen on the three stages of the soul, and Gregory of Nyssa on the relationship of soul and body.[12]

As with the earlier traditions in Christianity, East and West, William held that faith, as it became more and more interior and personally appropriated, purified the mind by evoking a more spiritual reading of and meditation upon the Scriptures, and purified the will by embracing the monastic ascetic practices of poverty, obedience, and chastity. For William, ascetic practices were not unnatural at all, as some critics of the monks charged. For William of St. Thierry, asceticism was as natural to the converted monk as constant — and often painful — practice is for the athlete, the musician, or the ballet dancer. These ascetic practices were hallowed by the traditional spiritual understanding (from Dionysius the Areopagite) of the soul's movement from purification (or purgation) to illumination (meditation) to union (loving contemplation).

In the first stage of William's spiritual journey, therefore, the soul (both mind and will) is purified until it is gradually reformed and transformed into a consciously loving soul, delighting in God's presence. At the limit of stage one, the soul moves on from this first purificatory stage. Then, in stage two, the soul's senses and affections are further healed and sanctified through grace and spiritual practice.

In the second stage, love guides reason, even more than reason guides love. The relationship of love and knowledge becomes deeply harmonized with every step taken forward in the meditative practices of stage two. Now the soul is capable of meditative readings of Scripture and meditative prayers. The soul finds itself in loving conversation with God now loved rightly, that is, purely for God's own sake. In this second stage, faith works through love. Indeed, in a foretaste of the afterlife, faith becomes love. In stage two, the soul now heals

---

12. Gregory of Nyssa, *De hominis opificio*, in Jacques-Paul Migne, *Patrologia Graeca* (1857–66), 44:123–256. This is probably the only text of Gregory's (in the translation Eriugena called *De imagine*) that William knew well.

its damaged but not lost *imago dei* — that is, its openness to, its capacity and desire for a Loving God. The soul thereby steadily departs from the region of dissimilarity to find a graced personal recovery of its *similitudo dei*. The soul then reaches a purified meditative understanding, more and more imbued with a purified, even pure love. In stage one, love is guided by *ratio fidei*. In stage two, *fides* itself becomes love, so that reason in turn is now guided by a purified love.

The soul never leaves the region of dissimilarity completely in this life, since one will always need to fight against never-ending temptations and distractions. As Peter Brown (2000, 108–25) observes about Augustine after his conversion, William remained a convalescent, not a completely cured soul. Nevertheless, in stage two, the soul now finds itself in a new, open space. One might even say that, for William, the soul now begins to find its love and understanding more and more harmonized and united into an ever-expanding, loving knowledge and understanding love. The soul begins to live in a *regio similitudinis*. The soul's capacity for and openness to God (the *imago*) is no longer merely a pre-unconscious unconscious trace of an unknown presence in the *memoria*. The soul is now somewhere else:[13] through the grace always informing its spiritual efforts, the soul touches and brings to consciousness the loving presence of God in flashes of eternity.

In the second stage, the soul now moves naturally through its spiritual practices. The soul's love is now purified enough to experience a pure love of delight in the presence of God, and unselfish love for the other as Other at transient moments. Like most Eastern spiritual traditions (the Hindu guru, the Zen Master, the Taoist sage), the Christian monastic traditions affirmed the need for a spiritual adviser to instruct and guide any person undertaking a spiritual journey (Corcoran 1985, 444–52). William named this need for a director the "obedience of necessity" appropriate to the early stages of the novice's inward journey.

In stage two, the obedience of necessity spontaneously yields to an obedience of *caritas*. Once faith has been transformed by grace and graced spiritual exercises into an ever more pure love of God and neighbor, an obedience of

---

13. William 1959a (*Aenigma fidei* 132, 134, par. 48): "Amat autem locutio sive inquisitio de Deo, humiles ac simplices in paupertate spiritus Deum querentes, quos ad inquirendum non curiositas agit, sed pietas trahit. Amat loqui non verbis precipitationis et alienis; sed ipsis quibus semetipsum et Patrem et Spiritum sanctum manifestavit mundo Verbum Dei ipso locutionis caractere, quo fidem Trinitatis propagaverunt in mundo homines Dei."

love takes over from an earlier obedience of necessity in a way reminiscent of William's mentor Augustine, who famously said, *"Ama et fac quod vis."* Freely, spontaneously, easily, the soul now lives no longer through duty and command but through love alone, "an obedience of charity." William's position here is sound not only spiritually and theologically but also psychologically. As William James (1978, 261–370) insisted, the "saint" performs good, loving acts spontaneously, easily, naturally. When the rest of us perform our good acts for our neighbors, we do so more out of duty than out of spontaneous love. We nonsaints live by one or another obedience of necessity; the saints, by an "obedience of *caritas.*"[14]

In the third stage of the spiritual journey, therefore, a person begins to understand the tradition named *unio.*[15] For William, in the third stage of union, the soul understands and experiences its *imago* and *similitudo* as an *imago* of the Trinity itself (*imago Trinitatis*). At this final stage, the soul finds that it consciously and lovingly participates in the Love who is God, that is, the loving God who is the Trinity. This new loving wisdom is made possible through the special sanctifying grace of the Holy Spirit, the *unitas Spiritus*, that allows the soul to live *in Spiritu.* Analogous to the manner in which faith's major theological discovery in stage one was the reality of grace through Christ, in stage three, love's major theological discovery is the reality of the love who is the tripersonal God present to us through the Holy Spirit in its new gift-grace to the soul of *unitas Spiritus.*[16] At the last stage, the soul discovers as fully as possible in this life the Spirit's presence, through a retreating, echoing sound of the thunder heard in the soul's transient moments experiencing eternity, as well as the lightning flashes of divine love experienced even in this life by the soul. Only then does the self know that its *imago dei* is not only the *imago* constituted by an openness to and capacity for God, but also something totally unexpected: the soul is *imago Trinitatis.* William's theology of mysticism (*unio*)[17] is also a

---

14. William 1959a (*Aenigma fidei* 130, 132, pars. 45–47).

15. Thus William (1959a, 178, par. 100) can conclude the *Aenigma fidei* with this remarkable sentence: "Sed ideo solus sufficit quia separari a Patre et Filio non potest, cum quibus inseparabiliter facit cuncta que facit."

16. William 1959a (*Aenigma fidei* 176, par. 98): "Cum ergo sit Spiritus sanctus spiritus Patris et Filii, et ab utroque procedat, sitque caritas et unitas amborum; manifestum est, quod non sit aliquis duorum, quo uterque conjungitur, quo genitus a gignente diligitur, genitoremque suum diligit, ut sint non participatione aliena sed propria essentia, nec alterius dono sed suo proprio *servantes unitatem spiritus in vinculo pacis.*"

17. For William's theology of mysticism as a spirit-centered mysticism, see McGinn 1994, 225–75.

theology of the Trinity. At this final stage, the soul feels and understands a harmony of love and knowledge so profound that they can almost seem one: love-knowledge is knowledge-love.

William ingeniously names the final grace *unitas Spiritus*. In discerning the Spirit's presence in us, we understand as deeply as we finite beings can *in* the Spirit, God's Triune presence. We understand, as Paul insisted, through a mirror in an enigma. In William's *Commentary on the Song of Songs*, as well as in the final section of his last work, *Golden Epistle*, William presents most firmly his new Trinitarian spirituality of the Spirit. Only one who has gone through all three stages of the spiritual life, culminating in the extraordinary grace of the *unitas Spiritus*, has experienced God's love powerfully enough to begin to understand the greatest of all revealed mysteries: the Trinity.

William insists on a theology of the experience of love as ultimately an experience of the Spirit, a theology grounded in living *in Spiritu*. In one of his most impressive theological insights, William wrote two complementary theses inspired by St. Paul's famous "We see now as through a mirror in an enigma but then we shall see God face to face" (1 Cor. 13:12). William designed the first treatise, *Mirror of Faith*, to show the contours of a theology and spirituality of love in the Spirit. In the second companion treatise, *Enigma of Faith*, William articulated his Trinitarian theology as the necessary theological expression of the spirituality of love expressed in *Mirror of Faith*, *Commentary on the Song of Songs*, and *Golden Epistle*, as well as earlier in *Nature and Dignity of Love* and almost everywhere in the twelve volumes we possess of his work.

As *Mirror* and *Enigma* demonstrate, for William there can be no separation of theology and spirituality. Only the theologian who is spiritual will be able to help the Christian community to begin to understand, as far as our finite minds are able, the ultimate mystery of Christian faith: God is Love; God is Triune. Some mystical theologians may reach the point of experiencing the triune God in moments of contemplation, in contemplative prayer, in spontaneous outbursts of pure love for both God and neighbor. Mystical theologians feel-understand our union *per Christum in Spiritu* as *imago Trinitatis* through the *unitas Spiritus* that envelops the soul in the stage of union. William daringly proposes that the soul, by the grace of the *unitas Spiritus*, experiences its participation in the loving union of the Trinity's own inner self. In the Trinity the Holy Spirit *is* the unity-harmony-communion of the Father and the Son. Thus the soul now experiences and begins to understand that the inner life of the Trinity is an inner life of love. Each person of the Trinity, for William as for the earlier Christian tradition (Lonergan 1964, 152–205), can be described as a distinct because related person (*pros-opon*; *per-sona*): the Father is origin and source; the Son as Son comes forth from the Father as Son and Eternal Word; the Spirit, as the eternal procession (as in breathing) of Father and Son is the *unitas* uniting all three persons in mutual love. Precisely as loving relationships, the Father, Son, and Spirit are distinct persons; as love through the eternal bond of the Spirit, the Trinity is One God — Trinity in Unity — the uniquely Christian Trinitarian monotheism.

William claims that, in the third stage of the spiritual journey, love and knowledge are so harmonized and unified through the grace of union, which is the *unitas Spiritus*, that the loving-knowing sanctified soul actually experiences a participation in the loving, harmonious unity of the Trinity's inner life. William's theological daring here is amazing: our contact in faith with the Incarnate Word (stage one) becomes ever more purified, interior, and meditative (stage two), until this life of intensifying union with God expands to become, in his bold claim, our experienced participation in the internal life of love of God's own Trinitarian self.[18] In the Trinity, the Spirit is the unity of love. In us, the final grace of our life through Christ in the Spirit is no less than a radical, deified participation in the Trinity's own inner life through the *unitas Spiritus* given to us as grace in the final moment of our graced spiritual journey. At this moment, William found further spiritual and theological meaning in one of his favorite New Testament texts, "We love because God first loved us." How does the soul know this? The soul knows that love through Christ in the Spirit. How does the soul interiorize this knowledge? Ultimately, the soul's final knowledge-love is the loving contemplation of God's own inner Trinitarian life made possible in the ultimate stage of union — made real by the *unitas Spiritus* Itself.

The gift mystically experienced as *unitas Spiritus* in the union with God allows the soul to experience and begin to understand a Trinitarian theology grounded in the Trinity's own life, the source of all life. For William of St. Thierry, the First Letter of John was absolutely accurate: God is Love. The early

---

18. William 1959b (*Speculum fidei* 88, 90, par. 78): "O ergo, quem nemo querit vere, et non invenit, quippe cum ipsa veritas te querendi in conscientia querentis non suspectam jam habeat responsum, aliquatenus invente veritatis, inveni nos, ut inveniamus te; veni in nos, ut eamus in te, et vivamus in te, quia vere non est volentis, neque currentis, sed tui miserentis. Tu prior inspira, ut credamus; tu conforta, ut speremus; tu provoca et accende, ut amemus; totumque de nobis tuum sit, ut bene nobis in te sit, *in quo vivimus, movemur et sumus*."

councils and theologians were equally accurate: through Christ in the Spirit we now know the Ultimate Mystery: God is Trinity in Unity. William's enduring contribution to the Trinitarian theology is his claim that a *full* Trinitarian theology should be a mystical theology of union and a mystical theology should be a Trinitarian mysticism. Deification is as real to William as it has traditionally been for all Eastern theologians. William's unique Christian optimism, beyond his earlier tragic humanism, about humanity is now clear: the final dignity and importance of the human being is her divinization. We can not only have conversation with God; we can also lovingly, conversationally live in God.

Thanks to William's fascinating account of the soul's three-staged spiritual journey, in part a synthesis of Augustine and Origen, our theological knowledge (understood as saturated by love) is now capable of a deeper theological understanding of the Trinity as the central mystery. For that very reason, our deeper knowledge of the Trinity is not an explanation, much less a proof, of the Trinity, but a more deeply apophatic insight into the ultimate mystery of the Real, the Triune God as actual, as mystery. Our love is the love of desire as possession and of desires never ending. Furthermore, in the stage of union, William's description of the rhythm of our desire-love suggests certain affinities to Gregory of Nyssa's notion of *epectasis*:[19] every new participation in God increases but never fulfills the desire of the soul. For Gregory of Nyssa, even in the life to come hereafter, *epectasis* never ends.

THE EXTENT OF WILLIAM OF ST. THIERRY'S CONTRIBUTIONS TO CONTEMPORARY TRINITARIAN THEOLOGY

For William, as for any Christian theologian, the mystery of the Trinity always remains a mystery. Even with its highest biblical cataphatic name for God — God is Love — theology remains apophatic. Trinitarian theology enhances and enriches our understanding of the mystery of God that is no less than the ultimate mystery of Ultimate Reality, which, as the uniquely One constituted by three persons, is the source, the sustainer, and end of all reality. The Triune

---

19. For Gregory of Nyssa's teaching, *epectasis* (always striving for those things that still lie ahead) is symbolized by Moses's constant attempt to rise higher (see Gregory of Nyssa 1978, 111–20).

God's Infinite Incomprehensibility is not only a comment on the finite limits of our knowledge. God's Infinite Incomprehensibility is even more a comment on the fully positive Incomprehensibility of God's Infinite, Triune Godhead, as in Karl Rahner. As Dionysius the Areopagite demonstrates, beyond our best cataphatic and our most apophatic knowledge of God lies a mystical experience of God.[20] William also wants to reflect theologically upon that mystical experience of God as Triune. For William, the theologian, through the very mystical experience of the Triune God, can also reflect on the possibility of a Trinitarian mystical theology of union (which Dionysius phenomenologically described) as the next theological step beyond Dionysius after a mystical experience of God. Here too, as with Maximus the Confessor's more Trinitarian and Christological reading of Dionysius, William's boldness and originality are remarkable.

Christianity is a Trinitarian monotheism: the Triune God is One Nature (*ousia, substantia*) in Three Persons (*hypostases, prosopa, personae*). For William, through the spiritual journey, the *memoria* in our wounded but intact *imago dei* (the traces of God in our subconscious and unconscious) has become fully conscious as a pure love of God for Godself, leading to a new, illuminated knowledge of ourselves as a restored *similitudo dei*, ultimately an unexpected *imago Trinitatis*. That *imago Trinitatis*, for William of St. Thierry, is who we ultimately are; that is our ultimate dignity as human beings. In fact, the *imago Trinitatis* in us is how we finally discover what is most deeply human about a human being—our participation in God's own inner life of love and pure intelligence-in-act. Beyond William's earlier tragic humanism, his amazingly optimistic, Trinitarian vision of who we are—an *imago Trinitatis*—is William's final vision of a full Christian humanism.

Like many (most?) theologians and unlike William of St. Thierry, I am not a mystic.[21] Nevertheless, that unhappy fact does not disallow my presuming to read William's texts, both theological and mystical. Theologians who are not mystics impoverish their theological thinking and their spiritual lives alike by hesitating to read and interpret the classic mystical theologies. Interpretations

---

20. This is the primary reason that Dionysius wrote a "Mystical Theology" (Pseudo-Dionysius 1987, 33–42) as a concluding text, after his cataphatic and apophatic analyses of "The Divine Names" (1987, 47–132).

21. Perhaps the main difficulty here lies in the fact that *mysticism* and, therefore, *mystic* remain essentially contested concepts (see McGinn 1994, 165–343). McGinn's own candidate for mysticism is a persuasive one: a consciousness of the constant presence of God to one.

are needed of such texts by all theologians. As Hans-Georg Gadamer rightly insists, our intellectual and spiritual interiorization-application of the truth we grasp in our hermeneutic efforts is necessary for interpretation itself. In my judgment, this hermeneutical key is also applicable to nonmystics interpreting mystical texts. As that generous pluralist, William James (1978, 370–418) argued, nonmystics (like James himself) should nevertheless read mystical texts. They could learn at least this much: something more than what modern, rational persons ordinarily think possible may be the case. For the psychological James, the mystics may well have been in touch with wider and deeper aspects of consciousness and preconsciousness, beneath and outside the usual, rather narrow limits of ordinary, rational consciousness. Jacques Lacan, unlike his mentor Sigmund Freud, shared James's fascination with and hermeneutical appropriation of earlier mystical texts as a possible entry into the Freudian unconscious — for example, in his analysis of mystical *jouissance* in Teresa of Ávila.[22] Julia Kristeva (1983), linguist, philosopher, and psychoanalyst, has also made important contemporary analyses of love-mysticism in, for example, Bernard of Clairvaux and Teresa of Ávila (although not yet in William of St. Thierry). Given this wide interest in mystical texts by so many nonmystical religious and secular thinkers, it is disconcerting to find so few Trinitarian theologians addressing William of St. Thierry, who was, after all, not only a mystic but also a first-rate mystical theologian. Presumably, the modern theological *gran rifiuto* to mystical theologies is another illustration of the lingering toxic effect of the centuries-old separation of theology and spirituality. Surely it is long past time for that separation to end. Trinitarian theology needs to recover its link to spirituality, as much as all Christian spirituality needs to recover its ultimately Trinitarian nature.

Most of us are not only not mystics; we are, alas, also not poets. The analogy of poetry and mysticism deserves reflection by all theologians hesitant to interpret mystical texts as an aid to their Trinitarian theologies. Most people instinctively and (when educated in reading poetry) intelligently respond to all great poetry. We have learned to internalize a poem's rhythms, its tone, its sensibility and, above all, its singular vision, as also happens for Muslim readers of the extraordinary rhythm of the Qur'an. This is similar to what happens in William's stage two.

---

22. Mitchell and Rose 1982, 137–49.

After learning in our youth to appreciate poetry by careful study,[23] we find ourselves both experientially and intellectually ever more deeply grateful for those poems that have become, often without premeditation, a part of our very lives. As T. S. Eliot suggested in his magnificent modern Christian poems, *Ash Wednesday* and *Four Quartets*, all experiences of human love, the beauty of nature, reading poetry, listening to music, seeing great paintings are one and all "hints and guesses, / Hints followed by guesses" of a realm of meaning beyond ordinary consciousness. As a Christian poet, Eliot also added to this list a line of poetry William of St. Thierry would have applauded: "The hint half guessed, the gift half understood, is Incarnation." In the final stage of the interiorizing of any great work of art, every person knows the truth of Eliot's claim about certain experiences of art, here music: "or music heard so deeply / That it is not heard at all, but you are the music / While the music lasts" (1943, "The Dry Salvages," lines 210–15). If we nonpoets can learn to love and understand great poetry, as most do, then we can also, without the experience of being mystics, learn from classical mystical-theological texts like those of William of St. Thierry. At a minimum, such texts should help Trinitarian theologians to find new ways to unite spirituality and theology.

In postmodern culture, many philosophers and theologians have become more open to poetry (Heidegger, Derrida), as well as to mystical and prophetic religious modes of thinking (Lacoste, Marion, Peperzak) and not only as modes of feeling. Modern culture, except for the Romantics, has had far narrower criteria of what is rationally possible. Several Enlightenment thinkers (Immanuel Kant among them) would not allow art or mysticism to count cognitively. In modern philosophy, for example, Kant's criteria of the conditions of possibility of rational knowledge in the *First Critique* did provide for (in the *Third Critique*) a role for experiences of the beautiful and the sublime (Kant 1951, 82–181). However, Kant's modern sublime, in contrast to postmodern understandings of the sublime like that of Jean-François Lyotard (1977, 176), became, at the end, Kantian reason's self-fascinated experience of its own remarkable powers in the presence of such awe-ful experiences as the Alps, or a waterfall, or the ocean. Only in postmodern philosophy and theology have Kierkegaard's dialectical arguments for a positive understanding of the cate-

---

23. The text suggests only the initial steps of learning to appreciate poetry; to interpret it adequately is of course a complex operation. For the fuller complexity of interpretation, see Ricoeur 1976.

gory "the Impossible" flourished in a manner directly analogous to the positive notion of God's Incomprehensibility (as discussed in chap. 2 above).[24] Some postmodern philosophers (e.g., Derrida 1992, Deleuze 2003, Levinas)[25] have allowed art, especially poetry, to challenge their philosophy intellectually, not merely to provide it with "feeling."

Every Trinitarian theologian, I suggest, can read and learn from William's classic texts: a love-focused, participatory, mystical theology of the Trinity that is simultaneously a Trinitarian mysticism. In meditating on William's Trinitarian theology, the reader's own desire stretches (Gregory of Nyssa's *epectasis*) while the reader's understanding is deepened both cataphatically (Love is God's highest name) and apophatically (the mystery of the Trinity has been enriched by theological understanding to become even more richly apophatic).

Any religiously sensitive reader of William's texts can sense the magnetic attraction of his highly spiritual Trinitarian theology. A reader gradually begins to sense how faithful William was to his oft-repeated aphorism: "To believe in Christ is to go to Christ by loving Him." Every practitioner of theology (that almost impossible discipline trying to understand something about God) also knows the truth of another aphorism of William's, "Love apprehends more by its ignorance than knowledge does by its [apophatic] ignorance because love rejoices to fade away into what God is" (McGinn 1994, 233).

Reading a theologian like William of St. Thierry is both disheartening and encouraging for any contemporary Western theologian living in the wake of the disastrous, centuries-old separation of theology and spirituality, along with the modern separation of philosophy and a way of life. That separation may have begun with a valuable distinction between theological theory and spiritual practice when mainline theology moved out of the monasteries into the universities of the cities. But within a century, the distinction deteriorated into a separation in nominalism.

William believed in the distinction between theology and spirituality; he feared and opposed the separation of the two. In fact, William's own early education was in the new, emerging dialectical methods, possibly at Laon with

---

24. See the essays in Matustik and Westphal 1995.

25. The influence of Russian writers, especially Dostoevsky, on Emmanuel Levinas's work is profound; the influence of Maurice Blanchot on Levinas's later work (and vice versa) is also noteworthy.

ANCIENTS, MEDIEVALS, MODERNS

Anselm of Laon or at a similar school at Rheims.[26] William's early conversion to a vocation away from the secular order to the monastery emancipated him to become one of the last and probably greatest of monastic theologians. William lived before the Scholastic revolution; he preferred the *douceur de vivre* of the earlier dialogical theology of Augustine of Hippo and the speculative beauty of Origen. For several of William's theological colleagues — William of Conches, Gilbert de la Porrée, Peter Abelard, Alain of Lille — the new intellectual methods produced, as noted above, a valuable, new, more humanistic theology: more optimistic about reason's role to forge an open conversation among God, nature, and humanity, within which the new rational tools of dialectic, logic, and dialogue could be employed without restriction.

Near the end of the theologically rich and pluralistic twelfth century, much theology became more urban, more university-grounded, more intellectualist, more Scholastic. Monastic theologies, mystical lay theologies (especially by women), and humanistic theologizing seemed to enter a twilight zone. By the thirteenth century, in the triumph of Scholastic theologies in the new universities, these earlier modes of theology were largely marginalized: monastic theologies to the monasteries; mystical lay theologies to the extraordinary mystics and poets (e.g., Dante) of the period, humanistic theologies to the memory of the later Renaissance. In the fourteenth and fifteenth centuries, moreover, much theology (with some exceptions, like the uniquely original genius Nicholas of Cusa) became more conceptualist rather than intellectualist, first with that genius of logic, Duns Scotus, and after Scotus with the even more refined and much more narrow in range logic and dialectics of the nominalists. Duns Scotus, like Thomas Aquinas before him, welcomed metaphysics for theology; the nominalists, like their student Martin Luther after them, rejected metaphysics. Jean Leclercq (1961), the leading twentieth-century historian of monastic theology, ironically called the dominance of the Scholastic method in Catholic theology from the thirteenth century until Vatican II the "long interruption" in Catholic theology.

Leclercq exaggerates but has a legitimate point. To describe Scholastic theology as a mere interruption in the history of theology ignores the fact that the

---

26. There is still a debate among specialists on which school William attended to learn dialectics, logic, and grammar before his conversion to the monastic life.

thirteenth-century major Scholastics made many enduring intellectual contributions to all theology: lucid definitions; intellectually refined *quaestiones*; the careful use of the rediscovered (through the Arabs) logic and dialectic of Aristotle; the new dialectic of authorities set forth in the *Sic et Non* in Abelard; the purifying intellectualist thrust of the Scholastic drive to system, first in *Sentences* like those of Peter Lombard and then, in the mid-thirteenth century, the arrival of the cathedral-like magnificent two *Summae* of Thomas Aquinas and several others (e.g., Alexander of Hales).

The great medieval Scholastics, unlike their Neo-Scholastic successors, were thinkers of the first order producing philosophies and theologies of the first order. Thomas and Bonaventure distinguished but did not separate theory and practice (way of life), theology and spirituality. As professors controversially representing the new mendicant orders in the University of Paris, Thomas and Bonaventure lived as mendicants in the world, not as monastics withdrawn from the world. Hence, Thomas and Bonaventure were intellectually and spiritually at home in the world of the university. Both struggled against the separation of faith and reason among some influential thinkers in the liberal arts faculty of the University of Paris, Bonaventure more angrily than Thomas.

Thomas too was so alarmed by the contemporary separation of faith and reason, as well as the fatal separation of philosophy and theology, and therefore also of spirituality and theology-philosophy, that he called his work against the professors in the liberal arts faculty (especially the radical Aristotelian Siger of Brabant) *Contra murmurantes*. Bonaventure is exemplary in his age by systematically attempting to keep theology and spirituality together — indeed, inseparable — in the new intellectual situation. Thomas Aquinas in his hymns and in the strong undertow of a wisdom spirituality in all his texts, worked hard to keep the distinction between spirituality and theology a distinction, not a separation. What did Thomas mean in the amazing words he is quoted as saying near the end of his too-short life (forty-nine years!): "Compared to what I have now experienced, all that I have written is as straw. I shall write no more"? Indeed, he did not write more; his great *Summa* is unfinished. Did some powerful mystical experience silence the Scholastic perfection of Thomas's theology? His Dominican intellectualist spirituality worked splendidly in Aquinas's work. Indeed, Thomas's wisdom spirituality was a strong spiritual undertow in all his pellucid and wonderful work. At the end, however, his theology was apparently not enough for Thomas, compared to the mystical experience he suffered near the end of his brief life when he was badly overworked and seriously ill. A "Cleopatra's nose" in the history of Thomas Aquinas is the unavoidable question: What kind of new theology would this unexampled philosophical and theological genius have produced if he had lived beyond his brief forty-nine years? Might Thomas have begun a new theology grounded in his new mystical experience? The "silence of St. Thomas" haunts theology to this day. Neither Thomas nor Bonaventure seemed to know William of St. Thierry's Trinitarian theology, even though some of William of St. Thierry's texts were, until fairly recently, considered texts of Bonaventure. For one thing, the new mendicant orders, the Franciscans (Bonaventura) and the Dominicans (Thomas), were not monastic but committed to living in the world through contemplation-in-action by preaching,[27] doing works of charity and justice, and university teaching.

Furthermore, a strange fate had overtaken the texts of William of St. Thierry by the time of Bonaventure and Thomas. William's theology was largely unknown outside the monasteries. Even within the monasteries, William's works were often listed as works by Bernard of Clairvaux and some later by Bonaventure, the two major theologians of love. Even the one work that continued to be read down through the centuries, William's *Golden Epistle* (*Epistola aurea*), was cited (e.g., by Bonaventure) as a work of Bernard of Clairvaux. William, the supreme monastic Trinitarian theologian and supreme mystical theologian of the Spirit, was not part of the canon of theological classics until, in the early twentieth century, some scholars, especially Déchanet (1940, 1942), rediscovered some well-known texts of William as William of St. Thierry, not Bernard of Clairvaux. Since that time, William's texts continue to be critically edited and variously interpreted by scholars. Until recently, William has hardly been mentioned in many histories of the Trinity. When William's work on the Trinity was mentioned at all, it was usually rather hurriedly interpreted — that is, *mis*interpreted. Moreover, in histories of spirituality before the twentieth

---

27. The new mendicant spiritualities differed among themselves: the Franciscans emphasized affective spirituality (Bonaventure); the Dominicans, intellectualist spirituality (Thomas Aquinas). Francis of Assisi himself famously opposed intellectualism among the early Franciscans. Dominic, founder of an order of preachers, just as famously approved of the Dominicans engaging in intellectual work. Within two generations the Franciscans had produced two of the greatest theologians in the history of Christian theology: Bonaventura and Duns Scotus. At the same time, the Dominicans gave birth to no less than both the Scholastic genius Thomas Aquinas and one of the most profound mystical theologians in all traditions (as Buddhists attest), the strange and wonderful Meister Eckhart.

century, some of William's texts were noted—but often as texts of Bernard. During the early to mid-twentieth century, when some fine scholars finally acknowledged William of Thierry's work as his work, an even more important discovery of a whole new genre of medieval theology was also being retrieved: neither the Scholastic nor the monastic theologies of the medieval period, but the recently named genre *lay theology*,[28] especially the at last recovered texts of the great female mystics of the period. Some medieval female theologians (e.g., Angela of Foligno), like some male theologians (Bernard, William of St. Thierry, Bonaventure), are more affective mystics; some female theologians are more intellectualist (e.g., Marguerite Porete); some female theologians resided in monasteries (e.g., Hildegard of Bingen); and some in *béguinages* (e.g., Hadewijch). All are now irreplaceable figures in the canon of theological and spiritual classics.

In contemporary theology the medieval mystical theologians are read along with William and the Victorines to demonstrate a crucial fact that needs constant repetition: theology without spirituality is too thin; spirituality without theology is too soft. On the whole, modern Enlightenment culture had little use for spirituality and even less for mysticism. The Enlightenment had many achievements: its democratic political theories and practices, its bold and all-important endorsement of tolerance and pluralism, its crucial development of critical methods to unmask all obscurantism and tyranny, whether in church or state. At the same time, the dark side of Enlightenment thought has lately been clarified, mainly thanks to postmodern thinkers. The Enlightenment widely ignored the fatal, contemporary European colonization project, begun in the sixteenth century, greatly expanded in the eighteenth and nineteenth centuries, mostly not dismantled until the twentieth century. Moreover, the Enlightenment continued and strengthened the separations already present in Western culture since the fourteenth-century nominalist crisis. The Enlightenment, in effect, not merely continued but reified and enforced the now-familiar modern separations: theory from practice (philosophical theory separated from a philosophical way of life, unimaginable to an ancient philosopher); theology from personal and spiritual experience (unintelligible to a monastic or to a lay mystical theologian); form from content (the moderns privileged the form of propositional definitions arrived at through logical and dialectical method;

---

28. For new lay theology, see McGinn 1998.

other forms — narrative, symbolic, poetic, aphoristic — were marginalized to *belles lettres*). The final separation of emotion and thought, feeling and thought, was the separation that both Bernard and William saw emerging in their own culture and presciently feared as presaging a benighted future for theology: the separation of the mystical experience of love from theological and philosophical theories of love; the separation of *ratio* and *intellectus*; the separation of *affectus* (feelings, affects, dispositions, passions) from *intellectus*, culminating in the separation of spiritual experience from theological understanding.

We still live in the intellectual ruins produced by fourteenth-century nominalist separations intensified in the eighteenth-century Enlightenment. Fortunately, postmodern culture, unlike the more narrow regime of Western modernity, is far more welcoming to difference, especially the now-valued differences of all those marginalized and rejected by modern culture, including mystics, prophets, visionaries, the poor who had no voice, the eccentrics. Indeed, the very word *mystical*, as Michel de Certeau (1992, 2015) argued, referring by example to ordinary spiritual practices and readings of Scripture, was once a familiar and honored adjective. However, the word *mystic* in the modern, centralizing seventeenth and Enlightenment centuries became a dismissive noun. A mystic was outside the center — strange, bizarre, seemingly irrational, unnerving to the majority. *Mystic* as a negative noun was used unjustly, especially for female mystics like Jeanne-Marie Bouvier de la Motte Guyon. Modern Neo-Scholastic theologians in the seventeenth and eighteenth centuries, with Catholic, Reformed, and Lutheran theologies alike, abandoned theology's roots in communal, especially liturgical experience (Buckley 1987), as well as in more personal spiritual practices. Modern Neo-Scholastic and several modern Cartesian theologies (but not Descartes himself) soon drifted into a vague attempt to function as modern semi-philosophies attempting to prove, through one or another version of modern rationality, some doctrine of traditional theology. In fact, the Catholic Neo-Scholastics of the seventeenth century through to the mid-twentieth century became obsessed with certainty in contradiction to what Thomas Aquinas considered theology's chief intellectual task: not certainty, but some partial, analogous, but real understanding of the great mysteries of faith. The modern Neo-Scholastics, especially the Suárezians, reduced the earlier Scholastic exercises in analogous understanding to mere corollaries of theology proper — that is, the kind of question worth considering only after the theologian had established "certainty" through scriptural "proofs," conciliar or magisterium definitions, earlier accepted theologies, and so on. As noted earlier, but worth repeating for its ironic accuracy, Bernard Lonergan (1972, esp. 267–355) once remarked that the modern Neo-Scholastics believed in clear and distinct ideas and very few of them! Whatever its own confusions and exaggerations, postmodernism is proving a boon to theology. On the whole, postmodern thinkers reject modernity's separations: theory from practice, content from form; *ratio* from *intellectus*; *affectus* from *intellectus*; spirituality from theology; philosophical theory from a philosophical way of life.

Many contemporary philosophers and theologians presently read the mystics and artists with new eyes. Moreover, there is now a widely recognized need for plural forms to express theological content. Contemporary theology also acknowledges that theory should analyze and articulate both reason and *affectus*, as Augustine always insisted. Among the texts and persons ripe for retrieval in this new, cultural postmodern situation are the theological and spiritual texts, including mystical texts, on Christian love: love as both relationship and postmodern excess.

William took the theology of the Trinity and gave it a new focus and form: love was the harmonizing focus for both spirituality and Trinitarian theology. The meditative, contemplative form of William's Trinitarian theology is still ignored by many Trinitarian theologians. Is contemporary Trinitarian theology condemned to stay in a modern model of theology, purely intellectualist, or, more exactly, conceptualist? When will the lay mystical Trinitarian theologies, the early Greek Trinitarian theologies, the monastic Trinitarian theologies begin to play a proper role in contemporary Trinitarian theology?

CONCLUSION: TWO CRITICISMS OF WILLIAM OF ST. THIERRY AND SOME SUGGESTIONS FOR HIS CONTRIBUTIONS TO CONTEMPORARY TRINITARIAN THEOLOGY

In any major thinker, there are always limits and critical problems. So it is with William of St. Thierry's spirituality and theology. First, the spirituality: William's account of the three stages of the spiritual journey to the experience of *unitas Spiritus* is, as I have argued above, profound and illuminating for any honest seeker, not only for William's fellow monks and mystics. However, too often William's journey is directed only to monks. This is especially true of his most widely read work, *Golden Epistle*. William seems to leave the rest of his readers (nonmonks) with some heavy work of translation to apply his monastic suggestions to their own lives in the world. Perhaps this is an inevitable problem in reading any monastic writing for any reader lacking a calling to the monastic life. Reading William's texts (like most theological texts — sometimes lucid, sometimes obscure, sometimes orderly, sometimes digressive) is, I have argued in this essay, well worth the effort for every theologian. As Hans-Georg Gadamer (1965, 29) reminds us, every interpretation includes application, as is hermeneutically witnessed most clearly in law and preaching. In William's meditative reading of the Scriptures, we sense anew that careful reading can also be a spiritual exercise. To learn to read a biblical, theological, or mystical text well is to become able to translate it for one's own interior development, dependent on one's present development: *quidquid recipitur per modum recipientis recipitur*. Like the monastic texts of Theravada Buddhism, William's texts need translation for nonmonks, unlike the texts written for lay Buddhists (not only monks) in the more open and inclusive forms of Buddhism in most Mahayana Buddhism. Unlike Christian texts written for all thinking persons, like Thomas Aquinas's *Summa Contra Gentiles* or William's own *On the Nature of Body and Soul*, most monastic texts in all traditions need an extra effort of translation from the monastery to the world. A hermeneutical translation is by no means impossible. Thoughtful readers can understand William's theological-spiritual texts as long as they are at all intellectually and spiritually receptive to mystical-theological writings. But the extra effort of translating and interpreting William's monastic texts from their original monastic context is necessary. The monastery is not the world: good monastic thoughts and practices, like all good persons, cross all borders.

My theological criticism of William, however, is not occasioned by his exclusively monastic focus. To prepare for this more substantial theological criticism, however, it is useful to recall William's singular and eminently retrievable achievements. William's contribution to Trinitarian theology is twofold. First, William made his theology explicitly and directly related to his spirituality; he shows us one way forward for contemporary Trinitarian theologians endeavoring to join their intellectual and spiritual tasks. William's lesson is an important one: a theologian's theoretical efforts in Trinitarian theology should be informed by spiritual practice, whether that practice is inchoate or, like William's, explicit, direct, and methodical: the three stages harmonizing faith, love, and reason. Reading William, one can be more alert to the limits of one's own journey and intellectual development.

Second, William notably enacted an alternative focus for understanding the

Trinity, regarding pure love as *unitas Spiritus*, rather than retaining Augustine's primary but not sole focus in *De Trinitate* on intelligence-in-act. Here is the crucial difference William's Trinitarian theology makes. By shifting the principal focus from reason to love-*affectus*, William provided new intellectual and spiritual resources for all Trinitarian theologies, even modern "social" models of the Trinity. The desire to know, intellectuals too easily forget, is a desire (*desiderium, affectus*). The desire to know is ultimately anchored in and is driven by the greatest of all desires: the desire for the Good. We desire to know because we desire the good of truth. The desire for the Good, in turn, is best understood, for Christians, as above all the desire for the pure, personal love of God, itself grounded in the mystical grace of *unitas Spiritus* that harmonizes reason and love, sense and mind, soul and body.

William did not shift his focus from intelligence to love without also strongly affirming and analyzing understanding like Augustine's own affirmation: *Intellectum valde ama* (see chapter 1 above, "Augustine Our Contemporary," and *Patrologia Latina* 33:458–59). As argued above, William at every stage of his journey shows the always-already interdependence of love and knowledge. Intelligence and love *are* eternally one in the Infinite Trinity. In human life and theology, love and understanding-knowledge are sometimes radically united by contemplative love, even though that interrelationship inevitably remains partial and participatory in finite beings. Human beings, as created and redeemed humans, desire to attain ever-greater spiritual and intellectual harmony by rediscovering their *similitudo dei* and *imago Trinitatis*. Through grace, human beings participate in the Trinitarian life of love and understanding. Of course we participate as finite beings. We participate in the Trinity, whereas the Infinite, Infinitely Loving God *is* that life. Human understanding of the Trinity, however far it may reach at the level of contemplative wisdom, remains and will always remain a finite, apophatic understanding of the Incomprehensible Triune God. Karl Rahner, like Gregory of Nyssa, argued that this apophatic understanding of God's Infinite Incomprehensibility will still be in force in the Beatific Vision. Human desire for the Good, however purified into a pure love of God for God's own sake, will never be fully satisfied, even in eternity. Desire for the good will always desire more. As noted above, Gregory of Nyssa speculated, in his fascinating interpretation of St. Paul's *epectasis*, that human beings will always be engaged in a constant process of desire-possession-desire, not only in this life but in the life hereafter! By its very deepening, human knowledge increases its apophatic sense, not only of the negative, finite limits of our knowledge, but also of God's positive Incomprehensibility. Human desire for the Good, by the purifying powers that allow it to become pure contemplative love for a God who is love, lives forever a life of contemplative *apophasis* and endless loving (*epectasis*).

For William, the constant deepening of faith and love, as well as the accompanying expansion of reason, is the kind of move needed by theologians, especially theologians of the Trinity. William's position remains, I believe, a profound contribution on how to approach a Trinitarian theology by understanding that faith and love so transform reason that reason itself can move past dialectic and all other exercises in ordinary reason to meditation and contemplation.

Nevertheless, in my judgment, William could also — and perhaps should — have spent more effort in understanding ordinary reason, beginning with Augustine's classic analysis of intelligence-in-act in *De Trinitate*. If William had studied Augustine on intelligence-in-act more thoroughly than he seems to have done, then he could also have understood the dialectic and logic used more extensively by Anselm and Abelard. Dialectic, logic, and grammar, after all, are also exercises of intelligence-in-act. Transformed reason (*ratio fidei*) need not lessen the need for ordinary forms of reason. Without weakening his own distinct position or the need in theology for a transformed reason, William could have affirmed a theological development of reason in cooperation with his more humanistic theological contemporaries, including Abelard as a *conversation* among diverse philosophers and theologians on the relationship of humans, nature, and God. Logic and dialectic, grammar and argument, function best when they function freely.

It is puzzling why William, so well versed in the main modes of medieval reason, found the conversation and argument model of Abelard and others so threatening to his own model of *ratio fidei*. Here William's main mentor on love, Bernard of Clairvaux, was too influential on William. Bernard of Clairvaux's rare, remarkable, still rightly influential writings on love (especially his multivolume *Commentary on the Song of Songs*) were clearly a major and positive influence on William of St. Thierry's own more conceptually clear theology and spirituality of love. Unfortunately Bernard of Clairvaux, the highly original, brilliantly poetic theologian of love, at times seems quite uncharitable, especially in his obsession to destroy Abelard, whose dialectic Bernard clearly misunderstood. Unfortunately William accompanied Bernard in this campaign against Abelard. As is the case with any original thinker (admittedly some more than others), just criticism could be directed against some aspects and applications of Abelard's methods. However, neither Bernard nor William raised much perhaps-needed criticism of Abelard. Rather they both engaged: Bernard more passionately, indeed angrily; William with greater detachment mixed with an atypical and unfortunate polemical streak. Ah well — all human beings are complex (sometimes only complicated). Who is/was Bernard of Clairvaux? On the one hand, he was the great theologian of experience and love; defender of the pluralistic, greatly gifted Hildegard of Bingen; the courageous denunciator of Rhineland Christians attacking the Jews. On the other hand, he was the deeply influential promoter of Crusades against Muslims; instigator of the wrongheaded attack on Peter the Venerable at Cluny and of the intransigence against Abelard allied to a refusal to debate Abelard publicly.

William possessed an exemplary knowledge of Augustine, as evidenced in his early works and in his continued fidelity to Augustine in his later works. Origen also became a real influence on William's formulation of the stages of reason and love from an animal to a rational to a spiritual state. William seemed not to have noticed that he also had at his intellectual disposal, in Augustine's own brilliant analysis in *De Trinitate*, a refined understanding of intelligence-in-act with far more precision, clarity, and depth than he himself usually accorded ordinary reflective reason as intelligence-in-act. William knew and used the old and new tools of reason: dialectic, logic, rhetoric, dialogue, metaphysical and mystical contemplation. Unlike Augustine, however, William does not enact a discussion of the power of reason as intelligence-in-act in both acts of direct understanding issuing through intelligence-in-act, not automatically, in concepts and acts of reflective understanding.

As Thomas Aquinas will argue in the century after William, Augustine's reflective analysis of intelligence-in-act yielding acts of concept and judgment was at the heart of Augustine's so-called psychological analogy. With his sharper Aristotelian tools, while not rejecting Neoplatonism (Verdeyen 1990; Lonergan 1971), Aquinas would demonstrate how Augustine's intelligence-in-act was metaphysically to be understood as act-act (i.e., intelligible emanations). Even granted certain limits in an analysis of ordinary reason, William was not a fideist. He clearly respected the dialectical, rhetorical, and logical uses of reason. He used them throughout his life. However, William believed that his notion of *ratio fidei* almost always provided theology with a new, improved form of transformed reason that sublated and held under its aegis all uses of "natural" or ordinary reason like dialectic. As we have seen above, William's position on the theological sense of "natural" reason was excellent, although more restrictive than Anselm's earlier notion of *intellectus* in his mode of theology as *fides quaerens intellectum*. Anselm's position on faith and reason would return, in highly refined, complex, and distinct forms later in Thomas Aquinas, Bonaventure, Duns Scotus, and others. In his own use of reason in theology, William seemed to fear far too much what he construed as the excessive role assigned to reason by William of Conches, Gilbert de la Porrée, and, above all, Abelard. Doubtless these more humanistic theologians occasionally erred on the side of what later centuries called rationalism. But their basic rational model of reasoned *conversatio* including dialectical arguments as a full medieval *disputatio* was not rationalist, despite the fears of Bernard and William.

A much-needed future theological task for Trinitarian theology, I suggest, is a newly thought-through union of the intelligence-in-act analyses in the Trinitarian theologies of Augustine, Aquinas, and Lonergan with the love-in-act analyses in the Trinitarian theologies of William, Richard of St. Victor, and Bonaventure. Through such a dual approach, the interdependence of love-knowledge — that is, of *affectus-intellectus* and *ratio-intellectus* — would find its full actuality in a new Trinitarian theology, based on the interdependence of reason and affect, with love as the primary drive: the desire to know as grounded ultimately in the desire for the Good. Such a union for love and knowledge for a new Trinitarian theology and spirituality remains a difficult but possible future task for Trinitarian theologians, at least those who know the intellectualist approaches in the Trinitarian theologies of Augustine and Aquinas, as well as the more love-centered and spiritual-experience-grounded Trinitarian theologies of William of St. Thierry and Bonaventure.

It seems a fair surmise that William of St. Thierry would have been fully capable of such a further development in his own Trinitarian theology if he had given more sustained attention in his description of stage one to his mentor Augustine's analysis of intelligence-in-act. If he had, perhaps he would have spared us the one major stain on his record: his rush to judgment, his refusal to provide a more judicious assessment of the more intellectualist but not necessarily rationalist positions of William of Conches, Gilbert de la Porrée, and, above all, Peter Abelard. Perhaps the unfortunate intellectual clash between

William and Abelard was inevitable — as inevitable as other theological clashes in the modern period, such as those between Luis de Molino and Domingo Bañez, between Martin Luther and Ulrich Zwingli, between Schleiermacher and Hegel, between Karl Barth and Paul Tillich, between Hans Urs von Balthasar and Karl Rahner. Rationalism may well have been Abelard's temptation, but his brilliant theology was reasonable and humanistic rather than rationalist. Rationalism was Abelard's temptation, only rarely his actuality. Fideism was William's temptation, but not his actuality.

Finally, my analysis of the Trinitarian theology of William of St. Thierry should not end on a negative note. We all always need greater theological balance in one form or another. At central moments in the history of theology, a balance of reason and faith, intelligence and love, experience and critique, *affectus* and *intellectus*, *ratio* and *intellectus*, *Vernunft* and *Verstand* has sometimes split apart into mutually unyielding clashes, often fierce, between different theological models. *Pace* Karl Barth, Christian theology should be far more both/and than either/or.

In the welcome pluralism of theologies in the twelfth-century Renaissance as in our own day, one hopes that diverse theologies will prove *diversa sed non adversa*. However, theologians too are "human, all too human": differences all too quickly can become intractable oppositions. *Odium theologicum* is real. We still need both critical theologies in the tradition of Abelard and experiential spiritual theologies in the tradition of Bernard and William. One often learns best from a theological tradition different from one's own, as I have tried in this essay to learn from and appropriate as much as I can of the spiritual profundity, intellectual acuity, and magnetic attraction of William of St. Thierry's Trinitarian theology and spirituality.

In William of St. Thierry, a Trinitarian theology should be mystical; a mystical theology should be Trinitarian. All contemporary Trinitarian theologians should consider anew how, by studying the complex and profound Trinitarian theology of William of St. Thierry, they too may discover some extremely fruitful suggestions on how to relate in explicit, stage-by-stage terms, Trinitarian theory to experience, *affectus* to *intellectus*, Trinitarian spirituality to Trinitarian theology. It is also not so difficult to imagine some further expansion by some future theologians of William's Trinitarian theology, which will be achieved by adding some more critical uses of reason in theology in the mode of Abelard and modern critical theology: a difficult task but not, in principle, an impossible one, when theology moves past its present impasse where at times *diversa sed non adversa* theologies seem utopian. Let the final words of William of St. Thierry serve as ideals for contemporary Trinitarian theology:

Amor ipse intellectus est.
Amor noster est Spiritus.

REFERENCES

Anselm, Saint, Archbishop of Canterbury. 1965. *St. Anselm's Proslogion, with a Reply on Behalf of the Fool by Gaunilo and the Author's Reply to Gaunilo*. Translated, with commentary, by Maxwell John Charlesworth. Oxford: Clarendon Press.

Bell, David N. 1984. *The Image and Likeness: The Augustinian Spirituality of William of Saint Thierry*. Kalamazoo, MI: Cistercian Publications.

Bouyer, Louis. 1958. *The Cistercian Heritage*. Translated by Elizabeth A. Livingstone. Westminster, MD: Newman Press.

Bredero, Adriaan H. 1996. *Bernard of Clairvaux: Between Cult and History*. Translated by Reinder Bruinsma. Edinburgh: T & T Clark.

Brooke, Odo. 1980. *Studies in Monastic Theology*. Kalamazoo, MI: Cistercian Publications.

Brown, Peter. 1967. *Augustine of Hippo*. Berkeley: University of California Press.

———. 2000. *Augustine of Hippo: A Biography*. Berkeley: University of California Press.

Buckley, Michael J. 1987. *At the Origins of Modern Atheism*. New Haven, CT: Yale University Press.

Certeau, Michel de. 1992. *The Mystic Fable: The Sixteenth and Seventeenth Centuries*. Vol. 1. Translated by Michael B. Smith. Chicago: University of Chicago Press.

———. 2015. *The Mystic Fable: The Sixteenth and Seventeenth Centuries*. Vol. 2. Edited by Luce Giard. Translated by Michael B. Smith. Chicago: University of Chicago Press.

Chadwick, Henry. 1981. *Boethius: The Consolations of Music, Logic, Theology, and Philosophy*. Oxford: Clarendon Press.

Corcoran, Donald, Sr. 1985. "Spiritual Guidance." In *Christian Spirituality: Origins to the Twelfth Century*, edited by Bernard McGinn, John Meyendorff, and Jean Leclercq. New York: Crossroad.

Déchanet, Jean. 1940. *Aux sources de la spiritualité de Guillaume de Saint-Thierry: Première série d'études*. Bruges, Belgium: Charles Beyaert.

———. 1942. *Guillaume de Saint-Thierry: L'homme et son oeuvre*. Bruges, Belgium: Charles Beyaert.

Deleuze, Gilles. 2003. *Francis Bacon: The Logic of Sensation*. Translated by Daniel W. Smith. Minneapolis: University of Minnesota Press.

Derrida, Jacques. 1992. *Acts of Literature*. Edited by Derek Attridge. London: Routledge.

Eliot, T. S. 1943. *Four Quartets*. New York: Harcourt.

Evans, Gillian R. 1989. *Anselm*. Wilton, CT: Morehouse-Barlow.

Gadamer, Hans-Georg. 1965. *Wahrheit und Methode: Grundzüge einer philosophischen Hermeneutik*. Tübingen, Germany: J. C. B. Mohr.

Gilson, Étienne. 1940. *The Mystical Theology of St. Bernard*. Translated by A. H. C. Downes Sheed. New York: Sheed and Ward.

Gregory, Pope. 1963. *Expositiones: In Canticum canticorum, In librum primum Regum*. Edited by Pierre-Patrick Verbraken. Turnholti, Belgium: Brepols.

Gregory of Nyssa. 1978. *The Life of Moses*. Translated and annotated by Abraham J. Malherbe and Everett Ferguson. New York: Paulist Press.

Hadot, Pierre. 1995. *Philosophy as a Way of Life: Spiritual Exercises from Socrates to Foucault*. Edited by Arnold Davidson. Translated by Michael Chase. Oxford: Blackwell.

Hick, John, and Arthur C. McGill, eds. 1967. *The Many-Faced Argument: Studies on the Ontological Argument for the Existence of God*. New York: Macmillan.

James, William. 1978. *The Varieties of Religious Experience*. Garden City: Doubleday.

Kafka, Franz. 1981. *Das Schloss*. Frankfurt am Main: Fischer Taschenbuch.

Kant, Immanuel. 1951. *Critique of Judgment*. Translated by John Henry Bernard. New York: Hafner.

Kristeva, Julia. 1983. *Histoires d'amour*. Paris: Éditions Denoël.

Lacan, Jacques. 2006. *Écrits: The First Complete Edition in English*. Translated by Bruce Fink, in collaboration with Héloïse Fink and Russell Grigg. New York: W. W. Norton.

Leclercq, Jean. 1961. *The Love of Learning and the Desire for God: A Study of Monastic Culture*. Translated by Catharine Misrahi. New York: Fordham University Press.

Lonergan, Bernard J. F. 1964. *De Deo Trino II: Pars Systematica seu Divinarum Personarum Conceptio Analogica*. Rome: Apud aedes Universitas Gregorianae.

———. 1971. *Grace and Freedom*. New York: Herder and Herder.

———. 1972. *Method in Theology*. New York: Herder and Herder.

Lyotard, Jean-François. 1977. *Rudiments païens: Genre dissertatif*. Paris: Union Générale d'Éditions.

Matter, E. Ann. 1990. *The Voice of My Beloved: The Song of Songs in Western Medieval Christianity*. Philadelphia: University of Pennsylvania Press.

Matustik, Martin J., and Merold Westphal, eds. 1995. *Kierkegaard in Post/Modernity*. Bloomington: Indiana University Press.

McGinn, Bernard. 1994. *The Growth of Mysticism: Gregory the Great through the 12th Century*. Vol. 2 of *The Presence of God*. New York: Crossroad.

———. 1998. *Flowering of Mysticism: Men and Women in the New Mysticism (1200–1350)*. New York: Crossroad.

McIntosh, Mark A. 1998. *Mystical Theology: The Integrity of Spirituality and Theology*. Oxford: Blackwell.

Migne, J.-P. (Jacques-Paul). 1841–55. *Patrologia Latina*. Paris: Garnieri Fratres, editores et J.-P. Migne successores.

———. 1857–66. *Patrologia Graeca*. Turnholti, Belgium: Brepols.

Mitchell, Juliet, and Jacqueline Rose, eds. 1982. *Feminine Sexuality: Jacques Lacan and the école freudienne*. Translated by Jacqueline Rose. New York: W. W. Norton.

Nietzsche, Friedrich. 1967. *On the Genealogy of Morals*. Translated by Walter Kaufmann and R. J. Hollingdale. New York: Random House.

Olivetti, Marco M. 1990. *L'argomento ontologico*. Padua, Italy: CEDAM.

Otten, Willemien. 2004. *From Paradise to Paradigm: A Study of Twelfth-Century Humanism*. Leiden: Brill.

Pseudo-Dionysius. 1987. *The Complete Works*. Translated by Colm Luibheid, with Paul Rorem. New York: Paulist Press.

Ricoeur, Paul. 1976. *Interpretation Theory: Discourse and the Surplus of Meaning*. Fort Worth: Texas Christian University Press.

Tracy, David. 2010. "God as Infinite Love: A Roman Catholic Perspective." In *Divine Love: Perspectives from the World's Religious Traditions*, edited by Jeff Levin and Stephen G. Post. West Conshohocken, PA: Templeton Press.

Verdeyen, Paul. 1990. *La théologie mystique de Guillaume de Saint-Thierry*. Paris: FAC-éditions.

William of St. Thierry. 1959a. *Aenigma fidei*. In *Deux traités sur la foi: Le miroir de la foi, l'énigme de le foi*, translated and annotated by Marie-Madeleine Davy. Paris: Vrin.

———. 1959b. *Speculum fidei*. In *Deux traités sur la foi: Le miroir de la foi, l'énigme de le foi*, translated and annotated by Marie-Madeleine Davy. Paris: Vrin.

———. 1983. *Epistola ad Fratres de Monte Dei* [*Epistola aurea*]. In *La Lettera D'Oro* [Italian and Latin], edited by Claudio Leonardi; translated by C. Piacentini and R. Scarcia. Florence: Sansoni.

CHAPTER 4

MARTIN LUTHER'S
DEUS THEOLOGICUS

Martin Luther, with riveting intensity and characteristic honesty, insisted that every aspect of theology is a desperate attempt, always inadequate, always necessary, to understand some aspect of the Unfathomable Mystery of God. Luther always held that theology is an analysis of the relationship between the Justifying God and the human sinner — above all, the relationship of the sinner now justified by faith alone, through the grace of the Gospel promise: the divine promise that imputes Christ's righteousness as forgiveness to any sinner, justified by grace through faith alone. The sinner thus becomes *simul iustus et peccator*: not *partim/partim*, but *totus/totus*.

The central Christic understanding of the justifying God who is Love is Luther's foundational insight into God's reality, as narrated and proclaimed in the New Testament itself, most clearly in the First Letter of John: God is Love.

For Luther, the understanding of the divine fullness revealed in Jesus Christ includes three principal dimensions. First, the fundamental insight into *Deus theologicus*, for Luther, was a glimpse of the reality of God as both revealed and hidden: revealed *sub contrario*, that is, in negativity, suffering, abjection, and abandonment, in the cross of Jesus Christ that paradoxically manifests God's loving promise of forgiveness. Christ's active righteousness is imputed as alien righteousness to us, Christ's righteousness experienced as our passive righteousness in faith alone. Hence, the first section below analyzes Luther's primary and central understanding of God's self-revelation in the cross of Jesus Christ as the revealed and hidden God of the Gospel.

At the same time, there is a second dimension to Luther's *Deus theologicus* and, therefore, another distinct (second) section in this essay. Martin Luther, in an uncanny, existentially fraught theological move, articulated a frightening experience of the utter majesty of God (*Deus nudus* to *homo nudus*), exposed by means of *Anfechtungen* (physical, psychological, spiritual, and satanic assaults upon the individual). These assaults occur both before and, at times, even after justification. At such sinister moments, the Christian experiences the radical hiddenness of God beyond even the word of forgiveness. In revelation, this experience of the inscrutable will of God is exposed and declared in the doctrine of double predestination.

Luther holds that the *fact* of predestination is revealed in Scripture (e.g., in the unnerving story of Jacob and Esau), but the *why* of predestination (indeed, as we shall see below, double predestination) is not revealed. The why of predestination is forever hidden in the inscrutable will of God, whose awesome majesty should be worshipped but not futilely speculated upon by a reason hopelessly beyond its limits. All the Christian can do in experiencing this second terrifying form of divine hiddenness is to flee back to the cross of Jesus Christ, where God's revelation of Godself as Love heals.

A third dimension (section 3) of God's reality, so the new Finnish school of Luther research maintains, had emerged in Luther's infrequent but pronounced appeals to justification as *theosis*—a category of divine union that is beyond the "marvelous exchange" of forensic righteousness and beyond even most understandings of Luther's lifelong appeals to *unio Christi*. The third dimension is further clarified by a non-Finnish contribution to Luther research: the recent scholarship on Luther's semantic, logical, and semiotic clarifications of such categories as relation, person, and eternity in the traditional Trinitarian understanding of God's nature. In his last dialogical, not usually polemical, *dis-*

putationes (formulated for the examinations of his doctoral students at Wittenberg), Luther analyzed with philosophical and theological finesse some central, traditional Trinitarian concepts for understanding God. Each of the sections of this essay, therefore, will analyze one of the three major dimensions of Martin Luther's complex *Deus theologicus*.

How these three major dimensions of Luther's theological understanding of God may correlate, one with another, is a task that this essay does not address explicitly, save for some brief Christological suggestions near the end. My major aim here is simply to demonstrate three dimensions of Luther's *Deus theologicus*. An attempt to show a complex theological unity of these three dimensions is for another time. This is also true for any critical assessment of Luther's rejection of a fully philosophical (i.e., metaphysical and/or contemplative, not only semantic and logical) approach to God's reality.[1] In sum, before any constructive critique of Luther's theology of God can be launched, it is first necessary to offer an interpretation of the three basic dimensions of Luther's complex *Deus theologicus*. Hence this essay.

GOD HIDDEN IN REVELATION: LUTHER'S THEOLOGY OF THE CROSS

Truth about the true God is not a human work or achievement. True knowledge of God comes only through faith, which is a divine — not human — work. Grace though faith alone is both God's *favor* through the righteousness of Christ, imputed to us as forgiveness, and *donum* (pure gift: i.e., passive incipient righteousness, which, through the Holy Spirit, can increase until the ultimate *donum* of our graced glory after this life).[2] The righteousness we receive is Christ's own active righteousness that endows upon us passive righteousness. We are reckoned righteous through Christ; his righteousness is imputed to us. We are now totally justified, since God's imputation covers over the many sins remaining. We are, therefore, *simul iustus et peccator*, totally just and totally sinful. Through faith, we have become entirely new creatures, formed, not by any

---

1. On Luther on reason, see Gerrish 1962; and Dragseth 2011, esp. the essays by Bayer (13–22), Janz (47–52), Hinlicky (53–60), and Bielfeldt (61–68).

2. This most important of Luther's theological insights is expressed everywhere in his work, most eloquently and fully, perhaps, in his magisterial *Lectures on Galatians* (1535). See Luther 1955, 26–27; and Luther 1883, 40, I, and 40, II, 1–184.

personal work or achievement, even works of love, but solely by Christ's grace through faith. The logic of justification is clear: *sola fides* made possible through *sola gratia*, made possible through *solus Christus*. Faith alone is the form of our passive righteousness, not, as for most of Luther's medieval predecessors, faith formed by our deeds of love (*fides caritate formata*). Jesus Christ alone is the form of our faith that then entails a faith active in the works of love. Works of love are the result — not the presupposition — of faith.

Before we receive the grace of faith, we are trapped in self-bondage. We struggle ever more desperately to escape from ourselves, but our deeply damaged selves are curved in upon themselves (*incurvatus in se*) with no exit. Faith grants God's unconditioned forgiveness. Faith exposes the failures of all works-righteousness: in all law, all ritual ceremonies, all penitential acts, all indulgences, and, above all, all those products of speculative reason that presume to describe the divine reality. The most basic framework for Luther's understanding of justification by faith alone is the dialectic of law and Gospel: the dialectical conflict of these mutually implying opposites lays bare the radicality of the conflict between works-righteousness and faith. The most basic role of law is to make us face our sinfulness — that is, our inability to keep the law, much less to find forgiveness through it. In contrast, the divine promise of the Gospel, grasped through Christ's grace by faith, is forgiveness.[3]

Luther's notion of dialectic, unlike Plato's or Aristotle's and far more like Heraclitus's and Hegel's, is structured as a conflict of opposites that not only clash but also imply and need each other. The Gospel rejects all works-righteousness — and yet at the same time implies the need of a work of law to force the sinner to face her sinfulness. On the other side of faith, the law returns with a valuable new function to order our political and ecclesial lives.

As Jaroslav Pelikan once observed, Western theology is a series of footnotes to Augustine: Catholic theologies, with their analogical language, are heirs to Augustine's nature-grace dialectic, especially in his early and middle works, but even in such relatively late texts as *De Trinitate* and *City of God*. It is important to understand that an analogical imagination is not a nondialectical method, as it is sometimes interpreted (e.g., by Karl Barth, who in his earlier work bizarrely named analogical knowledge of God an invention of the "Anti-Christ"!). True

---

3. Promise (of forgiveness) is persuasively considered the central category in Luther's theology in Bayer 2008 (esp. 50–58) and Bayer 2007 (esp. 125–39).

ANCIENTS, MEDIEVALS, MODERNS

theological analogy always includes negative dialectical moments. As the Fourth Lateran Council (1215) made clear, negative moments are intrinsic to all properly analogical language in theology: for every positive statement of similarity, an even greater negative statement of dissimilarity must be articulated in order to assure the proper use of analogical language in theology.[4]

Luther's fundamental understanding of *Deus theologicus*—from 1514 to 1546—is the God revealed by grace through faith in Jesus Christ. The Gracious, Infinitely Loving God of Jesus Christ is both manifested and hidden in the revelation of the cross of Jesus Christ. Once the favor and gift of true faith happens, authentic, *sub contrario* saving knowledge of God as Gracious simultaneously occurs. For Luther, any philosophical, metaphysical notions of God (natural knowledge of God) are now shattered by the revelation of the saving God revealed in the cross. Reason's presuppositions are now reason's self-exposure as deeply damaged. The bondage of the intellect for Luther, Susan Schreiner argues (2011, 324–32), is even deeper than the bondage of the will. For Luther, the Fall's damage to reason is far deeper than that imagined in Thomas Aquinas's notion of the Fall's resulting in a *vulnus ignorantiae*. Reason's wound for Luther, like the wound of Amfortas in *Parsifal*, is an open wound unhealed.

Nor is it the case, as Luther's later debates with John Agricola, and as the Antinomians clarified, that once faith takes over through a believer's faith as fundamentally trust (*fiducia*), indeed heartful trust (*fides cordis*), we no longer need the law in either church or state. On the contrary, Luther, in *Against the Antinomians*,[5] held that the earthly kingdom and the heavenly kingdom alike need laws for ordering life rightly. So much was this the case that the "early" Luther could even allow for the possibility that the institution of the church could, for purposes of order, continue with an external head—the pope—as long as the papacy was understood to be of a human—not divine—institution (i.e., law, not Gospel) and as long as the pope preached the Gospel.

Martin Luther's fundamental *Deus theologicus* is God's Hiddenness in revelation affirmed by the gift of faith in Christ's cross. Luther's *sola gratia* and *sola fides* are both grounded in *solus Christus*. Without faith in Jesus Christ as the crucified God-man incarnate, the death of Jesus of Nazareth on the cross is yet

---

4. For an analysis of the importance of negative dissimilarities in theological analogy, see the classical twentieth-century work, Przywara 2014, especially on the Fourth Lateran Council (349–72, 506–31).

5. Luther 1955, 47:107–19; 1883, 50:468–77.

another tragic murder of an innocent human being — tragic like the crucifixion of Spartacus and his followers, as well as countless others in the ancient world.

As early as his first *Commentary on the Psalms* (1515–16) and decisively in the *Heidelberg Disputation* of 1518 (esp. Thesis 20),[6] which was contemporary with his second *Commentary on the Psalms* (1518–19), Luther's theology of salvation by faith alone was a theology of the cross. Through the scandal and stumbling block of the theology of the cross, Luther theologically explained that the *Deus theologicus* revealed to faith is paradoxically revealed *sub contrario* in Christ's cross. The God who is Love is the Crucified God. God is revealed in Christ's passion and crucifixion on the cross as hidden in folly, godforsakenness: God is hidden both in the revolting physical sufferings of Jesus, as well as in the devastating spiritual *Anfechtungen* undergone by Jesus in his desperate prayer for release at Gethsemane, his humiliating public trial, his abandonment by his friends, his brutal scourging, the mocking of onlookers, and his cruel death — a death by crucifixion, an extremely painful and humiliating public death reserved for the worst criminals. Luther sharply highlights the Gospel accent in both Mark and Matthew that the crucified Jesus on the cross is abandoned, godforsaken — "My God, my God, why have you abandoned me?" In one of Luther's most profound theological moves, he insists with Paul that Jesus Christ has taken on our sin and has become sin himself. Christ has taken on our cursed status to become the accursed one himself. Our godforsakenness has become Christ's own on the cross, as he cries out into the thundering silence of his Father. Faith as divine favor happens through the cross of Jesus Christ, the crucified Jesus the Christ — that is, the unique one who alone is both true God and true human being. The revelation by faith in the promises of God's mercy enacted in the cross is the revelation of a true knowledge of the true God: God is Godself, the Infinitely Loving, forgiving, gracious God, the Hidden, Crucified God revealed in the cross of Jesus the Christ. For Luther, as for St. Paul, this philosophically and commonsensically unthinkable thought about the crucified God is the true scandal of Christianity.

It is difficult to imagine a more *sub contrario* (in fact, *sub contradictario*) way to describe Luther's *Deus theologicus* than to speak of the Hidden, Crucified God, revealed to faith in the cross of Jesus Christ. Here we do not find the Incomprehensible, Infinite God of the classical Greek contemplative theologians

---

6. Luther 1955, 31:52–53; 1883, 1:362.

(e.g., in Gregory of Nyssa).[7] In fact, Luther's theology of the cross is also beyond the medieval Franciscan emphasis on the humanity of the suffering Jesus. Luther did, in fact, have predecessors for several elements in his theology of the cross: first and most important, of course, Paul's insistence on Jesus Christ and Him crucified; second, Augustine, who also spoke in his *Commentary on the Psalms* of "the Crucified God," although not as frequently or foundationally as Luther did. Further influences on Luther's theology of the cross include the German mystical text *Theologica Germanica*, which the early Luther translated and the older Luther always honored, as well as Johannes Tauler.[8] In sum, in articulating the God revealed *sub contrario* on the cross, Luther did find some predecessors to lead him in that direction (above all else, of course, Paul in Romans and Galatians). But no Christian theologian since Paul himself has possessed the spiritual, theological, and rhetorical — indeed, poetic — power of Martin Luther to help all Christians, whatever their other theological and spiritual insights, to view God's Infinitely Loving nature as counterintuitively revealed in the negativity of the cross, to understand that God is not only Incomprehensible but also Hidden (*absconditus*). For Martin Luther, as later for Blaise Pascal, a treasured biblical text was Isaiah 45:15: "God is truly a Hidden God" ("How canst thou be a God that hidest thyself?" [Oxford New English Bible]). Martin Luther's concept of the Hidden and Revealed God is Luther's singular contribution to all Christian theological understanding of God. Other theologians have more refined Trinitarian theologies, deeper philosophical theologies, more profound mystical theologies, but no other theologian — not even the more orderly and more lucid John Calvin, nor the more deeply mystical John of the Cross, in his authoritative analysis of the "dark night of the soul" — has the theological power of Luther's theology of the cross revealing *sub contrario* the God who reveals Godself, not by means of speculative or mystical wisdom, but by means of the weakness and folly, the scandal of the cross.

Folly, not wisdom: against the humanist and philosophical expectation of his contemporaries, for Martin Luther, true knowledge of God is not to be found in speculative wisdom or in humanist rhetorical theologies (e.g., Eras-

---

7. I have analyzed this concept of Infinity in Gregory in "God as Infinite: Ethical Implications" (Renaud and Daniel 2017). See also Tracy 2020 (chap. 8).

8. On Luther's relationship to the German mystical traditions, see the judicious comments of Bernard McGinn (2017), in his magisterial history of Western Christian mysticism, that to understand Luther one must also interpret mystical elements in his theology without necessarily naming him a mystic. See also Luther 1980.

mus). Centuries later, Hegel, who claimed to be an orthodox Lutheran, used his own triumphal, unstoppable, rationally optimistic dialectical method to turn Luther's Hidden God into Hegel's own, utterly manifest, Absolute God. What Hegel turned into an abstract, speculative Good Friday was, on the contrary for Luther, the all-too-concrete Good Friday of the crucified Jesus, scandalously revealing the Hidden, Crucified God. Most first-century Greek philosophers were already shocked by the outrageous Christian claim that God in Godself became incarnate — much less incarnate in the person of an insignificant Jewish provincial who died a most disgraceful death of a criminal. That such a repellant death by crucifixion of an unknown Jewish colonial should be the revelation of God was too absurd to be considered as a serious option for knowledge of God. In Acts, the Athenians listened to Paul on the Unknown God for a while until they politely and contemptuously turned away. Later, Celsus did the same against Origen; Porphyry considered the very thought of a crucified God an intellectual, moral, and religious insult. Centuries later, Friedrich Nietzsche ironized the charges of the two Platonists (Celsus and Porphyry) by famously describing Christianity as "Platonism for the masses"!

God's naked majesty (*Deus nudus*) informed philosophy at its speculative and dialectical best (Plato, Aristotle, Plotinus, Celsus, Proclus): the thought (almost blasphemous for Porphyry) that the Glory of God — the Plotinian One Good — was to be found in the cross of Jesus of Nazareth was as outrageous to the Greek philosophers as it is today to their many, now far more secular modern successors. What artist, tragedian, or philosopher would dare this unnerving radical thought: the true God is the Crucified God of Infinite Love; the true knowledge of this God is only to be found revealed as hidden, *sub contrario*, in the cross of Jesus Christ?

Almost any philosophically inflected theology cannot but find Luther's theology of God hidden *sub contrario* in the cross of Jesus Christ exactly what Paul stated it would be, a scandal, a stumbling block, a foolishness, a weakness of mind and spirit — at the limit an insult to mind and imagination alike. It is not surprising, therefore, that although Christians of course always proclaimed the salvific cross of Jesus Christ, they rather timorously depicted the cross in images. Indeed, for the first four or five centuries the image of the cross was not the shocking central symbol of Christianity it became and remains, as much as the star of David is for Judaism, or the seated, serene Buddha is for Buddhism. In fact, in the seemingly endless hundreds of underground miles of early Christian tombs in the Roman catacombs, one finds far more images of the Good

Shepherd or the fish (*ichthus*), or the Eucharist as the central symbols of early Christianity, far more frequently than an image of the cross, much less a crucifix. The cross — however familiar the image has become — should not be domesticated; it remains a scandal for a major religion defiantly to proclaim and portray a cross as its central symbol.

More than any theologian before or since, Martin Luther is *the* theologian of the cross.[9] For Luther, the Gracious, forgiving, Infinitely Loving God — the true nature of the Christian God for Christians — is revealed at its deepest and most stark in hiddenness: the folly, scandal, and stumbling block of the cross. Any interpreter, attending primarily to other authentic but relatively marginal aspects of Luther's understanding of God is in danger of missing Luther's most singular contribution to a Christian theology of God: that God's deepest self-revelation is the deeply unsettling, uncannily disorienting Hiddenness of the Crucified, Gracious God, hidden as Infinite Love in the cross of Jesus Christ. As we shall see below, there are, to be sure, other important elements in Luther's *Deus theologicus*. But without acknowledging that the God Hidden in the revelation in the profound negativity of the cross of Jesus Christ is the central focus for any further insights into God's reality, one is in danger of turning Luther's theology of the cross into yet another theology of glory and all too cheap grace (Dietrich Bonhoeffer).

THE HIDDEN GOD BEYOND REVELATION

Luther never abandoned his primordial insight into the God Hidden in revelation (Gerrish 1982, 131–50; Dillenberger 1953; Bandt 1958).[10] However, in his later theology (after 1525), Luther moved into yet deeper theological waters with strange, disturbing insights into another dimension of the *Deus theologicus*. Especially in his classic text *De servo arbitrio* (1525), Luther contended, beyond the already sharp paradoxes of God's self-revelation *sub contrario* in the hiddenness of the cross, that there exists another frightening revelation of God's Hiddenness beyond, before, and behind the revelation of the Hidden, Crucified God of Jesus Christ. This strange, uncanny form of divine Hidden-

---

9. See Loewenich 1976; McGrath 1985; Forde 1997. For a particularly valuable book on modern theology's temptations to evade the scandal of the cross, see Westhelle 2006.

10. On satanic hiddenness *sub contrario* as an "angel of light," see Schreiner 2011 (293–96).

ness emerged partly out of Luther's closer attention to the implications for divine Hiddenness in the Augustinian and Pauline doctrine of double predestination — "the horrible decree," as Calvin named it. This frightening insight into God's Hiddenness was a matter of biblical revelation for Luther, as well as a matter of his intense personal experience of spiritual temptations, assaults, *Anfechtungen*.[11] This second sense of divine hiddenness assaulted Luther with radical doubt and despair, and with the thought that he might not be among the elect. These *Anfechtungen* (assaults and temptations) were, for Luther, not only subjective but also objectively satanic and even ultimately divine (since Satan's actions — as a creature — were, ultimately, under the control of the Creator). And with these assaults came a new experience, *coram Deo*, that often brought sheer terror for Luther.

Anfechtung (Lat. *temptatio* or *tentatio*) is a central category for Luther. *Anfechtung* is both a subjective and an objective reality. As a subjective experience, *Anfechtung* is the experience of a spiritual assault on an individual producing fear, even terror, in the face of the unfathomable majesty of God. *Anfechtung* is also an objective theological reality since, for Luther, its objective origin is a satanic reality (and, therefore, also an objectively divine reality, since God controls all and therefore permits Satan to tempt-assault an individual — as in the classical example of God tempting Job). Philosophically, Rudolf Otto (a Lutheran and a proto-phenomenologist) provided a persuasive phenomenological description of the holy as a combination of both subjective and objective phenomena in *The Idea of the Holy* ([1917] 1958): every authentic experi-

---

11. Luther's friends report his observing in a collegial conversation, "If I would live long enough I would like to write a book on *Anfechtung*, for without this nobody can understand the holy Scriptures or faith, or know the faith and love of God, indeed he or she cannot know what hope is" (see Luther 2000, no. 4777, 4:490, 24–491, 1). An especially familiar error of some interpretations of Luther is to read *Anfechtungen* as solely a matter of Luther's uniquely sensitive and often depressed temperament, as distinct from a reality more theologically objective than merely psychologically subjective. The subjectivist reading of Luther covers a large spectrum of interpreters, from Friedrich Nietzsche through Erik Erikson, as well as some Catholic interpreters, such as Heinrich Denifle and Hartmann Grisar. On Luther's life and character, the classic works on the crucial years in Luther's life remain Bornkamm 1969 and Brecht 1985. For the importance of Luther's belief in the *temptatio* placed in his mind and life by a fully objective Satan, read the fascinating study of Luther's life and thought in Oberman 1989. On the other hand, for a deliberately short and moving life of Luther that, among several salient points, fruitfully emphasizes Luther's fleshly joy in life (marriage, eating, drinking beer, singing, composing his splendid hymns, laughing, joking, enjoying sex, etc.), see Marty 2008. These life-affirming dimensions of the man Luther are too easily lost by a temptation (like my own) to overemphasize Luther's profound, subjective experiences of and objective understandings of *Anfechtung*.

ence of the uncanny holy is *mysterium tremendum et fascinans*. As mentioned earlier, in his "table talk" Luther once said that he wished, one day, to write a treatise on *Anfechtung*. Would that he had!

Theologically, Luther's concept of *Anfechtung* is likewise related to his unnerving sense that an apocalyptic battle always rages throughout history and in the heart of every Christian. Part of Luther's attraction for many postmodern thinkers is his profound sense of God, experienced at times as the interruptive Void through experiences of *Anfechtungen*. Luther's influence on postmodernity is more often indirect than direct: that is, through Heidegger, Sartre, Camus, and others, or by means of Søren Kierkegaard's notion of Angst, the major influence in both midcentury existentialist thought and postmodern fragmentary thought. A profoundly negative sense of the interruptive Void, in particular when a given thinker understands the Void as pure negativity (Sartre's *Nausea*; Camus's "the absurd"), the Void is also a paradoxical aspect of Nietzsche's tragic yes to reality as sheer Will to Power without purpose, without beginning, and without end.

On the other hand, the Void can be, for the enlightened Buddhist, an experience of a positive ultimate reality, if one can learn to stop grasping at false ultimacies, clinging to the ego and just letting go into the Void. Then the Void is experienced as ultimately trustworthy. Buddhists believe that the Void is erroneously experienced as pure negation only by those forever grasping egotists unable to let go of whatever reality they cannot cease clinging to in terror of what in fact is a positive enlightenment experience of *sunyata*, emptiness—the positive, trustworthy Void experienced by the enlightened Buddhist as embracing, enhancing, ultimate emptiness.

That Buddhist positive experience of the Void is in direct contrast to Luther's overpowering sense of the second form of the radical Hiddenness of God experienced as Void, meaninglessness, the frightening feeling-thought that all is an absurd Void of nothingness (Paul Tillich). Buddhists (especially Mahayana) and Martin Luther agree on our fundamental dilemma: our inability to escape our clinging egos (Luther's description of the ego as *incurvatus in se*). Moreover, Pure Land Japanese Mahayana Buddhists, unlike Zen Mahayana Buddhists, hold, again with Luther, that our situation (personal-existential and social-historical) is so bleak that only Other Power can emancipate us. From the Pure Land perspective, Zen Self-Power is less enlightened than self-deluding. Analogously, Martin Luther fiercely rejected all Pelagian, neo-Stoic, and humanist claims to sufficient self-powers through moral and religious self-discipline (works-righteousness, for Luther). Luther insisted that all such claims were pathetic exercises in self-delusion of our sin-damaged intellect and will. Only God through the gift-grace of Jesus Christ can save us.

Luther's sense of the Void is the hiddenness of God experienced *sub contrario* in the Word of the cross and even, at times, beyond the Word in the terror of hiddenness experienced in *Anfechtungen*. *Anfechtungen* are healed with joy by God's gracious forgiveness, paradoxically disclosed by God's gift of faith in the justifying cross of Jesus Christ.

Luther's theological category of *Anfechtung* is indeed important for understanding him. However, Oswald Bayer (2007, 57–65) exaggerates when he claims that *all* Lutheran theology finds its touchstone in an experience of *Anfechtung*. Clearly, that is the case with Luther's theology of the hidden God revealed *sub contrario* in the paradox of the cross. This is even more the case, of course, with Luther's experience and concept of the radical hiddenness of God, which Luther boldly asserts is beyond the Word. Beyond the Word for the Word of Christ–saturated Martin Luther! Nevertheless, *Anfechtung-temptatio* is not the touchstone of the theological *oratio* and *meditatio* traditions that are also present in Luther's theology of the full *Deus theologicus*—as, for example, in the distinct *oratio-meditatio* exercised in Luther's theology of God as Incomprehensible Love at times transiently experienced by the believer as including some sense of *unio Christi*. For that matter, neither is *temptatio* present in Luther's late dialectical disputations, in which, as we shall see below, Luther developed semiotic and semantic concepts (relation, person, eternity, etc.) for philosophically and theologically clarifying the traditional Trinitarian understanding of God.

Perhaps *Anfechtungen* did drive Luther's earlier more polemical disputations, such as his *Disputation against Scholastic Theology* (1517), or his fierce polemical disputes with Eck, Cajetan, Latomus, Carlstadt, Müntzer, Zwingli, and others. Admittedly, even in his later Wittenberg period—the period of his brilliant logical *disputationes* on the Trinity and Christology—Luther at times seemed driven (through *Anfechtungen*) to lash out against his adversaries, not only polemically but also virulently, in his two notorious, disgraceful treatises against the Jews and against the popes as anti-Christ: *On the Jews and Their Lies* (1543) and *Against the Roman Papacy, an Institution of the Devil* (1545).

In my judgment, these late outbursts are unworthy of so intellectually and existentially great a human being and so profound a Christian as Martin Luther. Anyone who admires Luther as much as I do, as that rare human phenomenon—both a religious and a theological genius—cannot but deeply regret his revolting, violent outbursts against Jews, along with his earlier, disgraceful outbursts against peasants. The old Luther did not hesitate to write that Pope Paul III (Farnese), the last Renaissance pope, an exceptionally intelligent, complex, pluralistic, ambiguous figure, partly reforming (he calls for the Council of Trent), was also partly corrupt. It would be difficult to engage in a genuinely dialogical *disputatio* if one's hoped-for conversation partner begins the disputation by announcing that his (Luther's) disputation opposite is not just wrong but is completely evil—that symbolically Paul III was the Antichrist! In this extreme case of Luther's polemics, it would be better to follow the weary suggestion of Richard Rorty and just change the subject: no dialogue but no violent polemic in particular, as in Luther versus the Jews; Luther versus the Turks. The best title I know for a polemical text is John Calvin's *To a Certain Useless Person*—one is hesitant even today to name the recipient.

Of course, Luther lived in a polemical age, when anti-Semitism was widely practiced by Christians (including Erasmus). The fact of the polemical character of most sixteenth-century theological exchanges (*not* dialogues) between intellectual adversaries (including humanists like Lorenzo Valla or Pietro Arentino) contextualizes, but does not excuse, Luther's at times beyond-the-limit polemical violence. Among his many gifts, Martin Luther, like Jonathan Swift and Friedrich Nietzsche in a later age, had a natural talent for passionate, brilliant polemic. The polemic of both Luther and Nietzsche sometimes illuminates a complex issue—for example, Luther on the Eucharist versus Zwingli, where Luther polemically slammed the table between the two principal participants on what was to be an important attempt to sort out the two very different theologies of the Eucharist of the Reformed Zwinglian theology of Eucharist as symbolic meaning (not that of Calvin, whose position was much more nuanced). Calvin's position on the Eucharist is a *tertium datur* between his fellow Reformed Zwingli's rather loose and not very carefully thought out, purely symbolic Eucharist and Luther's strong concept of consubstantiation (not, of course, Roman Catholic transubstantiation). In that famous nondialogical dispute on the Eucharist between Luther and Zwingli, one can remain haunted by the passion, power, and theological acumen of Martin Luther's shout, "*Hic est corpus meus*," as he slammed his fist on the table that would (now?) forever separate the Zwinglian although not the Calvinist Reformed theologies of the Eucharist from the Lutheran position, and both, of course, from the Roman Catholic position. Luther also polemicizes on the centrality of the Word versus the Zwickau prophets. At other times, Luther's polemics — like all polemics (e.g., those of Johann Eck, Thomas More, and Thomas Müntzer, with their increasingly violent *ad hominem* attacks on Luther's person, culminating in Müntzer's infamous 1524 pamphlet, *Speech against the Mindless, Soft-Living Flesh in Wittenberg*) — cloud rather than illuminate.

Luther found his equal in polemics in the person of Johann Eck, who clearly loved a brawl as much as Luther. Eck and Luther were each other's polemical double, although Luther was a far greater theologian than the "court theologian" Johann Eck. Moreover, the more detached theologian Cardinal Cajetan used up most of his careful Thomist arguments without budging Martin Luther as such ("Here I stand; I can do no other"). More surprisingly the humanist loyal Catholic Thomas More seemed to revel in *ad hominem* polemical attacks on Luther as violently as Luther did in his attacks on More.

Our own age may be characterized at its rare best by a turn to the Other (Levinas) and a turn to language culminating in what Charles Taylor called "the dialogical turn" of much contemporary, historically conscious hermeneutics, which he has rightly named the most important necessity for our day. This dialogical suggestion by Taylor is in radical distinction from Luther's polemically charged sixteenth century and the four centuries of polemical, intra-Christian confessional strife that followed. There is indeed need for a dialogical turn: dialogical ecumenism within Christianity, and within the gradual emergence of intercultural and interreligious dialogues globally. Polemics, to be sure, are sometimes necessary (e.g., against Nazism). Some polemicists partly cover over their strong criticism with wit. G. K. Chesterton, the charming successor to Dr. Johnson as the quintessential English commonsense thinker, rightly insisted: "To express some serious matter with wit in humor is not to cease to be serious."

Dialogue is ordinarily emancipatory, if at times too careful, even boring. The real difference between the two genres of dialogue (or dialogical disputation) and polemic is their conflicting attitudes toward the other: genuine dialogue always listens to the other as Other; polemics ignores the other, save consciously as a contemptible target for attacks and insults. There must be an Other for dialogue; there is no real other for polemics, only a target. The turn to the other is a dialogical, not a polemical, turn.

The doctrine of double predestination, unlike the doctrine of the theology of the cross, with its *sub contrario* revelation of God's Infinite Graciousness, exposed Luther to new experiences of doubt and despair. Even after justification,

Luther found himself at times in desperation. At those times, he seemed to live at the very edge of the abyss with that haunting question: Is God ultimately gracious *pro me*?

Luther clearly exists on the cusp between the medieval and early modern worlds. On his medieval side, Luther maintained an unusually strong belief in Satan as a person, a personal force of evil with whom he struggled constantly (Oberman 1989, 209–26). For Erasmus, on the contrary, Satan had become largely a powerful metaphor for objective evil, but was no longer an actual person. On both the medieval and early modern sides of Luther's sensibility — certainly before and not infrequently even after his overwhelming reformatory insight (the exact date and place of his conversion are still disputed among scholars) — there always breathed his peculiarly intense *Anfechtung* experiences, which he understood theologically as satanic assaults (Oberman). Those *Anfechtungen* manifested themselves as temptations to disbelieve that God had elected Martin Luther as one of the saved (a minority of humankind for Luther as for Augustine or Calvin, in any event).

Martin Luther, like Paul in Romans and Galatians, like Augustine in his late anti-Pelagian works, held to the doctrine of double predestination. The doctrine, for Luther as for Calvin, was in the Bible: found in God's hardening of Pharaoh's heart and God's election (in Rebekah's womb) of the younger son Jacob over the elder son Esau; and mentioned in the intractable Pauline metaphor of the potter and the clay. Luther emphasized the doctrine of double predestination far less than Calvin but in *The Bondage of the Will*, double predestination was indeed affirmed.

Erasmus's attempts in his *De libero arbitrio* to remove the sting of these scriptural statements of radical, even double predestination seem as strained as Augustine's opposite attempt to explain away the equally clear biblical passages on God's universal will for the salvation of all,[12] as in First Timothy — "This is right and acceptable in the sight of God our Savior who desires everyone to be saved and to come to a knowledge of the truth" (2:3). First Timothy has often served as the Magna Carta for all those theologians who argue for a biblically based hope (not, of course, knowledge) for universal salvation: Gregory

---

12. Augustine, *On Rebuke and Grace* (*De correptione et gratia*), chap. 44: "In What Way God Wills All Men to Be Saved," in Schaff 1887, 5:489.

of Nyssa, Eriugena, Karl Rahner, Karl Barth, Hans Urs von Balthasar, Paul Tillich, and many other contemporary Christian theologians, including myself. On no other central soteriological issue is a fuller Christological reading more needed than on the doctrine of predestination (e.g., as in Karl Barth) if one is to challenge the traditional understanding (Augustine, Luther, Calvin, et al.) of divine predestination as double predestination. Erasmus's evasiveness will not do, although his marshaling of biblical passages on free will is a real contribution to the debate. However, closer attention to the biblical message of *hope* for universal salvation, allied with a fuller Christology and pneumatology can, I believe, allow for the hope (not knowledge) of universal salvation that is neither Pelagian, nor semi-Pelagian, nor Origenist.

Luther's other warrant for the second form of God's terrifying Hiddenness is the Void that at times imprisons us and wears us down to despair. This sense of despair is beyond the revelation of God's graciousness hidden *sub contrario* in the cross of Jesus Christ. A sense of meaninglessness is existentially the phenomenon Luther appealed to so often — *Anfechtung*, both subjectively and objectively affirmed by Luther as bearing major theological import. This second sense of God's radical, frightening Hiddenness has, in the contemporary period, paradoxically proved one of Luther's most compelling insights, not only for Christians but for all those many persons who experience the Void — that is, those on the edge of an abyss of the seeming meaninglessness of life. A modern form of *Anfechtung* has occurred to many — whether Christians, as in Pascal's "Le silence éternel des ces éspaces infinis m'effraie" (Pascal 1965, #313, 172–73) and in Kierkegaard's probable translation of Luther's *Anfechtung* into modern *Angst* (Kierkegaard 1980), or non-Christians (all the secular existentialists, whether Sartre's "nausea" or Camus's "the absurd"). A sense of contemporary *Anfechtung* can also be found in many postmoderns who, through irony, parody, and pastiche, refuse not only Christian faith-hope but also any Romantic or modernist hopeful epiphanies. Postmoderns embrace chance, not fate or providence, much less divine predestination.

For secular, aleatory postmodernity, pure chance is the final truth of reality. For postmoderns on the whole, we live in an indifferent, purposeless, meaningless universe of pure chance. In science, consider the dispute between Steven Weinberg (the meaningless Void) versus Albert Einstein (the impersonal, Spinozist God). Postmodern *Anfechtungen* often take the form of either radical, bitter irony or an experience of excess, beginning with Georges Bataille

(Amy Hollywood), postmodernity's very influential failed prophet. Post-modernity's response to Blaise Pascal's wager on faith in the face of the eternal silence of an indifferent universe was nowhere more sharply, even sublimely, stated than in the very title of postmodernity's charter poem, Stéphane Mallarmé's "Un coup de dés jamais n'abolira pas le hasard" (Mallarmé 1965, 200–233). Martin Luther, who in *De servo arbitrio* rather surprisingly expressed his respect for the ancients' notion of fate, would have understood the new, post-modern *Anfechtung* now evoked not by fate but even more devastatingly by chance. Luther would, of course, have rejected with all the rhetorical force at his command what he would have named a delusional, postmodern evasive-ness through irony, parody, and pastiche (the three pillars of postmodernity). Luther would also reject any excess-laden form (or formlessness) of the aggressive nihilism in much postmodern art, especially poetry.

So powerful are Martin Luther's phenomenological descriptions of his various experiences of *Anfechtung* that many readers (early modern, late modern, or postmodern) can come to acknowledge such experiences as their own (John Calvin, John of the Cross, Søren Kierkegaard, Fyodor Dostoevsky, Emily Dickinson, Simone Weil, Dietrich Bonhoeffer, Ingmar Bergman, David Foster Wallace, and countless others). As Luther acknowledged, not all human beings experience the unnerving *Anfechtungen* that he himself endured. Melanchthon did not. Erasmus, although often melancholic, prayed for divine release from his experiences of weakness, lethargy, and weakness of heart. Erasmus experienced not *Anfechtung* but *pusillanimitas*, a word Erasmus borrowed from Jean Gerson's tract *De remediis contra pusillanimitatem* (Vial 2006; Ozment 1969). The Latin word does not translate well into English, since *pusillanimity* in English usually implies a weakness of character, whereas for Gerson, *pusillanimitas* is defined in almost but not quite *Anfechtung* terms as *maximum timor* (maximal fear) and *desperatio* (desperation). William James (1978, 138–96) famously distinguished between two basic human types: the "sick souls" who breathe *Anfechtung*, and the "healthy-minded" who know it not. These contrasting types tend not to understand one another—witness Pelagius and Augustine, Eriugena and Gottschalk, Arminius and the Synod of Dort, Erasmus and Luther, D. F. Strauss and Nietzsche, Turgenev and Dostoevsky, Jane Austen and Emily Brontë. The list could easily be extended.

The Christian theological debate on predestination has proved an important topic in Christian theology since Paul in Corinthians, Romans, and Galatians and, in Western theology, since Augustine.[13] Some version of the doctrine of predestination, especially one explicitly related to the doctrine of providence (as in Calvin), is usually a central Christian biblical belief. However, the doctrine of double predestination, affirmed in Augustine, was also affirmed in *De servo arbitrio* by Martin Luther, but not much dwelt upon after that. Double predestination was far more strongly affirmed and developed by John Calvin, but even there it was not Calvin's central doctrine about God. God's sovereignty and God's gracious mercy were the principal theological understandings of God for Calvin. The Calvinism defined in the Synod of Dort against Arminius is not the heart of Calvin's own theology, much less Luther's, even though both did hold to double predestination as implicit in the belief in the omnipotence and providence of God.

Most contemporary Christian theologians do not affirm Luther's doctrine of double predestination, since it seems inevitably to imply theological and philosophical determinism, which the doctrine of providence need not. Luther's *Anfechtung*, like the salvific faith to which it can point as the only hope for release, is both subjective (the "sick soul") and objective (Satan is a symbol of the objective power of radical evil—see Oberman's 1989 biography of Luther).

However powerful Luther's notion of the second form of God's Hiddenness is today in different Christian and secular forms, one must analyze further Luther's own account of God's Hiddenness behind or beyond revelation. Luther expressed this idea in several texts—for example, in his biblical commentaries on Isaiah and Genesis, and classically in his response to Erasmus, *De servo arbitrio* (Luther 1955, vol. 33; 1883, 600–787).[14]

Never in Christian history, save in the original conflict of Augustine and Pelagius, did such an influential and, at the time, somewhat unfocused theological debate occur as that between the volcanic Luther and the moderate, tolerant Erasmus. The temperaments of Luther and Erasmus were undoubtedly opposed, but their strong theological differences were far more important in the debate. A conflict of the theology on God, not merely a conflict of temperament, caused the Erasmus-Luther debate—a debate ultimately on the

---

13. For an excellent article on the history of the reception of Augustine's understanding of predestination, see Schreiner and Thompson 2013 (3:1591–99). On Luther's complex and changing relationships to Augustine, see Steinmetz 1995 (12–23) and Janz 2010 (110–12).

14. Both Erasmus's and Luther's treatises can also be found in English in Rupp 1969, vol. 17.

very reality of God: that is, the fuller meaning of the *Deus theologicus*. The conflicting treatises — Erasmus's *De libero arbitrio* and Luther's *De servo arbitrio* — could more accurately be named *De Deo*.

Erasmus, one of the greatest historical-philological scholars of Christian theology and the prime promoter of a Christian humanist theology of reform and tolerance in his crisis-ridden age, depicted in his many writings, including *De libero arbitrio*, a gracious portrait of a gracious God. An analysis of Erasmus's too-seldom-honored theology of God must await some other occasion (Gerrish 1982, 11–27; Boyle 1977 and 1983; Chantraine 1971).[15] How much richer, deeper, and more complex Luther's *Deus theologicus* is than Erasmus's writings is my present focus. *De servo arbitrio* is unique in its systematic theological power, combined with its deeply disturbing insights into a new, sinister form of God's hiddenness beyond or behind the always fundamental revelation of God's graciousness hidden in the cross of Jesus Christ.

Luther's more strictly philosophical (i.e., logical and semantic, not metaphysical) arguments in *De servo arbitrio* are mostly on the logic of the notions of divine "omniscience" and "omnipotence," along with a notion of noncompulsory divine necessity in human wills in order to deny "freedom of choice" — which Erasmus strenuously defended and Luther rejected as self-delusion. It is intriguing to wonder what difference, if any, the logically acute Luther would have found in some modern analyses of what divine "omniscience" and "omnipotence" can and cannot logically mean — as in Charles Hartshorne's logical analyses of these classical concepts (*inter alia*, Hartshorne 1973, esp. 118–91).

This famous debate between Luther and Erasmus is ultimately disappointing, partly because Erasmus, unlike Luther, did not know very much contem-

---

15. Erasmus's use of a more dialogical notion of *collatio* was intended to contrast with Luther's non-dialogical notion of *assertio*. To understand Erasmus's position more fully, one should also consult his post-Luther debate work, where Erasmus argues (against Luther's accusations) that his position is not in any way Pelagian in *Desiderie Erasmie Hyperaspistes Diatribae adversus servum arbitrium Martini Lutheri* (1526). *Liberium arbitrium* and *servum arbitrium* are more accurately translated as "freedom of choice" and "enslavement of choice," rather than as simply "free will" and "servile will," to emphasize that the issue is about freedom of choice solely in matters of salvation. Luther held that in other matters (e.g., everyday choices) the will is free; only in matters pertaining to salvation is there no freedom; that is, the "chief article" of Luther always was justification through grace by faith alone without any works-righteousness whatsoever: no merits whether condign or congruent. Erasmus, whose knowledge of Scholastic philosophical theology was as unsure as his contempt for it was all too sure, nevertheless appealed in the controversy to Thomas Aquinas's distinction between *necessitas consequentiae* and *necessitas consequens*. For Thomas's own gradually developed position, see Lonergan 1971 and Paluch 2004. For the Carolingian debate, see Gibson, Nelson, and Ganz 1981, 353–73.

porary, late medieval, scholastic, logical, and semantic nominalist philosophy, which Luther knew quite well indeed (White 1994; Oberman 1966). The Erasmus-Luther debate was at least as dependent on philosophical argumentation as on biblical hermeneutics (in which Erasmus held his own in his defense of several clear biblical texts on free choice). Luther's cry was "Let God be God." Erasmus's more hopeful humanist suggestion was "Let God be Good."

By any fair assessment, I think, Luther's theological position on the two forms of God's Hiddenness, even for those who reject his position on double predestination, is far more compelling than that of Erasmus.[16] Perhaps this famous debate was less a debate (it was certainly not a dialogue) but more like two ships passing in the night: one large, heavily armed destroyer (Martin Luther) filled the horizon with fire, thunder, and power; one (Desiderius Erasmus) more like an elegant, well-crafted, all too smoothly sailing humanist skiff, which, after a few well-aimed shots at the destroyer, spent the rest of its brief sailing time heading for the nearest safe port. He barely made it.

If Martin Luther could have found a way—inevitably, for him, a way paradoxical in language and dialectical in method—he might have contrived another brilliant dialectic to depict how the hiddenness beyond revelation described in *De servo arbitrio* dialectically implied the (Christological) need for God's Hiddenness in revelation. To my knowledge, he never did. Perhaps it cannot be done, and one must either *choose* the Gracious God hidden in revelation (as Karl Barth and several other interpreters of Luther suggest should be done, while rejecting the Hiddenness of God beyond the Word as sub-Christian— indeed, pagan) or be content simply to *juxtapose* these two very different, even conflictual theological insights into two irresolvably conflicting, incommensurate aspects of God's Hiddenness—in revelation and beyond revelation.

For my part, those Christians who, at one time or another, have experienced themselves at the edge of a Void of seeming meaninglessness, cannot but be deeply thankful to Martin Luther: first and above all, for his incomparable theology of the cross. In such situations, one must flee, as Luther advises, to

---

16. As I argued earlier, however, Luther's theological account of the experience of *Anfechtung* is both subjective-experiential and objective-theological. This dual concept is one of Luther's signal contributions in his understanding of *Deus theologicus*. However, to make an experience of *Anfechtung* necessary for every theologian, as Luther sometimes did and as Oswald Bayer always does, is exaggerated. Luther himself realized that some theologians he admired did not seem to experience *Anfechtung*, including his beloved mentor Johann von Staupitz and his Wittenberg younger colleague, Philip Melanchthon. On Staupitz, see Steinmetz 1986; on Melanchthon, see Kusukawa 1995.

ANCIENTS, MEDIEVALS, MODERNS

the cross of Christ—that cross which will disclose God's Hiddenness in negativity: that is, *sub contrario* in the suffering, weakness, and folly of the crucified Jesus Christ, revealing the Gracious, Loving, Crucified God. Second, for anyone suffering the inexplicable horror at times attendant upon life, Luther's brilliant and enduring phenomenology of *Anfechtung* can expose the human experience of a second, terrifying form of a divine hiddenness; in this situation, the only solution, as Luther himself maintained, is to flee back to the cross: *ad deum ex deo*.

LUTHER'S INCOMPREHENSIBLE GOD OF INFINITE, TRINITARIAN LOVE

Luther's two accounts of God's Hiddenness—in revelation and beyond revelation—are, in their theological depth and existential power, a singular, indeed uniquely profound contribution to a Christian theological understanding of God. However, there is a further richness and complexity in Luther's depictions of *Deus theologicus* still to be addressed. In this final case—God's Incomprehensible, Trinitarian mystery—it is less a matter of originality than of Luther's continuity with the classical tradition: first, the medieval tradition of the disputation that Luther reinstituted at the University of Wittenberg in his later years in order to address the classical Christological and Trinitarian questions anew, by means of the sharpened semantic and logical tools he had learned in his youth; and second, Luther's awareness of the living Christic tradition of various forms of mystical theology, especially among medieval German mystics. In those German mystical texts (especially those of Eckhart and Tauler), medieval Western mystical theology discloses the Infinitely Loving, Incomprehensible God and is often open to but reticent about the largely Eastern Christian understanding of justification as *theosis*. These two recent scholarly emphases are clearly different but, at times, are sufficiently akin to be treated in the same discussion, since, together, they provide additional elements constituting Martin Luther's labyrinthine *Deus theologicus*.

Therefore, in addition to the two forms of God's Hiddenness constituting Luther's *Deus theologicus*, there also exist his Trinitarian reflections in his late disputations—his logical and semantic late disputations on the Trinity, and his lifelong reflection on the many dimensions of Christ's presence to the justified (Helmer 1999). For Luther, Christ is above all present *to* the justified in a marvelous exchange: Christ's forgiving presence imputed *pro me* (God's favor through Christ). However, Christ is also present *in me*: that is, Christ is also present *in us* through the sanctifying power of the Holy Spirit (*unio Christi*). In other words, often but admittedly not always in the case of Martin Luther himself, Martin Luther's position on justification is not identical to that of his friend and companion in crisis, Philip Melanchthon, with Melanchthon's unyielding notion of a purely forensic justification. For Luther, justification not only externally imputes Christ's active righteousness to us forensically by the *favor* of the forgiveness of sins, but Christ is also present *in me* (*donum*) (see, among others, Mannermaa 2005, esp. 31 on *favor* and *donum*). The Christic presence in which the justified participate is also present on diverse occasions in Luther's sermons, especially in his rethinking of the traditional image of the *commercium admirabilem* — that is, that exchange whereby Christ on the cross takes on our sin, our accursedness, our godforsakenness, while, in the same wondrous exchange, the justified take on Christ's strength, Christ's wisdom. In addition, Luther also articulates a *commercium admirabilem* of Christ in the souls of the justified in other images and metaphors, especially his use throughout his life of the participation notion of *unio Christi*. At the limit, in several texts (thirty-seven, to be exact, the Finnish scholars claim), Luther's concept of *unio Christi* may also be read, in its final form, as *theosis*. The Orthodox tradition's concept of justification as deification was strongly held among the Greeks, including by Luther's most admired of the Greek Fathers, Athanasius of Alexandria in his *On the Incarnation*: "The Logos was made human so that we might be made God."[17] *Theosis* was also adopted, less frequently and more tentatively, in a good bit of Western theology, including that of Augustine.

Prior to some further reflection on this recent, now famously controversial, Finnish Lutheran scholarly reading of Luther's "justification" as *theosis*, I first briefly describe another recent and significantly related but distinct scholarly development in comprehending Luther's Trinitarian *Deus theologicus*: namely, a renewed scholarly attention to Luther's late disputations on the Trinity and Christology, involving extensive use of late medieval, nominalist, logical, semiotic, and semantic philosophy. By such means, Luther clarified certain complex logical issues for understanding the classical doctrines of the Trinity, such as the concepts of relation, essence, person, and eternity.

---

17. *De Incarnatione* 54, in Jacques-Paul Migne, *Patrologia Graeca* (1857–66), 25:192B; and Athanasius 2011, 167.

In rereading for this essay several excellent, earlier modern works on Luther's theology,[18] I was surprised to notice (which I had not in earlier readings some years ago) that these now almost classical studies of Luther's theology give very little attention, if any, to these later Trinitarian disputations of Luther, despite their obvious value for any full-fledged description of Luther's *Deus theologicus*. This lack has now been repaired by several scholars, especially Christine Helmer's (1999) study of Luther's developed Trinitarian *Deus theologicus* in hymns, sermons, and late disputations.

Furthermore, one can claim that Luther's late disputations illustrate how his theological analysis of *Deus theologicus* was enriched by observing how faith does not merely, as in his earlier disputations (e.g., the *Disputation against Scholastic Theology*), shatter reason's vain and self-deluding attempts to move beyond its own limits. Faith also paradoxically redeems reason for newly illuminated theological use. It is not merely that Luther always affirmed the classical doctrines of Christology and Trinity. In addition, Luther in these late disputations used all his considerable semantic and logical skills to help further understand the mystery of the Incomprehensible, Trinitarian God *as* mystery. Here Luther used all the late medieval logical and semantic tools at his disposal to do what the Scholastics of both the *via antiqua* (e.g., Thomas Aquinas and Duns Scotus) and the *via moderna* (e.g., William of Ockham and Gabriel Biel) always had as one of their principal goals: to locate as precisely as possible exactly where the mystery of the Trinity lies. Luther makes exactly the same kind of clarifying logical and grammatical (but never metaphysical) moves in his late disputations on the Trinity. As a result, the Trinitarian mystery becomes not merely affirmed but can also serve theologically as an integral dimension in Luther's *Deus theologicus*.

In my judgment, the central, encompassing affirmation of any genuinely

---

18. It is no disparagement of these important, indeed classic works on Luther, which earlier educated so many of us, to observe that, faithful to their period (the 1950s and 1960s), they mention but do not really analyze Luther's Trinitarian theology. On the other hand, Karl Barth's suggestion (*Church Dogmatics*, 1.2:76), despite his earlier overcriticism of Luther's two forms of divine hiddenness (1.1:479), argues that a Christological theology of election is a promising key to a possible theological resolution of debates on predestination: namely, that from all eternity, God was the electing God of Jesus Christ. (Karl Barth's is one of the major renovations of Reformed theology.) Indeed, for Barth, election is the very essence of God. Moreover, as God-man, Jesus Christ is both the electing God and the elect human being: the election of Jesus is the election of humanity. Barth's Christological route is surely a valuable one—particularly if, as I suggest, the full range of Christological symbols (incarnation-cross-resurrection-elevation-sending of the Spirit-promised second coming) are taken into account. On Barth on election, see McCormack 2000, 92–100.

Christian articulation of God is the Trinitarian affirmation: any method (whether mystical *theosis*, Neoplatonic metaphysics, nominalist logic and semantics, or, in contemporary thought, both analytic philosophy and phenomenological, hermeneutical, process, metaphysical, or contemplative philosophies) that can help Christians understand better (always incompletely and analogously) the Trinitarian mystery should always be risked. Martin Luther, in continuity with the classical Trinitarian tradition, did not hesitate to use all the many analytical philosophical aids at his disposal to help formulate the central Trinitarian character of his portrait with ever-greater depth and complexity. Luther's *Deus theologicus* was firmly a *Deus Trinitas*—the One God constituted in its very unity by the internal relations of Father, Son, and Holy Spirit, which paradoxically constitute the Trintarian monotheism of Christianity.

Recent scholarly studies of late medieval nominalist semantics and logic have greatly clarified Luther's expertise. Luther reintroduced the medieval *disputatio* (a genre he now used mostly less polemically, except, once again, against the papacy, especially the reigning humanist pope, Paul III) as a test of a doctoral student's theological knowledge and skill.[19] Luther, as professor, wrote the theses with other professors; the students (and, at the limit, the professors, including Luther himself) played the necessary roles of *opponens* and *respondens*. *Disputatio* as a genre was an impressive medieval transformation uniting ancient dialogue with dialectical and logical arguments. Furthermore, the late medievals (especially Ockham) developed techniques in logic and semantics beyond those of Aristotle.[20] These nominalist logical developments provided Luther with more precise tools than the earlier uses of Aristotelian logic (especially the syllogism) in the theology of the high-medieval Scholasticism of Thomas Aquinas, Bonaventure, and others, as well as the almost all-encompassing use of logic in the theology of Duns Scotus, Doctor Subtilis. When one reads Luther's later *disputationes*, Erasmus's earlier, not entirely unjust, ironic title for Luther, Doctor Hyperbolicus, evaporates. The late Luther, the university professor at Wittenberg, with the rigorous technical, logical, and

---

19. Hinlicky et al. 2008 contains three substantive essays with some important differences of interpretation of the later Luther's semantic and logical analyses of Trinitarian theology: see the chapters by Mattox (11–57), Bielfeldt (59–131), and Hinlicky (131–73). For a good example of Luther's later *disputatio*, see Luther 1883 ("Die Promotionsdisputation von Georg Major und Johannes Faber, 12 Dezember 1544"), 39, II, 284–386.

20. On the nature of the medieval genre of *disputatio* in the University of Wittenberg from ca. 1535–45, see Helmer 1999, 41–57.

         ANCIENTS, MEDIEVALS, MODERNS

semantic skills honed in his youth as a student at Erfurt, never rejected paradox as an important language for theology. However, Luther now clarified through logic, grammar, and a dialogically inflected disputation his portrait of *Deus theologicus* by analyzing important conceptual terms (especially *relation* and *person*) in classical Trinitarian theology.

Through the influential scholarship of Heiko Oberman (White 1994, esp. 144–220) on late medieval theology, followed by the more recent scholarship of Graham White, Dennis Bielfeldt, Paul R. Hinlicky, and Christine Helmer, one can understand the basic contours of Luther's Trinitarian *Deus theologicus* far better than earlier accounts were able to show. These new scholarly works have educated us all to see how important the Trinitarian doctrine of God was for Luther. Indeed, Luther articulated in his Trinitarian work a new Word-Spirit dialectic that may well prove his most profound theological contribution for understanding something about God in Godself, as Father, Son, and Holy Spirit.

Therefore, in the later Luther, reason — once illuminated and redeemed by faith — could have a new life in theology. For Luther, reason (here logic, semantics, and semiotics, but not metaphysics, which Luther always rejected) is no longer turned in upon itself, nor is it allied to a fatal blindness to its own self-bondage in its deeply wounded noetic state after the Fall. Logical and grammatical philosophy was now transformed by salvific faith to play what Luther considered a new (because redeemed) role, especially through a rigorous logical use of reason in the disputations. In his later years at Wittenberg, Luther used the genre of *disputatio* in a far more traditional way than in his early work — as a rational means to clarify theological truths logically and semantically and to argue for them nonpolemically.

The second recent scholarly innovation is the claim about *theosis* by the now famous Finnish school of Lutheran research. The Finnish scholars, beginning with Tuomo Mannermaa,[21] have been strongly influenced by their decades-long dialogue with theologians of the Russian Orthodox Church. As a result of the new research on Luther occasioned by these dialogues, the Finnish Lutheran

---

21. *Inter alia*, Braaten and Jenson 1998, Mannermaa 2010, and Puera 1994. An especially valuable work for comparative and possibly constructive theological purposes to relate the Finnish school to the more traditional interpretations of God's Hiddenness may be found in Juntunen 1996, which provides resources that could be employed in future work (preferably by the author Juntunen himself); White 1994 (27–32, 81–124), the classic work by Grabmann 1909–11; and Oberman 1963.

theologians and Luther researchers have paid more theological notice to those texts of Luther's on *theosis*, either previously ignored or underinterpreted. Many modern interpreters of Luther—neo-Kantians like Ritschl as well as existentialist hermeneutical thinkers like Ebeling—did always allow that, for Luther, justification meant not only that our sins were forgiven (*favor*) and no longer imputed to us, but that justification also included a *commercium admirabile* between Christ and the believer, which would become, in continuity with the wider tradition, a *unio Christi*, whereby Christ was also present to us as pure gift (*donum*). Until fairly recently, most Lutheran theologians, except those in the Osiander tradition, thought that any participation language to explicate that *unio* was too Platonic for understanding the clearly non-Platonic Luther.

So strong was the hold of the later Melanchthon's idea of a strictly forensic justification of imputed, not participatory, salvation—a position codified in the *Formula of Concord*—and so strong (so the Finns claim) was the neo-Kantian paradigm among many modern Luther interpreters that any ontological reading of Christ's presence, especially any participation language, was disallowed. For example, even those great Reformed thinkers who, like Albert Schweitzer, argued for a Christ-mysticism in Paul, would not allow for a God-mysticism in either Paul or Luther. For the Reformed Schweitzer, as for the Lutheran Anders Nygren, *unio mystica* was not appropriate to describe Luther's *unio Christi*. For them, a love-mysticism was too Catholic and too Neoplatonic-participatory (*eros*) to interpret Luther correctly.

I must leave to experts any further discussion of the many controversial claims of the Finnish theologians and researchers. However, one claim seems secure—at least to this non-expert. The texts on *theosis* clearly exist in Luther's admittedly voluminous texts and, therefore, should command some hermeneutical attention, either to disown them as not really representative of Luther's basic theological position, or to incorporate them into the singular, perhaps heterogenous and more capacious complexity of Luther's full theology of God, his *Deus theologicus*. These texts, although not prominent, are one of Luther's ways of articulating the *Christus praesens* to and in the justified—not only as *commercium admirabile*, not only as *unio Christi*, but also, however infrequently, as *theosis* (i.e., *unio mystica*). Why were these texts so long ignored, and why are the Finnish readings so quickly dismissed, especially by many German and American Lutheran scholars? Perhaps for the reason cited above: a Melanchthonian, purely forensic notion of justification is considered necessary by many

Lutheran theologians to prevent a new, Osiander-like reading from resurfacing. It is also possible that the Finnish interpreters may be exaggerating their discovery of *theosis*, overemphasizing the importance of the *theosis* texts, even oversystematizing the many-faceted excess of texts by Martin Luther under what seems to function for the Finns as almost a "new main article" to understand all of Luther: justification as *theosis*. As far as I can see, the many-faceted debate in Lutheran theology on the new Finnish interpretation of Luther has just begun. Like many non-experts, I look on the debate with an interest bordering on fascination.

In the meantime, this much is clear: Luther is undoubtedly original in his complex model for *Deus theologicus*: that is, in his unique and epoch-making description of the two forms of God's Hiddenness. By that double move, Luther does interrupt and, to a certain extent, disrupt the earlier traditions on adequate God-language by his singular — and, in my judgment, *pace* Karl Barth and many others, persuasive — concept of the double Hiddenness of God, both in and beyond revelation. At the same time, Luther's logically developed Trinitarian theology is not at all discontinuous with classical Trinitarian theology. In sum, Martin Luther is like any other deeply original mind — both innovative and therefore inevitably interruptive of one or the other dimension of prior Christian traditions and, at the same time, unmistakably continuous with the classical traditions: *simul traditionalis; simul interruptus*.

In the meantime, however, the classical understanding of God's Incomprehensibility in the *theosis* texts of Luther (early and late) possesses a mystical undertone that seems to me a promising component in any adequate, contemporary, full description of God. If these many faces of Luther's *Deus theologicus* could one day be correlated into some more encompassing theological unity without the loss of any of these vital components, it would be a major theological contribution for all Christian theology, not only for Lutheran theology. Otherwise, we are left — or, at least, I am left — with affirming each of these components as genuine dimensions of Luther's *Deus theologicus* without being able to correlate them into a single, clear unity.

My own belief is that Luther's diverse elements for his portrait of *Deus theologicus* are less likely, in a final estimate, to prove mutually contradictory, as distinct from uneasily and paradoxically mutually enriching, through a Christology that would expand Luther's emphasis on the cross to the fuller range of the central Christological and pneumatological symbols that can also be found in his work: incarnation-cross-resurrection-elevation-the sending of the Spirit, and the eschatological reality of the Second Coming. Some future attempt to coordinate these Christological symbols in Luther may prove the way forward to correlate Luther's twofold Hiddenness of God with his Incomprehensible, Trinitarian God. Perhaps.

A concluding suggestion: Luther's unique notion of the Hidden God should be brought into direct contact with Gregory of Nyssa's Infinite-Incomprehensible Trinitarian God.[22] Rethinking Luther's relationship to the early Greek theologians, especially to Gregory of Nyssa and not only to Athanasius and Augustine, could, I believe, be a breakthrough, encouraging further theological reflections on the issue of God as both Incomprehensible and Hidden. This is an ideal that is, for me at least, a central focus of the issue of an adequate model of *Deus theologicus* today: How can we best correlate the Incomprehensible God tradition with the Hidden God tradition and relate both to the Trinitarian God? There can be no doubt that Martin Luther must be a major voice in any such conversation. He is one of those very rare Christian theologians who belong to all Christian theology.

REFERENCES

Athanasius. 2011. *On the Incarnation*. Translated by John Behr. Yonkers, NY: St. Vladimir's Seminary Press.

Bandt, Hellmut. 1958. *Luthers Lehre vom verborgenen Gott: Eine Untersuchung zu dem Offenbarungsgeschichtlichen Ansatz Seiner Theologie.* Theologische Arbeiten, Band 8. Berlin: Evangelische Verlagsanstalt.

Barth, Karl. 2010. *Church Dogmatics*. Edinburgh: T & T Clark.

Bayer, Oswald. 2007. *Theology the Lutheran Way*. Translated and edited by J. G. Silcock and M. C. Mattes. Grand Rapids, MI: W. B. Eerdmans.

---

22. It would prove more fruitful first to relate Luther's Hidden God tradition to Gregory's Infinite-Incomprehensible God tradition, rather than immediately comparing, as I once thought, Luther's Hidden God tradition and Dionysius the Areopagite's Incomprehensible God tradition, especially given Luther's early approval but sudden fierce turn against Dionysius. The rich Dionysian tradition is presently having a major revival — all to the better, in my judgment. However, a comparison between the Hidden (*absconditus*) and Incomprehensible (*incomprehensibilis*) theologies of God would probably be best undertaken first (not last!) by comparing Luther to the relatively noncontroversial Gregory of Nyssa on God's Infinity and Incomprehensibility. On Gregory, see Tracy 2020, chaps. 2 and 8.

ANCIENTS, MEDIEVALS, MODERNS

———. 2008. *Martin Luther's Theology: A Contemporary Interpretation.* Translated by T. H. Trapp. Grand Rapids, MI: W. B. Eerdmans.

Bornkamm, Heinrich. 1969. *Luther in Mid-Career, 1521–1530.* Philadelphia: Fortress Press.

Boyle, Marjorie O'Rourke. 1977. *Erasmus on Language and Method in Theology.* Toronto: University of Toronto Press.

———. 1983. *Rhetoric and Reform: Erasmus' Civil Dispute with Luther.* Cambridge, MA: Harvard University Press.

Braaten, Carl E., and Robert W. Jenson, eds. 1998. *Union with Christ: The New Finnish Interpretation of Luther.* Grand Rapids, MI: W. B. Eerdmans.

Brecht, Martin. 1985. *Martin Luther: His Road to Reformation, 1483–1521.* Philadelphia: Fortress Press.

Chantraine, Georges. 1971. *«Mystère» et «Philosophie du Christ» selon Érasme.* Gemblou, Belgium: Duilot.

Dillenberger, John. 1953. *God Hidden and Revealed: The Interpretation of Luther's "Deus Absconditus" and Its Significance for Religious Thought.* Philadelphia: Muhlenberg Press.

Dragseth, Jennifer Hockenberry, ed. 2011. *The Devil's Whore: Reason and Philosophy in the Lutheran Tradition.* Minneapolis, MN: Fortress Press.

Forde, Gerhard O. 1997. *On Being a Theologian of the Cross: Reflections on Luther's "Heidelberg Disputation," 1518.* Grand Rapids, MI: W. B. Eerdmans.

Gerrish, B. A. 1962. *Grace and Reason: A Study in the Theology of Martin Luther.* Oxford: Clarendon Press.

———. 1982. "'To the Unknown God': Luther and Calvin on the Hiddenness of God." In *The Old Protestantism and the New: Essays on the Reformation Heritage.* Chicago: University of Chicago Press.

Gibson, Margaret T., Janet L. Nelson, and David Ganz, eds. 1981. *Charles the Bald: Court and Kingdom: Papers Based on a Colloquium, Held in London in April 1980.* Aldershot: Variorum.

Grabmann, Martin. 1909–11. *Die Geschichte der scholastischen Methode: Nach den gedruckten und ungedruckten Quellen.* 2 vols. Freiburg, Germany: Herder.

Hartshorne, Charles. 1973. *The Logic of Perfection.* Chicago: Open Court.

Helmer, Christine. 1999. *The Trinity and Martin Luther: A Study of the Relationship between Genre, Language and the Trinity in Luther's Works (1523–46).* Mainz, Germany: Philipp von Zabern.

Hinlicky, Paul R., et al., eds. 2008. *The Substance of the Faith: Luther's Doctrinal Theology for Today.* Minneapolis, MN: Fortress Press.

James, William. 1978. *The Varieties of Religious Experience*. Garden City, NJ: Doubleday.

Janz, Denis. 2010. "Predestination." In *The Westminster Handbook to Martin Luther*. Louisville, KY: Westminster John Knox.

Juntunen, Sammeli. 1996. *Der Begriff des Nichts bei Luther in den Jahren 1510 bis 1532*. Helsinki, Finland: Luther-Agricola-Gesellschaft.

Kierkegaard, Søren. 1980. *The Concept of Anxiety*. Translated and edited by R. Thomas. Princeton, NJ: Princeton University Press.

Kusukawa, Sachiko. 1995. *The Transformation of Natural Philosophy: The Case of Philip Melanchthon*. Cambridge: Cambridge University Press.

Loewenich, Walther von. 1976. *Luther's Theology of the Cross*. Translated by H. Bowman. Minneapolis, MN: Fortress Press.

Lonergan, Bernard. 1971. *Grace and Freedom: Operative Grace in the Thought of Thomas Aquinas*. Edited by J. Partout Burns. New York: Herder and Herder.

Luther, Martin. 1883. *D. Martin Luthers Werke*. Edited by J. F. K. Knaake et al. Kritische Gesamtausgabe. 57 vols. Weimar, Germany: Böhlau.

———. 1955. *Luther's Works*. American Edition, 82 vols. Philadelphia: Fortress; St. Louis, MO: Concordia.

———. 1980. *The Theologica Germanica of Martin Luther*. Translated and with an introduction and commentary by B. Hoffman. New York: Paulist Press.

———. 2000. *Weimar Ausgabe Tischreden*. Edited by Ulrich Kopf, Helmar Junghans, and Karl Starkmann. Weimar: Verlag Hermann Nachfolger.

Mallarmé, Stéphane. 1965. *Poems*. Bilingual ed. Translated by A. Hartley. Harmondsworth, UK: Penguin Books.

Mannermaa, Tuomo. 2005. *Christ Present in Faith: Luther's View of Justification*. Edited and with an introduction by Kirsi Stjerna. Minneapolis, MN: Fortress Press.

———. 2010. *Two Kinds of Love: Martin Luther's Religious World*. Translated by Kirsi Stjerna. Minneapolis, MN: Fortress Press.

Marty, Martin. 2008. *Martin Luther: A Life*. London: Penguin Books.

McCormack, Bruce. 2000. "Grace and Being: The Role of God's Gracious Election in Karl Barth's Theological Ontology." In *The Cambridge Companion to Karl Barth*, edited by John Webster. Cambridge: Cambridge University Press.

McGinn, Bernard. 2017. *Mysticism in the Reformation, 1500–1650: The Presence of God*. New York: Crossroad.

McGrath, Alister E. 1985. *Luther's Theology of the Cross: Martin Luther's Breakthrough*. Oxford: Basil Blackwell.

Migne, J.-P. (Jacques-Paul). 1857–66. *Patrologia Graeca*. Turnholti, Belgium: Brepols.

Oberman, Heiko A. 1963. *Harvest of Medieval Theology*. Cambridge, MA: Harvard University Press.

———. 1966. *Forerunners of the Reformation: The Shape of Late Medieval Thought*. New York: Holt, Reinhart and Winston.

———. 1989. *Luther: Man between God and the Devil*. Translated by Eileen Walliser-Schwarzbart. New Haven, CT: Yale University Press.

Otto, Rudolf. (1917) 1958. *The Idea of the Holy*. 2nd ed. Oxford: Oxford University Press.

Ozment, Steven E. 1969. *Homo Spiritualis: A Comparative Study of the Anthropology of Johannes Tauler, Jean Gerson, and Martin Luther (1509–1516) in the Context of Their Theological Thought*. Leiden, The Netherlands: Brill.

Paluch, Michał. 2004. *La Profondeur de l'amour divin: Évolution de la doctrine de la predestination dans l'oeuvre de Saint Thomas d'Aquin*. Paris: Vrin.

Pascal, Blaise. 1965. *Pascal's Pensées*. Bilingual ed. Translated and with notes and introduction by H. F. Stewart. New York: Random House.

Przywara, Erich. 2014. *Analogia Entis: Metaphysics, Original Structure, and Universal Rhythm*. Translated by J. R. Betz and D. B. Hart. Grand Rapids, MI: W. B. Eerdmans.

Puera, Simo. 1994. *Mehr als im Mensch? Der Vergöttlichung als Thema der Theologie Martin Luthers von 1513–19*. Stuttgart: Philipp von Zabern.

Renaud, Myriam, and Joshua Daniel, eds. 2017. *God: Theological Accounts and Ethical Possibilities*. London: Routledge.

Rupp, E. G., ed. 1969. *Luther and Erasmus: Free Will and Salvation*. Philadelphia: Westminster.

Schaff, Philip, ed. 1887. *A Select Library of the Nicene and Post-Nicene Fathers of the Christian Church*. New York: Christian Literature.

Schreiner, Susan. 2011. *Are You Alone Wise? The Search for Certainty in the Early Modern Era*. Oxford: Oxford University Press.

Schreiner, Susan, and Jeremy Thompson. 2013. "Predestination." In *The Oxford Guide to the Historical Reception of Augustine*, edited by Karla Pollman et al. Oxford: Oxford University Press.

Steinmetz, David. 1986. *Luther and Staupitz: An Essay in the Intellectual Origins of the Protestant Reformation*. Durham, NC: Duke University Press.

———. 1995. "Luther and Augustine on Romans 9." In *Luther in Context*. Grand Rapids, MI: Baker.

Tracy, David. 2020. *Fragments: The Existential Situation of Our Time*. Vol. 1 of *Selected Essays*. Chicago: University of Chicago Press.

Vial, Marc. 2006. *Jean Gerson: Theoricien de la théologie mystique*. Paris: Le Cerf.

Westhelle, Vitor. 2006. *The Scandalous God: The Use and Abuse of the Cross*. Minneapolis, MN: Fortress Press.

White, Graham. 1994. *Luther as Nominalist: A Study of the Logical Methods Used in Martin Luther's "Disputations" in the Light of Their Medieval Background*. Helsinki: Luther Agricola Society.

CHAPTER 5

MICHELANGELO AND THE CATHOLIC ANALOGICAL IMAGINATION

The history of Catholic theology is a rich and pluralistic one. Some eras gave rise to a theological colossus who is singular in achievement: Augustine in the fourth and fifth centuries; Thomas Aquinas in the Middle Ages; John Henry Newman in the nineteenth century; and Karl Rahner, Bernard Lonergan, and Hans Urs von Balthasar in the twentieth. Today, we have many brilliant phenomenological and hermeneutical theologians, feminist theologians, liberation theologians, political theologians, and Hispanic and African American theologians. Paradoxically, in some periods the leading Catholic thinkers are not the official theologians but rather the great artists. In the sixteenth and seventeenth centuries, for example, the most original Catholic theologians were the artists Michelangelo, Raphael, Leonardo da Vinci, Titian, Caravaggio, and Bernini.

To be sure, there were many talented, intelligent, and erudite Catholic theologians in the sixteenth and seventeenth centuries: Thomas Cajetan, Francisco Suárez, Francisco de Vitoria, and others. Above all, there were the great mystical theologians: John of the Cross, Teresa of Ávila, and Ignatius of Loyola; prophetic theologians, such as Bartolomé de las Casas, fighting with liberationist fever for the oppressed native peoples of the Americas; and some remarkable rhetorical, humanist theologians, most famously Desiderius Erasmus. However, the outstanding Catholic theological work of the sixteenth century was Michelangelo's Sistine Chapel ceiling (finished in 1512) and its later disruptive companion, the apocalyptic *Last Judgment* (finished in 1541) on the chapel's altar wall. Michelangelo endowed these monumental works with complexity, plurality, synthetic power, and a distinctly Catholic theological vision: incarnational, sacramental, metaphorical, and analogical.

Artistically, religiously, and theologically, the Sistine Chapel as a unit correlates the three major historical influences on Renaissance Catholic theology: Judaism, Greek and Roman culture, and, above all, the main Catholic tradition from the New Testament forward. (For important scholarship on Renaissance theology and Michelangelo's theological program, see Wind 2000.) The overarching emphasis on salvation through Christ was articulated most persuasively for Michelangelo by Augustine and Dante. The artist's theology of creation and incarnation was also deeply influenced by the mystically oriented Neoplatonism he absorbed as a young man, listening to the conversations of the philosophers Marsilio Ficino, Angelo Poliziano, and Giovanni Pico della Mirandola at the palazzo and in the gardens of his Florentine patrons, the Medici. During the same period, at the Dominican monastery of San Marco and at the Duomo itself, Michelangelo, like so many then in Florence, was willingly held captive by the fiery — indeed, the apocalyptic — sermons of Savonarola. The scholarly debate over which contemporary thinkers may have had the greatest influence on Michelangelo's theology continues unabated, but the most prominent appears to have been the Augustinian Giles of Viterbo, on the allegorical method, Neoplatonism, and even Kabbalah (O'Malley 1986, 92–148). In his later years in Rome, Michelangelo belonged to the ecumenical and humanist Catholic Reform movement. Promoting moderate reform, the movement was eventually swamped by the more rigorous and exclusivist Catholic Counter-Reformation and its decisive reforming Council of Trent (1545–1563); notably, however, the humanist Catholic Reform movement anticipated and was in harmony with the ecumenical Second Vatican Council of the early 1960s and the presently strong, post-Tridentine Catholic-Protestant-Orthodox ecumenical dialogue.

Michelangelo's theological vision of salvation is centered, as is all Christianity, on salvation through the event and person of Jesus Christ. His theology was also deeply influenced by his knowledge of the Hebrew Bible (or Old Testament). Hence, the predominance of the Old Testament in the nine central panels of the Sistine ceiling: the Division of Light from Darkness; the Creation of the Sun and the Moon; the Separation of the Waters; the Creation of Adam; the Creation of Eve; the Fall and the Expulsion; Noah's Sacrifice; the Flood; and the Drunkenness of Noah. Adjacent to these central panels are the famous Ignudi, the restless, athletic, male nudes whose presence both highlights the influence of ancient Greece and Rome on Michelangelo and suggests the uncontainable energy of God the Creator in all creation (Nagel 2000, 153–54; Nagel 2011, 233–35).

In a dazzling plurality, every space of the ceiling is crowded with biblical images and classical figures. The corners feature Old Testament scenes of miraculous salvation, prototypes of Christ: David and Goliath; Judith and Holofernes; the Punishment of Haman; the Brazen Serpent. The lunettes and coves depict the ancestors of Christ in brilliant colors; the medallions feature historical scenes from the books of Maccabees. Dominating the other figures are Michelangelo's monumental frescoes, pairing seven Old Testament prophets with five Greek and Roman prophets, the Sibyls (fig. 5.1); here the ancients unite to deepen Michelangelo's Catholic Renaissance theological vision and to convey Christianity's direct continuity with both biblical Judaism and classical Greek and Roman culture. Michelangelo's religious-theological vision of Christian salvation was inclusive, not exclusive, both Catholic and catholic. Like most Christians of the period (e.g., Martin Luther), Michelangelo interpreted Old Testament figures as prefigurations of New Testament figures. Christ, for Michelangelo, is implied in his paintings of Adam, Noah, Moses, the prophets, and the ancestors of Christ; Eve is a prefiguration of Mary and the church. Analogies proliferate among the types and prototypes that fill the ceiling.

The Sistine ceiling expresses the central symbols of Catholic Christianity in all their complexity. Its central panels on creation convey a High Renaissance optimism and humanism, reflecting on the harmony of nature with grace, although more tragic notes of sin and grace appear in the images of the Fall and

FIGURE 5.1 Michelangelo Buonarroti, *The Libyan Sibyl*, early sixteenth century (detail).
Ceiling fresco, Sistine Chapel, Apostolic Palace, Vatican City. Photograph: Erich Lessing /
Art Resource, New York.

FIGURE 5.2   Michelangelo Buonarroti, *The Creation of Adam*, early sixteenth century (detail). Ceiling fresco, Sistine Chapel, Apostolic Palace, Vatican City. Photograph: Erich Lessing / Art Resource, New York.

the expulsion of Adam and Eve, as well as in the frightening, panic-ridden portrait of the flood. Yet, in all his scenes of the creation of the universe, Michelangelo displays a gracious, majestic, utterly transcendent Creator God, culminating in one of the most famous images in Western iconography: the finger of the all-powerful God about to touch and to bring to life, as if through an electrifying bolt, the recumbent and languid Adam (fig. 5.2).

That image declares one of the deepest Catholic Renaissance beliefs: the dignity of the human being created in the very image and likeness of God's own self. For the Catholic High Renaissance, human beings are graced to live worthy lives of intelligence, creativity, justice, and love, since they bear the dignity of God's own self in their affects, their minds, their wills, and their very souls and hearts. This serene theology of creation and incarnation and a humanistic optimism about heroic, struggling humankind — even after the Fall and the flood — saturate the Sistine ceiling.

The optimism of the Renaissance was extinguished in the decades following the ceiling's completion, with the historic ruptures of the Protestant Reformation and the Catholic Counter-Reformation — the Christian tragedy of the split of Western Christianity into Protestant and Roman Catholic confessions — and the brutal sack of Rome in 1527. The contrast between the Sistine ceiling and the later *Last Judgment* is thus unsurprising. The former breathes with the bold, humanistic optimism of Pico della Mirandola, the Neoplatonism of Ficino, and the historical sensibility of Poliziano; its message is of creation and incarnation, leading to a salvation that is the re-creation of humankind. On the contrary, *Last Judgment* expresses the tragic, apocalyptic, yet hopeful vision of Savonarola, with the theological rigor of Dante and Augustine's later works. Michelangelo's fierce — even violent — rendition of the theme of judgment and resurrection sharply reminded contemporary viewers not only of their own failings and sins, but also of the horrors the Roman population had suffered in the 1527 sack of the city: rape, pillage, torture, murder, destruction, and the theft of artworks and irreplaceable ancient and medieval manuscripts.

The largest of all religious frescoes at that time, *Last Judgment* proclaims its monumentality, not only in its enormous size but also in its endless details: the saved and the damned, angels and demons, saints, martyrs, patriarchs. Unforgettable images crowd the composition: the pathos of the Reprobate (fig. 5.3), who covers one eye while he stares in horror with the other at his fate, as snakes and demons drag him down to hell; an angel lifting two of the saved by means of a rosary; a daring self-portrait on the flayed skin held by the martyr St. Bartholomew; the resurrection of the dead from their graves — some fleshed, some still skeletal. As a counterpart to that macabre scene at the bottom, at the very top of the fresco are scenes of angels lifting the symbols of Christ's salvific passion — the great weight of the cross and the column where Jesus was scourged.

But while Michelangelo's *Last Judgment* disrupts the Renaissance optimism about human beings conveyed in the Sistine ceiling frescoes, it does not annihilate it. Rather, it shifts that optimism to a theologically grounded, eschatological hope, tragic but graced. For Michelangelo and most Catholic theologians then and now, human beings are, to be sure, wounded in mind, will, and heart, but have not lost the image and likeness of God that define humankind. Despite its severity toward the condemned, Michelangelo's fresco manifests the hope of salvation for the many. It is worth noting that, here, the central figure of Christ is joined by the figure of his mother, the ever-merciful Mary — for Catholics, the traditional refuge of sinners (*refugium peccatorum*).

Theologically, the force of Christ's salvific and judging grace drives the fresco's relentless dynamism. The entire composition spirals around Jesus Christ the Judge of all the living and the dead: the saved concentrate on Christ as they

FIGURE 5.3   Michelangelo Buonarroti, *The Reprobate*, detail of *The Last Judgment*, early sixteenth century. Sistine Chapel, Apostolic Palace, Vatican City. Photograph: Alinari / Art Resource, New York.

ascend; even the saints, patriarchs, and martyrs concentrate upon the face of Christ with awe, fear, or surprise (fig. 5.4). Christ condemns the damned with one sweep of his arm, while the other hand points to the wounds of his passion, the instruments of salvation. This Christ is beardless, muscular, passionate — not angry, but rigorously just.

Unexpectedly, Michelangelo's Christ is a classical figure: Apollo, god of the sun, the ancients' Sol Invictus (the Unconquered Sun), is now become the biblical Sol Justitiae (the Sun of Justice). The entire composition is heliocentric, not geocentric, almost proto-Copernican: here salvation affects not only human history but also the immensity of the cosmos in space and time. Unlike most medieval *Last Judgments*, static and hierarchical, Michelangelo's huge fresco rushes with a hurricane force to release the grace of Christ as the deepest, most powerful reality raging through the cosmos.

In painting *Last Judgment*, Michelangelo — passionate and single-minded as ever — demanded more and more space to accommodate his full theological vision of Christ's salvation through his passion and the cross. He did not hesitate therefore to paint over existing paintings by such major artists as Botticelli and Perugino, and a few of his own paintings of Christ's earliest ancestors. Michelangelo also insisted that there be no frame to the colossal work, forcing spectators to enter fully into his fierce, apocalyptic vision and so feel Christ's judgment over their own lives. The overpowering, awe-inspiring fresco portrays a theological vision of Judgment that is not to be trifled with.

However distinct their theological visions, the ceiling and the altar wall paintings both convey the ineffability and ultimate incomprehensibility of God through their central images: the transcendent Creator God and the austere Christ the Judge, fully human and fully God. These majestic images utterly dominate their compositions: every figure in the ceiling is touched by the power of the Creator God; analogously, Christ the Judge sets in motion an irresistible dynamism, a cyclonic force that sweeps up all others — angels and demons, patriarchs and saints, saved and condemned.

As his work in the Sistine Chapel amply demonstrates, Michelangelo was that rarest of combinations: an artistic, a religious, and a theological genius.

FIGURE 5.4 Michelangelo Buonarroti, *Christ and the Virgin*, detail of *The Last Judgment*, early sixteenth century. Sistine Chapel, Apostolic Palace, Vatican City. Photograph: Scala / Art Resource, New York.

CLASSICS: RECEPTION AND PRODUCTION

Perhaps a better term than the too-romantic *genius* for understanding the shifting relationships of art, religion, and theology in works by a figure like Michelangelo is the quieter word *classic*. As genius is to talent, so a classic is to a period piece. A classic is a work (an event, a text, a symbol) in art, ethics, science, religion, philosophy, or theology, or even in everyday life (e.g., falling in love, or the birth of a child) that possesses such an excess of meaning that it resists definitive interpretation. Every classic must be reinterpreted anew in diverse periods. A classic likewise demands constant reinterpretation by any individual over the course of a lifetime. So rich is a classic's excess of meaning that the classic disallows any monolithic interpretations and, at the same time, possesses a universal, permanent meaning that commands ever-new interpretations. Some interpretations of classics will prove relatively adequate, some not adequate at all, but no interpretation of a classic will ever prove absolutely adequate. An interpreter can exhaustively interpret a period piece but can never exhaust interpretations of a classic. Our culture will never achieve a final, definitive interpretation of the works of Plato, Augustine, Shakespeare, Teresa of Ávila, Michelangelo, Rembrandt, or any other classic.

Any person's response to a classic changes over time. Later in life, one may discover a deeper interpretation of a beloved classic or may, alas, interpret it as more superficial than previously understood. One's reception of a classic at different periods of life depends on one's own development or lack thereof. A French friend once told me that he reread Marcel Proust every ten years to understand better what had happened to his own life over the last decade.

A key to understanding any classic is to follow the history of its reception in diverse cultures and periods or at different moments in one's life. For example, many of Michelangelo's contemporaries—including some popes, some theologians, a few fellow artists, and one major satirist (the hypocritical Pietro Arentino)—objected to the many nude bodies in so many of Michelangelo's sculptures and frescoes. Adrian VI (reigned 1522–1523) lashed out at the ceiling's "stew of nudes," while a later pope, the narrow-minded rigorist Paul IV (reigned 1555–1559), declared that Michelangelo's *Last Judgment* belonged in a tavern or brothel, not the papal chapel. The wish to whitewash the whole fresco (fortunately a minority opinion among popes) was impeded by some wise papal advisers and by Michelangelo's international reputation. However, shortly after Michelangelo's death, yet another pope ordered a minor artist to paint loincloths on as many nudes as possible. Michelangelo's critics failed to appreciate that the nude was an important aspect of Michelangelo's artistic and theological convictions. Even in today's art studies, the ability to sculpt or paint the female or male nude body is one of the central ways for an artist to depict the movements, the tensions, the twisted rhythms, and thereby the emotions of each distinct human figure.

Michelangelo's nudes sprang from an even deeper source. Theologically, a soul cannot be painted as such — it is, after all, invisible — but the soul can be painted or sculpted as it manifests itself in a visible, ensouled body. On this topic, as on so many others, Michelangelo had mainline Christian theological tradition behind him. The Gospel of John — the most spiritual, contemplative, even mystical of the four Gospels — begins, "And the Word became flesh and dwelt amongst us" (John 1:14). Christ became, not spirit or mind, but flesh. In his *Last Judgment*, Michelangelo strongly affirms the traditional Christian belief in the resurrection of the body — not simply the immortality of the soul (as in Socrates). The human soul is an embodied soul; the human body is an ensouled body. Rarely has this philosophical (Aristotle) and theological (Thomas Aquinas) belief received so strong an artistic and theological expression as in Michelangelo's sculptures, frescoes, and drawings.

Even more complex to understand than the reception of a classic by a culture or by an individual is the mystery of the creation of a classic. I tentatively suggest that the key to any classic's creation is paradoxical: namely, that the achievement of universality needs the intensification of an artist's deepest particularity. Was any sixteenth-century artist more insistent on realizing his singular vision than Michelangelo, who famously and ferociously defied his patrons? Yet only through such particularity did his masterworks gain a universality that increases with every passing century.

THE CATHOLIC ANALOGICAL IMAGINATION

It has become increasingly difficult for persons outside or even within Catholicism to describe, much less define, the uniqueness of the religious vision and common way of life distinguishing Catholic Christianity. What, if any, common vision is shared by such diverse Catholic theologies as, for example, Latin American liberation theologies; European transcendental, phenomenological, and hermeneutical theologies; and North American experiential theologies? How do you define the heart of a religion that includes such distinct forces as the many social justice movements; the charismatics; the vibrant, mainline, middle-class, urban and suburban Catholics; the several forms of traditional and modern spirituality; as well as the various forms of prophetic witness, such as that of Dorothy Day? Catholics tend to argue with one another, with all the marks of a family quarrel, over the best way to carry on the Catholic theological vision and to live an authentically Catholic life. In historical fact, Catholic Christianity is a multicultural, pluralistic tradition — starting with not one but four Gospels — grounded in commonly held beliefs and practices that are both described and lived in divergent ways. To appropriate a phrase from James Joyce, Catholicism means "here comes everybody." The common image of pre–Vatican II Catholicism as a monolith, with all Catholics sharing identical views on a wide range of issues, from politics through worship to doctrine, is no more — if it ever was. Catholic Christianity is, rather, an intense, complex, dialogical, and argumentative mosaic, alive with religious possibilities that can baffle, intrigue, and sometimes frustrate anyone attempting to define Catholicism.

Yet underneath this buzzing, vibrant Catholic pluralism lies a shared vision that can be named the Catholic analogical imagination. This analogical vision does not define the religious essence of Catholic Christianity but somehow holds together all its members with what Ludwig Wittgenstein termed "family resemblances." To list the explicit beliefs shared by Catholics is an entirely worthy enterprise. And yet, behind any set of beliefs or practices for any religious community lies some fundamental vision of the whole of reality informing all those beliefs: how to work out the relationships between God and cosmos, God and humankind; how to order the relationships of one human being to another and to society, to the cosmos, and ultimately to God; what fundamental attitudes of optimism or pessimism, hope or fatalism, comedy or tragedy ground any tradition's basic hopes and fears.

Catholics tend to agree with Albert Camus that there is more to admire in human beings than to despise. They believe that, in spite of all folly, stupidity, illusion, and sin, humanity is on the whole trustworthy. Furthermore, most Catholic scientists, artists, philosophers, and theologians believe that reason is to be trusted for discovering the order of things; that faith transforms but does not destroy nature. Catholics' image of God is ordinarily like that in the First Letter of John — God is Love (1 John 4:8) — and they believe that love in our ordinary lives deepens, not obliterates, reason. Catholic Christianity is a community of hope, not a ghetto of escape and fear. Catholics hold to an image of society that includes a hope that it can somehow be ordered through attention to the common good and to social justice. The image of the cosmos itself includes a trust that it too is somehow ordered by relationships established by God for all reality. Therefore, in spite of sometimes overwhelming evidence to the contrary, reality is ultimately benign. These beliefs are the essential thrust behind the constant Catholic search for analogies between faith and reason, human and divine love: the Catholic analogical imagination.

I use the word *imagination* to describe a basic theological horizon on the meaning of the whole. When we use imagination creatively, we do not simply report upon the reality we see, hear, taste, feel, and smell in the usual experience of the five senses. Rather, when one imagines creatively, especially when Christians imagine the reality inspired and nourished by the gift of faith in God's self-revelation in Jesus Christ, one redescribes the creative possibilities and actualities of *all* reality. In any theological analogical imagination (not confined to Catholics), one literally reimagines reality as a series of ordered possibilities; one chooses some central clue (a focal meaning, a prime analogate) for the whole of reality to order the relationships between God and humanity, the individual and society, society and the cosmos — for example, in the focal meaning of creation-incarnation as anticipation of salvation in the theology of the Sistine ceiling. Creation-incarnation in the Sistine ceiling is *the* theological secret informing the Catholic belief that all creation is good, and that the relationship of humanity and cosmos is a sacramental one and, theologically, an analogical one.

Every great religious tradition begins in some special occasion of revelatory insight, then proceeds through the centuries to expand that vision through ethical, artistic, philosophical, doctrinal, and logical efforts into an encompassing and, finally, classical theological vision of the whole of reality; and with that vision of the whole, some understanding of every major moment in that whole is ordered to the other moments. A combination of a focal meaning (the prime analogate) with ordered, proportional relationships determined by the focal meaning constitutes an analogical imagination.

Of course, Catholicism, like all secular and religious traditions, has a checkered history. Over the centuries, Catholic Christianity has created great truth, goodness, and beauty in individuals, as well as in whole cultures. Catholicism has also at times produced intellectual obfuscation, and even authoritarian cruelty toward both those outside its tradition and dissenters within it (e.g., Giordano Bruno and Galileo). Other evils, such as the Inquisition, historical anti-Semitism, and the horrifying present clerical sexual molestation and cover-up crisis, cannot be ignored; they are, in fact, matters for communal Catholic repentance. In my judgment, the goodness, beauty, and truth that Catholic Christianity has created in so many cultures, societies, and individuals ultimately outweigh the evil. However, the reality of evil in Catholic history cannot be denied, as Michelangelo's ferocious *Last Judgment* reminds all Catholics.

At its heart, Catholic theology is a deliberate, reflective working out of a series of analogous relationships, all theologically ordered with regard to that one central clue of God's incarnation-crucifixion-resurrection in Jesus Christ. The language of analogy articulates the significant differences and similarities between human beings and the rest of life in the cosmos; it also encompasses the relationships of love and justice between human beings and the God revealed in Jesus Christ. Analogy is to be distinguished from two other major candidates for a vision of the whole: an equivocal imagination, which asserts that all is difference, to the point of no order at all; and a univocal imagination, which asserts sameness, to the point of oneness or monism.

In less traditional but perhaps more helpful modern terms, an analogical imagination can be distinguished from a dialectical imagination. For an authentically analogical Catholic imagination, as well as other Christian analogical views (e.g., Orthodoxy, much of Anglicanism, much of Liberal Protestantism), there is always an order to be found in reality. The key to that order is discovered in some theological focal meaning (some prime analogate) that focuses one's mind as the underlying clue to the whole and then, by means of that clue, envisions all the relationships in reality itself. Analogy is an attempt to trace those relationships as ordered and sometimes harmonious.

For the dialectical mind, on the other hand, the authentic person's task in this life is to unmask illusions and idolatries, to admit one's radical self-delusion, and to be suspicious of all claims to a vision of the whole. Whether formulated by a Kierkegaard, a Marx, a Freud, a Nietzsche, or a de Beauvoir, each modern form of a dialectical imagination is fundamentally a hermeneutics of suspicion and negation, protest and prophetic witness. At its prophetic best (as in Kierkegaard and Dostoevsky), a dialectical imagination explodes all univocal visions as illusory; it exposes all equivocal visions as complacent. Moreover, a dialectical imagination challenges any analogical vision's temptations to underplay life's inevitable tragedies, its terrible suffering, its terrifying evil, its sin. Hence, the reminder issued by the Council of Lateran IV (1215) that analogical statements about God will always fall short, because analogy attempts to relate finite humankind to the infinite God. As Lateran IV insisted, for every similarity contemplated between humanity and God (especially intelligence-in-act and genuine love), there must always be added a greater dissimilarity.

ANALOGY AND DIALECTIC: JOHN AND PAUL

The Gospel of John and the letters of Paul articulate the two major theological attitudes that have dominated Christian history: the analogical imagination of John and the dialectical imagination of Paul. The theological analogical imagination in the Gospel of John is sacramental, contemplative-meditative, love-saturated, metaphoric, aesthetic. Analogical theologies of the Catholic tradition, grounded above all in the Gospel of John, were further developed in the early centuries of Christianity by Logos theologies, followed by several Neoplatonic theologies, and later still by medieval Scholastic, mystical, and lay theologies. All were profoundly analogical. For example, the Dominican Thomas Aquinas (1225–1274) held that, philosophically, intelligence-in-act is the principal focal meaning (prime analogate) that orders all analogical relationships between God and human beings. Thomas held this view with characteristic clarity and consistency from the beginning to the end of his magisterial works, especially in his *Summa Theologiae*.

The Western theological colossus Augustine of Hippo (354–430) represents the analogical imagination at its best, especially in his early dialogues and his later and greatest work, *De Trinitate*. In that text, Augustine employs all his intellectual and spiritual resources to express how intelligence and love become, through God's grace, analogous to the triune God. Even so, in his late anti-Pelagian work, Augustine emphasizes (perhaps overemphasizes) the concept of original sin. Augustine fascinates and influences all subsequent Western theologians by his unique ability to develop a fundamentally analogical theology that incorporates dialectical concepts of suffering, tragedy, evil, and sin (both personal and inherited) into his realistic, sometimes tragic, ultimately joyful theological Christian vision. As Augustine wrote in an Easter sermon: "We are an Easter people and our song is alleluia."

The final word in any analogical theology is a *yes* to reality, a *yes* that fully affirms life itself. A fundamental, Catholic analogical belief is that all human relations should be ordered by the focal meanings of love and intelligence, as revealed in the incarnation, cross, and resurrection of Jesus Christ. This Catholic imagination was set forth classically in the final line of Dante's *Divine Comedy*: "*L'amor che move il sole e l'altre stelle*" (The love that moves the sun and the other stars). It is not surprising that Michelangelo memorized much of Dante and read him on a nightly basis.

Aquinas's theological motto has become almost a mantra for Catholic analogical theologians (even non-Thomist theologians like myself): grace does not destroy but perfects nature. Grace establishes proportional relations between faith and reason, between ethics and aesthetics, and among science, mathematics, logic, philosophy, art, and theology. Love, intelligence, being and becoming are the fundamental realities in all analogical theologies. In analogical theologies, one also finds a grace-transformed understanding of both the beautiful and the sublime in the arts, including in costume: Michelangelo's draperies never merely decorate but always express each figure's distinct individuality. A Catholic analogical imagination pervades artworks in all media: fashion, architecture, sculpture, painting, music, poetry, literature, film. Note, for example, the unmistakable, Catholic analogical tonality in the films of Robert Bresson, John Ford, Alfred Hitchcock, Federico Fellini, Pier Paolo Pasolini, Martin Scorsese, Francis Ford Coppola, Andy Warhol, and many other Catholic filmmakers—whether they are practicing Catholics (like Bresson) or "cultural" Catholics strongly influenced by the images and memories of a Catholic upbringing and (like Scorsese) informed by erudition in the history of art.

Catholic theologians have articulated various forms of an analogical imagination over the centuries: from the foundational Gospel and letters of John, the later Pauline tradition, and the more moderate Luke-Acts to Origen, the Cappadocians, Augustine, Boethius, Eriugena, Anselm, Hildegard of Bingen, Thomas Aquinas, Bonaventure, Angela of Foligno, and Duns Scotus; from Nicholas of Cusa, Teresa of Ávila, John of the Cross to René Descartes, Jeanne Guyon, and François Fénelon; from John Henry Newman and the Tübingen school in the nineteenth century to the majority of Catholic theologians today. Furthermore, many modern Liberal Protestant theologians, from Friedrich Schleiermacher through Paul Tillich and beyond, articulated prominent analogical elements for Protestant theology. Schleiermacher's very definition of religion, as a sense and taste of the Infinite, opens itself to establishing an order of analogical proportions between the divine Infinite and our finite selves; Tillich insisted that all modern Christian theology should combine a Catholic (and thereby analogical) substance with a Protestant (dialectical) principle of critique and protest.

The analogical-dialectical distinction of theologies can be said to have originated with the analogical John and the dialectical Paul. The crucial theological truth is that their differences amount to a distinction, not a divide: a both/and, not an either/or. John articulated an analogical theology inexorably focused on love. At the same time, John's narrative never ignores the dialectical realities of the Passion and the cross. At the same time, John uniquely discerns that the very lifting up of Christ on the cross is the decisive manifestation of God's glory and beauty as infinite, salvific, unbounded love. The Gospel of John is a meditative, contemplative, love-intoxicated, analogical theological vision that develops its theological proportionalities by relating all to its primary focal meaning: God is Love.

In contrast, Paul's theology, especially in the Letter to the Galatians and in the Letter to the Romans, is dialectical through and through. Paul's highly original linguistic dialectic hurls readers about so they cannot evade their faults, sins, and self-delusions: "For I do not do the good I want, but the evil I do not want is what I do" (Rom. 7:19). Paul draws the Christian away from all complacency, sometimes even from all religious consolation. Paul demands that the believer face what for Paul is the ultimate dialectical contradiction: that God is best revealed not through glory but through the graced negativity of suffering, pain, the cross. For Paul (as for Luther and Pascal), we understand God best not through analogies to our own intelligence and love but through Christ's cross, revealing the shattering negations, conflicts, contradictions, innocent sufferings, and intellectual paradoxes in every human heart. At the same time, Paul and the Pauline tradition (compare Paul's own two early letters to the Corinthians with the later Pauline letters to the Colossians and to the Ephesians) affirm a dialectical imagination united to a John-like focal meaning of love: "Faith, hope, love abide, these three; but the greatest of these is love" (1 Cor. 13:13). Just as John's analogical theology of love demands for its full understanding the Gospel's narrated dialectical moments of pain, suffering, and the cross, so Paul's radical dialectical insistence on finding the true God in and through negativity, sin, suffering, and the cross opens Paul himself to a distinct analogical theology of interpersonal and cosmic love.

To return to our original example, Michelangelo's theology is classically Catholic because it is *both* an analogical theology of creation-incarnation as anticipation of salvation as re-creation (as depicted in the Sistine ceiling) *and* a profound theology of the cross and of eschatological "not-yet" in the dialectical, sometimes violent imagery saturating his *Last Judgment*. These two monumental frescoes exist together, somewhat uneasily in the same space, theologically clashing, even as they complement each other. Christianity cannot in fact be understood if one ignores either the beauty and goodness of all creation or the elements of suffering, evil, tragedy, and sin in all life. That is the Catholic analogical imagination.

REFERENCES

Nagel, Alexander. 2000. *Michelangelo and the Reform of Art*. Cambridge: Cambridge University Press.

———. 2011. *The Controversy of Renaissance Art*. Chicago: University of Chicago Press.

O'Malley, John W., SJ. 1986. "The Theology behind Michelangelo's Ceiling." In *The Sistine Chapel: The Art, the History, and the Restoration*, text by Carlo Pietrangeli, André Chastel, et al. New York: Harmony Books.

Wind, Edgar. 2000. *The Religious Symbolism of Michelangelo: The Sistine Ceiling*. Edited by Elizabeth Sears. Oxford: Oxford University Press.

Part 2

MENTORS

This section includes four studies of important mentors, not only for me but also for my theological generation. Two of these mentors — Reinhold Niebuhr and Karl Rahner — receive brief but properly affirmative attention in two essays published in journals for a wide, educated audience: *Commonweal*, for Karl Rahner; the *New Republic*, for Reinhold Niebuhr. The other two mentors — Paul Tillich and Bernard Lonergan — are treated at somewhat greater length.

REINHOLD NIEBUHR

Reinhold Niebuhr is second only to Martin Luther King Jr. as the major public theologian in the United States in the twentieth century. His amazing theological career began with his work as a minister for workers and their unions in Detroit, Michigan. Through his energetic years as professor of theological social ethics at Union Theological Seminary, his widely influential theological career expanded as he became, along with his brother H. Richard Niebuhr, a lustrous historian of the ironies of American history. Reinhold Niebuhr became, in effect, preacher and theologian to the nation behind Martin Luther King as an outstanding public theologian articulating a deeply influential Christian realism for contemporary politics (both Christian and secular). So successful was the public character of Niebuhr's position that some deeply secular thinkers (e.g., Arthur Schlesinger Jr.) declared themselves "atheists for Reinhold Niebuhr." Allied to the incomparable, game-changing, theological and political profundity of Martin Luther King, while also allied to the celebrated Jewish public theologian Abraham Heschel and the highly influential Roman Catholic public theologian John Courtney Murray Jr., Niebuhr served the public life of the United States with a range and depth unequaled by any of his contemporaries, save King himself. Today there is a great need for another public theologian like Niebuhr. There are some fine candidates for the role, especially the coruscating, brilliant, erudite Cornel West and the erudite, courageous, feminist Christian theologians Rosemary Radford Ruether and Elisabeth Schüssler Fiorenza, as well as some major womanist and *mujerista* theologians.

KARL RAHNER

Karl Rahner was the most profound and original Catholic theologian of the twentieth century. There was hardly a theological discipline or a major theological issue that Rahner did not address. He made major contributions, above all in fundamental and systematic theology with his groundbreaking transcendental method, which he employed in both philosophy and theology. He also contributed in major ways to pastoral theology, spirituality, and some strictly historical studies of history of theology (e.g., a whole volume on the early history of penance and a lapidary study of the still widely overlooked but important notion of the "spiritual senses" in Origen).

Karl Rahner's theology was a magnificent theological edifice that began with two Heidegger-influenced, fascinating philosophical studies (*Geist in Welt* and *Hörer des Wortes*), followed by a seemingly endless number of theological essays on most of the major issues of theology. I had the privilege of meeting Karl Rahner on several occasions. I was always struck by his irony about himself ("Some days I don't write at all," he once said, smilingly), and his exceptional somewhat melancholic modesty united to a fierce insistence on serious theology, including his openness to criticism of his own transcendental position as "too individualist and apolitical" (Johann Baptist Metz). Indeed, one of Rahner's last writings was to affirm liberation theology as articulated by Gustavo Gutiérrez. Besides Rahner's amazing erudition in the entire history of Catholic theology, as well as his wit, modesty, and generosity, I also sensed in him a melancholy strain that made him more — not less — believable as a great theologian who understood both the graced joy of faith in everyday life, and the need for hope in a world at once graced and tragic.

Rahner's important theological differences from the second major Catholic theologian of the last century, Hans Urs von Balthasar, are significant and continue to divide a good deal of modern Catholic theology. Eventually, many Catholic theologians have chosen which theological path is most valuable — Rahner or Balthasar — just as many modern Protestant theologians have chosen between the ways of Friedrich Schleiermacher and his many followers (including, among others, Rudolf Bultmann and Paul Tillich), and Karl Barth and his many followers.

For my part, the theologies of Schleiermacher, Tillich, Rahner, and Lonergan remain the best way forward for theology. But this choice should *never* mean that one does not read, over and over again, and learn from the amazing Karl Barth ("well-roared, lion"), and the deeply erudite and theologically aesthetic Hans Urs von Balthasar, who single-handedly restored the beautiful to its place in theology with the One, the True, and the Good. Those who think that the choice between Schleiermacher-Tillich-Rahner, on the one hand, and Barth-Balthasar, on the other, is an exclusivist choice impoverish themselves unnecessarily.

PAUL TILLICH

Paul Tillich's method of correlation is, for me, a valuable refinement of the Schleiermacher theological way and method. More exactly, Tillich's method of correlation, especially as practiced in his magisterial, three-volume *Systematic Theology*, can be helpfully reformulated as a method of "mutually critical correlations": that is, a critical correlation of, first, an interpretation of the Christian fact as expressed, above all, in the Bible (secondarily in the classics or "frag-events" of the Christian tradition); and, second, an interpretation of the main features of situation — the social, economic, political (i.e., in Tillich's early German political theology), psychological, and cultural situation (i.e., in Tillich's later American period). I have defended elsewhere (e.g., in the four essays on hermeneutics in volume 1 of my *Selected Essays, Fragments*, chaps. 6–9) the idea that theology is best understood as a hermeneutical discipline that can also be formulated as a theology of correlation. In fact, Tillich's method of correlation is a good way to clarify methodologically the reality of hermeneutics as a contemporary interpretation of every classic text, event, person, or symbol in the tradition, from the Bible forward. The Christian fact and the contemporary situation are a good Tillichian way to delineate theological method. Today, Tillich is unjustly neglected by many theologians as they continue to struggle to formulate an appropriate theological method. They would do well, I suggest, to reread and rethink (critically, of course) Paul Tillich's thought, especially in *Systematic Theology*, where he clarifies at proper length his understanding of his method of correlation while, even more importantly, he shows that method at work on *all* the major Christian symbols.

Furthermore, Paul Tillich was one of the few theologians of his generation who insisted on interpreting the Catholic "substance" of the tradition in creative tension with the Protestant "prophetic principle." The modern Protestant theological tradition, from Schleiermacher and Hegel to the inestimable F. O. Maurice, Karl Barth, Rudolf Bultmann, Paul Tillich, and their many younger successors is a series of major rethinkings of both the Christian Reformed Lutheran and Free Church theological traditions, and the contemporary situation in all its complexity, plurality, and ambiguity. Until the grand Catholic theological generation of de Lubac, Congar, Bouyer, Daniélou, Balthasar, Rahner, and Lonergan, there was no steady line of creative Catholic theologians — except for individual exceptions, like John Henry Newman, the outstanding rhetorical theologian of modernity (the "silver fox," as James Joyce once both ironically and positively called Newman, the great Ciceronian rhetorician), and the remarkable nineteenth-century Tübingen school, which was in deep contact with both the long and richly pluralistic Catholic theological tradition and the extraordinary German modern philosophical tradition, especially of Kant, Hegel, and, above all, of the Tübingen theologian Friedrich Schelling.

Until the generation of Rahner, de Lubac, Lonergan, and others (in fact, the two generations after Barth, Tillich, Bultmann, et al., and several generations after Schleiermacher, Hegel, Schelling, Newman, and Kierkegaard), Catholic theology was largely captured by an exceptionally narrow, unimaginative, defensive, modern form of Neo-Scholasticism (not to be confused with the august, creative high Scholasticism of Thomas Aquinas, Bonaventure, and Duns Scotus). Modern, Catholic, Neo-Scholastic philosophy and theology lasted from the sixteenth century — the brilliant "second Scholasticism" at sixteenth-century Salamanca through the ages of the great commentators in Thomas Aquinas, especially Cajetan and John of St. Thomas — to the late eighteenth century until Vatican II. To be sure, the Neo-Scholastic theologians were (and the few still active are) excellent logicians and metaphysicians who articulated their views with enviable precision in clear, largely doctrinal and dogmatic propositions. However, as Bernard Lonergan once ironically observed, the modern Neo-Scholastics believed in clear and distinct ideas — and very few of them. Would that nineteenth- and early twentieth-century Neo-Scholastic Catholic theologians had read more of John Henry Newman and the powerful modern Protestant philosophers and theologians, as did the Catholic theologians at Tübingen, with their creative interpretations of Schleiermacher, Hegel, and especially the late Schelling. Catholic theologians since the early twentieth century have become, in the *ressourcement* theologians, the theological equals of the enormously creative modern Protestant theologians from Schleiermacher to Barth.

The new Christian theological situation, I believe, is one where all Christian theologians, whatever their religious center of gravity (Roman Catholic, Anglican, Orthodox, Lutheran, Reformed, Free Church, American Evangelical, Pentecostal), should commit themselves to learning at least the major theologians, earlier and contemporary, of the three major Christian communions: Catholic, Protestant, and Orthodox. The church, to which the contemporary Christian theologian holds herself responsible, is the whole Christian church, constituted by valuably different church orders, spiritualities, and theologies, and resulting in principle in richer, pluralistic theologies for all, partly thanks to Paul Tillich's insistence on a theological method of correlation addressing in creative tension both Catholic substance and Protestant prophetic principle.

BERNARD LONERGAN

The final mentor on this list, Bernard Lonergan, was, in my own case as in that of very many others, my major mentor and teacher. I studied closely with Lonergan at the Gregorian University during Vatican II ("Bliss was it in that dawn to be alive, / But to be young was very heaven!" — Wordsworth). I have never before or since known so singular a thinker as Bernard Lonergan. His most intense intellectual love was for mathematics and physics. His legacy is distinguished in philosophy (in that remarkable work of sheer originality, *Insight: A Study of Human Understanding*), in theology (especially in the creation of theological method), and in systematic theology (his major contributions in Christology, grace, and Trinity). On method, he rethought what it *should* be: "A method is a normative pattern of recurrent and related operations yielding cumulative and progressive results." Lonergan's original reflections on method apply to all the human sciences and, properly reformulated in relation to the subject matter, to theological method. For Lonergan's method, theology becomes a collaborative enterprise with eight interacting functional specializations (research, interpretation, history, dialectic, foundations, doctrines, systematics, and communications).

As a careful student of the natural sciences (especially physics and biology), Lonergan was intent on making theology into a collaborative enterprise like the natural sciences. To my knowledge, this collaborative method has yet to be tested by any theological school. Most theologians (including me) plow on as more and more desperate individuals trying to learn the results of as many functional specialties as one can on one's own, as one *also* tries to find one's own voice and to articulate one's own theological vision. Can theology become a collaborative enterprise as are the sciences? If it ever does, Lonergan's uniquely collaborative method will show the way.

Lonergan first wrote two exemplary *explications de texte* studies of Thomas Aquinas: one on grace and freedom (a breakthrough interpretation that undid both Molinist and Bañezian traditional interpretations), and another, *Verbum: Word and Idea in Aquinas*. Lonergan also taught and wrote a two-volume work on Trinitarian theology (*De Deo Trino*), which clarifies the deeply introspective genius shown by Augustine in *De Trinitate* and the exceptionally subtle and persuasive theoretical refinement of Augustine's Trinitarian theology actualized by Thomas Aquinas, with his creative notion of "intelligible emanations" (as emanation from act to act, not potency to act). Lonergan also articulated a coruscatingly original understanding of several aspects of Christology, including the "law of the cross." In his later work Lonergan formulated an understanding of faith as "a new knowledge born of love" in *Method in Theology*. Lonergan also wrote a book on a new theory of economics, which has been praised by several economists but which I am not competent to judge.

Over the years, I have written several articles (and an early book) on my great teacher, Bernard Lonergan. They are mostly accurate about this demanding and complex thinker, I believe, except for a foolish, callously youthful 1970 criticism, which was as erroneous then as it is embarrassing now. Of these various writings, I have chosen one that suggests reading Lonergan anew in the light of Pierre Hadot's exceptional work on ancient and a few modern philosophies, not only as logic and theory (as most professional philosophy is done today), but also as exercises to aid a "way of life." That is exactly what *Insight* is: a set of intellectual exercises in mathematics, natural science, and philosophy, to allow the reader to appropriate oneself as a knower. *Insight* is a set of exercises and, as Lonergan states, something like a theory. In a similar manner, *Method in Theology* also comprises exercises for understanding the actual complexity of theology.

Bernard Lonergan, with his outstanding combination of mathematics, natural science, cognition theory, epistemology, metaphysics, and theology, was a unique genius.

CHAPTER 6

REINHOLD NIEBUHR

God's Realist

Elisabeth Sifton's splendid and strenuous book, *The Serenity Prayer: Faith and Politics in Times of Peace and War* (2003), was occasioned by a bizarre mistake: a famous prayer, composed by Sifton's father, Reinhold Niebuhr, was uprooted from its original context, reworded, and misappropriated. There is of course no copyright on prayers. Prayers are composed in the hope that they will help people, starting with the people who compose them. Most prayers are best left to the uses of personal piety. But some prayers strike a chord across traditions, cultures, individuals; and more than any prayer composed in English since the Elizabethans, Reinhold Niebuhr's "Serenity Prayer" is one of those extraordinary supplications: "God, give us grace to accept with serenity the things that cannot be changed, courage to change the things that should be changed, and the wisdom to distinguish the one from the other." The plain style of Niebuhr's meditation has enabled its genuine profundity to touch even the most secular among us, to provoke individuals who ordinarily avoid such a vocabulary to find a place for it in their lives. Sifton wisely suggests that her father's prayer may be both consciously prayed by believers, and unconsciously prayed even in the mere reading of it. Who does not want serenity, courage, and wisdom to deal with whatever chance, or fate, or providence has meted out?

Prayer, if it comes at all, usually comes as a surprise — as an unexpected gift from some hidden source in oneself or outside oneself. And the language of prayer discloses some awareness, however inchoate, of the ultimately real. Many names have been given to this greater reality: the Void, the Vast, the Good beyond Being, the Infinite, the One, the Way, Other Power, the gods, God. But the experience of prayer is always a limit-experience, in that the limit of our finitude is both reached and transgressed. Good prayers, like good religious poetry, are very rare. They need not be a matter of explicit belief, but only of a felt relationship to whatever the individual senses at privileged moments is on the other side of the actual and the possible. Good prayers can be powerful not only for believers in God, but also for almost anyone willing to allow the resources of the quiet language of genuine prayers to unlock the explosive power of their content.

Niebuhr was correct to acknowledge that the religious sentiments in his prayer were not original. Neither are the religious sentiments of John Donne and William Wordsworth, of Gerard Manley Hopkins, the Rossettis, or T. S. Eliot. Niebuhr's prayer should not be trifled with any more than we should change Donne's language to find something more palatable, more "relevant," more "customized." At the same time, Niebuhr was willing to let his prayer loose in the world without worrying too much about where it might land. Prayers, like poems, should be free to change sensibilities and even languages. Niebuhr endorsed the adoption of his prayer by Alcoholics Anonymous, even when the group substantially changed the wording. It seems that he was more amused than angered by less happy uses of the "Serenity Prayer" — sometimes as a new item of Christian kitsch throughout the world, as the prayer that appeared on tea containers, tacky banners, and silly balloons. Why worry about all that if the prayer helped? Would Antonio Allegri da Correggio have complained about all those Christmas cards? Kitsch in a religion (e.g., Hinduism or Catholicism) can often be a sign that a faith still lives, that it still serves the needs of all the sorts of people who live it.

Yet there are limits. Niebuhr's widow and his daughter were justifiably incensed by one particular appropriation of the "Serenity Prayer"; his daughter was provoked to write this book so as to correct it. In the aftermath of World War II, a German professor translated Niebuhr's prayer (which was used by American soldiers) into German. The translation was not a good one, and the lackadaisical professor added, as its possible author, the name Friedrich Christoph Oetinger, an eighteenth-century German Pietist who may have been a remote ancestor of the professor or his wife. So it was as a new German Pietist prayer that the German version of Niebuhr's supplication took off in postwar Germany. And this new German Pietist prayer was eventually carved grandiosely upon the walls of the Bundeswehr's cadet academy in Koblenz.

Sifton is justified to call this episode, from beginning to end, "sleazy." The shifty professor seemed unaware that Reinhold Niebuhr had spent a lifetime trying to free his religion from precisely this kind of anti-intellectual and non-political version of much pietism. Niebuhr knew, loved, and criticized the German cultural tradition in philosophy and theology. But like his contemporary Walter Benjamin, he was acutely aware that every document of civilization is at the same time a document of barbarism. He feared that militarism might be endemic to German culture, and he fought against it with prophetic fury. At the same time, unlike other progressives of his time, Niebuhr never seized upon the Nazi horror to reject German culture *tout court*. Niebuhr grew up speaking German in the Midwest. He did not speak English fluently until his years as a student in the divinity school at Yale University. He knew German culture and language from the inside of the German American enclave of his period as well as H. L. Mencken did. And Niebuhr knew from personal experience, as did Mencken, how German Americans were often demonized by other Americans in World War I. His brother, H. Richard Niebuhr, also a distinguished theologian, also rightly continued to honor German philosophy and theology in his work, although he did change his Midwestern, German American name from Helmut Richard Niebuhr to H. Richard Niebuhr. Reinhold Niebuhr remained Reinhold. So Niebuhr's prayer did not deserve to be adapted to a particular German pietistic tradition that he fought theologically all his life — much less to a German martial tradition that he despised.

The only good thing (indeed, a *felix culpa*) to have come out of this dreary episode is Elisabeth Sifton's book. Sifton is a natural writer, and also (not surprisingly, since she is one of the most distinguished editors in American publishing), a natural editor: the structure of her account is superb, both subtle and seductive. The reader only gradually becomes aware of the true scale of what is discussed here. Sifton has written a history disguised as a memoir. She begins, you might say, with serenity: the story of the rural place where Niebuhr found summer relief from his almost unbelievably active life of teaching, writing, organizing political committees, and circuit-riding (his phrase) throughout the country preaching to Protestant Americans and to anyone else who would listen about Christian political responsibility.

Sifton begins her story in a small town in northwestern Massachusetts called Heath. As she describes it, Heath in those days was not the usual summer place. To be sure, it was beautiful: the hills, the streams, the hardscrabble New England land. The tough soil of New England surprised both of Sifton's parents—her Midwestern father, who was used to the inordinately rich farmland of his childhood in Missouri and Illinois, and her English mother, who grew up in the gentler lands and rhythms of old England, where her mother's Anglican ancestors had stayed on, while the hard Puritans escaped to the hard, almost Puritanical, tough soil of New England. Heath does not sound delightful in Sifton's pages recalling it. The local farmers (apparently almost all Republicans) and the summer people, mostly progressive Protestant clergymen who favored social justice ("Too many clerics," thought their close friend W. H. Auden after a visit to the Niebuhrs), managed to coexist very well indeed. The summer intellectuals also included the occasional agnostic, including the indomitable Felix Frankfurter.

But for such a group, Heath could not be all serenity. These folks were not Buddhists. They were a brilliant and beleaguered group of progressive intellectuals who loved the ideal of America because America preached, and partly achieved, what Niebuhr liked to call "rough" justice. And they knew, in America in the 1930s, that too many Americans were left out of this American rough justice. The Heath summer people fought against every injustice that came to their attention. Sifton's recollections of a magical childhood place introduce a remarkable cast of characters who made up the summer community of Heath. Niebuhr and Frankfurter became lifelong friends who helped each other throughout their very active, very reflective lives. It was the agnostic Frankfurter who, in Niebuhr's frail and often depressed final years, reminded him of the need to accept with serenity what cannot be changed.

I must confess that as a reader, I eventually became somewhat keen to leave Heath behind. After a while, the place began to seem a little like Thornton Wilder's Grover's Corners. (The Heath chapters end with the memory of a local production of *Our Town*.) The great events of the day were happening elsewhere. The public story of Reinhold Niebuhr takes off in Sifton's stirring middle chapters. World War II overwhelmed whatever serenity the summer inhabitants of Heath had managed to find, and it is amazing what Niebuhr managed to accomplish in those overwhelming years. He produced his greatest theological work, his Gifford Lectures, which appeared with the excellent title *The Nature and Destiny of Man* in two volumes in 1941 and 1943. The concluding Gifford Lectures were delivered to the accompaniment of German bombs exploding near Edinburgh. Before the war, Niebuhr wrote article after article against American isolationism. Before and even during the war, he traveled as much as possible to England (and to Germany before the war) to help mobilize the anti-totalitarian struggle in the churches.

Niebuhr crisscrossed the United States, sometimes like a half-mad prophet, with a mission to call Protestant America to its ethical and political responsibilities. He taught Christian social ethics at Union Theological Seminary in New York for many years. He helped émigrés and refugees, such as Paul Tillich, find jobs in the United States. Even before the Allied victory was assured, Niebuhr joined Louis Brandeis, Felix Frankfurter, Isaiah Berlin, and others to argue forcefully for the establishment of a Jewish homeland after the war. At home, he continued to fight for human rights, and in those war years he also began to fight more vigorously for civil rights for black Americans. He became, in sum, one of the leading public intellectuals in America, and clearly the most significant theological voice in the land.

The structure of Elisabeth Sifton's narrative is borrowed from the structure of her father's prayer: from the brief periods of serenity in Heath, she moves to the courage and wisdom of the years before, during, and after the war, ending with the tough-minded and very difficult life of Niebuhr's last years, which were marred by a series of strokes. The great man died in 1971. Toward the end of his life, Niebuhr did not hesitate to fight Soviet totalitarianism. Elizabeth Sifton is wonderfully undiscomfited by her father's prominent role in American policy on the Cold War. Niebuhr, an anti-Communist liberal, fought in the postwar years for his theological ideals with the same fervor with which he had earlier fought Hitler's fascism. He exposed the naive and shameful self-delusion regarding Soviet Communism of too many American progressives of the time. For this honorable action, some progressives still dishonor Niebuhr, when they would be better off questioning their own part in making excuses for the horrors of Stalin and his successors. It goes without saying that in these same years Niebuhr was just as fierce in his opposition to Joseph McCarthy and all that he stood for.

Those were times in which many people, including many *good* people, made terrible errors of judgment. In this regard, Niebuhr's record (with some inevitable, honest errors of judgment) is admirable. He never lost his head. This rare, prophetic cleric turned out to be one of America's most tough-minded liberals. How many others denounced with Niebuhr's moral clarity the unjustified saturation bombings of German and Japanese cities, as well as the atomic bombings of Hiroshima and Nagasaki? How many other theologians were willing to take on Billy Graham, Cardinal Spellman, and Richard Nixon's prayer meetings, as well as the rabbis, priests, and ministers who officiated them? How many other Christian leaders had the courage to criticize the churches so ferociously for their ethical and political apathy? Like the prophet Amos, Niebuhr's favorite biblical prophet, Reinhold Niebuhr never hesitated to expose the delinquency of any political and ecclesiastical leaders who failed to take up the cause of the widow, the orphan, the stranger, the misfit, the marginalized.

Reinhold Niebuhr's theology was his own unique blend of two traditions: classical Protestant liberalism, and the mid-twentieth-century movement of Protestant neo-Orthodoxy. His theological liberalism, which goes back to Friedrich Schleiermacher, consists in reinterpreting all the major Christian symbols in direct relationship to the question of modernity. This is most ringingly expressed in Niebuhr's assertion that most religious symbols should be taken "seriously" but not "literally." The second source for Niebuhr's theology was the Protestant neo-Orthodoxy inspired by Karl Barth. Neo-Orthodoxy was an attempt to insist that the Christian tradition, if properly interpreted, challenged modern innocence about the adequacy of Enlightenment reason alone to solve our problems. For Niebuhr, this meant recovering such Christian traditional resources as the classical Christological symbols of the early councils, Luther's understanding of human nature as flawed and self-deluding, and Calvin's sense of history replacing nature as the main locus of God's covenantal presence.

Niebuhr's theological position can be more accurately described as neo-Reformation rather than as neo-Orthodox, since his main theological task was to recover the Reformation's reading of Augustine and Paul. For Niebuhr, Augustine serves as an unexpected and significant critical influence upon his political and ecclesial liberalism. Shorn of Augustine's strictly mythological elements, the classic Augustinian text on a theology of history, *The City of God*, with its profound grasp of the fallibility of the all-too-human darker side of historical reality, deserves to challenge and to inform modern liberal thought. Niebuhr never retreated from his defense of the accomplishments of modern reason in science, pluralism, and modern democracy; but he insisted that this was not the end of the story. Reinhold Niebuhr demanded in the name of the truth of historical reality that the liberal temper find a place for a grimmer, more realistic assessment of the tragic and sinful actuality of every society. Niebuhr argued passionately and tellingly that the tragic human situation is not soluble by modern secular reason alone, or by upbeat Christian liberal appeals to our "natural goodness." Niebuhr called this second reality the "realism" of the Reformation.

In this daring and original enterprise, Niebuhr rethought one of the most unlikely symbols in the whole Christian tradition: original sin. This symbol, fully articulated by Augustine in the West, unsettlingly portrayed the human predicament as a tangled combination of free will and the conflicts that it engenders. This situation seemed to bear no purely rational solution. Niebuhr's recovery of the Augustinian understanding of human complexity had remarkable resonance in a secular age that was appreciative of Freud's tragic vision in *Civilization and Its Discontents*.

By daring to retrieve a demythologized version of original sin, Niebuhr provided a critique of Protestant liberalism at its weakest: its naive understanding of the intrinsic goodness of human beings and its misplaced hope in the ability of love and understanding to overcome all personal and social conflicts. Niebuhr joined the liberals to insist that "original sin" could not be literalized: there was no literal "Eden," no "Adam," no "Eve," no serpent, no historical "Fall." Yet he fought the liberal dismissal of the tragic and sinful truth in the symbol of original sin. He was part of a larger movement in the philosophical and political culture of his time. Those were the years when Pascal's terror and Kierkegaard's dread were revered even by secular intellectuals, when Eliot and Auden were reading the modern world anew through Christian eyes. Barth had already insisted in his early German Expressionist theology that "revelation comes like a stone" to change not only our answers but our very questions. Reinhard Niebuhr concurred with Karl Barth's hard, lucid image of the stone; and he agreed even more with his colleague and friend, Paul Tillich, in his response to Barth, that "one does not receive answers to questions he has never asked."

For many in those "existentialist" days, it was time to recover, under the influence of Kierkegaard, the authentic individual. But Niebuhr had no time for the individualism of existentialism. There was moral and political work to be done. His realism was enlisted in the service of the prophetic call to justice. As Niebuhr would argue, love (which he nicely described as "the impossible possibility") was never enough to overthrow an entrenched, structural evil. Historical action and politics were needed, too. Niebuhr was able to develop a realism that was Christian in its source, but modern in its effect. So much was this the case that some secular American thinkers called themselves "atheists for Reinhold Niebuhr." Niebuhr helped them to overcome their earlier Deweyan belief in reason alone, as much as he helped Christian liberals to abandon "love alone" as a solution to an unjust society.

Niebuhr's tragic sensibility seemed exactly right for the struggle against fascism and, after it, against communism. His immense influence on American political thought, especially in the years following World War II, was largely due to his surprising use of the Christian symbols of grace and sin to illuminate our common passage through our ambiguous histories and societies. Once the category of original sin was extended beyond its literal meaning, it became an unexpectedly useful symbol for representing the dilemma of our wills inevitably trapping themselves, and therefore nullifying our best reasons and our best intentions by imprisoning them in the grasping confines of our possessive egos. It is little wonder that Martin Luther King Jr. always understood himself to be a Niebuhrian in his insistence on the need for both love and justice to fight the intolerable nature of American racism, and Niebuhr always encouraged King in the development of the realistic ideas and actions of nonviolent resistance that were needed for the noble struggle.

Reinhold Niebuhr was, I think, the finest American theologian since Jonathan Edwards, and perhaps the most profound religious realist in America since Abraham Lincoln. Like Edwards, Niebuhr never hesitated to summon explicitly Christian resources to understand the world and to explain his understanding to others. Like Lincoln, he never confined his insights to the orbit of Christianity, but instead employed a Christian vision to cast a powerful light on our common history in its frightening and tragic ambiguity. Recall Lincoln's extraordinary Second Inaugural Address, with its daring theism that sought not only to rally its listeners to their own cause but also to raise them above it. It is no surprise that Niebuhr considered the famously unchurched and theologically uneducated Lincoln the best theologian in American history. Abraham

Lincoln's realistic vision of the tragedy of the Civil War found a fully theological rendering in the later Christian realism of Reinhold Niebuhr.

Niebuhr's theological position was not without its shortcomings. It was constrained by the polemical and apologetic character of Christian thought in his period. Niebuhr's theology was also, from today's perspective, very narrow in its relative lack of interest in other religions, except for Judaism. To be sure, Niebuhr was a Christian ecumenicist, as in his very affirmative reassessment of Catholicism near the end of his life after Vatican II; and he was also unusual among Christian thinkers of his period in his very strong sense of the significance of contemporary Judaism. However, he was relatively uninterested in, and uninformed about, Islam and the great Eastern traditions of Buddhism, Taoism, and Hinduism, much less the indigenous traditions of Africa or parts of the Americas. But this is really to say no more than that he was a person of his time.

Elisabeth Sifton, truly her father's daughter, directs a good deal of criticism in this book at the ignorance of many secular intellectuals regarding religion in general and Christianity, Judaism, and now Islam in particular. She is surely right. On the complexities in understanding religion, American secular intellectuals too often content themselves with recalling the memories of their youth, which are often unhappy ones. If they took the same lazy way with the arts, they would still be lingering over *The Nutcracker Suite* and *The Exorcist*. Secular intellectuals would do well to heed Sifton's sometimes rightly angry advice to learn more before they speak so easily on religion.

But there are also other targets of Sifton's ire, and sometimes she exhibits a narrowness of view that is surprising in the author of such a wise book. Some of her comments on her fellow Christians, especially Catholics and Evangelicals, are troubling. Her peremptory remarks about Catholic matters — on the Catholic theology of baptism, and on John Courtney Murray's relationship with the Vatican — are both inaccurate and unfortunate. Furthermore, in her excellent description of the work of Protestant liberals for social justice in the 1930s and 1940s, she completely ignores the even more influential role that the Catholic social justice tradition played for many Catholic leaders of labor unions, for many Catholic workers (often a majority in the northern cities), and even for many Catholic bishops of the period. This omission is even stranger when one remembers that the Catholic social justice tradition had a powerful influence on President Franklin D. Roosevelt's formulation of some of the policies of the New Deal, and that Niebuhr himself applauded Catholicism for its social wisdom even before Vatican II. On Evangelical Christians, Sifton is at times inappropriately dismissive. In my own view, some of the most important theological work being done in the United States today is taking place within Evangelical Christianity. Some leading Evangelical theologians are developing principles of moral and social action that are clearly influenced by Niebuhr, and others are forthrightly rethinking their Evangelical heritage in relationship to modern problems. Aside from these unfortunate lapses, Elizabeth Sifton's *The Serenity Prayer* stands as an exceptionally fine study of a crucial moment in American history and a central figure in that history who is worthy not only of being remembered but also of being imitated. And now (2019) American idealism and American realism seem not to know each other any longer. Reinhold Niebuhr, where are you now that we so need you?

CHAPTER 7

"ALL IS GRACE"

Karl Rahner, a Rooted Radical

Since Karl Rahner's death on March 30, 1984, many of us have been stunned by the recognition of how much we all owe him. Part of what stuns us is, of course, his extraordinary energy and output: more than four thousand articles and books on every conceivable subject, ranging from Chalcedon to the Beatles and the grace of everyday life. Then there is his influence. There are few Catholic theologians writing today anywhere in the world who do not bear Rahner's imprint. More recently, there are many Protestant theologians who have felt the same impact.

Yes, he was a major influence on Vatican II and on much of the best that has happened in the church since then. Indeed, Rahner was the most influential Catholic thinker since Newman. Even those who could never quite follow the labyrinthine sentences and complex Germanic abstractions of his thought sensed that something important was at stake here, something worthwhile, something that would last.

He was, everyone says, a "theologian's theologian." And so he was. Yet Karl Rahner was something more. His prose, which many affected to find so tortuous, had a power and attraction peculiar to itself. There is a restless, driven quality to a Rahner essay that forces the reader to think. He always seemed to begin with a rhetoric reminiscent of Cicero: all the questions he would not ask, could not ask, had no time now to ask, hoped to know enough someday to be able to ask properly. So many unanswered, perhaps unanswerable questions. Then, exit Cicero, and enter pure Rahner: the question he *would* ask.

That question inevitably turned out to be one of the central questions we all wanted to ask all along: What can we know? What can we hope for? Who are we? Who is this Jesus Christ? What does it mean to speak the word *mystery*? What is grace? Who is God? Through all these questions, the religious quest of Karl Rahner became imprinted on the Catholic landscape. And as his work progressed, a curious sea change took place. The "later" Rahner insisted he knew less than he thought he knew at the beginning. God's reality became more incomprehensible the more comprehensible our best thoughts about God became. And we became more and more incomprehensible to ourselves the more we learned of ourselves. Our once-clear answers dissolved into unnerving questions. The questions multiplied and intensified to render theology a religious quest worthy of a lifetime of effort.

In Karl Rahner, thinking was a religious experience. Through those questions and under the pressure of that quest, mysteries, problems, and doctrines yielded a suddenly felt sense of radical mystery: the mystery we are, finally, to ourselves, before one another, before history and the cosmos, and, above all, before God. In that context, Jesus Christ was the event of disclosure, the decisive manifestation of both God and ourselves. Yet reflection on the reality of Jesus Christ did not dissolve but intensified the sense of radical mystery. Before any too-easy answer could emerge, the paradoxes, the aporias, the questions returned; who, then, in the light of this radical mystery of Jesus Christ, are we? Who is God? What is real?

"All is grace," he insisted over and over again. In Rahner, this response, this powerful faith, was fully believable. For no serious reader could miss that here, for once, theology preached no cheap grace, no fatuous optimism. Optimism and pessimism, Rahner knew, are natural vices; hope is a theological virtue. The brooding Rahnerian prose, its undertone, at once mystical and strangely ironic, even melancholic, its refusal of any easy comprehensibility, the surprising bluntness of his occasional concrete advice, the ability to face what we call reality and still be able to think, the willingness to pose a fundamental question rather than add yet another answer to the cluttered list—all these peculiarly Rahnerian motifs conspired to make a struggling reader willing to suspend the usual disbelief and find plausible the startling thought, "All is grace."

Rahner knew Thomas Aquinas as well as the mainline Thomists did. He knew the old manuals so well that he exploded their once-overpowering influence forever. Karl Rahner knew and loved the classic doctrines of the tradition. But he also knew some other realities that most Catholic theologians of his youth had long since forgotten: Augustine, the mystics, the promise and threat of modernity, the difference between thinking and problem-solving, and the power of theological questioning as an existential quest.

There are only four or five thinkers in the rich tradition of Catholic theology of whom it can be said: After that work, nothing can be the same again. Karl Rahner was one of those few. He knew in his very bones that God is God and we are not. And knowing this, he knew how little we actually know. Rahner also knew how much we can understand if we would stop clinging to our pathetic certainties and our brittle answers. Then we might learn to think again, to let go into radical mystery, to yield to what Karl Rahner did not hesitate to name the radical skepticism of the Christian: the deepening knowledge that all is mystery, the unexpected trust that all is grace.

We were blessed to have had Karl Rahner among us. He was rooted in the Catholic tradition in all its plurality and power. He was as restless as the rest of us in the incredible twentieth century. Yet somehow Rahner found a religious-theological way that was honest, courageous, and believable: All is grace.

CHAPTER 8

PAUL TILLICH AND CONTEMPORARY THEOLOGY

The Method of Correlation

The impact of Paul Tillich's work in contemporary theology is the influence not of a school but of an inescapable presence. It is impossible to speak of Tillichians in the same way one can speak of Barthians, Bultmannians, Rahnerians, Whiteheadians, Balthasarians, or Lonerganians. Perhaps the fact that there is no Tillichian school determines the major reason for Tillich's remarkable staying power as a live influence in contemporary theology. There are, to be sure, theologians whose work bears profound and explicit resonances of a Tillichian influence, above all, James Luther Adams, Langdon Gilkey, Nathan Scott, and Robert Scharlemann. Yet even these theologians, however great their debt to Tillich's work, clearly form no school. Although their work often shows the most explicit indebtedness to Tillich in contemporary theology, still, each of these theologians remains individual, creative, and, finally, unclassifiable as strictly Tillichian.

Perhaps Tillich's success (not failure!) in *not* producing a "school" can now be recognized, as it deserves to be, as one of his most enduring legacies. In a discipline too often marred by the false security of "schools," Tillichian influence has endured as a continuing set of concerns, a general method of approach, and a welcome inability to become too easily classifiable. Indeed, Tillich's influence pervades contemporary theology as surely as the "man in a macintosh" pervades James Joyce's *Ulysses*: he always seems to show up, but no one seems quite able to name or locate him with exactness. Yet there he is, again and again, invading the confines of every school, aiding every revisionary program, and forcing his concerns (which turn out, in the end, to be *our own* in the contemporary situation), upon all willing to risk the unending need for continual theological revision.

The most obvious impact of Tillich's program upon contemporary theology remains, of course, his famous method of correlation (esp. Tillich 1951, 59–66). Since that method and the strife of interpretation that still rages around it are already treated extensively (Adams, Pauck, and Shinn 1985), I shall here confine my own comments to a few brief observations. First, Tillich's choice of the word *correlation* over alternative possibilities was both logically and methodologically a brilliant stroke. To insist that the theologian "correlate" the interpretations of *both* "situation" *and* "message" into an ever-revisable, contemporary theological position puts exactly the right methodological demand upon every theologian. For however tempted by one's other religious convictions and theological commitments an individual theologian may be, the broad category of "correlation" implies that no one may simply assume an "identity," a "radical similarity," a "series of analogies," a radical "nonidentity," or only confrontation between the meanings in both situation and message. *Every* theologian should *start* her inquiry with the assumption only of *some* correlation between the fundamental questions and concerns of each "pole" of theological inquiry. In sum: any particular instance of "correlation" may prove to be only a single possibility on the fuller logical spectrum from radical identity through similarity to radical nonidentity.

The Tillichian insistence on a method of correlation reminds us that a particular case is always to be decided only on the basis of the particular subject matter under inquiry. We may believe that a radical nonidentity between message and situation prevails. Yet we cannot make that assumption prior to the hard effort of determining the actual correlation. Even Barthians ultimately correlate — if usually through a *Nein* to the situation. Even left-wing Hegelians among some political and liberation theologians correlate — if often through a just and much-needed exposure of a confrontational, radical nonidentity of reason, or the prophetic biblical message to the societal distortions in the present situation. Even "liberal" theologians of culture who lack Tillich's own dialectical sense for the presence of negations correlate — if usually through a too-sanguine assumption of the identity or radical similarity between the "highest values" of Christianity and the reigning liberal culture (Harnack). All theologians, whether consciously or unconsciously, employ some method of correlation. Since Tillich's work, all are better able to recognize that this matter of fact implies a matter of methodological principle: the need to formulate explicitly and employ critically a theological method of correlation.

Since the work of Hans-Georg Gadamer on interpretation, it has become still clearer that insofar as every authentic interpretation of any classic (including the religious classics of the theological tradition) involves application to the contemporary situation, every theological interpretation logically involves an implicit correlation of message and situation. At Gadamer's ineluctable insistence, every authentic interpretation will be a *new* interpretation (Gadamer 1975). In fact, there is no alternative to a correlating interpretation, save routinized repetition (in the manner of some naively anticorrelational models of "orthodox" fundamentalist theologies). In the present concern with hermeneutical theory, the enduring value of Tillich's insistence upon a method of correlation can be indicated by a few brief contrasts. Prior to the actual development of the technical resources of the post-Romantic hermeneutical theories of Gadamer (1975) and Ricoeur (1976),[1] Tillich's method of correlation already spoke to the need for every theological interpretation to include a moment of *application* to the situation and thereby prove to be a *new* interpretation. Moreover, Tillich formulated his method of correlation (and thereby, I suggest, his method of theological interpretation) in such manner that he avoided three crucial difficulties otherwise prevalent in theological methods.

First, Tillich did not formulate his developed position (in *Systematic Theology*) in the then-prevalent terms of the Romantic hermeneutical tradition from Schleiermacher through Dilthey: empathy, divinization, and reconstruction of

---

1. For the development from "Romantic" hermeneutics to Gadamer, see Palmer 1969.

the "mind of the author" or the social-cultural life-setting of the work. Second, Tillich did not allow what Gadamer has labeled "methodologism" to take over in formulating his theological method of correlation. Tillich's method is always an aid for interpretation (of an interpreted message and situation and their interpreted correlation), never a mechanical replacement of interpretation by method. Third, the "truth" of any particular theological interpretation of any particular symbol in the tradition with an emerging fundamental question in the present situation, or any hermeneutical correlation between the two (e.g., identity, similarity, analogy, nonidentity), is, in principle, always determined by the subject matter itself (the fundamental questions and responses in the symbols of both situation and message). Here is a method that renders explicit a matter-of-fact need for interpretation rendered as a need for some kind of application as correlation. Here is a method, as Gadamer might add, that does not sacrifice "truth" for "method."[2] Rather, the method of correlation formulates a very flexible method as a general guide for interpretive theological inquiry into particular questions and symbols demanding interpretation and application as correlation.

On more intra-theological grounds, moreover, Tillich's method of correlation deserves the explicit, and more often implicit, victory it has gained in much contemporary theology. Once again, a brief series of contrasts may serve to warrant this judgment. First, the method of correlation yields a post-neo-Orthodox, "dogmatic" theology. Indeed, the "correlation," as I suggested above, highlights the fact that every theology, as interpretation, involves application to the situation (hence "correlation"). Second, the ahistorical and ahermeneutical claims of traditionalist theologies are exposed in a stroke. On their own terms, fundamentalist, dogmatist (not dogmatic), and traditionalist (not traditional) theologies are mere repetitions of earlier theological (usually creedal) formulations. Thereby, such traditionalist theologies are not hermeneutical reflections on the tradition at all. When successful (against their own ahistorical and ahermeneutical claims), these theologies become no longer simple repetitions of earlier theologies but new interpretations of them. Thereby they become subject to the same rules of interpretation of both "message" and "situation" (alternatively of the contemporary "application" of the tradition to the contemporary situation).

---

2. The charge is often made by Gadamer against "methodologisms." Indeed, the title of Gadamer's famous work could just as well have been *Truth or Method*.

The neoconservative resurgence in both culture and church suggests that Tillich's method could once again prove liberating to all those frustrated by the ahistorical and ahermeneutical claims of the neoconservative crusaders. For the fact remains that insofar as theologians move past mere repetition into the risk of interpretation, they are attempting to apply the tradition to the situation — attempting, in sum, to correlate the fundamental religious questions and responses of both situation and message. Tillich's method of correlation, on these grounds alone, may be recognized for what it is: a way of rendering explicit the implicit, matter-of-fact, hermeneutical character of all theology.

Moreover, Tillich's actual employment of his method of correlation throughout his *Systematic Theology* suggests that, on intra-theological terms, he was fundamentally successful in formulating a theological position beyond the earlier confines of either liberalism or neo-Orthodoxy (see especially the prefaces to Tillich 1951 and 1957). Once again, the key may be found in Tillich's choice of the word *correlation*: a concept, to repeat, that allows for the full spectrum of logical possibilities, from identity through similarity and analogy to radical nonidentity. The "liberal" theologian is ordinarily concerned with whatever "identities" may obtain between message and situation, or, at the very least, with radical similarities between them — similarities and even a few identities can actually be discerned in both message and situation. The confrontations, the nonidentities, also always present tend to be obscured in liberal theologies, either notoriously, as in much of the Ritschlian tradition, or less obviously but no less fatally, as in many too-benign "theologies of culture." Neo-Orthodox theologies (which, as Wilhelm Pauck has observed, are in fact *not* traditional Orthodox theologies but modern, self-critical, liberal theologies) tend to emphasize the stark nonidentities between the full message and our present distorted, personal, political, social, or historical situation. The latter spectrum can range from an emphasis upon the distortions in the self exposed by the confrontation with the "kerygmatic word" (e.g., Rudolf Bultmann, in Tillich 1957), to the distortions in society, history, and culture exposed by the liberating message of Christian eschatology (e.g., Tillich 1963).[3]

What is striking about Tillich's formulation of the method of correlation and, above all, about his wide-ranging and striking use of that method, includ-

---

3. See also contemporary political theologians ranging from James Luther Adams through Jürgen Moltmann, Johann Baptist Metz, Dorothee Sölle, and the liberation theologians of the Third World or oppressed groups in the so-called First World.

ing in his earlier political theology in Germany, is that one cannot predict before the actual investigation of a particular subject matter what kind of correlation will be demanded by the subject matter itself. Sometimes, as in Tillich's interpretation of some modern works of art, the correlation discloses unexpected analogies. Even there, however, Tillich ordinarily chose works to analyze (like Picasso's *Guernica* or works by his beloved German expressionists) that show the presence of the negative *in* and sometimes *as* the very analogy (Lateran IV). Tillich's sensibility was almost always for art expressive in the style of contemporary existential estrangement. The works of "finitude" (a Raphael, a Renoir) he tended to note but rarely to study. At other times, a genuine (for Tillich, a dialectical) *confrontation* was the major form of "correlation." It might be a confrontation of contemporary estrangement through the New Being disclosed in the New Testament "picture" of Jesus the Christ (Tillich 1957, 118–38);[4] or it might be a confrontation of the Christian tradition itself as too unmindful of the profound negativities in its own history and its classic portrayals of humankind's actual state, as disclosed in the symbols of the Fall and the cross by a correlation with the self-illusions revealed by contemporary psychoanalysis and the distortions of the self exposed by existentialist thought (the "good luck" of Christian theology) (Tillich 1957, 27–28); or the structural, economic, and social distortions in society revealed by contemporary, socialist, "utopian" demands in the biblical eschatological symbols (Tillich 1977).

Such theological examples (which could be easily multiplied) may serve to warrant my earlier, methodologically formulated conviction: Tillich's method of correlation, in his actual pluralistic usage as distinct from some of his formulations (see below), allows for the full spectrum of logical possibilities from identity through similarity-analogy to radical confrontation. A Tillichian method of correlation really guides — but never determines — the results of any study of a particular theological issue. A logical possibility becomes an actuality only after the concrete study itself. The subject matter and the questions it evokes — and these alone — determine the final results. For, logically, the concept of correlation can allow for any one of the following possibilities: identity, similarity, analogy, confrontation, or polarity. And the method of corre-

---

4. Despite its well-known difficulties (*analogia imaginis*, etc.), Tillich's Christology, by its basic stand for the "picture" of Jesus in the New Testament, instead of the more familiar, historically reconstructed "historical Jesus," deserves restudy among contemporary hermeneutical and literary critical theologians. For a discussion of these issues in contemporary Christology, see Tracy 1980 (chaps. 6 and 7).

lation, substantively, as Tillich actually employed it, can sometimes produce a liberal insistence upon identity (rare) or radical similarity (common). The same method at other times produces a dialectical insistence on radical confrontation.

The method's fidelity to the actual demands of inquiry and interpretation (in other words, its fidelity to the demands of the particular subject matter under investigation) is its pluralistic strength. Tillich's own pluralistic use of the method and the distinct usages of later theologians demonstrate the enduring vitality of an approach that need not become a school, a method that need not yield to methodologism, a hermeneutical position that exposes the fundamentalist naïveté of fundamentalist theologies, a postliberal and post-neo-Orthodox position that allows the enduring hermeneutical achievements of both liberal and neo-Orthodox theologies to live a hermeneutically transforming existence ever anew. The range of logical possibilities allowed by the method of correlation is wide indeed. Yet the singular possibility relevant to a particular question only becomes an actuality after the hermeneutical study itself.

A final critical word on Tillich's method of correlation demands attention, however, before we shift our focus to less methodological and more substantive theological concerns. Since I have argued the point at length elsewhere (Tracy [1975] 1995), here I shall state my criticism more briefly and perhaps more pointedly. Any Tillich scholar will already have noted that in some of my earlier formulations of the method of correlation, I presumed to revise Tillich's own more usual formulation. The issue here is this: Is the final moment of correlation to be a correlation of the "questions" from the situation and the "answers" from the message (i.e., Tillich's usual formulation: *inter alia*, Tillich 1951, 62–64)? Or is a better formulation of the intent of the method (which, indeed, Tillich himself frequently employed) the one suggested above: namely, a correlation of the questions and answers of the situation and the questions and answers of the tradition?

Tillich's own more typical use of the method, as Langdon Gilkey argued, is more faithful to the reformulation suggested above than to his own accustomed formulation. The fact is that Tillich did at times rightly allow psychoanalysis, social theory, existentialism, and his own "self-transcending" naturalism to provide answers, not only questions, in his theology. Tillich's own brilliantly dialectical use of his method, as Robert Scharlemann (1969) has decisively shown it to be, demonstrates that his nondialectical formulation of "questions" from the situation and "answers" from the message is not adequate to his own dialectical uses of his method (see also Adams 1965; and Pauck and Pauck 1976, vol. 1). For example, Tillich's explicit refusal to allow "experience" to be a "source" for theology, while "culture" is allowed that position (Tillich 1951, 34–46), is confusing and perhaps confused. In sum: the method of correlation is better formulated, in justice to Tillich's own nuanced and subtle uses, not as Tillich formulated it but as he actually employed it: namely, as an interpretive correlation of the questions and answers of the message with the questions and answers of the situation.

This interpretation of Tillich's method is, I believe, not only more faithful to his own more usual use of the method, but also more in keeping with the hermeneutical character of contemporary theology. What Tillich has given us all is a general, guiding theological method that expresses in explicit terms the hermeneutical character of all contemporary theology. Each theologian, after all, must interpret the fundamental religious questions of the classics of the Christian tradition. In thus interpreting the tradition itself, each theologian also attempts to apply those questions and those responses to the contemporary situation. Thus does the tradition live as *traditio*, not as mere *tradita*. Thus does theology's own fidelity to its critically reflective task live in ever-revised forms. Thus does *applicatio* demand an interpretation of the questions and responses of the situation and, thereby, in that very application, some appropriate form of correlation (identity, similarity, analogy, confrontation, polarity) between the fundamental questions and the basic answers of both the tradition and the situation.

In this sense, the influence of Tillich's method of correlation seems widespread in contemporary theology. In a recent symposium, for example, both Edward Schillebeeckx and Hans Küng (explicitly not Tillichians) attempted to formulate a new consensus for contemporary "Catholic and ecumenical" theology (Küng and Schillebeeckx 1980). Their formulations are remarkably resonant with Tillich's earlier formulations: the task of the theologian is the attempt to provide "mutually critical correlations" between the tradition and contemporary experience. The words are the words of Edward Schillebeeckx; but the voice, like the voice of many theologians in our period, is the voice of Paul Tillich. By not founding *a* school, Tillich entered *all* schools. By formulating a method faithful to the theologian's task, a method genuinely guiding theology but never determining its results, Tillich aided *every* theologian. By insisting that the fundamental questions with which theology must deal are always the fundamental questions of the meaning and truth of our existence as human beings in the presence of the mystery of existence itself, Tillich listened to and still speaks to every questioning human being. His presence persists in contemporary thought because Tillich asked those fundamental questions that make a worthwhile existence authentically human. He asked those questions with the seriousness and the rigor they demand.

TILLICH'S QUESTIONS AND CONTEMPORARY THEOLOGY

Theology, as everyone knows, is too important to be left to the theologians. Theology presumes to ask certain fundamental questions incumbent upon every thinking being—questions of the meaning and truth of human existence in relationship to itself, to others, to society, politics, history, nature, and the encompassing whole. Some Russian Orthodox writers and theologians even name these fundamental questions the unavoidable, "accursed" questions of human existence. Many theologians may content themselves with other important but more narrow questions like those concerning church order. However, Paul Tillich recognized that fundamental questions and these alone are the religious-theological questions that grasp and are grasped by an "ultimate concern." He found himself most at home with those artists, philosophers, theologians, and political and cultural critics who risked asking those perennial questions in a time of broken, distorted, fragmented self, society, culture, and history. Tillich found himself most at home with the neo-Orthodox theologians' bracing rediscovery of the jarring, defamiliarizing, shattering power of the "kerygmatic" word in an age when what E. M. Forster mischievously named "poor, chatty, little Christianity" was in danger of becoming a nervous, well-meaning, but rather garrulous sentimentalist. And yet Paul Tillich was not at home with many of the "answers" his fellow rediscoverers of the power of the Word actually provided. Tillich discerned—and surely here he was correct—that the Word in our day forced upon our consciousness as many questions as answers, indeed, often questions *as* answers.

The answers forged for other situations—the *imago dei* for the patristic period; a cry for architectonic order in Aquinas, Calvin, and Melanchthon; a sense of profound need for forgiveness in Luther; a sense of the overwhelming, overflowing power of nature in Schelling (Tillich's major philosophical influence)—became, in Tillich's hands, a rediscovery of the fundamental questions lurking in each of those classic responses: finitude; estrangement; the clash of merely technical with properly ontological reason; a mystical, questioning sense of the whole. Paul Tillich could not in honesty write a *Church Dogmatics*. But Tillich could and did write a *Systematic Theology*: a theology structured by the method of correlation, ordered by the drive to the concrete from the necessary abstractions of essence (volume 1) through "existence" (volume 2) to the concrete actuality of "life" (volume 3); a theology empowered by the fundamental questions embedded in all the classic symbols of Christianity. As a series of answers, Tillich's systematics seem more what Whitehead called an assemblage than a system. Tillich's *Systematic Theology* is more comparable to the unsteady *Sentences* of Peter Lombard than to the architectonic whole of Aquinas's *Summae* or Schleiermacher's *Glaubenslehre*. Tillich's *Systematic Theology* is more faithful to the existential richness and partial order of the works of the Lutheran Tillich's true mentors—Martin Luther, Søren Kierkegaard, and Friedrich Schelling—than to the ordered and ordering patterns of Calvin, Schleiermacher, or Hegel.

Tillich's three-volume *Systematics* is a major, modern theological achievement. However, if one reads only Tillich's *Systematic Theology*, one may miss the liberating and defamiliarizing disorder lurking in those highly ordered volumes. Tillich's ontological language—at once analogical, symbolic, and dialectical—yields no single, final, second-order language for theology. Indeed, Tillich's other works—his brilliant essays on art, socialist politics, psychoanalysis, nature, and sacrament; his daring use of the concepts *Kairos* and the daimonic; his sermons and purely occasional pieces—all often reveal more powerfully than *Systematic Theology* the strength and accuracy of his insight and his authentic questioning of existence by means of Christian symbols.

The same phenomenon is true of Paul Tillich's most natural Catholic counterpart, Karl Rahner. Rahner's systematics volume *Foundations of Christian Faith* is a fine achievement, but Rahner's multiple essays on every imaginable theological topic are his best. The Christian pluralism so majestic in the entire Christian tradition should inform and transform the practice of contemporary Christian theologians. Who does not admit the need for responsible theologians to study Gregory of Nyssa and Augustine, Thomas Aquinas and Bonaventure, Martin Luther and John Calvin, François Fénelon and Blaise Pascal, Friedrich Schleiermacher and Georg Wilhelm Friedrich Hegel, Vladimir Lossky, and Sergei Nikolaevich Bulgakov? Why then the strange and all-too-often disturbingly ideological contemporary refusal of too many theologians to read Karl Barth and Paul Tillich, Hans Urs von Balthasar and Karl Rahner?

Christian theological pluralism does not cease in contemporary Christian theology. Of course each theologian has her critical preferences. And yet how can a serious Rahnerian not also learn from the erudite, aesthetic, theological genius of Hans Urs von Balthasar—and vice versa? How can a Tillichian not delight, however critically, in the sheer brilliance of the *Church Dogmatics* of Karl Barth? While of course each theologian must make critical decisions on every work of theology and on his own personally chosen direction, a theological pluralistic sensibility allied to a full hermeneutical sense (i.e., hermeneutics of retrieval, critique, and suspicion) is an appropriate theological virtue.

There is no reason to disparage Tillich's great achievement in *Systematic Theology*. Yet there is need to rediscover that the major legacy of his entire work there and elsewhere is his stunning ability to ask those hard, fundamental questions of ultimate concern; his acute sensibility at naming a *Kairos*, as well as the actuality of the daimonic in contemporary history; the necessity of attempting some rough order while facing the urgency and reality of the chaos in the self, society, history, and nature.

For both Tillich and Dostoevsky, the contemporary situation forces accursed questions upon the consciousness of every human being—for Tillich, the question of nonbeing, of possible meaninglessness and absurdity in existence itself (Tillich 1951, 188–99). Asking these questions frees the defamiliarizing, liberating classic responses of the Christian symbols to become retrievable responses once again (see also Tillich 1952). In some cases, for Tillich, these classic responses intensify the questions themselves. In all cases, those responses become genuine responses to authentic questions of human beings attempting to live worthwhile lives in an age of distortion, fragmentation, and, all too often, despair. In all cases, Tillich's questions of ultimate concern force the question of whether an honest, believable faith is possible in a nihilistic age, and whether an honest doubt, as an element in that very faith, is a positive element in the conscience of a contemporary Christian. Above all, Tillich's theology may teach any thinking person to ask those fundamental questions again, and to understand the classic symbols of Christianity for what they are: classic, hermeneutically retrievable responses to all questions of ultimate concern.

In our own post-Tillich situation, his favored questions are not necessarily ours. For many contemporary theologians, for example, the fundamental question of massive global suffering and oppression outweighs the Enlightenment questions of "reason and revelation" in a historically conscious age, as well as the early twentieth-century existentialist questions of absurdity, meaninglessness, and the alienation of the solitary human being in a mechanized age. There is little doubt that in *Systematic Theology* (or at least in the first two volumes) the existentialist question of authentic existence predominates. Like so many of the other classics of that period — Camus's *Stranger*; Eliot's *Waste Land*; Yeats's "widening gyre" in "The Second Coming"; Sartre's *No Exit*; Giacometti's emaciated, evocative sculptures; Hemingway's code of grace under pressure; Ortega's revolt of the masses; and Tillich's own German expressionists — Tillich's work (especially his essays on modern art and psychoanalysis, as well as the first two volumes of *Systematic Theology*) stands as a major candidate for a classic theological expression of existentialist modernity.

Even as the major attention of many contemporary theologians has shifted from questions of the solitary individual's sense of alienation and terror at possible meaninglessness to further questions concerning the global reality of a technological world that affects all communities and traditions, to the sense of the interconnectedness of all in a situation of massive global suffering and sinful social traditions and economic systems, it would still be foolish to dismiss Tillich's writings and other classics of that earlier existentialism as merely "personalist," much less as possessively "individualist." Rather, we honor these existentialist classics best as we honor all classic expressions of the human spirit: by attempting to reformulate their questions — their fundamental questions of ultimate concern — in our later, different situation. Paul Tillich honored many questions, both relativizing them and retrieving them: the questions of finitude and mortality from the patristic period; the question of radical fallenness and the need for forgiveness in Luther; the pointed questions of Enlightenment reason and revelation in Kant and liberal and modernist theologians; and the question of the depths of ontological reason in Schelling and Heidegger. Theologians of the present surely can continue to honor Tillich's existentialist questions of alienation, absurdity, and meaninglessness, even as we relativize and retrieve them for our post-existentialist situation.

For our own situation has become post-existentialist not because we have adequately answered those existentialist questions (we have not), much less because any thinker has now finally become an "authentic individual" in Kierkegaard's, Nietzsche's, or Tillich's demanding sense. Rather, the only real post-existentialist move forward has been the recognition that one cannot and should not become an individualist, an alienated, solitary self isolated from all the others — isolated, above all, from the oppressed who were privileged by the prophets and by Jesus — all those oppressed and marginalized persons and whole communities, too often ignored by official Christendom, and just as often scorned by the secular *scorners* of Christendom, who seemed unable to notice the colonialism grounding their Enlightenment. Political, liberationist, and feminist theologians continue Tillich's project, which included a political theology in his early German period, climaxing in his courageous, fierce criticism of the Nazi ideology, which resulted in his academic disgrace and exile. Of course contemporary theologians, especially political, liberationist, and feminist theologians, will critically revise the theological conversations of Tillich and his existentialist contemporaries, just as Tillich did not hesitate to revise quite critically the conversations of his liberal and dialectical predecessors.[5]

Although Tillich is best known for his "existentialist" theology, it is remarkable how diverse his posings of the fundamental questions in fact were. In his American period (and, therefore, in his *Systematic Theology*) Tillich's main concern was with the distortion in the individual self disclosed by existentialism, psychoanalysis, and classical Reformation theology (especially his own Lutheran heritage). The result is clear: Tillich's American period did disclose a relatively apolitical, personalist, existentialist thrust that differed from his earlier, German political and Schellingian philosophical theology.

The recent resurgence of interest in these earlier political (indeed Christian socialist) aspects of Tillich's work, it seems to me, is a very positive phenomenon. Not that Tillich's own inevitably dated solutions can be ours. Rather, his early work in political theology and the courage of his unyielding attack on Nazism show how every political theology that is a *genuine* theology must ask its political questions *as* fundamental theological questions.

In the contemporary theological situation, therefore, some of the earlier "political" aspects of Tillich's work (along with several social-political, theological aspects of volume 3 of *Systematic Theology*) demand further study: not, to be sure, as a proposed solution to our present questions, but as a retrievable example of how those questions can be posed theologically. Indeed, what most

---

5. Tillich's (1963) actual interpretation of the eschatological symbols differs notably, of course, from the contemporary retrieval by political and liberation theologians of the political import of biblical eschatology. Still, Tillich's interpretation of eschatology, for all its inadequacies by present exegetical and theological standards, did not allow eschatology to become purely vertical (Barth) or purely personalist-existentialist (Bultmann). Tillich's earlier interest in utopian symbols, in fact, shows some resonance with the influential work of Ernst Bloch on the political theologians and with Paul Ricoeur's reflections on ideology and utopia.

strikes a reader of Tillich is how single-mindedly theological his questioning remained throughout his many-faceted theological career, yet how diverse, and finally how radically pluralistic, his actual questions were.

CONCLUSION: TILLICH AND RADICAL PLURALISM

In our own situation, a distinctive note is the failure of any one situational fundamental question to command attention at all. Whether one interprets this situation in the European fashion as a conflict of interpretations (Paul Ricoeur) or in the Anglo-American mode as a dialogical pluralism of questions, responses, and traditions (William James) is a relatively minor point. What a contemporary analyst needs to note, above all, is that no single fundamental question (not even the fundamental question of meaninglessness of Tillich and his existentialist contemporaries) now dominates. Rather, we seem caught in a situation where all questions, often all at once, force themselves upon the attention of every theologian.

For some theologians, this seems to occasion the inability to ask *any* fundamental question at all. The question of meaningfulness can itself become meaningless as thinkers retreat to more manageable questions: manageable in terms of what Tillich and his onetime student Theodor Adorno aptly named "merely technical reason," with its revolt against all ontological or religious concerns. For other thinkers, this radically pluralistic situation occasions an unnerving sense of the uncanny, which releases a myriad of fundamental questions.[6] Here, Tillich remains a dependable guide. It is, in fact, striking how pluralistic Tillich's own work is, both in its questions and its answers. Despite the later dominance of the fundamental question of meaninglessness in an estranged world and its brilliant evocation of a possible response in the form of a New Being in Tillich's most famous later works, there is present throughout his work a constantly shifting analysis of the fundamental questions of ultimate concern in contemporary culture and in the symbols of classic biblical and traditional theologies.

---

6. I have tried to analyze this radical pluralism of fundamental questions within a horizon of the "uncanny" (Tracy 1980, chap. 8).

For example, Tillich's formulation of the question of "reason and revelation" (Tillich 1951, 71–105) shares both an Enlightenment concern for reason and a liberal theological concern for historical consciousness. Yet his formulation also shares the concerns of the Frankfurt school with the "dialectic of Enlightenment" reason, as one notes in Adorno and Horkheimer's devastating analysis of modern, exclusively "technical reason" (Adorno and Horkheimer 1971).[7] Like Adorno and Horkheimer, Tillich is concerned with forging concepts that, by incorporating the negative, are not reducible to mere categories. Like them, he insists upon the need for a negative dialectical moment — for him, theologically, as the Protestant Principle; for them, in a "post-theological" fashion, as the ancient Jewish refusal to name God or to provide an image for a future paradise. Unlike Adorno and Horkheimer, Tillich's retrieval of the possibility of a "theonomous" reason in the classic symbols of revelation and in the classic traditions of ontology frees dialectical language from both the overriding and impossible self-confidence of Hegel and the despairing critique of the solely negative dialectic of Adorno.

His early dialectics — theological, philosophical, and political — freed Tillich to incorporate the questions and concerns that other "dialectical theologians" found foreign to their single-minded concentration on the defamiliarizing, negative, purely vertical dialectic of the "kerygmatic" Word. For Tillich, the dialectic of the Word really did free one *from* the world and, by that negative freedom, freed one *for* the world. This freedom is a theological freedom for reason in its fully ontological, not merely ontic, sense;[8] for dialectically participatory symbols, not only dialectically negating signs;[9] for nature and its nonverbal manifesting powers, not only history illumined by the dialectical word (Tillich 1948); for Catholic substance and Protestant principle (Tillich 1963, 245).[10] Indeed, in his final extraordinary lecture, "The Significance of the History of Religions for the Systematic Theologian," Tillich expanded his concerns still further to suggest the need for a radical rethinking of his own and other

---

7. Note also that Tillich had direct connections with the Frankfurt thinkers, including his somewhat mysterious role as director of Adorno's thesis on Kierkegaard.

8. One of Tillich's major contributions to the theology of his period was his keeping alive the ontological concern in the ontic revolt against all ontology of the existentialist theologians.

9. For some formulations of this justly famous Tillichian distinction, see Tillich 1951, 235–41, and Tillich 1963, 111–29.

10. See also O'Meara in Adams, Pauck, and Shinn 1985, chap. 16.

Christian systematic theologies in the context of the world religions (Tillich 1966, 80–84).

A theological position that can incorporate such pluralistic concerns[11] without easy compromise and that can dialectically relate these questions into an ever-revised, onto-theological language, while never allowing the easy exit of eclecticism, should command universal theological respect. What is notable in Tillich's work is that the "and" in his famous polarities (reason and revelation, situation and message, Being and God, word and sacrament, nature and history, Catholic substance and Protestant Principle, Christianity and other religions, the existential and the political, the utopian and the eschatological, faith and doubt) is never an easily juxtaposed "and." The latter too-easy "and," so beloved by professional moderates in theology (e.g., A. Dulles), was well exposed in its timid and tedious eclecticism by the full force of the negative dialectics wielded by Tillich and the other theologians of the Word. Tillich knew that a theologian can never simply assent to any easy "and." Rather, each theologian must *earn* the right to affirm it.

With the intrinsically dialectical character of Tillich's own use of his method of correlation, with his retrieval of the dialectical and the participating power in the classic symbols, with his honest refusal to move forward into a new concern (psychoanalysis, "the Catholic substance," the "other religions") until the genuine Otherness of that "other" actuality was dialectically related through a tensive "and" to his own grounded religious core (the Protestant Principle),[12] Tillich earned the right to his theological "ands."

The welcome renaissance of interest in Tillich's work, I suspect, is not principally occasioned by a belief in his particular answers to our later and often different questions. Rather, that renaissance is occasioned by the belief that the mode of inquiry that Tillich brought to bear upon his ever-changing historical situation is what most needs retrieval today. That kind of theological inquiry, as I have tried to suggest in these reflections, is characterized above all by a fidelity to the kinds of questions of ultimate concern that the theologian must ask in every situation, by an honest sense that every answer is at best relatively adequate, that every question and response need constant revision as the question and the classic resources come more and more clearly into view, and that a radi-

---

11. For some good studies, see O'Meara and Weisser 1964.
12. See the insightful essay by Adams (1968, 304–34).

cal pluralism of both questions and responses is our actuality, while an earned, dialecticaly inflected, analogical "and" should be our ideal.[13]

Tillich achieved something more important than giving correct answers. He taught his contemporaries anew, as he can still teach any careful reader, how to ask a religious-theological question today. Paul Tillich did something more enduring than found a school; he set an example of how non-ultimate all our responses to the ultimate concerns in our fundamental questions are. Tillich teaches the most important lesson any contemporary theologian needs each day to relearn: what it means in the contemporary situation really to believe, and to think, and to act in the gifted clearing of that dialectically participatory, defamiliarizing "and."

REFERENCES

Adams, James Luther. 1965. *Paul Tillich's Philosophy of Culture, Science, and Religion.* New York: Harper and Row.

———. 1968. "Paul Tillich on Luther." In *Interpreters of Luther: Essays in Honor of Wilhelm Pauck*, edited by Jaroslav Pelikan. Philadelphia: Fortress Press.

Adams, James Luther, Wilhelm Pauck, and Roger Lincoln Shinn, eds. 1985. *The Thought of Paul Tillich.* San Francisco: HarperCollins.

Adorno, Theodor, and Max Horkheimer. 1971. *Dialectic of Enlightenment.* New York: Seabury Press.

Gadamer, Hans-Georg. 1975. *Truth and Method.* New York: Seabury Press.

Küng, Hans, and Edward Schillebeeckx. 1980. "Dialogue: The Way toward Consensus." In *Consensus in Theology? A Dialogue with Hans Küng and Edward Schillebeeckx*, edited by Leonard Swidler. Philadelphia: Westminster Press.

Lamb, Matthew. 1976. "Theory and Praxis in Contemporary Theology." In *Proceed-*

---

13. I have tried to study the relationships of these two classic theological languages in Tillich and other theologians in Tracy 1980, chap. 9. A major reason for Tillich's influence among theologians is the remarkable way in which his second-order, analogical-symbolic-ontological language always includes a negative dialectical moment, as well as the fact that his dialectical language always implies (e.g., through his emphasis on "participation" and his insistence on the need for a *"reunion* of the separated") an analogical-symbolic result. Karl Barth famously complained that Catholic theology was too saturated by both/and (e.g., revelation and reason). Barth, as was so often the case, was correct in his description but quite wrong in his too-hasty judgment. The later volumes of Barth's dogmatics, in fact, lean toward a dialectically informed both/and position.

ings of the Catholic Theological Society of America. Yonkers, NY: Catholic Theological Society of America.

O'Meara, Thomas, and Celestin Weisser, eds. 1964. *Paul Tillich and Catholic Thought.* Dubuque, IA: Priority Press.

Palmer, Richard. 1969. *Hermeneutics: Schleiermacher, Dilthey, Heidegger, Gadamer.* Evanston, IL: Northwestern University Press.

Pauck, Marion, and Wilhelm Pauck. 1976. *Paul Tillich: His Life and Thought.* Vol. 1. *Life.* New York: Harper and Row.

Ricoeur, Paul. 1976. *Interpretation Theory.* Fort Worth: Texas Christian University Press.

Scharlemann, Robert. 1969. *Reflection and Doubt in the Thought of Paul Tillich.* New Haven, CT: Yale University Press.

Tillich, Paul. 1948. "Nature and Sacrament." In *The Protestant Era*, translated by James Luther Adams. Chicago: University of Chicago Press.

———. 1951. *Systematic Theology.* Vol. 1. Chicago: University of Chicago Press.

———. 1952. *The Courage to Be.* New Haven, CT: Yale University Press.

———. 1957. *Systematic Theology.* Vol. 2. Chicago: University of Chicago Press.

———. 1963. *Systematic Theology.* Vol. 3. Chicago: University of Chicago Press.

———. 1966. *The Future of Religions.* Edited by Jerald Brauer. Chicago: University of Chicago Press.

———. 1977. *The Socialist Decision.* New York: Harper and Row.

Tracy, David. (1975) 1995. *Blessed Rage for Order: The New Pluralism in Theology.* Chicago: University of Chicago Press.

———. 1980. *The Analogical Imagination: Christian Theology and the Culture of Pluralism.* New York: Seabury Press.

CHAPTER 9

BERNARD LONERGAN AND THE RETURN OF ANCIENT PRACTICE IN PHILOSOPHY AND THEOLOGY

In this essay, I hope the reader will join me in a thought experiment. One reason for calling any hypothesis a thought experiment is, of course, that it is not verified (although thought experiments are verifiable). The other reason for the name, however, may also be important: a thought experiment is a hypothesis worthy of serious consideration because, if fully accurate, the hypothesis illuminates some genuine puzzles. Even if ultimately not true, the hypothesis suggests some questions and possibilities worthy of further development, refinement, and correction.

The major hypothesis in the present thought experiment is this: the time may be ripe for a second reception of the work of Bernard Lonergan. The first reception proved, in Lonergan's own lifetime, enormously fruitful: on the one hand, an emancipation (especially but not solely in Catholic theology and philosophy) of theological method from the increasing dead weight of Neo-Scholasticism. The Lonerganian emancipation, moreover, persuasively helped Catholic thinkers avoid the temptations of empiricism and idealism, of relativism and historicism: temptations that all-too-successfully awaited many a former Neo-Scholastic after the deluge. That first reception was exceptional in its fruits: witness the annual Lonergan Workshops and their publication; witness the many dissertations written every year on some aspect of Lonergan's work; witness the publication of Lonergan's complete work by the University of Toronto Press; witness the development, refinement, and sometimes corrections of Lonergan's positions on particular issues by so many excellent Lonergan scholars and thinkers. Even the corrections, after all, take place within the basic context of the invariant, self-structuring structure of consciousness and, thereby, of Lonergan's entirely original notion of "method." To read the annual papers of the Lonergan Workshop or keep informed by the many articles and books on Lonergan yearly (as the latter are reported in the valuable and informative *Lonergan Studies Newsletter*) is to observe how strong the legacy of Lonergan, based on his still astonishing personal intellectual achievement, continues to be. The first reception of Lonergan, in sum, is alive and well — indeed, flourishing.

And yet, at least to a relative outsider to this ongoing tradition of Lonergan scholarship like myself, something like a "second reception" of Lonergan's work by other than Lonergan scholars, specialists, and thinkers is perhaps necessary. Moreover, I believe that such a second reception is eminently possible in our present moment of philosophical and theological history. Although I have elsewhere defended the notion that our contemporary cultural time is better described as postmodern rather than as either modern or even late modern, I will not enter here into that highly contested debate. I will, however, recall that much of Lonergan's work is concerned with the challenges posed by modernity, from the scientific revolution through the modern turn to the subject and the rise of modern historical consciousness.[1] This is especially the case in *Insight* (1957), on modern science and cognitional theory, and in *Method in Theology* (1972), in the many sections on historical consciousness. This is also the case with many of Lonergan's essays on secularity, on the move from classical

---

1. See the many essays by Lonergan on these themes in the invaluable volumes of his essays in *Collected Works of Bernard Lonergan*, published by the University of Toronto Press.

consciousness to historical consciousness and from a classicist to an empirical notion of culture (see especially the essays in Lonergan 1974a, 1–11, 55–69, 231–39). I do not know another theologian as persuasive as Lonergan on the philosophical and theological implications of the modern scientific revolution. And what other theologian is more convincing on how the shift to interiority in the turn to the subject of modernity can open to a cognitional theory for philosophy — and therefore to a modern notion of method without methodologism — and to a modern notion of the subject without either Enlightenment notions of pure autonomy or Romantic notions of the expressive subject? At the same time, in the last four decades (when the more exact meaning of postmodern thought began to be clarified by various thinkers), some of the amazing alliances of Lonergan's work with some characteristically postmodern emphases of contemporary thought have also become clearer.

One characteristic of contemporary thought as postmodern is the widely acknowledged priority of praxis. This insistence on praxis has many, sometimes incommensurable, manifestations. At the moment, I want to focus on a single but important strand of postmodernity and Lonergan: the important praxis recovery of an ancient philosophical and theological notion of "spiritual exercises" for contemporary philosophy and theology (see Hadot [1983] 1995).

In theology, one of the most promising and puzzling developments of the last forty years has been the unexpected explosion of theological, and even some philosophical, interest in spirituality, allied to the desire to reunite a historically separated theology and spirituality, while still maintaining some distinction between them. This more general theological development seems paralleled by the new interpretations, expansions, refinements, and sometimes corrections of Lonergan's own work in this direction of explicitly relating theology and spirituality by the studies of Frederick Crowe (on the Ignatian spiritual exercises and Lonergan), Cathleen Going, Robert Doran, Sebastian Moore, Harvey Egan, Walter Conn, Bernard McGinn, Shawn Copeland, Richard Liddy, Bernard Tyrrell, and many others. In sum, many Lonergan scholars and thinkers have demonstrated the further power and promise of Lonergan's work by explicitly relating his theology to the practice and history of spirituality and to what might be named contemporary, psychologically informed spiritual exercises (see the works of Sebastian Moore, esp. Moore 1989).

Moreover, in philosophy, the issue is formulated with clarity in *Insight* itself (Lonergan 1957): before any authentic self-affirmation can occur, the reader must undertake a series of intellectual exercises of self-appropriation described in "Insight as Activity" (part 1 of *Insight*). This insistence on exercises was later summarized by Lonergan as the asking of the three related basic questions of philosophy: What am I doing when I am knowing? (cognitional theory); Why is doing that knowing? (epistemology); and What do I know when I do it? (metaphysics as a transcendental integration of heuristic structures) (Lonergan 1974b, 263–78).

Lonergan himself clarified the importance of this characteristic insistence on the performance of intellectual exercises in order to understand cognitional theory and, therefore, epistemology and metaphysics, in his response to a question raised at the Lonergan Congress of 1970 regarding *Insight*—whether it was a *way* or a *theory*, and how the exercise of self-appropriation to which it invites one also generates new horizons for spirituality.

> Now with regard to the business of *Insight*, *Insight* happened this way: my original intention was method in theology. *Insight* was an exploration of methods in other fields, prior to trying to do method in theology. I got word in 1952 that I was to go to the Gregorian and teach in 1953, so I cut down my original ambition to do method in theology and put this book together. It's both a way and something like a theory. Fundamentally it's a way. It's asking people to discover in themselves what they are. And as Fr. Heelan put it, "There's something liberating about that." The word *Lonerganian* has come up in recent days. In a sense there's no such thing. Because what I'm asking people is to discover themselves and be themselves. They can arrive at conclusions different from mine on the basis of what they find in themselves. And in that sense it is a way.
>
> But that self-appropriation can be objectified. It's a heightening of consciousness—as one moves from attention to intelligence, to reasonableness, to responsibility, to religious experience. Those modalities of consciousness, the *a priori* that they constitute, *that* can be objectified. Not in the sense of subject-object—in here now, out there now—but in the sense that objectivity is the fruit of authentic subjectivity. That self-appropriation can be objectified, and its objectification is theory.
>
> But it is not theory in exactly the same way physics is. Its basic elements—mass, temperature, electromagnetic fields—are not within the field of experience. They are, all of them, constructs. Temperature is not what feels hot or cold. You put your hand on something metal, on something wood and one feels warmer than the other. They're both the same temperature—they're in the same

room for a sufficient length of time. These fundamental concepts in physics are not data of experience.

But the fundamental terms and relations in cognitional theory are given in consciousness. The relations are the dynamisms of consciousness and the terms are the operations that are related through the dynamisms. So it is theory—but in a sense as totally different from theory (in physics) as Eddington's two tables. On one you can put your hands, rest your weight; you find it solid, brown, it weighs so much. The other consists mostly of empty space, and where the space isn't empty you have a wavicle; but what it's doing is very hard to say.

The exercise of self-appropriation gives you the structure that generates horizons. And because you have the structure that's generating horizon, because that structure is heuristic, you're anticipating. If the intelligible, the being, the good—what you mean by those terms—is what is correlative to the desire to understand, to be reasonable, to be responsible; then, in yourself, you have the subjective pole of an objective field. You have also, in intelligent reasonable responsibility, norms, built-in norms, that are yourself. They are not propositions about yourself; but yourself, in your spiritual reality, to guide you in working out what that objective horizon is, the objective pole of the horizon. It's normative, it's potential. Not absolute, in the sense that you have it all tucked away. But you have the machinery for going at it, and you know what happens when you do. (Lonergan 1974c, 213–14)

Hence my basic question for a distinct reading of Lonergan: Is it not plausible to read the first four chapters of *Method in Theology*, along with the two chapters in dialectics and foundations, as implicitly and sometimes explicitly engaging the careful reader in a set of exercises different from, but analogous to, those explicated in the whole of "Insight as Activity"? Admittedly the exercises of *Method in Theology* are more implicit than explicit (or, perhaps more accurately, more cryptic than developed in detail). The exercises necessary to Lonergan's theological method, after all, demand not only the intellectual exercises familiar to *Insight* (and recalled in chapter 1 of *Method in Theology* [Lonergan 1972, 3–22], hereafter cited as *MT* with page numbers), but demand as well modern psychological and therapeutic exercises, as well as what I shall name (following Pierre Hadot) "spiritual exercises" employed by the ancients. If this is indeed the case, then what I earlier called the possibility of a second reception of Lonergan's work is real: a reception in a changed intellectual climate, where modernity's typical suspicion of any union of theory with praxis, much less with spiritual exercises, is now itself under suspicion.

Recall some recent examples of this modern development. A first example is modernity's characteristic reading of Anselm's *Proslogion*. Modern thinkers, from Descartes and Kant through Hartshorne, have typically read Anselm's arguments and reflections on God as what Kant (not Anselm) named the ontological argument. A few contemporary interpreters of Anselm (e.g., Anselm Stolz, Karl Barth, Hans Urs von Balthasar, Jean-Luc Marion) take notice of the hermeneutical import of the prayers central to Anselm's text, as well as the intricate relationship of reflective thought and spiritual exercises in Anselm's Christian Platonism and Benedictine spirituality.

As a second example, consider three well-received intellectual biographies of contemporary philosophers: Simone Petrement's life of Simone Weil; Ray Monk's biography of Ludwig Wittgenstein, nicely titled *The Duty of Genius*; and James Miller's biography of Michel Foucault (Petrement 1979; Monk 1992; Miller 1993). What is striking about these three otherwise very different philosophers (and each, in turn, quite different from Lonergan) is a reality that Weil, Wittgenstein, Foucault, and Lonergan (unlike most philosophers of the modern West) shared: a belief in the importance of intellectual and even "spiritual" exercises for theory itself. Foucault is the most surprising here, since no such emphasis is present in his earlier and better-known work on archeological and genealogical methods. Only in his later works — partly because of the influence of Pierre Hadot and Peter Brown on ancient philosophy as a way of life, partly because of the impasses of Foucault's work on sexuality and of his own debate with the narrowness of modernity, partly because of Foucault's now widely shared belief in the need to recover the Hellenistic period of late antiquity as philosophically important (not only classic Hellenic thought). Following the groundbreaking work of Peter Brown on late antiquity, Foucault turned in his own thought, as in his life experiments, to the ancient notion of caring for and fashioning a self.

Or consider a third example, closer to hand: Lonergan's own self-correction placing the argument for the existence of God (originally in chapter 19 of *Insight*) within the context of systematic theology in *Method* (that is, of the self-appropriating, intellectual, moral, and religious subject). This famous Lonerganian shift on the relation between the philosophy of God and the "functional specialty" of systematic theology (articulated most clearly in his Gonzaga lectures, *Philosophy of God, and Theology*) (Lonergan 1973, esp. 45–69) corresponded to Lonergan's later, basic move to what he now named a fourth, existential level of intentional consciousness, and, thereby, to his new emphases on feeling, radical self-transcendence, and Christian faith as the dynamic state of being-in-love without restriction. This shift corresponds as well to Lonergan's realization that the intellectual exercises of *Insight* were necessary but insufficient conditions for formulating and assessing the question of God. This amazing self-correction, I suggest, can now be viewed as part of Lonergan's implicit recovery of another aspect of ancient philosophy and theology—the need for practice in the form of spiritual (including intellectual) exercises for developing an adequate theory on the relationship of reason and God.

I do not claim that Lonergan ever made this move to ancient "spiritual exercises" explicitly. I do claim, however, that only a move like the retrieval of ancient spiritual exercises for philosophy and theology can clarify the following three characteristic, indeed central, moves in *Method in Theology*: the insistence on exercises for sorting out basic conflicts in dialectics, allied to the emergent notion of intellectual, moral, and religious conversion for "foundations"; the development of exercises to clarify the positions in the first four chapters of *Method in Theology*; and, above all, the new and postmodern (even for the once "modern" Lonergan) character of Lonergan's thought on the typically postmodern importance of praxis and the full range of praxis—intellectual, aesthetic, emotional, and especially religious praxis. All these new moves have become central to Lonergan's notion of theological method. For Bernard Lonergan, method relates to self-structuring recurrent operations; operations are clarified by exercises (*MT*, 235–95).

The groundbreaking historical work of Pierre Hadot referred to above is illuminating on the role of "spiritual exercises" in ancient thought.[2] Given Lonergan's admiration for the work of Bruno Snell in classic Hellenic thought on *logos* and Eric Voegelin on both classic Hellenic and Hellenistic philosophy

---

2. See the insightful introductions and studies of Hadot's ([1983] 1995) work by Arnold Davidson, including the introduction to the English-language edition of Hadot's work. I am happy to express my thanks to my colleague and friend, Arnold Davidson, for introducing me to Hadot's work in Davidson's own writing (in *Critical Inquiry* and in his several introductions to Hadot's work, as well as several invaluable conversations). My own summary of Hadot's significance is, at several junctures, thankfully dependent on Davidson's work. Davidson's own work on modern spiritual exercises in the philosophies of Ludwig Wittgenstein, Simone Weil, and Stanley Cavell expands Hadot's work into contemporary philosophy.

(Snell 1960; Voegelin 1956–74), Lonergan would have been open, I believe, to Pierre Hadot's studies. At any rate, Hadot's work can illuminate crucial aspects of Lonergan's later work in *Method in Theology*.

In very summary form, Hadot advances several important claims, especially in his magisterial studies of Plotinus, but also in his more general studies of the role of "spiritual exercises" in the major ancient philosophical schools (Stoicism, Epicureanism, Aristotelianism, Platonism), and even in less-structured and noninstitutionalized movements (Skepticism and Cynicism), as well as in the great synthetic position of Neoplatonism.

A major difficulty for modern Westerners in reading the texts of the ancients and some medievals in Western culture, as well as the texts of other great cultures — for example, not only classical but also contemporary Buddhist texts in East Asian, South Asian, and now also Western forms — is the habitual belief of most modern Western philosophers and theologians that theory should be separate from practice, especially practice as specific as what an ancient thinker meant by the phrase "spiritual exercises." The ancients (and the monastic medieval schools — although not the Scholastics) would have found such a separation of theory and practical exercises not merely strange but also self-destructive for true philosophy.[3] *Philo*sophy, as Voegelin and Hadot both insist, was for the ancients above all a love of wisdom, a unity of thought, and a way of life. The philosopher as philosopher was unclassifiable in ordinary life, fitting nowhere in ordinary life as ordinary life is usually understood. The unclassifiable character of the philosopher-sage determined, Hadot maintains, all the major schools (Aristotelianism, Stoicism, Epicureanism, Platonism) and the two major philosophic movements (Skepticism, Cynicism) of the entire Hellenistic period, from the third century BCE (when the "sorting out" of the schools *as* schools occurred) to the third century CE (when the classic Neoplatonic synthesis of Aristotelian and Stoic logic and ethics with various forms of Platonism was achieved).

Each ancient school maintained itself (and its fidelity to its founding sage) by specific training in intellectual and spiritual exercises, including the traditional mathematical and dialectical exercises. Each school possessed its ideal of wisdom and a corresponding fundamental attitude or orientation (Lonergan's

---

3. More exactly, the Scholastics introduced a valuable set of distinctions (e.g., between philosophy and theology, faith and reason, spirituality and theology) that unhappily became, in later Neo-Scholastic formulations, separations.

"horizon" on the fourth level of intentional consciousness). These orientations, of course, differed depending on the ideal itself: for example, a tensive moral rigor in the spiritual exercises of the Stoics or a relaxation or letting-go set of exercises for the Epicureans. Above all, every school employed exercises to aid the progressive development in its philosophical participants of the ability to sense its particular ideal state of wisdom. At that ideal state, the transcendent norm of reason (e.g., as *Logos* for the Stoics) ultimately coincides with whatever name is given to Ultimate Reality by each philosophical and theological school: the One, the Good, *Logos*, Being, God. Note how this ultimate philosophical moment in each ancient school corresponds to Lonergan's argument on the relationship of complete intelligibility and God, if that argument of *Insight* (chapter 19, which is the ultimate conclusion of the intellectual exercises of *Insight*) is placed in the context of the feelings, and values — that is, the exercises for moral, religious (and the necessarily reenacted intellectual) conversion appropriate to progress in the fundamental religious orientation of being-in-love-without-restriction.[4] For Lonergan, faith was like new knowledge born of love (*MT*, 115).

Such exercises were understood by all the ancient schools as analogous to the exercises employed by an athlete for the body (thus the word), as well as analogous to the application of a set of exercises for a medical cure. In contemporary culture, one could expand the analogy, as Lonergan did, partly through the important work of Robert Doran, who clarified some of the exercises needed to appropriate one's feelings in contemporary therapies (*MT*, 30–34). Since the ancients, such exercises have included intellectual exercises: recall the use of mathematics to help the exercitant to move from the realm of the sensible to the realm of the purely intelligible — in Pythagoras and Plato (and Lonergan) (Lonergan 1957, 3–33). These exercises also encompassed more straightforward spiritual exercises, including the use of images in memory training, as well as continuous reflection on the basic doctrines or beliefs of the school and exercises for increasing one's attentiveness to the implications of those beliefs for both life and thought. Ancient philosophy and theology, unlike most contemporary, professionalized philosophy and theology, united a fundamental vision of life (often correctly expressed in terms of theory rather than common sense)

---

4. For Lonergan's own reflections here, see Lonergan 1973; for the Hadot summary, besides Hadot's own work, see Davidson, "Introduction," in Hadot (1983) 1995. See also Davidson 2001.

with a daily program for a way of life (unlike most modern philosophy, with some great exceptions: e.g., Fénelon, Pascal, Kierkegaard, Nietzsche, Wittgenstein, Weil, Foucault, and Lonergan). Through all such exercises, the exercitant can clarify her relationship to the ultimate norm: for example, through a Stoic exercise of intensifying lucid attentiveness to one's personal relationship to the *Logos* believed by Stoics to pervade the entire cosmos. Among the ancients, in sum, all reflection on the relationship between theory and practice must be understood from the perspective of such exercises — especially, but not solely, diverse forms of meditation and contemplation, each appropriate to a particular school.

Even on the very limited basis of this summary of Hadot's analysis of the link between ancient "spiritual exercises" and ancient theory, it is clear that Lonergan's *Insight* explicitly, indeed brilliantly, corresponds to the ancient insistence on the role of intellectual exercises for personal intellectual self-appropriation. The question recurs: does Lonergan's later work in *Method in Theology* also encourage a central role for something like spiritual exercises, not only the intellectual exercises of *Insight* (summarized in chapter 1 of *Method in Theology*), and the further spiritual-psychological exercises of chapters 3 and 5 and chapters 10 and 11? A complete answer would demand something like a book-length study of the exercises implicit and explicit in Lonergan's work. A briefer answer, conducted (as mentioned earlier) as a thought experiment, is all the present essay attempts.

ANCIENT EXERCISES IN CONTEMPORARY FORM: *METHOD IN THEOLOGY*

There can be little doubt that "Insight as Activity" demands that the reader engage in intellectual exercises in order to reach the intellectual self-appropriation of "I am a knower." What is surprising, from the perspective of ancient exercises in philosophy, is how many different kinds of exercises Lonergan actually employs in order to persuade the attentive reader to accept his philosophical claims: the move to the world of the intelligible via mathematics is one Lonergan shares with Pythagoras, Plato, and many ancients and moderns (e.g., Descartes); the exercises aiding the appropriation of the intelligence of common sense (as distinct from theory) are ones he has in common with the classical tradition of rhetoric of topics from Aristotle and Cicero to Lonergan's own rhetorical mentor, John Henry Newman; in *Insight* he appropriates modern science and its realm of intelligibility as expressed through both classical and statistical methods; and, finally, he brilliantly transposes the methods of Aristotle and Thomas Aquinas into exercises from experiencing, understanding, and judging one's experience.

There can also be little doubt that chapter 1 of *Method in Theology* nicely, if somewhat cryptically, recalls the intellectual exercises of *Insight*, even as the chapter also suggests the need to move beyond *Insight* to the fourth, existential level of intentional consciousness, which includes skills, feelings, emotions, spiritual practices, and beliefs—that new level, which is the principal object of attention of *Method in Theology*. Note, for example, Lonergan's comments in footnote 2 of chapter 1 of *Method*: "I have presented this pattern of operations at length in the book *Insight* and more compendiously in an article [entitled] 'Cognitional Structure.' But this matter is so crucial . . . that some summary must be included here [in *Method*]. Please observe that I am offering only a summary, that the summary can do no more than present a general idea, that the process of self-appropriation occurs only slowly, and, usually, only through a struggle with some such book as *Insight*" (*MT*, 7n2). Indeed, the word *struggle*—with its suggestion of effort and exercise—seems entirely appropriate here. There are many ways (even many accurate and complementary ways) to view the role of the first four chapters of *Method in Theology*. By observing certain details in chapter 2, as well as some similar factors in chapters 3 and 4 and the later chapters in dialectics and foundations, one can see how *Method in Theology* also encourages the reader to engage in a series of exercises for the appropriation of a fourth level of authentic self-transcendence. Although the ultimate ground of religious self-transcendence (as chapter 4 on religion clarifies) is the gift of grace, still, a graced self-appropriation of operative and cooperative grace is encouraged.[5] And prior to the clarification of that giftedness of religious self-transcendence lie the brilliant explanations and implicit exercises of chapters 2 and 3.

Recall, for example, the opening lines (cryptic even from Lonergan) of chapter 2, "The Human Good": "What is good, always is concrete. But definitions are abstract. Hence, if one attempts to define the good, one runs the risk of misleading one's readers. The present chapter, then, aims at assembling the various

---

5. See *Grace and Freedom* (2000), Lonergan's study of Thomas Aquinas.

components that enter into the human good. So it will speak of skills, feelings, values, beliefs, cooperations, progress, decline" (*MT*, 27). There are, of course, persuasive intellectual reasons for each of these elements and for the order in which Lonergan presents them. Moreover, there are also compelling reasons to believe that proper attention to each element encourages a reader to engage in both modern, psychological, therapeutic exercises and ancient spiritual exercises—often both together. Consider, as a first example, Lonergan's discussion of "skills" (*MT*, 27–30). Beginning the study with skills frees Lonergan to appropriate Piaget's work for his own purpose of clarifying the exact meanings of "mediated immediacy." That turns out to be somewhat more exercise-oriented than Piaget's own analysis of the skills necessary to group groups of differentiated operations. It resembles instructions for relearning basic skills in a manual of physical therapy.

If the early section on skills initiates the needed emphasis on exercises, the central section on feelings (*MT*, 30–34) shows why skills are necessary and what kinds of exercised skills are appropriate. The ancients, as noted above, needed intellectual and spiritual exercises to increase attention to the fundamental orientation opened by the ultimate vision of reality in a particular religion or philosophy. A contemporary thinker like Bernard Lonergan can clarify this ancient demand further: we need contemporary thinkers to learn better ways to be attentive to those feelings intentionally responsive to the vital, social, cultural, personal, and religious values at stake. Indeed, here Lonergan introduces just the right cautionary note of a good spiritual adviser: it is true that feelings are spontaneous, but they can be enriched and refined by "attentive study of the wealth and variety of objects that arouse them and so no small part of education lies in fostering and developing a climate of discernment and taste" (*MT*, 32). The dialectic of feelings, moreover, is never forgotten. For every development of good feelings, there are also possible aberrations, as Scheler's phenomenological analysis of the Nietzschean discovery of *ressentiment* shows so well.

The next section on values (*MT*, 34–36) marks Lonergan's transition to the fourth level of intentional consciousness, where value becomes a transcendental notion: the good, always concrete and intended in all questioning, is whatever is truly worthwhile. Section 4 on judgments of value completes this movement by showing how understanding values demands the existence of authentic, self-transcending persons, just as Aristotle insisted that a person seeking to be ethical must pay attention to the existence and activities of virtuous persons. Even those, like myself, who do not share Lonergan's admiration for the work of Carl Rogers or Abraham Maslow, agree with the basic reasons for his appeal to work like theirs in our period: the need for therapeutic skills and exercises for the development of authentic, self-transcending persons.

To be sure, the section on beliefs (*MT*, 41–47) in this chapter continues Lonergan's epistemological interests on the necessary role of belief for knowledge. Later in *Method in Theology*, Lonergan will even add "believing" to the list that includes experiencing, understanding, judging, deciding — indicative of his growing acknowledgment at the time of the role of beliefs in a sociology of knowledge. Still, I suggest the central role for beliefs in chapter 4 is exactly the kind of role that true beliefs possessed for the ancients: true beliefs as opinions (*doxai*) are worthwhile because they are expressive of those true judgments of value implied by the fundamental orientation of an authentic tradition of values, grounded in a vision of ultimate reality as good. (Recall the later relation between foundations, orientations, and horizons grounded in the three conversions — and doctrines or beliefs [*MT*, 267–93].) The section on the human good (*MT*, 47–52), moreover, brilliantly summarizes this whole development through an outline of the complex and developing order of the human good itself — an outline that could provide the basic framework needed for a new set of spiritual exercises faithful to the demands of spiritual traditions as well as modern psychological and sociological insight.

A similar analysis of the subsequent chapters of *Method in Theology* would also be needed to clarify the full complexity and ultimately religious, graced grounding of Lonergan's theological envisionment of all reality. But perhaps enough has been said to indicate why I believe that Lonergan (whether knowingly or not, I do not claim to know) appropriated from the ancients not only the crucial, emancipatory distinction between common sense and theory, but, as Lonergan's love for the early dialogues of both Plato and Augustine suggests, the even more emancipatory ancient insistence that theological theory is intrinsically related to the practices that demand spiritual exercises (intellectual, moral, and religious). Skills, feelings, values, judgments of value, beliefs: one and all can be viewed as contemporary (that is, psychologically informed) transpositions of the spiritual exercises of the ancients, no less clearly than Lonergan's self-transcending subject reinterprets Aristotle's virtuous person in order to clarify moral conversion, or than Lonergan's appropriation of modern mathematics and physics reinterprets Plato's exercises for clarifying intellectual conversion, or than his explicit turn to interiority radically transposes

Aquinas's systematic understanding of grace into terms of inwardness (*MT*, 343–44). These possibilities should encourage further developments of Lonergan's legacy in ways that some Lonergan scholars (e.g., Robert Doran, Frederick Lawrence) have already suggested.

But more is surely needed: somewhere, sometime, someone must develop the cryptically suggested exercises of the first four chapters of *Method in Theology* into the explicitness and fullness they both suggest and deserve. That task would be both a major contribution to modern thought and a fitting tribute to the incomparable Bernard Lonergan.

REFERENCES

Davidson, Arnold. 2001. *The Emergence of Sexuality: Historical Epistemology and the Formation of Concepts*. Cambridge, MA: Harvard University Press.

Hadot, Pierre. (1983) 1995. *Philosophy as a Way of Life: Spiritual Exercises from Socrates to Foucault*. Translated by Michael Chase, edited by Arnold I. Davidson. Oxford: Blackwell.

Lonergan, Bernard. 1957. *Insight: A Study of Human Understanding*. New York: Philosophical Library.

———. 1964. "Cognitional Structure," *Continuum* 2: 530–42.

———. 1972. *Method in Theology*. New York: Herder and Herder.

———. 1973. *Philosophy of God, and Theology*. Philadelphia: Westminster.

———. 1974a. *A Second Collection*. London: Darton, Longman and Todd.

———. 1974b. "*Insight* Revisited." In *A Second Collection*. London: Darton, Longman and Todd.

———. 1974c. "An Interview with Fr. Bernard Lonergan, SJ." Edited by Philip McShane. In *A Second Collection*. London: Darton, Longman and Todd.

———. 2000. *Grace and Freedom*. Toronto: University of Toronto Press.

Miller, James. 1993. *The Passion of Michel Foucault*. New York: Simon and Schuster.

Monk, Ray. 1992. *Wittgenstein: The Duty of Genius*. New York: Vintage.

Moore, Sebastian. 1989. *The Crucified Jesus Is No Stranger*. New York: Crossroad.

Petrement, Simone. 1979. *Simone Weil*. New York: Schocken.

Snell, Bruno. 1960. *The Discovery of Mind*. New York: Harper Torchbook.

Voegelin, Eric. 1956–74. *Order and History*. 4 vols. Baton Rouge: Louisiana State University.

Part 3

CONVERSATION PARTNERS

LOUIS DUPRÉ

The category *modernity* remains an essentially contested category. One of the major contributions to that debate is Louis Dupré's three-volume work on the emergence of modernity. Dupré locates modernity earlier than most intellectual historians do: for him, modernity begins with the emergence of the fourteenth-century nominalists and the fifteenth-century humanists. Dupré's first volume, *Passage to Modernity: An Essay in the Hermeneutics of Nature and Culture*, has already become a classic study of modernity on a par with such classics as John Herman Randall's *Making of the Modern Mind* and Hans Blumenberg's *The Legitimacy of the Modern Age*.

In this first volume, Dupré focuses on the centrality of form in Western thought and culture — ancient, medieval, and modern. There is no more persuasive study of the importance of form in the diverse, sometimes conflicting cultural expressions of Plato, Aristotle, and Plotinus; the Cappadocians and Augustine; Thomas Aquinas, Bonaventure, and Duns Scotus; Renaissance art and philosophy (Nicholas of Cusa, Ficino, Erasmus, Bruno); or the distinctly dialectical form of Martin Luther and its more moderate and systematic expressions in Philip Melanchthon and John Calvin.

The modern, more subject-oriented nature of form began with the mathematicized science of Galileo Galilei and reached its apex in Isaac Newton. That position was philosophically formulated in the quintessentially modern philosophies of Descartes, Pascal, Malebranche, Spinoza, Locke, Berkeley, and Hume. Modernity focused on the subject and climaxed in Immanuel Kant's new philosophical form of critique, not treatise. After Kant, different dialectical forms of thinking become prominent in Hegel, Schelling, Schleiermacher, and the Schlegels.

Moreover, by way of another contrast of form in the midst of the triumph of modern Cartesian philosophy, there were quietly revolutionary thinkers, such as Giambattista Vico, who recovered the classical forms of rhetoric against the new Cartesian forms. It was said of Vico that he thought out his position in the seventeenth century and largely wrote it in the eighteenth, and that people began to read it in the nineteenth, and only began to truly understand it in the twentieth century. Dupré's three volumes on modernity — especially the luminous and exceptionally well structured volume 1, *Passage to Modernity* — interpret all these ancient medieval and modern forms of form and more in all their *in*forming and *trans*forming power.

A crucial task for all contemporary thinkers is to enter the highly contested debate on what constitutes the nature of modernity and the difference it has made in all Western culture, including North and South American culture. Furthermore, modernity has new cultural forms in East Asian, South Asian, African, and Oceanic cultures. Some non-Western cultures (e.g., those of Japan, China, and Korea) are very successful indeed at integrating modern culture in an Asian form with traditional Asian culture (especially neo-Confucianism).

It is not possible to be a serious intellectual in our day without some position, implicit or explicit, on the deeply contested question "What is modernity?" Whether one describes oneself as "modern," "late modern," or "postmodern," it is important to remember that all three designations demand some notion of "modernity," whether "early" (fourteenth to sixteenth centuries), "classical," "late" (seventeenth, eighteenth, and nineteenth centuries), or "post" (twentieth and twenty-first centuries). A wise way to sort out one's own position on "the modern" would be to read together the already classic works on the passage-of and arrived-at modernity in the valuably clashing accounts of Hans Blumenberg's *The Legitimacy of the Modern Age* and Louis Dupré's *Passage to Modernity*.

FRANKLIN GAMWELL

To understand the continuing strength of a straightforward exercise in modern rationality for philosophy, ethics, and theology, the work of Franklin Gamwell is exemplary. Gamwell is in the modern tradition of process thought. Clearly, one of the major intellectual moves of all modern thought (scientific, philosophical, artistic, and theological) is the replacement of "substance" as the central concept for reality by "event." No philosophical tradition has been more committed to "event-thinking" than the largely American empirical tradition, in contrast with the British empiricist tradition of John Locke and David Hume. In the British empiricist tradition, the great exception to the nonmetaphysical empiricist enterprise is the inimitable, empirical, and idealistic Irish philosopher George Berkeley. The classical, modern British empiricism has been constituted by a fine British exercise of diversity: the purely empiricist Francis Bacon and John Locke were English, the uniquely metaphysical empiricist George Berkeley was Irish ("We Irish think differently"), and the skeptical, ironic, radical empiricist David Hume was Scottish.

In the United States, British empiricism was rethought into a notion of experience not limited to sense experience alone (as in most British empiricism), but far more inclusive of mood, feeling, and sensibility as intrinsic aspects of "experience," starting with Jonathan Edwards's critical response to John Locke's empiricism, with several analyses of experience beyond sense experience (such as Edwards's deep feeling for nature and his Reformed sense of religious affections). That tradition continued with Ralph Waldo Emerson's meditative philosophy on such diverse experiences as grief and a sense of "the Vast" in nature. That American tradition expanded further with Josiah Royce's experiential and idealist incorporation of a deep sense of community as a central experience (indeed for Royce far more central than empiricist and even experienced individualism). The tradition eventually reached its climax (a pluralistic one) with the incomparable William James's openness to and articulation of psychological, philosophical, and religious experience—as in his inimitable classic, *The Varieties of Religious Experience*.

This American empirical, not empiricist, tradition found a second climax, a metaphysical one, in the process philosophy of Alfred North Whitehead—the most ambitious, modern, systematic metaphysics of event ever attempted. Whitehead, a quintessentially English gentleman as scholar and thinker, co-wrote *Principia Mathematica* with Bertrand Russell. After such groundbreaking work in mathematics, logic, and philosophy of science, Whitehead emigrated to the United States—more precisely, to Harvard University. After studying the wide notion of "experience" in William James and recalling the importance of the concept *event*, and process, and relationality in modern physics and mathematics, Whitehead turned his attention to metaphysics. By that turn, as formulated with many philosophical neologisms in the formidable *Process and Reality*, he founded process philosophy and influenced process theology.

Many philosophers and theologians (e.g., Charles Hartshorne, Schubert Ogden, and John Cobb) strongly affirmed and articulated in properly technical terms the panentheistic understanding of the God-world relationship in contradistinction to both classical theism and modern pantheism. In the course of these penetrating developments in the ever-expanding American empirical philosophy and theology, there was one major lack: a modern ethics delineated in modern process terms in critical relationship to the two major Western philosophical ethics—Aristotelian teleology and Kantian deontology.

Enter Franklin Gamwell. Indeed, exactly here is where Gamwell's work is singular. Unlike any other process thinker (including Whitehead, Hartshorne, and Ogden), Gamwell developed a modern process ethics that was well correlated to process metaphysics and theology. Moreover, Gamwell, with an intellectual openness worthy of William James, formulated his process metaphysical and theological ethics in critical conversation with the two major Western ethical traditions: Aristotle and Kant. Gamwell strongly affirmed Aristotle's teleology but expanded and grounded it in a general teleology made possible by Whitehead's metaphysics. Gamwell also affirmed Kant's deontological demand for a transcendental categorial imperative in ethics, while criticizing Kant's anti-teleological standpoint.

Franklin Gamwell has developed a complex position, which deserves far more critical attention from his fellow ethicists. He has managed to articulate in several important books an intricate, modern, process philosophical and theological ethics, displaying all the strength of modern reason: hence the title of my essay on Gamwell's Aristotelian-Kantian-Whiteheadian ethics in this volume: "The Strength of Reason." I admit, as the other essays in these two volumes testify, that I am not as confident as Professor Gamwell in the full adequacy of modern rationality in its more familiar, nonlinguistic, non-hermeneutical forms (e.g., in analytical philosophy). However, any further hermeneutical position (as outlined in the four essays on hermeneutics in volume 1 of my *Selected Essays, Fragments*, chaps. 6–9), in no way lessens my admiration for and affirmation of the strength of modern reason as exemplified in the magisterial process ethics of Franklin Gamwell.

GEORGE LINDBECK

I regret that the essay on George Lindbeck's rich theology in this volume is almost entirely critical. I include the essay here simply as a historical document of an earlier debate in the 1980s and 1990s, a debate often referred to as the "Yale-Chicago debate" on the appropriate method for modern theology. This present essay is only one expression of the discussions occasioned by both Lindbeck in *The Nature of Doctrine* and his colleague Hans Frei on biblical hermeneutics. The argument was and is still a familiar one. The debate had two major areas for critical disagreement between "Yale" (Lindbeck, Frei, Kelsey) and "Chicago" (Ogden, Gilkey, Tracy, Ricoeur). In *The Nature of Doctrine*, Lindbeck strongly criticized the tradition of theology, starting with Friedrich Schleiermacher and continuing with Karl Rahner, Bernard Lonergan, Paul Tillich, Rudolf Bultmann, Edward Schillebeeckx, Hans Küng, Elisabeth and Francis Schüssler Fiorenza, Gordon Kaufmann, John Cobb, Schubert Ogden, Rebecca Chopp, and many other theologians, including me, and including most Liberal Protestant theologians and most progressive Catholic theologians.

George Lindbeck argued that the whole modern theological tradition, starting with Schleiermacher, is seriously mistaken. In Lindbeck's judgment, the whole liberal tradition is based upon a mistaken, experiential-expressive philosophical model or models that rendered Christianity merely one more "expression" of general religious experience. This charge was not unfamiliar, as it had been one of Karl Barth's frequent criticisms of Schleiermacher: in early Barth, Schleiermacher was treated very roughly; the later Barth was still critical but more nuanced, even including some positive readings of Schleiermacher on the doctrine of the Spirit. Basically, the same criticism was argued by Hans Urs von Balthasar against Karl Rahner, and has been argued in later theoretical discussions by John Milbank and other theologians involved in the radical theology movements, as well as in the passionate, exciting theological ethics of Stanley Hauerwas.

The critical set of issues raised by Lindbeck is certainly a real one, demanding every theologian's attention. Besides his largely negative criticisms, Lindbeck argues a positive case for a linguistic cultural model for theology based on the linguistic philosophy of Ludwig Wittgenstein and the cultural anthropology of Clifford Geertz. Theologically, both Lindbeck's and Frei's basic theological position is a distinct Wittgensteinian version of Karl Barth.

The second area of difference in the so-called Yale-Chicago debate was more properly hermeneutical, as formulated by Hans Frei. Frei, in several essays following his magisterial hermeneutical study of biblical interpretation, held that Chicago's position on a general hermeneutics was problematic—Ricoeur's above all, since he developed the general hermeneutical theory that I then employed in a somewhat revised way and more explicitly theological form. (For clarification, see the section on hermeneutics, chaps. 6–9, in volume 1 of my *Selected Essays, Fragments*.) Frei's hermeneutical criticisms were similar to Lindbeck's more general criticism, but now on more hermeneutical, not explicitly Wittgensteinian, grounds. Frei held that the general hermeneutics of Ricoeur in his philosophy and his biblical interpretations (e.g., of the parables of Jesus), as well as my employment of hermeneutics for a hermeneutical theology, were wrongheaded. For Frei, Christianity (beginning with the Synoptic Gospels) demands not a general hermeneutics but its own specific hermeneutics for an adequate theological interpretation, especially of the "history-like realistic narratives" of the reception of the Bible. Hence the importance of narrative theologies. Along with Lindbeck's criticism, Frei's hermeneutical criticism focuses on the major issue: how to interpret Christianity rightly and what method or methods are most appropriate for this delicate and difficult task.

For example, the Gospel of John includes a narrative of Jesus of Nazareth's ministry (deeds and works). However, the Gospel of John is also in the wisdom tradition: its narrative is carefully, indeed brilliantly structured (light-darkness, truth-falsity, etc.) for incorporation in the wisdom-like theological reflection typical of John. It is also worth noting that St. Paul's letters (the earliest letters, which precede the Gospels in time) do not express any particular interest in a narrative of the ministry of Jesus, since Paul's theological vision, from beginning to end, is focused on Christ — to be more exact, on Jesus Christ and Him crucified.

Elsewhere I affirm and gratefully learn from Frei's excellent articulation of the "history-like realistic narrative" of many — but not (as Frei at times seemed to think) of all — biblical narratives. Some Gospels (e.g., the Gospels of Mark and of John) do not quite fit the history-like, realistic narrative model; Matthew and Luke-Acts do nicely fit Frei's model, one based, perhaps, on the nineteenth-century realistic novel. On the contrary, not only John and Paul but also the Gospel of Mark do not fit a nineteenth-century (e.g., Tolstoy, Balzac, George Eliot, the Brontës, Hawthorne, Melville, Turgenev, et al.), history-like realistic model. In the history of reception, Mark, like all the Gospels, was received by Christian communities (as Kathryn Tanner persuasively argues) as a "literal" (i.e., history-like, realistic) narrative. However, Mark's Gospel is a very different kind of narrative than the classically realistic narrative of Luke-Acts. With its bizarre ending (or non-ending) and its frequently noncontinuous, constantly interruptive, uncanny narrative (e.g., Mark 13), Mark's Gospel paints a strange, apocalyptic portrait of Jesus — even stranger than the portraits in Luke, Matthew, and John.

Moreover, in Mark, the apostles are almost completely uncomprehending of Jesus's words and actions, in contrast to the demons, the ill, the psychologically troubled, the misfits — all of whom, unlike the apostles, do seem to understand this unnerving, apocalyptic prophet. Mark's narrative is, in fact, more like a discontinuous, haunted, apocalyptic Dostoevsky novel, or a modernist novel like Robert Musil's *The Man without Qualities*, or even a postmodern novel (like the dazzling, deep works of David Foster Wallace), rather than bearing much relationship to a realistic, history-like narrative of, say, a Jane Austen or a George Eliot, a Dickens or a Balzac, or even a Bellow or an Updike or a Toni Morrison. Luke-Acts is a history-like, realistic narrative, with well-articulated individual characters (Jesus, the apostles, and the "people" are clearly and distinctly portrayed in Luke-Acts). Mark's case of somewhat bizarre characters, including the disruptive, apocalyptic Jesus, in portentous contrast to the realistic, rather typical characters delineated in Luke-Acts and in Matthew, remind one more of Robert Browning than of characters in a realistic novel: "Our interest's on the dangerous edge of things. / The honest thief, the tender murderer, / The superstitious atheist."[1]

These brief comments do not, of course, respond adequately to either Lindbeck or Frei. Perhaps, however, they can indicate the direction in which an adequate response might be found. In the meantime, despite my rather sharp criticism of Lindbeck raised by his book, with its unpersuasive critique of all progressive theologians since Schleiermacher, who are lumped together by Lindbeck into his Procrustean, experiential-expressive model, I wish to affirm very strongly how much I admire George Lindbeck's groundbreaking work in ecumenical Christian theology, especially on the theological, foundational importance of Judaism for Christian self-understanding, and his subtle and finely honed ecumenical ecclesiology. Hans Frei's work, so erudite and elegant, was a major contribution both to a hermeneutic of the Bible and to theology more generally. I was privileged to teach at Yale Divinity School as a visiting professor for a semester in the midst of the Yale-Chicago debate of those now far-off days at the generous invitation of George Lindbeck and Hans Frei. The memory of those theological conversations and, even more, the memory of those two erudite, incisive, and gentlemanly persons, is a joyful personal memory. The theological and philosophical issues dividing the Yale and Chicago of those days were real, but the actuality of serious conversation of those days was even more real.

JEAN-LUC MARION

Since the mid-twentieth century, French thought has proved the most original and influential intellectual and cultural tradition in Western culture, not only in Europe, but also in both North and South America. Indeed, from the middle of the twentieth century until now, France has generated a staggering constellation of major thinkers. Consider the impact of an earlier French generation that included Simone de Beauvoir, Albert Camus, Maurice Merleau-Ponty, Gabriel Marcel, Simone Weil, Emmanuel Levinas, Claude Lévi-Strauss, and Paul Ricoeur — each a major thinker and each in critical conversation with

---

1. Robert Browning, *Bishop Blougram's Apology* (New York: Sheed and Ward, 1931), lines 417–19.

the others. In theology, the same generation gave birth to another constellation of original theologians: Henri de Lubac, Jean Daniélou, Yves Congar, Louis Bouyer, and, by French adoption, Hans Urs von Balthasar from Switzerland.

The succeeding generations expanded this amazing line of major French thinkers: Jacques Lacan, Louis Althusser, Michel Foucault, Giles Deleuze, and Jacques Derrida, followed in another generation by such exceptional philosophers as Jean-Luc Marion, Jean-Louis Chrétien, Rémi Brague, and Claude Romano, as well as such influential theologians as Jean-Yves Lacoste, Claude Geffré, Jean-Pierre Jossua, and, in his more recent turn to explicitly theological work, Jean-Luc Marion.

This French twentieth- and twenty-first-century intellectual renaissance has made French thought, for the first time since the age of Descartes, the leading European intellectual tradition. Even such classical modern German thinkers as Hegel, Husserl, and Heidegger, as well as Nietzsche, Marx, and Freud, have in the twentieth and twenty-first centuries received more original philosophical interpretations by French philosophers than by their contemporary German counterparts. This is surprising, since the extraordinary German philosophical tradition, from Leibniz and Kant to Fichte, Hegel, Schelling, Schleiermacher, the Schlegels, Nietzsche, Heidegger, Scheler, Arendt, and Habermas, is a tradition of such excellence and length of stay that it was surpassed in Western philosophy only by the Greeks themselves, from Thales through Aristotle, to Plotinus. To be sure, German scholarship on the history of German philosophy and theology remains unequaled for sheer rigor and thoroughness. However, German philosophy, except for Jürgen Habermas and Karl-Otto Apel, seems to have, in effect, ceded its modern, classical, philosophical tradition to interpretation by French thinkers while, paradoxically, turning much of its attention to Anglo-American analytical philosophy.

At the present moment, in the rich and pluralistic French philosophical tradition, it seems clear that Jean-Luc Marion is the most original and influential living phenomenologist (still the leading philosophical tradition in contemporary France, despite attacks from Alain Badiou et al.). It is just as clear that Jean-Yves Lacoste is the most original living French theologian.

Jean-Luc Marion, like Paul Ricoeur before him, is so productive — even prolific — a thinker and writer that very few readers have read all his remarkable works. In effect, Marion has had three distinct intellectual careers, each of which has resulted in major works. In his earliest intellectual career, Marion, influenced by his mentor, the major Cartesian scholar Ferdinand Alquié, has become the leading Descartes scholar in France — indeed, in the world. In a second intellectual career as a phenomenologist, Marion has been exceptionally creative, culminating in his philosophical magnum opus, *Étant donné: Essai d'une phénoménologie de la donation*, on the central phenomenological category of the given. In this second period, Marion presented his distinctive phenomenological analysis of "the gift" in critical dialogue with Jacques Derrida. Marion also developed in this period his most original phenomenological discovery: the category of the *saturated phenomenon*. In a third, more recent intellectual career, Marion has turned his always-present, implicit interest in theology to lecturing on and writing about explicitly theological works: a book on Augustine, earlier essays on Gregory of Nyssa and Dionysius the Areopagite, and his recent, fascinating interpretation of Basil of Caesarea (in his Gifford Lectures on revelation). Furthermore, in his lecture courses in both Paris (the University of Paris, the Sorbonne, and the Institut Catholique) and at the University of Chicago, Marion has undertaken a study of major theologians, beginning (thus far) with Justin Martyr, Tertullian, and Clement of Alexandria.

Actually, all three intellectual interests continue apace as more books on Descartes, on phenomenology, and now on theology pour forth from this unusually fecund scholar and thinker. He represents the best of the modern French philosophical tradition. In reading his many works and conversing with him frequently, sometimes critically (e.g., on Neoplatonism and on theological method), I cannot avoid the conclusion that Jean-Luc Marion is a singular enrichment of contemporary intellectual life.

CHAPTER 10

FRAGMENTS OF SYNTHESIS

*The Hopeful Paradox of
Louis Dupré's Modernity*

DUPRÉ AND THE CONTEMPORARY DEBATE ON MODERNITY

Louis Dupré has been one of the most trustworthy educators in our parlous times. More than any other contemporary philosopher of religion, Dupré has forced his fellow philosophers (and, for that matter, theologians) to pay serious attention to the philosophical and theological import of the spiritual traditions, especially the mystical traditions. From his earlier groundbreaking work, *The Other Dimension* (1972), through his studies of mystical traditions (especially his beloved Ruysbroeck) and his analyses of such thinkers as Kierkegaard, Hegel, Marx, Schleiermacher, and Duméry, to his constructive analyses of selfhood in modernity, Dupré has consistently instructed us all on the need to reconnect the spiritual traditions to the mainline philosophical and theological traditions. Moreover, he has achieved this work in Western traditions while remaining not merely open to, but also informed by, the often-greater success of non-Western (especially Eastern and South Asian) traditions in keeping united the classic ancient syntheses of cosmos, the ultimate, and the self (Dupré 1987, 245–61).

Dupré seems to possess a singular ability to rethink the contemporary dilemma, both intellectually and spiritually, by focusing his principal philosophical attention on the linked issues of transcendence and the self in contemporary philosophies and theologies (Dupré 1976, 1–31, 50–79). More sharply than any other contemporary philosopher of religion, Dupré shows how the loss of transcendence and the "small soul" (Nietzsche) of the contemporary "self" are indissolubly linked philosophical and theological issues. That intellectual linkage for Dupré, moreover, is grounded in an even more basic difficulty: the uncoupling, in contemporary Western thought, of critical intellectual (i.e., philosophical and theological) traditions and spiritual traditions.

For more than four decades, like many others, I have followed and been instructed by Dupré's unique and consistent project: to reunite what had been separated by modernity, both substantively — God, cosmos, self — and methodologically — the exercises and methods of our spiritual traditions and theories, and critiques of our philosophies and theologies. Dupré's work was already a substantial achievement before *Passage to Modernity* (1993). Furthermore, his oeuvre (beginning with an early book on Kierkegaard and *The Other Dimension*) has become ever more relevant, since now many contemporary philosophers and theologians have joined Dupré's earlier articulation of the kind of philosophical enterprise needed today. Many thinkers are now forging their own rethinking of the relationships of our philosophical-theological and our spiritual — especially mystical — traditions. Indeed, the recent important debate between Jacques Derrida and Jean-Luc Marion on the phenomenon of "gift" and the reflections on the "Good" in the Dionysian tradition are fine illustrations of a far more widespread philosophical and theological interest in rethinking the ordinarily marginalized mystical traditions as a resource that may be free of the onto-theological dilemmas of our intellectual traditions.[1]

---

1. On "gift," see Derrida 1992a and 1992b; on the Dionysian tradition, see Derrida 1994; also Marion 1977, 1991, and 1992.

Dupré made this argument on the intellectual import of the mystical traditions long before more recent thinkers began to sense the importance of that largely uncharted route (Dupré 1972, 484–547). Moreover, several other thinkers who also see how Western modern thought has impoverished its notions of the self by developing dominating attitudes toward nature and effectively eliminating or, at best, marginalizing any serious reflection on transcendence have now turned with fury against the modern project, sometimes excessively. Whatever their other crucial differences, both countermoderns (like Leo Stauss, Eric Voegelin, or Alasdair MacIntyre) and postmoderns (like Jean-François Lyotard, Michel Foucault, or Jacques Derrida) have forged powerful and, on the whole, persuasive (if profoundly conflicting) critiques of "modernity."

Dupré's recent entry into this charged debate on modernity provides, in my judgment, a new and important alternative to the usual analyses of modernity. Dupré sees as clearly as the countermodern and postmodern thinkers the impasse that modern thought, despite its remarkable achievements (too often ignored by its critics), now faces:[2] the devastating cultural and social consequences of an impoverished philosophical notion of the self, aligned with a social condition of increasing possessive individualism; a pervasive mechanistic and scientistic understanding of nature united to a still dominative attitude expressed in an often unbridled technology; a marginalization of any philosophical concern with transcendence, either as a general, central philosophical category or as centuries-old religious-theological questions about the transcendent and immanent God, united to a social marginalization and privatization of religion (e.g., *laïcité* in France); and a reifying of a once-emancipatory Enlightenment reason as a modern rationality that either continues to build an "iron cage" (Weber) or, less drastically, an increasing "colonization of the lifeworlds" (Habermas).

In this situation, Dupré presents an important alternative. He argues, as very few other contemporary philosophers have (whether they be defenders or critics of modernity), that the contemporary debate needs to focus on a careful hermeneutical reading of early (fifteenth-to-sixteenth-century) modernity and not just modernity's later, hardened, reified (eighteenth-century) Enlightenment version.

---

2. The formulations of these difficulties of "modernity" in this essay are my own, not Dupré's. Although I formulate the critique more strongly than Dupré usually does (at least in *Passage to Modernity*), the phrases are faithful to the spirit of his frequent criticisms of contemporary life, especially in *Transcendent Selfhood*.

A good deal of contemporary thought displays a kind of pervasive nostalgia for a lost, premodern unity paradoxically united to a radical hermeneutics of suspicion of all totality systems (whether modern or premodern). So does Louis Dupré. And yet, Dupré's most recent and clearly stunning major work, *Passage to Modernity: An Essay in the Hermeneutics of Nature and Culture* (1993), pays serious philosophical and theological attention to the missing link in most of the contemporary debate: the origins of modernity in the fourteenth, fifteenth, sixteenth, and early seventeenth centuries. In spite of other differences with Dupré's reading of the contemporary debate, I am thankful to have been enormously instructed by Dupré's hermeneutical essay on early modernity. Indeed, in my judgment, Dupré's reading of modernity significantly changes the terms of the more familiar debates between moderns and postmoderns. One need not accept Dupré's wholly negative reading of "postmodernity" (indeed, I do not, and I consider it a serious flaw in this otherwise penetrating philosophical study) to see the import of his work.[3] It is now possible to see that the understanding of "modernity" by both its defenders and its critics has been seriously misconstrued by ignoring, on the whole, the significance of the fourteenth-century nominalists and the fifteenth- and sixteenth-century humanists, as well as the major "early modern" formulations of two exceptional but very different geniuses, Nicholas of Cusa in the fifteenth century and Giordano Bruno in the sixteenth century, and, above all, the spiritual and religious resources that made early modernity not merely richer and more flexible than the eighteenth-century Enlightenment version but, above all, free of the set of problems that most contemporary versions of modernity share.

Of course, contemporary philosophical and theological thought was already informed by the now-classic works on early modernity in the tradition of scholarship from Ernst Cassirer through Hans Blumenberg (Cassirer 1963; Blumenberg 1983 and 1987). Moreover, Ernesto Grassi and other scholars of the humanist traditions in Italy have provided persuasive critiques of the widespread contemporary philosophical and theological ignorance of these Italian humanistic traditions as philosophical resources relevant to the contemporary debates so influenced by Heidegger.[4] Furthermore, we are all now the inheri-

---

3. It would be interesting to know what Dupré makes of the debate on postmodernity and negative theology in, for example, the following studies: Coward and Foshay 1992; Hart 1988; and Berry and Warnick 1992. My own readings of postmodernity and religion may be found in Tracy 1994 and 1995.

4. Among others, see Grassi 1983. Grassi's important work here has also been influential.

CONVERSATION PARTNERS

tors of the explosion of first-rate scholarship in the formerly marginalized Neo-platonic traditions in much modern thought, and, above all, the great spiritual and especially mystical traditions of our heritage. Though clearly an heir to this exceptional scholarship on early modernity, Louis Dupré is singular among contemporary philosophers of religion and intellectual historians for critically employing this classical history-of-ideas scholarship to provide a strictly philosophical hermeneutic of the "passage to modernity." Thereby Dupré allows both intellectual historians in the tradition of Hans Blumenberg, as well as contemporary philosophers and theologians, to rethink the philosophical import of early modernity for our contemporary problems.

As always, Dupré performs this hermeneutical-philosophical exercise with great modesty: he admits his (that is, our) intellectual and spiritual "poverty" (Emerson) on these issues; he insists (as does any clearheaded interpreter of our situation) that the best we can hope for today is the recovery of some intellectual and spiritual "fragments" (Dupré 1993, 253).[5] But note the shift in sensibility in Dupré's appeal to the familiar, contemporary metaphor of "fragments" to describe our situation. The neoconservative thinker T. S. Eliot will appeal to the image of "fragments" as all we have left to shore against our ruin as Eliot moves poetically, philosophically, and theologically from the completely fragmentary *Waste Land* to the moving, now Christian theological fragments of *Ash Wednesday* and the wondrous blend of Buddhist, Neoplatonic, and, above all, Christian incarnational fragments in *Four Quartets*. Walter Benjamin (that brilliant, dialectical, revisionist Marxist, oddly and uneasily united to a kind of revisionist Kabbalist) also appealed to the metaphor of "fragments," with very different resources and readings than Eliot's (or Dupré's): for Benjamin, the fragments in German baroque drama and the fragmentary character of the life of Baudelaire's *flaneur*, and even the fragments of hope (i.e., sparks of the divine) strongly embedded in Kabbalistic readings of Messianic Judaism, or in Franz Kafka's deeply unnerving readings of modern life, and in modern life as, itself, fragments manifested in the arcades of nineteenth-century Paris, the capital of modernity. Postmodern thinkers from Bataille to Kristeva also appeal to intense "fragments," now as expressions of excess and transgression, which may free us, however temporarily, from the asphalt highway of modern rationality. For many postmoderns, only the fragmentary and marginalized re-

---

5. For the full quotation from Emerson, see Dupré 1993, 253. See also Tracy 2020, chap. 1.

sources in our history — the avant-gardes, the mad, the hysterics, the misfits, the prophets, the mystics — will help us finally provide some glimpse of the emancipatory "otherness" and "difference" in subjugated countertraditions to modernity, and thereby free us from "more of the same" (Foucault).

These three distinct — even conflicting — appeals to "fragments" share with Dupré (as, indeed, with many of us) the sense that all we now possess are fragments of all our (and other) heritages and, through those fragments, some modest hope. But Dupré provides a genuinely new vision of a genuinely promising hope by his shifting of the usual terms of the debate: since the eighteenth-century Enlightenment, modernity has been read in terms of too-hardened a set of once-flexible, early modern categories, too narrow, even dogmatic, a way of understanding the meanings of modernity by both its proponents and its critics. This misreading has been intensified in our period by the sometimes stridently defensive moves of the proponents of modernity and the equally strident outcries of many antimoderns and postmoderns. We may need to step back for a moment and examine, as calmly and deliberately as we can, the origins of the modern age and the rich, flexible, still-amazing passage our culture first took to that age. Then our fragments — both premodern and modern — may not simply be shored against our ruin, nor merely help us undo the totality of the thinking and totalitarian and colonizing temptations of Western modernity. They may offer us some genuine hope. Dupré offers another kind of hope: more modest, more willing to admit our present poverty, more honest in insisting, with many other critics of modernity, that fragments are all we any longer possess. At the same time, Dupré shows how these fragments — premodern and modern alike, along with, in principle, the fragments of non-Western cultures now available to Western thinkers and postmodern thinkers as well — may become possible "bricks of a future synthesis" (Dupré 1993, 253).

A hopeful and plausible vision. We must await Dupré's next constructive philosophical volumes following the "hermeneutical" one to see more exactly what that envisioned "future synthesis" may prove to be. But on the basis of the philosophical-hermeneutical studies of *Passage to Modernity*, we know already how central a category *synthesis* is to Dupré. His reading of the ancient and medieval syntheses of cosmos-self-God (or the divine) is, as I shall argue below, one of the best on record. Dupré thereby shows new resources for contemporary thought from early modern thought: the humanists, like Ficino and Erasmus, as well as major, highly original thinkers like Cusanus and Bruno. Dupré displays the usually overlooked cultural resources of early modernity: the Renaissance as well as his anti-Benjamin, pro-Balthasar portrait of the Catholic Baroque. Above all, Dupré demonstrates how central (*pace* that fine tradition of intellectual historians from Burckhardt through Cassirer to Blumenberg) religion in fact was to early modernity, and thereby how necessary it is today to rethink the relationships of spirituality, philosophy, art, science, and theology. Dupré's vision is a paradoxical and intriguing one indeed: "fragments" and "synthesis" are not usually coupled together.

To understand how Dupré manages to render persuasive an appeal to "fragments" for a "synthesis," it is necessary to risk an interpretation of his interpretation. In my view, what modernity (in its dogmatic, reified Enlightenment form) broke was the premodern syntheses of form and content, feeling and thought, practice and theory. What Dupré's analysis helped me to see far more clearly than I ever did before is that none of these separations functioned in early modernity, even though the classical forms of both ancient and medieval substantive syntheses of God-cosmos-self were under critical study. Therein lies a tale (decidedly not a Whig history nor a "grand narrative") that provides a more complex, more reasonable, more hopeful vision for the present than the more familiar debates on "modernity": it may be possible to see, in early modernity, a way to rethink our options in the contemporary impasse on whether to name our present time "late modernity," "countermodernity," or "postmodernity."

MODERNITY: SYNTHESIS AND FRAGMENTATION

Since the critiques of Heidegger and Derrida, there have been few more pejorative words in contemporary thought than the word *onto-theology*. It is no small part of the intriguing character of Dupré's study that he retrieves a positive meaning for this word without denying the contemporary negative critique of modern philosophical onto-theology since Heidegger and Derrida.[6] Dupré's book is, above all, a subtle and rich study of how the ancient and Jewish-Christian-Islamic medieval synthesis of the cosmos, the divine, and the human rendered Western thought into a whole, in all its principal and very different

---

6. Dupré 1993, esp. 5 (where he clarifies his distance from Heidegger, Derrida, and Rorty).

religious, cultural, philosophical, and theological forms. For Louis Dupré, what most happened in early modernity was the fragmentation of the ancient and medieval synthesis of self, cosmos, and God. I cannot hope, in this short space, to do justice to the entirety of Dupré's rich, complex, and at times somewhat cryptic study. I therefore highlight only certain crucial aspects of his interpretation. The ancient, organic Greek and Roman unity was, of course, originally threatened by the Jewish-Christian notion of a Creator God transcendent to the cosmos, who was unlike the "gods" (Dupré 1993, 22–63; see also Burrell and McGinn 1990). Indeed, the greatest and (on the whole) most successful intellectual accomplishment of the Jewish, Christian, and Islamic medieval thinkers was the development of new syntheses designed to maintain the transcendent Creator God's profound immanence in the cosmos through the very transcendence of God and (through wisdom and grace) in humanity. Until the late medieval period, one or another version of an onto-theological synthesis of the cosmic, divine, and human realms held.

On Dupré's reading, first the fourteenth-century nominalist crisis, then the deluge: the nominalists redefined the traditional understanding of the transcendent God—defined anew, not by intelligence (*Ipsum Intelligere*) but by omnipotent will (and thereby by solely efficient, not formal, causality)—from both cosmos and the human. The ancient and medieval onto-theological synthesis was shaken. Dupré seems ambivalent toward the nominalists and their successors. Furthermore, Dupré misreads postmodernity, for example, as, basically, neo-nominalism. On the one hand, the nominalist reflections on words and referents did indeed help to prepare the way for modern science to use concepts more freely and flexibly than otherwise might have been the case, and to encourage a necessarily more empirical approach to modern science (Heiko Overmann). On the other hand, nominalism seriously fragmented the ancient synthesis of God, cosmos, and self, which had formed the most basic ideal of Western culture. In Dupré's reading of the late medieval nominalist crisis, the full ambiguity of modernity had already begun, therefore, as early as the late fourteenth century.

The daring character of Dupré's strategy now asserts itself. First, for Dupré, it is not enough, in any critique of modernity, to focus only on the dilemma of one of the major elements in the modern period: neither only the "self" (Taylor, Foucault, Kristeva, et al.), nor only reason or *logos* (Derrida and other critics of Western logocentrism), nor only God (the theologians, at least when they assume their proper role of articulating a *logos* for *theos*), nor only the cosmos, narrowed to "nature" by modernity.[7] The fragmentation of *any* onto-theological synthesis demands the most attention in order to comprehend what happened to the modern understanding of any single element: God, cosmos-nature, self, reason.

Second, it is not sufficient, in any description of modernity, to move immediately to a discussion of the seventeenth-century scientific revolution and the political and intellectual developments (perhaps all too easily understood, pro or con, in their doctrinal, eighteenth-century form) of the Enlightenment. One must *first* study the original "passage to modernity," from the end of the fourteenth century to the early seventeenth. An analysis of this rich, often over-looked period in debates on modernity provides a persuasive way to understand how the fragmentation originally happened. Dupré's study also suggests several examples of a "usable past" for our contemporary needs: the humanists; the new threshold synthesis of Cusanus and the early modern synthesis of Bruno; and the religious and spiritual forms and practices that underlay all these early modern movements, thereby allowing several new modern syntheses (e.g., the Baroque synthesis), not merely fragmentations of the old.

It may be the case that we late Westerners (whether we call ourselves late modern or postmoderns) do find ourselves without any synthesis at all—at least not one that adequately correlates God-cosmos-humanity. Some contemporary defenders of the "unfinished project" of modernity (like Jürgen Habermas and Karl-Otto Apel) insist on our "post-metaphysical" status and render religion fundamentally "private" and purely motivational, not "public" and rationally defensible for the culture (see Gamwell 1990, esp. 127–213). Contemporary critics of modernity from Heidegger through Derrida, moreover, read *all* Western thought from Plato through Hegel as ridden with an onto-theology. For them *onto-theology* has a purely negative meaning: namely, the claim that *all* Western syntheses of God-cosmos-self-reason are determined by Western logocentric reason—that is, reason controls the meaning of God, cosmos, and self. This reading of onto-theology is directly opposed to Dupré's. For them, that onto-theology is the fundamental problem of our intellectual tradition, not, as for Dupré, a sign of the need for a new synthesis.

Although an analysis of the conflicting meanings of onto-theology would demand a separate study of the sometimes conflicting texts of both Heideg-

---

7. This is the principal topic of Dupré 1993, part 1 (15–93).

ger and Derrida, this much, after Dupré's study, seems clear: no serious critic of Western "onto-theology" should presume to speak of this topic without addressing the possibility that Dupré's study of early modernity shows.[8] The onto-theology that has afflicted us with a mechanistic cosmos, an isolated, possessively individualist self, and a God who is either dead or so removed from cosmos, self, and history alike as to function as *deus otiosus* may prove to be a specific product of the dilemmas of modernity, not a necessary outcome of the Western turn to theory with the Greeks,[9] nor the outcome of the classical ontological syntheses of the ancients, the medievals, or the early moderns.

The stakes here are high, as Dupré himself insists in his narrative of early modernity: "Only when the early humanist notion of human creativity came to form a combustive mixture with the negative conclusions of nominalist theology," he writes, "did it cause the cultural explosion that we refer to as modernity. Its impact shattered the organic unity of the Western view of the real" (Dupré 1993, 3). As Dupré unfolds his interpretation of the humanists on human creativity, it becomes clear that the humanists, on the whole, kept some form of synthesis alive, either by grounding poetic (Dante) or rhetorical (Petrarch) understandings of human creativity in the divine Word creating *ex nihilo*, or by retrieving some new form of Neoplatonism (Marsilio Ficino, Pico della Mirandola) that allowed for God's radical immanence without the loss of divine transcendence, or by any number of other humanistic, intellectual strategies from Erasmus through Montaigne (Dupré 1993, esp. 93–119).[10] Each thinker found a way to free early modern humanist thought from the more radical fragmentation of the nominalists without retreating from the modern breakthrough on creativity, individuality, and expressivity.

Moreover, like Hans Blumenberg before him on early modernity, Dupré focuses on two outstanding thinkers of this period, Nicholas of Cusa (1401–1464) and Giordano Bruno (1548–1600).[11] Unlike Blumenberg, Dupré shows that Cusanus, with his pre-Copernican but already nongeocentric view of the cosmos allied to his equally original notion of God's absolute infinity, is not

---

8. Dupré's study is here allied to, among others, Jean-Luc Marion's studies of Descartes (Marion 1981 and 1986).

9. For two studies of how the question of God is thus affected, see Buckley 1971, 1989.

10. On Montaigne's humanist modern syntheses, see Toulmin 1990.

11. Dupré treats both Cusanus and Bruno at several crucial points in his narrative. Among the most significant are Dupré 1993 (59–62, 186–202) on Cusanus; and Dupré 1993 (61–66, 125–26, 183–85) on Bruno.

merely a premodern thinker but also a genuinely threshold figure. For Cusanus, in fact, reconfigured the onto-theological ancient and medieval synthesis in new (that is, modern) ways, both mathematical and metaphysical. Cusanus managed to articulate this originality while still maintaining a synthesis of God-self-cosmos. In that sense Cusanus held to a fundamental continuity with the classic ancient and medieval Neoplatonic tradition. Cusanus is the threshold thinker *par excellence* of early modernity. Moreover, Giordano Bruno (more indebted to Cusanus, in fact, than to Copernicus) worked out his own extraordinary, immanentist, pantheistic, or perhaps panentheistic, synthesis of God (no longer, to be sure, a Creator God), cosmos, and humanity by developing a philosophical vision that was both creative-expressive (i.e., poetic) and genuinely religious (hermetic).

Dupré succeeds in giving a more subtle and judicious reading of the syntheses of both Cusanus and Bruno than Blumenberg does, because he focuses attention on the character of their new onto-theological syntheses as *early modern* syntheses, related to yet different from the older syntheses, rather than simply stressing their relationships (implicit for Cusanus; explicit for Bruno) to the forthcoming Copernican world-picture. A good part of Dupré's success in this portrait of both Cusanus and Bruno, moreover, lies in his attention to the crucial religious components of their work. The understated subtlety of Dupré's interpretation is clear when one compares it not only (as above) to Blumenberg's famous portrait of "The Cusan and the Nolan" (Blumenberg 1983, 457–597),[12] but also to such well-known studies of Cusanus as those of Ernst Cassirer or Karl Jaspers (Cassirer 1963; Jaspers 1962, 116–273). Neither Cassirer nor Jaspers, in their otherwise admiring portraits of Cusanus, seems to know what to make of his religious — even mystical — dimension. For Cassirer, Cusanus's work, brilliant as it is, becomes a kind of "mystical" precursor to Kant's later, clear transcendental reflections on the limits and antinomies of reason.[13] Jaspers seems puzzled that so fine an analyst as Cusanus of the "symbolic ciphers" of both authentic existence and thought could still prove

---

12. For Blumenberg on Bruno and Copernicanism, see Blumenberg 1987 (353–86). It is also important to note that Dupré makes his argument for the importance of religion and theology in understanding early modernity without falling back into the "secularization" hypothesis of Karl Löwith, who is criticized strongly by Blumenberg (1983, 3–125).

13. For a useful study of Cassirer's neo-Kantian position, see Krois 1987.

so Christological in focus (Jaspers 1962, 193–95). The neo-Kantian teleology in the implicit grand narratives of modernity in both Cassirer and Jaspers,[14] and even the more cautious, more complex, neo-Copernican grand narrative of modernity in Blumenberg, lack the complexity and subtlety of Dupré's portrait of Cusanus, principally because they fail to provide an adequate account and analysis of the religious — even mystical — elements in Cusanus as other than somehow dispensable elements *en route* to either Copernicus or Kant.

Nor does Dupré exaggerate the import of these religious, even mystical, elements. As clearly as Frances Yates (1964), Dupré eliminates the nineteenth-century rationalist reading of Bruno. Unlike Yates, however, Dupré does not make the "hermetic" elements in Bruno so pervasive to his thought that the uniquely modern (including the Copernican) factors in Bruno are underestimated by a "hermetic-mystical" reading of this remarkable early modern thinker. Dupré's readings of Cusanus and Bruno persuade precisely by their insistence on the fuller complexity of both thinkers — both their novelty (hence modernity) and their equally genuine (and religiously inspired) commitment to the classical Western ideal of some kind of onto-theological synthesis. On Dupré's reading, both Cusanus and Bruno become plausible heuristic models for the kind of serious modern thought that wants to rethink rather than destroy the ancient onto-theological synthesis, even — perhaps especially — in the contemporary period. They are fragments that can now serve in our day, as Jaspers saw with clarity, as "ciphers" of a possible transcendence. More importantly, as Dupré shows, the efforts of both Cusanus and Bruno can function as heuristic fragments-ciphers of hope for some synthesis beyond our present fragmented impasse.

FORM AND FORMS: FOUNDATION AND EXPRESSION OF THE SYNTHESIS

What Hans Urs von Balthasar argued, on theological grounds, for theology, Louis Dupré argues for philosophy: no interpreter can understand the Western intellectual tradition without focusing on the importance of the phenomenon

---

14. This emphasis on the "grand narratives" of modernity is Jean-François Lyotard's well-known argument (Lyotard 1984).

of form in the Western tradition. Indeed, the central idea of Western thought from its beginning in Greece (even before classical Greece, as argued by Mircea Eliade) was the idea of the real as, in essence, its appearance in form. As Dupré interprets this Greek centrality of form (the principal leitmotif of his study of modernity), form grounds the ancient and medieval onto-theological synthe-ses (Dupré 1993, 150–93).[15] For the ancients, the essence of the real and our knowledge of it consist ultimately of form. Form, moreover, shows forth the real in harmonious appearance: whether in sensuous image, as in Greek sculp-ture; in mathematics, as in Pythagoras; in the forms of tragedy that render some aesthetic harmony to chaos and strife; and above all through the ancient philosophical turn to reflective form in the soul or mind. For the ancients, the real appears in an orderly way and thus becomes (even in tragedy) harmonious appearance. This aesthetic, that is, form-focused, understanding of the real pro-vided the ultimate grounding for any harmonious synthesis of the cosmic, the divine, and the human realms among the ancients and medievals. That is a dif-ficult thought to comprehend for us late twentieth-century heirs of the frag-mentation of all syntheses. It is even more difficult for us as inheritors of vari-ous hermeneutics of suspicion that every form may merely mask indeterminacy and power relations, and every appearance or manifestation may always-already hide a strife involving both disclosure and concealment.

Nevertheless, both critics and proponents of classical, medieval, and much modern thought (Bruno to Hegel) cannot grasp Western thought without dwelling on the centrality of form. For the premoderns, what appears or mani-fests itself through form is not our subjective construction but the very show-ing forth of the real itself, through form. For the Greeks, true being begins with intelligible form, that is, with multiplicity, chaos, strife rendered orderly and harmonious through form. The Jewish, Christian, and Muslim thinkers accepted the Greek centrality of form but could not accept the necessity of form in Greek and Roman thought. The Greek gods embody the form prin-ciple; indeed, the form is the divine and the divine is form for the Greeks. For the Jews, Christians, and Muslims, God creates form. But as long as God is not understood as exclusively a purely transcendent will (as with the later nominal-ists), and as long as God's actions are not read exclusively through efficient cau-

---

15. See Dupré 1993 for his most extended analysis of the form principle, whose richness I merely sug-gest in this summary. See also Balthasar 1982.

sality, form survives, indeed prevails: now through the Creator God's formal, efficient, immanent, and final causality. For Christian thought, moreover, the doctrine of the Word grounds this reality of form in the central Christian doctrines of Christology and Trinity.

The principle of reality manifested *as real* in and through harmonious form *informed* the Western philosophical, onto-theological tradition from Plato through Hegel. For Plato (see Dupré 1993, 167–68), despite all his constant rethinking of "form," especially in *Parmenides*, form in some manner resided within the appearing objects of which it constituted the intelligible essence. As the determining factor of that intelligibility (and thereby reality), form also surpassed the objects. In all Greek philosophy (including Aristotle, despite his critique of Plato on form and his ontology of form-matter and potency-act), being is defined in terms of form. Moreover, in Plato, form's dependence is to be understood primarily — not exclusively — in terms of participation. The same is also true, it might be added, of archaic and Greek religion as a religion of manifestation (Eliade), or, as Hegel nicely named Greek religion, the religion of beauty. The same centrality of form, as Hans Urs von Balthasar (1982, 429–685) so brilliantly shows, is true of any form of Christianity faithful to the incarnational principle and to a properly theological understanding of Word as Logos — that is, to manifestation in and through form. Above all, there is a profoundly Neoplatonic and even Hegelian tone to Dupré's reading of the centrality of form for all Western thought. Indeed, for Hegel, as Dupré justly observes, all content attains its truth in and through form (Dupré 1993, 44).

In my judgment, Dupré could (and perhaps should) render his own constructive philosophical position explicitly hermeneutical, in harmony with his brilliant historical-hermeneutical reading of the centrality of form in Western thought. On the basis of this first volume (1993) alone, it is sometimes difficult to know exactly where Dupré himself stands on the philosophical issues his study of modernity clearly involves. To be sure, the subtitle to his book is "An Essay in the *Hermeneutics* of Nature and Culture" (my emphasis). And yet it is difficult to tell how far to take this hermeneutical turn in Dupré. In one sense of the term (a sense Dupré explicitly endorses), there is clarity: we need a sound hermeneutics (i.e., description in the philosophical, not only history-of-ideas nor social history, sense) of the passage *to* modernity before we can attempt a worthwhile philosophical critique *of* modernity. Granted, but still the question recurs: Does Dupré's "essay in hermeneutics" function only as a study of how central "form" and "manifestation" are to the Western ideal of some synthesis of the cosmic, the divine, and the human realms? Or does Dupré's philosophical essay not also show how determinate a hermeneutical understanding of truth itself is to his entire philosophical enterprise?

Modern hermeneutics, after all, has articulated a position on truth very like that implicit in Dupré's hermeneutical-historical study in *Passage to Modernity*.[16] Indeed, at one point, Dupré interprets the ancients as holding that truth does mean "to be justified" (as for the moderns), but that justification can be found principally in the sense that truth means participation in being (not construction *of* it) as manifested through form. This ancient sense is also the one argued by modern hermeneutics: first by Hans-Georg Gadamer in his insistence in *Truth and Method* that truth is fundamentally disclosure, and it is best rendered through form (*Dar-stellung*, not *Vor-stellung*); and second, and most carefully, by Paul Ricoeur in his argument that truth is primordially manifestation, and only derivatively correspondence or even coherence, allied to Ricoeur's further hermeneutical question of how the world of possibility evoked by the manifestation is rendered through the forms of composition, genre, and style. Any philosopher who argues, on contemporary grounds, in favor of a hermeneutical understanding of truth as primordially manifestation through some form (as I also have elsewhere) cannot but be heartened by Dupré's reading of the centrality of form in the Western philosophical tradition.

At the same time, we cannot but wonder why Dupré does not also develop, in terms of contemporary hermeneutics, what seems to be his own constructive (and not merely descriptive) position: namely, truth as primordially manifestation through form. Perhaps we must await the next volume for this development. And yet, for this reader at least, this is somewhat disappointing. For the hints Dupré does give of what I can only surmise is his hermeneutical position on truth are indeed promising. Consider, for example, Dupré's implicit critique of Heidegger in his own anti-Heideggerian reading of manifestation (note that he does *not* use the Heideggerian formula of disclosure-concealment); or consider Dupré's interpretation of form in both Plato and the Renaissance (on the former, Dupré is with Gadamer against Heidegger; on the latter, he is with

---

16. This hermeneutical notion of truth is also in harmony with Dupré's analysis of "correspondence," "coherence," and "disclosure" models (the latter in Gadamer's sense) in Dupré 1990 (19–43). This discussion can be explicitly related to the discussion of form in *Passage to Modernity*, and then to Gadamer's relationship of disclosure and form in *Truth and Method* (1988) and to Paul Ricoeur (1976) on the role of form as composition, genre, and style.

Grassi against Heidegger); and his critique of Heidegger's notion of onto-theology as too general a thesis to allow for the profound differences between the ancient and medieval onto-theological syntheses and that modern onto-theological subjectivism which Heidegger so brilliantly exposed (on Heidegger, see Dupré 1993, esp. 5–8, 111, 118, 162).

Consider as well Dupré's subtle insistence that, although Jacques Derrida is both correct and helpful in his analysis of the logocentric character of West-ern Greco-Christian thought (Dupré 1993, 24), still Derrida misreads the full complexity of that thought as a purely negative one by failing to distinguish be-tween the ancient understanding of logos as participatory in being itself from the modern understanding of logos as exclusively constituted by the human subject that gives all being its meaning. The latter modern understanding de-mands, to be sure, theoretical, Western, logocentric culture. But that is a nec-essary, not a sufficient, condition for Derrida's understanding of logocentrism. The sufficient conditions for the modern form of logocentrism can only be found in the crisis of the original onto-theological synthesis from the late medi-eval nominalists forward. If I am correct in this reading, Dupré agrees more with Gadamer and Ricoeur than with either Derrida or the more radical side of Heidegger on this crucial issue of truth as manifestation through form. Hence the philosophical underpinnings of Dupré's hermeneutical-historical enter-prise are philosophically hermeneutical and should be rendered explicitly so in order to clarify how his hermeneutical-historical argument already (i.e., even before the further analyses of volumes 2 and 3 appear) bears a contemporary, strictly philosophical significance.

Dupré here does *not* agree with Hegel, despite his profoundly Hegelian af-finities. Dupré *does* want his work to allow the "fragments" of our culture's reli-gious, philosophical, and theological traditions to become once again "building blocks" for a new, onto-theological synthesis. However, Dupré clearly disowns any Hegelian ambition to find a form that would encompass all forms (the speculative proposition, the absolute *Begriff*) arrived at, as in Hegelian phe-nomenological terms, through a journey through all the principal forms of art, religion, and philosophy. One will have to await the further constructive developments of Dupré's position to see the fuller outline of his proposed new synthesis. But this much is already the case: Dupré advances some hope for a future, relatively modest onto-theological synthesis (perhaps like White-head's). But he offers no hope at all for the "mad and secret dream of Hegel"

(Karl Rahner): an ultimate onto-theological synthesis, indeed totality system, rendered in and through the ultimate form, the dialectically achieved, speculative proposition of the Absolute. Like Gadamer and Ricoeur, Dupré has long since abandoned this Hegelian rejection of finitude without forsaking his debts to Hegel throughout his entire oeuvre, including *Passage to Modernity*.

Like contemporary hermeneutical thinkers, therefore, Dupré is fully aware of finitude, with finite fragments trying to build a new, modest onto-theological synthesis. No ultimate system, no all-inclusive speculative proposition, no grand narrative can be allowed. Instead, Dupré leaves his attentive reader with something more valuable: a series of reflections on how different the onto-theological synthesis of the premoderns was from what many now name modern "onto-theology"; a stern and persuasive reminder of how form served, and can still serve, as the central ideal of our culture in manifesting and rendering intelligibility, truth, and reality; a welcome insistence on how early modernity cannot be understood without understanding the religious elements that pervaded and sometimes grounded modernity's new intellectual and cultural synthesis from Cusanus and Bruno through the humanists, the Reformers, and the Baroque. Dupré has written an intriguing narrative encompassing the many forms of early modernity worthy of retrieval: many early modern images, symbols, hymns, and myths; the Renaissance retrieval of rhetoric and poetics; the forms Cusanus and Bruno forged primarily by developing formal, not efficient, causality to show the nondualistic relationship between the finite and the Infinite; new forms for the use of light as form in Duccio and Giotto; form as individuating in Dante; Ficino's aesthetical philosophy; Erasmus's narrative theology; Luther's dialectical theology, so expressive of early modern unresolved tensions and oppositions; Ignatius of Loyola's rendering of a form for ancient spiritual exercises, now translated into a modern method; and, most surprisingly of all, Dupré's brilliant defense of the moving, transient, elusive form of Baroque culture as a genuinely modern achievement.

Throughout Dupré's careful interpretations of all these forms (and more) lies his pervasive analysis of the centrality of form itself to our culture. Dupré leaves his reader with something far grander than one more grand narrative of modernity, or one more familiar critique of modernity. Dupré leaves one amazed anew at the radical newness of modernity by thinking in new historical, hermeneutical, and philosophical ways about our culture's original passage to modernity. He persuades us to take that passage again, not merely as our fate but also our chosen destiny. At least, modernity could be acknowledged as our welcome destiny, if we would but make the effort to understand first the rich, complex terms of early modernity, and not the more dogmatic terms for the modern of the eighteenth and nineteenth centuries, or most of the twentieth. Like the best historians, Louis Dupré in *Passage to Modernity* helps us to see an entire period afresh. Like very few philosophers, Dupré also helps us to think through again the most central issues of philosophy (form, nature, culture, the self, transcendence, reason, truth) by rethinking our culture's history. No small accomplishment, that.

REFERENCES

Balthasar, Hans Urs von. 1982. *The Glory of the Lord: A Theological Aesthetics.* Vol. 1. *Seeing the Form.* Edited by Joseph Fessio and John Riches, translated by Erasmo Leiva-Merikakis. San Francisco: Ignatius Press.

Berry, Philippa, and Andrew Warnick, eds. 1992. *Shadow of Spirit: Postmodernism and Religion.* London: Routledge.

Blumenberg, Hans. 1983. *The Legitimacy of the Modern Age.* Cambridge, MA: MIT Press.

———. 1987. *The Genesis of the Copernican World.* Cambridge, MA: MIT Press.

Buckley, Michael. 1971. *Motion and Motion's God.* Princeton, NJ: Princeton University Press.

———. 1989. *At the Origins of Modern Atheism.* New Haven, CT: Yale University Press.

Burrell, David, and Bernard McGinn, eds. 1990. *God and Creation: An Ecumenical Symposium.* Notre Dame, IN: University of Notre Dame Press.

Cassirer, Ernst. 1963. *The Individual and the Cosmos in Renaissance Philosophy.* Oxford: Oxford University Press.

Coward, Howard, and Toby Foshay. 1992. *Derrida and Negative Theology.* Albany: State University of New York Press.

Derrida, Jacques. 1992a. *Given Time: I. Counterfeit Money.* Translated by Peggy Kamuf. Chicago: University of Chicago Press.

———. 1992b. *Donner la mort.* Paris: Métailié-Transition.

———. 1994. "How to Avoid Speaking: Denials." In *Languages of the Unsayable,* edited by Sanford Budick and Wolfgang Iser. New York: Columbia University Press.

Dupré, Louis. 1972. *The Other Dimension: A Search for the Meaning of Religious Attitudes.* New York: Doubleday.

———. 1976. *Transcendent Selfhood: The Loss and Rediscovery of the Inner Life.* New York: Seabury Press.

———. 1987. "Mysticism." In *Encyclopedia of Religion*, edited by Mircea Eliade. New York: Macmillan.

———. 1990. "Truth in Religion and Truth of Religion." In *Phenomenology of the Truth Proper to Religion*, edited by Daniel Guerrière. Albany: State University of New York Press.

———. 1993. *Passage to Modernity: An Essay in the Hermeneutics of Nature and Culture.* New Haven, CT: Yale University Press.

Gadamer, Hans-Georg. 1988. *Truth and Method.* New York: Crossroad.

Gamwell, Franklin I. 1990. *The Divine Good: Modern Moral Theory and the Necessity of God.* San Francisco: Harper.

Grassi, Ernesto. 1983. *Heidegger and the Question of Renaissance Humanism.* Binghamton, NY: Medieval and Renaissance Texts and Studies.

Hart, Kevin. 1988. *The Trespass of the Sign: Deconstruction, Theology, and Philosophy.* Cambridge: Cambridge University Press.

Jaspers, Karl. 1962. *The Great Philosophers.* New York: Harcourt, Brace and World.

Krois, John Michael. 1987. *Cassirer: Symbolic Forms and History.* New Haven, CT: Yale University Press.

Lyotard, Jean-François. 1984. *The Postmodern Condition.* Minneapolis: University of Minnesota Press.

Marion, Jean-Luc. 1977. *L'Idole et la distance.* Paris: Grasset.

———. 1981. *Sur la théologie blanche de Descartes.* Paris: Presses Universitaires de France.

———. 1986. *Sur le prisme métaphysique de Descartes.* Paris: Presses Universitaires de France.

———. 1991. *God without Being.* Translated by Thomas A. Carlson. Chicago: University of Chicago Press.

———. 1992. "Le phénomène saturé." In *La Phénoménologie et théologie*, edited by J. F. Courtine. Paris: Criterion.

Ricoeur, Paul. 1976. *Interpretation Theory: Discourse and the Surplus of Meaning.* Fort Worth: Texas Christian University Press.

Toulmin, Stephen. 1990. *Cosmopolis: The Hidden Agenda of Modernity.* Chicago: University of Chicago Press.

Tracy, David. 1994. *Plurality and Ambiguity.* Chicago: University of Chicago Press.

———. 1995. *On Naming the Present*. Maryknoll, NY: Orbis Books.

———. 2020. *Fragments: The Existential Situation of Our Time*. Vol. 1 of *Selected Essays*. Chicago: University of Chicago Press.

Yates, Frances S. 1964. *Giordano Bruno and the Hermetic Tradition*. Chicago: University of Chicago Press.

CHAPTER 11

THE STRENGTH
OF REASON

*Franklin Gamwell's Philosophical
Theology and Moral Theory*

In 1987, there was a course titled "The Philosophical Grounding of Ethics: Aristotle and Kant" at the University of Chicago. The professors were Paul Ricoeur, Franklin Gamwell, and myself. Each of us gave three lectures and responded to the lectures of the others. It became a memorable dialogue and a genuine argument.

The three trajectories of the course, if memory serves me well, can be described as follows: Paul Ricoeur, by his own account, enacted a return to Kant through Hegel (and, therefore, also through Aristotle); Franklin Gamwell enacted a critical affirmation of the major claims of both Aristotle and Kant, along with a critical correction of each by means of the other, as well as arguing for a constructive general teleology of the Divine Good largely inspired by

Whitehead; and I pursued the claim that Aristotle's lack of a transcendental argument can be largely corrected by correcting Aristotle's misinterpretation of his teacher Plato on the moral-metaphysical Good. On this issue, moreover, Kant likewise held to a similar preference of Plato over Aristotle.

In retrospect, the course was an indication of a major move in the work of both Ricoeur and Gamwell. After Ricoeur's books on metaphor and narrative (both of which Ricoeur first taught as lectures), this collaborative course on ethics became the occasion for Ricoeur's pronounced turn to ethics in his later works (especially some years later in *Oneself as Another* [1992], *The Just* [2000], and *Reflections on the Just* [2007]). In the case of Gamwell, three years later he published his magisterial book, *The Divine Good* (1990) — an original and sustained argument against several dominant positions in contemporary moral theory. Several histories of ethics have divided a good deal of modern moral theory into an ineradicable opposition: Kant or Aristotle. By this reading, Western moral theory is either strictly deontological (Kant and neo-Kantians) or strictly teleological (Thomists, most Whiteheadians, and neo-Aristotelians, like Stephen Toulmin, Martha Nussbaum, Alasdair MacIntyre and, in theological form, Stanley Hauerwas). Gamwell's book provided a radical rethinking of both Kant and Aristotle, where each was argued to possess a major philosophical insight that, despite their intentions, could be dialectically related into a modern, metaphysical, transcendental teleology of the Divine Good.

First, on Kant: Gamwell argues that Kant's transcendental method should be employed by any modern philosopher taking the turn to the subject. Any responsible, modern moral philosopher needs, by the very demands of reason itself, to fulfill Kant's transcendental-critical insistence on analyzing the transcendental, rationally necessary conditions of subjectivity for every moral act as moral — that is, as a result of purely rational moral duty, not mere desire. Kant strongly rejects, as lacking a transcendental, necessary rational ground, any teleological account of desire and purpose like Aristotle's ethics. Gamwell argues in favor of Kant's transcendental grounding of moral theory, while also arguing against Kant's denial of the role of desire and purpose in ethics. Gamwell, therefore, argues that every transcendentally moral act is also, when analyzed, a purposeful act. As purposeful, therefore, every moral act is not only an efficient cause, but also a final cause. In sum, Aristotle's much earlier call for a teleological ethic, once metaphysically grounded, is affirmed.

To put a complex position too starkly, Gamwell argues that Kant's transcendental notion of subjectivity is too limited to intellectual consciousness alone, as distinct from Whitehead's more complex account of common human experience and reason (an account that includes the lure of feeling, a sense of valued importance, and purposeful desires). Gamwell argues persuasively that Whitehead's more inclusive account of human experience and reason can be formulated into a modern metaphysical account of moral theory.

Whitehead's fundamental principle of Creativity—with its inclusion of feeling, desire, and intrinsic value, as well as its metaphysically implied principles of event and relationality—constitutes, therefore, a purposeful, metaphysical, moral teleology, wherein "the many become one and are increased by one." Without Whitehead's metaphysics, the Kantian account of transcendental ethics, once united to the important account of exclusively efficient causality in a great deal of modern natural science, followed by a great deal of modern philosophy, has virtually eliminated final causality (and, thereby, teleological purpose) from modern moral philosophy.

It would be difficult to overstate how influential the reduction of all causality (i.e., Aristotle's material, formal, efficient, and final causes) to a narrow and purely externally related notion of efficient cause has been for all modern thought—including moral theory and philosophy of science—culminating in a rejection of any teleological metaphysics and, at the limit, metaphysics itself. Without final and formal causality, even the nature of efficient causality is so reduced that reality is no longer metaphysically construed as relational or purposeful Creativity, but as more like a series of purposeless and merely externally related events. Correlative to this loss of final causality is the fatal loss of the role of desire in Kant and many post-Kantians, including Heidegger, and of the lure of feeling in any metaphysical understanding of full authentic existence as the teleological metaphysical ground of the moral self.

In sum, Gamwell's argument for final causality, purpose, desire, and value allows him, as it earlier allowed Hegel in his own post-Kantian ethics, to incorporate a form of Aristotle's teleological ethics into a Kantian position. Again, like Hegel in relation to both Kant and Aristotle, Gamwell develops a non-Hegelian—but still Whiteheadian—teleological metaphysics. In my judgment, moreover, the long Neoplatonist tradition can be construed as partly incorporating both Hegel and Whitehead as modern and critical Platonic avatars. Be that as it may, Gamwell's distinctive (indeed, unique) contribution to a metaphysical moral theory, within the process tradition itself, has effectively called into critical question the all-too-familiar reading of moral theory as largely divided between Kant and Aristotle. Gamwell's own subtle series of arguments, especially in *Divine Good*, has argumentatively united Kant's transcendental moral theory of rational duty to Aristotle's teleological-empirical moral theory by means of Whitehead's teleological metaphysics of Creativity and the Divine Good. On Gamwell's revisionary reading, Kant and Aristotle remain opposites — but opposites that can now be dialectically related by joining the major accomplishment of each to the major accomplishment of the other, while simultaneously rejecting (through arguments internal to each thinker) the further inconsistent claims of each: namely, Kant's inconsistent rejection of a teleological metaphysics and Aristotle's inconsistent refusal to ground his empirical-teleological morality metaphysically (or, in modern Kantian terms, transcendentally).

Most modern neo-Aristotelians (e.g., Toulmin, Nussbaum, MacIntyre, and, in theology, Hauerwas) argue for Aristotle's ethics, but do not attempt to provide a transcendental grounding of that ethics any more than did Aristotle himself. One exception is Iris Murdoch, who employs a version of Aristotelian virtue ethics while turning to arguments from Plato and from Kant for a metaphysics to "guide" (her word) morality.

Gamwell's critical exchange with Murdoch (over whether to name Ultimate Reality "the Good" or the "Divine Good" — that is, the neoclassical, dipolar God) is a fine example of how two philosophers can argue on the common ground of a metaphysically defended morality, or, to use Murdoch's phrase, from the title of her Gifford Lectures, "metaphysics as a guide to morality." In fact, both Murdoch and Gamwell are committed by argument to "a metaphysics as a guide to morals." Hence, both are prepared to address the final, metaphysical moral question, What is the proper name for the Ultimate Reality: the Good or God? Murdoch, like Plotinus, argues for the Good and, unlike Plotinus, considers God an incoherent concept. Gamwell, instructed here principally by the work on the dipolar concept of God developed first by Whitehead and revised and refined by Hartshorne and Ogden, agrees that traditional notions of God as the solely necessary, eternal, and unqualifiedly all-powerful individual (classical theism) are finally incoherent. For example, how can God be literally (i.e., actually) all-powerful, given that there are other centers of power (e.g., free, intelligent human beings), as distinct from the coherent concept that God is all-powerful, not actually, but in the logically correct sense that God — and God alone — affects all individuals and is affected by all individuals. Gamwell argues in all his work that the neoclassical concept of God as dipolar is not only coherent but also allows the thinker to affirm the Divine Good as a clear and coherent concept, distinct from the relatively vague concept "the Good" of classical Neoplatonism and of Iris Murdoch.

Before leaving Aristotle (whose work, in my judgment, is as important for Gamwell as Plato's was for Whitehead), two further, purely scholarly rather than strictly philosophical issues deserve attention in order to clarify how solid and textually sound Gamwell's reading of Aristotle on teleology is. First, there is as yet no scholarly consensus on the nature of the texts of Aristotle that we possess. Some of these texts seem to be notes from students; others seem like Aristotle's own lecture notes in various degrees of finished form. Fortunately, the principal Aristotelian text relevant to Gamwell's analysis, *Nicomachean Ethics*, is the most well-formed treatise of all the texts we do possess of Aristotle, even though some textual puzzles remain (e.g., the lengthy, interruptive, and excessive discussion on friendship in the middle). Gamwell reasonably avoids many textual issues as unnecessary to resolve for his hermeneutical and philosophical purposes of clarifying the basic lines of Aristotle's moral teleology.

Second, consider the scholarly issues regarding Aristotle's texts. We know that Aristotle wrote not only treatises and lecture outlines, but also dialogues. Although we possess only fragments of Aristotle's dialogues, centuries later Cicero and Quintilian possessed Aristotle's dialogues and judged them quite well formed indeed. Cicero, for example, informs us that although Aristotle's dialogues did not demonstrate the artistic and philosophical genius of Plato's incomparable dialogues, Aristotle's dialogues were nonetheless clear, flowing, and polished (perhaps in dialogues Aristotle was Salieri to Plato's Mozart). Some ancients held that Aristotle's dialogues were meant for a popular communication of his philosophy, in contrast to the more sophisticated, complex arguments of his treatises, meant for students in Aristotle's Lyceum.

Furthermore, contemporary scholars of Aristotle are also left with a major hermeneutical puzzle: How should we relate the several texts of Aristotle to one another? The long history of the reception of Aristotle's texts complicates the problem still more. The ancient Neoplatonist philosophers considered Aristotle's texts on logic his most important texts for understanding his other texts; the Muslim, Jewish, and Christian medievals usually considered Aristotle's metaphysics the principal key to his texts; and some contemporary philosophers (e.g., Marjorie Grene and Stephen Toulmin) consider Aristotle's deep biological interests in teleology the key, even to his metaphysical and ethical teleology. Aristotle, after all, modeled a good deal of his philosophy on the teleological, organic forms he first studied in a field that today would be called marine biology. Among others, Marjorie Grene has argued that Aristotle's profound, lifelong interest in biology influenced every aspect of his teleological philosophy on several issues, as much as Plato's commitment to mathematics as providing an ideal model for metaphysics influenced much philosophy, from Plato (and Pythagoras before him) until Descartes and Leibniz.

In this intellectual, Platonic-Aristotelian tradition, moreover, Whitehead is particularly distinguished among modern metaphysicians for grounding his metaphysics in both mathematics and biology, and in natural science more broadly, thus allowing him to develop his unique teleological metaphysics. (Whitehead was, after all, the coauthor with Bertrand Russell of the magisterial *Principia Mathematica* [1910–13].) Gamwell, probably wisely, avoids these scholarly debates on strictly textual problems. For example, Gamwell interprets and argues both pro and con with Aristotle's teleology in the text of *Nicomachean Ethics*, while avoiding extended discussion of Aristotle's *Metaphysics*. This Gamwellian textual decision is especially important because, given Gamwell's own metaphysical proclivities, he may well have been tempted to correlate the teleology of Aristotle's ethics with Aristotle's metaphysics more explicitly — as Thomas Aquinas and even Hegel had done before the modern scholarly conflicts on the interrelationships of Aristotle's texts. That scholarly conflict — on how to correlate, if we can, the many diverse Aristotelian texts — continues since Werner Jaeger's still-debated claim to have discovered a chronological key to the ordering, and thereby the interrelationships, of Aristotle's texts. Some recent claims also debated among scholarly experts insist that Aristotle's texts are related on neither strictly philosophical nor chronological grounds, but rather on pedagogical ones: that is, Aristotle's texts are ordered to help a student in Aristotle's Lyceum to study in his early years the arguments appropriate to many subject matters (e.g., biology, logic, poetics, or rhetoric) in order, eventually, to be able think metaphysically. In other words, only after some years was a student in Aristotle's Lyceum capable of becoming a genuine philosopher.

For the ancients, after all, the philosopher was a unique human type. The philosopher was the one person in the community whose life was devoted to reason; in Aristotle's case, to knowing the nature of argument on almost every important subject. Hence the ancient need for distinct schools of philosophy to prepare young men (and also women, at least in the garden school of Epicurus and, possibly, in Plato's Academy, given what Plato says in *Republic* about the need for equal education of men and women) either to become genuine philosophers themselves or at least to know enough philosophy to help guide the city morally and politically and to stop the democratic populace from exiling (Anaxagoras) or killing (Socrates) the philosophers, as Leo Strauss has argued. Aristotle's pedagogy shows how to sort out different kinds of argument and, eventually, to engage in transcendental and metaphysical arguments on the necessary general characteristics of reality, as well as to use modern terminology on the limit questions of the human desire for life as meaningful and on value as not divorced from fact.

The singular importance of Aristotle for Western culture can best be found in his amazing ability to sort out the kinds of arguments needed for different questions, and the kinds of evidence appropriate to those questions. Aristotle's biological-teleological arguments, for example, in the fascinating treatise *On the Parts of Animals* clearly influence but in no way determine the metaphysical teleology of *Metaphysics* or the teleology of *Ethics*. Each Aristotelian teleological claim demands a distinct kind of argument. The logical arguments in *Prior Analytics* and *Posterior Analytics*, and the setting forth of rhetorical and dialectical topical arguments in *Topics* (i.e., *topoi* — or places where different kinds of argument can be found), clearly help to place but not determine the fuller rhetorical arguments employing both topics and tropes in *Rhetoric* and *Poetics*.

Aristotle's ability to sort out the kinds of argument needed for different disciplines and different questions within a given discipline (e.g., the argument on the primacy of plot over character in the form of tragedy in *Poetics*) made Aristotle's texts, whatever their provenance, a collection of treatises (and sometimes manuals) to teach, even today, the right kind of general argument needed for different questions in different disciplines: for example, in contemporary theology, historical arguments cannot be resolved by philosophical arguments, and vice versa. Intellectual integrity across the disciplines demands attention to the kinds of arguments and evidence appropriate to the many different questions in each discipline. Aristotle still remains a guide here — as Franklin Gamwell has been for more than thirty-five years in the Divinity School at the University of Chicago, especially in his always-pertinent questions on arguments advanced by students and colleagues alike. Gamwell is too much the Yankee gentleman to have served as an interruptive Socrates, but he has been our discursive Aristotle.

Even with the far greater sophistication of the modern sciences, as well as of modern logic and mathematics, we are all heavily indebted to Aristotle's singular ability to clarify the nature of rational argument: it must involve no self-contradiction; it demands consistency and coherence among the concepts employed; and it must honor the different kinds of evidence needed in each argument. Argument must also honor the needs for warrants, when evidence is challenged as irrelevant; and for backings, when warrants themselves are challenged (Toulmin 1958). Argument demands both truthfulness (mean what you say and say only what you mean) and truth redeemed through argument. As Gamwell frequently asserts in his writings, making a claim about a conceivable object demands an argument appropriate to justify that claim.

Dante was not wrong to call Aristotle "the master of those who know" (*il maestro di color che sanno*) — the master, in other words, of those who know the necessity of the self-correcting power of argumentative reason in the many different forms of argument. Anyone who has had the intellectual pleasure of reading the several texts of Franklin Gamwell (especially the magisterial *The Divine Good* [1990] and *Democracy on Purpose* [2001]) will agree with me that, for these many years at Chicago, Franklin Gamwell has served in the role of an Aristotelian maestro, as *the* principal colleague who has aided students and colleagues alike to sort out the kinds of argument needed for redeeming their different claims.

THEOLOGY AND THE POLITICAL PUBLIC REALM

Franklin Gamwell has consistently argued (both implicitly and explicitly) for argument itself; that is, for argumentative reasoning as the kind of reasoning needed in both philosophy and theology. Besides new questions and new intellectual developments (most recently on the problem of evil) in Gamwell's work, as far as I know, there have been no real ruptures and no notable detours or digressions in his work in philosophical theology and ethics. Gamwell is, therefore, well poised to encounter further conversation partners in relationship to his well-grounded philosophical theology: namely, the possible future relationships between his model of argumentatively based philosophical theology and some other models, perhaps complementary, perhaps competitive.

Some further discussion would be valuable, I suggest, on models of reason alternative to the traditional and argumentative model dominant from Aristotle forward to contemporary analytic philosophy and Anglo-American metaphysics already functioning in different kinds of contemporary philosophical theology. Other, not necessarily conflictual, models include a phenomenological analysis of excessive or saturated phenomena in the work of Jean-Luc Marion, Jean-Louis Chrétien, and others; the dialogical model of inquiry initiated by Plato and developed into a hermeneutical theology in modern thought by Gadamer, Ricoeur, and others; the emergence of modern critical theories as distinct from traditional theories to uncover not conscious errors but unconscious and systemically operative distortions in our thought (on sexism, racism, classism, etc., as was performed by the Frankfurt school); and finally, the return of contemplative thinking in some philosophical theology (Peperzak, Coakley), partly occasioned by the late Heidegger's turn to what he called meditative (as distinct from "calculative") reasoning. The turn to contemplative thinking in several Western theologies is also occasioned by new interest in the combinations of contemplative thinking and logical and metaphysical arguments in Plotinus and in such earlier Christian philosophical theologians as Gregory of Nyssa, who is truly inclusive, since he includes both logical and transcendental arguments within his fundamentally mystical-contemplative thinking.

Gamwell, who already knows a great deal of Paul Ricoeur's work, possesses a widely admired ability to provide, if he so decides, fair-minded interpretations of positions alternative to his own. He is eminently qualified to engage in the conversation on models of philosophical reasoning for contemporary philosophical theology noted above. But allow me to be clear: my suggestion for yet another intellectual journey for Gamwell's retirement years (may they be many!) is perhaps more my desire than his: namely, to hear his distinct voice of argumentative reason in the continuing debate on models of reasoning.

The Gamwellian rethinking of a metaphysical moral theory in relation to philosophical theology of a neoclassical understanding of God as the Divine Good has led to a second remarkable achievement: Gamwell's argument against the dominant consensus on the role of religion in the public realm, together with his uniquely formulated arguments for a discussion-debate in the public realm on comprehensive visions of the Good (i.e., on religion broadly construed). On this set of issues on religion and the public realm, Gamwell argues for a singular model for an authentically public theology that is opposed to the two influential alternatives. The first alternative argued against by Gamwell is any understanding of religion as purely private: that is, the belief that religion is merely another instance of personal preference in a society ruled by personal preference. The second alternative argued against by Gamwell is the resurgent Christian Right's attempt to impose traditional Christian personal values on a pluralistic and democratic society in order to "save" society from the debasement construed to be caused by a secularist reduction of the Christian values — values said to have earlier held American society together.

The Christian Right, in Franklin Gamwell's limited and precise meaning of the term, does *not* mean a Christian political conservative, as distinct from a Christian political liberal. Rather, Gamwell's Christian Right is a Weberian ideal type. Here are some of the central characteristics of the Christian Right as an ideal type according to Franklin Gamwell. First, the Christian Right depends on an erroneous reading of the original separation of church and state. They understand the original separation to endorse a state-sponsored setting for the Christian church to hold society together by developing such traditional and admirable Christian Reformed personal virtues as honesty, integrity, responsibility, self-discipline, a traditional work ethic, and compassion for the weak.

Second, this belief of the new Christian Right on how to interpret the original separation of church and state is often allied to a traditional theological belief that the United States is "a light upon the hill," chosen by God to lead humankind to a Christian democratic future.

Third, Gamwell argues that, in the recent past, the Christian Right generally held that "religion and politics do not mix." On this reading of the complex, pluralistic, and ambiguous American past, the Christian church was already fulfilling its separate constitutional role by providing a Christian populace, educated by the Christian churches, to incarnate those personal virtues mentioned above. Those virtues make for a virtuous and harmonious society — which, according to this interpretation of the Constitution, was exactly what the Founders intended by their separation of church and state. Therefore, with the occasional exception (e.g., the temperance movement's promotion of Prohibition in the early twentieth century), the Christian Right has, until the last thirty years or so, largely kept to the idea that "religion and politics do not mix."

Fourth, in sum, for Gamwell the Christian Right, as an ideal type, includes any Christian who holds to the above interpretation of the meaning of the separation of church and state and to the concomitant belief that Christian political theology should be focused on replacing present secular values of personal preference with such Christian personal virtues as honesty, integrity, responsibility, self-discipline, a traditional work ethic, and compassion for the poor. Gamwell holds, as do most of us, that there is every good reason to endorse the traditional virtues listed above — although, whether these virtues are *only* Christian virtues is, in my judgment, unlikely (ancient and contemporary Stoics, as well as participants in other religions, consider most of the same traditional personal virtues important for both the individual *and* the wider society), and within Christianity itself, there are different ways of understanding and correlating these Christian virtues, especially love and justice (e.g., the sophisticated Roman Catholic social justice tradition).

However, for those of us who do not accept the interpretation of the separation of church and state promoted by the Christian Right, there is a notable absence in the Christian Right's otherwise admirable list of personal virtues: namely, the public virtue of the common good and, allied to it, the public egalitarian virtue of equal justice for all. The public virtue of justice resists all forms of injustice, not only out of compassion but also out of a democratic sense of justice that all persons are created equal before God. Justice as a virtue resists *any* unjust social structures (e.g., involving race, gender, or class) that have consciously or unconsciously systemically enforced injustice in a society (e.g., segregation). The traditional Christian personal virtues are indeed virtues. However, without the public virtue of democratic justice ("all are created equal"), based on a sense of the common good, the democratic ideal is lost. Politically, Gamwell strongly argues, as he has throughout his work on moral theory and metaphysics, that individuals (more exactly, "persons") are constituted by relations. Individuals as such, therefore, are directed to a political ethics emphasizing community and the common good, not merely the personally virtuous good of an individual. Moreover, the ethical ideal of the common good leads one naturally to affirm what Martin Luther King Jr. called "The Beloved Community" — which concept, in turn, leads to the vision of the comprehensive Good of the political community and to the ultimate relation, the Divine Good.

For Gamwell, the opposite option is equally troubling: the widely held conviction (especially but not solely among secular thinkers) that personal preference is what the state is fundamentally designed to aid, especially preferences in material, economic matters. The separation of church and state, in this reading, reduces religion to merely another personal preference. Religion, therefore, is unwelcome in the public realm, since, like other cultural choices (e.g., for jazz, horror movies, or eggs over easy), religion *as* a private preference of some individuals is protected by the state, just as any other private cultural or economic choice is. This personal preference option affects both the political Right and Left. For example, in the 1970s, the economist Milton Friedman was asked at a public university forum to reflect on the following question regarding the activities of members of the University of Chicago's Department of Economics in Pinochet's Chile: "Should we all at the University of Chicago not be ethically troubled by the Business School's economic aid to a regime infamous for its fierce oppression of the people, including widespread imprisonment of opponents as well as documented cases of torture and murder?" Friedman answered that he and other economists help Chile with purely economic matters. Whatever their own moral qualms may be about Pinochet's regime, the Chicago economists in Chile do not discuss morality and politics with the Chilean government in their purely economic dealings with them. Economics, after all, is rational and thereby discussable; moral issues are not. Morality cannot be discussed rationally and is strictly a matter of personal preference.

Some thinkers on the Left sometimes give roughly the same answer: all is, finally, personal preference. For example, Richard Rorty, and even John Rawls in his later work, did not believe that it is possible to argue philosophically for a defense of democracy. Democracy, like other regimes, is a matter of historical (or even geographical) contingency. Neither democracy nor any other political regime is philosophically defensible as morally the best regime for human beings. Furthermore, in this Rortyan reading, both personal morality and democratic politics are, in effect, personal preferences of particular individuals and societies at particular historical times: for example, the direct democracy of ancient Athens, or the representative democracy of the United States. Rorty makes clear that he admires and is thankful to live in a democratic regime. However, all that is luck, contingency; it is not, perhaps regrettably, a philosophically defensible option.

This is even more the case when the question of religion in the public realm of a democracy is raised: Rorty's response on this question seems to be that it is better to change the subject. No conversation on a comprehensive Good for a society (i.e., religion in the broad sense or Rorty's own, fine humanistic vision) can ultimately be a rational one: "Change the subject." Franklin Gamwell refuses "to change the subject" on the question of religion and the public realm in a democracy and has explicitly argued to that effect in his major works. Despite their deep political differences, Friedman and Rorty agree that moral, political, and religious convictions are solely matters of personal preference and cannot be publicly — that is, rationally — defended.

Franklin Gamwell's analysis of the present, seemingly dominant American opinion on morality and religion in the public realm, as largely divided between the Christian Right and the "personal preferential" thinkers, is an intriguing and, I think, persuasive analysis of why neither of the two major options presently informing contemporary societal questions of morality, politics, and religion in our battered public realm is persuasive. Of course, Gamwell admits that there are other options besides these two (e.g., the early, more Kantian John Rawls), but the two former options are so powerful in our contemporary American culture that he does not exaggerate in calling their combination the dominant consensus of our present society. The option of the Christian Right clearly remains a powerful force in our politics and society. Even stronger is the alternative option: the viewpoint (especially in the media) that religion is solely a private option that some individuals may freely choose to engage in, but that this private option should have no real role in discussion in the public political realm.

In his further reflections, especially in the book *By the People, for the People* (2010), Franklin Gamwell makes several striking points about the two main conflicting forces within this dominant consensus: the personal preferential view; and the view of the Christian Right. Each position is indeed in direct opposition to the other. Neither position encourages engaging in public discussion on comprehensive views of the Good for American democracy. The seeming inability of either side to listen to the other, much less actually dialogue and argue with each other, Gamwell insists, beclouds a fact unacknowledged by both parties: both sides share a surprising ground—possessive individualism.

Throughout his work, Gamwell has consistently argued that the possessive individualism shared by both opposed parties in the dominant consensus is philosophically, ethically, and politically erroneous. Each of us is an individual insofar as we are related to others. In certain societal and political circumstances (e.g., the effects of sexism and racism), it *is* morally important to emphasize the need for individualism. This need becomes acute for ensuring the human rights of all those individuals who, for reasons of race, gender, ethnic origin, sexual orientation, class, or economics, have been deprived of their full individuality, their personal dignity, and their individual rights. This need for individual rights has rightly occasioned several amendments to the Constitution to redress injustices based on race, gender, class, and economic or ethnic status. Thus also the continuing need for economic redistribution of resources to the weak, marginal, and poor in society, in accordance with principles of justice and the common good, in a society where the gap between the very rich and the very poor widens every year.

In his recent writings on evil, furthermore, Gamwell argues against both

Augustine's and Reinhold Niebuhr's insistence that pride is necessarily the principal sin for human beings. Gamwell, instructed here by feminist thought, states that pride may well be the principal sin of the successful and the empowered, but not of the disempowered. Self-abasement rather than pride often becomes the principal sin of the disempowered, who can internalize the societal, even structural denials of their full human individuality to the point where they endorse, in their own self-understanding, a false understanding that can amount to sinful self-abasement.

Americans can too easily forget that, even at the beginning of the Republic, the democratic ideal classically articulated in the Declaration of Independence and the Constitution did not allow that democratic ideal—"all men [*sic*] are created equal"—to apply to women, to slaves, or to the poor and less-well-off economically. It has taken several amendments to the Constitution to partly undo these injustices—and in the case of race, it took a shockingly bloody civil war that still haunts American memory as deeply as the Trojan War once haunted the memory of classical Greece.

The democratic ideal construed by Franklin Gamwell, as by John Dewey before him, includes the affirmation of both the dignity and equality of each citizen, and, through the individual's persistent philosophical, moral, and political relationships with the community, the democratic ideal *also* implies a relationship to a comprehensive good. Just as Gamwell earlier argued for a metaphysical moral teleology, so too, in *Democracy on Purpose*, he argues for a correlative metaphysical political teleology, within which argument takes place in the public realm on various claims of articulating a vision of the comprehensive good for society.

Franklin Gamwell argues forcefully that every comprehensive vision of the Good for society—*contra* both the "personal preference" option and the personal Christian virtue option of the Christian Right—should be argued in a public realm. In philosophy proper, Gamwell may be interpreted as providing the metaphysical grounding that John Dewey's noble defense of the democratic ideal needed but did not provide. In theology, moreover, Gamwell has consistently argued that philosophical theology is, by definition, a public theology. In his view, therefore, public theology is not an extra theological task, undertaken after the real thing—systematic theology—is finished in order to relate the results of systematic theology to the public realm. On the contrary, for Gamwell, public theology is intrinsic to the theological task *as such*. Public philosophical theology is not the luxury item that many theologians think it to be; it is a *necessity* for all theology.

Franklin Gamwell's political, philosophical public theology also makes eminent sense of the original meaning of the separation of church and state as formulated by Thomas Jefferson in his argument against those who held that the religious diversity promoted by any political endorsement of religious freedom would inevitably lead to societal conflict: "Truth is great and will prevail if left to herself," Jefferson wrote. "She is the proper and sufficient antagonist to error, and has nothing to fear from the conflict unless . . . disarmed of her natural weapons, free argument and debate; errors cease to be dangerous when it is permitted freely to contradict them" (quoted in Gamwell 2010, 10).

The public realm, as Thomas Jefferson argued in his day and as Franklin Gamwell nobly does in ours, should include public debates on different claims of distinct issues for understanding a comprehensive good for society — both penultimate arguments on the common good and ultimate metaphysical arguments on the comprehensive Good inclusive of this society and of all reality. No comprehensive vision for society, traditionally religious or traditionally secular, is irrelevant to the public debate on the common good for a genuinely democratic society. Without that public debate, we are left in a situation of turbulent chaos and increasing pathos: a set of possessive individuals, not relational distinct persons, largely defined by personal preferences, uneasily jockeying for power with little or no sense of a common good. In the end, the result will be the one Thomas Hobbes described: "a war of all against all." Has the majestic democratic ideal of the American Republic yielded to empire, oligarchy, and possessive individualism?

A concluding note: Franklin Gamwell's intellectual contributions have been joined by his deep and unrelenting commitments, not only to think for the public good in his philosophical theology, but also to act for the public good in season *and* out of season — in his earlier ministerial work for the good of the people of his different parishes; in his political work on civil rights; in his judicious guidance on public issues in his years as an adviser at the Rockefeller Foundation; in his exceptionally thoughtful and genuinely democratic earlier collegial role as Dean of the Divinity School at the University of Chicago for ten years; and in his tireless efforts helping to organize and work with that new organization, Protestants United for the Common Good. So much first-rate intellectual and public practical work — how does he manage it all? Perhaps, like Aristotle himself, Gamwell has never been able to decide definitively on what, ultimately, is the greater good life — the life of contemplation, or the life of political action. Aristotle could never quite decide the issue, so he practiced both contemplation and politics. So has Franklin Gamwell. He, too, like his mentor Aristotle, has chosen to excel at both: the committed intellectual life *and* the committed political life.

For us, here at the University of Chicago, Franklin Gamwell's work has served and will continue to serve as the best kind of example of intellectual integrity. As I mentioned earlier, Dante held that Aristotle provided for Western culture as a whole the model of argumentative reason by formulating the different kinds of argument that a genuinely intellectual culture will always need. For more than thirty years in Chicago's divinity school, Franklin Gamwell served an analogous role. He has become for all of us *il maestro di color che sanno* — the master of those who know.

REFERENCES

Gamwell, Franklin I. 1990. *The Divine Good: Modern Moral Theory and the Necessity of God.* San Francisco: Harper San Francisco.

———. 2001. *Democracy on Purpose: Justice and the Reality of God.* Washington, DC: Georgetown University Press.

———. 2010. *By the People, for the People: A Political Voice for Progressive Christians.* Eugene, OR: Wipf and Stock.

Ricoeur, Paul. 1992. *Oneself as Another.* Translated by Kathleen Blamey. Chicago: University of Chicago Press.

———. 2000. *The Just.* Translated by David Pellauer. Chicago: University of Chicago Press.

———. 2007. *Reflections on the Just.* Translated by David Pellauer. Chicago: University of Chicago Press.

Toulmin, Stephen E. 1958. *The Uses of Argument.* Cambridge: Cambridge University Press.

CHAPTER 12

LINDBECK'S NEW PROGRAM FOR THEOLOGY

A Critical Reflection

George Lindbeck's *The Nature of Doctrine: Religion and Theology in a Post-liberal Age* (1984) has become an important and influential book. In a sense, he has written two books. One study (as the main title indicates) is on the nature of doctrine. There his original and suggestive "rule-theory" reading of doctrine is developed. The second study (as the subtitle indicates) is yet more ambitious. Here Lindbeck articulates a new paradigm (a "cultural-linguistic" paradigm, "borrowed" principally from Ludwig Wittgenstein and Clifford Geertz). This paradigm is geared to understanding religions as analogous to languages and cultures, as well as to understanding theologies as largely grammatical enterprises. No minor ambition, this. The book, therefore, is not simply a modest, programmatic statement of the new "Yale school" — however couched in the typically modest and cautious prose we have all become accustomed to from Lindbeck.

I forgo a summary of the argument of the book as a whole and instead confine my remarks to three major moves in this argument. Two issues I shall discuss at some length: first, Lindbeck's interpretation of the major alternative model for theology as "experiential-expressive"; and, second, Lindbeck's own cultural-linguistic approach to "truth-claims" in theology. A third issue I discuss very briefly is his suggestive interpretation of doctrine by means of rule-theory. All these issues are clearly major strands in his overall argument.

It must be clearly stated, however, that, even if Lindbeck is erroneous (as I shall suggest he is) in his interpretation of what he names experiential-expressive theologies, he might still claim that his cultural-linguistic model for theology is more adequate than alternative models. He could still claim, for example, that a cultural-linguistic model is more comprehensive in its scope or more attuned to some contemporary social-scientific and some linguistic-philosophical analyses of religion than alternative models. Similarly, even if his model has problems that the present book does little to resolve (e.g., regarding truth-claims), Lindbeck could still claim that the interpretation of doctrine, as principally second-order rules, not first-order referential propositions, could still stand. My own beliefs, indeed, can be summarized as follows: first, Lindbeck's analysis of the alternative model he names experiential-expressive is seriously, even fatally flawed; second, his own cultural-linguistic model needs to manifest, far more than the present work does, an ability to handle the question of truth-claims in theology to avoid (as he himself sees) the obvious charges of relativism, confessionalism, and fideism; and third, Lindbeck's interpretation of the nature of doctrine is nonetheless both original and suggestive, although questions on the nonpropositional character of the "rules" he enunciates are, to me at least, not yet clear.

To state my own conclusions thus bluntly should not indicate that even I (experiential-expressivist, as Lindbeck clearly believes I am) should be unable to learn from this learned and careful, programmatic work. Indeed, I believe, as my second and third beliefs cited above suggest, that, even if my other criticisms are correct, Lindbeck has nevertheless aided us all by his interpretation of doctrines as principally second-order rules, rather than simply first-order propositions. If that is true, then the main title of the book (*The Nature of Doctrine*) and, thereby, the sections of the book on doctrine, are his most important and enduring contribution. The sections discussing the subtitle (*Religion and Theology in a Postliberal Age*) are the most problematic.

To provide a new paradigm for interpreting doctrine is a major contribution. It is an especially welcome contribution from George Lindbeck, *the* major theological contributor in North America to ecumenical dialogue among the major Christian confessions. Although Lindbeck's interpretation of doctrine clearly does cohere with his interpretation of religion and theology, I fail to see how his grammatical reading of doctrine entails a grammatical reading of theology or a cultural-linguistic reading of religion. But just this question of "coherence" or "entailment" between the title and subtitle of this programmatic work seems to me the greatest puzzle of Lindbeck's argument as a whole. In fact, this book is really two books that roughly cohere with one another. The first book (on doctrine) is, I believe, one that any theologian, however different her paradigm for theology, can and should learn from. The second book (on religion and theology in a postliberal age) is, at least for this theologian, provocative but thoroughly unpersuasive.

The first issue is Lindbeck's analysis of what he calls the "dominant" liberal theological paradigm since Friedrich Schleiermacher, the liberal trajectory he describes as using an experiential-expressive model for theology. He has many comments on and critical descriptions of this model. But all these sometimes-disparate descriptions seem geared to make, as the name indicates, one principal point: that all these models are based on a typically modern liberal "turn-to-the-subject" paradigm. All of them are grounded in the mistaken belief that "inner experiences [are] prior to expression and communication" (36). Indeed, "whatever the variations, thinkers of this tradition all locate ultimately significant contact with whatever is finally important to religion in the prereflective experiential depths of the self and regard the public or outer features of religion as expressive and evocative objectifications (i.e., nondiscursive symbols) of internal experience" (21). In sum, the theologians in this dominant "liberal" tradition understand inner prereflective experience as "foundational," and all language and culture as merely "expressive" of that foundational, nondiscursive experience. They possess a unilateral understanding of the relationship of experience and language, as well as of experience and culture, when what we need is a dialectical understanding of these complex relationships.

The problem with Lindbeck's descriptions of the "dominant" theological model is not that his analyses do not point to real problems within the tradition from Schleiermacher to Paul Tillich, Mircea Eliade, Karl Rahner, Bernard Lonergan, and others. The problem is that Lindbeck is apparently unaware that thinkers in the very tradition he targets for criticism have addressed *precisely* these issues as their own major questions for at least fifteen years prior to the publication of this book. Indeed, the turn to an explicitly hermeneutical position by many theologians in this dominant tradition, as well as the turn to a radical "de-privatizing" of the same tradition by political, liberation, and feminist theologians, are the major attempts within the general liberal paradigm to address both the "linguistic" (hermeneutical theologies) and the cultural (de-privatizing social-political theologies) issues that Lindbeck announces as news.

In fact, anyone who has read modern hermeneutics in either philosophy or theology can discover that the major claim from Hans-Georg Gadamer (whom Lindbeck does not mention) through Paul Ricoeur (whom Lindbeck bizarrely lists as one more experiential-expressivist) has been to rethink the dialectical (not unilateral) relationship between experience and language. They have, to be sure, attempted to do this without abandoning the classical liberal insight into a non-empiricist notion of experience that both the Continental tradition and the American tradition (William James, Alfred North Whitehead, John Dewey, et al.) first forged. But such attempts, if successful, would prove "dialectical" — indeed, far more dialectical than a seemingly new, "unilateral" move from "experience" to "language" in Lindbeck's cultural-linguistic model. In fact, the major argument of the hermeneutical tradition since Gadamer has been against Romantic expressivist understandings of language's relationship to experience. This work, in turn, has been what has allowed a major transformation of the Schleiermacher-Tillich-Rahner-Lonergan experiential paradigm into an explicitly hermeneutical one. Moreover, this hermeneutical transformation has been continuous with the major "correlation" schema of the liberal theological tradition, and with it the discovery of a non-empiricist notion of experience. Hermeneutical theologians (in the broad sense) have also argued for the correctness of the linguistic-experiential performance of the classical liberals and neo-Orthodox as distinct from some of their theories on experience and language: witness Brian Gerrish's work on Friedrich Schleiermacher and Ernst Troeltsch, or Langdon Gilkey's work on Paul Tillich and Reinhold Niebuhr.

The argument among explicitly hermeneutical theologians has been consistent: one can maintain the richer and broader understanding of experience, forged by the liberals (both European and American), only by dialectically relating it to recent understandings of language (and thereby, inevitably, also to history and society). Experience cannot be understood on a Romantic, expressivist model (or any other purely expressivist model). But this crucial insight does not mean that we should, in effect, abandon half the dialectic by simply placing all experience under the new guardianship of and production by the grammatical rules of the codes of language. Insofar as these familiar hermeneutical claims hold, theologians can continue the liberal analyses of the broader notion of experience, without yielding to the earlier expressivist temptations of that tradition. To do so, of course, theologians in the liberal tradition must become both explicitly hermeneutical and explicitly social-political-cultural. But this, indeed, is exactly what most of them have become: consider Edward Schillebeeckx's recent work in hermeneutics and critical theory in relation to his own earlier work; consider Schubert Ogden's use of Stephen Toulmin; and, more recently, Jürgen Habermas and Karl-Otto Apel in relation to Whitehead and Charles Hartshorne. Consider also, if I may cite it, my own explicitly hermeneutical turn in *The Analogical Imagination* (1998), in contrast to the hermeneutically informed but underdeveloped position on "common human experience" in *Blessed Rage for Order* (1975).

Hermeneutically informed theologians, moreover, usually also find themselves called to become (via their own analyses of the dialectical relationships of experience and language) more cultural-historical-political. At the same time, explicitly "political" theologians like Johann Metz and Jürgen Moltmann, as well as "liberation" theologians like José Bonino and Gustavo Gutiérrez, and feminist theologians like Elisabeth Schüssler Fiorenza have found it necessary to concern themselves with hermeneutics in order to achieve an adequate political theology. These theologians, to be sure, would not describe their positions as cultural-linguistic, as distinct from something like "hermeneutical-political." For the moment, it seems sufficient to state that the *bêtes noires* of Lindbeck's position should hardly feel overwhelmed by his charge of experiential-expressivism when their own work has challenged the expressivist and "privatist" tendencies of the earlier liberal experiential traditions. They have done so by developing explicitly hermeneutical-political theologies critical of the earlier liberal accounts of language and experience, and even critical of some of their own earlier formulations. But they have also done so without abandoning the noble, correlative enterprise of the classical liberals and their self-critical successors, such dialectical or neo-Orthodox theologians as Tillich, Bultmann, early Barth, Rahner, and Lonergan. To recognize an "anomaly" is not necessarily to abandon a paradigm completely. It is to rethink the paradigm in such manner that its accomplishments are not rejected in the transformation of its problems.

Lindbeck's problems with this liberal tradition, I suspect, are finally less methodological or formal than his paradigm analysis would suggest. His problems are substantive or material. As his frequent references to Karl Barth and his colleagues at Yale (Hans Frei and Paul Holmer) make clear, Lindbeck's substantive theological position is a methodologically more sophisticated version of Barthian confessionalism. The hands may be the hands of Wittgenstein and Geertz, but the voice is the voice of Barth.

In sum, the label *experiential-expressivism* does not fit as an accurate philosophical or theological description of the alternative liberal theologians Lindbeck paints in such broad strokes. For Lindbeck's real problem, I repeat, is theological: like Karl Barth (of *Church Dogmatics* rather than *Romans*) and like some of his colleagues at Yale, Lindbeck is theologically deeply troubled by the liberal tradition. He wants theology to be done purely from *within* the confessing community. He wants a new, ecumenical, confessional theology. He does not, therefore, finally approve even of such "dialectical" methods of correlation as Tillich's or Rahner's or Lonergan's, nor even the next generations' hermeneutical-political models. He wants something purer, cleaner, more economical—a cultural-linguistic model from the social sciences become a "confessionalist" model for theology. Lindbeck's cultural-linguistic model is, I fear, less a new paradigm that eliminates the anomalies of the old than a new paradigm that first denies the accomplishments of the old and then develops new-old anomalies of its own (as on "truth-claims"). In his own Lutheran tradition, Lindbeck's confessionalist theological model is more like Melanchthon's confessional theology than it is like Luther's own existential theology.

Moreover, Lindbeck's cultural descriptions of the need for our American theologies to become "Anglo-American empiricist," rather than remaining trapped in "nineteenth-century" German idealism and Romanticism and twentieth-century existentialist phenomenology, are curious as cultural descriptions. Such analyses of what constitutes Anglo-American culture conveniently overlook three cultural facts. First, as mentioned above, the very traditions he cites as the problem have all been involved for some years in rethinking hermeneutically and politically-culturally precisely the issues he requests that they address. Second, even the Anglo-American, linguistic-philosophical tradition, in many of its major proponents (e.g., Richard Rorty, Hilary Putnam, Stuart Hampshire, Stephen Toulmin, Stanley Cavell), no longer understands itself as culturally alienated from the Continental tradition in its explicitly hermeneutical form. And third, the major accomplishment of the American experiential philosophical tradition (from William James through John Dewey) has been to challenge the British empiricist traditions' narrow understanding of experience as sense experience alone (John Smith) — further cultural proof, perhaps, that the "American" part of Lindbeck's "Anglo-American empiricist culture" needs rethinking.

In sum, I am not persuaded by Lindbeck's interpretation of the alternative theological paradigm as experiential-expressive. That title, as Wittgenstein might say, is a good example not of "naming" but of "language idling." Lindbeck may, of course, have good reasons to dispute my claim that the hermeneutical-political model works in addressing the issues of language and experience, and the related issues on language-experience-history-culture. But until he interprets the easily available and familiar texts employing that model, I and others must remain as unpersuaded by his charge of experiential-expressivism as I remain unpersuaded by his theological call for a new confessionalism.

The second issue is the "cash value" of Lindbeck's own cultural-linguistic model for the crucial issue of truth-claims in theology. Perhaps George Lindbeck would claim that, even if his description of the alternative model I name hermeneutical-political and he calls experiential-expressive is inadequate, nevertheless his own cultural-linguistic model is still preferable. His reasons for that preference would perforce have to be different from those he actually gives for rejecting his own experiential-expressive construction. What those reasons might be is, unfortunately, a guessing game. The fact is that a fruitful and critical discussion between Lindbeck's cultural-linguistic model and a hermeneutical-political model has not yet been posed sharply by anyone — and surely not by Lindbeck's description of the alternative as experiential-expressive.

Lindbeck's puzzling and rather begrudging comments on the transcendental theologies of Rahner and Lonergan (i.e., that they are too "complicated" and "hybrid" or not "economical" enough) lead me to infer that the paradigm I name hermeneutical-political would prove, for Lindbeck, too "complicated" and "non-economical" for his Ockham-like tastes. These hermeneutical-political models are "complicated" (like reality itself). They do demand the employment of several disciplinary approaches, including ones (e.g., transcendental analysis or metaphysics) that Lindbeck seems to find without argument ready candidates for Ockham's razor. Moreover, he also seems to believe that any theologian who agrees with the basic thrust of Rahner or Lonergan (as I clearly do) must also end up agreeing with Rahner's "anonymous Christian" position or Lonergan's belief that Friedrich Heiler had located certain essential characteristics in all religions. If this material theological issue of the possible unity of religion is the real theological problem for Lindbeck (he devotes considerable space to it), this difference, at least, is easily resolved. For no one of their later hermeneutical-political descendants agrees with the positions of their great predecessors on this "unity of essence" issue: witness Troeltsch vis-à-vis Schleiermacher, or Gilkey vis-à-vis Tillich, or Metz or Küng vis-à-vis Rahner, or Burrell or myself vis-à-vis Lonergan, on these crucial issues of "dialogue," "essence," and "unity-plurality."

But, Lindbeck might then say, Why work with the complexities of hermeneutics, metaphysics, and critical theory if all theology really needs is a clean, cultural-linguistic model? We can understand religion as like a language or a culture (i.e., "a comprehensive interpretative scheme with an interest in the maximally important!"). We can understand theology as a grammatical analysis of the depth grammar or logic of the religion. This seems, and indeed is, one plausible, social-scientific way to describe religions and to analyze one crucial task of theology. The question for theology is: Is it adequate for the full range of theology's task? Lindbeck, with his admirable desire to avoid relativism and fideism, is fully aware of this larger theological task. Indeed, he devotes two crucial sections of his compact book to addressing these issues: his "Excursus on Religion and Truth" (63–73) and the entire last chapter, "Toward a Postliberal Theology." I regret to say that I do not believe that he has resolved the issues he has set for himself (i.e., relativism and fideism) — at least on the basis of the analysis set forth in those sections.

There the strength of his cultural-linguistic model, to be sure, does come through. It is the strength of the truth of "intra-systematic" coherence to interpreting the tradition by maintaining a rigorous notion of "intratextuality." No theologian should deny that one major task of all responsible theology is to show how it is the centuries-old, rich, pluralistic Christian tradition itself that is being interpreted, and not interpreted away or invented. Lindbeck's grammatical model for this task is illuminating. This remains the case, even if hermeneutical-political theologians like myself would hold that, on Lindbeck's own grounds, grammar alone is not sufficient. Theologians also need rhetorical analysis (i.e., the ancient discipline that is the correlate of modern hermeneutics): rhetorical analysis (which includes grammatical analysis) is needed to encompass adequate interpretations of the concrete, plural, traditional narratives, symbols, doctrines, and so forth, and not only of the narratological (or doctrinal or symbolic) codes. Indeed, Gadamer is exactly right: modern hermeneutics is a historically conscious and more linguistically sophisticated form of ancient rhetoric of both the topics and the tropes of classical rhetoric. Moreover, Lindbeck's long footnote (136) on the Yale deconstructionists leads me to believe that he has not reflected very much on the rhetorical (hermeneutical and/or deconstructive) aspects of the question of interpretation of texts and, thereby, on how grammar and rhetoric (like code and use) inevitably interact in all concrete interpretations — even of grammatical codes. But even this important issue, however central to many modern discussions of the interactive relationships of grammar and rhetoric (e.g., Paul de Man and Wayne Booth), need not detract from the power of Lindbeck's partial but real contribution: his kind of grammatical analysis *does* illuminate one way to analyze the rules and codes, especially of "doctrines." Further rhetorical-hermeneutical analysis can illuminate how those codes become actual discourse.

But however pressing is the concern with the relationship of grammar and rhetoric for interpreting the concrete discourse of the tradition, the major problem lies elsewhere: How can theologians assess the truth-claims of Lindbeck's grammatically analyzed traditions? Lindbeck is fully aware of this set of problems and tries many ways to meet it: by distinguishing between the intrasystematic truth of coherence and performative ontological truth; by agreeing with the need for *ad hoc* apologetics; by appealing to the need for skill and practice over theory; by disputing illusory claims to pure neutrality; by developing a notion of applicability as futurology; and so forth. Even those who agree that a "purely neutral" theory of rationality is never purely neutral, and who agree that skill and practice are crucial ingredients in any attempt to assess rationally all theological claims, will remain unpersuaded that Lindbeck's "epistemological realism" is other than relativism with a new name, or that his cultural-linguistic grammatical model for theology is other than confessionalism with occasional *ad hoc* apologetic skirmishes.

Professor Lindbeck's position, as far as I can see, is a new linguistic version of one side of classical pragmatism. More exactly, the one aspect of pragmatism's response to assessing truth-claims that he clearly holds is an analysis of "consequences" in life as criteria of assessment of either an individual or a confessing community (note his analysis of assessing the truth-claim of God-language exclusively by seeing how that claim "performs" to order a life). Two other aspects of William James's pragmatic position receive, at best, shorter shrift. First, consider James's insistence on assessing whether one's present religious belief is an illuminating suggestion (or, as James put it, a "luminous possibility") or not. Here, at least in post-James hermeneutics, the understanding of truth as manifestation (with the categories disclosure-concealment and recognition) is, I believe, available — and in non-Romantic-expressivist ways. Second, recall James's insistence on assessing whether what we believe through our religious tradition coheres or not with what we otherwise know, practice, and believe.

This latter nest of issues, it should be emphasized, does not necessitate a capitulation of traditional religious beliefs to contemporary secular beliefs. Rather, as the revised correlation model for theology implicitly or explicitly involved in all hermeneutical-political positions suggests, any correlation should be, in principle, one of *mutually critical* correlations of an interpretation of the meaning and truth of the tradition, and the interpretation of the meaning and truth of the contemporary situation. Such a hermeneutically revised correlational model provides a heuristic guide; no more, no less. The model, like all models, guides. The concrete subject matter at issue alone rules. And there all the rational and religious skills available are needed to discern the proper response here and now. On the correlation model, a response may, logically, be one of identity, similarity-in-difference, or pure nonidentity (existentially, confrontation) between the meanings of tradition and situation. That heuristic and hermeneutical correlation is one way to keep alive the noble project of both our liberal and neo-Orthodox predecessors, without claiming either control through purely neutral, ahistorical notions of "rationality," or purely Romantic notions of expressing "inner feelings," or deceptively "economical" notions of the purely grammatical task of theology.

To conclude: I have discussed only two crucial aspects of Lindbeck's provocative and programmatic book. If I have contributed suggestions that Lindbeck himself may find helpful for developing or revising his program, I shall be very content. In turn, I have learned much from his book. This is especially the case on two questions that have aided me greatly in my own distinct theological program: namely, Lindbeck's sophisticated and illuminating analysis of one way to formulate the grammatical aspect of theology's wider task; and Lindbeck's original interpretation of the nature of doctrine via rule-theory. I hope to continue to learn on these and other questions from the careful, compact writings and ecumenical spirit of George Lindbeck.

I wish to emphasize these gains as strong and solid ones. For even if I believe that any interpretation of the Christian tradition, as suggested above, must be more complex than a grammatical analysis alone can encompass, any hermeneutical thinker can and should still learn from Lindbeck's analysis of one way that grammatical analysis can function in theology. On Lindbeck's analysis of doctrine, moreover, I still have some lingering questions as to the adequacy of his rule-theory interpretation of doctrine: for example, the "rules" he actually cites, as implied by Nicaea and Chalcedon, do make sense as rules; however, at least the first two rules (on the "one God" and on "Jesus of Nazareth") are also clearly referential propositions. Nevertheless, the interpretation of doctrines as *regula fidei* is genuinely illuminating. Lindbeck's interpretation of doctrine does seem a way forward out of several propositional-confessional impasses.

As for the rest, I have given some reasons why I cannot count myself among those for whom Lindbeck wishes, in the final line of his book, "May their tribe increase." But then, I have not experienced "from within" the cultural-linguistic world of the present Yale school. Can we meet? Can we converse critically? Can we even "translate" our positions to one another? I believe we must try—as I have here, however inadequately. Despite protestations against "translation" to the contrary, so does Lindbeck. That is why he wrote *The Nature of Doctrine*. That is why the rest of us read it. That is why others read reviews like this along with the book itself. That whole critical-conversational process is what theological hermeneutics is, finally, all about. And no labels of his or my minting (whether experiential-expressive or hermeneutical-political or cultural-linguistic, or Yale school, or Chicago school) should becloud our common ethical and religious-theological responsibility to converse and translate. George Lindbeck is foremost among those who have proved themselves those rarest of theologians—confessionally and doctrinally deeply ecumenical. I hope he can also carry that same rare, ecumenically confessional spirit into also becoming more ecumenical with the alternative liberal traditions in theology from Schleiermacher to Schillebeeckx. Then a genuinely new paradigm for theology, and not only for doctrine, might be forthcoming.

CHAPTER 13

JEAN-LUC MARION

Phenomenology, Hermeneutics, Theology

There are many ways to approach the thought of Jean-Luc Marion. Some have focused on such intra-phenomenological debates as those with Derrida on gift, Ricoeur on two notions of givenness, and Levinas on the philosophical relationship of justice and love. These debates are highly significant ones in which I, too, like the other contributors to the edited volume *Counter-experiences* (Hart 2007), have offered a judgment. But none of these intra-phenomenological debates (save later in this essay, where I reflect on the dispute surrounding the relationship of phenomenology and hermeneutics) claim my attention here. Rather, I consider Marion's work as it contributes to the age-old issue of the relationship of philosophy (here, phenomenology) and theology. I do so principally because I believe that Marion's work, if I read him correctly, is enormously fruitful for theology. I also take this focus because I believe his work has, at times, been seriously misread in two opposite ways: either as a philosophy that is a covert theology, or as a proposal to control theology by philosophy. Since I do not find either reading persuasive, I feel obliged to give my own reading—influenced no doubt by my own positions in both philosophy and theology. I, too, will inevitably raise some questions, but they remain, as far as I can see, more in the nature of further questions than internal criticisms. But of that, the reader—and Jean-Luc Marion—must judge.

To complete this task, I shall begin with my own assessment of the major developments in Marion's impressive intellectual journey, and then suggest what questions need further attention to clarify and advance Marion's enterprise as it affects the relationship of philosophy and theology. In view of Kevin Hart's (2007, 1–56) outline of the chronological stages in Marion's thought, therefore, I shall be silent on several issues in order to concentrate on the philosophy-theology relationship—at times implicit, at other times explicit, in his thought.

MARION'S FIRST STAGE: THE REREADING OF DESCARTES

Marion's first stage of thought was principally a reading of Descartes. In his magisterial interpretation of Descartes, Marion (1999b), influenced initially, I believe, by his mentor Ferdinand Alquié and by Levinas's reading of the category of the Infinite in Descartes's *Third Meditation*, spelled out Descartes's complex position on the *cogito* in terms of all the relevant texts of Descartes. In brief, the more familiar reading of Descartes was as a turn to the subject that instituted a modern onto-theological claim to ground all reality in the subject rather than premodern substance. Marion, far more than Heidegger or even Levinas, spelled out the fuller complexity of Descartes's texts and his influence (1999a). In historical context, Descartes's position on God and causality (*causa sui*) was deeply influenced by Francisco Suárez's controversial attempt to unite the Scotist *ens commune* and the Thomist analogy. Étienne Gilson (1982) had already argued against Suárez, and Bernard Lonergan (1957) consistently argued for the disastrous intellectual influence of Suárez, both in the interpretation of Thomist analogy and in the misinterpretation by modern thought of causality as only efficient causality.

However, it is Marion who articulated the full-fledged intellectual debacle that followed in Descartes's wake regarding the understanding of God in both philosophy and the Cartesian theology that Michael Buckley (1987) had also delineated in seventeenth-century French thought. In sum: for Buckley this was the historical moment when theology lost its roots in religious life — liturgy, spirituality, prayer, faith — and became, in effect, a second-rate Cartesian philosophy. Neo-Scholasticism was regnant in Catholic theology before the *ressourcement* movement of de Lubac, Congar, Chenu, Balthasar, Rahner, and Lonergan. Meanwhile, the Neo-Scholastics continued their control of Catholic thought under the ironic rubric of responding to Descartes in Cartesian terms and not, as they claimed, on Thomist principles.

Modern philosophy before Marion's groundbreaking work on Descartes missed the significance of Descartes's *Third Meditation* and his argument that the category of the Infinite is ontologically prior to the category of the finite, and thus breaks all our finite categories and therefore is contrary to the univocity in the *Fifth Meditation* and "common being" that Descartes elsewhere — with his egology and his understanding of causality and God as *causa sui* — employed in the *Meditations*. This neglect of the *Third Meditation*, I suggest, was unfortunate, and not just for Catholic theology.

That history of effects of the misreading of the *Meditations* has also proved disturbing for secular philosophical thought and much Protestant theology. In much modern philosophy, this reading of Descartes by means of the *cogito* alone is foundational. Here, the influence of Spinoza is crucial. Spinoza's impersonal understanding of God is fully dependent on his interpretation of Descartes's notion of causality and, therefore, Suárezian "common being" and "univocal language." Moreover, Vincent Carraud (2002) has demonstrated the Suárezian formulation of the principle of "sufficient reason" and its enormous influence in modern philosophy, especially in Leibniz. The "atheism controversy" of Jacobi and Fichte, and (above all) the Kantian formulation of God as a noumenal limit-concept that can be thought but not known, determined much secular and Protestant thinking about God in the modern period.

Levinas (1961), brilliantly but somewhat impressionistically, rediscovered the importance of the Infinite in Descartes. And Marion (2018) demonstrated the complexity of Descartes's thought by a careful textual analysis of several meanings of God in Descartes. Moreover, there is the contrast in Descartes between the Infinite (in principle, not compatible with Suárezian univocity and causality) and *causa sui* — in principle fully compatible with Suárez and the major thinkers (Spinoza, Leibniz, Wolfe, and Kant) who followed in Descartes's wake. This study of Descartes by Marion (1999a) is far more persuasive than the grand narratives of the problems of Western thought since Plato, articulated in distinct but related terms by Heidegger and by Derrida. For Marion's narrative is the more modest narrative of modern Western thought, not an indictment of all Western philosophy since Plato as onto-theological (Heidegger) or logocentric (Derrida). Marion, Carraud, Henry, Chrétien, Lacoste, and other "new phenomenologists" delineate with Heidegger the need for a non-onto-theological position for both philosophy and theology. Unlike Heidegger and with Levinas, they shift phenomenological attention from the self to the Other and, with Marion in particular, to his rich phenomenological notion of the saturated phenomenon allied to a new, non-Heideggerian understanding of givenness related to reduction (which the later Heidegger largely ignores). But this is to push the Marion development further along, perhaps, than the arc of his actual trajectory.

MARION'S SECOND STAGE: A PHENOMENOLOGY OF THEOLOGICAL LANGUAGE

It is interesting, certainly for the theologian, that Marion's next move was not to provide the strictly phenomenological (i.e., philosophical) series of reductions needed to defend his phenomenological description of givenness or his original notion of the fourfold saturated phenomenon. That would come later. In the second stage of his thought, Marion was concerned to recover the Dionysian tradition in Christian theology. A probable influence here was Balthasar's defense of the Dionysian tradition (1984) and the insistence on the liturgical-eucharistic setting of Dionysius's reflections on God, whereby neither cataphatic nor apophatic moves are definitive for understanding Dionysius's insistence in *Mystical Theology* on the Incomprehensible God revealed beyond predication and beyond cataphatic and apophatic readings alike in mystical, liturgical, and personal prayer. To show this, Marion developed phenomenologies on the distinction of "icon" and "idol," and above all his refutation of all onto-theology in his influential *God without Being* ([1995] 2012). The latter work should be read not as a theology but as a phenomenology of theological language in the Dionysian tradition. Aside from a too-narrow reading of Thomas Aquinas on God as *Esse* (a reading Marion later largely corrected) and a claim that the bishop alone is the authentic theologian, Marion insightfully argued that the Dionysian tradition — once so influential not only in Eastern theology but also in Western theology prior to Thomas (Balthasar rightly claims that Dionysius is second in influence only to Augustine in Western theology) — did suffer a setback by Aquinas's choice of *Esse* as the principal cataphatic name for God over the Dionysian "the Good."

Even those of us who believe that Aquinas was far more subtle in this matter (especially in his commentary on Dionysius) than Marion has thus far allowed can still agree with Marion that the Thomist loss of the cataphatic name "the Good" as the principal name for God (as it remained in Bonaventure) did bear some consequences that became unfortunate, even for the presumably Thomist Neo-Scholastics, after Suárez's linking of the Thomist analogical *Esse* to the Scotist *esse commune*.

As we shall see later, beyond Marion's excellent reading of Dionysius, the recovery of the Dionysian apophatic and mystical-theological tradition also allows, in principle, for a Levinasian recovery of Plato's "Good beyond Being," which, like Descartes's Infinite, provides a new way to think of God that is philosophically and theologically freed of the modern "isms": theism, atheism, agnosticism, pantheism, and panentheism — all dependent on modern metaphysical causality and onto-theology.

I have suggested elsewhere that an equally important shift away from the Dionysian tradition in Western Christian theology occurred when Luther, once an admirer of Dionysius, turned violently against him to rethink *Deus Absconditus*, not as the "Incomprehensible God" of the Dionysian tradition but as the doubly "Hidden God" of the Reformation tradition. The latter Lutheran and Calvinist positions (reformulated for modernity in Catholic Augustinian terms in Pascal's *Pensées*) can be read in two ways: first, as a violent and unfortunate rejection of the Dionysian tradition in almost all Protestant theology until recently, with the exception of Anglicanism — a major misfortune, occasioned if not caused by Luther's rejection of that tradition; and, more modestly, as a healthy corrective to the Dionysian tradition, by insisting on the major lack in that tradition (and in Marion's retrieval of it, thus far) — namely, a theology of the Cross, attentive, as in Luther, Pascal, and Balthasar and Lonergan, to Paul's law of the cross (Lonergan) disclosing Christ Crucified (and not just John's Glory manifested in the givenness of the Lifting Up of Christ on the Cross).

Again, as in Pascal, this attention to the theological phenomenon of the Cross of Christ can also allow for more phenomenological attention than Marion has thus far given to Pascalian *misère* — that is, in its full Pascalian sense of *misère* as sin, *misère* as suffering, and *misère* as ineluctable, tragic fate (the aspect emphasized by Jean Racine). These too are saturated phenomena that deserve — indeed, demand — attention in any full attempt to do justice to the icon of Christ, the incarnate, crucified, resurrected one who will come again. Could not the recovery of the Dionysian *Dieu sans l'être* also become the occasion for the God without Being, manifested and hidden in the suffering and negativity of Christ Crucified as the Crucified God? Without that retrieval, we do not have the full Jesus Christ. Without the Cross, we do not have an adequate response to Levinas's poignant question: Can any philosophy that does not address innocent suffering provide any adequacy today? With the full range of Christological symbols — Incarnation, Cross, Resurrection, Second Coming — contemporary theology might be able to render a fuller and yet more saturated icon of Jesus Christ beyond not only Being but also beyond even the Dionysian tradition of God's Incomprehensibility. That icon would look to the excessive giving, generosity, love — even *kenosis* — of the Dionysian God, while also realizing, with Pascal, that the excessive kenotic love of God in Christ must be understood not only by incarnation but also by the cross; not only by resurrection, but also by the eschatological, not-yet event of the Second Coming.

But these questions, to be sure, are more strictly theological than philosophical-phenomenological. They seem appropriate, however, as comments on the second stage of Marion's work. Hence, in that stage, we find a phenomenology of idol and icon and "God without Being" that may be described not as theology but as a phenomenology of theological language and iconic image. There are, therefore, some further questions that do not call into question the analyses of "God without Being" and the icon as distinct from the idol but instead ask for their completion by attention to the "dark side" revealed in the Cross in order to be faithful, beyond Dionysius, to the fuller Christian understanding of Jesus Christ in Incarnation-Cross-Resurrection-Second Coming.

MARION'S THIRD STAGE: THE NEW PHENOMENOLOGY OF THE SATURATED PHENOMENON

In Marion's third and present stage of thinking, he has left behind (only momentarily, one presumes) his phenomenology of theological language and has returned to phenomenology proper. Influenced partly by the debate with Derrida on the possibility of gift, but more by the exigencies of his own thought on phenomenological reduction and givenness, Marion has worked out in his major philosophical work, *Étant donné* (1997), what his work on Descartes implied and his work on the icon and the Dionysian theology needed: a strictly phenomenological defense of givenness, related to a critique of both Husserl's notions of intentionality and constitution and Heidegger's formulation of the *es gibt*. Marion has paid less attention to the Levinas-Blanchot discussion of the relationship of *es gibt* and *il y a*. Perhaps Marion's relative silence on the latter discussion is partly occasioned by his most original phenomenological breakthrough: the formulation of the "saturated phenomenon" — saturated in all four senses.

Surely the work *Being Given* (2002) and the allied text *In Excess* (2004), as well as his exceptional study of the visible in painting and his recent and daring study *The Erotic Phenomenon* (2006), constitute Marion's major, strictly philosophical contributions to the "new" phenomenology. The phenomenology of *Being Given*, moreover, establishes phenomenologically the categories of both "revealability" and revelation as the "saturated phenomenon *par excellence*."

Quite consistently from a theological viewpoint, Marion never presumes that philosophy can establish the fact of an actual revelation, especially the Christian revelation. Here, surely, his philosophical and theological hesitation is exactly right. The phenomenological defense of revealability shows the condition of possibility of the "Impossible" revelation to be rather surprisingly like Karl Rahner's argument in *Hörer des Wortes*. But only the actual divine revelation itself — the saturated phenomenon *par excellence* — could ever establish revelation. The actual revelation of God by God is, in Christian Trinitarian terms, the revelation of the Father through the Son in the Spirit. The latter, in Christian terms, is clearly a matter of faith — itself, a gift/grace from God. Marion is clear that no philosophy could in principle establish that. Even Hegel did not really claim to, since his absolute *Begriff* as *Vorstellung* was possible only because of the existence of an absolute Christian revelation as *Vorstellung*. The time spent by many theologians in the modern period on metaphysical "proofs" for the reality of God is a tale with few breakthroughs (e.g., Charles Hartshorne) before the Catholic *ressourcement* theologians recovered premodern resources for such thought: Balthasar, Lonergan, Rahner, Schillebeeckx, and Küng, as well as the many different neo-Reformation theologians, especially Barth and Tillich. There were also, however, other theological and philosophical breakthroughs: Pascal, Kierkegaard, and in more contemporary terms, Franz Rosenzweig and Mikhail Bulgakov.

PHENOMENOLOGY AND HERMENEUTICS FOR THEOLOGY

Much more could — and should — be said about the relevance of the new phenomenology to theology. As an enterprise, systematic theology is a hermeneutics of revelation. Systematic theology is distinct from fundamental philosophical theology that rationally argues for the revealability of Christian revelation (Rahner). Christian systematic theology is fully dependent on an actual revelation, as well as the pure gift of faith in revelation to become *fides quaerans intellectum*. As a hermeneutic, theology as faith seeking understanding is also dependent not only on a hermeneutics of retrieval of the primordial revelation, but also on a faith-transformed intelligence (the latter, in sum, not only as the human image as *microcosmos*, but also as *imago dei*). In hermeneutical theology, a hermeneutics of critique is, at times, also necessary. Sometimes critique, not retrieval alone, is the best way to read the witnesses (the Scriptures, creeds, doctrines, symbols, liturgies, prayers, etc.) appropriately (e.g., in not reading Genesis as science). Moreover, when necessary, theology also needs a hermeneutics of suspicion (e.g., on the sexist character of the biblical witnesses). This hermeneutical character of theology in its full sense — retrieval, critique, suspicion — is not caused only by modern needs (even if they occasion it — e.g., Darwinian science in the first case, secular feminist movements in the second), but also by the prophetic character of the revelation itself. Prophecy criticizes itself.

To argue adequately my own position here on theology as a combination of hermeneutics of retrieval, critique, and suspicion, I realize, would take another essay. For the moment, it is perhaps enough to state that theology should, indeed, abandon all modern onto-theological attempts and content itself with its philosophical side — with a phenomenology first, as a way to describe the givenness of the actual revelation of God as witnessed to us in the texts we name Scripture, in the liturgy and in all prayer, communal and personal. The fact that Christian revelation is the event and person of Jesus Christ, and the fact that contemporary Christians believe *in* Jesus Christ *with* the apostles, also shows the inevitably hermeneutical character of theology — beyond the original phenomenology of the actual revelation as the saturated phenomenon *par excellence*. In my judgment, hermeneutical theology welcomes and can eventually encompass phenomenological theology, not (as in Marion and Sokolowski) the reverse.

However, any hermeneutical theology divorced from the givenness of revelation and the transforming gift of faith will soon stumble — even on hermeneutical grounds alone, which, after all, are dependent on a receptivity to the gift of revelation for any hermeneutical conversation. For this move, the kind of phenomenology proposed by Marion in *Being Given* and *In Excess* is invaluable — even, perhaps especially, not only for phenomenological theologies (like Marion's own recent work) but for hermeneutical theologies as well. Indeed, Marion himself suggests that the phenomenality of actual saturated phenomena (the Other, face, flesh, gift, *eros*, etc.) issues forth into what he nicely names "an endless hermeneutic." That is even more the case in theology (e.g., for such extremely saturated phenomena as Incarnation, Cross, Resurrection, Second Coming, etc.).

If this be so, then I suggest that another step for Marion is not to return only to a phenomenology of strictly theological language (Dionysius, Thomas, Augustine, Luther, Bonaventure, Balthasar, et al.), but that he might spend more phenomenological time on the original revelation itself, as witnessed in the Scriptures, insofar as Scripture both *in*forms and *trans*forms all later theologies. This he is clearly doing in his recent theological work, both phenomenological and historical (Justin Martyr, Tertullian, Clement of Alexandria, Basil of Caesarea, etc.). Hence my final proposal: once scriptural revelation is more fully described by Marion's brilliant phenomenology, then a phenomenology of the voice will become at least as necessary as any phenomenology of the visible (face or icon). No one can see the face of God and live, as Exodus insists. But the voice of God — for Moses, even for Job in the whirlwind — is always there. And in the New Testament, the fact that the Word becomes flesh also means that, in Jesus the Christ, the voice becomes face. A phenomenology and a hermeneutics — of voice and face in the God-man, Jesus the Christ — remain a major task for any contemporary fully Christian systematic theology. Both the new phenomenology and the hermeneutics of the ancients and the moderns have become indispensable philosophical tools for the modern theologian — as indispensable as Platonism was for the patristic period.

A phenomenology of the face connected to a phenomenology of the voice; iconic manifestation and prophetic proclamation; incarnation and cross; Dionysius and Pascal. Can we not hope that Jean-Luc Marion, after contributing so much on these constant polarities, can be encouraged to turn his attention more fully to the second of these polarities as well?

REFERENCES

Balthasar, Hans Urs von. 1984. *The Glory of the Lord: A Theological Aesthetics.* Vol. 2. San Francisco: Ignatius Press.

Buckley, Michael J. 1987. *At the Origins of Modern Atheism.* New Haven, CT: Yale University Press.

Carraud, Vincent. 2002. *Causa sive ratio: La raison de la cause, de Suárez à Leibniz.* Paris: Presses Universitaires de France.

Gilson, Étienne. 1982. *La liberté chez Descartes et la théologie.* Paris: Éditions Vrin.

Hart, Kevin, ed. 2007. *Counter-experiences: Reading Jean-Luc Marion.* Notre Dame, IN: University of Notre Dame Press.

Levinas, Emmanuel. 1961. *Totality and Infinity: An Essay on Exteriority.* Translated by Alphonso Lingis. Dordrecht, The Netherlands: Kluwer Academic.

Lonergan, Bernard. 1957. *Insight: A Study of Human Understanding.* London: Longmans, Green.

Marion, Jean-Luc. (1995) 2012. *God without Being: Hors-Text, Second Edition.* Translated by Thomas A. Carlson. Chicago: University of Chicago Press.

———. 1997. *Étant donné: Essai d'une phénoménologie de la donation.* Paris: Presses Universitaires de France.

———. 1999a. *Cartesian Questions: Method and Metaphysics.* Chicago: University of Chicago Press.

———. 1999b. *On Descartes' Metaphysical Prism: The Constitution and the Limits of Onto-Theo-Logy in Cartesian Thought.* Translated by Jeffrey L. Kosky. Chicago: University of Chicago Press.

———. 2002. *Being Given: Toward a Phenomenology of Givenness.* Translated by Jeffrey L. Kosky. Stanford, CA: Stanford University Press.

———. 2004. *In Excess: Studies of Saturated Phenomena.* Translated by Robyn Horner and Vincent Berraud. New York: Fordham University Press.

———. 2006. *The Erotic Phenomenon.* Translated by Stephen E. Lewis. Chicago: University of Chicago Press.

———. 2015. *Negative Certainties.* Translated by Stephen E. Lewis. Chicago: University of Chicago Press.

———. 2018. *On Descartes' Passive Thought: The Myth of Cartesian Dualism.* Translated and with an introduction by Christina M. Gschwandtner. Chicago: University of Chicago Press.

Part 4

PROPHETIC THOUGHT

FEMINIST THEOLOGIES

Feminist scholarship and philosophy have been major forces in Christian theology. Feminist hermeneutics is unequaled in its demands for the full range of modern hermeneutics. First of all, feminist historical hermeneutics of retrieval has recovered so many major female theologians — once marginalized and often even forgotten female theologians like Hildegard of Bingen, Angela of Foligno, Mechthild of Magdeburg, Hadewijch, and others.

Second, feminist hermeneutics has exposed the patriarchal character of every known culture and major religion, including, of course, Christianity. Indeed, in the patriarchal, institutional forms of Christianity, especially in Eastern Orthodoxy and Roman Catholicism, women are still denied their full equality in the institutions, including ordination.

Third, feminist theological hermeneutics has moved beyond a critique of Christian patriarchal wrongs to an even more subtle, more profound, and more necessary analysis, issuing in a hermeneutics of suspicion of the unconscious but systemically functioning, tragic, even sinful, reality of a pervasive, unconscious sexism. Sexism, like racism, is not a conscious error like patriarchy, which can be undone by pointed and sustained criticism. On the contrary, an unconscious systemic sexism unconsciously drives and sustains all conscious patriarchal structures. There has been a profound need, therefore, for a feminist hermeneutics of suspicion to uncover the unconscious systemic power of ingrained sexism.

In sum, feminist theologies have demonstrated a rare ability to employ all three major types of hermeneutics: a historical feminist hermeneutics of retrieval, in order to recover so many forgotten, ignored, and marginalized female theologians in Christian history; a feminist hermeneutics of critique, in order to uncover and fight the patriarchy still endemic to so many church structures and statements; and a feminist hermeneutics of suspicion, to expose the unconscious but systemically functioning distortions that affect all Christianity, just as that poisonous reality affects all religions and all cultures.

Feminist theologies (always in the plural for there is no one, monolithic feminist theology) have proved one of the most emancipating movements in the entire history of Christianity. Feminist theologies, therefore, have changed all theology — indeed all scholarship, culture, and everyday life — in a manner now as ineluctable as it was historically inevitable.

First, Anne Carr, Sarah Coakley, Maria Clara Bingemer, and many other feminist theologians have justly argued that the separation of spirituality and theology is a tragedy in the history of both Catholic and Protestant theology. This was not the case among Orthodox theologians of the East, from Greece through several Slavic countries, culminating in the exceptional speculative-contemplative theologies of Russian Orthodoxy. The separation of spirituality and theology has adversely affected the canon of the history of theology, which, until recently, marginalized the role of the great female mystical theologians, from the ancient church through the many major medieval mystical theologians. The tragic separation of theology and spirituality is gradually being overcome, in large part, because of the recovery of largely ignored female mystical theologians who more consistently refused any such separation: for example,

St. Macrina is now acknowledged as the "fourth Cappadocian," alongside Basil the Great, Gregory of Nyssa, and Gregory Nazianzen.

Second, feminist theory has also been entirely right to insist that theology and ethics (i.e., theological ethics) should never have been separated (e.g., Valerie Saiving, Rosemary Radford Ruether, Elisabeth Schüssler Fiorenza, Judith Plaskow, and many others). Once again, the critical theory theologies of several feminist theologians in the last fifty years have been a major force for re-uniting ethics and theology, not only in Christian theology, but in *all* theology. The critical feminist analyses of conscious patriarchy and, even more deadly, the systemic but largely unconscious sexism in Christianity, have been exposed once and for all by various feminist hermeneutics of suspicion (e.g., in Elisabeth Schüssler Fiorenza's groundbreaking biblical exegesis and theology, and Ellen Wondra's powerful feminist theology). In sum, the history of Christian theology is widely being rectified by various forms of critical feminist theologies.

A third separation presently being healed by the vast effort of ecumenical feminist theologies is the insistence that students of theology should be edu-cated as Christian theologians responsible for a basic theological understand-ing and use of all three major forms of Christianity: Catholic, Orthodox, and Protestant. Inevitably—and positively—each Christian theologian will have some religious center of gravity (Reformed, Lutheran, Anglican, Free Church, Catholic, or Orthodox), but each theologian will no longer allow a separation of one's personal religious-theological center of gravity from the other great Christian religious and theological traditions. Every Christian theologian of the future, one hopes, will prove a full-fledged Christian theologian.

Indeed, it is no exaggeration to observe that feminist hermeneutics of all three major kinds of hermeneutics (retrieval, critique, suspicion) has led the way to enforce the kinds of major changes noted above for *all* Christian the-ology. Every thoughtful theologian, both female and male, is a feminist theo-logian today.

ARTHUR COHEN

How can any theologian—Jewish or Christian—attempt to think about the most horrific and most radically evil event of the twentieth century, the Jew-ish Holocaust? At the same time, how can any serious theologian—Jewish or Christian—fail to face this horror? To claim anything like an adequate answer, or any answer, to this overwhelming evil seems absurd—in fact, somewhat obscene. There *is* no answer. Both Jewish and the Christian traditions of theodicy, that is, the neuralgic issue of God and innocent suffering, are shattered by the incomprehensible abyss of the overwhelming evil and suffering, and the inevitable existential question for believers of why God did not somehow act when his chosen people lived this horror. The Holocaust has become a major question for many Jewish theologians and thinkers (e.g., Emil Fackenheim, Irving Greenberg, Cynthia Ozick, Elie Wiesel, Susan Shapiro), including Arthur Cohen. Cohen, a theologian of the first rank as well as a distinguished novelist, articulated in his groundbreaking book, *The Tremendum: A Theological Interpretation of the Holocaust*, with his characteristic theological directness, creativity, theological depth, and literary skill, a very original theological interpretation of the Holocaust by daring to name it the "subscending *tremendum*." This move is a paradoxical transformation of Rudolf Otto's famous naming of the "holy" as a positive, inexplicable mystery that both "fascinates and frightens" to Cohen's naming of the Holocaust as the subscending abyss of evil, the "*tremendum*."

Prior to this explosive work in *The Tremendum*, Arthur Cohen had established his reputation as a leading Jewish theologian with such daring earlier work as *The Natural and the Supernatural Jew* and his highly critical treatment of the all-too-familiar and too-consoling fixed phrase "the Judeo-Christian tradition" in a book that upset many Jewish, Christian, and secular readers, *The Myth of the Judeo-Christian Tradition*. Arthur Cohen was also very well known, particularly in his native New York literary circles, as a singularly subtle novelist, producing such major novels as *Simon Stern*, *A Hero of His Time*, *Acts of Theft*, and the exceptional intellectual novel, clearly modeled on the life and work of Hannah Arendt, justly entitled *An Admirable Woman*. Nevertheless, none of these excellent theological or literary works prepared one for the powerful, indeed, explosive short work *The Tremendum*. As Cynthia Ozick rightly wrote, "*The Tremendum* is at once meticulous in its thinking and explosive in its effect, as a precarious, trembling, daring, prodigious book on the God-condition after the Holocaust." A good, deceptively modest phrase, that: "the God-condition after the Holocaust." To radically rethink the God-condition after the *tremendum* is exactly what Arthur Cohen did. All traditional theodicies, Jewish and Christian, as well as all traditional, secular anthropodicies, collapse in the face of the Shoah.

In place of all attempts to name the Holocaust, even the attempt to use one of Western culture's most dignified and recondite names, tragedy, is found wanting to name this abyss. Even the most unnerving book of the Hebrew Bible, the book of Job, does not here suffice. The philosophical name, "radical evil," familiar since Kant formulated it, somehow pales in attempting to name the Holocaust. One may honestly think only silence is appropriate in this situation. Certainly, silence is preferable to the thoughtless chatter that can trivialize the horrific nature of this reality. Arthur Cohen discovered a dangerous mean between silence and theodicy: the uncanny, deliberately troubling name *the tremendum*.

Furthermore, Arthur Cohen did not set out on his courageous journey of radical theological rethinking in his attempt to name this unique event without deliberate attention to the Jewish theological traditions—biblical, rabbinic, Kabbalistic, philosophical, and theological. In fact, Arthur Cohen, especially in his deeply intriguing last chapter, appeals over and over to the great traditions of Jewish thought, especially to the several distinct Jewish traditions of negative theology. He incorporates an original reading of both the Kabbalah, promoted by the extraordinary scholarship of Gershon Scholem, and the philosophical and liturgical theology of the commanding, incomparable, pre-Holocaust, modern, Jewish philosophical theologian, Franz Rosenzweig.

Arthur Cohen's last, speculative chapter was clearly introduced as a first formulation of what he planned as a post-Holocaust, Rosenzweig-inspired, major speculative work, his theological magnum opus. Cohen's early death tragically cut short that possibility, although his notes toward that end await a young Jewish theologian ready to take on that much-needed, speculative, Rosenzweigian task.

Arthur Cohen's book demands at least as much critical attention from Christian theologians as from Jewish theologians. After all, Christian theology also faces the need to rethink the God-condition after the *tremendum*. In fact, the Christian theological need here is even greater, since Christian theologians need first to attempt to face the *tremendum* honestly, engaging with the disgusting, centuries-old tradition of Christian anti-Semitism, which provided a good deal of historical backing for the completely secular Nazis. The silence of most theologians, both Catholic and Protestant, on the Holocaust as the horror unfolded before their very eyes is a cause for strong Christian repentance. There were, of course, some honorable exceptions among Christian theologians, clergy, and laypersons. However, most Christian theologians seemed perhaps too unconsciously, habitually embedded in the centuries-long, deep-rooted tradition of Christian anti-Semitism to leave a state somewhere between indifference and apathy. Christian theologians today should join their Jewish theologian colleagues by first listening attentively to Jewish theological reflections on the Holocaust and then attempting some modest, probing, Christian theological response (as in the work of Johann Baptist Metz).

Fortunately, some Christian theologians (such as Paul van Buren, Gregory Baum, Rosemary Radford Ruether, John Pawlikowski, Hans Küng, Johann Baptist Metz, Cardinal Lustiger of Paris, Elisabeth Schüssler Fiorenza, Francis Schüssler Fiorenza, Anthony Godzieba, and many younger theologians) have taken on this necessary Christian theological task. In this still-unfolding series of theological attempts first to listen to their Jewish colleagues as they attempt to find some theological way of naming the Holocaust (e.g., Cohen's *tremendum*), younger theologians like Susan Shapiro are tentatively attempting to articulate the disturbingly new theological need to rethink the God-condition after the Holocaust. In this situation of theological crisis, the bold, groundbreaking, creative theological work of Arthur Cohen should hold a major place of honor for *all* theologians, Jewish and Christian alike.

GUSTAVO GUTIÉRREZ

Very few theologians in the long, two-thousand-year history of Christianity can be said to have inaugurated a new way of theologizing. Gustavo Gutiérrez, the rightly named "father of liberation theology," is one of those few.

Although the enduring presence of Gutiérrez, along with one of his central categories, "a preferential option for the poor," pervades chapter 16, the chapter itself is concentrated on the Christology that I claim can best inform that option. Gutiérrez's profoundly biblical theology possesses a fascinating "working canon" (not an exclusivist "canon within the canon"), which highlights certain central biblical texts — especially Exodus, Deuteronomy, Amos, Micah, Isaiah, Luke-Acts, Mark, and Galatians, and, above all, Matthew 25 — the Magna Carta of all liberation theology. These biblical texts, explicitly or implicitly, endorse the option for the poor both in the First Testament (e.g., Exodus and Deuteronomy, Amos, Micah, Isaiah) and in the New Testament (Luke-Acts as the Gospel most focused on social justice; Mark's focus on the marginalized, the poor, the outcasts, the ill, the mentally troubled; and Matthew's great call to the option for the poor).

The Christology I propose in the chapter is influenced by Gutiérrez's biblical account of a necessary, theological, preferential commitment to the poor (perhaps better than "option" for the poor) — that is, a *solidarity* with the poor. The notion of poverty is interpreted with powerful originality by Gutiérrez as principally but not solely the economic poor and the economic-social political structures ("sinful structures") that not only allow but also enforce the economic-social poverty of masses of peoples in Latin America (Gutiérrez's primary focus), in Africa and Asia, as well as in minority peoples in rich countries like the United States — Native Americans, African Americans, and many oppressed Hispanic persons and communities. Instructed by the strong criticisms of male machismo, all too familiar in Latin culture, criticisms made by Latin American and Hispanic *mujerista* and feminist theologians — for example, by *mujerista* theologian María Pilar Aquino in the United States, and such powerful Brazilian feminist theologians as Ivone Gebara and Maria Clara Bingemer — Latin American liberation theologians and US Hispanic theologians have come to see the need to denounce widespread and entrenched machismo and to join in the struggle for the liberation of women in Latin and Hispanic societies — as indeed, in all societies — and to face two overwhelming facts: women and children are the majority of the poor but, so often in every culture, economically and socially are marginalized as insignificant (another central aspect of "the poor," as Gutiérrez has insistently argued). These women are not only doubly oppressed — as poor and as women — they are often triply oppressed, by class, gender, and race, through the all-too-powerful fatalisms of sexism, racism, and classism.

Gustavo Gutiérrez has consistently held that the central problem for Christian theology should no longer be the still-unresolved and important problem of the nonbeliever (revelation, faith, and reason), but rather the problem of the nonperson — namely, the poor and the marginalized as insignificant, nonpersons who do not count: the outcasts, the misfits, and the mentally troubled. The Christian Gospel has an unmistakable option for the poor: the nonpersons who are the overwhelming majority of the listeners and followers of Jesus of Nazareth, the prophet of the poor.

To return to the Christology of the present chapter on Gutiérrez, I defend both the "option for the poor" (especially in Gutiérrez's careful interpretation of the wide range encompassed by the category of "the poor" and his authoritative, liberationist interpretation of this option) and the Christian necessity of solidarity with the poor. Any theological affirmation of the "option for the

poor" intensifies the eschatological "not-yet" present in any adequate Christology, constituted by a sense that it has *already happened* in Jesus Christ and
that redemption-liberation has not yet happened (the terrible state of the world
with the massive suffering of the poor as a result of sinful economic, social,
political, and cultural structures). The positive side of the Christological not-
yet is the New Testament, eschatological-apocalyptic divine promise of a Second Coming of Jesus Christ. Hence any adequate Christology is constituted
by four interacting Christological symbols: incarnation-cross-resurrection (i.e.,
the true symbols that redemption-liberation has already come) in creative tension with the not-yet of the situation of the poor, so in need of liberation,
especially in the poor's own active voice and actions. The important fourth
Christological symbol is the mysterious, apocalyptic-eschatological Christological insistence to remember always that not-yet, while still living in Christian hope and joy for the decisive Second Coming of Jesus Christ. Only when
that already-not-yet tension is kept alive can an adequate Christology result.
The great Christological symbols, incarnation and resurrection, declare that,
in "Jesus the Christ, redemption has already come." This is especially clear in
the Logos Christology of the Gospel of John and the Logos Christologies of
early theologians like Justin Martyr, Clement of Alexandria, and, most powerfully, the biblical and Platonist Logos theology of the first major theologian of
genius, Origen of Alexandria.

The eschatological not-yet of an adequate Christology is not merely, as I
held in my earlier book, *The Analogical Imagination*, the tripartite Christology
constituted by incarnation, cross, and resurrection. That tripartite Christology
of *Analogical Imagination* needs not just a corrective, but also, as a fourth con-
stitutive element, the Christological symbol, the Second Coming. Even in
Paul's Christology, this is the case. To be sure, Paul's dialectical Christology
focused on the cross of Jesus Christ and Him crucified. Nevertheless, with the
apocalyptic tone in much of Paul's theology, starting with First Thessalonians,
Paul never seemed to abandon his belief in an imminent Second Coming of
Christ in his own lifetime, despite increasing evidence to the contrary.

History did not end but continued its inexorable journey. Christian theologians therefore had to rethink their belief in an imminent Second Coming.
Unfortunately, some of that rethinking so compromised the eschatological-
apocalyptic not-yet of Christology that theologians could be left with only
an incarnation Logos theology choice, stripped of its eschatological not-yet.
Among modern theologians, Johann Baptist Metz, another theologian allied

with Gutiérrez, has retrieved the Markan-Pauline apocalyptic decisively, demonstrating the memory of suffering in the passion of Christ and all the suffering of history, especially of the poor.

No theologian in our time has provided a more resonant and powerful liberating vision for all theology than has Gustavo Gutiérrez. Gutiérrez's influence daily increases as more and more theologians, both progressive and traditional, are deeply changed by liberation theology, with its insistence that *all* properly Christian theologians join Gutiérrez and his many liberationist colleagues (e.g., Alejandro Nava and his many very productive Hispanic theological colleagues) in affirming, without hesitation, a solidarity with the poor, because that preferential option should inform *all* theology.

JAMES CONE

Racism is the original sin of America: toward the native peoples of the continent by theft of their land, massacres, lying treaties, and the confinements to demoralizing reservations; toward African peoples during the disgraceful centuries of chattel slavery, from the disgusting treatment of Africans on the ships of the horrifying Middle Passages, through the auction blocks and the revolting conditions of slave labor (including the breakup of families, floggings, and more inhumane treatment for three centuries until the Civil War), only too rapidly followed by a brief Reconstruction period and a long Jim Crow period; toward many Hispanic people in the wake of the completely unjust Mexican-American War (which resulted in the appropriation of one-third of Mexico to create much of present-day Texas, New Mexico, Arizona, Colorado, and California), as well as the emergence of ever-new forms of white racism against brown-skinned Hispanic people; toward East and South Asian peoples, whose wretched treatment culminated in prison camps for Japanese Americans in World War II; and toward immigrants through a history of prejudice and imperialist treatment. The United States, founded on an original and noble ideal of freedom for all, also includes a frightening history of endemic, racist oppression of all nonwhite peoples that has scarred forever the American experiment. All in all, the United States, like all empires, is a complex, plural, and deeply ambiguous heritage, still attempting to work out its ideals and struggling, sometimes very successfully, against its all-too-often racist, classist, and sexist mixed ancestry. All reality is complex, pluralistic, and ambiguous; some political entities, especially those republics that become empires (Rome, the United States, France), are the most ambiguous of all.

Without a doubt, the four American centuries have been characterized by the inhuman treatment of black Americans, first as slaves and then as victims of the racism and classism that followed their emancipation. Despite the attempts of reformers since the Civil War, during Reconstruction and beyond (especially the inestimable Frederick Douglass), new forms of black oppression and lynchings, associated with Jim Crow laws and the too-often-successful attempts by the Ku Klux Klan to deprive black Americans of the vote, continue to this day. The Klan, with its shocking symbolism of cross-burnings, mainly directed its violence toward African Americans, although the Klan initially included Jews and Catholics as secondary targets. As a result of the Jim Crow laws and Klan violence, thousands upon thousands of Southern blacks fled for jobs and some relief to the Northern cities, where many found themselves largely confined to urban ghettos in crumbling, rat-infested tenements. Some substantial relief, at least for voting in the South, came through the civil rights movements of the 1960s, led by Martin Luther King Jr., and the black power movements of Stokely Carmichael and Malcolm X.

Fortunately, real progress has been made through the civil rights movements in the desegregation of Southern institutions and the opening of the vote to all African American citizens, culminating in the first election of an African American, Barack Obama, as president of the United States. However real the ever-increasing gains by African Americans, the United States of America is not, as many citizens naively hoped after Obama's election, a post-racist society. The ghettoizing in Northern cities, the injustice still imposed on poor blacks ("I can't breathe"), and the national scandal of the inordinate number of blacks in the overcrowded, violence-ridden, systematically unjust US prison system continues — a scandal that "cries to heaven" for a justice that thus far has not come. Meanwhile, the shocking indifference toward the plight of Native American peoples (better named in Canada "First Nations") remains unabated.

It is little wonder, therefore, that the leading African American theologian of our time, James Cone, devoted his entire distinguished career to confronting racism, from his game-changing first major book, *Black Theology and Black Power* (1969), to his later works. Cone employs critical theories as well as the rich cultural resources of African American culture, including slave narratives and slave hymns from the earliest black struggle for freedom. His penetrating study, *The Spirituals and the Blues: An Interpretation* (1972), reflects on the most original forms of American music: the spirituals, the blues, and jazz (with its improvisational genius and its unbroken link to the black artists of Chicago, New Orleans, and Harlem), followed by rap and hip-hop, now a worldwide phenomenon after its founders in the South Bronx.[1]

As James Cone's autobiographical *My Soul Looks Back* (1985), at once poignant and tough-minded, testifies, Cone was the child of parents of exceptional integrity and courage in the small Southern town of Bearden, Arkansas. There Cone learned two life lessons on a daily basis, as did all African Americans, South and North, East and West: first, the everyday actualities of white oppressive segregation — separate (that is, segregated) water fountains, separate waiting rooms at doctors' offices, separate seats on buses, exposed by the wondrous Rosa Parks's refusal to change seats in 1955. Second, Cone and his siblings learned from their intrepid, courageous, working-class father and equally strong mother to resist and refuse to bow to white oppression and oppressive white power structures. Like his father and mother, James Cone has never compromised. Nor have his siblings. Indeed, his brother Cecil Cone also became a distinguished black theologian whose critical work on James's theology directed James himself to employ fewer European and North American philosophical and theological resources than he had learned to employ while earning his doctorate in white seminaries — where not a single book on black history or black religion was in the curriculum, which, at the time, consisted of largely European (especially German) and American white theology.

James Cone's work on black theology related initially to the contemporary black power movement and, more and more, to retrieving the enormous and diverse resources of African American culture. Furthermore, Cone kept learning from his African American critics to the point where he made three further decisive, necessary steps forward for his black theology. First, Cone attended international conferences of liberation theologians. This international experience allowed Cone to understand and learn from the similarities (namely, a common theological commitment to a theology of liberation focused on solidarity with all the poor, oppressed, and marginalized throughout the world), and from the differences among the believers' liberation theologies. For ex-

---

1. See Alejandro Nava, *In Search of Soul: Hip-Hop, Literature, and Religion* (Oakland: University of California Press, 2017).

ample, the initial conversations between US African American theologians and Latin American liberation theologians were not very promising, since the African Americans emphasized race as the issue needing most liberating attention in intractably racist American culture. The Latin Americans initially tended to downplay race in favor of class analyses, including Marxist analyses.

Both sets of liberation theologians, of course, held the all-important common goal of forging a liberation theology using the social sciences, not just philosophy, as the necessary conversation partners for theology as in more traditional theology. Moreover, both Latin American liberation theology and North American black liberation theology were deeply biblical theologies.

Eventually, largely thanks to the mutual respect and listening abilities of those two dialogical theologians, James Cone and Gustavo Gutiérrez, the dialogue between Latin American theology and US black theology became a real one. The African American theologians began to include much more class analysis (including Marxist analysis — as in Cornel West) in their never-abandoned racial focus in order to better explain the important class factors in African American life. The Latin American theologians, in turn, led by Gutiérrez (a native Peruvian indigenous Amerindian), added racial analysis to their liberation program, especially in countries (e.g., Brazil) with large black populations, as well as countries (e.g., Peru and Mexico) with large native populations. Leading Brazilian liberation theologians (Leonardo Boff, Dom Hélder Câmara, Ivone Gebara, Maria Clara Bingemer, et al.) were helpfully instructed by black theologians' insistence on the need to struggle for liberation from both class and racist elements, and, in the case of poor black, Amerindian, and mestizo Latin women, the triple oppression of class, race, and gender. The gain for both liberation theologies — Latin American and African American — is clear in James Cone and other African American theologians.

The major Latin American liberation theologians (e.g., Leonardo Boff, Jon Sobrino, Maria Clara Bingemer) and several Asian liberation theologians (e.g., Korean Minjung theologians and Chinese liberation theologians, especially in Hong Kong and the western United States, including Stephen Chan at Seattle University) are fully aware of the importance of racial analysis to combat racism in every form, in every culture and society. Thanks largely to the liberation theologians of Asia, Africa, and Latin America, all liberation theologians analyze the persistent ugly traces of an earlier, imperialist-sponsored political and socioeconomic colonialism, as well as the "second colonialism": the cultural colonization of a largely American, popular consumerist colonialism culture, where a cozy, rich, middle-class population is in danger of being entertained to death by an all-encompassing popular culture with a fatal global reach.

The many diverse liberation theologies around the planet (e.g., that of Aloysius Perris's powerful Asian liberation theology in Sri Lanka), besides being grounded in the usual liberationist realities, are also constituted by the results of Christian dialogue with the majority of Buddhist and Hindu traditions of South Asia—especially the new "social activist" Buddhists.

In the meantime, James Cone has expanded his theology to include class analysis in his rightly dominant racial focus. Cornel West, the leading practitioner of revisionary Marxist analysis in the United States, like so many Latin Liberation theologians (e.g., Enrique Dussel), has proved intellectually, existentially, and politically both a powerful public philosopher and an eloquent liberation theologian. West's courageous, controversial, erudite, and intellectually penetrating voice is now heard throughout the United States as the best known, most energetic proponent of liberation theology and public philosophy. West's critics, mostly on the right politically and ecclesiastically, can rarely respond to West's devastatingly accurate and erudite analyses of the dour and tragic American condition. The fairly desperate responses of more traditional theologians to Cone and West, as well as the bold genius of Toni Morrison and their many liberationist allies—black, white, Hispanic, white progressive, and Amerindian—usually miss the point. In the Amerindian case, the best title I know for a book of liberation theology is Vine Deloria Jr.'s *We Talk, You Listen*. Indeed.

Many enemies of liberation theology have fought it with barely disguised power (e.g., in the 1980s, Reagan's Washington and John Paul II's Vatican). Dom Hélder Câmara, that courageous, remarkable, indeed awe-inspiring bishop in Brazil, spoke for all besieged liberation theologians when, with his fine ironic smile, he once stated, "When I talk about the poor, they call me a saint; when I talk about the cause of their poverty, they call me a Communist." An American liberation theologian in all but name, Dorothy Day, founded *The Catholic Worker* newspaper and the Catholic Worker Movement, which still works for the poorest of the poor. Like Dom Hélder Câmara, Dorothy Day would not allow anyone to sentimentally label her a saint. For example, when a young *New York Times* reporter was sent by his superiors (apparently shocked to hear there might be a saint in New York City of all places) to interview "the saint," the reporter innocently enough did not expect "the saint's" reply to his question about how it *feels* to be a saint. Day silenced that line of questioning quickly: "Young man, do not trivialize me; ask some serious question."

With fierce anger toward the white racism infecting America, James Cone argued, especially in his early works like *Black Theology and Black Power*, as well as his brilliant book, *Martin and Malcolm and America: A Dream or a Nightmare*, for the need to take seriously both Martin Luther King Jr.'s hopeful American *I Have a Dream* and Malcolm X's nightmare vision of the reality blacks face every day in "the land of the free." Only James Cone could make the case for listening to both Martin Luther King Jr. and Malcolm X so persuasively. The United States needs to hear both these murdered prophets. Cone builds his strong case through both social analysis and liberationist theology. He also highlights a fact too seldom attended to: not long before the brutal assassinations of both Martin Luther King Jr. and Malcolm X, the two began to influence each other in fascinating ways. Both King and Malcolm X began to see their positions, however different, as not just oppositional but as dialectical: that is, as each position dialectically implied important aspects of the other.

Another major advance in James Cone's later position was beholden to his womanist theological critics (some of his colleagues at Union Theological Seminary): Delores Williams, in her book *Sisters in the Wilderness: The Challenge of Womanist God-Talk*; Jacqueline Grant, in *White Women's Christ and Black Women's Jesus: Feminist Christology and Womanist Response*; and Katie Cannon in *Black Womanist Ethics*. Cone began to learn to listen to the triple oppression (race, class, gender) endured by poor black women, whose number is legion. Womanist theologians, major innovators in theology, begin with a twofold affirmation and critique. First, they strongly affirm the radical feminist critique of the patriarchal and sexist nature of Western (and other) cultures, including the theologies and philosophies begot by such cultures. Second, they strongly affirm the radical black theological critique of a violently and systemically oppressive white attitude toward black liberation theology, especially that of James Cone, the major figure in black theology. At the same time, the womanist theologians criticize both of these theological movements on new critical grounds: they critique white feminists for their earlier indifference to the race issue and, therefore, to the fact that black, womanist liberation theologians are triply oppressed (by gender, class, and race) and that the latter fact is central to a black woman's daily existence.

Furthermore, the womanist theologians criticize the black male theologians in the same way as we earlier saw Latin *mujerista* theologians criticize the male Latin American and Hispanic liberation theologians. The basic, womanist criticism is clear and persuasive: black men do indeed experience the double oppression of race and class. However, male black liberationist theologians previously failed to recognize the triple (race, class, gender) victimization of most black women. To ignore this triple oppression (and a fourth one, if she is also gay — as liberationist queer theology has persuasively argued) is to ignore the very existence of the structures of oppression in the culture and society from which black male theologians are committed to liberate black peoples.

Besides these important affirmative and critical moves vis-à-vis both white feminist liberationist theology and black male theology, diverse womanist theologians, like black male theologians, have made some distinctive theological moves. First, most womanist theologians are usually rooted in the liberating forms of the black church. Second, like most liberation theologians, womanist theologians are strongly biblical theologians — but with a difference. For example, Delores Williams argues that most theologies of the cross from St. Paul through Martin Luther to Jürgen Moltmann are trapped by a "sacred aura" put around the cross by a patriarchal culture. As an alternative to a Pauline theology of a cross-affected redemption, Williams turns to the portrait of the ministry of Jesus, his words and life, as revealing a redemption through Jesus's "ministerial vision of right relationships."

Jacqueline Grant is also deeply rooted in the black church (in her case, as in James Cone's, in the African Methodist Episcopal church). Unlike Williams, Grant accepts the traditional faith of the black church that Jesus died on the cross to save us from our sins. At the same time, influenced by Sojourner Truth and by her experiences as a woman in the biblically based black churches, Jacqueline Grant does not hesitate to write, "For me today, this Christ, found in the experience of Black women, is a Black woman."

Katie Cannon, in her book *Black Womanist Ethics*, is influenced by her scholarly studies of Zora Neale Hurston. Perhaps as a result, Cannon, far more than Williams or Grant, has been quite critical of the black church for the "objectification, degradation, and subjection" of the female in black preaching.

All the womanist theologians are deeply biblical theologians informed by their scholarship and the exceptional tradition of biblical preaching in the black churches. The male black theologians have mainly appealed to rethinking the story of freed slaves in Exodus in the Bible as the story the freed black slaves themselves had told in their magnificent hymns and narrations.

The womanist theologians, like the male black theologians and the Latin American theologians — indeed all liberation theologians — have made the call to solidarity with the poor, the insignificant, the marginalized, the misfits in our consumer societies in Matthew 25:44–45 a clarion call for all serious Christian thinking: "Lord, when did we see thee hungry, or thirsty, or a stranger, or naked, or sick, or in prison, and did not minister to thee?" He will answer them, saying, "As long as you did not do it for one of these least ones, you did not do it for me."

Furthermore, several Catholic womanist theologians (Toinette Eugene, Diana Hayes, Shawn Copeland, et al.) have articulated powerful womanist theologies, clearly Catholic in tone and texture. Love is a major theological theme among the Catholic womanist theologians, especially in Toinette Eugene, with her fascinating reinterpretation of the figure of Mary as the empowering woman in the Christian tradition, as witnessed in Mary's *Magnificat*. Theologically they hold that love is greater and deeper than justice but that love can never be less than justice. The love-justice relationship is one of the classic concerns of Christian theology, as it is in the Bible itself. Moreover, womanist theologian Diana Hayes has developed an immensely creative use of the methodology of the Canadian theologian Bernard Lonergan in order to articulate a powerful theoretical form of womanist theology that is also rooted in the concrete experience of black women.

In sum, it is impossible to understand modern American Christian theology (Protestant, Catholic, Orthodox, and Mormon) without paying close attention to the enormously creative and morally, politically, prophetically diverse forms of black male liberation theology and black female womanist liberationist theologies.

CHAPTER 14

FEMINIST THEOLOGY

The Unexampled Challenge

There can be little doubt that feminist theory and feminist theology represent one of the most important advances in all Christian theology of the last few decades. There are no theological symbols, no theories of symbol itself, and no theological methods that are not challenged from within by feminist thought.

Consider, for example, theological method. The exposure of the German idealism of so much theological method in favor of an insistence on a critical theoretical analysis of the social location of the theologian has, to a large extent, been the achievement of feminist, womanist, and *mujerista* theologians. Through that influence, I and many other theologians have come to acknowledge the contextual character of all theology, including my own male, white, academic theology. The need to add a more "materialist" version to theology and, indeed, any theological method is the result of the developments in political, liberation, and feminist theologies.

This emphasis on the contextual character of theological inquiry has, moreover, intensified the major intellectual dilemma of *all* forms of theology in our period. For insofar as theology continues to be God-centered, as Daphne Hampson's book *Theology and Feminism* (1990) persuasively insists it should, and insofar as theology also acknowledges its own deeply contextual character, then the intellectual dilemma is clear. On the one hand, theology as either theology or thealogy must claim universality for the reality it *reflects* upon and, thereby, for its basic claims *for* that reality. On the other hand, theology, like all forms of critical reflection, remains partly bound to its historical context. This dilemma — as exchanges among feminist theologians in the *Journal of Feminist Studies in Religion* shows — has been sharpened by the overwhelming consensus in feminist theology on the contextuality of all thought, as that analysis is sometimes uneasily joined with the insistence on the universal ethical claims of feminism. At the same time, the intellectual problem expands to include an understanding of the clearly universal character of the Divine Reality affirmed in most — but not all — forms of feminist and womanist theology. Here Hampson's criticism of some forms of Christian feminist theology as more humanistic than theological seems accurate. At the least, there sometimes seems to be too little theological attention to the nature of the Divine Reality as the principal referent of all theological language in some forms of Christian feminist theology as, indeed, in many other forms of theology.

There is every good reason to expect that this complex intellectual dilemma (which cuts across the disciplines) will intensify for all of us over the coming years. There is also good reason to believe that feminist thought is likely to lead the way in critical reflection on this contextuality-universality issue. The clash of contextuality and universality is perhaps nowhere as acute as in the question of criteria for the meaning and truth of theological claims in theological methodology. Since I have been asked to comment on how feminist theology has had an impact on my own theology, the question of criteria in theological method is one place to focus.

Allow me to expand further on the full force of the new methodological problem exposed by feminist analysis. On the one hand, one cannot ignore the quite material realities of gender, race, and class in analyzing the concrete reality of the theologian involved or implied in any particular form of theology. This critical theoretical bent, I repeat, is central to any form of feminist theology.

Moreover, in my judgment, this same materialist insistence should now be present in *every* form of theology. On the other hand, Christian feminist theology, in all its forms, is clearly and systematically committed to certain ethical claims of justice and equality on gender issues. So are post-Christian feminist theologies, as well as Jewish and post-Jewish theologies. This ethical commitment to justice is nonnegotiable in Christian theological prophetic terms — and, therefore, in principle, not construed as reducible to social location alone. These ethical (more exactly, ethical-religious) demands of justice are understood as universal in their applicability to all theology, no matter how particular the origin of these ethical demands.

In short, all the grave intellectual dilemmas of modern ethics return in a full-fledged way to all forms of that at once most contextual and most universally ethical form of theology in our period: feminist theology. Despite some puzzling appeals to pragmatic criteria here, the dilemma holds: feminist theology (and therefore, in principle, all theology) cannot without self-contradiction — indeed, self-destruction — let go of *either* its intellectual-ethical insistence on the full material (gender, race, class) contextuality of all theology, *or* its intellectual conviction that its ethical demands for justice and equality are universal in their applicability.

Or consider a second dilemma posed for all Christian theology by feminist analysis. Every symbol of Christian theology has, minimally, been interpreted in and through a patriarchal culture and tradition, and with a systemically operative, if often unconscious, sexist agenda. Maximally, as several post-Christian feminist theologians insist, every major symbol may be irretrievably both sexist and patriarchal. The values of justice that we have all inherited partly but not solely from the prophetic heritage of Judaism and Christianity may seem to demand a rejection of the heritage itself. As the full force of this problem surfaced in the Christian and post-Christian debates within feminist theology, the ethical dilemma noted above has resurfaced with even greater force.

At the same time, every theory of symbol employed, implicitly or explicitly, in contemporary theology and in philosophy of religion forces *all* interpreters to acknowledge the unconscious power of religious symbols on persons in any tradition. If our symbols turn out to be not only far more pluralistic but also far more ambiguous than most theologians (including theologians of symbol) once realized, then all the problems of theological interpretation of *every* major symbol are opened anew. They certainly have been thus reopened for me, as the realities of sexism have been exposed in every major symbol of the tradition by feminist hermeneutics of both critique (patriarchy) and suspicion (sexism). One of the most difficult problems of my own recent work on God has been the profoundly gendered character embedded even in our most relational (i.e., Trinitarian) understanding of the Divine Reality. Once we acknowledge that fact, any constructive step forward is far more difficult than previously thought.

At the very least, a new, explicitly feminist hermeneutics of suspicion has been forged by feminist thought to spot and answer not only the errors but also the systemic, unconscious distortions likely to be present in all our traditions and theologies. In sum, the question of theological criteria for meaning and truth increases in complexity. For example, let us say, first, that hermeneutics may be able to provide criteria of truth as manifestation, that is, as disclosure and concealment of meaning and truth through forms, like symbols. Second, let us further state that we can also analyze how any hermeneutical claims to meaning and truth in such symbolic manifestations do or do not cohere with what we otherwise know or, more likely, believe to be the case. Third, let us also analyze what ethical and political consequences all such meanings and truths entail in order to judge whether they are ethically desirable or not.

In fact, these three hermeneutical and ethical criteria are ones that, elsewhere, I have tried to spell out and defend as comprising a complex and interrelated set of criteria — criteria of relative adequacy that, once fully articulated, could provide criteriological warrants for an adequate theological method. But notice how feminist theory profoundly complicates this already complex set of methodological concerns.

For example, is there any adequate hermeneutics of both retrieval and suspicion to account for the ambivalence of our present response to our pluralistic, ambiguous, and, perhaps, overdetermined traditions? Is there an adequate ethical theory that can, without denying contextuality, adequately account for the ethical demands of feminism as universal ethical demands? There may be other routes to reach the intellectual and moral aporias of all contemporary theology, but feminist theory and feminist theologies force any theologian to face these problems squarely. Those theologies cannot but hurl all of us into those problems, sometimes called postmodern, with full force. For we know anew what Christian theology as critical reflection should always know: the fact that something is Christian does not, by itself, make it true; the fact that something is claimed to be Christian (e.g., patriarchy) does not, by itself, make it Christian.

Feminist theology, more systematically and self-consciously than other forms of theology, forces this dual demand upon all theology. As French feminist thought has justly been called the conscience of postmodernity, so too has feminist theology become the intellectual conscience of all Christian theology in our period. In that sense, the debates within feminist theology (Christian or post-Christian; feminist, womanist, or *mujerista*; humanistic or theocentric; modern or postmodern; Anglo-American empirical, historical, and ethical, or French psychoanalytic, antiempirical, and hermeneutically suspicious) are among the most significant questions even as they have become the most complex, for all serious theological reflection in our time.

CHAPTER 15

ARTHUR COHEN

The Holocaust as the Tremendum

To read Arthur A. Cohen's *The Tremendum: A Theological Interpretation of the Holocaust* (1993) is to believe anew in the necessity of theology. So accustomed can we become to the debasement of both secular and theological currencies that we can be startled in the face of one of the rarest of human achievements: genuine theological thinking. The reader of Cohen's singular work will find there thinking on its ownmost ground.

To think the "*tremendum*" is to think an actuality of our history that cannot — yet must — be thought. To think theologically in this situation means to demand a new kind of "thought-full" language. That newness may sometimes prove to be an old language radically revised because genuinely rethought. So it is here in Cohen's revisionary retrieval of Rudolph Otto's language for the holy as the uncanny *mysterium fascinans et tremendum*: that fascinating and frightening mystery that transcends all thought and history. As Cohen rethinks Otto, an unnerving sea change occurs for both our religious experience and our theology. For Otto's "transcending" *mysterium tremendum* is deconstructed and rethought into Cohen's "subscending" *tremendum*. To think the Holocaust as the *tremendum* of the overwhelming power of radical evil that subscends thought and action alike is to force theologians to think anew. To think, with Cohen, of the "caesura" erupting in all traditions through the power of the *tremendum* is to dare to think a tradition through again. Through that caesura, we must undertake a deconstructive journey that our more usual, domesticated language of "rupture" or "break" no longer yields.

This demand for new theological language like the language of *tremendum* and caesura empowers Cohen's initial reflections. Through such thought-full language, Cohen helps us resist the kind of "thought-less-ness" which, as Hannah Arendt insisted, inflicts our doxic, language-ridden moment. Surely both Arendt and Cohen are correct here. We cannot think theologically about the Holocaust if we simply continue to use the exhausted languages of the traditions. Even the expression "radical evil" cannot provoke the demand for thought that the unsettling, unexpected phrase "the *tremendum*" will. To declare that a rupture or a radical break has occurred in our culture and our thought can tempt us to a sense of *déjà vu*, evoking a thoughtlessness that the deconstructive word *caesura* resists.

As our language collapses in upon itself to disclose the banalization of much existence, our concepts can become mere categories, our best theological paradoxes mere *doxai*. We begin to sense the need for both language and thought to be deconstructed *before* constructive theology can occur again. Only then might we be freed to think again. For the theologian, this pervasive sense of an exhausted language geared to thoughtlessness intensifies to an anxiety that all may be lost. For theology is nothing if it cannot think. Theology is spent if it cannot think the limit-concept of all our thought — the limit-concept empowering what should be the ultimate limit-word, "God." What happens in a thoughtless situation to thinkers committed to *logos* on *theos*, to theo-logy? What indeed? What word in our language now seems more banalized, less disclosive, less frightening or gracious than the one limit-word that bespeaks the single reality theology dares to think — the uncanny, dangerous word "God." And what intellectual enterprise within traditional theology can seem more one-dimensional, more beside the point in the age of the *tremendum* than traditional theodicies? Those theodicies were once expressions of the risk of genuine thought. Now they appear as Piranesi-like ruins, exposing the shattered fragments of the words "God" and "evil" alike.

Arthur Cohen's instincts for the heart of the contemporary theological dilemma are profoundly right. Only a new defamiliarizing and deconstructive language, one forged in the process of thought upon those linked, incommensurable realities, the *tremendum* and God, can free us to think again. Only a language impelled by the caesura from within, a language expressive of the abyss in our culture (both secular and religious), the caesura in our domesticated religious thoughts and our battered liturgies, can free theological thought to speak again.

It is history itself—our history, that history which smashed against itself in the Holocaust—that has exposed the pathos of earlier liberal theologies. Those earlier liberal theologies were courageous and disclosive expressions of enlightenment and emancipation. But simply to repeat them now is to issue the theological equivalent of a Hallmark card of condolence—well-intentioned, sad, tired, pathetic. Even the more recent Jewish and Christian neo-Orthodox theologies—those splendid and liberating expressionist outbursts of paradox, ambiguity, and negation impelled by a sense of the radical verticality of divine transcendence—have now crashed upon the inverse verticality, the subscension of individual historicity by the sheer force of the *tremendum* of the Holocaust as global history.

As the reader of this daring book soon discovers, we can find no easy way out of our uncanny dilemma. Cohen will force us to feel and, through that feeling, to think the *tremendum*. He will honor earlier liberal and neo-Orthodox theologies (including his own earlier work) in the only honorable way left to those who confront the *tremendum*. He will deconstruct their innocence, expose their illusions, and retrieve their intent to think. He will insist that the great heritage of Jewish orthopraxis and Jewish theology must be accorded new hermeneutical reflection now. Cohen will commit himself to rethink and retrieve the classic Jewish responses to earlier catastrophes and survivals of the Jewish people: the rabbinic tradition's response to the destruction of the Temple and the beginning of the long exile, and the Kabbalists' response to the expulsion of Spanish Jewry. He will honor his great predecessors as the classic thinkers they are: Philo, Maimonides, Mendelssohn, Buber, and, above all, Rosenzweig. He will pay heed to the reflections of his contemporaries: the Mishnaic research of Jacob Neusner; the post-Holocaust reflections of Elie Wiesel, Emil Fackenheim, Irving Greenberg, and others; and the extraordinary recovery of the Kabbalistic tradition in Gershom Scholem. Above all, as the final chapter of *The Tremendum* clarifies, Cohen will insist upon speaking to and from the heart of all properly Jewish theology—the reality of the Jewish people, to whose praxis and thought he holds himself and his thought accountable.

Like all genuine thought, Arthur Cohen's theology is grounded in a historicity that is both the history of a people and the retrieval of a heritage of certain fragments of classic religious thought and praxis. To think theologically in a post-Holocaust situation is to live and think historically. And yet, as *The Tremendum* makes clear, to think historically *cannot* become the kind of easy exercise in "historicist consciousness" long since exposed by Nietzsche and Benjamin as a failure to think. To think *historically* is also to *evaluate*. To think historically is to develop a hermeneutics of suspicion, focused upon the illusions and the not-so-innocent theories of both ourselves and our predecessors. Only through such radical suspicion is a full retrieval of any tradition possible. The chapter devoted to historical theology is, therefore, fully as much a part of the constructive theological argument of the work as a whole as the phenomenology of the *tremendum* in chapter 2 and the constructive reflection on God in chapter 4. As Hans-Georg Gadamer insists, "To understand [the past] at all is to understand [it] differently." Historical theology is not a "history" of theological opinions. Historical theology *is* theology. It is thinking. It is thought-full conversation with the classics on the fundamental questions about the meaning of our existence before God. Those same questions have found responses in the classic texts, images, symbols, events, persons, rituals, and thoughts of every classic religious tradition. If those questions are to be asked anew, and those responses are to be retrieved as thought, not merely repeated as opinion, they must be understood differently. Otherwise they will not be understood at all.

To understand any tradition after the *tremendum* is to retrieve its genius through a retrieval that is also suspicion. Through that kind of hermeneutics, we may find hidden, forgotten, even repressed aspects of the tradition for thought now. A hermeneutical enterprise like this occurs in the powerful theological reflections of the final chapter of Arthur Cohen's book. There the reader will find Cohen's own constructive rethinking on the reality of God in a post-*tremendum* age. Unless I misread him, Arthur Cohen moves in this section through a powerful hermeneutics of suspicion to an equally powerful hermeneutics of retrieval. By that dangerous route, he retrieves for thought the deconstructive mode of thinking of the Jewish Kabbalistic traditions, historically retrieved by Scholem; the negative theology in the Gnostic-Kabbalistic tradition, from Boehme through Schelling; and, above all, the unthought that must now be thought in the mystic epistemology and ontology of the incomparable Franz Rosenzweig.

Cohen does not allow himself simply to repeat the solutions of his chosen classics, those defamiliarizing trajectories of the tradition. His choice of these particular classics is both liberating and courageous. For precisely these classic modes of deconstructive thought, let us recall, were and are still often despised, when not altogether forgotten or repressed by both Jewish and Christian theologians in favor of some "clearer" or "more orthodox" aspect of the traditions. As Cohen's creative rethinking of the position of Franz Rosenzweig makes especially clear, he understands this subterranean tradition of negative, deconstructive theological reflection on God only by understanding it differently. He must so understand it, for he understands it post-*tremendum*. Traditional deconstruction must itself now be deconstructed in order to be retrieved at all. By this complex and daring strategy, Cohen aids us all to break through the thoughtlessness of so much contemporary Jewish and Christian theology. He demands a rethinking of the most difficult, complex, unnerving, and uncanny traditions in all Western theological reflection on God — traditions of thought where the radically negative is intrinsic to all self-deconstructing thought in theology, and may well be internal to the reality of God's own self.

By forcing this deconstructive retrieval upon the attention of contemporary theology, Cohen unsettles our usual options. Even those contemporary theodicies that most share Cohen's own clearly "bipolar" vision of God's reality (like process theodicies) now also stand accused of not facing in thought the radical power of evil disclosed for all to see in the *tremendum*.

Arthur Cohen is also respectful toward but unsatisfied with the more familiar options for serious post-Holocaust thought in contemporary Jewish religious thought. He respects but will not accept either the "eclipse of God" of Martin Buber, or the "death of God" of Richard Rubenstein. As one who both insists upon narrative in thought and has made his mark as one of our foremost novelists, Cohen clearly honors the turn to narrative-as-thought. But he does not share Elie Wiesel's hesitancy to move through narrative to explicitly conceptual theological thought. Cohen's move to retrieve Rosenzweig and Schelling distances his position as well from the Hegelian, post-Holocaust reflections of Emil Fackenheim. Just as surely, Cohen's lack of emphasis on retrieving the complex covenant traditions in the history of Jewish thought distinguishes his position from Irving Greenberg's radically revisionary, post-Holocaust covenant theology.

As a Christian theologian, I cannot presume to comment further on this intra-Jewish theological discussion. This much, however, I will presume to say. I have become convinced that contemporary Jewish theologians are thinking both for and in their tradition, to be sure; yet they are also thinking on behalf of *all* theologians in *all* traditions, as they risk deconstruction and rethinking of the actuality of our relationship to God in a post-*tremendum* age. The seriousness and richness of the kind of thought already present in contemporary Jewish theology is now intensified by the original proposals of this work: a work by means of which Arthur Cohen honors the entire theological community. To force us all to face and feel the Holocaust, to demand that we dare to think in the presence of that abyss of unspeakable evil, to unmask our temptations to thoughtlessness by forging new language for thought — the *tremendum*, the caesura, the negative, deconstructive, mystical epistemology and ontology in the actuality of all thought on God that is faithful to the disclosure and concealment of God's reality in our day — to risk this enterprise, I repeat, is to accomplish a task of genuine theological thinking that every thoughtful theologian will honor by engaging it critically, and every thoughtless one had best now find more clever ways to try to evade.

One final word. I write as a Christian theologian and, as such, a few reflections addressed to the Christian readers of this work may perhaps be in order. My first question must be a blunt one: Why do so many Christian theologians still refuse to face the *tremendum*, which the Holocaust discloses? (I include most of my own work in this indictment.) When the reason is, as it often is, that the Christian sense of repentance and guilt for the revolting history of Christian anti-Semitism is the cause for Christian theological silence, the option can be respected. And yet, guilt and repentance and the noble religious praxis empowering both cannot become the occasion to avoid thought. Silence is possible, as silence, only to a speaker. Theology lives or dies as serious thinking on God and all things, including ourselves, in relationship to God.

When those Christian theologians most committed to thinking in relationship to the frightening history of our age (especially the admirable liberation theologians) can ignore both the Holocaust and the history of Christian anti-Semitism, something is profoundly awry. When the subject of the *tremendum* becomes a subject only discussed in the context of the "Jewish-Christian dialogue," then the subject is quietly trivialized by Christian theologians as an intra-Christian theological challenge. No less than for Jewish theology does the *tremendum* and the caesura demand new Christian theological reflection. Our classic and our contemporary theodicies are now speechless. Our serious theological reflections on the reality of God must now occur within the uncanny realm of recognition of the *tremendum*. The courageous, revisionary, and still largely unheeded post-Holocaust Christological reflections of such Christian theologians as Gregory Baum, Roy Eckardt, Franklin Littell, Johann Baptist Metz, Jürgen Moltmann, John Pawlikowski, Rosemary Radford Ruether, and Paul van Buren should be listened to and seriously reflected upon by all Christian theologians. Yet even these revisionary Christological proposals cannot be enough. For, as this work of Arthur Cohen makes clear, even the best revisionary theological reflections on the central symbols of each tradition (the covenant symbol for Jewish theologians; the Christ symbol for Christian theologians) must finally yield to the kind of thought that constitutes all properly theological reflection: thought on the reality of God.

Only when Christian theologians join their Jewish theological colleagues to think the reality of God post-*tremendum* will a genuine dialogue really begin. Only then will the thoughtlessness that threatens to engulf us all cease. The critical response of the entire theological community — Jewish and Christian — to this extraordinarily thoughtful work of Arthur Cohen will prove a singularly good test of whether theology does indeed still dare to think post-*tremendum*.

CHAPTER 16

GUSTAVO GUTIÉRREZ AND THE CHRISTIAN OPTION FOR THE POOR

To my good friend Gustavo Gutiérrez, whose theology and person have illuminated all Christian theology

Some years ago, I wrote a small book titled *Plurality and Ambiguity*. One reviewer of that book, the philosopher Richard Bernstein, stated that the entire book was a reflection on a single sentence of Walter Benjamin: "Every great work of civilization is at the same time a work of barbarism" (Bernstein 1989). That seemed to me accurate.

This essay is *also* only a reflection on the theology of another prophetic-mystical thinker of our period, Gustavo Gutiérrez. The central theological problem of our day is not the problem of the nonbeliever but the problem of those thought to be nonpersons by the reigning elites (Gutiérrez 1987). That also strikes me as right. This does not mean, for Gutiérrez or for me, that the theological problem of the nonbeliever, including the nonbeliever *in* the believer, is now resolved. But it does mean that only when the issue of those others explicitly or implicitly thought of as nonpersons takes priority will the problem of the nonbeliever receive new thought. This means that within Christian theology, as within the Christian churches, the option for the poor should be at the heart of every serious Christian theology today.

Just as Emmanuel Levinas has argued that philosophy today should begin not with the modern problem of the self but with the problem of the Other, so too should Christian theology, in its distinct turn to the Other — especially the oppressed, repressed, and marginalized Other — make the contemporary turn-to-the-Other, as opposed to the modern turn-to-the-subject, the starting point, not the conclusion, of all genuine Christian thought (Levinas 1969).

This issue is, of course, too large and complex — both philosophically and theologically — to treat in a single essay. I will instead treat two central aspects of it. First, I address the basic paradigm that Gutiérrez and others have named the "mystical-political" dimension of all Christian theology, and that I name the "mystical-prophetic" dimension. Second, I show how a move into a rethinking of Christology in this paradigm, with the additional expansion of the prophetic to the apocalyptic Second Coming (e.g., in Metz and Ashley), strengthens and focuses the kind of Christology needed for a theological defense of the option for the poor (Metz 1980; Ashley 2000, 22–43). First, however, a reflection on the basic paradigm itself.

THE MYSTICAL-PROPHETIC PARADIGM

Awareness, wide-awakeness, and right mindfulness of our participation in the whole and, for Christians, our participation in God — these are basic characteristics of any mystical form of theology. The term *mystical* is accurate enough, in a general sense. But in a more *exact* sense, the word is meant to refer not only to the intense awareness of the presence of God, as described by the great mystics, but also to practices of reflective, even argumentative modes of theological awareness, as well as to contemplative or fully enlightened states of awareness that are usually understood to be beyond meditation, which still needs language, concepts, and images, as in Ignatius Loyola's use of images in his *Spiritual Exercises* (Loyola 1987).

The same kind of difficulty with naming the basic option "mystical-prophetic" occurs in our second choice for this more self-aware mode of the basic polarity of all religions: namely, distance and participation. In the history of Western religions, the word *prophetic* first reminds most readers of the great prophetic traditions of ancient Israel and their continuation in rabbinic Judaism, Christianity, and Islam.

Indeed, a peculiarity of *any* prophetic sense that makes it unlike mysticism, unlike contemplation, as well as (for different reasons) unlike apocalypticism is the desire for clear language to express, in terms the ordinary person can understand, the obligations of the individual, the responsibilities of the community, and the honor to be accorded those communal responsibilities "under God." Language and history are central here, and a religious sense of participation, through distancing oneself before some primordial whole, renders one responsible to the community, family, ancestors, the cosmos, and God. For the ancient prophets of Israel, language should be clear so that the call of God, its promise and threat, can be understood by all. To be sure, for the prophetic consciousness, some transcendent, distancing Other speaks through the prophet to *both* the people *and* the rulers. The prophet is aware of a great distance from that Other who demands to be heard, whether the prophet wishes it or not (witness Lamentations, or Jeremiah, or Isaiah). Yet the prophet must speak—and with sufficient clarity, so that "all who have ears to hear may hear." The mystic speaks from participation in the immanence of God; the prophet speaks, with hesitation and fear, in the awe-ful presence of the utter transcendence of God.

Several—though not all—of the classical prophets, Amos and Isaiah especially, could not be more clear in the demand for justice for the destitute and the oppressed in an unjust society. Neither could the Jesus of Luke's Gospel, nor, implicitly, of Mark's. Neither could Martin Luther King Jr., Elisabeth Schüssler Fiorenza, Ellen Wondra, or Gustavo Gutiérrez. Prophets must use the power of language, a power at once distancing them from a primordial sense of the whole and allowing them to speak to a people in a particular historical situation in words that anyone can understand. It is not difficult to understand Amos. Prophets are often impatient with mystics. They accuse them, usually wrongly, of a lack of social awareness. Prophets are usually also impatient with apocalyptic writers. They accuse them, often rightly, of uttering a language so obscure that it cannot be understood by all—indeed, can lead to a ridiculous fundamentalism (let us calculate the days to the end time on the basis of the symbolic numbers of the text; let us make Russia "the beast of the North" that will hasten Armageddon; when should the thousand-year reign of Christ begin?). Prophets, on the other hand, usually want clear, direct speech to empower their call from the transcendent God, and their demands are for action now. They claim not to speak their own words but instead testify to the distant, disruptive, proclamatory Word of the Transcendent Other: "Thus says the Lord." But prophets must use language, that most necessary of distancing phenomena, clearly and cleanly, so that the people may hear and act, responding with ethical-political responsibility to the summons of the God to whom the prophet witnesses. Prophets often denounce iconic images as idols or as pagan. Just as a mystical contemplative's main temptation is to withdraw from social action, so the prophet's main temptation is to see any icon, any image, any sense of participation as idolatry.

The questions recur: Must the mystical and prophetic types finally prove to be dialectical opposites, such that the twain can never meet? Or are the mystical and prophetic forms, like the religious sensibilities of participation and distance and the religious forms of manifestation and proclamation empowering them, finally polarities? That remains one of the most important questions of any religion, attempting to live authentically in a multireligious world, with both self-respect and a willing self-exposure to the Other.

Every religion is grounded in some manifesting or proclamatory event. In the prophetic biblical traditions, this could not be clearer. We cannot understand Judaism without the founding revelatory events of Sinai and Exodus. It would be impossible to understand Christianity without the revelatory event of Jesus as the Christ. It would be equally impossible to understand Islam without understanding that the central revelatory event is not a historical-religious event like Sinai and Exodus, or a religious-historical event and person like the unsubstitutable Jesus as the Christ, but a text, the Qur'an, given by God to be recited by the last of the prophets, Muhammad. Both Judaism and Christianity also need a text, the Bible, but that text, unlike the Qur'an, is understood not as the revelation but as the canonical witness to the revelatory event. In Islam alone among the three radically monotheistic religions, the revelatory event *is* a text: the Qur'an, to which the prophet Muhammad canonically witnesses. All three religions, in my judgment, are fundamentally proclamation-prophetic religions, whose power of distancing moves religion from the earlier emphasis on manifestation through nature and cosmos of the so-called pagan religions of the country people (the *pagani*) to proclamation in and through history.

The move, within Christianity, is from the disruptive, proclamatory, and prophetic Word, as in the prophet Jesus's own eschatological sayings, parables, and proverbs, to the manifesting, meditative Word of Logos in the Gospel of John, or from the dialectical, prophetic Paul of Thessalonians, Romans, Corinthians, and Galatians to the later Pauline tradition in Colossians and Ephesians. This trajectory to mystical participatory form had already begun, of course, in the classical Wisdom traditions of the Jewish Scriptures (now named, for Christians, the First or Old Testament). Greek reflective questions (*pace* all anti-Hellenizers) are already being posed in intra-Jewish, Christian, and Islamic terms (e.g., the Sufis). Sometimes these questions took a critical turn. The extraordinary achievement of Jewish, Christian, and Muslim readers was their insight that belief in a transcendent Creator God need not destroy, though it does indeed disrupt and transform, the ancient conception described in all the ancient, Greek-inspired philosophies of a participatory, manifesting synthesis of the human, cosmic, and divine realms and of the *plenum* implied in those philosophies and religions.

There was no need to choose between the Jewish Creator God and the ancient synthesis of those early Jewish, Christian, and Muslim hermeneutics. When these reflective strands came together in Christian and medieval thought, they manifested the wide-ranging, reflective inquiry of the Greeks in new forms. God's creative act did not have to be understood in terms of only efficient causality, nor through the emanation imagery of the Neoplatonists. The transcendent Creator God would be, in that case, the cause of, but completely transcendent to, not immanent in, the created human and cosmic realms. But what if the causality of creation is not purely efficient but also final and formal or, perhaps more exactly, quasi-formal? Then the Creator God of the Scriptures is not only the origin of all but, as origin, also the sustainer of all and the final end, final cause, of all reality.

This remarkable Jewish-Christian-Muslim, reflective, medieval achievement could comprehend philosophically, and thereby theologically, how the Creator God of the Bible is both transcendent to all creation and, as such, immanent in all creation. These thinkers were aided by the almost biblical reading they accorded to Plato's *Timaeus* and its creation account (Plato 1959). These readings saved the ancient, manifesting, participatory synthesis of the human, the cosmic, and the divine, and the *plenum* within it, for thought and life (e.g., the manifesting-proclamatory Christian sacraments). The challenge of the nonreality of creation was as difficult for the medieval Jewish, Christian, and Islamic thinkers to resolve — and they did resolve it — as the crisis of the nonperson is today for all prophetic, political, liberationist Jewish, Christian, and Islamic thinkers.

Religion as proclamatory Word posits itself by implying its Other, the manifesting participatory Sophia, as feminist theologians have rightly insisted. In Christianity, combining the Logos of Wisdom traditions, the Gospel of John and its attendant Logos theologies, with recent Sophia theologies, as well as the classical retrievals of the ancient synthesis and the *plenum*, deeply enriched the liturgical-sacramental lives of Christians and produced Greek- and Latin-inspired creation theologies of the transcendent-immanent God, whether formulated in earlier, Neoplatonist, Christian theological terms or in the medieval terms of Aristotle's four causes. In Judaism, a similar mingling of traditions produced Maimonides's conception of the theological-sacramental power of the law and Rosenzweig's conception of the philosophical-theological importance of the Jewish liturgical year. In Islam, a belief in the one and transcendent God, Allah, grounded the ancient synthesis in the philosophies and theologies of such thinkers as Ibn Sina and Ibn Rushd. The ancient philosophical synthesis, and the participatory religious *plenum* pervading it, was not destroyed but disrupted, transformed, and reposited by the Jewish, Christian, and Muslim thinkers in the Middle Ages. The prophetic Word posits itself by implying its Other: the reflective-contemplative, at times, the mystical.

The prophetic *optum* for the poor, proclaimed by Luke's Jesus, and the apocalyptic disruptions of all religious elites, including the original disciples, proclaimed by Mark's Jesus, posit themselves by implying the participatory, mystical Wisdom of John's Logos. There is no choice, for Christians, between the love emphasis of John's Gospel, that "love-intoxicated Gospel," as Augustine called it, and the justice emphasis of Luke and Mark. In my judgment, by rendering explicit the option for the poor as central to their self-understanding, Christians have a great opportunity to rethink the issue at the heart of Christianity: namely, the relationship between love and justice. Love can become too vague if its demand for equality does not include the demand for justice for all rendered unequal, especially the poor and all marginalized persons, communities, and classes. There is no Christian justice if it is not grounded in the participatory love of God made manifest in Jesus the Christ. Neither justice nor love, and therefore neither the prophetic nor the mystical, can live without implying each other. It does little good to speak, as some Christian elites now do, of a "charity" for the poor. The only special love worth mentioning here is one that includes a demand for justice. Love is greater than justice but never less than justice. One sound way to ensure the demand for justice is to speak plainly and clearly of an option for the poor. Only then, I have come to believe, will the ethical-political dialectic of love and justice, like the prophetic-mystical polarity empowering it, find its proper Christian focus. This can be seen even more clearly in the return of apocalyptic, not only prophetic, language in Christian thought today.

APOCALYPTIC AND CHRISTOLOGY

Christian apocalyptic thought, with its dualisms, its sense of an end, its sense of an interruptive not-yet, and often its violence, can seem an unlikely contributor to a contemporary theological enterprise affirming the option for the poor. Better to speak, most theologians seem to think, of eschatology, as Augustine did. Better to rely on prophetic, not apocalyptic, language as the disruptive language we need, since we do indeed clearly need prophetic language. That is the reasonable case most Christian theologians, even eschatologically oriented ones, tend to make; there are grounds for this ancient and modern Christian theological suspicion of apocalyptic, as opposed to eschatological, language. If apocalyptic language, which so fragments the continuity of history, does not also fragment itself through the deliteralization upon which Augustine insisted in *City of God* (1945), and upon the insistence of such theologians after Augustine as Rudolf Bultmann (1951), Reinhold Niebuhr (1943), Karl Rahner (1978), Cyril O'Regan (2014), and Mathew Levering (O'Regan and Levering 2019), then much could be lost for Christians. For all that Christians would then possess would be a diminished and incomplete form of apocalypticism that could seem to protect them from experiencing the void revealed in the terror of history as that history has been experienced by marginalized and oppressed peoples. By literalizing when the end will occur, and by violently dividing all reality into two opposing forces on behalf of a community's sense of injustice, such apocalypticism hardens, finally, into a fundamentalist self-righteousness.

Ernst Käsemann may indeed have exaggerated in detail, but in principle his famous statement remains properly provocative: "Apocalyptic is the mother of all Christian theology" (Käsemann 1969, 40). It is impossible to understand the New Testament without apocalyptic, and I do not mean this only in the obvious sense of the important apocalyptic texts: Thessalonians, Matthew 25, almost the whole of Mark, and especially the *fascinans et tremendum* power of the book of Revelation. The New Testament does not merely begin chronologically with Mark's strange, apocalyptic Gospel. It ends, not in triumphalist closure, even after the Resurrection, but with the plaintive unsettling cry, "Come Lord Jesus, come" (Rev. 22:20). The Christian Bible ends with that cry of the eschatological always/already/not-yet "Come!"

The New Testament cannot be adequately understood without that apocalyptic tone of "Come!" One always needs, with the historical, critical exegetes of our time, to remember the historical settings and the social locations of these New Testament texts. The fall of Jerusalem in 70 CE as a tragedy, indeed an apocalyptic tragedy, was important not only for Jews but also for Jewish Christians and for all the Gospels, including Mark. The importance of the historical mission to the Gentiles and all the other major historical events that influenced the texts we now read is embedded in the four New Testament Gospels — five if you add Paul (as one should). But above all, we need to have great attentive sensitivity, which is too often lacking, to the event that did *not* occur, the Second Coming of Jesus Christ, the Son of Man, and what that might mean for a reading of the New Testament itself.

For example, when theologians and the whole Christian church employ the great symbols for Christology, they usually employ the three classical Christological symbols: Incarnation, Cross, and Resurrection. Because these symbols reveal who Jesus Christ is, and thus, for Christians, reveal who God is and who we human beings might become, each of them has received hundreds of interpretations from the very beginning of Christian theology.

Without the symbol of Incarnation, for example, where is the Christian affirmation of Jesus Christ as God? Where is the affirmation of the disaster still attendant upon much Christian denigration of the body, and especially sexuality — a clear case of Christianity forgetting both body and creation? An incarnational perspective, as in Francis of Assisi and Clare, is crucial for any further Christian understanding of how we actually participate in nature and history and owe justice to our fellow creatures — not only human creatures. For myself, Buddhists gave me the best insight on Francis of Assisi, whom they consider the most radical religious figure in the entire West since Francis clearly saw salvation not only for human beings but all living creatures. Moreover, recent Christian feminist, womanist, and *mujerista* theologies have persuasively shown how historical Christianity seems to have trapped itself in Hellenistic categories of soul and body, male and female, mind and passion. Without challenging these binary oppositions, Christianity could again lose its biblical, Jewish, antidualistic roots.

With the classic Christian symbol of Incarnation, even the cross becomes differently understood, or, at the least, more deeply understood. For the cross of the Crucified One, as viewed through the symbol of Incarnation can also be seen (as Mircea Eliade argued) as the cosmic tree of the ancients and of so many ancient religions. The tree — the cosmic tree in Hinduism, for example, and in so many indigenous religions — manifests the synthesis of the divine, the cosmic, and the human realms, for the cosmic tree reaches with its branches to the whole cosmos in the air and reaches with its roots to the power and joy of Earth itself (Eliade 1959). With the Incarnation, belief in resurrection becomes genuinely not a belief in Greek immortality of the soul but, with Luke and Paul in their distinct ways, a resurrection of the body, reminding Christians over and over that the body is good. Redemption does not replace the goodness of creation affirmed in Genesis. Furthermore, Christians must be in communion with all the living and the dead.

Without the classic symbol of the Cross, Christian life and thought are always in danger of sentimentalizing Christianity into a "have a nice day" greeting card without suffering, without a sense of evil, and without remainder. For the lifting up of the cross may well be, as John insists in his incarnationally oriented Gospel, and as Hans Urs von Balthasar's theology attempts to express, the manifestation of God's beauty and glory. Even in John, who, against any nonnarrative speculation and abstract Gnostic readings, grounds the crucifixion in a history-like, realistic Passion narrative, Christology is cross-centered. Cross, suffering, pain, negativity, death, disgrace, Godforsakenness also attend the Johannine Jesus, although less intensely than with Paul of Romans and Galatians. Certainly Paul almost obsessively refused to let go of the thought that neither a Christian nor anyone else can think of God except as the crucified God revealed in Jesus Christ and Him crucified.

Without the cross, where would the great movements in the theologies of liberation find a way to understand the conflict, the pain, and the negativity in every historical struggle for justice? Without the cross, could Christians even *begin* to face the ruptures of all history, with its betrayals and self-delusion through the centuries — the void exposed in the Shoah and in the horrifying Middle Passage of enslaved African peoples and every other instance of the useless, innocent, unjust suffering of whole peoples, in what even the optimistic Hegel called the "slaughter-bench" of history (Hegel 1944, 21)?

With the cross, one need not worry that Christianity will descend to what Nietzsche believed with some hint of his own *ressentiment* that Christianity was a reactive, weak, finally somewhat embarrassingly sentimental religion that cannot bear to face life's suffering, tragedy, evil, sin, and abuse of power. On the contrary, through the Crucified God of the Cross of the crucified Jesus Christianity is able to face and resist the reality of force that, as Simone Weil insisted, eventually affects every human life, even the life of the privileged, for each of us must die alone, and each of us was born alone. Force, as Weil argues in her brilliant essay on the *Iliad* as the poem of force — physical force, intellectual force, spiritual force, affects us all through sickness, old age, disease, and death; force is the power that proleptically draws us all further into what? — either the Void or the Good or God (Weil 1977, 439–68). With the cross, any Christian belief in resurrection will be shorn of all temptations to individual and historical triumphalism, and all nonsense about the ease of death. Like Paul, we face death as the final, fearsome earthly power, to which each of us must one day yield.

The equally necessary symbol of Resurrection presents its own demands in relation to Incarnation and Cross. Against any fatalism and all *dolorism* (suffering for its own sake), in every struggle for justice or for material life itself, the Resurrection empowers the kind of hope that is believably actual in the struggle against injustice. Hope is neither optimistic nor pessimistic. Optimism and pessimism are largely matters of temperament and response to life's experiences. Resurrection hope does not know but endures; one continues the struggle in the hope for all (1 Tim. 4:10) in the vindication of the life and death of this unsubstitutable Jesus Christ, the incarnate, crucified, and risen One. With Resurrection, the incarnational trust in body, flesh, and creation is strengthened and moved past any temptation to nature romanticism into a struggle for affirming the basic goodness of the body and for the entire earth — indeed, as Paul expresses it, for all creation groaning to be free. With Resurrection, Cross will never give in to a temptation to fatalism or to ultimate despair.

The theological necessity for each of these classic symbols (Incarnation, Cross, Resurrection) for understanding Christ, and, thereby, naming God by naming the Jesus narrated and confessed by Christians as the Christ, has never been more clear. We need all three symbols and their inner tensions and their tensions with each other. The ever-changing need to relate these classical Christological symbols to one another in ever-new combinations, in fidelity to the Christian pluralism beginning in the New Testament itself and continuing throughout the entire pluralistic history of Christianity and now alive in a global, post-Eurocentric Christianity, shows once and for all how no theology and no naming of God through Christ Jesus can be built on only one of these symbols. The cry of faith, hope, and love resounds through Incarnation and Resurrection. The cry of "justice now" as the option for the poor resounds through Cross and Second Coming. Only all four symbols — united, of course, to the life and message of Jesus that they interpret — can bring Christian theology to greater clarity on the full-fledged option it now needs: the option for the poor.

With so intense a struggle to understand who Jesus Christ is for Christians, and thereby how to name God, and with hope for what might be embedded in the classical Christological symbols of Incarnation, Cross, and Resurrection, it may seem strange to plead, as I now do, even against my former self on the role of apocalyptic in Christian theology. All I have formerly written on Christology has been on the four central symbols — Incarnation, Cross, Resurrection and Second Coming — with the apocalyptic serving only as a "corrective," not part of the foundational symbol system of Christian theology. Now I hold that the fourth symbol (and, since Augustine, a fourth too-often-neglected symbol) of Christology, the interruptive apocalyptic symbol of the Second Coming of Christ, must also be attended to for a full Christian self-understanding. The unsettling symbol of an apocalyptic Second Coming of Christ is not, I have come to believe, a luxury item for Christian self-understanding or for the naming God. Apocalyptic is what Jacques Derrida nicely calls "a certain tone in contemporary culture and thought" (Derrida 1993, 117–71). It is a tone that must be heard by Jews and Christians, especially by Christians attempting to live a Christian life and to think a fully Christian vision of history and time. The radical "not-yet" of the interruptive, apocalyptic power alive in the symbol of the Second Coming destabilizes all Christian thought, and that for the better. Once deliteralized and stolen *back* from the date-setting literalists, the Second Coming is as powerful and as central a symbol for Christian self-understanding through Jesus Christ and for naming God as are the incarnation, cross, and resurrection.

The New Testament as a whole unfolds between its two great destabilizing, fragmenting, and fragmented texts: the fragmentary, interruptive, apocalyptic text of the Gospel of Mark, as distinct from the continuous, realistic narrative of the Gospel of Luke-Acts. Moreover, what does one find concluding the New Testament? The fragmentary book of Revelation, that strange and deeply ambiguous text possessing at one and the same time some of the most liberating lines and images in the entire New Testament, as well as some of the most violent and ethically and religiously revolting images of a vengeful

Christ. Mark's brief account of the Resurrection, which he clearly affirms, disallows any Christian triumphalism with its interruptive note of apocalyptic and ends, most scholars agree, with the women at the tomb fleeing in fear and terror (Mark 16:8). The book of Revelation, the last book of the Christian Bible, that unsteady collection of fragments from ever-new genres, hymns, warnings, epistles, heavenly journeys, mediating angels, narratives, nonclosures, ruptures, and interruptions of history, seems held together, if it is at all as a text, at times only by what appears to be the obsession of the author or authors to cry, "Not yet, not yet," to any complacent Christian and to have the radical apocalyptic not-yet of the fiercest great Christological symbol, the Second Coming join the Incarnation, the Cross, and the Resurrection to disclose the always-already not-yet time of Christian salvation.

To be sure, in one powerful sense the end times have already happened in Jesus Christ. They have already begun, but they are just as strongly "not yet." For Christians, the Bible does not end like a classical folktale with "and they lived happily ever after." It ends rather with a cry, a plea, a prayer, a passion: "Come Lord Jesus, come." Perhaps the unjust marginalization of those honest persons who join fundamentalist groups may have tempted them into their literalist love of the book of Revelation, a love that shares the obsessive quality of parts of the book itself: the numbers to count, the symbols, the literalized geography, countdowns for what Hal Lindsay, the most prominent fundamentalist spokesman of the apocalypse, has named "the late, great planet Earth."

I cannot share any fundamentalist readings of the book of Revelation. However, I have also now come to appreciate its apocalyptic Second Coming. Why do we reject Revelation (the Apocalypse), when our name for the liturgical season of Advent is one of the few words left in the English language that speaks of that other notion of the future — of God's coming from the future to the present — *Adventus, advenir, Zukunft*? The season of Advent is not just a rather relaxed preparation for the Incarnation and Christmas. What of all the apocalyptic readings in the liturgies of the four weeks of Advent? What does one do with them? At the same time, the violence of language and imagery in Revelation remains deeply disturbing — on intra-Christian grounds.

The embarrassment, if that is what it is, of many theologians like Rudolf Bultmann and Karl Rahner regarding the disruptive, not-yet category of apocalyptic has effectively handed over this great symbolic text of Revelation and the apocalyptic power pulsating like a bloodstream throughout the whole New Testament to Christian fundamentalists who are all too certain about what this symbol must mean, not only for the individual but also for bizarre historical countdowns. The fact is that the New Testament ends in nonclosure; the New Testament ends with a prayer, a passionate cry of "Come." The Christian Bible ends with a fragmented text that barely holds itself together, save by the power of its demands for justice now shouted by a persecuted people. The New Testament begins with Mark's strange Gospel, the strangest of the four, apocalyptic through and through. The New Testament ends Christologically, having already affirmed the symbols of Incarnation, Cross, and Resurrection, with a fourth symbol that we too easily forget: the apocalyptic Second Coming of Christ, which destroys at its core any Christian temptation to triumphalism, such as any mistaken theological attitude toward the Jews, as in supercessionism. Without the symbol of the Second Coming, and without that symbol read apocalyptically, Christianity would settle down into a religion that no longer is driven by the constant New Testament complex understanding of salvation of "already/not yet" most clearly expressed as in Gustavo Gutiérrez's great and liberating theology as the option for the poor and the marginalized.

REFERENCES

Ashley, J. Matthew. 2000. "Apocalypticism in Political and Liberation Theology: Toward an Historical Docta Ignorantia." *Horizons* 27 (Spring): 22–43.

Augustine. 1945. *City of God.* Translated by John Healey. London: J. M. Dent.

Bernstein, Richard J. 1989. "Radical Plurality, Fearful Ambiguity, and Engaged Hope." *Journal of Religion* 69 (January): 85–91.

Bultmann, Rudolf. 1951. *Theology of the New Testament.* Translated by Kendrich Grobel. New York: Charles Scribner's Sons.

Derrida, Jacques. 1993. "On a Newly Arisen Apocalyptic Tone in Philosophy." In *Raising the Tone of Philosophy: Late Essays by Immanuel Kant, Transformative Critique by Jacques Derrida.* Edited by Peter Fenves. Baltimore: Johns Hopkins University Press.

Eliade, Mircea. 1959. *The Sacred and the Profane.* Translated by Willard R. Trask. New York: Harcourt Brace.

Genovese, Eugene D. 1974. *Roll, Jordan, Roll: The World the Slaves Made.* New York: Pantheon Books.

Gutiérrez, Gustavo. 1987. *On Job: God-Talk and the Suffering of the Innocent.* Translated by Matthew J. O'Connell. Maryknoll, NY: Orbis Books.

Hegel, Georg Wilhelm Friedrich. 1944. *Lectures on the Philosophy of History*. Rev. ed. Translated by J. Sibree. New York: Wiley.

Käsemann, Ernst. 1969. "The Beginnings of Christian Theology." *Journal for Theology and the Church* 6.

Levinas, Emmanuel. 1969. *Totality and Infinity: An Essay on Exteriority*. Translated by Alphonso Lingis. Pittsburgh, PA: Duquesne University Press.

Loyola, Ignatius. 1987. *Spiritual Exercises of St. Ignatius Loyola*. Translated by Elizabeth Meier Tetlow. Lanham, MD: University Press of America.

Metz, Johann Baptist. 1980. *Faith in History and Society: Toward a Practical Fundamental Theology*. Translated by David Smith. New York: Seabury Press.

Niebuhr, Reinhold. 1943. *Nature and Destiny of Man*. New York: Charles Scribner's Sons.

O'Regan, Cyril. 2014. *Anatomy of Misremembering: Von Balthasar's Response to Philosophical Modernity*. New York: Crossroad.

O'Regan, Cyril, and Matthew Levering. 2019. *The Achievement of Hans Urs von Balthasar: An Introduction to His Trilogy*. Studies in Early Christianity. Washington, DC: Catholic University of America Press.

Plato. 1959. *Plato's "Timaeus."* Translated by Francis M. Cornford. Indianapolis, IN: Bobbs-Merrill Educational Publishing.

Rahner, Karl. 1978. *Foundations of Christian Faith: An Introduction to the Idea of Christianity*. Translated by William V. Dych. New York: Seabury Press.

Tracy, David. 1987. *Plurality and Ambiguity: Hermeneutics, Religion, Hope*. Chicago: University of Chicago Press.

Weil, Simone. 1977. "The Love of God and Affliction." In *The Simone Weil Reader*, edited by George Panichas. Wakefield, RI: Moyer Bell.

CHAPTER 17

JAMES CONE
AND AFRICAN
AMERICAN THOUGHT

A Discovery of Fragments

In developing the category of *fragments* for contemporary reflection on philosophy and theology, I have been reading African American thought for many years, starting with, of course, James Cone and Cornel West, and have been driven *back* to "fragments," which, as far as I can see, were in American culture first employed in African American culture and thought, especially in the improvisations of jazz to the unstoppable fragmenting power of rock, rap, and hip-hop. That at least is my hypothesis. I believe that it is not only significant to acknowledge the importance of black theology; it is also important for white theologians to acknowledge the profound ambiguity of the cultural category *whiteness*, which is embedded in white philosophy and theology, where it is too often thought *not* to be (Nilson 2007).

POSTMODERNITIES

If postmodernity is to avoid essentialism, the great enemy that it hopes to rout, a necessary first step is to admit that there is no single phenomenon identifiable as postmodernity. There are only postmodernities. And if modernity is ever to free itself from the trap of totalizing that it has unconsciously set for itself, its first step is not only to continue the great modern experiment, the political democratic pluralism experiment, the still-unfinished project of modernity, as Jürgen Habermas calls it, but also to admit, at the same time, that there are, in fact, modernities. The shift to the plural for both postmodernity and modernity does not imply only the obvious differences, of which everyone is now aware: namely, between the forms of Western modernity and the forms of modernization taking place in Asian and African cultures. More importantly for our own American culture, the shift requires us to rethink the categories of modernity and postmodernity in relationship to the many traditions—especially the African American traditions—that demand a reformulation of the category.

To expand the cultural, philosophical, and religious horizons of the discussion between modernity and postmodernity, so prominent across the disciplines today, is also partly to let go of a category that has been my own favorite: namely, pluralism. Pluralism is a correct word as far as it goes (viz., to affirm the plurality that exists) but it still seems to assume that there is a center with margins. In fact, anyone who is aware of the contemporary discussion now knows that there is no longer any such center. Pluralism is no longer adequate to describe our global, post-Eurocentric, post-"white" situation. We need a word like *polycentrism* (Johann Baptist Metz)—a word that tries to articulate the reality of the many centers now present in our culture, which no longer has a dominant center and margins. Many forms of postmodernity are, indeed, exposing once-forgotten, marginalized, repressed, and opposed traditions, including their usually unacknowledged colonialist presence in Enlightenment modernity. The Enlightenment, with a few exceptions (e.g., Diderot), did not seem to know how much its successes depended upon colonization, as Paul Gilroy in his superb book *The Black Atlantic* (1993) demonstrates. It is no surprise that the initial categories employed by postmodern thought, the "Other" and the "different," very quickly led to a recognition that all of us are now "Others" in a polycentric world.

Hence the category *fragments*. Fragments show the need to shatter any reigning totality system, such as the "white" understanding of modernity and culture. And at the same time, fragments embody a quite positive meaning: a break out of totality into infinity by negating all totality systems as one discovers one's own, once marginalized traditions, as well as all the others and the different as possible disclosures of infinity. Perhaps these elements of the modern Enlightenment were somewhat less repressed in early modernity — that is, the sixteenth and early seventeenth centuries, especially in a figure like Bartolomé de las Casas. Indeed, early modernity is now far more significant for understanding the secure achievements and the too-often-ignored ambiguity of modernity than the classical Enlightenment modernity — that is, the late seventeenth and eighteenth centuries, when the categories of modernity tended to be reified as the very word and concept *the modern* was.

The key cultural phenomenon needing new study in this new situation by both philosophers and theologians is the phenomenon of religion, especially religion in what William James called its "intense forms," for example, the intense religion of the black church traditions. It may well be, as several contemporary philosophers claim, that religion is the most nonreductive (*saturated* is one favored word) phenomenon of all. Indeed, I have come to believe that to be the case. And yet, even before that contemporary case can be made, it may be necessary to clear the decks of some additional cultural debris.

Religion has always been the unassimilable Other (as distinct from the conquered or colonized Other in indigenous cultures and religions) in many versions of Enlightenment modernity. And just as one can see this reality (thanks partly to feminist critique of how Freud's critique of religion is curiously and troublingly similar to his critique of woman), so too I believe one can see in "mainline" American intellectual life how the critique of religion was often linked to the ignorance of — even indifference toward — black religious traditions of this country. Any saturated form of the religious phenomenon seemed suspicious to Enlightenment modernity: from Romantic symbols to the recovery of African rituals (Charles Long), to the discovery in the nineteenth century of the Hindu excessive erotic forms for the sacred (Wendy Doniger).

Above all in American Christian theology, African American and Hispanic thought (especially in black religions, in philosophy, theology, cultural studies, history, and social science) has led the way to recover repressed, intense, saturated, and fragmentary religious forms of American religion. This can be seen in the recovery of the slave narratives, as in Dwight Hopkins's work (1993, 1999), and through new attention to the theology of the gospel songs and the distinct theologies of the spirituals and the blues, as in Matthew V. Johnson's profound *Cicada's Song*. Above all, in James Cone's work one witnesses the intensity of the religious experience of the black churches and the power of demanding liberation, justice, and struggle as the heart of prophetic Christianity. The God of black religion is a prophetic, fragmenting, liberating God for all oppressed peoples.

All these clearly religious, intense, often excessive fragmentary phenomena are presently being rediscovered and employed anew. Why does one otherwise observe the bizarre parade in classical modernity (i.e., the eighteenth century) of the invention of modern "isms" for naming God? This is the case, whether it be, as it first was, in the Enlightenment, *deism*, or even *theism* or *atheism* in its modern forms, or *pantheism*, or the greatest discovery and development of modern thought on God in the twentieth century, *panentheism*.

Can the question of God, when now asked in ways that refuse to engage simply in the modern Enlightenment discussion on what is the correct "ism" for naming God, really be controlled as a question by any of these modern "isms"? Before the categories of the "Other" and the "different" became such central philosophical, cultural, ethical, religious, and theological categories in contemporary philosophical thought (Levinas, Derrida, Deleuze), African American thought never gave in to the dominant temptation to reduce all reality (as Foucault states about Western modern thought) to more of the same; or, at best, to the similar.

The German Romantics in the early nineteenth century (the Schlegels, Novalis, and others) sensed this difficulty but could not do too much with it, even with their fine development and privileging of the metaphor "fragments" over any category of totality. Unfortunately, Romantic thoughts on fragments, as Derrida and others correctly argue, never quite broke out of the modern totality, because the Romantic metaphor always suggested a broken-off fragment involving a nostalgia for a lost totality, rather than negating all totality, breaking through into open infinity, and thereby calling into question all notions of totality itself. However, the fragment does become, in African American thought, exactly what the Romantics wanted but could not achieve: a shattering of any totality system and the possibility of positive rediscovery of the intense presence of infinity in fragmenting religious forms, especially musical forms.

African American thought, better than any other American tradition of thought in the last century, succeeded at exposing the pretensions of any modern system of totality and the contingent, deeply ambiguous cultural character of *all* claims to universality, especially "modernity" and "whiteness." Christianity as a totality system becomes Christendom. Christendom could not and cannot survive any experiment with authentic Christianity. This was not just Kierkegaard's insight in his brilliant attack upon Christendom. It was clearly the insight that one can find without exception in the African American thinkers — male and female (womanist theologies), straight and gay (James Baldwin), even those who were not particularly favorable to or inclined toward religion in its Christian form (Malcolm X's defense of Islam).

One witnessed this African American fragmentary force earlier with Frederick Douglass in the three extraordinary autobiographical narratives of his life: the deeply fragmenting *Narrative* (1845), *My Bondage and My Freedom* (1855), and the final versions of these autobiographical accounts in *The Life and Times of Frederick Douglass, Written by Himself* ([1881; 1892] 1962). One also witnessed this insight in the pathbreaking social-scientific work of W. E. B. Du Bois. Both Douglass and Du Bois, unlike many other thinkers of their periods, did indeed demand a study of the most intense forms of religious experience in the black churches in order to understand the complexity of American culture at all. Each of them (Du Bois more than Douglass) was, in fact, also very much involved in the modern Enlightenment intellectual project and in attempts to understand God and religion from that point of view.

Unlike many white thinkers of their period, however, Douglass and Du Bois never ignored the fragmenting and saturated character of the phenomenon of religion. They were never naive enough to think that a thinker could possibly understand American culture — or any culture — without attending (as Du Bois's colleague William James also insisted) to the intense, saturated, fragmentary cases of religion, especially as they are described in Du Bois's classic work on religion and the gospel songs and religious spirituals, *The Souls of Black Folk* (1997). It is instructive that Douglass and Du Bois, however modern they were in their basic philosophical positions in their distinct ways, nevertheless (unlike so many other contemporary modern intellectuals) could not let go of analyzing the phenomenon of religion in its most intense forms (e.g., slave songs, gospel songs, spirituals — the earliest expressions of African American music deeply influencing later expressions like jazz, blues, rock and roll [first inspired by Little Richard!], rap, and hip-hop [now a global phenomenon, first formulated among Hispanic and African American people in the South Bronx]).

Douglass and Du Bois never made totality claims. It is not surprising, therefore, to find Du Bois drawn not to a system, but to ever-new experiments in thought, both social, scientific, and philosophical, to comprehend how African American fragments might relate to a whole but never to a totality. Likewise, it is not surprising that Zora Neale Hurston did the same, both in her social-scientific work and in her influential literary work (1983, 1978a, 1978b) — a role that the incomparable Toni Morrison has perfected in her exceptional novels.

FRAGMENTS: THREE APPROACHES

There are three kinds of contemporary thinkers for whom the category *fragments* tends to be crucial. The first are conservatives who, often with depth, witness fragments as moments of cultural regret and nostalgia, as all that is left of what they view as a once-unified Western culture. This is perhaps best expressed in T. S. Eliot's famous words in *The Waste Land* (line 431) that all we now have are "These fragments . . . shored against my ruins." However, fragments need not have merely nostalgic meaning, either among the Romantics or the major conservative thinkers of our day, including such African American thinkers as the fine literary and theological critic Nathan Scott.

The second group of thinkers appealing to fragments are the postmoderns, almost all of whom see fragments not as an occasion for nostalgia but as emancipatory from the deadening hand of all reigning modern totality systems, especially those systems that have tried to hide their own complicity in how the totality works against its victims.

The third group of thinkers (explicitly philosophical and theological) see fragments even more positively than the postmoderns as bearers of hope for some form of redemption in our own time — if we would but attend to them. This is especially the case in contemporary intellectual history, among such Jewish thinkers as Franz Rosenzweig and Walter Benjamin, and in such Christian thinkers as Simone Weil and Cornel West, as well as in the secular African American thought after W. E. B. Du Bois. Fragments first entered the postmodern sensibility through the use of fragments in so many forms of post–World War I modernist writers. These fragments were intended to undo the domesticating power of modern rationality's claim to universality and totality, and to provide something that was finally excessive toward or transgressive of the modern totality systems (Bataille).

However, contemporary thought has moved on beyond the literary modernists, whether under the explicit banner of some version of postmodernity or some other rubric. For the love of excess and transgression in practically every postmodern thinker is obvious. Some of them tend to be somewhat nervous, like Jacques Derrida, regarding the explicit category *fragments*, since they fear that an appeal to fragments could be trapped in a nostalgia for a lost totality, either in the German Romantic or conservative modes. But if one follows the recoveries that are being made in contemporary thought of traditions that were once not considered "major" traditions by most "white" thinkers, one can observe what has really happened. Think, for example, of the recoveries I cited earlier in James Cone's work, from his earlier influential book, *Black Theology and Black Power* ([1969] 1997) to his theologies of the spirituals and the blues in *The Spirituals and the Blues: An Interpretation* (1972) and his stunning analyses of both Martin Luther King and Malcolm X in *Martin and Malcolm and America: A Dream or a Nightmare* (1991). Likewise, many other African American theologians, philosophers, and cultural theorists, especially the womanist theologians like Delores Williams (1993), are recovering other slave narratives, spirituals, blues, and gospel songs, as well as the preaching, rituals, and customs of black churches, with their fragmentary, liberating, tragedy-inflected Christianity.

Perhaps, like the Jesuits of Voltaire's imagination, religion must always enter the rooms of modernity without warmth and leave without regret. But that is not real religion. For religion is vibrant—usually in its most transgressive and excessive forms, such as those found in the great gospel songs, in the prophets and intellectual love mystics of all the traditions, in the Kabbalists, in the Sufis, and in the marginalized, repressed, and ignored traditions, like the radical apophatic traditions of the Eastern Orthodoxy (Lossky) and the traditions of African American thought that, so often, have an apophatism on the incomprehensibility and tragic but ultimately healing hiddenness of God's actions for the oppressed.

Such fragmentary, saturated religious phenomena were often ignored by many intellectuals as not bearing intellectual weight. That is *exactly* what is now clear as a deep, devastating error. There are many ways to dismiss such phenomena, but all now know (or should know) what great religious figures Sojourner Truth and Harriet Tubman were. But we all also know that they, too, were too easily described as simply "saints" (which too often implies that the rest of us do not have to take them too seriously). Dorothy Day was right when a reporter called her a saint in her own lifetime and she replied, "Don't trivialize me." Real "intense" religion (William James) has become a central phenomenon to be described and analyzed, as in so much of African American thought, and a central topic in postmodern thought.

For religion can never really be contained. It can only be conquered or colonized, as indeed it was; or rendered a once-necessary form, on the route to absolute knowledge, as in Hegel and his modern idealist successors; or made into pleasant narratives and symbols that may help moderns feel again, as best they can, their own way to some ethical position and some aesthetic consolation in the face of death. Religion is too often thought of as really some other phenomenon than religion. Perhaps it is really ethics, or bad science, or disguised metaphysics. Perhaps religion was once real, even fierce, but it has now become just one more captive of the universalist strains of onto-theology. Practically no major secular thinkers — save William James and W. E. B. Du Bois, at the beginning of the century — predicted either the catastrophes of the century or that religion would do anything else than quietly die away by century's end.

The many strategies of modern thought with regard to religion are like those of people who refuse to admit their own "whiteness" and any other rubric of false universality or totality: strategies of benign neglect, strategies of indifference, and strategies like Schleiermacher's nonaggression pact between theology and philosophy. These were strategies for those who seemed unable or unwilling to describe the phenomenon of religion or even to try to think about it. The phenomenon seemingly most other to and different from what counted as real and reasonable was, in fact, religion. The phenomenon that was, in fact, the one most ignored or, more exactly, repressed, was race. Both of these phenomena — religion and race — have returned and often returned together to force all serious thinkers in our period to rethink their position.

But it is not just the postmodern love of extremes, transgression, and excess that is now needed to study religion. It has, of course, almost become a truism by now that literary modernism, whatever else it was, preferred the unfinished, the syntactically unstable, the semantically malformed. Literary modernism produced and savored discrepancy and what it shows and how it shows it, since the highest wisdom is often knowing that things and pictures do not add up. Literary modernism had also been employed and brilliantly rethought by the thinkers and writers of the Harlem Renaissance. This occurred at the very time in the 1920s and 1930s when Ezra Pound and Gertrude Stein were trying to break out of the bounds of the language once approved as standard English in order to destabilize it. This took place at the same time Zora Neale Hurston and the Harlem Renaissance were rethinking the possibilities of black dialect and such syntactic breaks for thinking and writing itself.

What African American thought principally added to the familiar portrait of modernist writers on fragments is something like a theological and philosophical theory of the modernist image. The contemporary image, after all, is a fragment, as information technology makes even clearer. Film, the most important art form of the period is fragments rushed together to produce moving pictures. History does not yield to the continuity of a grand narrative, once envisioned by philosophers and theologians alike. History, including intellectual history, breaks up into images. Such images can be found in all the major African American theologians, particularly the womanist theologians Jacquelyn Grant, Linda E. Thomas, and Emilie M. Townes (Hopkins 1999, 126–37, 105–25, 178–89, respectively), who seem to have an exceptional ability to deal with and make clear the need for a constellation of messianic, Jesuanic, fragmenting, apocalyptic images. In African American thought, images seem quite naturally to become fragments that not only destroy all claims of totality but also yield to fragments of hope, suggestions, redemption, infinity. The images that African American thinkers blast from past experiences of suffering and joy put dialectic at a standstill, as Walter Benjamin had hoped.

Above all, one must avoid modernity's (and not only Hegel's) central temptation: the drive to totality, the drive to try to eliminate differences in order to produce, once again, a totality system that can claim universality as it levels all difference and otherness. To attempt any totality system is inevitably to try to efface every fragment from every culture, to try to deny the singularity of each culture, to try to eliminate those discrete and potentially explosive images that one finds in such works as slave narratives, in classical gospel songs, in hip-hop and rap (see Nava 2017). If one carries out this modern temptation, one ends up in favor of some larger conceptual architectonic, of which the fragment would be made a mere part. Even the category of historical context (i.e., the favored category of the nineteenth-century discovery of history) is too often conceived as itself a kind of totality that disallows the experience of a historical event as a unique fragment of time disrupting the present. Thus read, the fragments of marginal, forgotten, repressed traditions were always used by "tricksters," who were too often made tricksters because they were forced to live the lie of a reigning totality system.

In Christian terms, this would suggest an odd privileging of a Gospel like Mark's: that fragmentary, discontinuous, nonclosure Gospel centered on the suffering of this uncanny apocalyptic prophet, Jesus, who never seems to be understood by his own followers, although he is understood by the marginal, the deeply psychologically troubled, and demons. Luke-Acts can lend itself much more readily to continuous history, like all history-like, realistic narrative. Mark cannot; there, history itself is fragmentary. In the African American theological terms of James Cone, a radically eschatological — indeed, messianic and apocalyptic — understanding of history is constituted by a series of fragments interrupting the usual narrative as blasted from a repressed past.

This third meaning of fragments is also to be found in the work of many African American writers. Why is it that, for many of us, Toni Morrison is not only the best living American writer, but also one of the most experimental in her forms — forms that always seem to be willing to try almost any image to see how such fragments may *also* yield new light? Consider this famous fragmenting passage from *Beloved* (1988, 214):

> I am Beloved and she is mine. Sethe is the one that picked flowers, yellow flowers in the place before the crouching. Took them away from their green leaves. They are on the quilt now where we sleep. She was about to smile at me when the men without skin came and took us up into the sunlight with the dead and shoved them into the sea. Sethe went into the sea. She went there. They did not push her. She went there. She was getting ready to smile at me and when she saw the dead people pushed into the sea she went also and left me there with no face or hers. Sethe is the face I found and lost in the water under the bridge. When I went in, I saw her face coming to me and it was my face too. I wanted to join. I tried to join, but she went up into the pieces of light at the top of the water. I lost her again, but found the house she whispered to me and there she was, smiling at last. It's good, but I cannot lose her again. All I want to know is why did she go in the water in the place where we crouched? Why did she do that when she was just about to smile at me? I wanted to join her in the sea but I could not move; I wanted to help her when she was picking the flowers, but the clouds of gunsmoke blinded me and I lost her. Three times I lost her: once with the flowers because of the noisy clouds of smoke; once when she went into the sea instead of smiling

at me; once under the bridge when I went in to join her and she came toward me but did not smile. She whispered to me, chewed me, and swam away. Now I have found her in this house. She smiles at me and it is my own face smiling. I will not lose her again. She is mine.

After his first two, more traditionally written theological books, James Cone's theological essays have also adopted a similar use of fragments and fragmentary forms. Thus we see his fine forays into the kind of fragments that speak for themselves in their singularity. Thereby do they generate new meaning and new tensions as they work with and against all other fragments into an ever-new constellation, much like Cone's constellation of emancipating fragments from both Martin Luther King Jr. and Malcolm X. As fragments, opposites meet.

More and more, Cornel West, the best theological public intellectual in the United States today, has performed prophetic actions (including hip-hop) and fragmenting philosophical theology. West's philosophy and theology yield to something like the Toni Morrison passage, a phantasmagoric collage of brilliant theological fragments from the African American past. Every womanist theologian knows well how to write liberating fragmentary work on both race and gender together.

The now-familiar academic debate of modernity versus postmodernity needs to question itself; at least it needs to make two crucial, new theological and spiritual moves. First, we need to shift the contemporary debate from an eighteenth-century version of modernity and from the late twentieth-century dominant cultures' version of postmodernity, which can often seem too relaxed and too unaware that the fragments they pick up include ethical demands for justice. Too many postmodern thinkers fail to develop an ethics of justice; Derrida happily does so under the very Jewish rubric of a messianic ethic. Justice, for Derrida now, as for all African American thought at all times, is the one phenomenon that cannot be deconstructed.

Second, we must shift our attention away from any false hope for any totality system and focus instead upon the actuality of the explosive, marginal, liberating fragments of our many heritages—but not in the conservative fashion so familiar today, which seeks to shore up some perceived past unity against our present seeming ruin. On the contrary, sometimes this spiritual search for fragments must demand a destructive moment. We must be willing to fragment or shatter whatever reigning totality system we find: economic, cultural, religious, social. We need more moments not only of critique but also of deep suspicion of all totalities and of all claims to innocence.

We can do so by finding the spiritual fragment that can expose the pretense that lies lurking in our untroubled and inaccurate claims to universality. Thinkers such as Cornel West (1988) accomplish this feat through an amazing ability to produce a constellation of fragments. Who else could put fragments like tragedy, prophecy, and pragmatism together into a new, believable constellation as West does? We also need to rethink other thinkers of our culture in terms of the fragments that they either try to deny or could not release themselves from. Think of the one fragment that Kant's classical modern three critiques could not and did not contain—radical evil. Notice how Immanuel Kant, in his later superb essays (his essays on history and the singularities of history and religion), honestly rethinks the fragments that did not fit his critical system.

Why did Hegel, that greatest and most confident of the moderns even at the end of his life, after not only *Phenomenology of Spirit* (1977) but also *Logic* (1892), find it necessary to rethink again and again (as the different editions we now have of his lectures on philosophy of religion show) the religious fragments that kept rendering his totality system incomplete. Regarding Judaism, Hegel could not contain it except by the lie that, after the biblical period, Judaism became a dead religion. On the other hand, Hegel wisely kept changing the basic contours of his philosophy of religion as a result of his repeated attempts to understand Buddhism in its formlessness. Moreover, he repressed the African religious traditions because they did not and could not seem to fit the system.

And surely it is time for all of us to face the fragments that lurk as land mines in all the classical modern systems; for example, the great flexibility and modesty of the speculative fragmentary power of such extraordinary modern thinkers as Frederick Douglass and W. E. B. Du Bois who, driven by their reflections on black religion, turned against major aspects of their own understanding. For me, as I suspect for most people, it is Douglass's first fragmentary autobiography that is the most powerful one. Douglass, of course, became and was a great man. But it is the first autobiography of his escape from slavery, that fragmentary, disturbing, unnerving narrative, that lurks in the imagination of anyone who has ever read it. No major African American thinker has ever attempted or even wanted a system. African American thinkers have left us, all of them (such as James Cone in his theology, Cornel West in his philosophy, and Tony Morrison in her literature), with something far more valuable than a system. They have left to us fragments that break and undo any pretense to totality, that evoke hints and guesses of hope for our culture and our society. They have therefore left to us fragmentary glimpses of light and redemption. These are the crucial resources that African American thought, if heeded, can provide to our desiccated public realm for all those who have ears to hear.

REFERENCES

Cone, James. 1972. *The Spirituals and the Blues: An Interpretation*. New York: Seabury Press.

———. 1991. *Martin and Malcolm and America: A Dream or a Nightmare*. 1991. Maryknoll, NY: Orbis Books.

———. (1969) 1997. *Black Theology and Black Power*. Maryknoll, NY: Orbis Books.

Douglass, Frederick. (1881; 1892) 1962. *The Life and Times of Frederick Douglass, Written by Himself*. Introduction by Rayford W. Logan. New York: Collier Books.

Du Bois, W. E. B. 1997. *The Souls of Black Folk*. Boston: Bedford Books.

Gilroy, Paul. 1993. *The Black Atlantic: Modernity and Double Consciousness*. Cambridge, MA: Harvard University Press.

Hegel, G. F. W. 1892. *The Logic, Second Edition*. Oxford: Clarendon Press.

———. 1977. *Phenomenology of Spirit*. Oxford: Clarendon Press.

Hopkins, Dwight. 1993. *Shoes That Fit Our Feet: Sources for a Constructive Black Theology*. Maryknoll, NY: Orbis Books.

———, ed. 1999. *Black Faith and Public Talk: Critical Essays on James H. Cone's "Black Theology and Black Power."* Maryknoll, NY: Orbis Books.

Hurston, Zora Neale. 1978a. *Their Eyes Were Watching God*. Urbana: University of Illinois Press.

———. 1978b. *Mules and Men*. Bloomington: Indiana University Press.

———. 1983. *The Sanctified Church*. Berkeley, CA: Turtle Island.

Johnson, Matthew V. 2006. *The Cicada's Song: A Novel*. Atlanta, GA: Publishing Associates.

———. 2010. *The Tragic Vision of African American Religion*. New York: Palgrave Macmillan.

Morrison, Toni. 1988. *Beloved*. New York: New American Library.

Nava, Alejandro. 2017. *In Search of Soul: Hip-Hop, Literature, and Religion*. Oakland: University of California Press.

Nilson, Jon. 2007. *Hearing Past the Pain: Why White Catholic Theologians Need Black Theology*. Mahwah, NJ: Paulist Press.

West, Cornel. 1988. *Prophetic Fragments*. Grand Rapids, MI: W. B. Eerdmans.

Williams, Delores S. 1993. *Sisters in the Wilderness: The Challenge of Womanist God-Talk*. Maryknoll, NY: Orbis Books.

Part 5

SEEKERS OF THE GOOD

SIMONE WEIL

Two essays in this volume begin to describe a few of the dimensions of Simone Weil — a remarkable, paradoxical, puzzling, and unnerving person and thinker. Some further reflections on how she actualized both the prophetic and the contemplative-mystical dimensions of thought seem to be in order.

Weil was, at one and the same time, two separate types of thinker: a philosopher and a prophet/mystic. As a philosopher, she was a mathematical Pythagorean and a Platonic-Cartesian-Kantian of a rigorously exact sort. As a philosopher, she engaged in discursive argument and exacting mathematical-logical analysis. As a prophet, like all prophets, Weil did not argue but asserted her ethical-political demands. As a mystic, Weil abandoned discursive, argumentative reason for a contemplative vision that embraced her conviction (like that of later liberation theologies) that Christianity was a religion of the poor (her first mystical vision was evoked by the poor in a small fishing village in Portugal). Philosophy for Weil included her overwhelming love for mathematics (though she lacked the rare mathematical genius of her brother André). Her love of geometry caused her to fall to her knees in her second contemplative-mystical vision, standing before the geometric, mystical beauty of Giotto's frescoes in Assisi. At the monastery of Solesmes, Simone Weil had her third and decisive mystical vision listening to the Gregorian chant of the monks and reciting George Herbert's great poem, "Love." From that moment on, Weil sensed a constant awareness of the presence of God.

These three mystical experiences did not lessen but intensified Weil's philosophical and prophetic work. As a philosopher, of course, she never abandoned discursive reason, argument, and strict logical-mathematical reason. However, more and more, she became like her major philosophical mentor, Plato. After all, Plato, unlike the more purely discursive Aristotle, honored the mathematical Pythagoreans and considered mathematics, as did Weil, the most important entry into a purely intellectual world — alternatively, the spiritual dimension of reality. Like Plato in the intractable arguments of her dialogues, Weil too, as her brilliant notebooks attest, never abandoned the rigorous argumentative power she learned from Alain and, above all, from Descartes and Kant. Again, like Plato, the mystically experienced Weil allowed her philosophy to become more contemplative and intuitive rather than solely discursive. Her newfound experiences were surprising to Weil, who had never read any mystics, and whose thought and action up to that time was purely secular. As Hannah Arendt acutely observed, Weil's magisterial, critical social theory was the only highly developed social-political theory of the Left that was not Marxist.

Simone Weil's mystical experiences and her new, more contemplative philosophy intensified her ethical-political, indeed, prophetic work. When prophecy grasped her consciousness, she was relentless, even ruthless, with herself and others in hard ethical demands. This ethical-prophetic insistence was also characteristic of Weil's singular actions: her exceptionally difficult work in a factory for a year; her tough labor on a farm; her advocacy in Spain for the Republican forces in the Spanish Civil War, cut short by a bizarre accident; her untiring efforts to bring her beloved parents to safety in the United States; her return to Europe to work with the Free French forces stationed in London; her reasonable plan, rejected by General de Gaulle, to parachute herself and other women into occupied France as frontline nurses to aid the male troops in any way needed; and her typically intransigent insistence, while in Great Britain, to eat only as much as the strictly rationed people in France ate — a decision that, for a tubercular individual, proved fatal and resulted in a loss for a world that needed her thought and person (as Albert Camus justly observed).

Simone Weil, without any internal conflicts, continued her work as a philosopher. Philosophically, she was an unusual Platonist indeed — one who insisted that Platonism was wrong to disparage manual work. Such difficult, steady work in the factory, on the farm, and in everyday life represented for Weil rigorous action, a necessity for rigorous thought.

Unlike Nietzsche (whose Dionysian interpretation of Greek tragedy Weil strongly rejected), Weil attempted to relate the Greek tragic vision, starting with Homer and culminating in Aeschylus and Sophocles (unfairly, not Euripides), to the classic Greek philosophical vision of the incomparable Plato. In her often extraordinary philosophical reflections, now published in several volumes, Weil also attempted to correlate her version of the classical Greek tragic and philosophical vision with a version of Christianity focused on Mark's Gospel and the cross, even as she remained relatively silent on the resurrection. As far as I can see, Weil was also attempting in her all-too-short life to correlate not only Greek tragedy with Greek philosophy, but also the Gospel of Mark with the Gospel of John. This was a brilliant if never completed attempt to articulate a Weilian version of the tragic (Mark) and the contemplative-mystical (John) in the New Testament.

It is deeply unfortunate that Weil possessed a strange, foolish, in fact repulsive position on Judaism. Weil's bizarre position kept her from appealing, as surely she should have, given her prophetic position on the evil of colonization, either to Exodus (the story, after all, of the liberation of enslaved people) or the classical, social justice prophets of Israel (Amos, Micah, Isaiah). Weil wrongly read the entire Hebrew Bible (or at least the lengthy historical parts) as an extended book of Joshua. Joshua and Judges are indeed troubling today in their disturbing portrait of Yahweh commanding the ancient Israelites to slay all their enemies, especially (but not solely) the Canaanites, in order to take control of the Promised Land. However ethically troubling some sections of the Hebrew Bible (for Christians, as the First Testament) may be, Weil did strongly affirm in her life, if not in her thought, the overwhelming effect of the Hebrew Bible, that most extraordinary collection of books — Genesis, Exodus, Deuteronomy (choose life; love your neighbor as yourself), the major prophets, the majority of the Psalms (the traditional prayer book of Jesus and Christians alike), the Wisdom Books (especially Job).

The New Testament, which Simone Weil knew well, is itself divided in a creative tension between major prophetic narrative works (Mark, Matthew, Luke-Acts) and contemplative-mystical works (John and a great deal of the otherwise prophetic Paul and the Pauline tradition). All three radical mono-theisms (Judaism, Christianity, Islam) are, at heart, prophetic, practical, action-oriented expressions of faith in God. All three radical monotheisms are focused on God's actions in history. Nevertheless, all three traditions have included contemplative-mystical works—as in the Wisdom tradition of the First Testament, the prophetic-mystical reflection of John and Paul in the New Testament, and in Sufi readings of the Qur'an.

Simone Weil, who chose not to be baptized (except, some friends claim, on her deathbed), was nevertheless the new kind of saint the modern, secular world can hear. No one is likely to agree with all her opinions (e.g., the rather Gnostic notion of God and creation), but no one should resist facing this singular, splendidly disturbing person—philosopher, prophet, mystic.

IRIS MURDOCH

The history of the reception of Plato in modern philosophy has been a mixed one. On the positive side, no philosopher has equaled Alfred North Whitehead's astounding statement that the history of Western philosophy is a series of footnotes to Plato (!). On the negative side, both Friedrich Nietzsche and Martin Heidegger (save for his essay *The Sophist*) wrote fierce criticisms of Plato—critiques continued by Gilles Deleuze and Jacques Derrida. In a rare departure from his mentor Heidegger, Hans-Georg Gadamer, in several essays, brilliantly defended Plato against his former teacher. Even more significantly, Emmanuel Levinas called for a renewal of Platonic philosophy as a major task for modern philosophy. Earlier, Simone Weil had consistently argued for Plato's predominance in philosophy. Indeed, Weil's influence was a major contribution to Iris Murdoch's strong turn to Plato's metaphysics and ethics.

In the English-speaking philosophical world, philosophers (especially those in the wider analytical tradition) produced several distinguished recoveries of Aristotle in diverse forms of philosophy (Alasdair MacIntyre, Martha Nussbaum, Stephen Toulmin)—and in theology (Stanley Hauerwas). Notable, however, is the fact that the Aristotle recovered by most modern Aristotelians, with the exception of the neo-Thomists, is the Aristotle of *Ethics, Politics*, and *Rhetoric*, but not *Metaphysics*, unlike the Aristotle recovered by the many medieval Aristotelians like Thomas Aquinas. Iris Murdoch's strong defense of Plato and Neoplatonism has proved as distinctive in the Anglophone philosophical world as Hans-Georg Gadamer's defense of Platonism has proved in German philosophy and Emmanuel Levinas's Neoplatonic insistence has proved in some French philosophy. Murdoch's Platonism has a twofold focus. First, for Murdoch (as for Whitehead), Plato is the paradigmatic philosophical thinker. He is a metaphysical, ethical, spiritual, and even at times mystical exemplar who shows how our muddled energies and desires can be clarified and purified, both by intellectual exercises (like mathematics and dialectics) and ethical exercises, as well as disciplined spiritual exercises (e.g., meditation and contemplation).

Second, Murdoch has philosophically developed a Platonic metaphysics of the Good, analogous to the great earlier Neoplatonists, from Plotinus to Proclus. In a way, Murdoch's religious philosophy of the Good (especially in *The Sovereignty of Good* and *Metaphysics as a Guide to Morals*) is a deliberate response to ethical voluntarism, wherein only the individual will—indeed, often only individual acts of the will—bears ethical weight. In contrast to the individualist and voluntarist ethics of both existentialist philosophy (e.g., as Murdoch dissected it in her first book, *Sartre: Romantic Rationalist*) and that of several fellow analytical philosophers, Murdoch strongly argues against all possessive, basically ahistorical, individualism and voluntarism.

In contrast to many modern emphases on the individual act alone, Murdoch, partly influenced by her fellow Platonist, Simone Weil, argued for an ethics guided by obedience to the Good. Further, Murdoch concretizes the magnetic role of the Good in all human life in her brilliant, philosophically informed novels. Accordingly, the earlier novels often display a conflict between "artists and saints," "existentialists and mystics," while in her later, more complex novels, the conflict she portrays becomes one not so much *among* characters but *within* each complex, plural, and ambiguous particular character.

Iris Murdoch's religious metaphysics of the Good also calls to mind classical Christian Neoplatonists Gregory of Nyssa and Augustine. In contemporary philosophy and theology, she has also reignited attention to the major classical pagan Neoplatonists Plotinus, Porphyry, and Proclus by her philosophical defense of the principal name for Ultimate Reality as "the Good," not "God." If I may presume to be briefly autobiographical: I shall never forget a three-hour discussion with Iris Murdoch many years ago at my apartment over the central issue of God or the Good as the necessary or correct name for Ultimate Reality.

Murdoch's eloquent defense of our personal need to purify our desires and order our energies in a manner like Plato's (especially in *Symposium* and *Theaetetus*) led her to be open to—and influenced by—some Buddhist practices of an even more radical purification of the ego than that proposed by Plato. From Murdoch's sometimes important occasional attentions to Buddhism, she learned the classical practice of ceasing to cling to the ego, to let go to the Void, which, like the Good for Murdoch, is trustworthy and not to be feared. I do not read Murdoch as holding to the radical "no-self" of some Buddhists. Her own de-selfing insistence in both her philosophy and her novels leads at times to a more Buddhist rather than Platonic direction for the necessary de-selfing of the modern voluntarist individual.

Iris Murdoch was a *rara avis*: she possessed an exceptional philosophical mind, a profound spiritual, even mystical sensibility, and a major artist's ability to portray her philosophical-spiritual way in her many grand novels. As both philosopher and artist, and as religious thinker, Iris Murdoch deserves the sustained attention of every serious reader.

T. S. ELIOT

In an essay on Baudelaire, T. S. Eliot astutely noted how differently Baudelaire was read from the Swinburnean 1890s through the years after World War I until today. One can note the same kind of phenomenon in the poetry of Eliot himself: from the explosive modernism of *The Waste Land* in 1929 through the poetry inflected by his conversion to Anglican Christianity, culminating in the penitential sequence of *Ash Wednesday* and the musicality and bewitching beauty of the visionary and auditory imagination of his last long poem, *Four Quartets*.

In the reception of Eliot, the differences are also notable. Eliot's first emergence as the great modernist poet was established in the unforgettable lines and images in "The Love Song of J. Alfred Prufrock" ("I have heard the mermaids singing, each to each. / I do not think that they will sing to me."), through "Gerontion" ("Here I am, an old man in a dry month, / Being read to by a boy, waiting for rain."), to the emblematic long poem, *The Waste Land*. The best

SEEKERS OF THE GOOD

poetry of T. S. Eliot, both early and late, will last as long as the English language is spoken.

On the other hand, Eliot's later social, political, and ecclesiastical criticism now seems dated and not very interesting. Even Eliot's literary criticism, which once ruled the critical world, remains brilliant in his interpretations of individual poets, especially Dante and the seventeenth-century metaphysical poets. However, his then-famous critical generalizations linger but no longer rule critical theory on literature: "the objective correlative," "the dissociation of sensibility," the "impersonality" of the work of art, and several others. In some of his later essays, Eliot became trapped in the quagmire of his declarations against the modern world and in an exclusivist reading of Christianity that belies his open generosity, especially to Buddhism (e.g., "The Fire Sermon," section 3 of *Waste Land*), and to the prominent Hindu *Upanishad* entries in *Waste Land*, especially its famous final lines — "Datta. Dayadhvam. Damyata. / Shantih."

Moreover, chapter 21 in this volume argues that, unlike the restricted Christianity portrayed in many (happily not all) of Eliot's late social, political, and literary essays, his deepest and most persuasive articulation of his profound Christian vision, *Four Quartets*, includes major Buddhist and pagan elements (e.g., the lotus in the empty, full pool of section 1 of "Burnt Norton," the Platonic "still point," etc.). The *Four Quartets* also appeals to animist and "pagan" religions inspired by Eliot's reading of modern anthropology and comparative religion. Paradoxically, Eliot's Christianity in his great poetry was as inclusivist as many of his essays on Christianity were exclusivist.

On the other hand, Judaism is ignored as a religion, save for some brief appeals to some prophets like Ezekiel and Jeremiah in *Waste Land*. Eliot's closed attitude to Judaism, unlike his open attitude to Buddhism, Hinduism, and early Greek, Egyptian, and Roman religions, even yields to an occasional, repellent anti-Semitism in some of the imagery of his early poems: for example, "Burbank with a Baedeker: Bleistein with a Cigar," and the essays in *After Strange Gods*, which, fortunately, Eliot refused to allow to be published in later years.

Eliot's religious vision usually included the best of the Anglican theological tradition. Anglicanism has the enviable position among Christian communions of officially declaring itself both Catholic and Reformed, along with a genuine opening to Orthodoxy grounded in the Anglican strong affirmation and knowledge of the theology of early centuries of Christianity, both Latin and Greek. Eliot's poetry often expresses the Reformed emphasis on sin-grace.

His poetry also articulates a powerful Catholic emphasis of the continuity of nature and grace (e.g., the wondrous images of the "hints and guesses" of grace in the third section of *Four Quartets*, "The Dry Salvages" — "the unattended / Moment . . . in and out of time . . .").

Eliot's Christian vision in *Ash Wednesday*, *Four Quartets*, and the dramas (such as *The Cocktail Party* and *Murder in the Cathedral*) bespeaks the genius of Anglican Christianity, both the Catholic emphasis on nature-grace (more exactly grace-nature-grace) and the Protestant emphasis on sin-grace (more exactly, grace-sin-grace). That is the gracious Christian vision for which Eliot should be remembered with gratitude, not the narrow, exclusivist version that surfaces in some of the late social-political-ecclesiastical essays. At the same time, some of Eliot's discerning insights on individual writers surely continue to deserve honor. Here, for example, from Eliot's *Selected Essays*, is Eliot on Dante, his major poetic model: "The *Divine Comedy* is a complete scale of the depths and heights of human emotion; the *Purgatorio* and the *Paradiso* are to be read as extensions of the ordinarily very limited human range. Every degree of the feeling of humanity, from lowest to highest has, moreover, an intimate relation to the next above and below and all fit together according to the logic of sensibility."[1]

Eliot once observed that the best critical method is to be very, very intelligent: Eliot surely was that. Recall his retrieval of the metaphysical poets and the critical genius of John Dryden; his reading of Pascal as obsessed with Montaigne; his honest retraction of his earlier reading of Milton; his insistence on reading the poetry and the criticism of Dr. Johnson together, not (as is more usual) separately; the strong affirmation of James Joyce's *Ulysses*; his nicely complex reading of Baudelaire; his recovery of the genius of Lancelot Andrews in his sermons; his defense of the widely forgotten philosophy of F. H. Bradley; his exceptionally fine reading of William Blake; and many more. It is, perhaps, also worth mentioning that Eliot's language usually sounds more American than British tones (the speech of more open, broad American vowels; fewer English clipped consonants), as can be heard in his splendid recordings of his poems. Eliot's acceptance (in 1930) of British citizenship, of course, must be acknowledged as very important to him. At the same time, as he admitted, his work is English to be sure but finally more American — Mid-Atlantic perhaps?

---

1. T. S. Eliot, *Selected Essays* (New York: Harcourt Brace, 1959).

However, even T. S. Eliot as critic sometimes nods: his reading of Hamlet is bizarre and wrongheaded; his defense of the sensationalist dramas of Seneca seems off-target; his early reading of Yeats's splendid early Celtic poems was negative (although, happily, he later withdrew it); he atypically refused to allow for the beauty of Walter Pater's prose, seemingly because Eliot, faithful perhaps to his New England Puritan ancestors, found Pater's "art for art's sake" amoral. On the other hand, Eliot wisely observed that most versions of "art for art's sake" erroneously make art a substitute for religion. In the modern world, Eliot noted, art is often a substitute for religion — but then, he added, sometimes so is modern religion.

T. S. Eliot, along with W. B. Yeats and Wallace Stevens, was one of the twentieth century's truly commanding Anglophone poets. T. S. Eliot was also, at his frequent best (in essays like "Tradition and the Individual Talent" and "Poetry and Drama"), a major twentieth-century literary critic. T. S. Eliot helps one to hope, with Julian of Norwich, that "All shall be well, and all manner of things shall be well."

CHAPTER 18

SIMONE WEIL AND THE IMPOSSIBLE

A Radical View of Religion and Culture

SIMONE WEIL AS MYSTICAL-POLITICAL

Is there a unity to Simone Weil's religious thought? I do not see that there is. Her thought was so multiple — on topics, on sources, on various fragmentary attempts — that it is difficult if not impossible to propose a single unity for a thinker who wrote so much on such varied topics and in such largely fragmentary forms in so brief a life. That Weil was one of the major religious thinkers of the twentieth century is secure. If I were forced to try to claim a unity to her thought, I would choose political-mystical philosophy (Nava 2001). Indeed, she was the foremost predecessor of all the recent attempts — in political and liberation theologies and, more recently, in many other new forms of Christian thought — to reunite the mystical and prophetic strands of the Christian tradition into a coherent, mystical-prophetic philosophy and theology. Of course, her thought cannot be reduced to her life. But her life experiences, so varied and united only by her singular, radical sensibility, do provide some signal clues to her remarkable flashes of pure thought (Fiori 1989).

Consider, for example, her three famous mystical experiences. Here we find clues to some tenuous unity to her thought and life and to their uncanny power to lure us like a magnet into her presence. In her first mystical experience, while hearing some Portuguese fishermen's wives sing their songs of sorrow and joy, Weil believed that she saw the heart of Christianity: it is the religion of slaves and cannot live except in fidelity to that insight. For Weil, this is Christianity's most distinctive trait: what will later be called its "preferential option for the poor" in the midst of a radical egalitarianism ("God rains on the just and the unjust," as she loved to quote from the Bible).

In her second mystical experience at the church of San Francesco at Assisi, yet another element of her thought showed itself: the light of the Good in the poverty and purity of God's fool, Francis, as well as the light of the Good, radiant in the necessity disclosed to intelligence by the beauty in the play of geometric shapes and light in Giotto's frescoes at Assisi. In her third mystical experience, at the singing of Gregorian chants at the monastery of Solesmes while reading George Herbert's marvelous metaphysical-theological poem "Love," Weil experienced even more intensely her central vision in mystical terms, at once Platonic and Christian: first, as with Giotto, the play of light and mathematical geometric forms, yielding the harmony and proportion heard in the West, from Pythagoras through Plato, Gregorian chant, and Giotto to Simone Weil. At the same time, and pervading all this light and intelligence in thought, beauty, and religion for Weil was what George Herbert articulates in his poem — the reality of the Good, Love, God as the Ultimate Reality, if we could but learn to be attentive to the Good.

These three famous visions were neither random nor arbitrary. She stated, in *Gravity and Grace* (1987b), that the meaning of life often depends on which word we use to describe what happens to us: chance, fate, fortune, or providence. Her three mystical visions (perhaps like the three allotted to Plotinus, if we only knew what his were) can provide some central clues, not only to her exceptional life (which is from beginning to end a wonder of interiority), but also to her thought. That thought is, again from beginning to end, a search for an order in the relationship of the Good and necessity in all its forms; an order in the relationship of the Impossible order of charity to the actual order of human wretchedness; and the relationship of creation and incarnation to the cross. The order of intelligence, charity, and action for the poor might, if conceived and practiced by others, help to heal the three great disorders of modernity: passion separated from intelligence (never in her); practice divorced from theory — a modern insult to this Platonic activist, who even insisted on the importance of manual labor for the purity and accuracy of thought itself; and form separated from content. These Weilian forms are, in part, Descartes-like in their form of logical, rigorous meditations and, in part, Montaigne-like and, even more, Pascal-like in the form of essays as attempts (*essais*), forays, thought experiments. Platonic thought for Weil also needed new forms to prove adequate to its new modern content — work, history, body — that is, matter. Indeed, Weil is more materialist than any other Platonist, even as she shares Plato's love for the purely intelligent forms from mathematics to dialectics and to mythological and mystical thought (*Republic*). She is often as materialist as Lucretius and as dialectically materialist as Marx and the later revisionist Marxists of the Frankfurt school. Walter Benjamin is her Jewish Marxist Other and may prove her best modern conversational counterpart. Would that Weil had learned from Benjamin, as he learned from Scholem, and thus spared herself and her admirers her narrow, willful, ignorant reading of Judaism. Emmanuel Levinas, who both shared and praised the force of Weil's insistence on the Other, not the self, as the proper starting point (a prophetic-ethical one) for contemporary thought, was nevertheless right in his anger at Weil's mistreatment and misreading of Judaism. He hurled his violent charge at her: "Simone Weil, you understand everything except the Bible!"

The Montaigne-like form of Weil's essays and Descartes-like form of her treatises on work, body, and politics made it possible for Weil to find new, non-Marxist forms for her leftist thought and actions in the period between the world wars. Her other preferred form could be called *pensées*, in honor of Pascal. She shared so much with Pascal that she seemed destined to criticize him, even as she rethought and reformulated some of his greatest insights into her own: insights on the wretchedness of the human condition; the centrality of the cross in Christianity; the centrality of suffering for understanding the cross — physical, psychological, and spiritual agony — what she renamed "affliction"; the importance of the category *order*; and, above all, the need to acknowledge the Pascalian three orders of existence and to consider their relationships. The first Pascalian order is the order of the flesh. Force and its rule for Weil constitute, as she argued eloquently in her essay, "The Iliad, or The

Poem of Force," the kingdom of the necessity of force that affects all human lives, as we all must suffer the deaths of those we love and must ourselves one day die. But force affects some (slaves) for their entire lives, not just at death. The second Pascalian order is the order of intelligence — logic, mathematics, science, metaphysics — the place where most genuine thinkers live their lives as much as possible. At the same time, Weil typically said that *intellectuals* is an ugly word, but one we deserve. The third order for Weil, again with Pascal, is the order of charity — an order as different from the order of intelligence as the order of intelligence is from the order of the flesh. It is just as difficult for those who live principally in the order of intelligence to understand those in the order of charity as it is for those who live only in the order of the flesh to understand those in the order of intelligence.

More than Pascal, but in his spirit, Weil showed how intertwined these three orders are, even for those in the order of charity. The order of charity is one where body — flesh — is still very much present (even for Christ). Her mysticism is intellectually — in spite of the perhaps accurate claims that she was anorexic — also a body mysticism, of intelligence and body working together. Indeed, that vision of the ensouled body and embodied soul is the central reason why, for Weil, thinkers should practice manual labor. Theologically, for Weil, there is the vision of the overwhelming reality of her kenotic understanding of God's bodily incarnation and her deeply embodied understanding of the passion and cross as affliction: physical, psychological (abandonment by his disciples save his mother, two Marys, especially the beloved Magdalen, and John), and spiritual (Godforsaken, "My God, my God, why have you abandoned me?"). The crucifixion, for Weil, is a bodily, psychological, public, and spiritual humiliation. It is the personal suffering of Christ as a slave, a criminal, a reject from the body of society. Jesus — stripped, scourged, naked, and in overwhelming pain — must suffer, not merely in spirit but also in body so that his soul may suffer in real affliction. Jesus, for Weil, undergoes the horror of human and decisive abandonment. She paradoxically insists that Jesus's cry from the cross, "My God, my God, why have you forsaken me?" shows the divine character of Christianity! The order of intelligence, she argued, must find a way to be attentive to and active in the order of charity as well. She refused to call her own thought "theology." Perhaps she had good reasons for that refusal. But Weil did always insist on the need for the keenest use of intelligence (logical, rigorous, demanding, speculative, and contemplative) in reflecting on the order of charity. Recall her fine suggestion that John of the Cross developed a genuinely scientific account of the stages of the spiritual life. Only high intelligence participating within and yet distancing itself from the order of charity could count for Weil as the right kind of theology. Recall that her theological references were often to Teresa of Ávila and John of the Cross, rather than to officially designated theologians. She did not admire greatly Thomas Aquinas — he was too Aristotelian on reason and not sufficiently mystical in spirit for her.

Any attentive reader (how rare those readers are, she writes) soon notes throughout her reflections that, for Simone Weil, attention is the most necessary spiritual practice, as it was for the Stoics whom she admires. Weil's prose forms — treatises, essays, *pensées* — achieve the lucidity, rigor, clarity, and elegance of the classical French moral tradition, and they do so not only on questions of the body, mechanical necessity, and the structure of society, but also on the divine mysteries, understood now as mysteries in the order of charity. Weil's entire work is characterized by a prose and thought on limits. Hence her admiration for Kant on the limits of reason. Simone Weil left us forms appropriate to her content, perhaps even, in one of her favorite words, *necessary* for that content. She left thought that never, as in the Enlightenment, divorces passion and intelligence any more than Pascal did. She left a form of Platonism that, by its insistence on a theory of work, changed Platonism into a traditionally idealist position that also became a materialist one. Simone Weil insisted on body, social conditions, history, and matter far more than most Platonists do.

Which leaves us where, then? Simone Weil was a thinker whose very forms of thinking often act like searchlights amid our contemporary confusions; a thinker who articulated, better than anyone else of her time, why Christianity must be a mystical-political religion of and for the oppressed. A thinker who, in my judgment, stands with Walter Benjamin in the period between the wars (and who, like him, was finally destroyed *by* the war) as that rare kind of thinker who dared to expose the self-delusions of most confident thinkers of that period and ours. For myself, Weil and Benjamin will one day be recognized as the crucial thinkers between the wars who fragmented the ego of the twentieth century just as, in postmodern thought, Nietzsche and Kierkegaard are now acknowledged as the thinkers who were best suited to expose and smash the self-deluding modern systems of the nineteenth century and of ours.

And yet I cannot claim that even this suggestion of a mystical-political reading does justice to the multifarious character of Weil's thought. Some other focus is also needed. Here, reflection on her as a Christian Platonist *does* advance the discussion of a possible manifold unity to her thought. For Simone Weil was profoundly both Christian and Platonist. Therefore, it is just to call Weil a Christian Platonist, as long as this title is not placed above the wider category of mystical-political, and as long as we acknowledge that even Christian Platonism does not account for the full range, originality, and power of Weil's thought. She was indeed a radical, even at times a strange Christian and odd Platonist.

WEIL'S CHRISTIAN PLATONISM: THE SEA CHANGE OF TRAGEDY

Simone Weil was neither a very orthodox Christian nor an orthodox Platonist. On the Christian side, she was reticent, when not silent, on certain doctrines and symbols of the Christian symbol system: especially the resurrection, perhaps because of her acute fear of any Christian triumphalism. Weil was also reticent on the eschatological tradition, perhaps because of her fear of how quickly any imagination — including the eschatological when literalized — can delude us by trying to fill the historical void with fundamentalist fantasies.

Weil's double reticence on resurrection and apocalypse in the New Testament became fierce when Weil turned her attention to the Torah, or Hebrew Bible, which is, for Christians, also their Scripture (i.e., their First or Old Testament). To be sure, she accorded some parts of the Old Testament more attention than many Christian thinkers do to this day: above all, Job, certain of the Psalms (esp. Lamentations), Isaiah's suffering servant, and, most surprisingly, the creation accounts of Genesis.

But it remains a puzzle why this exceptionally open and attentive mind and soul, so prophetic in her person and thought, would prove so deaf to the prophets like Amos and their demand for what she so cared about — justice for the oppressed. It remains an even greater puzzle why Weil did not read Exodus more attentively: not just as a book of triumphalism, as in the book of Judges and the book of Joshua — that is, not just as a triumphalist book of victories and land-grabs by the Israelites over the Canaanites and other peoples (although triumphalism is also there).

Above all, she missed the central point of the book of Exodus. It is a prophetic book of liberation of and for the slaves and victims of history — as oppressed peoples throughout the centuries have readily sensed (e.g., as in the moving, prophetic-mystical African American gospel songs). Even the more

Hellenized wisdom literature of the Old Testament does not receive the attention one would expect from the Grecophile Simone Weil, who once admitted that ancient Greek philosophy and tragedy were her "Old Testament."

Whatever the peculiarities of Weil's own history—born to a highly assimilated (indeed, by her parents' generation, completely secular) Jewish family, Weil herself was very open to Buddhism and Hinduism (she even learned Sanskrit), Confucianism and Taoism. Her closedness to and willful ignorance of the riches of the Jewish tradition, in its biblical form as well as in its later history, remain a mystery (the only exception: Weil may have read some of the Kabbalists). That mystery is not solved, in my judgment, by deciding in prosecutorial style that Weil was a "self-hating Jew." She did, like Pascal, find the "I," the *"moi"*—her own—hateful and in constant need of decreation, but as an egotist, not as a Jew. However, how can one explain her surprising insensitivity to the massive suffering of the greatest victims in Europe of her day, her fellow Jews?

Simone Weil's problem here—and it is a grave problem for those of us who have learned so much from her in her insistence that Christianity should *always* be on the side of the oppressed in *any* period—involves, I suspect, psychological and historical reasons beyond our reach but not beyond our disrespect. After all, she never allowed the excuses of others whenever it came to justice. She rightly denounced Christianity's involvement in the Crusades, the Inquisition, the treatment of the Cathari, whom she greatly admired, as well as the indifference of the majority of the rich and cultured "Christians" of every century toward the poor in their midst. She despised Corneille for praising the grandeur and glory of France in the imperialist and, for her, revolting *"grand siècle"* of Louis XIV. The list of the historical figures she judged harshly is a long one. Her only equal here is Nietzsche (whose reading of tragedy she violently rejected).

Weil's intellectual-spiritual problem with some versions of Jewish "exceptionalism" or "election" was shared by some Jewish thinkers (as she should have known) in her own day. It is even more widely shared in our day (e.g., the Orthodox Jewish theologian, David Hartmann) by many Jewish thinkers who never cease fighting the problems of triumphalist interpretations of election, including those at some points in the Bible, especially the slaying of the Canaanites and other peoples by the conquering Israelites. This cruel strand of the Bible is for many Jewish thinkers—as she should have known—as deep and troubling as the exclusionist triumphalism and complacent sense of election and super-

cessionism of many Christians, which she did know and straightforwardly denounced. Why, then, did Weil fail to denounce anti-Semitism, when she saw
with such clarity that Christianity's temptation to triumphalism and totality-
thinking is a betrayal of Christianity on intra-Christian terms? She always insisted that the stern reality of the cross and the clearly prophetic vocation of
Christianity was to privilege the oppressed, the victims of history, not the victors of what Hegel called the "slaughter-bench" of history. Why, then, did she
not credit her fellow Jews, whose prophets (including Jesus of Nazareth) taught
that Christianity now involves "the prophetic option for the poor"?

Simone Weil somehow refused to see how the same prophetic principle,
the same liberationist drive for the victims of history that she found that day
in Portugal among the mourning women in Christianity, is grounded in the
Hebrew Bible and in the Christian reading of it as the Old or, better, the First
Testament. The Hebrew Bible is not, as she seemed to think, a long book of
Joshua. The ancient Hebrews, driven by their prophetic and legal traditions
alike, were not the ancient Romans, as she imagined. Indeed, some of the ancient Romans — Virgil above all — were not the vulgar triumphalists she makes
them out to be. Her reading of Judaism is a very sad chapter in a life otherwise
driven by a sense of justice and a demand for compassion.

However, the real Simone Weil, I continue to believe, is elsewhere than in
her unexpected readings of the Hebrew Bible. The real Simone Weil is in her
readings of the ancient Greeks (whose writings as noted above effectively functioned for her as her own Old Testament) and in her partial but extraordinary readings of the New Testament. Who except Simone Weil could move
so subtly between two profoundly different accounts of the passion of Jesus:
the Gospel of Mark, whose afflicted Jesus (as Weil never tired of reminding
Christians) screams from the cross the shattering words of physical affliction
and spiritual abandonment, "My God, my God, why have you forsaken me?";
and the Gospel of John, where, by contrast, the very lifting up of Jesus on the
Cross discloses God's Beauty and Glory in the last words (words of necessity,
not triumph) of John's Jesus, "It is consummated." Simone Weil affirms both
Gospels as she affirms how beauty in the *Iliad* is seen most clearly on the other
side of intense suffering of force. She affirms both Mark and John as readily
and as subtly as she affirms (*contra* Nietzsche) both tragedy and philosophy,
both Sophocles and Plato, among the Greeks. The key to Weil's readings in
both cases — Christianity and Platonism — is her unerring sense of necessity,
justice, and the Good — in a word, her insistence vis-à-vis both Platonism and

Christianity that a tragic sensibility must be maintained. Otherwise Platonism is only one more purely philosophical system brilliantly incorporating, as historically Neoplatonism did, elements not only of Plato, but also of the Stoics and the Aristotelians. Otherwise Christianity is a triumphant Christendom. Simone Weil insists on the betrayal of Christianity by Christendom over and over again: for example, in the orthodox Christian triumphalist cry against the Cathari and anyone else unlucky enough to live among them: "Kill them all; God will know His own."

More clearly than Pascal, Weil understood that the true wretchedness of humanity must include not only sin (she is always clear how real and pervasive that is) but also tragedy—that is, fate as (in her words) the necessity of suffering in life (Aeschylus). She sometimes refers to the consequences of sin as tragedy—the curse of fate in Oedipus—and even, in the way of innocent substitutionary redemption, of the "fate" of Christ.

Simone Weil's thought is a profound, personal Christian theological reading that affects her interpretations of all the central doctrines of Christianity. God becomes, at times for her, as much as for Luther, the awe-ful Hidden God of the Void. The incarnation becomes, in the light of the cross, kenotic for Weil, as for St. Paul. She believed deeply in the puzzling declaration in Revelation, "The Lamb is slain from the foundation of the World." Even more, Weil's speculations on the intra-Trinitarian relationships of Father and Son suggest such speculation as that of Hans Urs von Balthasar or Jürgen Moltmann. Above all, Weil's Christian anthropology was formed neither by traditional (e.g., Thomist) interpretations of nature and grace (although she too affirms our essential goodness—our natural attraction, in spite of our egoism, to the Light), nor by the traditional Reformation interpretation of sin and grace (although she affirms, as strongly as the later Augustine, or Luther, or Pascal, the power and reality of sin in our personal, social, and historical lives). Weil is ruled by neither the nature-grace paradigm nor the sin-grace paradigm. She is somewhere else.

Simone Weil sees the wretchedness of humanity (almost more like Racine than Pascal) as comprising, first, our greatness (our intelligence, our intrinsic drive to the light, our graced ability to love, our sense of justice); second, our tragic sensibility: the necessity of force that must eventually invade every human life (Allen and Springstead 1994). From these arises our sense of a need for justice—as an equilibrium emerging from tragedy. As she insists, if this be my last day—as it was in the *Iliad* for so many of its characters—then the beauty of the sunset or the beauty of family, friends, life itself is more intense and more beautiful than ever. Such a sense evokes compassion toward literally all — toward victims and victors alike, as she sees in her beloved *Iliad* or in Aeschylus's *The Persians*. The tragic reality comprises for Weil aspects of our greatness and not only our wretchedness: justice, compassion, and intelligence, as well as sin (ours and the consequences of others' sin — our fate, our curse, as with the families of Atreus and Oedipus). She affirms, I repeat, the reality of sin. She also affirms that sin, both as personal and as a consequence of the actions of others, is present for all Christians; we should attend to our own sin by attending to the kenotic incarnation-cross of Christ, the only purely innocent, sinless human being and the one and only God.

This reading on the centrality of the cross and the reality of the tragic (as something like a paradoxical *metaxu* — a medium between our greatness and our tragic wretchedness) frees Simone Weil's Christian vision from the sin-pessimism of the later Augustine, or Calvin (we are "lumps of sin," for Augustine), just as the cross and the tragic free her from the vulgar optimism about humanity of too much Christian humanism. Weil arrived, in my judgment, at a deeper Christian vision of God as hidden, of Christ as incarnate and crucified, of ourselves as wretched (i.e., as great, tragic, and sinful all at once), and of creation as sparks of the Good let loose in the world. Hers is an exceptional and original Christian vision, one that can be understood partly as a revised (i.e., tragic) form of a Christian Platonism. Weil's Platonism, transformed by a tragic sensibility and her insistence on work, is perhaps the deepest philosophical formulation of her Christian vision. But Platonism is not Weil's only option for a usable past. Witness her love for the Stoics and their spiritual practices of attentiveness; her deep respect for the logical, rigorous, and meditative power of Descartes; her reverence for Kant's thoughts on reason acknowledging its powers, and, through that very acknowledgment, its own limits. Indeed, Weil called the greatest use of reason an acknowledgment, like Kant's, of its limits. Recall as well Weil's sometime sympathy even for the Manicheans. Did any other twentieth-century Christian thinker share these diverse sympathies? Outside Christianity, recall Weil's love of certain texts of the Buddhists, the Hindus (especially the *Bhagavad-Gita*), and the Taoists (especially the understanding of religion as a "way" of nonactive action). If Christianity had traveled East rather than West, Simone Weil, in spite of her love of the Greeks, would not have been deeply disturbed: Buddhist thought would have strengthened her kenotic Christology; the *Gita* would have become her new *Iliad*; and Taoism would have shown her a way to understand Christ as way, truth, and life.

But that historical possibility, like Pascal on Cleopatra's nose, is merely a great "what if." Christianity did not move East; Christianity turned West and entered the Hellenistic world. For Weil, that meant that Christianity entered the luminous world of pre-classical (note her love for pre-classical Greek folklore and myth — as strong as that of Mircea Eliade) and classical Greece. Recall, above all, her love of both tragedy and philosophy, both Homer and Aeschylus, Sophocles and the *Hippolytus* (little more) of Euripides and, of course, all of Plato.

In sum, Simone Weil was indeed a Platonist, but one with a difference. The difference again comes through her joining Plato, unlike the Plato of most other Christian Platonists, not only to philosophy (Socrates and, for her, the so-called pre-Socratics, especially Heraclitus and Parmenides), but also to tragedy — a remarkable achievement for an interpretation of the Greeks. Since the Romantic rediscovery of the Greeks and the seemingly endless debates, especially in German thought, on *which* Greeks (Aristotle and Neoplatonism for Hegel; tragedy for Nietzsche; the pre-Socratics for Heidegger), the interpretation of the Greeks by Simone Weil is a singular one. For her, the greatness of ancient Greece (which, like many before and after her, she partly romanticized) included not one singular choice but practically all the great forms and expressions: the folklore, the myths (especially the Christlike myth of Prometheus); the poems of Pindar, the epics (above all, the *Iliad*, the "poem of force"); the pre-Socratics, especially Heraclitus; the tragedies (especially Aeschylus as well as Sophocles and the *Hippolytus* of Euripides); Plato and his Socrates; and the Stoics. The almost sole exceptions to her praise of the Greeks were, for distinct and, for me, unpersuasive Weilian reasons, the *Odyssey* and Aristotle. For Weil, the *Odyssey* is partly good (i.e., the part like the *Iliad*); and Aristotle is acceptable (i.e., when he is like Plato). On the later Platonists, she is more reticent but, especially on Plotinus, greatly approving.

She did not look for which item of Greek culture could serve as the clue to Greece's greatness. Greek tragedy or philosophy; Heraclitus or Plato; folklore-myth: she embraced almost all. And therein lay her genius, as a kind of Christian Platonist with a difference. For she consistently reads Plato as related not only to the Pythagoreans and their religious and ritualistic desire for the world of intelligibility in mathematics and music (proportion and harmony), but also to the excessive and transgressive, not harmonious, religious, ritualistic (for her mystical) Eleusinian mysteries. Both these sources, mathematics and the mysteries, influenced her reading of the rational and mystical Plato. Moreover, she reads Plato as not simply against "the poets," as he famously called Homer and the tragedians, but as himself possessing a tragic sensibility. Witness her reading of the speech of Agathon in *Symposium*, and her reading of the tragic theme of *Republic* and *Timaeus*, before other scholars argued for the harmony of the tragic-hopeful sensibility between Aeschylus, *Oresteia*, and *Timaeus*. For, as in *Timaeus*, intelligence persuades (*peitho*) but never compels necessity (*ananke*).

With all their extraordinary achievements, the early Christian Platonists reflected too little on the tragedies and the tragic sensibility in either the Greeks or Christianity. They did see clearly the rational texts and mystical character of Plato in the works that we possess—the dialogues (which Weil dared to name Plato's popularizations of his discoveries). At any rate, Simone Weil's singularity as a Christian Platonist is, I believe, partly occasioned by her use of tragedy to rethink Christianity (especially the Gospel of Mark in contrast to the Gospel of John), just as she rethinks the relationship of Homer and the tragedians (Mark-like) to Plato (John-like). I do not know why the early Christian Platonists could be so right on the Christian theological relevance of Greek philosophy—especially Plato, whom they cherished, developed, and, when necessary, challenged (e.g., through the Christian notions of creation and incarnation) while at the same time, being at best so reticent, at worst wrong, on the Christian theological relevance of the tragedies. A partial exception is Augustine. His Platonism is clear and never abandoned (as *De Trinitate* shows and *Retractions* makes ever clearer). Augustine's later tragic sensibility gave rise to his profound anti-Pelagian reflections on the effects and the consequences of "original sin." But so convinced was Augustine that the ancient tragic concept of fate denied God's omnipotence that he never developed what he could have for his own Christian Platonic anthropology: a Christian Platonist tragic sensibility on our own, weird human combination of essential goodness and both sinful and tragic actuality.

Simone Weil did what Augustine might have done but never did: she restored tragedy to a prominent place in both the reading of Plato and the reading of Christianity. She accomplished this remarkable feat without exaggerating the claims for the range and power of tragedy over philosophy (as did Nietzsche), and without denying our drive to justice as natural to us (indeed, she finds a sense of justice as equilibrium in the *Iliad* itself). Weil strongly affirmed the power and goodness of our intelligence (as in the worlds of intelligibility opened by mathematics, logic, and philosophy). She affirmed the power and essential goodness of our rare experiences of love, not as ego-love, but as love of the other (the neighbor), especially the oppressed other in the order of *caritas*. She never flinched from a vision of the all-pervasive reality of sin — both personal sin (the ego, as she interprets its dilemma, is Luther's ego "*curvatus in se*") and the societal effects of sin. Here Augustinian concupiscence is not her category, but the category of fate: fate understood always, as she insists, with the sense of a curse for past sins, our own and those of others — the family (Aeschylus and Sophocles), history (Thucydides), the entire race (Augustine).

That Weilian anthropology is consonant with — indeed, analogous to — her Christology. There incarnation and cross (always thought together) play central roles that she does not deny, but she is relatively reticent on resurrection. A Weilian anthropology is consonant as well with her willingness to name God both Love and Hidden-as-Void. Her anthropology is also consonant with her highly speculative Kabbalah-like understanding of a certain cleavage in God at creation, where "the sparks of the good are let loose in the world," and her even more speculative reflection on the incarnation as so kenotic that it suggests a cleavage in God (i.e., in the Trinity).

Even when one disagrees (as I basically do with her "cleavage" metaphor and her Kabbalistic leanings, as distinct from her "kenotic" metaphor for creation and incarnation), one cannot but be stunned by the purity of her intelligence, the power and the courage of her Christological speculations — at once Christian, and Platonist, and something more. That "something more" in Simone Weil's rather odd Christology occurs above all through her singular readings of both Plato and Christianity. Nor did she stay intellectually and spiritually with Platonism and Christianity alone. She found the same kind of Weilian vision of our situation in her readings of Taoism, the *Bhagavad-Gita*, and Buddhism. She kept these traditions distinct from and yet reconcilable with her Christian Platonism. She neither simply Christianizes nor Platonizes. Rather she shows how those other traditions can aid, develop, and challenge aspects of both Platonic and Christian self-understanding. She did this in the same spirit as she elsewhere insists that atheism — a real atheism (e.g., that portrayed in Dostoevsky), not the relaxed intellectual hypothesis of some intellectually lazy modern intellectuals — may be a necessary ascetic purification for any authentic faith in God.

The complex Weilian vision seems (even to many traditional Christian Platonist eyes) too radical, even excessive, as her critic Bataille sensed — indeed, impossible. In an exact sense, her vision is impossible. Like Kierkegaard, Simone Weil implicitly understood faith, in Kierkegaard's words, as a "passion for the Impossible." Weil understood the Impossible to be a category for both the limits of our reason (Kant) and the *es gibt*, the sheer givenness and gift of the Impossible. For Weil, the Impossible is best discerned in the kenotic incarnation and cross of Jesus Christ.

Implicitly, Weil understood God as the Impossible. Explicitly, she named humankind not merely the Pascalian paradox of *grandeur et misère* but ultimately incomprehensible. Above all, she clarified the Impossibility of Jesus Christ as not only the kenotic incarnation and not only the cross but, impossibly, as both together—each understood properly only through the other. Many contemporary thinkers now attempting to recover the category of the Impossible as a major category for thinking on God and/or the Void (Levinas, Derrida, Meltzer, Caputo, Kearney, et al.) can find Simone Weil a great ally. Like Kierkegaard, she was an early "apostle of the Impossible." Moreover, unlike the rest of us, even Kierkegaard, Simone Weil was not only an apostle of the Impossible. In her strange and unnerving thought, and in her even stranger and most unnerving life, Simone Weil was Impossible.

REFERENCES

Allen, Diogenes, and Eric O. Springstead. 1994. *Spirit, Nature, and Community Issues in the Thought of Simone Weil*. Albany: State University of New York Press.

Fiori, Gabriella. 1989. *Simone Weil: An Intellectual Biography*. Translated by Joseph Berrigan. Athens: University of Georgia Press.

Nava, Alejandro. 2001. *The Mystical and Prophetic Thought of Simone Weil and Gustavo Gutiérrez: Reflections on the Mystery and Hiddenness of God*. Albany: State University of New York Press.

Weil, Simone. (1945) 1977. "The Iliad, or The Poem of Force." Translated by Mary McCarthy. In *The Simone Weil Reader*, edited by George Panichas. New York: Moyer Bell.

———. 1951a. *Waiting for God*. Translated by E. Craufurd. New York: Harper and Row.

———. 1951b. *La condition ouvrière*. Paris: Gallimard.

———. 1962. *Selected Essays*. Translated by Richard Rees. London: Oxford University Press.

———. 1970. *La Connaissance surnaturelle*. Translated by R. Rees. In *First and Last Notebooks*. London: Oxford University Press.

———. 1973. *Oppression and Liberty*. Translated by A. Wills and J. Petrie. Amherst: University of Massachusetts Press.

———. 1986. *Simone Weil: An Anthology*. Translated by S. Miles. New York: Weidenfeld and Nicholson.

———. 1987a. *Intimations of Christianity among the Ancient Greeks*. Translated by E. Craufurd. London: Ark Paperbacks.

———. 1987b. *Gravity and Grace*. Translated by E. Craufurd. London: Ark Paperbacks.

———. 1987c. *The Need for Roots*. Translated by A. Wills. London: Ark Paperbacks.

CHAPTER 19

SIMONE WEIL

The Mask, the Person

Simone Weil's thought demonstrates that contradictions spur thinking. Her thought also shows that dialectically achieved paradox, rather than any compromised dialectical synthesis, is the proper form for rigorous thought on reality and on the ultimately Real—the Good and/or God. At the same time, there is a strange paradox in the reception of Simone Weil. The paradox, perhaps even contradiction, is between her life and her work. Weil's thought includes an original, modern social theory and a modern, original form of Platonic-Cartesian-Kantian philosophy; her life includes a radical, mystical, and prophetic religious vision and way of action. Her thought is classical in form, but modern in content. Her thought is both rigorously conceptual and punctuated throughout by newly coined images and surprisingly new uses of traditional images—light, looking rather than eating, the sun, the void, the cave.

As in ancient philosophies, Weil's philosophy is clearly a mode of thinking that unites theory to a way of life. Indeed, the union of theory and way of life in ancient philosophy is one of the principal reasons for Weil's attractions to ancient philosophy, especially the Stoics and the Platonists. Her philosophy itself, however paradoxical and modern, is formulated in measured, lucid, precise, and rigorous terms. It is, in a word, classical. On the other hand, her person is one of extremity. She lived a life of excess. The result is clear: for many thinkers, Weil's philosophy is too often ignored in favor of what came to seem her exemplary life of extremity. Her more recent entry into postmodern thought is more as an iconic person of excess than as a thinker of measure, mediation, and *metaxu*. We must, she insists, leave behind our perhaps most cherished modern reality, our self-fashioning personality, which is, in fact, a false mask. Personality is a disguise over our authentic, decreated selves. The decreated self is a reality in ever-deepening touch with what is most real about us — the desire to know the necessity of the world (as in the Stoic *amor fati*), and the desire to become an authentic self through loving contact with others and through actions resisting every injustice. To be authentic is to contemplate attentively every good or beautiful form of the Formless Good beyond Being and beyond intelligibility.

Certainly, Weil's life is *fascinans et tremendum*. That exceptional life fully merits close attention, especially by artists and religious thinkers, as a new, radical form of an ascetic-mystical vision and way of life. Her person and her life are intense, remarkable, unforgettable, even iconic. And yet her person is not her thought. Her life and thought are not opposites, but her thought (classical, lucid, measured) and her life (extreme, mysterious, excessive) are not easily harmonized. Despite several fine biographies of Simone Weil and some excellent studies of her social theory, her philosophy of work, her philosophy of *metaxu*, her philosophical analyses of the two ultimate realities in her philosophy (Necessity and the Good) we still lack a single study that unites her life and her thought seamlessly. Perhaps we always will. No matter. Paradox, for Weil, can be a sign of rigorous thought. Even contradictions, for Weil, can give rise to a rethinking of matters we thought we had long ago resolved but had not.

Some thinkers — Georges Bataille, Maurice Blanchot, Susan Sontag, and T. S. Eliot, among others — have been so mesmerized by Weil's life of extremity that they have virtually ignored her demanding and original philosophical thought. Once a thinker pays attention to Weil's thought rather than her life, however, a philosophical reader is forced to rethink several traditional concepts (the Good, God, necessity, the self), while struggling at the same time to understand several new concepts of Weil's philosophy (affliction, decreation, *metaxu*, the Impossible, work).

Simone Weil's philosophical interests include the problem of the self or person as related to the impersonal forces within and outside the self (e.g., health or illness, sexuality, heredity, culture, gender, economics). As she argued in her famous article on human personality, she did not believe that there is a "metaphysical person." More Marxist than metaphysical, Weil argued that our cherished personalities are not central; "person" is not the metaphysical reality that Jacques Maritain and contemporary personalists believed it to be. She always fought, alongside Maritain and others who defended the rights of the individual, for the human dignity of each person. Our first moral obligation, she insisted, was not to hurt any other individual human being. In that sense, she strongly defended the rights of the individual. At the same time, she judged erroneous any metaphysical notions of the "person" as the central reality in human beings. In Weil's thought, we are indeed individual persons with rights but, even more, we become authentic persons by our relations to and obligations to others and to the Good by means of our innate desire for the Good, sometimes repressed. The desire for the Good may often be silenced by social, historical, and temperamental conditions. Nevertheless, the desire for the Good, not the person, is the central metaphysical reality within us as it struggles to be released by our actions for the other, eventually constituting our authentic selves. The true self is literally *trans*formed from an illusory personality into an authentic individual person, grounded in its attentive contemplation of the Good and consenting freely to actions on behalf of others by the power of its innate desire for the Good.

In Weil's thought as in Marx's, the modern cult of "personality" is less a result of metaphysics than it is of particular economic-social-cultural conditions. For example, Weil wrote, watch a factory worker in court; you will notice two things: the judges and lawyers use the language of educated persons, even technical legal language with little to no regard for the uncomprehending facial expressions and stumbling (because uneducated) speech of the worker. The judges, lawyers, and journalists, in effect, do not acknowledge the uneducated worker as an equal person. They mechanically act as members of their class, despite their official rhetoric that they treat all persons as equals. Not metaphysics but social reality—class—intervenes and separates many of the educated and bourgeois class from even knowing their obligation to respect the equal, intrinsic human dignity of those they consider "lower class."

Simone Weil discovered this truth for herself when she lost a sense of her own personal rights and individual personality in her experimental year in factory work. Persons, therefore, are constituted by their relationships to others and by economic-social-historical forces that Karl Marx rightly, in Weil's view, taught philosophers to acknowledge and analyze in any psychological or philosophical study of persons. I am not some mysterious entity called a "personality," however vaunted "personality" has been since Renaissance thinkers, the Romantics, and *fin-de-siècle* artists. Weil always acknowledged—with gratitude—her debt to Karl Marx, even as, in her early life, she developed a post-Marxist social theory. Weil never abandoned that social theory, even after her religious turn. Still less did Weil abandon her unending activities against social injustice. Gradually, in her later, more strictly philosophical work, Weil developed her highly original philosophy, including studies on how impersonal and personal forces interrelate to constitute a self. She strongly fought against the societal form that many social scientists name "possessive individualism" as the central blight of Western democratic societies: a society where individual selves tend, by the power of a culture encouraging possessive individualism, to disown all others as others and replace them with the narcissistic illusion that we are all self-created "personalities."

One way to rethink the paradox of person and work in Simone Weil, I suggest, is to retrieve the ancient notion of the mask, a notion directly contrary to modern notions of a mask. For moderns, to wear a mask is to hide one's "true" self. One of the greatest of the moderns, René Descartes, stated as his personal maxim, *Larvatus prodeo*. For ancient cultures, on the contrary, a mask does not hide but rather reveals by re-presenting (rendering present) some otherwise hidden reality—a god, a *daimon*, a ghost.

As early as the Roman republic, the word for an "individual," a "person" (*persona*), was derived from the word for "mask" (*persona*). For the Romans, a person is a mask in the sense that each of us, every day, must adopt several social roles, just as masked actors in drama must take on theatrical ones. Cicero, for example, says that each person in everyday life needs to perform as many as thirteen different social roles daily. The American sociologist Erving Goffman describes our lives as, in effect, a series of ever-shifting social roles, depending on context: for example, now I must perform the role of a responsible writer as best I can, while you kindly engage in the role of responsible, attentive, and critical reader. These two related roles are merely two of the many roles that each of us must perform daily in our multiple social relationships with others.

In the ancient Etruscan and Roman theater, *persona-mask*, whether comically grotesque or tragically riveting, was for the Romans the means whereby an actor's voice sounds through (*per-sonare*, to sound through) the open mouth of the mask to reach the ears of the other characters in the play and to reach the ears of the audience. The Latin *persona* (originally, theatrical mask) gradually evolved into an ordinary word for "person" in daily Latin usage: *mask* became a word for an "individual person" (*persona*). In Roman cultures, the individual is always constituted as such by her social roles in civic society, not as a modern personality of our societies of possessive individualism.

At roughly the same time in Greek Hellenistic culture, the Greek word for "mask" (*pros-opon*) became an ordinary Greek word for "person." For example, by the fourth century CE, Greek Christian theologians and philosophers developed the Greek ordinary word *prosopon* into a new philosophical word. Just as with other Greek philosophical concepts, as the early Heidegger demonstrated was the case with Aristotle's concepts, the ordinary word *prosopon* (person-mask) was formed into a new relational concept for *person* by the Greek theologians. For philosophical theologians like Basil of Caesarea and his brother Gregory of Nyssa, the philosophical-theological concept *prosopon* was used to indicate a distinct individual, constituted as such by his relations to others. Literally, *pros-opon* means "toward the eyes of the other." As we saw above, the Latin *persona-mask* was directed to the ears of others (originally the audience in the theater). Eventually, as we noted in Cicero, *persona* designated the many social roles and relations that constitute a Roman citizen. In contrast, the Greek *prosopon* (mask-person) is directed not to the ears but to the eyes of the other. An individual becomes a person, in this Greek reading, only by being related to others. The Latin *persona* makes the same relational point but, in a Roman culture of oratory and rhetoric, the relations to others is to the ears of others, in keeping with the Roman "person" as defined by her social roles. On the other hand, the ordinary Greek word *prosopon* served the less rhetorical, more philosophical-dialectical culture of the Greeks as a new philosophical concept—a person who, as a distinct entity, is a distinct individual only by being related to others. In modern philosophical parlance (e.g., that of both Emmanuel Levinas and Simone Weil), the Other both ethically and metaphysically precedes and constitutes the self—not the reverse. The postmodern turn to the Other and alterity replaces the modern turn to the subject from Descartes through Husserl.

Simone Weil's love of ancient Greece led her to make frequent appeals, as did Heidegger, to the etymologies of Greek words to forge contemporary philosophical resources. I feel confident, therefore, that she would have approved of my finding yet *another* Greek verbal resource in the word *pros-opon*. *Prosopon* was a normal word in classical Greek for "mask" and, later, for "person." *Prosopon* was a word constructed from theatrical and social life, not originally from metaphysics. However, in Greek culture, *prosopon* was later forged into a new philosophical concept: a person became a distinct individual by being constituted as such by her relations to other persons. The Greek individual, the person, is therefore a distinct individual as an intrinsically relational reality.

Weil even goes so far as to claim that only a Christian, theological-philosophical, Trinitarian notion of person (i.e., a distinct individual is constituted as a distinct reality only by its relation to the other) displays the true notion of person. In the Christian Trinity, God is relational; that is, one God in three persons. The Father is distinctly and properly Father, only by being related to Son; the Son is a distinct individual Son, only by being related to the Father. In a daring move in her philosophical theory of person, Weil held that an authentic person is analogous to a Trinitarian person. In monotheistic religions, for Christians just as for Jews and Muslims, God is one. For Christians, however, unlike other monotheists, God is one by being constituted as one relationally; that is, by mutual relations of love among Father, Son, and Spirit. The central Christian metaphor in First John 4:16 is endorsed strongly by Simone Weil — God is Love. In Christian intellectual history, the metaphor "God is Love" became the central Christian doctrine, the Trinity: God is three persons (*prosopa*) in one nature; God is internally, not only externally, relational.

Moreover, in Weil's thought, the desire for the Good is beyond, even as it grounds and drives, our desire to know. The desire to know the necessity of the world and to love the beauty of the order of the world can be found, Weil held, not only in Spinoza and modern science, but also in the ancient Stoics. Driving that desire to know the necessary order of the world in mathematics, science, and philosophy is the desire to know as it is energized by the desire for the Good: here the beauty of the order of necessity is a good to be embraced — the Stoic *amor fati*.

The primacy of the impersonal desire for the Good is, in my judgment, the key to all Weil's social theory and philosophy. The impersonal desire for the

Good is also the key to her critique of the modern idea of a purely autonomous, self-created personality. The soul of every person, in Weil's philosophy, contains an infinitely small part of the soul (as in some Gnostics and Kabbalists) that is a spark of the Good given by the Good/God. The spark in us longs for the Good, both by contemplating the Good and by acting for the good of all others. At the same time, Weil is not naive about the self's goodness. Like Spinoza, Weil knows that the desire to discover one's own place for the Good is often suppressed by the innate drive of the ego to possess all things, to grasp a space of one's own. Simone Weil was sympathetic to Augustine's theory of some mysterious flaw in us that kept us from the Good. She was even more sympathetic to the ancient tragic sense that we possess a basic disorientation to evil rather than to the Good. Our egocentric graspings and clingings to our personality are the basic but not sole reasons for our tragic sufferings. We have all become the House of Atreus, bearing some mysterious inherited flaw. Here Aeschylus and Augustine unite in their bleak portraits of our tragic destinies.

The Good beyond Being is impersonal. The Good attracts us like a magnet to release the repressed, the innate impersonal desire for the Good in us. God, for Weil, is the impersonal Good. God is correctly called personal, in her judgment, only as tri-personal (that is, in Christian Trinitarian monotheism). Only through a Trinitarian monotheism is even God constituted as one by the divine relationships of each distinct divine person to the other two. However, Weil more often speaks of the ultimate reality as the impersonal, generous Good beyond Being.

The ego, often despite itself, experiences the Good that attracts it out of itself to others. In Weil's philosophy of the person, we experience the magnetic lure of the Good in many forms, many mediations, many *metaxu* of the Good — in the life of the senses, the life of the mind, the life of the spirit. Especially after her mystical visions, along with her consistently tragic reading of the human situation, Simone Weil found mediations of the Good everywhere: in saints and sages; in the beauty of the order of the world; in all beautiful works of art; in the joy of exercising our intelligence; in mathematics, science, and philosophy; in the release to the Good, available in every religious ritual; in spiritual disciplines designed to open us to the Good, as she herself discovered in the spiritual exercises of the Stoics, the Buddhists, the Taoists, the Hindus, the Christians, and, especially, in the scientific subtlety and poetic grandeur of St. John of the Cross. Weil found the Good sensed as present in the very absence of God in modern life. Indeed, modern atheism, in Weil's judgment, served as a good; that is, it was a necessary purification of our naively anthropomorphic ideas of God. Weil found the Good alive and attended to in all mystical experience in all religious traditions, not only in her own center of gravity, the Catholic Christian tradition. Above all, Weil found the Good in other persons, especially the marginalized and outcasts of society.

The desire for the Good, once released, can shatter the self-deluding, self-centered ego, the narcissistic personality. The desire for the Good, like the desire to know, is an impersonal power. The desire for the Good frees the ego from itself for the other. Our "personal" role (as an individual person slowly transformed by the desire for the Good) is to consent freely and attentively to the desire for the Good, just as we learn to consent freely to our innate desire for knowledge. Both of these grounding desires are impersonal; all consent is personal, individual, and fully possible to an intellectually and ethically transformed self. Otherwise the Good is experienced only transiently as the Impossible, which haunts our memories and goads our actions for justice. A fascinating and paradoxical relationship between an impersonal desire for the Good and personal consent is central to Weil's complex theory of the person. Weil's authentic person can be interpreted as a modern development of the ancient Greek notion of person as *prosopon*, an intrinsically relational individual directed to and loving the other by means of the impersonal power of the desire for the Good within us. A person, for Simone Weil, is therefore a mask, a *prosopon* rendering present a true, relational self, not a disguise for a self-fashioning personality.

As anthropologists and historians of religion have demonstrated, it is important to remember that the mask is an important reality in many ancient cultures and many contemporary indigenous cultures. The Greek and Latin notions of the mask harmonize with other ancient notions of the mask. The ancient mask represents, it does not hide. Mask (*prosopon*) re-presents (i.e., renders present, enacts) an absent reality: a god, a spirit, a hero, a ghost, or, especially in masked rituals, an event, such as the origin of the cosmos or the origin of the community. Here one may appeal to the familiar German philosophical distinction between *Vorstellung* and *Darstellung*: a mask is not *Vorstellung*; that is, an image standing in for some other absent reality through the image-mask. The ancient mask is not *Vorstellung*; it is *Darstellung*—a rendering present of a reality through the very image-mask.

For a large number of cultures—African, Oceanian, Native American, and Asian, in ancient Egypt and Mesopotamia, and in much of the ancient

European world—the mask was a central clue for an understanding of some reality beyond the ordinary. Through masks in a ritual, participants enacted the presence of other realities beyond the ordinary or natural realm: gods, spirits, ghosts, ancestors, and events, like the founding of the community in relationship to the origin of the cosmos.

Some modern artists have recovered the ancient sense of the mask as enactment, not disguise: Picasso with his use of African masks in his paintings; contemporary Japanese Noh theater continuing that great dramatic tradition; William Butler Yeats's attempts to create a modern Irish theater with masks modeled on Noh theater. Several other dramatists experimented with masks in early twentieth-century Russian and French theater. In these modern forms of art, the ancient sense of the mask returns. That ancient sense of mask-person (*prosopon*) also returns in Weil's notion of the person: a distinct individual constituted by its relationships to others and grounded in its desire for the Good.

Of all the great masks-persons of classical tragedy, Simone Weil herself most resembles Antigone. From her school days to the end of her short life, many friends and observers called her Antigone. Whether her friends called her Antigone seriously or ironically matters little. Weil's mask-person, her *prosopon*, was Antigone. To understand Simone Weil's person better, it is worth recalling the Antigone of Sophocles's tragedy. As a Sophoclean hero, Antigone is a *daimon*—an excessive, mediating figure between mortals and the immortal gods. The Sophoclean hero is not just a larger-than-life person of high standing and strength, like Clytemnestra, Cassandra, and Agamemnon in Aeschylus, or like Phaedra and Hippolytus in Euripides. In my judgment, alone among the tragedians Sophocles interprets the hero as a *daimon*. In Sophoclean drama, the daimonic hero can help us understand our tragic human situation because the *daimon*-hero cannot but act excessively—that is, beyond the human measure and beyond even the enlarged actions of the Aeschylean and Euripidean heroes. In Sophoclean drama, one glimpses Ultimate Reality only through the actions of a *daimon*-hero. Through observing the driven actions of the daimonic hero, one can begin to sense some (tragic-hopeful) response to the inevitable limit questions of life: Is life just? Is life meaningful? Is the ultimate reality the Void (as in most of Euripides) or a Zeus of ultimate justice (as in most of Aeschylus), or are we tragically condemned to be forever uncertain about the ultimate justice and meaningfulness of life, although sometimes (i.e., in some of Sophocles' dramas) hope-ful? Is there any meaning at all to this incomprehensible confusion we call life: an inseparable mixture of transient joys and often intense suffering, a sense of the Good in so much darkness, the seeming injustice of the fate of the daimonic hero along with quiet suggestions of some possible ultimate Jovian justice? Sophoclean tragedy sometimes ends in hope; sometimes, despair. We sometimes forget, in a culture that uses the word *tragic* as a synonym for hopeless, that half the Greek tragedies end in hope, half in despair. The Sophoclean hero, as a *daimon*, is driven by impersonal, unstoppable forces to thoughts and actions beyond the ordinary measure proper to mortals. Therein Sophocles hopes to find out whether daimonic mortals who transgress the human measure might reveal something of the ultimate mystery of all our lives as hopeful — or not.

Sophocles's most powerful *daimon*-hero, Antigone, is both like and unlike his other great daimonic hero, Oedipus. Like Oedipus, Antigone is a typical Sophoclean hero in her strength of character. Again like Oedipus, Antigone is a person-mask driven by an ineluctable impersonal force, more relentless even than the fatal desire to know the truth, whatever it costs that drives the daimonic Oedipus. Antigone is driven not by the desire to know the truth (she already knows and accepts it) but by the deeper desire for the Good — that Good beyond Being, the Good that grounds all reality and all intelligibility. Antigone is more than willing to go beyond the human measure. Antigone is also at times willful, intransigent, and thoughtless toward others, even those she loves. Recall Antigone's fierce rejection of her weak but well-meaning sister, Ismene, or her thoughtlessness toward the suffering of her fiancé, Haemon.

What is the clue to Antigone, this extraordinary, tragic, daimonic personage? Antigone is indeed the heroic figure that Hegel claimed was perhaps the most beautiful creature in our literature. Antigone is the figure that Jacques Lacan rightly named as *the* tragic figure, greater even than the Oedipus of his master Freud. The clue to Antigone, I hold, is her daimonic mask-person, her unique *prosopon*. Antigone cannot stop herself from burying her brother (a traitor to the city), despite all the rules of the city and the openly declared penalty for such action — death. No one (not even the prophet Teiresias) seems to understand what drives Antigone so one-sidedly, so stubbornly, so fatally to this action for her dead, traitorous brother. In a single, moving line (523), Sophocles reveals the secret, when Antigone responds to the contemptuous inquiry of Creon, and quietly says: "I was not born for hate but for love." It is love, the impersonal desire for the Good, that fiercely and relentlessly drives Antigone forward. She *must* perform this just action for her dead brother. Even though her brother is dead and was a traitor to the city, Antigone insists that, at this moment and place, her dead brother is the Other who must receive the Good, the respect due any human being, living or dead.

Inevitably, we are both fascinated and terrified by such daimonic figures as Antigone and Oedipus. Perhaps Sophocles was correct: only by observing the lives of these excessive, daimonic heroes who are beyond the human measure, like Oedipus and Antigone, can we catch some glimpse of what life is finally about. As Bataille, Sontag, Eliot, and many others observed, Simone Weil was such a figure of excess. Like Antigone, Weil was at times willful, intransigent, unintentionally and intentionally thoughtless to those she loved, especially her long-suffering parents.

To understand Simone Weil's person as a mask-*prosopon* is to refuse to allow her person and her work to be separated as an insoluble paradox, between the extremes of which one must choose. In fact, Weil's philosophy of measure is grounded in her central idea that the deepest reality in us, if we allow it, is the excessive desire for the Good. The desire for the Good grounds all measure and helps one discern when measure itself demands a move beyond the human measure to a new daimonic plane, where measure and excess, thought and action, measured thought and excessive action, the rose and the fire—are one.

With the matchless Antigone, Simone Weil as person and as thinker had the right to say, "I was not born for hate but for love."

CHAPTER 20

IRIS MURDOCH AND THE MANY FACES OF PLATONISM

THE UNLIKELY RETURN OF PLATO

There is something courageous in Iris Murdoch's decision to develop a form of Platonism in the late twentieth century. Among the ancients, Aristotle, that sometime Platonist, can always return, even if in our own period he returns not as a metaphysician but more often as a practical philosopher (Toulmin 1990; Nussbaum 1986). But Plato? Consider his critics. For many philosophers in the Continental tradition from Nietzsche through Heidegger to Deleuze, Plato is where the Greeks took a wrong turn — either away from the honest aesthetic world of tragedy (Nietzsche), or away from the nonforgetfulness of Being in the pre-Socratics (Heidegger), or away from the more daring language studies of some of the Sophists (Deleuze). At the same time as these not insignificant Continental criticisms leveled at Plato argue, we find that, for many Anglo-

American analytical philosophers, Platonism — especially in the modern form of a Hegelianized Platonism (Bradley) — is exactly the kind of muddled, vague, overambitious, implausible kind of philosophy that analytical philosophy in its earliest, more strictly observant mode was supposed to undo forever. From that perspective, only a few of Plato's arguments — analyzed through conceptual analysis and decontextualized from their concrete settings — seem of much logical interest. Even many of the internal critics of analytical philosophy (e.g., Richard Rorty, Bernard Williams, Alasdair MacIntyre) do not return to Plato or Platonism. They are more likely to turn either to rethinking the relationship of philosophy and literature (Rorty), or tragedy (Williams), or tradition (MacIntyre), rather than attempting to recover any notion of the Good in Plato.

Nor are most contemporary theologians more likely to recover Plato or Platonism. The Thomists — even the transcendental ones like Rahner, Coreth, and Lonergan — are more likely to find Plato on the Good as an interesting but dispensable way station on the road to Being and God — and Thomas Aquinas. The Barthians have never found much to approve of in Plato or the Platonists. It is almost enough for Karl Barth to remember that Schleiermacher was one of the great Plato translators and scholars to find that door closed. Barth's successors seem so concerned to restore a realistic, narrative form of theology that Plato's experiments with other forms seems, one gathers, irrelevant to their researches. The process theologians are, to be sure, always ready to quote Whitehead's famous statement that Western philosophy is a series of footnotes to Plato. However, even they seem less interested in noting, as Whitehead himself did note, that his *Process and Reality* (1929) can be read as a modern scientific rewriting of Plato's *Timaeus*.

There are, of course, philosophical and theological exceptions to this general picture. Most notably, some contemporary French thinkers — especially Emmanuel Levinas — have reread and rethought aspects of the Platonic heritage while critically retrieving it. Levinas's insight into Plato is notably similar to, yet finally different from, Iris Murdoch's reading of Plato. For Levinas, Plato helps one to break out of totality (including the totality of any Platonism, especially that of the last great Neoplatonist, Hegel) into the completely open concept of absolute (not quantitative) Infinity.[1] Plato achieves this kind

---

1. See especially Levinas 1969 reflecting on Plato's famous expression in *Republic* 6.509B: "The Good beyond Being" (*agathón epékeina tês ousías*).

of breakthrough, for Levinas, through his brilliant move in the *Republic* to the "Good beyond Being" (*agathón epékeina tês ousías*). Levinas's critique of Heidegger on Plato, as well as his insistence that ethics, not ontology, is first philosophy, is surprisingly similar to Murdoch's critique of Sartre.[2] Both involve, moreover, a rethinking of the Good in Plato as a necessary resource for contemporary ethics. Marion rethinks the category of the Good in relationship to the notion of gift (grace), well-articulated, for Marion, by Dionysius the Areopagite (Marion 1991, esp. 215–17).[3] This move allows Marion to challenge Thomism as well as most metaphysical namings of God as Being in favor of the Good as the primary cataphatic name for God, as in Dionysius and Bonaventure, but not in Thomas or Suárez (Marion 1991, esp. 32, 74–82).[4] Indeed, like Levinas's readings of Plato on the Good, Marion's reading of Dionysius on the gift bears a striking similarity to, and just as striking a difference from, Murdoch's reading of the Platonic Good as a resource for contemporary thought. Iris Murdoch's reading of the Good, with her fascinating metaphor for the Good as distant, impersonal, strong, magnetic power,[5] could prove one of the most important intra-Platonic challenges to the contemporary French philosophical debate over the Good as gift—a metaphor bearing both more personal and theistic overtones.

The French philosophical retrieval of and new debate upon Plato and the Good is surely the conversation that Iris Murdoch (with her criticisms of Sartre and Derrida and her affinity for Simone Weil) could profitably address (and vice versa).[6] For therein lies a genuine internal challenge to her critique of God

2. For Levinas here, besides the discussion in Levinas 1969, see also Levinas 1981 and the discussion of Heidegger in Levinas 1985. See also Peperzak 1993 and Wyschogrod 1974. On Sartre, see Murdoch 1953 and 1993 (154–56, 260–61, 266–67). Notice, for example, Murdoch's frequent appeals to Simon Weil's understanding of *attention* (as "a just and loving gaze directed upon an individual reality"), in contrast to Sartre's oppressive, controlling "gaze" at the Other (e.g., in Murdoch 1970, 34–35). It is puzzling that Murdoch's work does not refer to Levinas, with whom, in my judgment, she has much in common, despite obvious and important differences. A critical comparison of the two thinkers on the "Other" and "ethics" would be a valuable contribution.

3. It is, however, rather strange that Marion denies the importance of Neoplatonist philosophy even for Dionysius or Augustine, even though he employs it, as they do, throughout his reflections on the Good and gift.

4. See, however, the important qualifications on Thomas Aquinas in the preface (Marion 1991, xiv–xv).

5. The metaphor occurs throughout Murdoch 1993 (see, e.g., chap. 15, "Martin Buber and God," on the reasons why Murdoch argues against "personal" [i.e., "god"] language in favor of the impersonal [magnet-like] language of the Good). See also the essay "On 'God' and 'Good'" in Murdoch 1970 (46–77).

6. On Derrida, see Murdoch 1993 (185–216). For Derrida himself on ethics, see his important recent development of a "Messianic ethics" (Derrida 1994).

and the Good, and the major internal difference from her magnetism model for Plato's understanding of the Good. In the meantime, there have been other retrievals of Plato and the many kinds of Platonism in our period. In hermeneutical philosophy, for example, Hans-Georg Gadamer's most significant critique of his mentor Heidegger lies in their conflict of interpretations on Plato. Moreover, Gadamer's interpretation that there is a fundamental agreement between Plato and Aristotle on the meaning of the Good for ethics deserves far more attention from the many neo-Aristotelians of our day than it ordinarily receives (Gadamer 1987).

In Christian theology, moreover, the increasing influence of Hans Urs von Balthasar has led to a rereading of Plato and the Platonists (Christian and non-Christian) by many contemporary Christian theologians. Surely Balthasar — especially in his superb studies of Plotinus and Dionysius, of Bonaventure, and of Dante[7] — is right to insist that Platonism has provided Christian theology with a much greater sense of participation and an insistence on the centrality of form in Christian theology than the Scholasticism and Reformation theologies that largely replaced Platonism. Among contemporary theologians, John Macquarrie and Bernard McGinn have also developed arguments grounded in the kind of rigorous scholarship, at once historical and constructive, that a revival of Plato and Platonism in contemporary theology needs (Macquarrie 1985; McGinn 1991). These new movements have surely retrieved aspects of Platonism for contemporary needs. They are clearly important in themselves and, as readings of Plato and Platonism, promising for the future of any theology prepared to rethink the understanding of God beyond both classical theism and beyond modern forms of deism, pantheism, and even panentheism, although the latter can have a Platonic reading, as in Whitehead himself. And yet, even these new Platonic theologies need to meet the kinds of challenges of Plato and Platonism that Iris Murdoch's affirmation of the Good and the negation of God address.

I have no idea if Murdoch's strategy is a deliberate or an intuitive one, but, as I read her, both her novels and her philosophical books (from *The Sovereignty of Good* through *The Fire and the Sun* to *Metaphysics as a Guide to Morals*) reply

---

7. For Balthasar on form, see Balthasar 1982. For the separate studies, see Balthasar 1984 ("Dionysius and Bonaventure"), 1986 ("Dante"), 1989 ("Plotinus"). For good studies of this important contemporary Christian Platonist theologian (my description, not his), see Riches 1986 and Schindler 1991.

to the critics of Plato by employing a clever strategy, first named by another troubled Platonist in another deeply troubled age, Augustine of Hippo: the strategy of despoiling the Egyptians. Most contemporary defenders of Plato choose one or another of his critics (usually within the disciplines of philosophy or theology) to move their argument forward (e.g., Gadamer on Heidegger). Fair enough. But Murdoch's multilayered strategy, especially (but not solely) in *Metaphysics as a Guide to Morals*, is a more expansive, daring, and subtle one. She attempts to turn the critics — or, at least, their major intellectual resources — into new resources for her own Platonic understanding of the human search for the Good and the Platonic understanding of the Good as the impersonal, distant, unavoidable, ultimate reality, magnetically drawing all to itself, especially through beauty and love, as both are provoked by and provocative of the Good.

This is clearly Murdoch's strategy in the signal case of Freud and the Freudians.[8] Outside the strictly philosophical and theological debates, and indeed influencing them (as Paul Ricoeur [1970] persuasively argues), is the all-pervasive influence of Freud in our culture. For our culture is one where, as W. H. Auden observed, Freud is no longer so much a particular position as a whole climate of opinion. Part of that climate is the belief, widely shared by practically all of us, that traditional notions of the human search for the Good (including the Platonic pilgrimage from appearance to reality — that is, to the Good as a therapy for the soul) may finally prove too optimistic, even at times naive, a portrait of the profound ambiguities in the human situation. Recall how Peter Brown (1967, 261) sharply compares the shock that Augustine gave to the Platonists of his day by his disturbing portrait of the self always trapping itself in its own egoistic madness, to the shock that Freud gave to contemporary, optimistic Viennese psychologists, or, one may add, that Freud *still* gives to those able to see (as Jacques Lacan so persuasively does) past Freud's domesticating, ego-psychology successors.

Iris Murdoch, like Jacques Lacan, never domesticates Freud's steady, indeed

---

8. See the many discussions of Freud carefully indexed in both Murdoch 1970 and Murdoch 1993. This interest in and use of Freud occur throughout the novels; see especially Murdoch 1961. I have been especially guided for Murdoch's use of Freud as a novelist by the studies of Deborah Johnson (1987, esp. 14–18, 33–40); and Elizabeth Dipple (1982, esp. 93–94, 152–57, 272–73). Johnson's study is also very instructive for analyzing Murdoch's work from a feminist perspective, including discussion of feminist critiques of Freud and Freudianism.

relentless, insistence on the powerful influence of the unconscious on all consciousness, nor his vision of the fragility of the ego in any search for the good life—or even, as in *Civilization and Its Discontents*, in any human search for a decent, civilized life. It would be difficult to name a contemporary novelist (think of *A Severed Head* as merely the most explicitly Freudian of Murdoch's tales) who takes Freud more seriously in his unyielding portrait of the delusions of the ego,[9] especially as the ego searches for some good. Recall, for example, how *A Severed Head*, a very contemporary Freudian narrative, without loss of its tragic sense, becomes suffused—and to an extent, diffused—by a brilliant Murdochian comedy of errors. For Iris Murdoch insists, in her novels as much as her philosophy,[10] that Freud was entirely right to see libidinal energy at the base of all artistic and spiritual experience, although still distinct from those energies for Murdoch; less clearly for Freud, as in his reductionist reading of Leonardo da Vinci. However, Freud was right to show how ideals of the good (such as self-sacrifice) can sometimes function as illusions hiding deeper sadomasochistic drives.

But what Murdoch shows is that these Freudian insights are devastating only to those forms of Platonism and understandings of the search for the Good that have forgotten Plato. It is not just Freud; it is also Plato who insists that *eros* is a universal energy, a profoundly ambiguous force that can work either for destruction or for the good. What Murdoch shows is not merely the Freudian tone of Plato's analysis of *eros* and the Good but, just as paradoxically, the Platonic tone of Freud's analyses of *eros*, of the soul, and of therapy. Indeed, Freud was never reluctant to admit his affinity with and, at times, his debt to his ancient mentor. He declared his debt to Plato for the exposure of the illusions created by the ego, as well as for the self's need for a therapy that moves beyond the fragile, self-deluding ego to the full reality of the self or soul. It is Plato who first enunciated the classic Freudian portrait of the full complexity of our situation in his extraordinary picture of the tyrant as the one who does, in reality, what the rest of us do in dreams.[11] It was Plato who insisted that only a full-scale therapy of the soul could be trusted to allow anyone to happen upon an occasional glimpse of the Good (Plato, *Sym-*

---

9. See the analyses of Murdoch 1961 in Johnson 1987 (esp. 17–18).

10. See especially Murdoch 1993, 20–24, for one of her many intriguing Plato-Freud comparisons.

11. I am indebted for this insight to David Grene (see Grene 1967), with whom I jointly taught a course on the *Republic*.

SEEKERS OF THE GOOD

posium 210E). A glimpse, notice, no more than that — not a union with the One, as with Plotinus and many later Platonists.

Of course, neither Murdoch nor any other careful interpreter of *eros* and the Good would claim that Plato and Freud share the same view of our situation. But Iris Murdoch does show their ready affinities by her careful interpretation of central aspects of both Plato's and Freud's different but oddly akin notions of the need for therapy in the soul before any objective truth or goodness can be claimed. Her basic argument is that Plato is never as optimistic on the search for the Good as many later Platonists now seem in a post-Freudian age.[12] Murdoch demonstrates this reading of Plato's subtlety on the complex, ambiguous self both by philosophical argument and, perhaps above all, by showing how such a search for the Good moves forward in and through the strange, tragicomic interactions of the characters in her novels. Her personae, so contemporary and yet so ancient, seem driven by madness in the ego, its self-delusions and illusions regarding what constitutes the genuine Good. At the same time, this madness in the ego accompanies (rather than opposes) the desires of the id — both being magnetically attracted to the Good. This unique combination of Freud and Plato on *eros* and the Good, therapy and truth, is what renders Murdoch's philosophical novels so captivating and her late twentieth-century philosophical retrieval of Plato's Good so important a post-Freudian candidate for serious contemporary philosophical and theological reflection.[13]

FORMS OF THOUGHT AND THE FORM OF THE GOOD

The other charge against Plato, most forcefully articulated by Heidegger, is that Plato initiated the onto-theological reign of metaphysics. To my knowledge,

---

12. This was already, of course, the insight (vis-à-vis Porphyry and Plotinus) of that deeply troubled Platonist St. Augustine, the clearest analogue to Freud's portrait of the deeply divided self.

13. This also renders Murdoch's philosophy curiously analogous to the debates among the earlier Frankfurt thinkers (especially Adorno and Horkheimer) on the exemplary role of Freudian psychoanalytical theory as an initial example of a contemporary philosophical critical theory — that is, a theory grounded in practice (e.g., the Freudian case studies) that both explains, as all theory does, and emancipates, as critical theories do (while traditional theories rarely do). In the sense that the Christian theological understanding of sin-grace from Augustine through Kierkegaard and beyond is more a critical than a traditional theory, it both explains and emancipates.

Murdoch does not directly address this central contemporary attack on Plato and Platonism — an attack, as noted above, first forged by Nietzsche, sharpened by Heidegger, and resharpened in our own period by Jacques Derrida.[14] Although Murdoch addresses other issues raised by Martin Heidegger and Jacques Derrida (each, for her, daimonic and poeticizing philosophers), she addresses their central charge against Plato rather indirectly.[15] In fact, in *Metaphysics as a Guide to Morals*, she basically ignores this charge, only to attempt to show — both by her interpretations of Plato's experiments with genres and forms for rendering the Form of the Good,[16] as well as by her own daring experiments with genres and forms — how plausible and, one might add, now non-onto-theological Plato's account of the Good is.

It is, for example, no small matter that Plato chooses the dialogue form to articulate his philosophy.[17] Indeed, if Plato's Seventh Letter (341B–E) is genuine (as I believe it is likely to be), Plato not only meant but he also *wrote* that to understand his philosophy, all we have are the dialogues.[18] *Elenchus*, dialectic, and *dianoia* are, to be sure, crucial even for Plato, who holds *noesis* as beyond all those discursive forms of reasoning. But Plato did not leave us a treatise — that is, a systematic collection of arguments like the treatises of Aristotle, a few of which are probably Aristotle's own creation, while most are lecture notes of his students. Nor did Plato have collections of almost Koan-like meditations combined with strong dialectical arguments, both ready to be arranged by others into the fascinating nonchronological form of Plotinus's *Enneads* provided by Porphyry. This difference between Plotinus and Plato possibly arises because, for Plotinus, a union with the One is possible, whereas, for Plato, all we can hope for is an occasional glimpse of the Good (*Republic*), or

---

14. See Johnson 1987 for an illuminating analysis of what can be called the implicitly feminist elements (especially in the portraits of male and female characters) in Murdoch's novels.

15. Indeed, Murdoch's description and critique of these "daimonic" philosophies intensifies in her readings in Murdoch 1993. Her reading of Jacques Derrida is especially severe — and, in my judgment inaccurate, uncharacteristically unfair. Perhaps a reading of Derrida's recent work on ethics (e.g., Derrida 1994) might have helped to modify Murdoch's reading.

16. This analysis of Plato's own artistry, despite his famous banishment of "the poets," already begins in Murdoch 1977. Note the even stronger case made throughout Murdoch 1993 on Plato on the Good in comparison with the earlier analyses in Murdoch 1977 and 1970.

17. For a more detailed defense of my position here, see Tracy 2020, chap. 13. For further studies here, see Friedlander 1969 (154–71, 230–36) and Gadamer 1980.

18. See the eloquent and persuasive reading of the importance of this letter for understanding Plato by David Grene (1967, 95–124).

the Beautiful (which appears suddenly in *Symposium*), and possibly the One (in *Parmenides*).[19]

Above all, the form of a Platonic system — the kind of systematic, ordered form in Neoplatonism that was forged so well by Proclus and rethought centuries later in Thomas Aquinas's *Summa*[20] — was never a temptation for Plato. Indeed, I personally doubt if, *pace* Aristotle and others, Plato ever gave a lecture on the Good at all (Cornford 1967, 28–47). In that case, there is no other text for Plato's philosophy than the dialogues themselves. It is all in the dialogues. On my reading, the Seventh Letter, whether written by Plato himself or not, is hermeneutically sound: What we possess for understanding the philosophy of Plato, including his understanding of the Good, are the dialogues. And I believe we can show that the dialogues are all any interpreter of Plato, including Aristotle, ever possessed in texts.

Happily, as some analytical philosophers still refuse to see, but Iris Murdoch clearly does, the dialogues more than suffice. For in Plato's dialogues one can find not only formal arguments (some good, some bad, some middling), but also arguments as they actually occur for concrete human beings in concrete settings with particular conversation partners. The link between argument and character in the dialogues helps any attentive reader to learn that an understanding of the Good will come about only for those engaged in the kind of therapy for the soul that Plato's dialogues provide: a therapy that clarifies the world of intelligibility (e.g., through mathematics), a therapy that takes one to a world of developing ideas and forms by constructing ever-finer and more complex hypotheses, through ever more demanding dialectical arguments, before any *noesis* of the true can occur. In the greatest dialogues, there is a world where the beauty of particular persons and particular art objects is both affirmed as an emblem of the Good and suspected as a distraction from the pure search for the Good. In the dialogues lives a world where myths are both demythologized and invented wholesale, sometimes to forge a dialectical point (as in the Myth of Er at the end of *Republic*), at other times to become the principal form of logos itself (as in *Timaeus*, that brilliantly dialectical myth that

---

19. On Plotinus, see Hadot 1973. I have already cited the relevant passages in *Republic* and *Symposium*. The Question of "the One" in *Parmenides* (so influential on the Neoplatonists) remains extremely difficult to interpret with anything like surety, especially on the question of whether "the One" of that uniquely dialectical dialogue is really analogous to the Good (in *Republic*) or the beautiful (in *Symposium*, as I believe, but cannot prove it is), or is a sole exercise in logic alone: hence my cautionary adverb "possibly" here.

20. For the influence of Proclus in the systematic form of the *Summa*, see Hankey (1987, esp. 1–19).

is perhaps Plato's greatest vision of how the Good has been made concrete in both cosmos and history).[21]

The wondrous middle dialogues—especially *Phaedrus, Symposium,* and *Republic*—seem modeled as dramas of the intellectual journey of the soul to the Good and the Beautiful. They function, for Plato, as alternatives to the dramas of the soul in Homer and in the tragedians (especially Aeschylus).[22] But the early aporetic dialogues and even, perhaps, the less dramatic, more dialectical later dialogues like *Parmenides* and *Sophist* seem not so much dramatic in structure as mimetic; that is, as Aristotle suggests, the early dialogues of Plato may be modeled not on the dramas of the tragedians but on the ancient mimes. This is not an insignificant point, especially, as I shall suggest, for understanding the form not only of Plato's dialogues but also Iris Murdoch's own Platonic philosophy. For the ancient mimes, as David Grene has suggested,[23] were, in their genre or form, very much like many of Plato's early dialogues. The mimes, unlike the dramas, do not drive to dramatic closure. The mimes, unlike the dramas, occur in the midst of everyday life, where inquiring human beings simultaneously search for the good and delude themselves. At other times, however, we are involved in some more drama-like troubled journey from birth to death and, if fortunate, discover some way to move, at least on occasion (e.g., when in the presence of a beautiful body evoking love), from appearance to reality. The mimes are not dramatic in form and not necessarily too significant in content. The mimes are usually, to use the more familiar word, aporetic. They give

---

21. It is true that myth is usually demythologized in the early aporetic dialogues. However, beginning with the myths of the dramatic middle dialogues, especially *Phaedrus, Symposium,* and *Republic,* and culminating in the extraordinary dialectical-mythic *Timaeus,* one cannot justly claim that Plato is only a demythologizer. In fact, Plato is also one of the great re-mythologizers. In one sense, it is, of course, anachronistic to discuss Plato in terms of modern (i.e., post-Romantic) notions of myth. As is well known, in Plato (including *Timaeus*) *muthos* and *logos* are often used interchangeably, not as contrasting terms. This is important to recall, even though the hermeneutical point holds: Plato develops (in the examples cited above), for philosophical purposes, what one can justly name *myth.*

22. There is a striking affinity, at times, between the sensibilities of Aeschylus and Plato: witness the role of *peitho* (persuasion) and necessity in *Oresteia* and, in Plato, of abstract (and mythic) terms in the "likely story" of *Timaeus.* For some fruitful reflections in the Plato-Aeschylus comparison, see Cornford 1948, esp. 361–64.

23. See the public lecture delivered at Hobart and William Smith Colleges (Geneva, New York) in April 1989 titled "The Importance of Conversation; or, The Dialogues of Plato" (an unpublished manuscript in the David Grene Papers, Special Collections, University of Chicago). The location of the model of the mimes in only the early dialogues is my suggestion, not David Grene's. In my judgment, the middle dialogues seem modeled on tragic dramas, and most of the later dialogues (save the "likely story" of *Timaeus*) in a series of interrelated dialectical arguments.

glimpses of the Good in the midst of everyday life to ordinary, thoughtful, troubled, both self-deluding and honestly searching human beings.

Surely David Grene is illuminating and original to recall Aristotle's usually overlooked comment that the mime was the model for Plato's dialogues or, at least, for the large majority of the early dialogues. Indeed, most of the early, aporetic Platonic dialogues are like the mimes in the sense of how questions (such as, What is courage? What is piety, etc.) occur to human beings in very ordinary circumstances as they try to make some sense of their lives and catch some glimpse of some ideal, some reality greater than themselves that is magnetically drawing them forward to the truth.

To return to Iris Murdoch's retrieval of Plato for the present: Some critics have suggested that Iris Murdoch's Gifford Lectures (*Metaphysics as a Guide to Morals*) lack the systematic character they expected or at least desired. A systematic drive seems more available in the briefer but more methodical arguments of *The Sovereignty of Good* and the highly focused interpretations of Sartre in *Romantic Rationalist* or of Plato himself in *The Fire and the Sun*. (This is especially true of the relatively "tight" argument of *The Sovereignty of Good*.) However, on my reading at least, it is no disparagement of those earlier fine works by Murdoch to say that they lack not merely the ambitiousness but also the elaborate range of forms in *Metaphysics as a Guide to Morals*.

The latter book — even more than Murdoch's explicitly Platonic dialogues in *Acastos* (1988) — seems to me more faithful to the kind of form needed for rendering a Platonic theory of the Good in the late twentieth century — the century that has read not only Plato and the great Platonists but also Freud, Marx, and feminist theory, and such powerful philosophical critics of Plato as Nietzsche, Heidegger, and Derrida. For *Metaphysics as a Guide to Morals*, in spite of its occasional appearance of meandering formlessness, seems less a treatise and more like several Platonic dialogues, at once mimetic, dramatic, and dialectical. From the very beginning of this strange, intriguing book, *Metaphysics as a Guide to Morals*, the reader finds herself in the midst of a wider and unhurried conversation on unities and forms, on the Good and the search for the good; on illusion and the ego; or on art, religion, love, and death; on the Good and on the Void — on questions, in short, that any thoughtful human being is likely at some point in life to ask oneself. In this meditative and meandering book, one sometimes finds oneself in the midst of extended arguments (e.g., the chapters on consciousness) or of brilliant, extended interpretations (e.g., the wonderful chapter restoring Schopenhauer to the serious philosophical consideration he deserves and almost never receives) (Murdoch 1993, 57–80). At other times, the reader finds not extended argument at all but brief and telling reflections with favored Murdochian conversation partners who seem to keep returning like characters in a novel into the odd conversation that is this uncanny, novel-like, philosophical book. At times the same characters seem to linger only to leave all too abruptly, again as in novels, mimes, and life itself (Wittgenstein, Kant, Freud, Weil, and, of course, Plato). Sometimes, something like closure may occur to a particular train of thought. More often, the argument dissolves or ends abruptly, as when the reflections on the need in our day for meditation, or at least for keeping silent, become the charmingly abrupt advice, "Teach it to your children." End of discussion. This is rather like the ancient mimes, that is, rather like ordinary life and its incomplete conversations. And through it all, the somewhat labyrinthine search for the Good yields to a magnetic pull, on rare occasions, to a glimpse of something real, distant, unavoidable, transcendent, pure, oddly believable — the Void, the Infinite, perhaps the Good, perhaps God.[24] In spite of a final brief summary, there is in fact no dramatic closure to this open-ended, multiple dialogue-like work (Murdoch 1993, 504–13). As a philosopher, Iris Murdoch here has indeed found the proper form for articulating her particular vision of the Good, for she remembers what some of the critics seem to forget: both Plato's mime-like, dramatic, and dialectical dialogues, and her own mime-like novels, to which I now briefly turn.

The digressive, sometimes self-disrupting order of Iris Murdoch's novels seems to suggest that any ordinary, realistic ordering of both experience and understanding in her novels, as in life and thought, is in fact a falsification. The shifting and mixed genres of her novels also seem faithful to a vision of the slippery, indeed treacherous, nature of language. The multivoiced (one might also say Bakhtinian) character of her novels rejects any dominant single narrative voice in favor of many different, often conflicting voices. This mime-like set of characteristics suggests how Iris Murdoch may have found the modern novel more congenial than even the ancient dialogue for her Platonic view of the human search for the Good. Indeed, the most widely acknowledged

---

24. I am tempted to suggest that the nearest Platonist in terms of a labyrinthine form to Murdoch is her Irish predecessor John Scotus Eriugena. We can hardly miss, in so many Celtic works, realities like the labyrinthine beauty of the *Book of Kells* (which James Joyce always traveled with) or the endlessly complex, wondrous forms of *Ulysses* and *Finnegans Wake* of that strangely Aristotelian-Thomist James Joyce. Most Platonists and almost all Aristotelians prefer a clearer, more straightforward form, except, it seems, Irish ones (such as Eriugena, Joyce — and Murdoch — a splendidly complex, plural tradition).

strengths of her novels bear striking family resemblances to some of the classic strengths of the Platonic dialogues: the sharply focused detail of the settings; the moments of tensive interaction between the characters; the frequent surprises, intellectual and emotional; the play between the ideas and arguments themselves with the self's mixture of understanding and egoistic self-delusion (Dipple 1982, esp. 36–80; Johnson 1987, 20–56). At the same time, Murdoch's novels, like Plato's early aporetic dialogues, tend not to reach closure but to dissolve or sometimes explode or implode as the truth at stake becomes both unavoidable and unbearable, both undeniable and unavailable.

Her modern psychological novels—like Plato's dialogues—demand an active response from an attentive reader. Unlike the form of the treatise, the dialogue's very open-ended form demands the reader's response. Unlike the realistic novel,[25] which Iris Murdoch's novels both resemble and dissolve, her novels' characteristic open-endedness demands an active questioning response on the part of the reader. Alasdair MacIntyre is right to insist that "Iris Murdoch's novels are philosophy, including her own,"[26] when their mime-like, drama-like form, their omnipresent dialectical arguments, their modern, novel-like genre replacing the mime-like dialogues of the ancients, are taken as the signal clues to the philosophical content of her philosophy as a glimpse of the Good in the midst of actual human life. One can probably never separate form and content as readily as most philosophers and theologians are still wont to believe.[27] Not only Derrida and Nietzsche but also Plato thoroughly knew that unique combination of great philosopher and great artist. So did Augustine, Søren Kierkegaard, and Saul Bellow. So does Iris Murdoch—which is part of her great strength as both philosopher and novelist. Indeed, it is often difficult and sometimes impossible to know in her work where literature ends and philosophy begins, or where philosophy ends and art begins. And that fruitful paradox can now be acknowledged for what it always was: a strength, not a

---

25. Here I am once again informed by Johnson's (1987) feminist and Bakhtinian reading in her short but illuminating study of Murdoch's fiction. Johnson, in her turn, seems most influenced by the French feminist critic Luce Irigaray for her study of multiplicity and subversion in Murdoch's novels. Besides Johnson and Dipple (my principal literary guides to Murdoch's fiction), see also Byatt 1965 and Conradi 1986. In terms of Murdoch's novels, my own readings here are especially indebted to Murdoch herself: Murdoch 1973, 1974, and 1978. Among her more recent novels, Murdoch 1990 and Murdoch 1994 have been especially helpful to me in my attempts to compare her philosophical and novelistic works.

26. Cited in Johnson (1987, 86), from MacIntyre's review of Dipple (1982).

27. I have argued this, with proper reference to relevant philosophers and theologians, in Tracy 1994, 302–19.

weakness, especially for any thinker concerned to render a plausible view of the Good not simply as a historical subject but as a contemporary need.

THE GOOD AND THE RETURN OF SPIRITUAL EXERCISES

Iris Murdoch does not wish to promote a new institutionalization of a Platonic school for therapy of the soul in the search for the Good. In her portraits of our human condition in her novels, as well as in her frequent appeals to various kinds of intellectual and spiritual exercises in *Metaphysics as a Guide to Morals*,[28] Murdoch clearly believes that we need not a new institution but greater attentiveness to the practices we are already actively engaged in or passively engaged by. Throughout her work, Iris Murdoch reminds us of the ethical and metaphysical import of our most everyday practices. For example, our ordinary human interactions, as her novels show, are often our best opportunity for both self-delusion and for spotting those self-delusions as we clumsily feel our way through the very attractions and confusions of our interaction with others, even as we often subconsciously sense some magnetic pull of the Good.[29] A second example: Erotic love can wrench us from our usual self-interest to face some other reality, possibly the Good (Murdoch 1993, 20–25). A third example: Art can, at times, free us to consider the possibility, as Murdoch (1977, 76–77) nicely says, of "a pure transcendent value, a steady visible enduring higher good, and perhaps provides for many people, in an unreligious age without prayer or sacraments, their clearest *experience* of something grasped as separate and precious and beneficial and held quietly and unpossessively in the attention. Good art which we love can seem holy, and attending to it can be like praying. Our relation to such art, though probably never entirely pure, is markedly unselfish."

Not only love and beauty are signals of the presence of our attraction to the Good. As the ancients insisted, intellectual practices function this way as well. Mathematics and dialectic direct our attention out of ourselves by their demand that we acknowledge some other purely intelligible power by intellec-

---

28. The reader is encouraged to reread the discussion of Pierre Hadot on ancient spiritual exercises in chapter 9 of this volume. Hadot's work is as relevant to Murdoch as to Lonergan.

29. Perhaps the point, as well, of Stendhal's observation: "We can achieve everything in solitude save character."

tually entering a world of pure intelligibility. Indeed, learning anything really well — any genuine, painstaking work of scholarship, any careful attention to learning another language well[30] — takes us immediately out of ourselves to a different kind of call and demand. That call is to a sense of objectivity as we painstakingly learn to pay virtuous attention to particular realities outside ourselves. Moreover, as Iris Murdoch's many appeals to Simone Weil suggest (esp. Murdoch 1993, 500–506), explicitly spiritual exercises are also available to anyone. Above all, we can cultivate moments of tact, silence, and attentiveness to the world outside ourselves as ways of decreasing our natural egoism. We can learn to pay attention in nature and in scientific inquiry to the image of necessity as the law in nature. Such careful attentiveness to nature and its necessities (especially through the natural sciences) can help exhibit the futility of selfish purposes. Such attention can also promote a focused attentiveness to the Void — that encroaching reality can open suddenly in and through our very use of language.[31]

Iris Murdoch's hope for the reunion of thought and exercises is not focused upon a Kantian abrupt call for the will to abide by duty, or upon a Kierkegaardian, radical, sudden leap of faith, or even to a radical transformation or conversion of the self from evil to good. Instead, Iris Murdoch's hope is directed to a slow shift of our attachments, a painstaking education of desire and thought — an education like that which Plato foresaw as our best, perhaps our only hope for both living and thinking well. Even metaphysics for Murdoch serves not only its intellectual purpose but also a spiritual one, another great barrier against our natural egoism.[32] There is no shortcut to enlightenment.

The words most frequently used in Murdoch's account of spiritual exercises — *detachment* and *attention* — suggest not so much Stoicism or Christianity, although both include exercises of attentiveness and detachment (e.g., Meister Eckhart), but some new form of Platonized Buddhism. Clearly, Christianity's classic narrative of creation, fall, and redemption, given Iris Murdoch's Quaker and Anglican heritages, is deeply embedded in her own imagination of the human drama. How else to account for her appeal, even after her denial of a

---

30. The examples are Murdoch's own (Murdoch 1993).

31. Derrida's work, in my judgment, can also be read fruitfully in this way. Such a reading could, for Murdoch, allow for a more positive assessment of Derrida than the solely negative one she gives in Murdoch 1993 (esp. 185–216).

32. Indeed, this seems to be a principal point of Murdoch's "Metaphysics: A Summary" (Murdoch 1993, 504–12), as well as the title of the work itself, *Metaphysics as a Guide to Morals*.

personal God, to a Christ-mysticism that discloses the approachable, even consoling, aspect of the Good?[33] Indeed, it is striking how suspicious Iris Murdoch (like Simone Weil) is of almost any consolation in religion.[34] Murdoch's problems with Jewish, Christian, or Muslim radical monotheistic understandings of God seem to me to have less to do with familiar metaphysical difficulties than with what can only be called a problem of sensibility or even spirituality. She fears that any acceptance of a personal God, unlike the impersonal Good, will tempt us to ways which will allow us to escape facing reality — reality as what must be endured, what cannot be denied as there, what breaks through our natural egoism and fantasizing imagination by its unrelenting necessity.[35] For Murdoch, a belief in God can function as another veil created by our anxiety to hide away what is terrible and absurd in life and reality.

Surely an observer of any of our Western religions will agree that such a scenario can be the case. Moreover, Christian, Jewish, and Muslim thinkers can be thankful for Murdoch's pushing them in the direction of greater austerity of thought and practice. There is a need in our period, I have long believed as a Christian, for what might be named a more Buddhist sensibility of greater detachment in Christian God-talk (Tracy 1990, 68–94). Meister Eckhart now seems, even to many of his fellow Christian theologians, to have developed a far more believable God-language, even on intra-Christian grounds, than that of many of his supposedly more consoling orthodox critics. Even when a Christian theologian like myself turns away with gratitude from both Buddhist *sunyata* and the Platonist impersonal Good to God, a turn to the practice of radical detachment is profoundly necessary for any adequate contemporary Christian theological understanding of the relationship of God and the Good.[36]

A final question here: Is the Good best conceived through Iris Murdoch's

---

33. Murdoch seems most influenced here by Simone Weil's Christ-mysticism, although perhaps Murdoch's own Quaker background is also influential here.

34. This "hermeneutics of suspicion" upon all consolation in religion (in both Weil and Murdoch) seems to me true in its suspicion of how false the consolations of a "personal God" can become, cloying and clinging to anthropomorphic pictures of an all-consoling God, and how, at times, grace can be, as Dietrich Bonhoeffer famously suggested, merely "cheap grace." Nevertheless, the spiritual states of peace, quiet, and serenity (all of which Murdoch endorses) are not far from authentic spiritual understandings of "consolation" in the monotheistic traditions.

35. On necessity, see Simone Weil's wondrous essay, "The Iliad, or The Poem of Force" (Weil [1945] 1977, 153–84).

36. I hope to expand upon and defend this position in a forthcoming book on naming and thinking God.

metaphor as a magnet powerfully attracting us despite ourselves? Or is Platonic Good best conceived through the metaphor of gift, the other great Platonist metaphor that I and others now attempt to retrieve? That question needs to be asked first, I believe, in order to provide the necessary refinement of a contemporary Platonic entry to the question of God and the Good. In the meantime, even those trying to grasp the full power and range of the reality of the Good as gift can likewise affirm the power of Murdoch's metaphor of the Good as a magnet, forcibly drawing one to itself despite oneself, attracting us by its beauty, its objectivity, and its goodness. Here too the old Italian proverb applies: A good heart crosses all borders. That magnetic force of the Good is just what any thoughtful reader can experience in Murdoch's novels that read so much like good philosophy and these stunning, meandering philosophical books that read so much like good novels. In both Iris Murdoch's novels and her philosophy lurks a magnetic power that allows the reader an occasional glimpse of the Good.

REFERENCES

Balthasar, Hans Urs von. 1982. *The Glory of the Lord: A Theological Aesthetics*. Vol. 1. *Seeing the Form*. Translated by Erasmo Leiva-Merikakis. Edited by Joseph Fessio and John Riches. San Francisco: Ignatius Press.

———. 1984. *The Glory of the Lord: A Theological Aesthetics*. Vol. 2. *Studies in Theological Style: Clerical Styles*. Translated by Andrew Louth, Francis McDonagh, and Brian McNeil. Edited by John Riches. San Francisco: Ignatius Press.

———. 1986. *The Glory of the Lord: A Theological Aesthetics*. Vol. 3. *Studies in Theological Style: Lay Styles*. Translated by Andrew Louth, John Saward, Martin Simon, and Rowan Williams. Edited by John Riches. San Francisco: Ignatius Press.

———. 1989. *The Glory of the Lord: A Theological Aesthetics*. Vol. 4. *The Realm of Metaphysics in Antiquity*. Translated by Brian McNeil, Andrew Louth, John Saward, Rowan Williams, and Oliver Davies. Edited by John Riches. San Francisco: Ignatius Press.

Brown, Peter. 1967. *Augustine of Hippo*. Berkeley: University of California Press.

Byatt, A. S. 1965. *Degrees of Freedom: The Novels of Iris Murdoch*. London: Chatto and Windus.

Conradi, Peter J. 1986. *Iris Murdoch: The Saint and the Artist*. London: Macmillan.

Cornford, F. M. 1948. *Plato's Cosmology: The "Timaeus" of Plato, Translated with a Running Commentary*. London: Routledge and Kegan Paul.

———. 1967. *The Unwritten Philosophy and Other Essays*. Cambridge: Cambridge University Press.

Derrida, Jacques. 1994. *Specters of Marx*. Translated by Peggy Kamuf. London: Routledge.

Dipple, Elizabeth. 1982. *Iris Murdoch: Work for the Spirit*. Chicago: University of Chicago Press.

Friedlander, Paul. 1969. *Plato: An Introduction*. Vol. 1. Translated by Hans Meyerhoff. Princeton, NJ: Princeton University Press.

Gadamer, Hans-Georg. 1980. *Dialogue and Dialectic: Eight Hermeneutical Studies in Plato*. Translated by P. Christopher Smith. New Haven, CT: Yale University Press.

———. 1987. *The Idea of the Good in Platonic-Aristotelian Philosophy*. Translated by P. Christopher Smith. New Haven, CT: Yale University Press.

Grene, David. 1967. *Greek Political Theory: The Image of Man in Thucydides and Plato*. Chicago: University of Chicago Press.

———. 1989. "The Importance of Conversation; or, The Dialogues of Plato." Unpublished paper in Special Collections, Regenstein Library, University of Chicago.

Hadot, Pierre. 1973. *Plotinus on the Simplicity of Vision*. Translated by Michael Chase. Chicago: University of Chicago Press.

Hankey, W. J. 1987. *God in Himself: Aquinas' Doctrine of God as Expounded in the "Summa Theologiae."* Oxford: Oxford University Press.

Johnson, Deborah. 1987. *Iris Murdoch*. Bloomington: Indiana University Press.

Levinas, Emmanuel. 1969. *Totality and Infinity*. Translated by Alphonso Lingis. The Hague, The Netherlands: Martinus Nijhoff.

———. 1981. *Otherwise Than Being or Beyond Essence*. Translated by Alphonso Lingis. The Hague, The Netherlands: Martinus Nijhoff.

———. 1985. *Ethics and Infinity*. Translated by Richard A. Cohen. Pittsburgh, PA: Duquesne University Press.

Macquarrie, John. 1985. *In Search of Deity: An Essay in Dialectical Theism*. New York: Crossroad.

Marion, Jean-Luc. 1991. *God without Being*. Translated by Thomas A. Carlson. Chicago: University of Chicago Press.

McGinn, Bernard. 1991. *The Presence of God*. Vol. 1. New York: Crossroad.

Murdoch, Iris. 1953. *Sartre: Romantic Rationalist*. Cambridge: Bowes and Bowes.

———. 1961. *A Severed Head*. London: Chatto and Windus.

———. 1970. *The Sovereignty of Good*. New York: Routledge.

———. 1973. *The Black Prince*. New York: Viking Books.

———. 1974. *The Sacred and Profane Love Machine*. New York: Viking Books.

———. 1977. *The Fire and the Sun: Why Plato Banished the Artists*. Oxford: Oxford University Press.

———. 1978. *The Sea, the Sea*. New York: Viking Books.

———. 1988. *Acastos: Two Platonic Dialogues*. New York: Penguin Books.

———. 1990. *The Message to the Planet*. New York: Viking Books.

———. 1993. *Metaphysics as a Guide to Morals*. London: Penguin.

———. 1994. *The Green Knight*. New York: Viking Books.

Nussbaum, Martha. 1986. *The Fragility of Goodness*. Cambridge: Cambridge University Press.

Peperzak, Adrian. 1993. *To the Other: An Introduction to the Philosophy of Emmanuel Levinas*. West Lafayette, IN: Purdue University Press.

Riches, John, ed. 1986. *The Analogy of Beauty: The Theology of Hans Urs von Balthasar*. Edinburgh: T & T Clark.

Ricoeur, Paul. 1970. *Freud and Philosophy*. Translated by Denis Savage. New Haven, CT: Yale University Press.

Schindler, David L., ed. 1991. *Hans Urs von Balthasar: His Life and Work*. San Francisco: Ignatius Press.

Toulmin, Stephen. 1990. *Cosmopolis*. Chicago: University of Chicago Press.

Tracy, David. 1990. "The Buddhist-Christian Dialogue." In *Dialogue with the Other: The Inter-Religious Dialogue*. Leuven, The Netherlands: Eerdmans/Peters Press.

———. 1994. "Literary Theory and Return of the Forms for Naming and Thinking God in Theology." *Journal of Religion* 74 (3):302–19.

———. 2020. *Fragments: The Existential Situation of Our Time*. Vol. 1 of *Selected Essays*. Chicago: University of Chicago Press.

Weil, Simone. (1945) 1977. "The Iliad, or The Poem of Force." In *The Simone Weil Reader*, edited by George Panichas. New York: David McKay.

Whitehead, Alfred North. 1929. *Process and Reality: An Essay in Cosmology*. Cambridge: Cambridge University Press.

Wyschogrod, Edith. 1974. *Emmanuel Levinas: The Problem of Ethical Metaphysics*. The Hague, The Netherlands: Martinus Nijhoff.

CHAPTER 21

T. S. ELIOT AS RELIGIOUS THINKER

Four Quartets

THE CONFLICT OF INTERPRETATION ON ELIOT

The conflict of interpretations on T. S. Eliot has reached an impasse.[1] The first reception of Eliot as poet, critic, and thinker during his lifetime was one kind of exaggeration. Practically everything he then said (no matter how confused or foolish) was either explained away or placed on tablets of stone for further "New Critical" reflection. The present widespread rejection of Eliot is just as exaggerated: every foolish act, every obnoxious opinion (even if later repudi-

---

1. This essay, originally delivered at Northwestern University and later at Boston College, is the result of a course I had the honor to teach with David Grene.

ated), is taken as the signal clue to his person and his work. What is lost in all this conflict is the poetry itself — that is, the one reality that should concentrate any reader's attention, the one phenomenon that made Eliot one of the greatest poets of the twentieth century. The poetry, not the criticism, not the private person, is what most needs new modes of reflection, new openness, new readings. Otherwise it will be lost in the contemporary conflict of ideological interpretations, from which there can seem to be no honorable exit for any thinker or poet who, like Eliot, believed in and tried to show another dimension of reality (sometimes called a religious or spiritual dimension). That dimension, to be sure, can imply but is not reducible to the ideologies affecting it.

Eliot's critical writings, sometimes brilliant and sometimes wrongheaded, are not the key to the one great mystery of Eliot: the greatness of his poetry — its range from "Prufrock" through *Four Quartets*; its multiple voices; its auditory genius; and its effortless ability to reach beyond all one's views about T. S. Eliot the man and the formerly influential opinion-maker. In my judgment, anyone with an ear for the peculiar, plural rhythms of the English language cannot reject Eliot's poetry. Anyone with any taste at all for the poetics of the spirit in the twentieth century, a century so tentative, restless, and violent, senses the integrity of the spiritual and philosophical aspects of Eliot's poetry. His best thinking is not in his criticism (although some of that remains very good indeed). Eliot's best thinking is in his poetry. It *is* the poetry.

It is impossible to understand Lucretius as the great poet-philosopher he is without knowing how to unite his full-fledged materialism to the noble journey of the Epicurean way. It is impossible to understand Dante without sensing something of the rational, formal spirituality of his exceptional vision of medieval Christianity. It is equally impossible to understand T. S. Eliot without some sense of how his spiritual vision (mainly Christian, but also Platonist and Buddhist) does not close in upon itself into a narrow dogmatic view of religion and culture (as do a few of his essays). Rather, Eliot's poetry opens up into a grounded spiritual vision of multiplicity, subtlety, and tentativeness. Not to understand how materialism can be an integral view of all reality is not to understand either the poetry or the thought (more exactly, the poetry *as* thought) of Lucretius (whom Eliot, it should be recalled, admired). To understand only materialism as an adequate view of life is to hinder one's understanding of Dante, Eliot, W. B. Yeats, and so many other poets. In any case, we impoverish our experience foolishly under some rubric of what constitutes the "really real" — the one thing, as Nabokov insisted, that should always be enclosed in quotation marks. Eliot came to full maturity as a poet and thinker in *Four Quartets*. There we find how a twentieth-century poetics of the spirit informed — indeed, *trans*formed — by an enormous range of Western and non-Western religious and philosophical ideas came to be rendered plausible for any honest, open mind. In that sublime poetry is Eliot's artistic and religious integrity.

There is need, therefore, to reconsider what kind of religious thinker T. S. Eliot actually was. This need can be pressing, since so many of Eliot's interpreters and some of his own more doctrinal essays, have contributed to a reading of him as simply a conservative Christian apologist — more complex and subtle in his strategies and thoughts than C. S. Lewis and Hilaire Belloc to be sure, but in the same stream of Christian doctrinal and apologetic tradition. No matter that Lewis and Eliot both resisted this reading of the common Christian stance. Nevertheless, it has become a commonplace both of Eliot's critics and of some of Lewis's admirers (e.g., Dale 1988). Eliot has also been read as a finer, more subtle, less comically paradoxical Christian apologetic thinker than G. K. Chesterton, with Chesterton's inimitable, delightful, charming version of Christian orthodoxy. Eliot strongly resisted Chesterton's too-joyful reading of Christianity, just as Chesterton always maintained a wide distance from Eliot's too-modernist and, for Chesterton, too-bleak version of Christianity.

My own belief is that Eliot's greatest religious poetry, *Four Quartets*, firmly establishes his position as a major modern religious thinker — not a version of Christian apologetics at all but something quite other. Indeed, *Four Quartets*, although as deeply Christian in sensibility as they are exceptionally musical in tonality even for Eliot's often praised auditory imagination, render a version of religious thought that is deeply Christian but also sometimes closer to ancient Neoplatonism, at times even to Buddhism than it is to traditionalist Christian orthodoxy. The final vision of *Four Quartets* — the vision of annunciation and incarnation — is profoundly Christian. But the form of that Christian thought in its amazing Neoplatonic vision of God as both personal and impersonal, bears more resemblance to the thought of that other great and troubled Christian thinker and contemporary of Eliot — Simone Weil — than it does to that of either Chesterton or Lewis. More puzzling still is its dissimilarity to the arbitrarily other T. S. Eliot of some of the early, pointedly polemical essays — especially the exclusionary, anti-Semitic *After Strange Gods* (1943) or the more inclusive but rather narrow visions of Christianity in *The Idea of a Christian Society* (1939), or *Thoughts after Lambeth* (1931).

We have, then, no small puzzle: the most famous explicitly Christian poet in Anglo-American literature since Gerard Manley Hopkins and Christina Rossetti is not what many critics or admirers or, perhaps, Eliot himself believed that he was. In my judgment, Eliot (in *Four Quartets* specifically, but not in the essays and not even in that other major Christian poem *Ash Wednesday*) presents something richer, stronger, indeed altogether more unsettling for any thoughtful reader than most interpretations of his religious thought suggest.

To call the poet Eliot a thinker is not to deny his insistence that his mentor Dante taught him to find spatial forms for time and to make words "sensuous embodiments" of ideas (Eliot 1950a, 199–241). *Four Quartets*, more than any other of his poems or plays, realizes this best. Dante also taught Eliot how to see poetry not as a replacement for intellection (including doctrines as abstract summaries of thought) but as a profound intellectual aid for any reader or listener. In other words, through Dante's example, T. S. Eliot could attune his readers to feel and realize what believing some doctrine or abstract thought felt like. This almost tactile, experiential, felt knowledge is indeed pure Eliot — and, to be sure, an all-important aspect of Dante himself. There are, however, certain other realities to be noted if one is to sense how Eliot in *Four Quartets*, without ever breaking Dante's basic rubrics, freed both himself and his readers not only to *feel* thought but to *think through* his poetry.

The first reality is Eliot's inheritance from both Dante and Donne: meditative poetry (as distinct from such splendid devotional poetry as that of George Herbert) helps the poet to render and the reader/listener to sense how poetry can evoke abstract thought once poetry finds an appropriate poetic form (as in Dante's pictorial form; as in the musical form of *Four Quartets*). For Eliot, Dante has the good fortune to write before the modern dissociation of sensibility; that is, before the seventeenth-century split between feeling and thought, with which Eliot (here joining many countermoderns and postmoderns alike) charged Enlightenment modernity (Eliot 1950b, 247–48).

The second rubric for understanding Eliot's poetry as religious thought is his reading of how a poet can function best once the modern split had occurred. Recall Eliot's recovery of a poetics of detachment and impersonality, as well as his affirmation of the metaphysical poets, the French symbolists, and his fellow modernists, especially Joyce and Pound. The modern symbolists and literary modernists were Eliot's principal modern poetic models, just as Dante was his great premodern mentor. For Eliot, metaphysical poetry "elevates sense for a moment to regions ordinarily attainable only by abstract thought." That is exactly what purely devotional poetry rarely does and what *Four Quartets* quintessentially enacts for the reader. Eliot possessed a sensitive and deeply intellectual temperament. He was, after all, a very well-educated philosopher and a self-educated Anglican theologian.

Eliot learned from Mallarmé that poetry could never replace the absence of mystical experience nor the complex thought attendant upon that experience. However, by evoking a feeling of the absence of a mystical experience of God and by provoking the feelings that abstract religious thought allows (including the abstractions of the great fourteenth-century English mystics), Eliot, both poet and religious thinker, went as far as any twentieth-century poet in the English-speaking world has ever done to evoke and provoke both ancient and new, both Eastern and Western spiritual thinking. *Ash Wednesday* is a truly great poem based on traditional Christian imagery and thought. However, *Four Quartets* is something else again. Much of its power lies not only in the wondrously musical rhythms and leitmotivs of the sections within each quartet and their brilliant Dantesque use of words and images as sensuous embodiments of often highly abstract thoughts on time, history, and eternity, but also in the poems' odd, puzzling, unsettling, often untraditional, but eminently thoughtful, complex religious vision.

To understand Eliot's thought as *religious* thought more fully, I propose the following strategy. First, I recall how, in "Burnt Norton," notes of religious thinking enter, which, although not unfamiliar to Christian orthodoxy, are marginal to it, even somewhat destabilizing to orthodox belief. The moment in the rose garden of "Burnt Norton" is the first, and perhaps even the central "unattended moment" in the *Quartets*. These are moments of intuition of another dimension to time which happens in and out of time: timeless intuitions of temporal reality that can be recollected only in time.

It is striking that the central imagery of the entire crucial passage in the rose garden in "Burnt Norton" is, through and through, Buddhist, not Christian. One cannot but recall that Eliot, as a young man, almost became Buddhist, save, as he later recalled, "for reasons practical and sentimental." In terms of an explicit religious way, Eliot became a deeply committed Anglican Christian but without ever losing his sense of the genius and importance of Buddhism as a live option for a contemporary spiritual way. The subtle undertow of a kind of Buddhist transformation of consciousness that often pervades Eliot's poetry is present in the marvelous imagery of the rose garden scene in "Burnt Norton": the lotus, the clouds, the emptiness (*sunyata*) of the pool. These images function not as a direct Buddhist source or influence (like the Hindu "Fire Sermon" in *The Waste Land*), but as something far more important: a central vision, in keeping with Mahayana Buddhist teaching on formlessness as form — that the heart of reality is transience. Buddhism, after all, is the only religion or philosophy in which what is construed as the central problem for humankind (the transience of all reality) is also understood to be the central spiritual solution for all those who will cease craving and clinging to surrounding actualities or possibilities and let go into *sunyata*, the emptiness-fullness-transience of all reality. Most human beings (even many Buddhists) cannot achieve *nirvana*. "Humankind cannot bear very much reality." But there are always moments like these in the rose garden of "Burnt Norton," as well as many other unattended moments in *Four Quartets* (especially the "Third Quartet") to help us recall this other spiritual dimension of reality.

As Cleo McNelly Kearns persuasively argues,[2] Buddhism, for Eliot, was less a set of teachings than an extremely subtle method of transformation of consciousness that shifted all perception by its highly refined sense of how consciousness is transfigured by proper attention to the smallest particulars of experience — especially all unexpected, initially unattended experiences like that in the rose garden with the cloud and the full/empty pool. Eliot's imagery in the rose garden and the words, I suggest, are worthy of a Zen Buddhist Haiku. Eliot's images and words help one to sense — through close attention, awareness, and awakeness — how the clarifying, dissolving, fragmenting forms in the poem display the fundamental Buddhist thought that reality is emptiness (*sunyata*). Eliot's fine use of the Buddhist spiritual ways, not only of dissolving images but even fragmenting language itself, can be seen in the syntactic difficulty a reader has in asserting whether the pool is empty or full, the unclarity in the exact subject-verb-object structure of the sequence, the indefiniteness of all fixed identities ("they") in the scene. The startling power of Buddhist spiritual exercises, the suspicion of all false consolations as illusions to which we compulsively cling — Eliot renders this profound Buddhist insight as a felt thought through the fine imagery of the manifestation of nonbeing in the rose garden in "Burnt Norton." The rose may be the rose of Dante's *Paradiso*, and the chil-

---

2. Here, as throughout these reflections, I am indebted to Cleo McNelly Kearns (1987; 1994, 77–94), as well as to several other commentators, especially the sensitive and erudite commentary of Derek Traversi (1976, 85–215); A. David Moody (1979, 203–64); and Helen Gardner (1959, 1978).

dren in the trees may be the dead/alive children of Kipling's story "They" — but the voice is the voice of the Buddha.

This Mahayana Buddhist teaching of the spiritual practice of attention to "this here now," I am convinced, is what most attracted Eliot to Buddhist practices and doctrines. Moreover, Eliot found very precise images to entice any attentive reader to this awareness. Eliot's "still point of the turning world" passage in "Burnt Norton" is in harmony with Buddhist teaching on nonbeing, but even more suggestive of a different philosophical-spiritual vision of reality: the Heraclitean "coincidence of opposites" disclosed in the quotations from Heraclitus that introduce "Burnt Norton," as well as Eliot's nice transformation of the Mallarmé image ("Garlic and sapphires in the mud") to begin the next movement after the Neoplatonic "still point" passage. Indeed, only in this long movement of the poem does one reach the central image of "Burnt Norton" and perhaps of the entire *Quartets*: the still point of the turning world (Traversi 1976; Cornwell 1962, 17–64).

Eliot's imagery here cannot but alert the reader to Platonic thought when philosophically and theologically constructed through the moving imagery. The image, strictly speaking, is neither Buddhist nor Christian, although it does cohere with some versions of both Christianity (e.g., Gregory of Nyssa) and Buddhism. In fact, there is a clear, non-Buddhist insistence in Eliot (as in classical Platonism) on an ordered determinateness: order, balance, the ordered reconciliation of opposites. This Heraclitean-Platonic image still holds, but now in a still more explicitly ordered whole, far more reminiscent of the central role of form in Neoplatonism than of a Buddhist sense of radical formlessness, indeterminacy, nonbeing, emptiness.

Any reader — especially one aware of the explicitly Christian language of *Ash Wednesday*, as well as within the doctrinal orthodoxy of Eliot's essays and within *Four Quartets* itself, cannot miss the pervasive Christian sensibility and imagery culminating in the explicit language of "The hint half guessed, the gift half understood, is Incarnation." It would surely not be foolish to read the image of the still point in Christian theological terms. The impersonality of the image itself makes one hesitate to interpret the still point in only Christian terms (except, perhaps, those of Meister Eckhart). Indeed, the still point — this abstract spiritual center outside both the self and history — seems to be a strictly impersonal reality, one from which emanate all movement and pattern. Eliot's still point is, to be sure, the source of all energy, pattern, and movement, where opposites are reconciled (as in Heraclitus and most Neoplatonism). What the image is *not* is personal — unlike most interpretations of the Jewish, Christian, or Islamic personal God.

I do not claim, of course, that Eliot's impersonal center, this still point, cannot be reconciled with some understanding of the Christian God. (The Christian Neoplatonists, in their various ways, attempted exactly that, no one more successfully than the daring Meister Eckhart.) But in "Burnt Norton," no such reconciliation occurs. Analogous to Iris Murdoch in her Platonized Buddhism and Simone Weil in her Platonized Christianity,[3] Eliot in "Burnt Norton" distances himself from conventional concepts of a personal deity and, perhaps, for the moment, from orthodox Christianity's personal categories for ultimate reality. Thus does the Eliot of *Four Quartets* leave the Eliot of most of his essays on Christianity far behind to join himself to the tradition of the apophatic Christian Platonist thinkers from Dionysius the Areopagite through John Scotus Eriugena, Marguerite Porete, and Meister Eckhart. This apophatic legacy is intensified rather than lessened when Eliot turns to the more explicitly Christian images of the later sections of *Four Quartets*. History itself — the divinely empowered heart of prophetic Judaism, Christianity, and Islam — becomes, for Eliot, a manifestation of "a pattern of timeless moments." In the later sections of *Four Quartets* ("Little Gidding," sec. 5), Eliot's religious thought in its now explicitly Christian form sometimes transforms itself into some vision just as puzzling and radical as that pervading the central images of "Burnt Norton" (the Buddhist imagery of the lotus, the pool, the emptiness, and the Heraclitean-Platonic imagery of the still point).

ELIOT'S RELIGIOUS IMAGINATION: MANIFESTATION AND MEDITATION

There are various ways to make useful distinctions among the most basic forms of religious expression.[4] When one is attempting to highlight the reality of the participation of human beings in the cosmos and, in Jewish, Christian, and

---

3. Murdoch 1993, esp. 80–90, 461–92; Veto 1994. A study is needed of the possible influence of Weil on Eliot here.

4. I have clarified and defended these distinctions in writing elsewhere, especially Tracy 1985, 1990.

Islamic faiths, in the relationship to God and history, the most basic distinction is that between religion as manifestation and religion as proclamation (Paul Ricoeur).

Religion as manifestation signifies the sense of radical participation of any person in the cosmos and in whatever is construed as the divine reality. A felt sense of God's radical immanence in cosmos, nature, and self is strong in Eliot. This sense of religion as manifestation is in sharp contrast to religion as proclamation. In the latter case (and the three great prophetic and monotheistic traditions of Judaism, Christianity, and Islam are all proclamation traditions at their religious hearts), a sense of God's transcendent, radically Other power is also a source of the divine disclosure as principally in history, not nature. Indeed, the proclamation traditions introduced a deeper sense of distance between God and human beings and a strong sense of an interruption of the once-powerful (indeed fundamental) sense of belonging to or radical participation in the cosmos and human deification.

In my judgment, the most intriguing aspect of Eliot's Christian view in his poetry is how Eliot's "religion as manifestation" instincts affect even his Christian view of history. In some of his best prose, Eliot displays a characteristically prophetic (i.e., proclamation) view of history — as in his fine essay on Joyce, where, prophet-like, he denounces contemporary history as "the immense panorama of futility and anarchy" (Eliot 1975, 177). Moreover, throughout *Four Quartets* — especially but not solely in the third movement of each quartet (except "Little Gidding") — Eliot continues the imagery of *The Waste Land* on history as chaotic, anarchic, and possibly futile. And yet *Four Quartets* as a whole (which, after all, clearly bears the marks of the cataclysmic events of World War II, including Eliot's own activities as a warden during the London Blitz) shows a more manifestation-oriented understanding of religion, and even of history. It is not merely that the Western, indeed Eurasian, cultural tradition becomes more unified and ordered for Eliot in *Four Quartets*; neither the fragmented vision of *The Waste Land* nor the narrow orthodoxy of such essays as *After Strange Gods* prevails.[5] Rather, in *Four Quartets*, history (now

---

5. It is true that Eliot never allowed *After Strange Gods* to be republished. It remains, nonetheless, a disgraceful performance — especially because of what can only be called its anti-Semitism. I agree fully with Cynthia Ozick's melancholy conclusion that "it is now our unsparing obligation to disdain the reactionary Eliot" (Ozick 1989, 154). On the debate on this troubling issue, see also Ricks 1988 and Scott 1994, 60–77.

seen in the context of the still point) becomes manifestation; that is, history as a pattern of timeless moments, not as a series of interruptive, prophetic-proclamatory movements.

This is clearly the case in the powerful Dantesque history-as-manifestation imagery of "Little Gidding" (especially the familiar compound-ghost of the fourth movement, which brilliantly unites Dante's *Purgatorio*, the London Blitz, and a good deal of English history). History is manifestation in both "East Coker" and "The Dry Salvages." In "East Coker," Eliot's personal time of a visit to this "sacred" place becomes the manifestation time of both solar time (the cycle of the seasons) and the biological time of a single human life. Time also becomes historical time, in which all cultures and movements rise and decay, the centuries pass, and, in memory *sub specie aeternitatis*, all historical actors and actions can unite in a theological sense of history. Charles I and Milton, the experiment of East Coker, Eliot's own English ancestors, and Eliot himself in his pilgrimage to East Coker: all now yield, at the last, not to the conflicts of their own historical moment but to the rhythm and stillness of history as a pattern of timeless moments in time. Moreover, in "The Dry Salvages," the archaic religious imagery displays another form of religion as manifestation, as well as Eliot's personal American history: the river as "within," the Mississippi of his St. Louis childhood, the sea all "around" us, the sea of the New England summers of his youth. The imagery of all these realities — indeed of all history — in *Four Quartets* is not finally Jewish-Christian prophetic proclamation (although that is real in *The Waste Land* and remains real at selective times even in *Four Quartets*, especially in the third movements of the first three *Quartets*). In *Four Quartets*, history becomes more a manifestation of timeless moments in time. In our beginning is our end; in our end, is our beginning.

Of course, the sense of participation in nature does not die in prophetic traditions, as the Jewish liturgical year, the Christian sacraments, and Islamic ritual make clear. However, the prophetic traditions, with their strong sense of God's transcendence allied to the powerful prophetic sense of an ethical responsibility to resist evil and face historical suffering, have their own ways of responding to evil, suffering, and hope (including straightforwardly ethical-political ways), as Eliot's essays *The Idea of a Christian Society* (1939) and *Notes towards the Definition of Culture* (1948) argued in largely prophetic, not meditative, terms.

Many indigenous religious traditions, however, have never lost the earlier religious sense of radical participation in nature and the cosmos. Those traditions — once named "pagan" by Jews, Christians, and Muslims — return to haunt the conscience, the always ethical conscience, of the prophetic, proclamation-oriented traditions, as they so brilliantly do in Eliot's imagery of the peasant "dancing around the bonfire" in the first movement of "East Coker" or the wonderful, archaic image of the Mississippi river as "a strong brown god — sullen, untamed and intractable" of the first movement of "The Dry Salvages."

Indeed, it is difficult to overemphasize the importance of such a religious sense of manifestation with its felt synthesis of the human, cosmic, and divine realms for most ancient and medieval thinkers and for the Eliot of *Four Quartets*. I agree fully with Louis Dupré in *Passage to Modernity* (1994) that the most important and widely overlooked consequence of modernity (which he persuasively dates as beginning as early as the nominalist crisis of the fourteenth century and the humanist developments of the fifteenth century) is the breakup of both the ancient and the medieval senses of a synthesis of God, self, and cosmos.[6]

Clearly all ancient and even most Jewish, Christian, and Islamic understandings of a felt synthesis of God, cosmos, and self (in contrast to Dupré's more intellectualist formulation) are principally religious expressions of participatory manifestation, not disruptive proclamation. The ancients may indeed have had a sense of cosmos that encompassed an understanding of the divine realm (the gods, even Zeus), as well as the human realm now understood as *microcosmos*, and of human reason as the Stoic *logos* participating in both the cosmic and the divine realms of *logos*. The ancient syntheses (notice again how *Four Quartets* begins with Heraclitus) were, one and all, felt syntheses of the dialectical relationality of the cosmos, the divine, and the self. Those syntheses were grounded in various forms of religion as manifestation — that is, in a sense of our radical participation in the cosmos.

Eliot saw clearly that the monotheistic traditions changed but never broke this ancient, "pagan" sense of a felt synthesis and the intrinsic relationality among God, self, and cosmos and the radical participation of the self in the cosmos and in God. The Christian doctrine of redemption and its focus on

---

6. I should note that the interpretations of modernity in this section of the text are my own interpretations of contemporary, post-Eliot debates on modernity. I believe this reading of the problematic of modernity to be in harmony with Eliot's reflections, but it is not his own more neoconservative reading. I have also noted in the text those places where I am explicitly interpreting Eliot himself on modernity. See chapter 10 on Dupré in this volume.

evil, suffering, and transformation do not prevail in *Four Quartets* (as they do in *The Waste Land*). Here again, following his principal mentor Dante, Eliot sees both the patristic and medieval periods (even aspects of Augustine) as being dominated by reflection — not on redemption, but on creation. How can any radically monotheistic tradition with its doctrine of a Creator God assume the continuance, in a new, transformed configuration, of a synthesis of God, self, and cosmos? Here was the great challenge of the patristic and medieval thinkers. On the whole they succeeded, and they never lost a sense of radical participation and ordered relationship — the sense I called above a sense of the felt synthesis of God, self, and cosmos.

Especially through Platonic resources, the medievals (even the champions of Aristotle, like Aquinas) managed to maintain God's radical immanence in nature and humanity without loss of God's transcendence. Recall, for example, the subtlety of medieval discussions not only of efficient causes but also of formal and final causes, as well as an understanding of causality lost in much modern thought, where only efficient causality is usually considered as causality. Recall, above all, how reason (*logos*) for the Christian thinkers like Anselm and Aquinas — and Augustine before them — was never equivalent to modern rationality. Reason for the ancients and medievals was ordinarily understood (and, it seems, experienced) as reason proving radically participatory in the cosmic and divine (note again Eliot's use of Heraclitus on the common *logos* of all humanity at the very beginning of *Four Quartets*). For most patristic and medieval theologians, the human being — including human reason as participatory *logos* — was still *microcosmos* (as for the ancients) as well as *imago dei* for the Christians. Reason was a profoundly participatory reality related to God, cosmos, and self. This patristic and medieval sense was kept alive in Eliot's Anglo-Catholic tradition, a Christian tradition centered on manifestation and meditation, sacrament, liturgy, and high culture.

Modernity changed all this. No synthesis — whether ancient or medieval — any longer held. As modernity advanced in its more scientific, seventeenth-century form and, even more so, its more reified, eighteenth-century form, the sense of any radical participation of humanity in an increasingly mechanized cosmos failed. Ancient *logos* and medieval *ratio* became modern rationality. According to Eliot, in one of his most famous formulations, the late seventeenth-century "dissociation of sensibility" (i.e., the separation of feeling and thought) set in. The medieval synthesis could not hold. Each element split away and was forced to function increasingly on its own. Cosmos became "nature" as science adopted a more and more dominating attitude toward it. Eliot, a fine interpreter of the British idealist philosopher F. H. Bradley, always distrusted scientism. For many modern thinkers, God withdrew from the synthesis into ever-greater transcendence and hiddenness. The self was divested of its former state as *microcosmos* and possessed increasingly vague memories of its reality as *imago dei*. The self became ever more purely autonomous, isolated from any sense of radical participation in the cosmos or any felt relationship to God as creator. Ancient and medieval reason-as-*logos* was cut off from the cosmos in any participatory sense. Moreover, the divine itself was relegated to a narrower and narrower range of what would count as rational and, thereby, real.

Consider, for example, the relative narrowness of most modern debates on rational approaches to God (i.e., what becomes the conflict of the "isms"): deism, modern theism and atheism, modern pantheism and panentheism. Whoever had the best set of rationally endorsed abstract propositions, backed by modern forms of argument, could be taken seriously on the question of God. It is no surprise that modernity's first major innovation here was the explicitly nonparticipatory notion of the God-self-world relationship named deism. Deism, in fact, was a halfway house to atheism, or what moderns named agnosticism. Certainly modernity was not simply a disaster on this crucial issue of reason as participatory in the cosmos and the divine. But consider the difficulties.

Understanding itself is not merely distinguished from but also separate from feeling and experience (again, Eliot's "dissociation of sensibility"). Theological rationality often separated itself from religious sentiment and communal religious experience (Buckley 1990); hence the import for Eliot of those forms of early modern religion that resisted this separation: the communal experiment of East Coker or Donne's metaphysical poetry, among others.

Second, the only form considered appropriate by some theologians for developing an authentically modern theology was the form of highly abstract modern theory: analytical definitions, rigorous logical argument, and, clear and distinct ideas. No other forms—certainly not the laments, the songs, the narratives of suffering peoples, like the magnificent spirituals and blues of African American culture and other premodern forms (especially those of oppressed peoples, which united spirituality and theology), the experiment with fragmenting forms of the great modernists, or, for that matter, scriptural forms themselves — were adequate, on this modern analytical reading, for a genuine theology. Neither Dostoevsky nor Dante, neither the biblical Ruth nor Job, need apply. They possessed the wrong form for modern theology.

Third, explicitly spiritual exercises — especially those developed, for example, by Origen, Gregory of Nyssa, or Augustine, to help transform the mind and cleanse the vision in order to understand suffering, evil, hope, and God — no longer found a place in the functioning of modern philosophical and theological rationality. At its (alas, not so rare) worst, modernity bequeathed us a mechanistic notion of the cosmos; a dominating attitude toward nature; an ever more narrow notion of rationality, culminating in positivism and scientism; an increasingly solely autonomous self become a possessive individualism; and a deistic God — sometimes a warm kind of deism, perhaps, but deism all the same. The prospects for any kind of modern theology that agreed with these aspects of modernity were not promising. For Eliot, unlike many "modern" Christian liberal apologists, the once-emancipatory hopes of modernity were clearly spent.

For Eliot, modern thought at its best (e.g., that of F. H. Bradley) made us realize that there is no turning back, in hopeless and intellectually helpless nostalgia, to a simple retrieval of any of the syntheses of the ancients or the medievals. Eliot was never, for example, a neo-Thomist philosophically, in spite of his admiration of Jacques Maritain. T. S. Eliot consistently held that the achievements of modernity — in science and technology, in democratic politics and cultural pluralism — should not be denied and should be strongly defended. And Eliot *did* defend them: not always, but at his most lucid and best moments. He was a typically responsible conservative thinker intractably opposed to both Fascism and Communism, especially in their usually antimodernist positions. Eliot knew that any response that religious thought might achieve in the contemporary world could be found only by moving through, not around modernity. Furthermore, Eliot always remained a literary modernist. He never joined C. S. Lewis or G. K. Chesterton in their antimodernist positions but continued with the other, now classical, great modernists (Joyce, Woolf, Proust, Pessoa) in their brilliant attempts at new forms and new, quiet hope: Joyce's "epiphany," Woolf's "luminous moments," Proust's "involuntary memories," Pessoa's pseudonyms, and Eliot's own "unattended moments." The Eliotic, moving "unattended moments" evoke attentiveness in any awake reader, even as they offer some alternative to the solely materialist and scientistic expressions that are, for many (perhaps most) modern thinkers, never equivalent to modern science, which Eliot, like all reasonable persons, unhesitatingly affirms.

PHILOSOPHY AND THEOLOGY AS WAYS
OF VISION AND WAYS OF LIFE

The most fragmented of the many fragments Eliot found to shore against our ruin was the modern self. For modern culture, the self serves simultaneously as the most privileged and the most fragmented of realities. The modern self's privilege also becomes its cul-de-sac; after the collapse of the ancient and medieval syntheses, all culture for Eliot suffered a dissociation of sensibility whose chief victim was the fragmented self—the complex, pluralistic, ambiguous self of the modern sensibility in too much modern thought. Not only is feeling separated from thought but so, too, is form from content and practice from theory. The Harvard professors William James and Josiah Royce were two major exceptions on the separation of practice and theory, just as Eliot's dissertation subject, F. H. Bradley, with his holistic Hegelianism and stylistic philosophy, was an exception to the separations of feeling from thought and form from (philosophical) content.[7] Indeed, perhaps one may suggest that Eliot's philosophical position was what today would be named hermeneutics.

T. S. Eliot's problem with philosophy lies deep: like Kierkegaard or Nietzsche, everything in Eliot resisted the professionalization of philosophy in the modern academy. He had no hesitation in embracing the professionalization of banking, in his work in a bank, without ever abandoning his multifaceted sociopolitical critique of the culture-leveling imposed by modern capitalism. Like most of us, Eliot acknowledged that banking must be professionalized to function well. He was, from all reports, a good banker. And yet Eliot resisted, with all the considerable cultural power he possessed in his lifetime, the professionalization of modern philosophy. He never resisted a philosophical insistence on precision, care, and conceptual clarity in either modern analytical philosophy (he admired that side of Bertrand Russell's logical atomism) or Aristotle, Aquinas, and all good forms of modern Scholasticism, like Jacques Maritain's. Eliot believed, as the ancients did, that philosophy was as much a

---

7. On Eliot's philosophy, see the helpful studies by Peal 1989 and Shusterman 1994, 31–48.

way of life as a way of thought. The professionalization of philosophy presents philosophy as a solely modern academic discipline. Philosophy as a guide to life, unlike among the ancients and unlike contemporary Buddhist philosophers (e.g., the Kyoto school), now lives an underground life, occasionally surfacing as a new philosophical "ism," as in the existentialism contemporary with Eliot.

Eliot wanted a philosophy as both an explanatory theory of reality and a vision of life that could unite feeling and thought again (Bradley) but could render that union in authentically realized ideas in poetry (Dante, the metaphysical poets, the modernists, the symbolists). T. S. Eliot desired all this, moreover, in a manner that reunited theory and practice, including such specific practices as the kinds of "spiritual exercises" that had become so central to his personal life. Instinctively, he turned to Plato, Lucretius, Dante, Donne, Hooker, and Andrews. Expansively, Eliot turned quite naturally to the "whole" Eurasian cultural context, ancient and modern, as he recalled his earlier scholarly immersion in Buddhism and Hinduism and his more recent study of archaic traditions by means of anthropology and history of religions, as well as his acquaintance with the Christian mystics, from Julian of Norwich to John of the Cross.

If Eliot were living now, he would surely have applauded the work of Pierre Hadot on the ancient philosophy as a way of life (Hadot 1995). Like the otherwise very different Michel Foucault, who also insisted that the modern self is at once privileged and fragmented by the modern cultural regime, Eliot would have welcomed Hadot's erudite studies of how all ancient philosophers (Stoic, Epicurean, Aristotelian, Platonist, Skeptic, and Cynic) practiced spiritual exercises (Hadot 1995, 79–145) in direct and correlative relationship to their philosophical theories. Not until modernity did Western philosophy split theory from such spiritual practices. Only in Western modernity did philosophy (aside from David Hume, Jean-Jacques Rousseau, Denis Diderot, and a few other Enlightenment thinkers) help reinforce the fragmentation of the modern self allied to the related split of form from content: systematic treatise has replaced philosophical dialogue in modern philosophy and, in the even more fatal analytical split of feeling from thought, feeling became merely private and emotivist.

This detour into Pierre Hadot's work is worth recalling if we care to understand T. S. Eliot's philosophical and theological achievement in *Four Quartets*. It is not just that Eliot enacts, as did his mentor Dante, how it feels to believe a particular religious doctrine. Eliot also incorporates in *Four Quartets* very diverse traditions of spiritual exercises (Buddhist, Hindu, Platonist, Christian, archaic, indigenous, secular) in order to reunite spiritual practice and philosophical, theological thought. By his poetic practice, therefore, T. S. Eliot helps his reader to realize his ideas by showing how philosophy-theology is *both* a vision of life *and* a way of life. Each spiritual and philosophical way demands rigorous, constant, full awareness and vigilant attentiveness, as well as purifying intellectual (e.g., mathematical) and moral exercises. Classical Christian doctrines (like "annunciation" and "incarnation") are marvelously realized poetically (in both thought and feeling) in *Four Quartets* not for apologetic reasons but to show, not merely state, how the Christian incarnational-sacramental vision is experienced by Christians as both a felt idea and a disciplined way of life. Eliot insisted throughout *Four Quartets* on a center outside of the self: in everyday glimpses of another dimension to reality; in his brilliant series of "unattended moments"; in the still point; in the impersonal imagery of Eliot's Buddhist, Hindu, Platonist, and Christian mystical resources allied to Christian personal incarnational imagery. Indeed, every one of the central images from "Burnt Norton" through "Little Gidding" frees the alert reader/listener both to see and to feel each of the many different forms of philosophy-theology T. S. Eliot so winningly relates. The "still point of the turning world" and "the hint half guessed, the gift half understood" (Incarnation) are, in *Four Quartets*, not one but, as Hindus say, perhaps not two either. Inclusivity of the religious vision, not exclusivity, reigns in T. S. Eliot's Christian poems far more than in his more exclusivist Christian essays.

The central and pervasive exercise of *Four Quartets*, however, is not to be found even in such crucial spiritual exercises as Buddhist detachment or Christian *caritas*. Eliot displays both detachment and *caritas* as visions of life and ways of life through all the marvelous musical, visual, and verbal means at his disposal. He manifests the final vision of "Little Gidding" where the Fire and the Rose are one, just as Dante manifested in *Paradiso* that the Christian vision and the way of love are one, or just as a classic Japanese Zen haiku displays the two great Buddhist virtues, detachment and compassion. And yet *Four Quartets* teaches another sharp lesson: the fear that to insist on experiencing love and detachment here would be to "hope for the wrong thing" ("East Coker," sec. 3). On the contrary, "The only wisdom we can hope to acquire / Is the wisdom of humility: humility is endless" ("East Coker," sec. 2). And humility, for T. S. Eliot, was the most important spiritual exercise we late arrivals at any form of spirituality can learn to practice, if we too would understand and experience classical philosophies and religions at all—that is, as spiritual dimensions of life. T. S. Eliot was both a poetic genius and a genuinely humble man.

In *Four Quartets*, and there alone, Eliot forged a contemplative poetry worthy of comparison with his beloved principal mentor, Dante. But Eliot achieved this vision not in the premodern terms of Dante but in the modernist forms of Eliot's own twentieth century, that century at once so horrifying and so luminous. After *Four Quartets*, Eliot wrote no further major religious and philosophical poetry. His best religious thought—his splendid Anglican inclusivity; his moving, religious, philosophically expansive, pluralistic range—can best be found in *Four Quartets*. *Four Quartets* concentrates our attention upon a kind of religious thought that can make great sense to many of us today: great artistry evocative of a genuine experience of both an aesthetic and a spiritual dimension to life, united to a philosophy that helps one reflect critically upon and find plausible the actuality of that other dimension to life, which both religion and art disclose in their different but related ways. Heraclitus and the Buddha, Plato and Dante, and many others communicate all this. So too does T. S. Eliot in the wondrous power of *Four Quartets*.

REFERENCES

Buckley, Michael. 1990. *At the Origins of Modern Atheism*. New Haven, CT: Yale University Press.

Cornwell, Ethel F. 1962. *The "Still Point."* New Brunswick, NJ: Rutgers University Press.

Dale, Alzina Stone. 1988. *T. S. Eliot: The Philosopher Poet*. Wheaton, IL: Harold Shaw.

Dupré, Louis. 1994. *Passage to Modernity*. New Haven, CT: Yale University Press.

Eliot, T. S. 1939. *The Idea of a Christian Society*. London: Faber and Faber.

———. 1948. *Notes towards the Definition of Culture*. New York: Harcourt, Brace.

———. 1950a. "Dante." In *Selected Essays: New Edition*. New York: Harcourt, Brace, and World. Orig. pub. 1929.

———. 1950b. "The Metaphysical Poets." In *Selected Essays: New Edition*. New York: Harcourt, Brace, and World.

———. 1975. "Ulysses, Order and Myth." In *Selected Prose of T. S. Eliot*, edited by Frank Kermode. New York: Farrar, Straus and Giroux.

Gardner, Helen. 1959. *The Art of T. S. Eliot*. New York: Dutton.

———. 1978. *The Composition of "Four Quartets."* New York: Oxford University Press.

Hadot, Pierre. 1995. *Philosophy as a Way of Life.* Edited and with an introduction by Arnold Davidson. Oxford: Blackwell.

Kearns, Cleo McNelly. 1987. *T. S. Eliot and Indic Traditions: A Study in Poetry and Belief.* Cambridge: Cambridge University Press.

———. 1994. "Religion, Literature, and Society in the Work of T. S. Eliot." In Moody 1994.

Moody, A. David. 1979. *Thomas Stearns Eliot, Poet.* Cambridge: Cambridge University Press.

———, ed. 1994. *The Cambridge Companion to T. S. Eliot.* Cambridge: Cambridge University Press.

Murdoch, Iris. 1993. *Metaphysics as a Guide to Morals.* London: Penguin.

Ozick, Cynthia. 1989. "T. S. Eliot at 101." *New Yorker,* November, 119–54.

Peal, Jeffery. 1989. *Skepticism and Modern Enmity.* Baltimore: Johns Hopkins University Press.

Ricks, Christopher. 1988. *T. S. Eliot and Prejudice.* London: Faber.

Scott, Peter Dale. 1994. "The Social Critic and His Discontents." In Moody 1994.

Shusterman, Richard. 1994. "Eliot as Philosopher." In Moody 1994.

Tracy, David. 1985. *The Analogical Imagination.* New York: Crossroad.

———. 1990. *Dialogue with the Other.* Leuven, Belgium: Peeters Press.

Traversi, Derek. 1976. *T. S. Eliot: The Longer Poems.* New York: Harcourt Brace.

Veto, Miklos. 1994. *The Religious Metaphysics of Simone Weil.* Albany: State University of New York Press.

ACKNOWLEDGMENTS

For their encouragement to publish: Donald Burgo, Wendy Doniger, Franklin Gamwell, Kevin Hart, Hans Küng, Jean-Luc Marion, Gaspar Martinez, Bernard McGinn, Françoise Meltzer, Adriaan Peperzak, Richard Rosengarten, and Bernard Rubin.

For their critical readings: John McCarthy and Cyril O'Regan.

For their critical encouragement over many years: Maria Clara Bingemer, James Buchanan, Carolyn Chau, Peter Conley, Hugh Corrigan, Paul D'Andrea, Anthony Godzieba, Franz Gruber, Eric Holzwarth, Werner Jeanrond, Julius-Kei Kato, Steven Kepnes, Joseph Komonchak, Julia Lamm, Frederick and Sue Lawrence, Richard Liddy, Martin Marty, Patricia McGinn, Alejandro Nava, Stephanie Nelson, Elias O'Brien, Stephen Okey, Barnabas Palfrey,

Jennifer Rike, Francis and Elisabeth Schüssler Fiorenza, Mark Shacklette, Susan Shapiro, Dennis Sheehan, Andreas Telser, Zoran Turza, Bengt Uggla, Ellen Wondra, and many others.

Above all, for their extraordinary editorship: Alan Thomas, Randy Petilos, Christine Schwab, and Nicholas Murray.

For all their welcome aid: Thomas Levergood, John Buchmann, and Bonny McLaughlin.

And to the many individuals who commented on the individual lectures and articles in their original settings, as well as many acquaintances, friends, students, conversation partners, and critics not mentioned above.

To all, my profound thanks.

I also wish to thank the following institutions, editors, and publishers for the chance to think through the ideas in these essays, in earlier form, first as lectures and later in the pages of their publications. The essays have been revised with corrections, clarifications, and necessary additions but remain substantially the same.

Chapter 1 was presented as a lecture at the University of Chicago and at St. Vincent de Paul Seminary, Boynton Beach, Florida, and was published in *Augustine Our Contemporary: Examining the Self in Past and Present*, ed. Willemien Otten and Susan E. Schreiner (Notre Dame, IN: University of Notre Dame Press, 2018).

Chapter 2 was presented as a lecture at Fordham University and was published in *Orthodox Readings of Augustine*, ed. George E. Demacopoulos and Aristotle Papanikolaou (Crestwood, NY: St. Vladimir's Seminary Press, 2008), used with permission.

Chapter 3 was published in *Rethinking Trinitarian Theology: Disputed Questions and Contemporary Issues in Trinitarian Theology*, ed. Giulio Maspero and Robert Wozniak (Edinburgh: T & T Clark International, 2012), used by permission of Bloomsbury Publishing Plc.

Chapter 4 was presented as a lecture at Wabash College, Crawfordsville, Indiana, and was published in *Luther Refracted: The Reformer's Ecumenical Legacy*, ed. Piotr Malysz and Derek R. Nelson (Philadelphia: Fortress Press, 2015).

Chapter 5 was published in *Heavenly Bodies: Fashion and the Catholic Imagination*, by Andrew Bolton (New York: The Metropolitan Museum of Art, 2018), © 2018 The Metropolitan Museum of Art, reprinted by permission.

Chapter 6 was published in *The New Republic*, April 26, 2004.

Chapter 7 was published in *Commonweal* 111 (April 20, 1984). For more information, visit http://www.commonwealmagazine.org.

Chapter 8 was presented as a lecture at the Paul Tillich Archive, New Harmony, Indiana, and was published in *The Thought of Paul Tillich*, ed. James Luther Adams, Wilhelm Pauck, and Roger Lincoln Shinn (San Francisco: HarperCollins, 1985), © 1985 American Academy of Arts and Sciences, reprinted by permission of HarperCollins Publishers.

Chapter 9 was presented as a lecture at Boston College and was published in *Lonergan Workshop* 10, ed. Fred Lawrence (Boston: Boston College, 1994).

Chapter 10 was presented as a lecture at Harvard University and was published in *Christian Spirituality and the Culture of Modernity: The Thought of Louis Dupré*, ed. Peter J. Casarella and George P. Schner (Grand Rapids, MI: Wm. B. Eerdmans, 1998).

Chapter 11 was presented as a lecture at the University of Chicago, February 4, 2011.

Chapter 12 was published in *The Thomist* 49 (July 1985): 460–72.

Chapter 13 was presented as a lecture at the University of Notre Dame and was published in *Counter-experiences: Reading Jean-Luc Marion*, ed. Kevin Hart (Notre Dame, IN: University of Notre Dame Press, 2007).

Chapter 14 was published in *Journal of Feminist Studies in Religion* 7, no. 1 (Spring 1991): 122–25.

Chapter 15 was published as the foreword to *The Tremendum: A Theological Interpretation of the Holocaust* (New York: Crossroad, 1981).

Chapter 16 was presented as a lecture at the University of Notre Dame and was published in *The Option for the Poor in Christian Theology*, ed. Daniel G. Groody (Notre Dame, IN: University of Notre Dame Press, 2007).

Chapter 17 was presented as a lecture at the University of Chicago and was published in *Black Faith and Public Talk: Critical Essays on James H. Cone's "Black Theology and Black Power,"* ed. Dwight N. Hopkins (Waco, TX: Baylor University Press, 1999), © 2007, reprinted by permission of Baylor University Press.

Chapter 18 was presented as a lecture at the University of Notre Dame and was published in *The Critical Spirit: Theology at the Crossroads of Faith and Cul-*

ture, ed. Andrew Pierce and Geraldine Smyth (Dublin: Columba Books, 2003).

Chapter 19 was presented as a lecture at the Bibliothèque nationale de France, Paris, and was published in *Christian Platonism: Simone Weil*, ed. Emmanuel Gabellieri and François L'Yvonnet (Paris: Les Cahiers de l'Herne, 2014).

Chapter 20 was presented as a lecture at the University of Chicago and was published in *Iris Murdoch and the Search for Human Goodness*, ed. Maria Antonaccio and William Schweiker (Chicago: University of Chicago Press, 1996), © 1996 by The University of Chicago, all rights reserved.

Chapter 21 was presented as a lecture at Boston College and was published in *Literary Imagination, Ancient and Modern: Essays in Honor of David Grene*, ed. Todd Breyfogle (Chicago: University of Chicago Press, 1999), © 1999 by The University of Chicago, all rights reserved.

INDEX OF NAMES

Page numbers in italics refer to figures.

10, 34, 60, 61, 86–87, 138; and original sin, 10–11, 38, 39, 46, 55, 56–57, 181, 199, 386, 387; overdetermined model of self, 19–20, 40–41, 43, 61; pastoralism, 39, 82–85; on Paul, 23, 34, 46, 82; and Pelagius, 28, 36–37, 151, 152; as philosopher and artist, 415; and philosophy for all, 24; Platonism, 386; and power of music, 31; and reason, 434; reception of, 61, 71–73; and *regio dissimilitudinis*, 99; relationships to Plotinus and Porphyry, 23, 69; as rhetorician, 26–28, 72; on salvation of all, 149; and self as *deinos* and *daimon*, 60; sermons and letters, 39, 68, 82–84; sin-grace paradigm, 10, 19, 34–42, 41–42, 60, 87, 100, 108, 383, 384, 409n13; and sin-saturated self, 34, 36–37, 41–42; and St. Anthony, 60; theocentrism and Christomorphism, 11, 74–86, 86; and *theosis*, 156; as thinker-artist, 26, 68, 368; and tragedy-grace paradigm, 19, 42–61, 397; Trinitarian analogy of God, 71; underdeveloped pneumatology, 77, 86; and Virgil and Homer, 45, 46; will, concepts of, 19, 28–34. *See also* Augustine of Hippo, works of

Augustine of Hippo, works of: *The Bondage of the Will*, 36, 71n1; *The City of God*, 10, 27, 45, 53, 69, 138, 198–99, 343; *Confessions*, 10, 20–22, 28, 28n4, 29–30, 35, 45, 69, 71, 89, 98; *Contra Julianum* (*Opus Imperfectum*), 38n7; *De civitate Dei*, 82; *De doctrina christiana*, 33, 52; *De libero arbitrio*, 21, 28; *De Magistro*, 84; *De sermone Domini in monte*, 81–82; *De Trinitate*, 10, 11, 21, 22, 23, 27, 69, 73, 76, 78, 82, 126, 127, 138, 181, 190, 386; early dialogical writings from Cassiciacum and Thagaste, 22–23, 47, 70; *Enarratio-*

nes in Psalmos, 27, 45, 46, 77, 78, 82, 85, 88–90, 141; *In evangelium Ioannis tractatus*, 82; *On Free Will*, 71n1; polemical texts, 38–40, 69, 86; *Retractions*, 28, 70, 73, 386; *Tractatus in epistolam Ioannis*, 82

Austen, Jane, 29, 151, 245

Bacon, Francis, 241
Badiou, Alain, 247
Bakhtin, Mikhail, 40
Baldwin, James, 355
Balthasar, Hans Urs von, 2, 13, 167, 188, 217, 247, 305; *analogia caritatis*, 16, 105; on Augustine's *De vera religione*, 72; critical response to Nygren's attack on Augustine, 33; defense of Dionysian tradition, 300–301; on form, 260, 262; and love-centered theology, 96; and Plato and Platonism, 406; and Rahner, 130, 187, 244; refusal of contemporary theologians to read, 216; and *ressourcement* theology, 12, 81, 299, 303; on separation of theology and spirituality in Western Christian theologies, 4, 6, 11; and theology of the Cross, 301; and tragedy, 47, 51; and Trinity, 383; and universal salvation, 150

Balzac, Honoré de, 245
Bañez, Domingo, 130, 190
Barth, Karl, 2, 33, 187, 189; and *analogia fidei*, 105; on analogical knowledge, 138; on Anselm, 104; on Catholic theology, 223n13; *Church Dogmatics*, 157n18, 216, 217, 290; criticism of Schleiermacher, 243–44; and doctrine of predestination, 150; and eschatology, 219n5; as fragmentary writer, 73; and German Expressionist theology, 199; Lindbeck and, 290; and Luther's hiddenness of God, 154,

Barth, Karl (*continued*)
161; and Plato, 404; and Protestant neo-
Orthodoxy, 188, 198, 289, 303; refusal of
contemporary theologians to read, 216;
response to Nygren's attack on Augustine, 33; and sin-grace paradigm, 10; and
theory of election, 157n18; and Tillich,
130; and tragedy, 47, 51; and universal
salvation, 150
Basil of Caesarea (Basil the Great), 77, 248,
305, 309, 395
Bataille, Georges, 150–51, 253, 357, 387, 392,
401
Baudelaire, Charles, 71, 253, 372
Baum, Gregory, 12, 312, 335
Bayer, Oswald, 138n3, 146, 154n16
Belloc, Hilaire, 425
Bellow, Saul, 245, 415
Benedict XVI (pope), *Deus Est Caritas*, 33
Benjamin, Walter, 359, 377, 379; and historicist consciousness, 332; and the
metaphor of "fragments," 253, 356; and
tragedy, 47, 49; and *Trauerspiel*, 50, 71;
and works of barbarism, 195, 337
Berdyaev, Nikolai, 48, 50, 51
Bergman, Ingmar, 151
Berkeley, George, 240, 241
Berlin, Isaiah, 197
Bernard of Clairvaux, 2, 16, 77, 94–95, 122;
Commentary on the Song of Songs, 98,
127; obsession with Abelard, 95, 127–
28; poetic-rhetorical style, 26, 97, 98,
107; theologian of love, 33, 95–96, 116,
128; and twelfth-century monastic the-
ology, 14, 95, 96
Bernini, Gian Lorenzo, 17, 167
Bernstein, Richard, 337
Biel, Gabriel, 157
Bielfeldt, Dennis, 159
Bingemer, Maria Clara, 12, 17, 308, 313, 318

Blake, William, 73, 372
Blanchot, Maurice, 118n25, 303, 392
Bloch, Ernst, 219n5
Blumenberg, Hans, *The Legitimacy of the
Modern Age*, 239, 241, 252, 253, 259,
260
Boehme, Jakob, 333
Boethius, 2, 16–17, 105, 182
Boff, Leonardo, 12, 318
Bolton, Andrew, 15, 17
Bonaventure, Saint, 2, 77, 104, 216, 305;
and analogical imagination, 16, 182; and
Anselm, 129; and Aristotelian logic,
158; and Augustine, 33, 100; Balthasar
on, 406; and Bernard of Clairvaux, 96;
distinctions rather than separations of
theory from practice, 6, 12, 80, 94, 96,
120; and form, 240; and the Good as
principal name for God, 301, 405; high
Scholasticism, 189; *Itinerarium men-
tis in Deum*, 13, 80, 94; love-centered
theology, 96, 129; as mendicant in the
world, 120, 121; and mysticism, 122
Bonhoeffer, Dietrich, 151, 418n34
Bonino, José, 289
Bonner, Gerald, 36
Booth, Wayne, 293
Bornkamm, Heinrich, 144n11
Botticelli, Sandro, 17
Bouchard, Lawrence, 47, 51
Bouyer, Louis, 12, 13, 16, 188, 247
Boyle, Marjorie O'Rourke, 153
Braaten, Carl E., 74
Bradley, F. H., 372, 435, 437, 438
Brague, Rémi, 13, 247
Brandeis, Louis, 197
Brecht, Martin, 144n11
Bresson, Robert, 182
Brontë, Emily, 151
Brontë sisters, 29, 245

Brown, Peter, *Augustine of Hippo*, 37, 39, 73, 83, 90, 110, 407

Browning, Robert, 246

Bruno, Giordano, 180; early modern synthesis, 252, 254, 257, 259, 265; and form, 240

Buber, Martin, 16, 331, 333

Buckley, Michael, 298–99

Bulgakov, Sergei, 16, 47, 48, 51, 216, 303

Bultmann, Rudolf, 2, 33, 189, 289; and apocalyptic language, 343, 348; and eschatology, 219n5; and "kerygmatic word," 211; Lindbeck on, 243; and modern Protestant theological tradition, 188

Burckhardt, Jacob, 255

Burnaby, John, 33

Burrell, David, 256, 292

Byatt, A. S., 415n25

Byron, George Gordon, 30

Cahill, Lisa Soule, 12

Cajetan, Thomas, 146, 168, 189

Calderón, Pedro, 17, 49, 50, 54, 60

Calvin, John, 2, 41, 67, 77, 141, 198, 215, 216; and Augustine, 35, 72; and Bernard of Clairvaux, 94, 96; on doctrine of providence, 152; and double predestination, 36, 144, 149, 150, 152; on the Eucharist, 147; experiences of *Anfechtungen*, 151; and form, 240; and reason, 36; and sin-grace paradigm, 10, 100, 384; *To a Certain Useless Person*, 147

Câmara, Dom Hélder, 318, 319

Camus, Albert, 50, 145, 150, 178, 246, 367

Cannon, Katie, *Black Womanist Ethics*, 320, 321

Caputo, John, 388

Caravaggio, Michelangelo Merisi da, 17, 167

Carlstadt, Andreas Rudolf Bodenstein von, 146

Carmichael, Stokely, 316

Carr, Anne, 308

Carraud, Vincent, 299, 300

Cassirer, Ernst, 252, 259–60

Cavell, Stanley, 50, 290

Celsus, 142

Certeau, Michel de, 123

Cézanne, Paul, 75

Chan, Stephen, 318

Chantraine, Georges, 153

Charles I, 432

Chaucer, Geoffrey, 17

Chekhov, Anton, 40

Chenu, Marie-Dominique, 12, 299

Chesterton, G. K., 148, 425, 436

Chopp, Rebecca, 243

Chrétien, Jean-Louis, 247, 277, 300

Chrysostom, Saint John, 26

Cicero, 70, 204, 394, 395

Clare of Assisi, 344

Clark, Katerina, 40

Clark, Kenneth, 18

Claudel, Paul, 17

Clement of Alexandria, 106, 248, 305, 314

Coakley, Sarah, 16, 277, 308

Cobb, John, 16, 74, 242, 243

Cohen, Arthur, 309–12, 329–35; and "caesura" through the power of the *tremendum*, 330; and demand for new theological language to address the Holocaust, 330–31, 333–35; and historical theology, 332; and Jewish traditions of negative theology, 311; *The Myth of the Judeo-Christian Tradition*, 310; *The Natural and the Supernatural Jew*, 310; novels of, 310, 333; and post-Holocaust thought in contemporary Jewish theology, 332–34; retrieval of Rosenzweig and Schelling, 333; *The Tremendum*, 310–12, 329

Cohen, Herman, 16

Coleridge, Samuel Taylor, 16

Collins, Mary, 12

Colonna, Vittoria, 18

Cone, Cecil, 317

Cone, James, 315–22, 351; *Black Theology and Black Power*, 316, 320, 357; and class analysis, 319; and intensity of religious experiences of African American churches, 354; and international conferences of liberation theologians, 317–18; *Martin and Malcolm and America*, 320, 357, 361; *My Soul Looks Back*, 317; social analysis and liberationist theology, 320; *The Spirituals and the Blues*, 317, 357; theological essays using fragments and fragmentary form, 360, 361, 363; and womanist theological critics, 320

Congar, Yves, 12, 81, 188, 247, 299

Conradi, Peter J., 415n25

Contarini, Cardinal Gasparo, 18

Copeland, Shawn, 322

Copernicus, 259, 260

Coppola, Francis Ford, 182

Coreth, Emerich, 12, 404

Corneille, Pierre, 17, 54, 381

Cornford, F. M., 412n22

Cornwell, Ethel F., 429

Correggio, Antonio Allegri da, 194

Crétien, Jean-Louis, 13

Cusanus. *See* Nicholas of Cusa

Cyprian, 48

Dale, Alzina Stone, 425

Daniélou, Jean, 12, 13, 32n5, 81, 188, 247

Dante Alighieri, 17, 27, 119, 172, 258, 424, 438; on Aristotle, 276, 284; and Augustine's interpretation of will as love, 31, 33; Balthasar on, 406; and Christianity as a *commedia*, 50; and *Divine Comedy*, 182; and form, 265; and modern theology, 436; *Paradiso*, 428, 439; *Purgatorio*, 432; and salvation through Christ, 168

Day, Dorothy, 319–20, 358

de Beauvoir, Simone, 180, 246

Déchanet, Jean-Marie, 121

de Gaulle, Charles, 366

Deleuze, Gilles, 118, 247, 354, 368, 403

Deloria, Vine, Jr., *We Talk, You Listen*, 319

de Man, Paul, 72, 293

Denifle, Heinrich, 144n11

Derrida, Jacques, 88, 247; and the apocalyptic, 347; critique of onto-theology, 255, 257–58; critique of Plato, 368, 410, 413; critique of Western logocentrism, 256, 264, 300; debate with Marion on phenomenon of "gift," 250; and ethics of justice, 361; and the Impossible, 117–18, 388; and "Messianic ethics," 405n6; and the Other, 354; as philosopher and artist, 415; and poetry, 117, 118; and rhetoric of tropes, 27, 72; and Romantic thought on fragments, 354, 357

Descartes, René, 68, 104, 123, 240, 247, 396; analogical imagination, 16, 182; and the Infinite, 299, 301; *Larvatus prodeo*, 394; Marion on, 247–48, 298–300; misreadings of the *Meditations*, 299; and Plato, 274

Dewey, John, 29, 282, 288, 291

Dickens, Charles, 245

Dickinson, Emily, 16, 73, 151

Diderot, Denis, 3, 352, 438

Dilthey, Wilhelm, 209

Dionysius the Areopagite, 27, 51, 55, 305; apophatic theology, 430; and ascetic practices, 109; Balthasar on, 406; "The Divine Names," 115n20; and the Good, 405; and Incomprehensible God,

162n22, 300, 302; *Mystical Theology*,
115n20, 300; and notion of gift, 405
Dipple, Elizabeth, 407n8, 415
Doniger, Wendy, 353
Donne, John, 16, 27, 33, 435, 438
Dostoevsky, Fyodor, 16, 17, 27, 118n25, 387,
436; and "accursed questions," 217; *The
Brothers Karamazov*, 40; and dialecti-
cal imagination, 180; experiences of
Anfechtungen, 151; and tragedy, 51; and
Turgenev, 151
Douglass, Frederick, 316, 356, 362; *The Life
and Times of Frederick Douglass, Writ-
ten by Himself*, 355; *My Bondage and My
Freedom*, 355; *Narrative*, 355, 362
Dryden, John, 372
Du Bois, W. E. B., 356, 358, 362; *The Souls
of Black Folk*, 355
Duccio di Buoninsegna, 265
Dulles, Avery, 13, 222
Duméry, Henry, 249
Duns Scotus, 2, 121n27, 157; and analogical
imagination, 16, 182; and Anselm, 129;
and form, 240; and logic in theology,
119, 158; and metaphysics, 119; Scholastic theory, 13, 189; separation of spirituality and theology, 12, 94
Dupré, Louis, 239–41; on Baroque culture,
265; and centrality of form in Western
thought and culture, 240, 261, 262–63,
265; critique of Heidegger, 263–64; on
Derrida's understanding of logocentrism, 264; and issue of truth as manifestation through form, 262–64; and
metaphor of fragments, 253–55; and
the mystical traditions, 249, 251;
on nominalist crisis, 256; and onto-
theological synthesis, 254–60, 264–65;
and origins of modernity, 239, 252, 257;
The Other Dimension, 249, 250; *Passage*

to Modernity, 239–40, 241, 250, 251n2,
252, 253, 254, 262–63, 265–66, 433;
and postmodernity, 252; readings of
Nicholas of Cusa and Bruno, 258–60,
258n11; and selfhood in modernity, 249,
250, 251; *Transcendent Selfhood*, 250,
251n2
Dussel, Enrique, 319

Ebeling, Gerhard, 160
Eck, Johann, 146, 148
Eckardt, Roy, 335
Eckhart, Meister, 12, 121n27, 155, 417, 418,
429, 430
Eddington, Arthur, and two tables, 229
Edwards, Jonathan, 50, 54, 200, 241
Egidio of Viterbo, 18
Einstein, Albert, 150
Eliade, Mircea, 261, 262, 288, 345, 385
Eliot, George, 245
Eliot, T. S., 16, 27, 194, 199, 401; and Anglican theological tradition, 371; attitude
to Judaism, 371; on Baudelaire, 370,
372; and Buddhism and Hinduism, 371,
427–29, 438; conflict of interpretation
on, 423–30; conversion to Anglicanism, 370; as critic, 372–73; and Dante,
371, 372, 426, 434, 438, 440; on "dissociation of sensibility," 371, 426, 434,
435; and F. H. Bradley, 372; and "hints
and guesses," 30, 74, 117, 429, 439; and
humility, 439–40; on Joyce, 431; as literary modernist, 436; and Mallarmé,
427; and metaphysical poetry, 426–27;
and modern self, 437; and philosophy
as both vision and way of life, 437–40;
polemical essays, 425; and religion as
manifestation, 431–32; religious imagination, 430–40; resistance to professionalization of philosophy in modern

influence of on modern culture, 407; interpretation by French philosophers, 247; and Leonardo da Vinci, 408; and *Oedipus Rex*, 47; and overdetermination, 29; and Plato, 408–9; psychoanalytic theory as philosophical critical theory, 409n13; and the unconscious, 29, 37, 108, 116, 407–8

Friedman, Milton, 279–80

Gadamer, Hans-Georg: and Augustine, 72; and dialectical relationship between experience and language, 288; and Hegel, 265; hermeneutics, 116, 125, 209, 277, 293; and methodologism, 210, 210n2; and Plato, 368, 369, 406, 407; and tragedy, 47, 49; *Truth and Method*, 263; truth as rendered through form, 263; and understanding of the past, 332

Galileo Galilei, 180, 240

Gamwell, Franklin I., 74, 257; *By the People, for the People*, 281; critical exchange with Murdoch, 272; definition of Christian Right, 278–79; *Democracy on Purpose*, 276, 282; development of metaphysical moral theory through reanalysis of Aristotle and Kant, 269–74; *The Divine Good*, 270, 272, 276; model for authentically public theology, 277–83; and need for argumentative reasoning in both philosophy and theology, 276; and neoclassical concept of dipolar God, 272–73; and "The Philosophical Grounding of Ethics," 269–70; on possessive individualism, 281; process ethics correlated with process metaphysics and theology, 241–43; on self-abasement as principle sin of the disempowered, 281–82; on Whitehead's account of human experience and reason, 271

Gardner, Helen, 428n2

Gautama Buddha, 26

Gebara, Ivone, 313, 318

Geertz, Clifford, 285

Geffré, Claude, 247

Gerrish, Brian A., 153, 288

Gerson, Jean, *De remediis contra pusillanimitatem*, 151

Gilbert de la Porrée, 119, 129

Giles of Viterbo, 168

Gilkey, Langdon, 207, 213, 288, 292; and "Yale-Chicago debate," 243

Gilroy, Paul, *The Black Atlantic*, 352

Gilson, Étienne, 13, 74, 298

Giotto, 17, 265

Godzieba, Anthony, 312

Goethe, Johann Wolfgang von, 27, 47, 49

Goffman, Erving, 394–95

Gogol, Nikolai, 40

Gordon, Mary, 17

Gottschalk of Orbais, 151

Grabmann, Martin, 13

Graham, Billy, 198

Grant, Jacqueline, *White Women's Christ and Black Women's Jesus*, 320, 321, 359

Grassi, Ernesto, 252, 264

Greeley, Andrew, 16, 17

Greenberg, Irving, 310, 331, 334

Greene, Graham, 17

Gregory I (pope; Gregory the Great), 31, 33, 105, 106

Gregory Nazianzen, 2, 26, 47, 68, 98, 309

Gregory of Nyssa, 74, 216, 248, 429; Cappadocian, 309; and concept of *prosopon*, 395; *Contra Eunomium*, 98; conversation with Macrina, 98; *De hominis opificio*, 109n12; and Infinite-Incomprehensible Trinitarian God, 140–41, 162, 162n22; and metaphysics of the Good, 369; mystical-

290; *The Nature of Doctrine*, 285–95; on need for Anglo-American empiricist theologies, 290–91

Lindsay, Hal, 348

Littell, Franklin, 335

Little Richard, 355

Locke, John, 240, 241

Lonergan, Bernard, 33, 68, 113, 167, 187, 188, 190–91, 288, 289; analogical imagination, 16; and Aquinas, 12, 71, 72; and Augustine, 72; collaborative method, 190; *De Deo Trino*, 190; and desire to know, 31; Diana Hayes and, 322; and Heiler, 292; *Insight*, 72, 190, 191; *Ipsum Intelligere*, 74; and "law of the cross," 191, 301; Lindbeck on, 243; and love-centered theology, 96, 129; *Method in Theology*, 191; method of correlation, 290; on Neo-Scholasticism, 81, 124, 189; and Platonism, 404; response to Nygren's attack on Augustine, 33; and *ressourcement* theology, 299, 303; on Suárez, 298; transcendental theology, 291; and unity of essence issue, 292; *Verbum*, 72, 190

Long, Charles, 353

Lossky, Vladimir, 48, 216

Lössl, Josef, 37

Lottin, Joseph, 13

Löwith, Karl, 259n12

Loyola, Ignatius, *Spiritual Exercises*, 105–6, 338

Lubac, Henri de, 13, 16, 188, 247; and *ressourcement* theology, 12, 81, 299

Lucretius, 27, 94, 377, 424, 438

Luke, Gospel of, 52, 245, 312, 339, 342, 345, 347, 360, 368

Lustiger, Cardinal Jean-Marie, 312

Luther, Martin, 14–15, 41, 77, 100, 169, 216, 305; *Against the Antinomians*, 139;

Against the Roman Papacy, an Institution of the Devil, 15, 146–47; belief in Satan as person, 149; and Bernard of Clairvaux, 94, 96; *The Bondage of the Will*, 35–36, 149; *Commentary on the Psalms*, first and second, 140; concept of consubstantiation, 147; conversion, 149; and *curvatus in se*, 60, 108, 138, 145, 387; and debate with Erasmus on reality of God, 151, 152–54, 153n15; *De servo arbitrio*, 143, 151, 152, 153, 154; dialectical form, 240, 265; and Dionysius, 301; *Disputation against Scholastic Theology*, 146, 157; disputations on the Trinity and Christology, 136–37, 146, 155–59; and doctrine of double predestination, 136, 144, 148–49, 150, 152; experiences of *Anfechtungen*, 136, 140, 144–46, 144n11, 149, 150–51, 154n16, 155; and Fall's damage to reason, 139; Finnish school of Luther research and Luther's justification as *theosis*, 74, 136, 156, 159–61; and forgiveness, promise of, 138, 138n3, 215, 218; *Heidelberg Disputation*, 140; and hiddenness of God beyond revelation, 143–55; and hiddenness of God revealed by faith in Christ's cross, 139–40, 142, 146, 383; and Incomprehensible God of Infinite, Trinitarian Love, 146, 155–62; and justification by faith alone, 15, 137–38, 140, 153n15, 155–56, 160; *Lectures on Galatians*, 137n2; and logic and grammar as tools of theology, 12, 157–59; *On the Jews and Their Lies*, 146–47; and participation notion of *unio Christi*, 156, 160; polemical disputes and texts, 15, 146–48; reality of God as both revealed and hidden, 136, 139, 141; and reason, 35–36; rejection of metaphysics, 119, 159; rejection of

Luther, Martin (*continued*)
works-righteousness, 145–46, 153n15; and sin-grace paradigm, 10, 35, 108, 383; theology of the cross, 15, 137–43, 154–55, 301, 321; as thinker-artist, 68; two senses of the Hidden God, 15, 86, 143–44, 154, 155, 161–62, 301; understanding of human nature, 198; and Zwingli, 130

Lyotard, Jean-François: and Augustine, 72, 88; critique of modernity, 251; emphasis on rhetoric of tropes, 27; and the sublime, 117

Macarius, 32

MacIntyre, Alasdair, 251, 270, 272, 368, 404, 415

MacKinnon, Donald, 47, 51, 54–55

Macquarrie, John, 406

Macrina the Younger, 98, 309

Madac, Gouven, 82n9

Maimonides, Moses, 331, 342

Malcolm X, 316, 320, 355, 361

Malebranche, Nicolas, 29, 240

Mallarmé, Stéphane: Eliot and, 427, 429; "Un coup de dés jamais n'abolira pas le hasard," 151

Mannermaa, Tuomo, 155, 159

Marcel, Gabriel, 50, 246

Marcus Aurelius, 47, 94

Maréchal, Joseph, 12

Marion, Corinne, 13

Marion, Jean-Luc, 13, 117, 246–48; *Being Given*, 303, 305; and Dionysian tradition, 300–301; *The Erotic Phenomenon*, 303; *Étant donné*, 248, 303, 405; *God without Being*, 300; and the Good, 405; *In Excess*, 303, 305; intraphenomenological debates, 250, 297, 302; and Neoplatonism, 405n3; phenomenological analysis of the gift, 248,

300; phenomenology of theological language, 300–302, 304; reading of Thomas Aquinas on *Esse*, 300; refutation of onto-theology, 300; rereading of Descartes, 247–48, 258n8, 298–300; and saturated phenomenon, 248, 277, 300, 301–5

Maritain, Jacques, 393, 436, 437

Mark, Gospel of: apocalyptic narrative, 245–46, 343–44, 347–48, 349, 360; elements of tragedy, 52, 367; focus on the marginalized and poor, 312, 339, 342; Passion narrative, 140, 382, 386; as prophetic narrative, 368

Marty, Martin, 144n11

Marx, Karl, 180, 247, 249, 377, 393–94; Marxist analysis, 318, 319

Matter, E. Ann, 98

Matthew, Gospel of, 52, 140, 245, 312, 322, 343, 368

Maurice, F. O., 16, 188

Maximilla (prophet of Montanism), 51

Maximus the Confessor, 115

McCarthy, Joseph, 198

McGill, Arthur C., 104

McGinn, Bernard, 81, 115n21, 118, 256, 406

Mechthild of Magdeburg, 14, 16, 307

Melanchthon, Philip, 35, 151, 154n16, 215; confessional theology, 290; and form, 240; *Formula of Concord*, 160; and notion of justification, 156, 160

Meltzer, Françoise, 388

Melville, Herman, 50, 245

Mencken, H. L., 195

Mendelssohn, Moses, 16, 331

Mendes-Flohr, Paul, 16

Merleau-Ponty, Maurice, 246

Messiaen, Oliver, 17

Metz, Johann Baptist, 12, 292, 338; Christian theological response to Holocaust,

312, 335; as political theologian, 211n3, 289; and polycentrism, 352; and suffering of the passion and throughout history, 314–15

Michelangelo Buonarroti, Sistine Chapel: Catholic theological vision, 17–18, 168–69, 179, 183–84; and central symbols of Catholic Christianity, 169; *Christ and the Virgin*, detail of *The Last Judgment*, 172, *175*; classical figure of Christ, 174; correlation of Christianity, Judaism, and Greek and Roman culture, 168, 169; *The Creation of Adam*, *171*; draperies, 182; heliocentric composition, 174; High Renaissance optimism and humanism, 169; Ignudi, 169; and knowledge of Hebrew Bible, 169; *Last Judgment*, 35, 168, 172–74, *175*, 177, 180, 184; *The Libyan Sibyl*, 169, *170*; and Neoplatonism, 17, 18, 168, 172; predominance of Old Testament in nine central panels and corners, 169; reception by contemporaries, 176–77; *The Reprobate* (detail of *The Last Judgment*), 172, *173*; scenes from books of Maccabees, 169; scenes of creation of universe, 169, 171; and theme of judgment and resurrection, 172, 177; tragic notes of sin and grace, 169, 171; and ultimate incomprehensibility of God, 174

Milbank, John, 16, 244
Milton, John, 17, 54, 58, 60, 372, 432
Molino, Luis de, 130, 190
Moltmann, Jürgen, 211n3, 289, 321, 335, 383
Montaigne, Michel de, 34, 258, 372
Montanus, 51
Moody, A. David, 428n2
More, Thomas, 148
Morrison, Toni, 245, 319, 356, 360–61, 363
Moses, 53
Mozart, Wolfgang Amadeus, 17

Muhammad, 51
Müntzer, Thomas, 10, 146, 148
Murdoch, Iris: *Acastos*, 413; and Aristotelian virtue ethics, 272, 368–70; and Buddhist practices, 370, 430; critique of Derrida, 405, 410n15; feminist elements in novels of, 410n14; *The Fire and the Sun*, 406, 413; and forms of thought and form of the Good, 409–16; and Freud, 407–9, 407n8; and hermeneutics of suspicion upon consolation in religion, 418, 418n34; and magnetic role of the Good, 369, 405n5, 406, 418–19; *Metaphysics as a Guide to Morals*, 272, 369, 406, 407, 410, 413–14, 416; mimelike novels, 414–16; and Plato and Platonism, 369, 370, 386, 403–9, 412, 413; and Plato's Good beyond Being, 74, 272, 273, 369–70, 405, 409; rejection of possessive individualism and voluntarism, 369; *Sartre*, 369, 405, 413; *A Severed Head*, 408; *The Sovereignty of Good*, 369, 406, 413; spiritual exercises of detachment and attention, 416–19; and Weil, 369, 405, 405n2, 417, 418n33

Murray, John Courtney, Jr., 186, 201
Musil, Robert, *The Man without Qualities*, 245

Nabokov, Vladimir, 29, 41, 424–25
Nagel, Alexander, 169
Nava, Alejandro, 315, 375
Neusner, Jacob, 331
Newman, John Henry, 12, 167, 189; and analogical imagination, 182; *Grammar of Assent*, 98; *Plain and Parochial Sermons*, 98; Platonism, 27; rhetorical theology, 26, 188; as thinker-artist, 68; and tragedy, 54
Newton, Isaac, 240

Nicholas of Cusa, 119, 252, 254; and analogical imagination, 182; and form, 240; and recovery of the onto-logical synthesis, 257, 258–59, 264, 265; as thinker-artist, 68

Niebuhr, H. Richard, 186, 195, 343

Niebuhr, Reinhold, 185–86; "atheists for Reinhold Niebuhr," 29, 200; as Christian ecumenicist, 201; and Christian realism, 72, 186, 200–201; *The Nature and Destiny of Man*, 29, 197; and original sin, 199, 200; recovery of Reformation's reading of Augustine and Paul, 44, 198–99; on religious symbols, 198; and "Serenity Prayer," 193–95 (*see also* Sifton, Elisabeth); and struggle against totalitarianism and injustice, 197–98, 200; theology as blend of classical Protestant liberalism and neo-Reformation, 198–99; tragic sensibility, 47, 51, 54, 199, 200, 386; and the will, 32–33

Nietzsche, Friedrich, 382, 437; and Augustine, 33; and "authentic individual," 218; on Christianity, 142, 345–46; critique of Plato, 368, 410, 413; and D. F. Strauss, 151; and dialectical imagination, 180; Dionysian interpretation of Greek tragedy, 367; *Genealogy of Morals*, 102; on German philosophy and Lutheranism, 47, 144n11; and historicist consciousness, 332; influence on postmodern thought, 88, 379; interpretation by French philosophers, 247; and *Oresteia*, 47; as philosopher and artist, 68, 415; polemic, 147; and the self, 250; and tragedy, 49n9, 381, 385, 403; and the Void, 74; and the will, 32–33, 145; and will to power as eternal return, 75

Nilson, Jon, 351

Nixon, Richard, 198

Novalis, and tragedy, 47, 49

Nussbaum, Martha Craven: and Aristotle, 368, 403; and teleological moral theory, 270, 272; and tragedy, 50

Nygren, Anders, 160; attack on Augustine's *caritas* synthesis, 33

Obama, Barack, 316

Oberman, Heiko A., 144n11, 149, 152, 154, 159, 256

O'Connor, Flannery, 17

Oetinger, Christoph, 194

Ogden, Schubert, 74; dipolar concept of God, 272; and panentheistic understanding of God-world relationship, 242; process philosophy, 242; and Toulmin, 289; and "Yale-Chicago debate," 243

Olivetti, Marco M., 104

O'Malley, John, 18, 168

O'Regan, Cyril, 343

Origen of Alexandria, 2, 24, 26–27, 99, 119, 142; and analogical imagination, 182; and *gnosis*, 106; Logos theology, 314; and Song of Songs, 52; "spiritual senses," 186; stages of spiritual journey, 100, 106, 109; and William of St. Thierry, 128

Ortega y Gasset, José, 50

Osiander, Andreas, 160, 161

Otten, Willemien, 10, 95

Otto, Rudolf, *The Idea of the Holy*, 144–45, 310, 329–30

Ozick, Cynthia, 310, 431n5

Ozment, Steven E., 151

Palamas, Gregory, 67

Palestrina, Giovanni Pierluigi da, 17

Parks, Rosa, 317

Parmenides, 385

Pascal, Blaise, 2, 108, 150, 216, 240, 303, 305;

and Augustine's interpretation of will
as love, 33; and Cleopatra's nose, 121,
385; Eliot on, 372; and faith, 151; and
Hidden God, 141; and human state as
grandeur et misère, 102, 301; and love-
centered theology, 96; Nietzsche on, 33;
Pensées, 98, 301, 377; Platonism, 27; rhetorical theology, 26; and sin, 383; and
terror of silence of infinite space, 86,
199; and theology of the Cross, 183, 301,
302; as thinker-artist, 68; three orders
of existence, 377–78; and tragedy, 54,
55, 383
Pasolini, Pier Paolo, 182
Pater, Walter, 373
Pauck, Marion, 214
Pauck, Wilhelm, 208, 211, 214
Paul, Saint, 30, 57, 345, 346; Colossians and
Ephesians, 341; conversion, 102; and
crucified Jesus Christ, 50, 140–41, 142,
183, 245, 301, 314, 321; and dialectical
imagination, 181, 183, 314; Epistle to
the Romans, 14–15; First Tessalonians,
314, 340; First Timothy, 149; and meta-
phor of potter and clay, 149; and "mir-
ror in an enigma," 112; Philippians, 84;
prophetic-mystical reflections, 368; in
Romans and Galatians, 35, 141, 149, 151,
183, 340–42, 345; and Second Coming,
314; and Unknown God, 142
Paul III (pope), 147, 158
Paul IV (pope), 176
Pawlikowski, John, 312, 335
Péguy, Charles, 17, 54
Pelagius, 30, 47; and Augustine, 36–37, 69,
151, 152; moralism, 29, 36, 41, 42
Pelikan, Jaroslav, 47, 138
Peperzak, Adriaan Theodoor, 117, 277
Pessoa, Fernando, 436
Peter Lombard, *Sentences*, 120, 216

Petrarch, 69, 258
Philo, 52, 75, 331
Picasso, Pablo, 73, 399; *Guernica*, 212
Pico della Mirandola, Giovanni, 168, 172,
258
Piero della Francesca, 17
Pindar, 385
Plantinga, Alvin, 74
Plaskow, Judith, 309
Plato, 68, 142, 176, 299, 382, 440; Academy,
274; and Aeschylus, 412n22; contemporary attack on, 409–10; dialogues,
277, 366, 386, 410, 411–13; and *eros*,
408; and form, 240, 262; and Good Beyond Being, 22, 74, 75, 301, 405, 410–11,
418; history of the reception of, 368;
and mathematics, 274, 377; on moral-
metaphysical Good, 270; and myth,
412n21; and *noesis*, 410, 411; *Parmenides*, 22, 262, 410, 411, 411n19, 412; *Phaedrus*, 412, 412n21; as philosopher and
artist, 415; *Republic*, 22, 274, 377, 386,
405, 410, 411, 412, 412n21; Seventh Letter, 410, 411; *Sophist*, 412; *Symposium*,
22, 30, 75, 408–9, 411, 412, 412n21; and
"the poets," 386, 410n16; as thinker-
artist, 68; *Timaeus*, 341, 386, 404, 411–
12, 412n21, 412n22
Plotinus, 30, 142, 247, 376, 406; and Augustine, 69, 409n12; combination of
contemplative thinking and logical and
metaphysical arguments, 277; *Enneads*,
410; and form, 240; Neoplatonism, 369,
411; and *nous*, 21–22; and One Good,
22, 74, 79, 272, 369, 409, 410
Pole, Cardinal Reginald, 18
Poliziano, Angelo, 168, 172
Porete, Marguerite, 12, 14, 122, 430
Porphyry, 79, 409n12, 410; and Augustine,
69; and concept of crucified God, 142;

Russell, Bertrand, 242, 274, 437
Ruysbroeck, Jan van, 249

Saiving, Valerie, 309
Sartre, Jean-Paul, 50, 145, 150, 405n2
Savonarola, Girolamo, 168, 172
Scharlemann, Robert, 207, 213
Scheler, Max, 33, 47, 247
Schelling, Friedrich, 188, 189, 215, 218, 219, 240, 247, 333
Schillebeeckx, Edward, 12, 17, 214, 243, 289, 295, 303
Schiller, Friedrich, 47, 49
Schlegel, August Wilhelm, 47, 49, 240, 247
Schlegel, Friedrich, 240, 247
Schleiermacher, Friedrich, 2, 187, 189, 198, 216; analogical imagination, 16, 182; and dialectical forms of thinking, 240; Dupré on, 249; *Glaubenslehre*, 98; and Hegel, 130; and hermeneutics of recovery, 2; interpretation by French philosophers, 247; Lindbeck on, 243, 288, 295; and love-centered theology, 96; and modern Protestant theological tradition, 188; and relation of spirituality and theology, 6; and relation of theology and philosophy, 358; and Romantic hermeneutical tradition, 209; *Speeches*, 98; as translator and scholar of Plato, 404; and unity of essence issue, 292
Schlesinger, Arthur, Jr., 186
Scholem, Gershon, 311, 332, 333, 377
Schopenhauer, Arthur, 32, 47, 413–14
Schreiner, Susan, 10, 139, 152n13
Schweitzer, Albert, 160
Scorsese, Martin, 182
Scott, Nathan, 207
Scott, Peter Dale, 431n5
Scotus. *See* Duns Scotus

Seneca, 47, 53, 61, 373
Shakespeare, William, 34, 49, 176
Shapiro, Susan, 310, 312
Shinn, Roger Lincoln, 208
Sifton, Elisabeth, *The Serenity Prayer*, 191–97, 201–2
Siger of Brabant, 120
Simplicianus, 36
Smith, John, 291
Sobrino, Jon, 12, 47, 51, 318
Socrates, 56, 177, 275, 385
Sokolowski, Robert, 304
Sölle, Dorothee, 211n3
Soloviev, Vladimir, 16, 48
Sontag, Susan, 392, 401
Sophocles, 27, 56, 57, 367, 382, 385, 387; *Antigone*, 47, 58–59, 399–401; and hero as *daimon*, 399–401; *Oedipus at Colonus*, 59–60; *Oedipus Rex*, 46–47, 58, 383, 385, 400; *Oedipus Tyrannus*, 59; *Trachiniae*, 59
Spark, Muriel, 17
Spartacus, 44
Spellman, Cardinal Francis, 198
Spinoza, Baruch, 240, 299, 396, 397
Springstead, Eric O., 383
Stalin, Joseph, 197
Staupitz, Johann von, 154n16
Stauss, Leo, 251
Stein, Gertrude, 359
Steinmetz, David, 36, 152n13
Stendhal, 416n29
Stevens, Wallace, 373
Stock, Brian, 69
Stolz, Anselm, 104
Strauss, D. F., 151
Studer, Basil, 79
Suárez, Francisco, 80, 168, 298, 299, 301, 405
Swift, Jonathan, 147

and universal salvation, 150; and "Yale-
Chicago debate," 243, 244
Traversi, Derek, 428n2, 429
Troeltsch, Ernst, 288
Truth, Sojourner, 321, 357
Tubman, Harriet, 357
Turgenev, Ivan, 151, 245
Tyconius, 48

Unamuno, Miguel de, 50
Updike, John, 245

Valla, Lorenzo, 147
Van Buren, John, 72
van Buren, Paul, 312, 335
van der Meer, Frederik, *Augustine the
Bishop*, 82
van Gogh, Vincent, 75
Vial, Marc, 151
Vico, Giambattista, 240
Virgil, *The Aeneid*, 42, 45, 53, 61
Vitoria, Francisco de, 168
Voegelin, Eric, 251
Voltaire, 3, 44
von Speyr, Adrienne, 16

Wagner, Richard, 33
Wallace, David Foster, 151, 245
Warhol, Andy, 182
Waugh, Evelyn, 17
Weber, Max, and "iron cage" of modern
rationality, 251
Weil, André, 366
Weil, Simone, 68, 246, 365–68, 425; and
Antigone, 399; ascetic-mystical vision
and way of life, 392, 397; and atten-
tion as necessary spiritual practice, 379,
405n2; attitude to Judaism, 367–68,
377, 381; and Augustine's interpreta-
tion of will as love, 33; centrality of cross

and reality of the tragic, 47, 51, 54, 367,
382–86, 387, 388, 397; Christian Platonism, 379–87, 430; contemplative vision
of Christianity as religion of the poor,
365–66; critical social theory, 366, 394;
criticism of historical figures, 381; and
cult of personality, 393–94; and desire
for the Good, 393, 396–98, 401; and
Eastern traditions, 381, 384–85, 387,
397; experiences of *Anfechtungen*, 151;
failure to denounce anti-Semitism, 381,
382; and fragments, 356; *Gravity and
Grace*, 376; "The Iliad, or The Poem
of Force," 45, 47, 346, 377–78, 382,
383–84, 385, 386; materialism, 377;
on modern atheism, 387, 397–98; and
the Other, 377, 395; and Pascal's three
orders, 378–79; philosophical interests, 393; Plato as philosophical mentor,
366, 368; Platonic-Cartesian-Kantian
philosophy, 27, 365, 366, 379, 384, 391;
prophetic ethical-political work, 365,
366–67, 375–80, 391, 394; readings of
ancient Greeks and New Testament,
382–83, 385–86, 392, 396; on sin and
fate, 387; three mystical experiences,
366, 376; and true notion of person, 396
Weinberg, Steven, 150
West, Cornel, 186; fragmenting philosophical theology, 351, 356, 361, 362, 363; revisionary Marxian analysis, 318, 319
White, Graham, 154, 159
Whitehead, Alfred North, 68, 264, 270; account of human experience and reason,
271; analogical imagination, 16; comparison of Buddhism and Christianity,
5; dipolar concept of God, 272; distinction between assemblage and system-
atization, 216; metaphysics grounded
in mathematics and biology, 274; and

Whitehead, Alfred North (*continued*)
non-empiricist notion of experience,
288; and Plato, 273, 368, 369, 404, 406;
Principia Mathematica (with Russell),
242, 274; principle of Creativity, 74,
271, 272; *Process and Reality*, 242, 404
Whitman, Walt, and filaments, 1, 73
Wiesel, Elie, 310, 331, 333
Wilder, Thornton, 196
William of Conches, 95, 100, 102, 103, 119,
129
William of Ockham, 94, 157, 158
William of St. Thierry, 14, 16; *amor ipse
intellectus est*, 31; and ascetic practices,
109; and Augustine, 100; and Bernard
of Clairvaux, 98, 127–28; as Christian
in convalescence, 110; clash with Abelard, 129–30; *Commentary on the Song
of Songs*, 97, 98, 112; contributions to
contemporary Trinitarian theology,
114–24; conversion to monastic life,
103, 119; distinction, but not separation, between theology and spirituality,
118; *Enigma of Faith*, 97, 98, 112; *Golden
Epistle*, 97, 103, 112, 121, 124; healing
of *imago dei* and restoration of *similitudo dei* through stages of spiritual life,
101, 108–11, 115; humanistic optimism,
99–100, 114; and interdependence
of love and knowledge, 126; *Mirror
of Faith*, 97, 98, 112; monastic focus of
spiritual journey, 124–25; *Nature and
Dignity of Love*, 97, 112; *On the Nature
of Body and Soul*, 125; and *regio dissimilitudinis*, 107–8; and spirituality of
love, 33, 95, 97, 107, 112–13; and spiritual journey from faith to *ratio fidei* to
unitas Spiritus, 97–98, 101, 103–15, 124;
theology of mysticism (*unio*), 111–12,
115; and tragic humanism, 100, 102, 114;
Trinitarian theology, 96–114, 118, 124,
125–30; and understanding of ordinary
reason, 127–29; works of attributed to
Bernard and Bonaventure, 121–22
Williams, Bernard, 50, 404
Williams, Delores, *Sisters in the Wilderness*,
320, 321, 355, 357
Williams, Rowan, 16, 47, 51
Wills, Garry, 26, 86
Wind, Edgar, 18, 168
Wittgenstein, Ludwig: on Augustine's *Confessions*, 69; and Catholic analogical
imagination, 178; as fragmentary writer,
73; lack of separation between ethi-
cal and spiritual concerns, 7; "language
idling," 291; Lindbeck and, 285
Wondra, Ellen K., 6, 309, 339
Woolf, Virginia, 40, 299, 436
Wordsworth, William, 73, 190, 194

Yannaras, Christos, 48
Yates, Frances, 260
Yeats, William Butler, 373, 399, 424

Zizioulas, John, 48
Zwingli, Ulrich, 130, 146

INDEX OF SUBJECTS

agnosticism, 301, 435

Alcoholics Anonymous, and Niebuhr's Serenity Prayer, 194

Alexandria, 48

American empirical tradition: and "event-thinking," 241; and notion of experience, 241–42; and process philosophy of Whitehead, 242

Amos, book of, 198, 312, 339, 367, 380

analogical imagination, 16–17, 138–39, 177–82; versus dialectical imagination, 180, 183

analogy, 180

analytical philosophy and theology, 6, 243, 276, 404, 435–37

ancients: misreading of by modern philosophers, 93; need for distinct schools of philosophy, 274–75; notion of mask, 394–95, 398–99; philosopher as unique human type, 274; philosophical synthesis and participatory religious *plenum*, 255–60, 341–42, 433–35; and reason, 434; understanding of logos, 264. *See also* Greek philosophy; Greek tragedy

Anfechtungen, 136, 140, 144–46, 150–51

Anglicanism, 180, 301, 371–72

Anglo-American linguistic-philosophical tradition, 290–91

Anglo-American metaphysics, 276

Antinomians, 139

anti-Semitism, 3, 146–47, 180, 181, 311–12, 431n5

apocalyptic thought, 343–49

Arians, 69, 78

Asian liberation theologians, 318

atheism, 301, 354, 387, 435

"atheists for Reinhold Niebuhr," 29, 186, 200

Babylonian Exile, 52

Baroque synthesis, 257, 265

béguinages, 122

Bhagavad-Gita, 384, 387

Bible: New Testament, 343–44, 347–49; texts endorsing option for the poor, 312; tragic elements, 51–53, 55. *See also specific books*

black power movement, 316

blues music, 317, 354, 355, 357

Book of Kells, 414n24

Brazilian feminist and liberation theologians, 313, 318

British empirical tradition, 241, 291

Buddhism: central symbol of serene Buddha, 142; and Francis of Assisi, 344; Japanese Pure Land Buddhism, 41, 75, 145; Mahayana Buddhism, 125, 145, 428–29; social activism Buddhists, 319; spiritual exercises, 397; and *sunyata*, 145, 418, 428; theory and practice as distinct, but not separate, 3; Theravada Buddhism, 125; Zen Buddhism, 86, 87, 110, 145

Calvinism, 50, 152. *See also* Calvin, John

Cappadocia, 48

Cappadocians, 182, 240, 309

Cathari, 381, 383

Catholic Christianity: charismatics, 178; and clerical sexual molestation crisis, 180; as community of hope, 179; denial of full equality for women, 308; image of God, 178–79; multicultural, pluralistic tradition, 177–78; prophetic witness forms, 178; and reality of evil in history, 179–80; social justice tradition, 201–2, 279. *See also* Catholic theology

Catholic Counter-Reformation, 168, 171–72

Catholic-Protestant-Orthodox ecumenical dialogue, 169

Catholic theology: *caritas* synthesis, 33; medieval, 13–14; and Neo-Scholasticism, 189, 299; *ressourcement* theology, 12, 81, 189, 299, 303; and Scholasticism, 119; and Second Vatican Council, 12–13; separation of spirituality and theology, 12; understanding of love, 33

Catholic Worker Movement, 319

Chalcedon, Council of, 78, 81, 295

China, integration of modern culture with traditional Asian culture, 240

Christendom, 355, 383

Christian anti-Semitism, 311–12, 334–35

Christian mysticism. *See* medieval female mystics; mystical-prophetic paradigm

Christian Right: and imposition of personal values on society, 277–79; and interpretation of original separation of church and state, 278–79

Christian theology and tradition: and the apocalyptic, 343, 347; cross as central symbol of, 50–51, 142–43, 345; essence of God as love, 4–5; and love-justice relationship, 4, 5, 322, 342–43; move from proclamatory and prophetic to mystical participatory form, 340–41; and need to rethink God-condition after Holocaust, 311–12, 334–35; and pluralism, 216–17, 346; and retrieval of ancient synthesis and *plenum*, 341–42; and revelatory event of Jesus Christ, 340; shepherd or fish as early central symbols of, 143; thoughtlessness of contemporary, 330, 333; and tragedy, 50–51, 54; and turn to the Other, 338

Christian triumphalism, 381–82

Christology: Christological symbols, 314, 344–47; dialectical, of Paul, 314; and eschatological-apocalyptic "not-yet,"

314, 344, 347, 348, 349; tripartite, 115, 314, 397

Christomonism, 77

church and state, separation of: Christian Right interpretation of, 278–79; original meaning of as formulated by Jefferson, 283; and religion as personal preference, 279–80

classics: defined, 176; excess of meaning, 71, 176; mystery of creation of, 177; reception and production, 176–77

classism, 3, 42

climate change, 43

Commonweal, 185

Communio, 12–13

Concilium, 12–13

Constantinople, 48

consumerist colonialism culture, 319

conversio, recovery of in humanist theologies, 95

cosmic tree, 345

Counter-experiences (Hart), 297

countermoderns, 251, 255, 426

creation theologies, 342

Creativity, 74, 87

critical theories, 42, 277, 409n13

cross, as central Christian symbol, 50–51, 142–43, 345

Cynics, 438

daimonic hero, 58–60, 399–401

deinos, 58–60

deism, 354, 406, 435

deontological ethics, 242

Deuteronomy, book of, 312

dialectical imagination, 180–81

dialogical disputation versus polemic, 148

Dominicans, 121, 121n27

Donatists, 48, 69, 339

Dort, Synod of, 36, 151, 152

double predestination: Augustine and, 24,
45, 100, 150, 152; Calvin and, 36, 144,
149, 150, 152; Luther and, 136, 144,
148–49, 150, 152; and Synod of Dort,
36
Duomo, 168

Eastern Orthodox thought: denial of full
equality for women, 308; and justification as *theosis*, 155, 156; and nature-grace
paradigm, 47, 77; and ontological of the
Holy Spirit, 77; radical apophatic traditions, 357; rarely separated theory and
practice, 81, 308
Ecclesiastes, book of, 51
ego-psychologists, 29
elitism, 42
Enlightenment: and colonialism, 122, 219,
352; and effects on early modern categories, 251–52, 254, 255, 257, 352; and
"isms" for naming God, 354; and reason,
198, 217–18, 221, 251; rejection of saturated religious forms, 122–23, 353; and
religion as Other, 353; and separations
of theory from practice, form from
content, and emotion from thought,
122–23, 426
Ephesus, Council of, 78
Epicureans, 25, 438
es gibt, 303, 388
ethical voluntarism, 369
Etruscan theater, 395
Eucharist, as central symbol of early Christianity, 143
Evangelical Christianity, 202
event-thinking, 241
evil: natural, 43–44, 47; radical, 43, 48–49,
311, 330; and reality of in history, 179–
80

existentialism, 218, 369, 438
Exodus, book of, 52, 312, 367, 380

feminist, womanist, and *mujerista* theology,
219, 413; arguments against separation
of spirituality and theology, 308; and
binary oppositions of historical Christianity, 344; call for inclusion of all
major forms of Christianity in Christian theological education, 309; as contextual and universally ethical form of
theology, 309, 324–25, 326; and hermeneutics, 289, 307–9, 326; as intellectual conscience of Christian theology,
327; and the interpretation of Christian
symbols through patriarchal cultures
and traditions, 325–26; and theological
method, 323–24. See also *mujerista* theologies; womanist theologies
"First Nations," 316. *See also* Native
Americans
form: centrality of in Western thought
and culture, 240, 260–65; and classical
forms of rhetoric, 240; in Greek philosophy, 261–62; in the monotheisms,
261–62; and Neoplatonism, 429; and
new forms in East Asian, South Asian,
African, and Oceanic cultures, 239; and
the real, 261; subject-oriented nature
of, 240
form and content, separation of, 3, 122,
438
Fourth Lateran Council, 16, 139, 181
fragmentary, as distinct from fragment,
73n5
fragments: Cornel West's fragmenting
philosophical theology, 351, 356, 361,
362, 363; and cultural regret and nostalgia, 356; and emancipation from totality

systems, 353, 354–56, 359, 361–62; as "frag-events" or "filaments," 1, 71; and hope and redemption, 356; of marginal, repressed traditions, 359–60; postmodern thought and, 253–54; and post-WWI modernist writers, 356–57; and womanist theologians, 361

France, twentieth- and twenty-first-century intellectual renaissance, 246–47

Franciscans, 121, 121n27

Frankfurt school, 221, 277, 377, 409n13

Free Church theological traditions, 188

French feminist thought, 327

French Revolution, terror of, 49

French symbolists, 426

fundamentalism, 339, 348–49

Galatians, book of, 312

German expressionists, 212

German Romantics, and nostalgia for lost totality, 71, 354, 357

German transcendental philosophy and theology, 12, 398

Gnostic-Kabbalistic tradition, 333, 345, 397

gospel music, 354, 355, 357, 359, 380

Greek philosophy: and form, 261–62; *prosopon* in, 395, 396, 398–99

Greek tragedy, 44, 45–47, 399–401; and definitions of tragedy, 46–47; and French philosophy, 50; and Greek Christian theologians, 47; and hope, 55; and Iberian philosophy, 50; in post-Kantian German philosophy, 47–50

Harlem Renaissance, 359

"Heavenly Bodies," New York Metropolitan Museum of Art, 15, 17

Hebrew Bible, 169, 367–68, 382

hermeneutics, 5; and correlation model for theology, 294; of critique, 3, 304; and dialectic between experience and language, 288–89; and "dialogical turn," 148; and disclosures of conscious errors, 3; and feminist, womanist, and *mujerista* theology, 289, 307–9, 326; grounded in conversation with genuine Other, 2; and notion of truth, 263, 263n16; of recovery, 2–3; of retrieval, 304; of revelation, 304; Romantic tradition, 209–10; of suspicion, 41, 180, 261, 304, 332; and transformation of experiential paradigm into hermeneutical, 288; and unconscious distortions, 3, 42

Hinduism, 110; and cosmic tree, 345; and erotic forms for sacred, 353; and spiritual exercises, 397

hip-hop music, 317, 355–56, 359

Hippo, Vandal seizure of, 39

Hiroshima and Nagasaki, atomic bombings of, 198

Hispanic communities, economic-social poverty among, 313

Hispanic theology: male machismo, and struggle for liberation of women, 313; and recovery of saturated and fragmentary religious forms, 353

historical theology, 332

Holocaust. *See* Jewish Holocaust

homophobia, 42

House of Atreus, 44, 57, 384

humanistic theologies, 14, 94–96, 168; and Erasmus, 94, 141–42, 153, 168, 258; and recovery of *conversio*, 95; and synthesis, 254, 258; and William of St. Thierry, 99–100, 114

Iberian philosophy, and tragedy, 50

il y a, 303

logos, ancient versus modern understandings of, 264

Logos theologies, 6, 181, 314

love mystics, 33, 357

Magnificat, 322

Mahayana Buddhism, 125, 145, 428–29

Manicheans, 48, 69, 86, 346, 384

manifestation religions, 340, 431–32

mask, ancient notion, and modern recovery of, 394–95, 398–99. See also *prosopon*, in Greek theology and philosophy

medieval female mystics, 33, 81, 116, 119, 122, 160, 308–9, 357

mendicant orders, 120, 121, 121n27

Mexican-American War, 315

Micah, book of, 312, 367

microcosmos, self as, 304, 433, 434, 435

Middle Passages, 315, 345

modernity: academic debate of modernity versus postmodernity, 361; as contested category, 239; debates over rational approaches to God, 354, 435; difficulties of, 251; drive to totality, 359; and loss of ancient and medieval synthesis, 255–60, 433–35; mechanistic notion of cosmos, 436; misreading of, 254; notion of rationality, 3–4, 251, 434, 436; possessive individualism, 436; reformulation of in relation to traditions of in Asian and African cultures, 352; separation of feeling and thought, 123, 426, 434, 435, 438; separation of form and content, 3, 122, 438; separation of theory and practice, 80–81, 93–94, 118, 122–23, 377, 436, 438; Weil's three great disorders of, 377

monastic traditions, 14, 110, 119

monotheistic religions: and form, 261–62; and God's self-revelation, 4; as proc-

lamation religions, 340, 431, 432–33; prophetic, existential faith, and ethical-political acts for the Other, 5; same one God of all three with different emphases, 5; and synthesis among God, self, and cosmos, 433–34

mujerista theologies, 186, 313, 320–21

music, original forms of American, 317

mystical-prophetic paradigm, 14, 181, 338–43; and distance and participation, 338–41; and Dupré, 249, 251; and Gospel and letters of John, 177, 368; and Gregory of Nyssa, 27, 53, 277; and medieval German mystics, 155; and poetry, 116–17; and Weil, 365, 366–67, 375–80; and William of St. Thierry, 111–12, 115

mysticism and mystics, as contested concepts, 115n21, 123. *See also* medieval female mystics

Native Americans: economic-social poverty among, 313; indifference toward plight of, 316

natural evils, 43–44, 47

nature-grace paradigm, 42, 383; Augustine and, 10, 34, 60, 61, 86–87, 138; in Eastern Orthodox thought, 47, 77; in medieval and High-Renaissance thought, 19, 35

neo-Aristotelians, modern, 270, 272, 406

neo-Confucianism, 240

neoconservative resurgence, 211

neo-Kantians, 160, 260, 270

neo-Orthodox theologies, 198, 211, 213, 215, 288–89, 294, 331

neo-Palamite, 81

Neoplatonism, 341, 383, 385, 430; analogical, 181; Aquinas and, 128; and Aristotle's texts of logic, 273; and concept